Data Mining Techniques

Third Edition

Data Mining Techniques

For Marketing, Sales, and Customer Relationship Management

Third Edition

Gordon S. Linoff
Michael J. A. Berry

Wiley Publishing, Inc.

Data Mining Techniques: For Marketing, Sales, and Customer Relationship Management

Published by
Wiley Publishing, Inc.
10475 Crosspoint Boulevard
Indianapolis, IN 46256
www.wiley.com

Copyright © 2011 by Wiley Publishing, Inc., Indianapolis, Indiana

Published simultaneously in Canada

ISBN: 978-0-470-65093-6
ISBN: 978-1-118-08745-9 (ebk)
ISBN: 978-1-118-08747-3 (ebk)
ISBN: 978-1-118-08750-3 (ebk)

Manufactured in the United States of America

10 9 8 7 6 5 4

For general information on our other products and services please contact our Customer Care Department within the United States at (877) 762-2974, outside the United States at (317) 572-3993 or fax (317) 572-4002.

Wiley also publishes its books in a variety of electronic formats. Some content that appears in print may not be available in electronic books.

Library of Congress Control Number: 2011921769

To Stephanie, Sasha, and Nathaniel. Without your patience and understanding, this book would not have been possible.

– Michael

To Puccio.

Grazie per essere paziente con me.

Ti amo.

– Gordon

About the Authors

Gordon S. Linoff and Michael J. A. Berry are well known in the data mining field. They are the founders of Data Miners, Inc., a boutique data mining consultancy, and they have jointly authored several influential and widely read books in the field. The first of their jointly authored books was the first edition of *Data Mining Techniques*, which appeared in 1997. Since that time, they have been actively mining data in a wide variety of industries. Their continuing hands-on analytical work allows the authors to keep abreast of developments in the rapidly evolving fields of data mining, forecasting, and predictive analytics. Gordon and Michael are scrupulously vendor-neutral. Through their consulting work, the authors have been exposed to data analysis software from all of the major software vendors (and quite a few minor ones as well). They are convinced that good results are not determined by whether the software employed is proprietary or open-source, command-line or point-and-click; good results come from creative thinking and sound methodology.

Gordon and Michael specialize in applications of data mining in marketing and customer relationship management — applications such as improving recommendations for cross-sell and up-sell, forecasting future subscriber levels, modeling lifetime customer value, segmenting customers according to their behavior, choosing optimal landing pages for customers arriving at a website, identifying good candidates for inclusion in marketing campaigns, and predicting which customers are at risk of discontinuing use of a software package, service, or drug regimen. Gordon and Michael are dedicated to sharing their knowledge, skills, and enthusiasm for the subject. When not mining data themselves, they enjoy teaching others through courses, lectures, articles, on-site classes, and of course, the book you are about to read. They can frequently be found speaking at conferences and teaching classes. The authors also maintain a data mining blog at `blog.data-miners.com`.

Gordon lives in Manhattan. His most recent book before this one is *Data Analysis Using SQL and Excel*, which was published by Wiley in 2008.

Michael lives in Cambridge, Massachusetts. In addition to his consulting work with Data Miners, he teaches Marketing Analytics at the Carroll School of Management at Boston College.

Credits

Executive Editor
Robert Elliott

Senior Project Editor
Adaobi Obi Tulton

Production Editor
Daniel Scribner

Copy Editor
Paula Lowell

Editorial Director
Robyn B. Siesky

Editorial Manager
Mary Beth Wakefield

Freelancer Editorial Manager
Rosemarie Graham

Marketing Manager
Ashley Zurcher

Production Manager
Tim Tate

Vice President and Executive Group Publisher
Richard Swadley

Vice President and Executive Publisher
Barry Pruett

Associate Publisher
Jim Minatel

Project Coordinator, Cover
Katie Crocker

Proofreaders
Word One New York

Indexer
Ron Strauss

Cover Image
Ryan Sneed

Cover Designer
© PhotoAlto/Alix Minde/GettyImages

Acknowledgments

We are fortunate to be surrounded by some of the most talented data miners anywhere, so our first thanks go to our colleagues, past and present, at Data Miners, Inc., from whom we have learned so much: Will Potts, Dorian Pyle, and Brij Masand. There are also clients with whom we work so closely that we consider them our colleagues and friends as well: Harrison Sohmer, Stuart E. Ward, III, and Michael Benigno are in that category. Our editor, Bob Elliott, kept us (more or less) on schedule and helped us maintain a consistent style.

SAS Institute and the Data Warehouse Institute have given us unparalleled opportunities over the past 12 years for teaching. We owe special thanks to Herb Edelstein (now retired), Herb Kirk, Anne Milley, Bob Lucas, Hillary Kokes, Karen Washburn, and many others who have made these classes possible.

Over the past year, while we were writing this book, several friends and colleagues have been very supportive. We would like to acknowledge Diane and Savvas Mavridis, Steve Mullaney, Lounette Dyer, Maciej Zworski, John Wallace, Paul Rosenblum, and Don Wedding.

We also want to acknowledge all the people with whom we have worked in scores of data mining engagements over the years. We have learned something from every one of them. Among the many who have helped us throughout the years:

Alan Parker	Gary King
Dave Waltz	Tim Manns
Craig Stanfill	Jeremy Pollock
Dirk De Roos	Richard James
Michael Alidio	Georgia Tourasi
Michael Cavaretta	Avery Wang
Dave Duling	Eric Jiang
Jeff Hammerbacher	Bruce Rylander
Andrew Gelman	Daryl Berry

Doug Newell

Adam Schwebber

Ed Freeman

Tiha Ghyczy

Erin McCarthy

Usama Fayyad

Josh Goff

Patrick Ott

Karen Kennedy

John Muller

Ronnie Rowton

Frank Travisano

Kurt Thearling

Jim Stagnito

Mark Smith

Stephen Boyer

Nick Radcliffe

Yugo Kanazawa

Patrick Surry

Xu He

Ronny Kohavi

Kiran Nagarur

Terri Kowalchuk

Ramana Thumu

Victor Lo

Jacob Hauskens

Yasmin Namini

Jeremy Pollock

Zai Ying Huang

Lutz Hamel

Amber Batata

And, of course, all the people we thanked in the first edition are still deserving of acknowledgment:

Bob Flynn

Marc Goodman

Bryan McNeely

Marc Reifeis

Claire Budden

Marge Sherold

David Isaac

Mario Bourgoin

David Waltz

Prof. Michael Jordan

Dena d'Ebin

Patsy Campbell

Diana Lin

Paul Becker

Don Peppers

Paul Berry

Ed Horton

Rakesh Agrawal

Edward Ewen

Ric Amari

Fred Chapman

Rich Cohen

Gary Drescher

Robert Groth

Gregory Lampshire

Robert Utzschnieder

Janet Smith

Roland Pesch

Jerry Modes

Stephen Smith

Jim Flynn

Sue Osterfelt

Kamran Parsaye

Susan Buchanan

Karen Stewart

Syamala Srinivasan

Larry Bookman

Wei-Xing Ho

Larry Scroggins

William Petefish

Lars Rohrberg

Yvonne McCollin

Lounette Dyer

Finally, we would like to thank our family and friends, particularly Stephanie and Giuseppe, who have endured with grace the sacrifices in writing this book.

Contents at a Glance

Contents

Introduction

Fifteen years ago, Michael and I wrote the first version of this book. A little more than 400 pages, the book fulfilled our goal of surveying the field of data mining by bridging the gap between the technical and the practical, by helping business people understand the data mining techniques and by helping technical people understand the business applications of these techniques. When Bob Elliott, our editor at Wiley, asked us to write the third edition of *Data Mining Techniques*, we happily said "yes," conveniently forgetting the sacrifices that writing a book requires in our personal lives. We also knew that the new edition would be considerably reworked from the previous two editions.

In the past 15 years, the field has broadened and so has the book, both figuratively and literally. The second edition, published in 2004 and expanded to 600 pages, introduced two key new technical chapters covering survival analysis and statistical algorithms that had then become (and still are) increasingly important for data miners. Once again, this version introduces new technical areas, particularly text mining and principal components, and a wealth of new examples and enhanced technical descriptions in all the chapters. These examples come from a broad section of industries, including financial services, retailing, telecommunications, media, insurance, health care, and web-based services.

As practitioners in the field, we have also continued to learn. Between us, we now have about half a century of experience in data mining. Since 1999, Michael and I have been teaching courses through the Business Knowledge Series at SAS Institute (this series is separate from the software side of the business and brings in outside experts to teach non-software-specific courses), the Data Warehouse Institute, and onsite classes at many different companies. Our role as instructors in these courses has introduced us to thousands of diverse business people working in many industries. One of these courses, "Business

Data Mining Techniques," was based on the second edition of this book. These courses provide a wealth of feedback about the subject of data mining, about what people are doing in the real world, and how best to present these ideas so they can be readily understood. Much of this feedback is reflected in this new edition. We seem to learn as much from our students as our students learn from us.

Michael has also been teaching a course on marketing analysis at Boston College's Carroll School of Management for the past two years. The first two editions of *Data Mining Techniques* are also popular in courses in many colleges and universities, including both business courses and, increasingly, the data mining programs that have appeared at various universities over the past decade. Although not intended as a textbook, *Data Mining Techniques* offers an excellent overview for students of all types. Over the years, we have made various data sets available on our website, which instructors use for their courses.

This book is divided into four parts. The first part talks about the business context of data mining. Chapter 1 introduces data mining, along with examples of how it is used in the real world. Chapter 2 explains the virtuous cycle of data mining and how data mining can help understand customers. This chapter has several examples showing how data mining is used throughout the customer lifecycle. Chapter 3 is an outline of the methodology of data mining. This overall methodology is refined by Chapters 5 and 12, for directed and undirected data mining, respectively. Chapter 4 covers business statistics, introducing some key technical ideas that are used throughout the rest of the book. This chapter also has an extended case study from MyBuys, showing the strengths and weaknesses of different methods for analyzing the results of A/B marketing tests.

Earlier editions placed all the data mining techniques in a single section. We have decided to split the techniques into two distinct categories, so directed and undirected techniques each have their own sections. The section on directed data mining starts by refining the data mining methodology in Chapter 3 for directed data mining. The following chapters cover directed data mining techniques, including statistical techniques, decision trees, neural network, memory-based reasoning, survival analysis, and genetic algorithms.

The directed data mining techniques were all covered in the second edition. However, we have enhanced them in several important ways, particularly by including more examples of their use in the real world. The decision tree chapter (Chapter 7) now includes a case study on uplift modeling from US Bank and also introduces support vector machines. The neural network chapter (Chapter 8) discusses radial basis function neural networks. The memory-based reasoning chapter (Chapter 9) now has two very interesting case studies, one on how Shazam identifies songs and another on using MBR to help radiologists determine whether mammograms are normal or abnormal. Chapter 10 on survival analysis includes a much-needed discussion on customer value. Chapter 11 on genetic algorithms includes swarm intelligence, another related concept from the world of "computational biology" that has promising applications for data mining.

The third section is devoted to undirected data mining techniques. Chapter 12 explains four different flavors of undirected data mining. Clustering algorithms have been split into two chapters. The first (Chapter 13) focuses on the most common technique, k-means clustering and three variants, k-medians, k-medoids, and k-modes. It also has an enhanced discussion of interpreting clusters, which is important regardless of the technique used for identifying them. The second chapter on clustering (Chapter 14) introduces many techniques, including hierarchical clustering, divisive clustering, self-organizing networks, and Gaussian mixture models (expectation maximization clustering), which is new in this edition. Chapter 15 on market basket analysis has been enhanced with examples that extend beyond association rules, including a case study on ethnic marketing. Chapter 16, "Link Analysis," the last chapter in the undirected data mining section, was almost peripheral in the 1990s when we wrote the first edition of this book. Now, it is quite central, as exemplified by the three case studies in this chapter.

The final section of the book is devoted to data — data mining's first name, so to speak. Chapter 17 covers the computer architectures that support data, such as relational databases, data warehouses, and data marts. It also covers Hadoop and analytic sandboxes, both of which are used to process data not suitable for relational databases and traditional data mining tools. The two earlier editions had one chapter on preparing data for data mining. This subject is so important that this edition splits the topic into three chapters. Chapter 18 is about finding the customer in the data and building customer signatures, the data structure used by many data mining algorithms. Chapter 19 covers derived variables, with hints and tips on defining variables that help models perform better. Chapter 20 focuses on reducing the number of variables, whether for techniques such as neural networks that prefer fewer variables or for data visualization purposes. One of the key techniques in this chapter, principal components, is new in this edition.

Chapter 21 covers a topic that could be a book by itself — text mining. Analyzing text builds on so many of the ideas found earlier in the book that we felt that the chapter covering text mining had to go later in the book. Its position at the end highlights text mining as the culmination of topics covered throughout the book. The final case study from DIRECTV is not only an interesting application of text mining to the customer service side of the business, but also an excellent example of data mining in practice.

Like the first two editions, this book is aimed at current and future data mining practitioners and their managers. It is not intended for software developers looking for detailed instructions on how to implement the various data mining algorithms, nor for researchers trying to improve upon these algorithms, although both these groups can benefit from understanding how such software gets used. Ideas are presented in nontechnical language, with minimal use of mathematical formulas and arcane jargon. Throughout the book, the emphasis is as much on the real-world applications of data mining as on the technical explanations, so the techniques include examples with real business context.

In short, we have tried to write the book that we would have liked to read when we began our own data mining careers.

— Gordon S. Linoff, New York, January 2011

What Is Data Mining and Why Do It?

In the first edition of this book, the first sentence of the first chapter began with the words, "Somerville, Massachusetts, home to one of the authors of this book…" and went on to tell of two small businesses in that town and how they had formed learning relationships with their customers. One of those businesses, a hair braider, no longer braids the hair of the little girl. In the years since the first edition, the little girl grew up, and moved away, and no longer wears her hair in cornrows. Her father, one of the authors, moved to nearby Cambridge. But one thing has not changed. The author is still a loyal customer of the Wine Cask, where some of the same people who first introduced him to cheap Algerian reds in 1978 and later to the wine-growing regions of France are now helping him to explore the wines of Italy and Germany.

Decades later, the Wine Cask still has a loyal customer. That loyalty is no accident. The staff learns the tastes of their customers and their price ranges. When asked for advice, the response is based on accumulated knowledge of that customer's tastes and budgets as well as on their knowledge of their stock.

The people at the Wine Cask know a lot about wine. Although that knowledge is one reason to shop there rather than at a big discount liquor store, their intimate knowledge of each customer is what keeps customers coming back. Another wine shop could open across the street and hire a staff of expert oenophiles, but achieving the same level of intimate customer knowledge would take them months or years.

Well-run small businesses naturally form learning relationships with their customers. Over time, they learn more and more about their customers, and they use that knowledge to serve them better. The result is happy, loyal customers and profitable businesses.

Larger companies, with hundreds of thousands or millions of customers, do not enjoy the luxury of actual personal relationships with each one. Larger firms must rely on other means to form learning relationships with their customers. In particular, they must learn to take full advantage of something they have in abundance — the data produced by nearly every customer interaction. This book is about analytic techniques that can be used to turn customer data into customer knowledge.

What Is Data Mining?

Although some data mining techniques are quite new, data mining itself is not a new technology, in the sense that people have been analyzing data on computers since the first computers were invented — and without computers for centuries before that. Over the years, data mining has gone by many different names, such as knowledge discovery, business intelligence, predictive modeling, predictive analytics, and so on. The definition of data mining as used by the authors is:

> *Data mining is a business process for exploring large amounts of data to discover meaningful patterns and rules.*

This definition has several parts, all of which are important.

Data Mining Is a Business Process

Data mining is a business process that interacts with other business processes. In particular, a process does not have a beginning and an end: it is ongoing. Data mining starts with data, then through analysis informs or inspires action, which, in turn, creates data that begets more data mining.

The practical consequence is that organizations who want to excel at using their data to improve their business do not view data mining as a sideshow. Instead, their business strategy must include collecting data, analyzing data for long-term benefit, and acting on the results.

At the same time, data mining readily fits in with other strategies for understanding markets and customers. Market research, customer panels, and other techniques are compatible with data mining and more intensive data analysis. The key is to recognize the focus on customers and the commonality of data across the enterprise.

Large Amounts of Data

One of the authors regularly asks his audiences, "How much is a lot of data?" when he speaks. Students give answers such as, "all the transactions for 10 million customers" or "terabytes of data." His more modest answer, "65,356 rows," still gets sighs of comprehension even though Microsoft has allowed more than one million rows in Excel spreadsheets since 2007.

A tool such as Excel is incredibly versatile for working with relatively small amounts of data. It allows a wide variety of computations on the values in each row or column; pivot tables are amazingly practical for understanding data and trends; and the charts offer a powerful mechanism for data visualization.

In the early days of data mining (the 1960s and 1970s), data was scarce. Some of the techniques described in this book were developed on data sets containing a few hundred records. Back then, a typical data set might have had a few attributes about mushrooms, and whether they are poisonous or edible. Another might have had attributes of cars, with the goal of estimating gas mileage. Whatever the particular data set, it is a testament to the strength of the techniques developed in those days that they still work on data that no longer fits in a spreadsheet.

Because computing power is readily available, a large amount of data is not a handicap; it is an advantage. Many of the techniques in this book work better on large amounts of data than on small amounts — you can substitute data for cleverness. In other words, data mining lets computers do what computers do best — dig through lots and lots of data. This, in turn, lets people do what people do best, which is set up the problem and understand the results.

That said, some case studies in this book still use relatively small data sizes. Perhaps the smallest is a clustering case study in Chapter 13. This case study finds demographically similar towns, among just a few hundred towns in New England. As powerful as Excel is, it does not have a built-in function that says "group these towns by similarity."

That is where data mining comes in. Whether the goal is to find similar groups of New England towns, or to determine the causes of customer attrition, or any of a myriad of other goals sprinkled throughout the chapters, data mining techniques can leverage data where simpler desktop tools no longer work so well.

Meaningful Patterns and Rules

Perhaps the most important part of the definition of data mining is the part about meaningful patterns. Although data mining can certainly be fun, helping the business is more important than amusing the miner.

In many ways finding patterns in data is not tremendously difficult. The operational side of the business generates the data, necessarily generating patterns at the same time. However, the goal of data mining — at least as the authors use the term — is not to find just any patterns in data, but to find patterns that are useful for the business.

This can mean finding patterns to help routine business operations. Consider a call center application that assigns customers a color. "Green" means be very nice, because the caller is a valuable customer, worth the expense of keeping happy; "yellow" means use some caution because the customer may be valuable but also has signs of some risk; and "red" means do not give the customer any special treatment because the customer is highly risky. Finding patterns can also mean targeting retention campaigns to customers who are most likely to leave. It can mean optimizing customer acquisition both for the short-term gains in customer numbers and for the medium- and long-term benefit in customer value.

Increasingly, companies are developing business models centered around data mining — although they may not use that term. One company that the authors have worked with helps retailers make recommendations on the web; this company only gets paid when web shoppers click on its recommendations. That is only one example. Some companies aggregate data from different sources, bringing the data together to get a more complete customer picture. Some companies, such as LinkedIn, use information provided by some people to provide premium services to others — and everyone benefits when recruiters can find the right candidates for open job positions. In all these cases, the goal is to direct products and services to the people who are most likely to need them, making the process of buying and selling more efficient for everyone involved.

Data Mining and Customer Relationship Management

This book is not about data mining in general, but specifically about data mining for customer relationship management. Firms of all sizes need to learn to emulate what small, service-oriented businesses have always done well — creating one-to-one relationships with their customers. Customer relationship management is a broad topic that is the subject of many articles, books, and conferences. Everything from lead-tracking software to campaign management software to call center software gets labeled as a customer relationship management tool. The focus of this book is narrower — the role that data mining can play in improving customer relationship management by improving the company's ability to form learning relationships with its customers.

In every industry, forward-looking companies are moving toward the goal of understanding each customer individually and using that understanding to make it easier (and more profitable) for the customer to do business with them rather than with competitors. These same firms are learning to look at the value of each customer so that they know which ones are worth investing money and effort to hold on to and which ones should be allowed to depart. This change in focus from broad market segments to individual customers requires changes throughout the enterprise, and nowhere more so than in marketing, sales, and customer support.

Building a business around the customer relationship is a revolutionary change for most companies. Banks have traditionally focused on maintaining the spread between the rate they pay to bring money in and the rate they charge to lend money out. Telephone companies have concentrated on connecting calls through the network. Insurance companies have focused on processing claims, managing investments, and maintaining their loss ratio. Turning a product-focused organization into a customer-centric one takes more than data mining. A data mining result that suggests offering a particular customer a widget instead of a gizmo will be ignored if the manager's bonus depends on the number of gizmos sold this quarter and not on the number of widgets (even if the latter are more profitable or induce customers to be more profitable in the long term).

In a narrow sense, data mining is a collection of tools and techniques. It is one of several technologies required to support a customer-centric enterprise. In a broader sense, data mining is an attitude that business actions should be based on learning, that informed decisions are better than uninformed decisions, and that measuring results is beneficial to the business. Data mining is also a process and a methodology for applying analytic tools and techniques. For data mining to be effective, the other requirements for analytic CRM must also be in place. To form a learning relationship with its customers, a company must be able to

- *Notice* what its customers are doing
- *Remember* what it and its customers have done over time
- *Learn* from what it has remembered
- *Act* on what it has learned to make customers more profitable

Although the focus of this book is on the third bullet — learning from what has happened in the past — that learning cannot take place in a vacuum. There must be transaction processing systems to capture customer interactions, data warehouses to store historical customer behavior information, data mining to translate history into plans for future action, and a customer relationship strategy to put those plans into practice.

Data mining, to repeat the earlier definition, is a business process for exploration and analysis of large quantities of data in order to discover meaningful patterns and rules. This book assumes that the *goal* of data mining is to allow a company to improve its marketing, sales, and customer support operations through a better understanding of its customers. Keep in mind, however, that the data mining techniques and tools described in this book are equally applicable in fields as varied as law enforcement, radio astronomy, medicine, and industrial process control.

Why Now?

Most data mining techniques have existed, at least as academic algorithms, for decades (the oldest, survival analysis, actually dates back centuries). Data mining has caught on in a big way, increasing dramatically since the 1990s. This is due to the convergence of several factors:

- Data is being produced.
- Data is being warehoused.
- Computing power is affordable.
- Interest in customer relationship management is strong.
- Commercial data mining software products are readily available.

The combination of these factors means that data mining is increasingly appearing as a foundation of business strategies. Google was not the first search engine, but it was the first search engine to combine sophisticated algorithms for searching with a business model based on maximizing the value of click-through revenue. Across almost every business domain, companies are discovering that they have information — information about subscribers, about Web visitors, about shippers, and payment patterns, calling patterns, friends and neighbors. Companies are increasingly turning to data analysis to leverage their information.

Data Is Being Produced

Data mining makes the most sense where large volumes of data are available. In fact, most data mining algorithms *require* somewhat large amounts of data to build and train models.

One of the underlying themes of this book is that data is everywhere and available in copious amounts. This is especially true for companies that have customers — and that includes just about all of them. A single person browsing a website can generate tens of kilobytes of data in a day. Multiply that by millions of customers and prospects and data volumes quickly exceed the size of a single spreadsheet.

The Web is not the only producer of voluminous data. Telephone companies and credit card companies were the first to work with terabyte-sized databases, an exotically large size for a database as recently as the late 1990s. That time has passed. Data is available, and in large volumes, but how do you make any sense out of it?

Data Is Being Warehoused

Not only is a large amount of data being produced, but also, more and more often, it is being extracted from the operational billing, reservations, claims processing, and order entry systems where it is generated and then fed into a data warehouse to become part of the corporate memory.

Data warehousing is such an important part of the data mining story that Chapter 17 is devoted to this topic. Data warehousing brings together data from many different sources in a common format with consistent definitions for keys and fields. Operational systems are designed to deliver results quickly to the end user, who may be a customer at a website or an employee doing her job. These systems are designed for the task at hand, and not for the task of maintaining clean, consistent data for analysis. The data warehouse, on the other hand, should be designed exclusively for decision support, which can simplify the job of the data miner.

Computing Power Is Affordable

Data mining algorithms typically require multiple passes over huge quantities of data. Many algorithms are also computationally intensive. The continuing dramatic decrease in prices for disk, memory, processing power, and network bandwidth has brought once-costly techniques that were used only in a few government-funded laboratories into the reach of ordinary businesses.

Interest in Customer Relationship Management Is Strong

Across a wide spectrum of industries, companies have come to realize that their customers are central to their business and that customer information is one of their key assets.

Every Business Is a Service Business

For companies in the service sector, information confers competitive advantage. That is why hotel chains record your preference for a nonsmoking room and car rental companies record your preferred type of car. In addition, companies that have not traditionally thought of themselves as service providers are beginning to think differently. Does an automobile dealer sell cars or transportation? If the latter, it makes sense for the dealership to offer you a loaner car whenever your own is in the shop, as many now do.

Even commodity products can be enhanced with service. A home heating oil company that monitors your usage and delivers oil when you need more sells a better product than a company that expects you to remember to call to arrange a delivery before your tank runs dry and the pipes freeze. Credit card companies, long-distance providers, airlines, and retailers of all kinds often compete as much or more on service as on price.

Information Is a Product

Many companies find that the information they have about their customers is valuable not only to themselves, but to others as well. A supermarket with a loyalty card program has something that the consumer packaged goods industry would love to have — knowledge about who is buying which products. A credit card company knows something that airlines would love to know — who is buying a lot of airplane tickets. Both the supermarket and the credit card company are in a position to be knowledge brokers. The supermarket can charge consumer packaged goods companies more to print coupons when the supermarkets can promise higher redemption rates by printing the right coupons for the right shoppers. The credit card company can charge the airlines to target a frequent flyer promotion to people who travel a lot, but fly on other airlines.

Google knows what people are looking for on the Web. It takes advantage of this knowledge by selling sponsored links (among other things). Insurance companies pay to make sure that someone searching on "car insurance" will be offered a link to their site. Financial services pay for sponsored links to appear when someone searches on a phrase such as "mortgage refinance."

In fact, any company that collects valuable data is in a position to become an information broker. The *Cedar Rapids Gazette* takes advantage of its dominant position in a 22-county area of Eastern Iowa to offer direct marketing services to local businesses. The paper uses its own obituary pages and wedding announcements to keep its marketing database current.

Commercial Data Mining Software Products Have Become Available

There is always a lag between the time when new algorithms first appear in academic journals and excite discussion at conferences and the time when commercial software incorporating those algorithms becomes available. There is another lag between the initial availability of the first products and the time that they achieve wide acceptance. For data mining, the period of widespread availability and acceptance has arrived.

Many of the techniques discussed in this book started out in the fields of statistics, artificial intelligence, or machine learning. After a few years in universities and government labs, a new technique starts to be used by a few early adopters in the commercial sector. At this point in the evolution of a new technique, the software is typically available in source code to the intrepid user willing to retrieve it via FTP, compile it, and figure out how to use it by reading the author's Ph.D. thesis. Only after a few pioneers become successful with a new technique does it start to appear in real products that come with user's manuals, help lines, and training classes.

Nowadays, new techniques are being developed; however, much work is also devoted to extending and improving existing techniques. All the techniques discussed in this book are available in commercial and open-source software products, although no single product incorporates all of them.

Skills for the Data Miner

Who can be a data miner? The answer is not everyone, because some specific skills are needed. A good data miner needs to have skills with numbers and a basic familiarity with statistics (and a stronger knowledge of statistics is always useful). Chapters 4 and 6 cover many of the key statistical concepts required for data mining. Having a good working knowledge of Excel is also very useful, because it is the predominant spreadsheet in the business world. Spreadsheets such as Excel are very useful for analyzing smallish amounts of data and for presenting the results to a wide audience.

Of course, familiarity with data mining techniques is critical for a data miner. The bulk of this book is devoted to various techniques. Understanding the techniques themselves is important; more important is understanding when and how they are useful. Perhaps as important as the technical details is the demystification of data mining techniques. Although many are quite sophisticated, they are often based on a very accessible foundation. These techniques are not magic. Even when you cannot explain exactly how they arrive at an answer, it is possible to understand them, without a Ph.D. in mathematics or statistics. The techniques are better than magic, because they are useful and help solve real-world problems.

Another very important skill for a data miner is really an attitude: lack of fear of large amounts of data and the complex processing that might be needed to squeeze out results. Working with large data sets, data warehouses, and analytic sandboxes is key to successful data mining.

Finally, data mining is not just about producing technical results. No data mining model, for instance, ever really did anything more than shift bits around inside a computer. The results have to be used to help people (or increasingly, automated processes) make more informed decisions. Producing the technical results is the end of the beginning of the data mining process. Being able to work with other people, communicate results, and recognize what is really needed are critical skills for a good data miner. Throughout this book are many examples of data mining in the business context, both in the next two chapters and throughout the technical chapters devoted to each technique. Data mining is a learning process based on data, as described in the next sections, and any good data miner must be open to new ideas.

The Virtuous Cycle of Data Mining

In the first part of the nineteenth century, textile mills were the industrial success stories. These mills sprang up in the growing towns and cities along rivers in England and New England to harness hydropower. Water, running over water wheels, drove spinning, knitting, and weaving machines. For a century, the symbol of the industrial revolution was water pouring over wheels providing the power for textile machines.

The business world has changed. Old mill towns are now quaint historical curiosities. Long mill buildings alongside rivers are warehouses, shopping malls, artist studios, and sundry other businesses. Even manufacturing companies often provide more value in services than in goods. The authors were struck by an ad campaign by a leading international cement manufacturer, Cemex, that presented concrete as a service. Instead of focusing on the quality of cement, its price, or availability, the ad pictured a bridge over a river and sold the idea that "cement" is a service that connects people by building bridges between them. Concrete as a service? Welcome to the twenty-first century.

The world has changed. Access to electrical or mechanical power is no longer the criterion for business success. For mass-market products, data about customer interactions is the new waterpower; knowledge drives the turbines of the service economy and, because the line between service and manufacturing is getting blurry, much of the manufacturing economy as well. Information from data focuses sales and marketing efforts by targeting customers, improves product designs by addressing real customer needs, and enhances resource allocation by understanding and predicting customer preferences.

Data is at the heart of many core business processes. It is generated by transactions in operational systems regardless of industry — retail, telecommunications, manufacturing, health care, utilities, transportation, insurance, credit cards, and financial services, for example. Adding to the deluge of internal data are external sources of demographic, lifestyle, and credit information on retail customers; credit, financial, and marketing information on business customers; and demographic information on neighborhoods of all sizes. The promise of data mining is to find the interesting patterns lurking in all these billions and trillions of bits lying on disk or in computer memory. Merely finding patterns is not enough. *You must respond to the patterns and act on them, ultimately turning data into information, information into action, and action into value.* This is the virtuous cycle of data mining in a nutshell.

To achieve this promise, data mining needs to become an essential business process, incorporated into other processes including marketing, sales, customer support, product design, and inventory control. The virtuous cycle places data mining in the larger context of business, shifting the focus away from the discovery mechanism to the actions based on the discoveries. This book emphasizes *actionable* results from data mining (and this usage of "actionable" should definitely not be confused with its definition in the legal domain, where it means that some action has grounds for legal action).

Marketing literature makes data mining seem so easy. Just apply the automated algorithms created by the best minds in academia, such as neural networks, decision trees, and genetic algorithms, and you are on your way to untold successes.

Although algorithms are important, the data mining solution is more than just a set of powerful techniques and data structures. The techniques must be applied to the right problems, on the right data. The virtuous cycle of data mining is an iterative learning process that builds on results over time. Success in using data will transform an organization from reactive to proactive. This is the virtuous cycle of data mining, used by the authors for extracting maximum benefit from the techniques described later in the book. Before explaining the virtuous cycle of data mining, take a look at a case study of data mining in practice.

A Case Study in Business Data Mining

Once upon a time, there was a bank with a business problem. One particular line of business, home equity lines of credit, was failing to attract enough good customers. There are several ways the bank could attack this problem.

The bank could, for instance, lower interest rates on home equity loans. This would bring in more customers and increase market share at the expense of lowered margins. Existing customers might switch to the lower rates, further depressing margins. Even worse, assuming that the initial rates were reasonably competitive, lowering the rates might bring in the worst customers — the disloyal. Competitors can easily lure them away with slightly better terms. The sidebar "Making Money or Losing Money" talks about the problems of retaining loyal customers.

MAKING MONEY OR LOSING MONEY?

Home equity loans generate revenue for banks from interest payments on the loans, but sometimes companies grapple with services that lose money.

As an example, Fidelity Investments once put its bill-paying service on the chopping block because this service consistently lost money. Some last-minute analysis saved it, by showing that Fidelity's most loyal and most profitable customers used the service. Although it lost money, Fidelity made much more money on these customers' other accounts. After all, customers that trust their financial institution to pay their bills have a very high level of trust in that institution. Cutting such value-added services may inadvertently exacerbate the profitability problem by causing the best customers to look elsewhere for better service.

Even products such as home equity loans offer a conundrum for some banks. A customer who owns a house and has a large amount of credit card debt is a good candidate for a home equity line-of-credit. This is good for the customer, because the line-of-credit usually has a much lower interest rate than the original credit card. Should the bank encourage customers to switch their debt from credit cards to home equity loans?

Continued

MAKING MONEY OR LOSING MONEY? *(continued)*

The answer is more complicated than it seems. In the short term, such a switch is good for the customer, precisely because it is bad for the bank: Less interest being paid by the customer means less revenue for the bank. Within the bank, such a switch also causes a problem. The credit card group may have worked hard to acquire a customer who would pay interest every month. That group doesn't want to lose its good customers.

On the other hand, switching the customer over may build a lifetime relationship that will include many car loans, mortgages, and investment products. When the focus is on the customer, the long-term view is sometimes more important, and it can conflict with short-term goals.

In this particular example, the bank was Bank of America (BofA), which was anxious to expand its portfolio of home equity loans after several direct mail campaigns yielded disappointing results. The National Consumer Assets Group (NCAG) decided to use data mining to attack the problem, providing a good introduction to the virtuous cycle of data mining. (The authors would like to thank Lounette Dyer, Larry Flynn, and Jerry Modes who worked on this problem and Larry Scroggins for allowing us to use material from a Bank of America case study.)

Identifying BofA's Business Challenge

BofA needed to do a better job of marketing home equity loans to customers. Using common sense and business consultants, it came up with these insights:

- People with college-age children want to borrow against their home equity to pay tuition bills.

- People with high but variable incomes want to use home equity to smooth out the peaks and valleys in their income.

These insights may or may not have been true. Nonetheless, marketing literature for the home equity line product reflected this view of the likely customer, as did the lists drawn up for telemarketing. These insights led to the disappointing results mentioned earlier.

Applying Data Mining

BofA worked with data mining consultants from Hyperparallel (then a data mining tool vendor that was subsequently absorbed into Yahoo!) to bring a range of data mining techniques to bear on the problem. There was no shortage of data. For many years, BofA had been storing data on its millions of retail customers in a large relational database on a powerful parallel computer from

Teradata. Data from 42 *systems of record* was cleansed, transformed, aligned, and then fed into the corporate data warehouse. With this system, BofA could see all the relationships each customer maintained with the bank.

This historical database was truly worthy of the name — some records dated back to 1914! More recent customer records had about 250 fields, including demographic fields such as income, number of children, and type of home, as well as internal data. These customer attributes were combined into a customer signature, which was then analyzed using Hyperparallel's data mining tools.

Decision trees (a technique discussed in Chapter 7) derived rules to classify existing bank customers as likely or unlikely to respond to a home equity loan offer. The decision tree, trained on thousands of examples of customers who had obtained the product and thousands who had not, eventually learned rules to tell the difference between them. After the rules were discovered, the resulting model was used to add yet another attribute to each prospect's record. This attribute, the "good prospect for home equity lines of credit flag" flag, was generated by a data mining model.

Next, a sequential pattern-finding technique (such as the one described in Chapter 15 on market basket analysis and sequential pattern analysis) was used to determine *when* customers were most likely to want a loan of this type. The goal of this analysis was to discover a sequence of events that had frequently preceded successful solicitations in the past.

Finally, a clustering technique (described in Chapter 13) was used to automatically segment the customers into groups with similar attributes. At one point, the tool found fourteen clusters of customers, many of which did not seem particularly interesting. Of these fourteen clusters, though, one had two intriguing properties:

- 39 percent of the people in the cluster had both business and personal accounts.

- This cluster accounted for more than a quarter of the customers who had been classified by the decision tree as likely responders to a home equity loan offer.

This result suggested to inquisitive data miners that people might be using home equity loans to start businesses.

Acting on the Results

With this new insight, NCAG (the business unit for home equity lines of credit) teamed with the Retail Banking Division and did what banks do in such circumstances: They sponsored market research to talk to customers. Four times a year, BofA would circulate a survey to the bank branches to find out what was actually happening on the frontline. With the knowledge gained from data mining, the bank had one more question to add to the list: "Will the proceeds of the loan be used to start a business?" The result from the data mining study was one question on an in-house survey.

The results from the survey confirmed the suspicions aroused by data mining. As a result, NCAG changed the message of its campaign from "use the value of your home to send your kids to college" to something more on the lines of "now that the house is empty, use your equity to do what you've always wanted to do."

Incidentally, market research and data mining are often used for similar ends — to gain a better understanding of customers. Although powerful, market research has some shortcomings:

- Responders may not be representative of the population as a whole. That is, the set of responders may be biased, particularly by the groups targeted by past marketing efforts (forming what is called an *opportunistic sample*).

- Customers (particularly dissatisfied customers and former customers) have little reason to be helpful or honest.

- Any given action may be the culmination of an accumulation of reasons. Banking customers may leave because a branch closed, the bank bounced a check, and they had to wait too long at ATMs. Market research may pick up only the proximate cause, although the sequence is more significant.

Despite these shortcomings, talking to customers and former customers provides insights that cannot be provided in any other way. This example with BofA shows that the two methods are compatible.

TIP When doing market research on existing customers, using data mining to take into account what is already known about them is a good idea.

Measuring the Effects of Data Mining

As a result of a marketing campaign focusing on a better message, the response rate for home equity campaigns increased from 0.7 percent to 7 percent. According to Dave McDonald, vice president of the group, the strategic implications of data mining are nothing short of the transformation of the retail side of the bank from a mass-marketing institution to a learning institution. "We want to get to the point where we are *constantly* executing marketing programs — not just quarterly mailings, but *programs* on a consistent basis." He has a vision of a closed-loop marketing process where operational data feeds a rapid analysis process that leads to program creation for execution and testing, which in turn generates additional data to rejuvenate the process. In short, the virtuous cycle of data mining.

Steps of the Virtuous Cycle

The BofA example shows the virtuous cycle of data mining in practice. Figure 1-1 shows the four stages:

1. Identifying business opportunities.
2. Mining data to transform the data into actionable information.
3. Acting on the information.
4. Measuring the results.

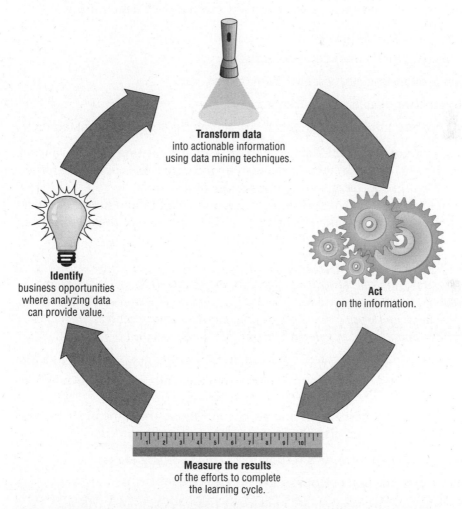

Figure 1-1: The virtuous cycle of data mining focuses on business results, rather than just exploiting advanced techniques.

As these steps suggest, the key to success is incorporating data mining into business processes and being able to foster lines of communication between the technical data miners and the business users of the results.

Identify Business Opportunities

The virtuous cycle of data mining starts by identifying the right business opportunities. Unfortunately, there are too many good statisticians and competent analysts whose work is essentially wasted because they are solving problems that don't help the business. Good data miners want to avoid this situation.

Avoiding wasted analytic effort starts with a willingness to act on the results. Many normal business processes are good candidates for data mining:

- Planning for a new product introduction
- Planning direct marketing campaigns
- Understanding customer attrition/churn
- Evaluating results of a marketing test
- Allocating marketing budgets to attract the most profitable customers

These are examples of where data mining can enhance existing business efforts, by allowing business managers to make more informed decisions — by targeting a different group, by changing messaging, and so on.

To avoid wasting analytic effort, it is also important to measure the impact of whatever actions are taken in order to judge the value of the data mining effort itself. As George Santayana said (in his full quote, of which only the last sentence is usually remembered):

> *Progress, far from consisting in change, depends on retentiveness. When change is absolute, there remains no being to improve and no direction set for possible improvement: and when experience is not retained, as among savages, infancy is perpetual. Those who do not learn from the past are condemned to repeat it.*

In the data mining context, this also applies: If you cannot measure the results of mining the data, then you cannot learn from the effort and there is no virtuous cycle.

Measurements of past efforts and ad hoc questions about the business also suggest data mining opportunities:

- What types of customers responded to the last campaign?
- Where do the best customers live?
- Are long waits at automated tellers a cause of customer attrition?
- Do profitable customers use customer support?
- What products should be promoted with Clorox bleach?

Interviewing business experts is another good way to get started. Because people on the business side may not be familiar with data mining, they may not understand how to act on the results. By explaining the value of data mining to an organization, such interviews provide a forum for two-way communication.

One of the authors once participated in a series of meetings at a telecommunications company to discuss the value of analyzing call detail records (records of completed calls made by each customer). During one meeting, the participants were slow in understanding how this could be useful. Then, a colleague pointed out that lurking inside their data was information on which customers used fax machines at home (the details of the resulting project are discussed in Chapter 16 on link analysis). This observation got the participants thinking. Click! Fax machine usage would be a good indicator of who was working from home. For the work-at-home crowd, the company already had a product bundle tailored for their needs. However, without prodding from the people who understood the data and the techniques, this marketing group would never have considered searching through data to find a work-at-home crowd. Joining the technical and the business highlighted a very valuable opportunity.

TIP When talking to business users about data mining opportunities, make sure they focus on the business problems and not on technology and algorithms. Let the technical experts focus on the technology and let the business experts focus on the business.

Transform Data into Information

Data mining, the focus of this book, transforms data into actionable results. Success is about making business sense of the data, not using particular algorithms or tools. Numerous pitfalls interfere with the ability to use the results of data mining:

- Bad data formats, such as not including the zip code in the customer address.
- Confusing data fields, such as a delivery date that means "planned delivery date" in one system and "actual delivery date" in another system.
- Lack of functionality, such as a call-center application that does not allow annotations on a per-customer basis.
- Legal ramifications, such as having to provide a legal reason when rejecting a loan (and "my neural network told me so" is not acceptable).
- Organizational factors, because some operational groups are reluctant to change their operations, particularly without incentives.
- Lack of timeliness, because results that come too late may no longer be actionable.

Data comes in many forms, in many formats, and from multiple systems, as shown in Figure 1-2. Identifying the right data sources and bringing them together are critical success factors. Every data mining project has data issues: inconsistent systems, table keys that don't match across databases, records overwritten every few months, and so on. Complaints about data are the number one excuse for not doing anything. Chapters 17, 18, and 19 discuss various issues involving data, starting with data warehousing and working through the transformations into a format suitable for data mining. The real question is, "What can be done with available data?" This is where the techniques described later in this book come in.

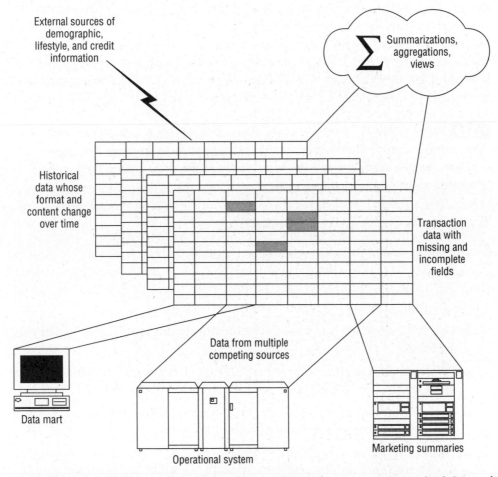

Figure 1-2: Data is never clean. It comes in many forms, from many sources both internal and external.

A wireless telecommunications company once wanted to put together a data mining group after having already acquired a powerful server and a data mining software package. At this late stage, the company contacted the authors to help investigate data mining opportunities. One opportunity became apparent. A key factor for customer attrition was overcalls: new customers using more minutes than allowed by their rate plan during their first month. Customers would learn about the excess usage when the first bill arrived — sometime during the middle of the second month. By that time, the customers had run up large bills for the second month as well as the first and were even more unhappy. Unfortunately, the customer service group also had to wait for the same billing cycle to detect the excess usage. There was no lead time to be proactive.

However, the nascent data mining group had resources and had identified and investigated the appropriate data feeds. With some relatively simple programming, the group was able to identify these customers within days of their first overcall. With this information, the customer service center could contact at-risk customers and move them onto appropriate billing plans even before the first bill went out. This simple system was a big win, and a showcase for data mining. Simply having a data mining group — with the skills, hardware, software, and access — was the enabling factor for putting together the appropriate triggers to save at-risk customers.

Act on the Information

Taking action is the purpose of the virtuous cycle of data mining. As already mentioned, action can take many forms. Data mining makes business decisions more informed. Over time, better-informed decisions should lead to better results.

Sometimes, the "action" is simply doing what would have been done anyway — but with more (or less) confidence that the action will work. Even this is a success for data mining, because reducing the level of worry is a good thing.

More typically, actions are in line with what the business is doing anyway:

- Incorporating results into automated recommendation systems, when customers appear online
- Sending messages to customers and prospects via direct mail, e-mail, telemarketing, and so on; with data mining, different messages may go to different people
- Prioritizing customer service
- Adjusting inventory levels
- And so on

The results of data mining must feed into business processes that touch customers and affect the customer relationship.

Measure the Results

The importance of measuring results has already been highlighted, although this is the stage in the virtuous cycle most likely to be overlooked. The value of measurement and continuous improvement is widely acknowledged, and yet less attention than it deserves, because it has no immediate return-on-investment. How many business cases are implemented without anyone going back to see how well reality matched the plans? Individuals improve their own efforts by comparing and learning, by asking questions about why plans match or do not match what really happened, and by being willing to learn when and how earlier assumptions were wrong. What works for individuals also works for organizations.

Commonly, marketing efforts are measured based on financial measures — and these are very important. However, modeling efforts should also be measured. Consider what happened once at a large Canadian bank that had a plan to cross-sell investment accounts to its customers. This marketing message was all over the bank: in television and radio advertisements, in posters in the branch, in messages printed on the back of ATM receipts, in messages while customers were on hold for customer service, and so on. Customers could not miss the messages.

This story, though, concerns a different channel, direct mail. A data mining effort identified customers most likely to respond to an investment campaign offer. A marketing campaign was designed and targeted at customers who were likely to respond. In this case, though, the bank included a special holdout group: This group was predicted to respond well, but did not receive the direct mail. (The sidebar "Data Mining and Marketing Tests" discusses this idea in more detail.) Holding out potential responders is a rather controversial action for the direct mail manager. The data miners are saying, "This is a group that we think will respond, but don't contact all of them; leave some out so we can learn from this test."

What was learned was quite worth the cost of not contacting some good customers. Among customers who scored high for the investment account offer, the same proportion opened accounts regardless of whether they received the offer or not. The model did, indeed, find customers who would open the accounts. However, the marketing test also found that the marketing communication was superfluous. Given all the other marketing efforts, this particular direct mail campaign was not needed.

The time to start thinking about measurement is at the beginning when identifying the business problem. How can results be measured? A company that sends out coupons to encourage sales of its products will no doubt measure the coupon redemption rate. However, coupon-redeemers may have purchased the product anyway. Another appropriate measure is increased sales in particular stores or regions, increases that can be tied to the particular marketing effort. Such measurements may be difficult to make, because they require more detailed sales information. However, if the goal is to increase sales, there needs to be a way to measure this directly or indirectly. Otherwise, marketing efforts may be all "sound and fury, signifying nothing."

DATA MINING AND MARKETING TESTS

Marketing tests are an important part of analytic marketing, as is data mining. The two often complement each other, and marketing tests are an important part of understanding whether data mining efforts are working. Typically two things should be tested when using data mining for a marketing treatment. First, is the marketing message working? Second, is the data mining modeling working?

The key is to use holdout groups intelligently to understand these two factors. In practice, four potential groups exist:

■ **Target Group:** Receives the treatment and has model scores indicating response.

■ **Control Group:** Receives the treatment and is chosen either at random or based on lower model scores.

■ **Holdout Group:** Does not receive the treatment and is chosen either at random or based on lower model scores.

■ **Modeled Holdout Group:** Does not receive the treatment and has model scores indicating response.

These four groups are indicated in the following figure:

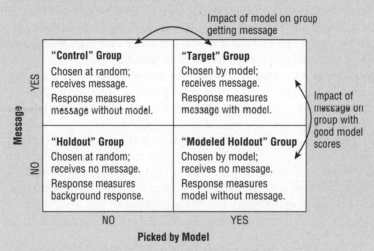

These four groups are used for measuring the effectiveness of both the message and the modeling effort.

The responses from these four groups then provide useful information. Using these groups for modeling is called *incremental response modeling* and is discussed in more detail in Chapter 5.

In the example where the Canadian bank learned that the direct mail effort was unnecessary, the response rates for the Modeled Holdout were the same as for the Target Group. This indicates that the treatment is not having an effect. The difference between the Target Group and the Control Group measures whether or not the modeling is working.

Continued

DATA MINING AND MARKETING TESTS *(continued)*

The following chart is an example from another bank that uses such charts to measure the effectiveness of its campaigns. This chart is the actual chart from the bank:

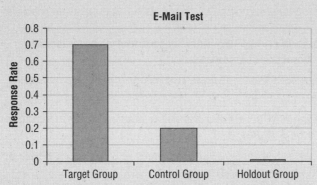

This chart readily shows the difference in response to determine whether the treatment works and whether the modeling works.

The first two bars show that the Target Group has a higher response rate than the Control Group, indicating that the modeling is working. The second two bars show that the Control Group has a higher response rate than the Holdout Group, indicating that the marketing treatment is working.

Just measuring these four groups is really the beginning of measuring the effectiveness of data mining. For instance, model scores are often broken into deciles. In such cases, it is important to include a sample from all deciles in the campaign to be sure that the model is working. Of course, everyone in the top deciles gets included in the effort (because this achieves the business goal). For the lower deciles, only a sample is included. The sample should be big enough to determine whether the deciles are really working — something that is quite important when using models. Chapter 4 explains the statistics background for determining the right size for such tests.

Standard reports, which may arrive weeks or months after marketing interventions have occurred, contain summaries. Marketing managers may not have the technical skills to glean important findings from such reports, even if the information is there. Understanding the impact on customer retention means tracking old marketing efforts for even longer periods of time. Well-designed reporting applications can be a big help for marketing groups and marketing analysts. However, for some questions, even more detail is needed.

Thinking of every marketing effort as a small business case is a good idea. Comparing expectations to actual results makes it possible to recognize promising opportunities to exploit on the next round of the virtuous cycle. You are often too busy tackling the next problem to devote energy to measuring the success of current efforts. This is a mistake. Every data mining effort, whether successful or not, has lessons that can be applied to future efforts. The question is what to measure and how to approach the measurement so it provides the best input for future use.

As an example, let's start with what to measure for a targeted acquisition campaign. The canonical measurement is the response rate: How many people targeted by the campaign actually responded? This leaves a lot of information lying on the table. For an acquisition effort that uses a model score (where a high score indicates a higher likelihood of response), some examples of questions that have future value are:

- Did this campaign reach and bring in profitable customers?
- Did a higher model score indicate a higher response rate?
- Were these customers retained as well as would be expected?
- What are the characteristics of the most loyal customers reached by this campaign?
- Did the newly acquired customers purchase additional products?
- Did some messages or offers work better than others?
- Did customers reached by the campaign respond through alternate channels?

All of these measurements provide information for making more informed decisions in the future. Data mining is about connecting the past — through learning — to future actions.

One particular measurement is *lifetime customer value*. As its name implies, this is an estimate of the value of a customer during the entire course of his or her relationship (or perhaps for some fixed period in the future, such as for the next two years). In some industries, quite complicated models have been developed to estimate lifetime customer value. Even without sophisticated models, shorter-term estimates, such as value after one month, six months, and one year, can prove to be quite useful. Customer value is discussed in more detail in the next chapter.

Data Mining in the Context of the Virtuous Cycle

Consider a large telecommunications company in the United States. Such a company has millions of customers. It owns hundreds or thousands of switches located in central offices, which are typically in several states in multiple time zones. Each switch can handle thousands of calls simultaneously — including advanced features such as call waiting, conference calling, call-forwarding, voice mail, and digital services. Switches, among the most complex computing devices yet developed, are available from a handful of manufacturers. A typical telephone company has multiple versions of several switches from each of the vendors. Each of these switches provides volumes of data in its own format on every call and attempted call — volumes measured in tens of gigabytes each day. In addition, each state has its own regulations affecting the industry, not to mention federal laws and regulations that are subject to rather frequent changes. To add to the confusion, the company offers thousands of different billing plans to its customers, which range from occasional residential users to Fortune 100 corporations.

How does this company — or any similar company with large volumes of data and large numbers of customers — manage its billing process, the bread and butter of its business, responsible for its revenue? The answer is simple: very carefully! Companies have developed detailed processes for handling standard operations; they have policies and procedures. These processes are robust. Bills go out to customers, even when the business reorganizes, even when database administrators are on vacation, even when computers are temporarily down, even as laws and regulations change, even when switches are upgraded, and when hurricanes strike. If an organization can manage a process as complicated as getting accurate bills out every month to millions of residential, business, and government customers, surely incorporating data mining into decision processes should be fairly easy. Is this the case?

Large companies have decades of experience developing and implementing mission-critical applications for running their business. Data mining is different from the typical operational system (see Table 1-1). The skills needed for running a successful operational system do not necessarily lead to successful data mining efforts.

Problems addressed by data mining differ from operational problems — *a data mining system does not seek to replicate previous results exactly*. In fact, replication of previous efforts can lead to disastrous results. It may result in marketing campaigns that target the same people over and over. You do not want to learn from analyzing data that a large cluster of customers fits the profile of the customers contacted in the previous campaign. Data mining processes need to take such issues into account, unlike typical operational systems that want to reproduce the same results over and over — whether completing a telephone call, sending a bill, authorizing a credit purchase, tracking inventory, or other countless daily operations.

Data mining is a creative process. Data contains many obvious correlations that are either useless or simply represent current business policies. For example,

Table 1-1: Data Mining Differs from Typical Operational Business Processes

TYPICAL OPERATIONAL SYSTEM	DATA MINING SYSTEM
Operations and reports on historical data	Analysis on historical data often applied to most current data to determine future actions
Predictable and periodic flow of work, typically tied to calendar	Unpredictable flow of work depending on business and marketing needs
Focus on individual items, one at a time (the needle in the haystack)	Focusing on larger groups at one time, trying to make sense of the haystack
Limited use of enterprise-wide data	The more data, the better the results (generally)
Focus on line of business (such as account, region, product code, minutes of use, and so on), not on customer	Focus on actionable entity, product, customer, sales region
Response times often measured in seconds/milliseconds (for interactive systems) while waiting weeks/month for reports	Iterative processes with response times often measured in minutes or hours
System of record for data	Copy of data
Descriptive and repetitive	Creative

analysis of data from one large retailer revealed that people who buy maintenance contracts are also very likely to buy large household appliances. Unless the retailer wanted to analyze the effectiveness of sales of maintenance contracts with appliances, such information is worse than useless because the maintenance contracts in question are only sold with large appliances. Spending millions of dollars on hardware, software, and data miners to find such results is a waste of resources that can better be applied elsewhere in the business. Analysts must understand what is of value to the business and how to arrange the data to bring out the nuggets.

Data mining results change over time. Models expire and become less useful as time goes on. One cause is that data ages quickly. Markets and customers change quickly as well.

Data mining provides feedback into other processes that may need to change. Decisions made in the business world often affect current processes and interactions with customers. Often, looking at data finds imperfections in operational systems, imperfections that should be fixed to enhance future customer understanding.

Lessons Learned

Data mining is an important part of customer relationship management. The goal of customer relationship management is to re-create, to the extent possible, the intimate learning relationship that a well-run small business enjoys with its customers. A company's interactions with its customers generate large volumes of data. This data is initially captured in transaction processing systems such as automatic teller machines, telephone switch records, and supermarket scanner files. The data can then be collected, cleaned, and summarized for inclusion in a customer data warehouse. A well-designed customer data warehouse contains a historical record of customer interactions that becomes the memory of the corporation. Data mining tools can be applied to this historical record to learn things about customers that will allow the company to serve them better in the future. This chapter presented several examples of commercial applications of data mining such as better targeted couponing, making recommendations, cross selling, customer retention, and credit risk reduction.

Data mining itself is the process of finding useful patterns and rules in large volumes of data. To be successful, data mining must become an integral part of a larger business process, *the virtuous cycle of data mining*.

The virtuous cycle of data mining is about harnessing the power of data and transforming it into actionable business results. Just as water once turned the wheels that drove machines throughout a mill, data must be gathered and disseminated throughout an organization to provide value. If data is water in this analogy, then data mining is the wheel, and the virtuous cycle spreads the power of the data to all the business processes.

The virtuous cycle of data mining is a learning process based on customer data. It starts by identifying the right business opportunities for data mining. The best business opportunities are those that will be acted upon. Without action, little or no value is to be gained from learning about customers. Also very important is measuring the results of the action. This completes the loop of the virtuous cycle, and often suggests further data mining opportunities.

The next chapter puts data mining in the context of customers themselves, starting with the customer lifecycle and following with several examples of the virtuous cycle in action.

Data Mining Applications in Marketing and Customer Relationship Management

Data mining techniques do not exist in a vacuum; they exist in a business context. Although the techniques are interesting in their own right, they are a means to an end. This chapter is about the business context.

The chapter starts with a description of the customer lifecycle and the business processes associated with each stage. Every stage of the customer lifecycle offers opportunities for customer relationship management and data mining, as described throughout the chapter. The customer lifecycle is a central theme because the business processes supported by data mining are organized around that lifecycle.

The business topics addressed in this chapter are presented in roughly ascending order of complexity of the customer relationship. This relationship starts with customers as prospects, moves through the established customer relationship, and ends with retention and winback. In the course of discussing the business applications, the chapter introduces technical material as appropriate, but the details of specific data mining techniques are left for later chapters.

Two Customer Lifecycles

The term *customer lifecycle* can refer to two different things — the customer's own personal lifecycle, or the lifecycle of the customer relationship. From a data mining point of view, the latter is usually more important.

The Customer's Lifecycle

Customers, whether they are individuals, households, or businesses, change over time. Startups become established firms. Some become takeover targets. Some continue to grow independently. Eventually, many fail. An individual's lifecycle is marked by life events, such as graduating from high school, having kids, getting a job, and so on.

These life stages are important for marketing and customer relationship management. Moving, for example, is a significant event. When people move, they might purchase new furniture, subscribe to the local paper, open a new bank account, and so on. Knowing who is moving is useful for targeting such individuals, especially for furniture dealers, newspapers, cable companies, and banks (among others), especially within a few days or weeks after the move. This is true for other life events as well, from graduating from high school and college, to getting married, having children, changing jobs, retiring, and so on. Understanding these life stages enables companies to define products and messages that resonate with particular groups of people.

Some businesses are organized around particular life stages. A bridal shop specializes in wedding gowns; such a business grows not because women get married more often, but through reputation and recommendations. Similarly, moving companies do not need to encourage their recent customers to relocate; they need to bring in new customers.

For most businesses, the customer's individual lifecycle is less important. In any case, managing customer relationships based on life stages is difficult, because:

- Identifying events in a timely manner is challenging.
- Many events are one-time, or very rare.
- Life-stage events are generally unpredictable and out of your control.

These shortcomings do not render them useless, by any means, because life stages provide a critical understanding of likely customer needs. However, most business processes are organized around a different lifecycle — the lifecycle of the customer relationship.

The Customer Lifecycle

The business relationship with a customer evolves over time. Although each business is different, the customer relationship places customers into five major phases, as shown in Figure 2-1:

- *Prospects* are in the target market, but are not yet customers.
- *Responders* are prospects who have exhibited some interest — for instance, by filling out an application or registering on a website.

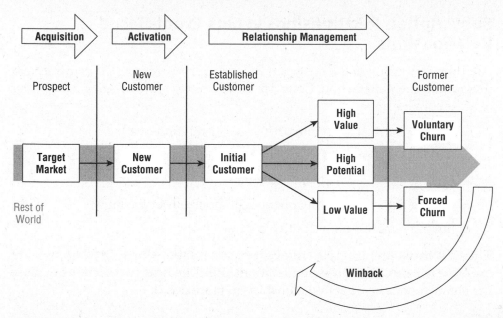

Figure 2-1: The customer lifecycle progresses through different stages.

- *New customers* are responders who have made a commitment, usually an agreement to pay, such as having made a first purchase, having signed a contract, or having registered at a site with some personal information.

- *Established customers* are those new customers who return, for whom the relationship is hopefully broadening or deepening.

- *Former customers* are those who have left, either as a result of voluntary attrition (because they have defected to a competitor or no longer see value in the product), forced attrition (because they have not paid their bills), or expected attrition (because they are no longer in the target market; for instance, because they have moved).

The precise definition of the phases depends on the business. For an e-media site, a prospect may be anyone on the Web; a responder, someone who has visited the site; a new customer, someone who has registered; and an established customer, a repeat visitor. Former customers are those who have not returned within some length of time that depends on the nature of the site. For other businesses, the definitions might be quite different. Life insurance companies, for instance, have a target market. Responders are those who fill out an application — and then often have their blood taken for blood tests. New customers are those applicants who are accepted, and established customers are those who pay their premiums for insurance payments.

Subscription Relationships versus Event-Based Relationships

Another dimension of the customer lifecycle relationship is the commitment inherent in each interaction. Consider the following ways of being a customer of a telephone company:

- Making a call at a payphone (if you can still find one!)
- Purchasing a prepaid telephone card for a set number of minutes
- Buying a prepaid mobile telephone
- Buying a postpay mobile phone with no fixed-term contract
- Buying a mobile phone with a contract

The first three are examples of event-based relationships. The last two are examples of subscription-based relationships. The next two sections explore the characteristics of these relationships in more detail.

> **TIP** An ongoing billing relationship is a good sign of an ongoing subscription relationship. Such ongoing customer relationships offer the opportunity for engaging in a dialog with customers in the course of business activities.

Event-Based Relationships

Event-based relationships are based on transactions. The customer may or may not return; tracking customers over time might be difficult or impossible. In the earlier examples, the telephone company may not have much information at all about the customer, especially when the customer pays in cash. Anonymous transactions still have information; however, clearly little opportunity exists for providing direct messages to customers who provide no contact information.

When event-based relationships predominate, companies usually communicate with prospects by broadcasting messages widely (for instance, advertising, Web ads, viral marketing, and the like) rather than targeting messages at specific individuals. In these cases, analytic work is very focused on product, geography, and time, because these are known about customers' transactions.

Broadcast advertising is not the only way to reach prospects. Couponing through the mail or on the Web is another way. Pharmaceutical companies in the United States have become adept at encouraging prospective customers to visit their websites for more information — while the company gathers a bit of information about them. Also, many companies employ the Web and social networking to communicate with otherwise anonymous customers.

Sometimes, event-based relationships imply a business-to-business relationship with an intermediary. Once again, pharmaceutical companies provide an example, because much of their marketing budget is spent on doctors, rather than on the patients who pay for the drugs.

Subscription-Based Relationships

Subscription-based relationships provide more natural opportunities for understanding customers. In the list given earlier, the last two examples all have ongoing billing relationships where customers have agreed to pay for a service over time. A subscription relationship offers the opportunity for future cash flow (the stream of future customer payments) and many opportunities for interacting with each customer.

Subscription-based relationships may take the form of a billing relationship, but they also might take the form of a retailing affinity card or a registration at a website. In some cases, the billing relationship is a subscription of some sort, which leaves little room to up-sell or cross-sell. A customer who has subscribed to a magazine may have little opportunity for an expanded relationship. There is *some* opportunity. The magazine customer could purchase a gift subscription or buy branded products. However, the future cash flow is pretty much determined by the current product mix.

In other cases, the ongoing relationship is just a beginning. A credit card company may send a bill every month; however, nothing charged, nothing owed. A long-distance provider may charge a customer every month, but it may only be for the monthly minimum. A cataloger sends catalogs to customers, but most will not make a purchase. In these examples, usage stimulation is an important part of the relationship.

The beginning and end of the relationship are the two key events for defining subscription-based relationships. When these events are well defined, then survival analysis (see Chapter 10) is a good candidate for understanding the duration of the relationship. However, sometimes defining the end of the relationship is difficult:

WARNING Defining the end of a customer relationship can be difficult. Different definitions produce different models and, at times, lead to different conclusions. Get agreement on when the relationship is considered over before defining a target variable.

- A credit card relationship may end when a customer has no balance and has made no transactions for a specified period of time (such as three months or six months).

- A catalog relationship may end when a customer has not purchased from the catalog in a specified period of time (such as 18 months).

- An affinity card relationship may end when a customer has not used the card for a specified period of time (such as 12 months).

Even when the relationship is well understood, there may be some tricky situations. Should the end date of the relationship be the date the customer calls to cancel or the date the account is closed? Should customers who fail to pay their last bill, after voluntarily requesting termination of service, be considered the same as customers who were stopped for nonpayment?

These situations are meant as guidelines for understanding the customer relationship. Figure 2-2 maps out different stages of the customer experience for the simple case of newspaper subscription customers. These customers basically have the following types of interactions:

- Starting the subscription via some channel
- Changing the product (weekday to seven-day, weekend to seven-day, seven-day to weekday, seven-day to weekend)
- Suspending delivery (typically for a vacation)
- Complaining
- Stopping the subscription (either voluntarily or involuntarily)

In a subscription-based relationship, understanding the customer over time is made possible by gathering all these disparate types of events into a single picture of the customer relationship.

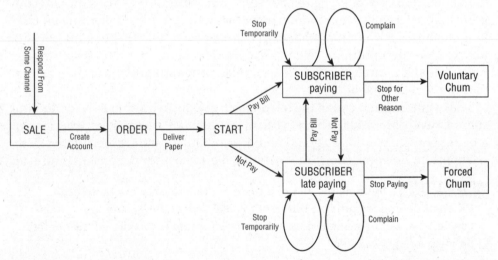

Figure 2-2: (Simplified) customer experience for newspaper subscribers includes several different types of interactions.

Organize Business Processes Around the Customer Lifecycle

Business processes move customers from one phase of the customer lifecycle to the next. These business processes are important because they lead to making customers more valuable over time. This section looks at these different processes and the role that data mining plays in them.

Customer Acquisition

Customer acquisition is the process of attracting prospects and turning them into customers. This is often done by advertising and word of mouth, as well as by targeted marketing. Data mining can and does play an important role in acquisition.

There are three important questions with regards to acquisition: Who are the prospects? When is a customer acquired? What is the role of data mining?

Who Are the Prospects?

Understanding prospects is important because messages should be targeted to the appropriate audience. One of the challenges of using historical data is that the prospect base may change over time:

- Geographic expansion brings in prospects, who may or may not be similar to customers in the original areas.

- Changes to products, services, and pricing may bring in different target audiences.

- Competition may change the prospecting mix.

These types of situations bring up the question: Will the past be a good predictor of the future? In most cases, the answer is "yes," but the past has to be used intelligently.

The following story is an example of the care that must be taken. One company in the New York area had a large customer base in Manhattan and was looking to expand into the suburbs. It had done direct mail campaigns focused on Manhattan, and built a model set derived from responders to these campaigns. What is important for this story is that Manhattan has a high concentration of neighborhoods with wealthy residents, so the model set was biased toward the wealthy. As expected, the responders were much wealthier than the prospects in surrounding areas. However, the non-responders were wealthier as well.

When the model was extended to areas outside Manhattan, what areas did the model choose? It chose a handful of the wealthiest neighborhoods, because people in these areas looked, demographically, like the responders in Manhattan. Although there were good prospects in these areas, the model missed many other pockets of potential customers, which were discovered through the use of control groups in the mailing — essentially random samples of names. The areas with high response rates were wealthy areas, but not as wealthy as the Manhattan neighborhoods used to build the model.

WARNING   Be careful when extending response models from one geographic area to another. The results may tell you more about similar demographics than about response.

When Is a Customer Acquired?

There is usually an underlying process for the acquisition of customers; the details of the process depend on the particular industry, but some general steps are as follows:

- Customers respond in some way and on some date. This is the "sale" date.
- In an account-based relationship, the account is created. This is the "account open date."
- The account is used in some fashion, and this is the "activation date" or "first purchase date."

Sometimes, all these things happen at the same time. Complications invariably occur — bad credit card numbers, misspelled addresses, buyer's remorse, and so on. The result is that several dates could be the acquisition date.

Assuming that all relevant dates are available, which is the best to use? That depends on the business need. After a direct mail drop or an e-mail blast, seeing the response curve to know when responses are expected to come in might be interesting, as shown in Figure 2-3. For this purpose, the sale date is the most important date, because it indicates customer behavior and the question is about customer behavior.

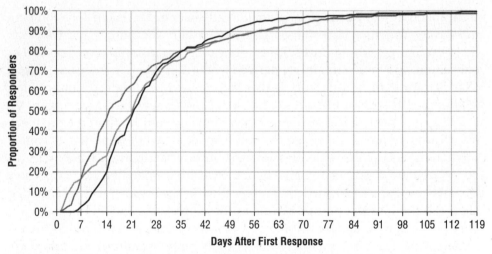

Figure 2-3: These response curves for three direct mail campaigns show that 80 percent of the responses came within five to six weeks.

A different question might have a different answer. To compare response rates of different groups, for instance, the account open date might be more important. Prospects who register a "sale" but whose account never opens should be excluded from such an analysis.

What Is the Role of Data Mining?

Available data limits the role that data mining can play. Response modeling is used for channels such as direct mail and telemarketing, where the cost of contact is relatively high. The goal is to limit the contacts to prospects that are more likely respond and become good customers. Data available for such endeavors falls into three categories:

- Source of prospect
- Appended individual/household data
- Appended demographic data at a geographic level (typical census block or census block group)

The purpose here is to discuss prospecting from the perspective of data mining.

A good place to begin is with an outline of a typical acquisition strategy. Companies that use e-mail, direct mail, or outbound telemarketing purchase lists. Some lists are historically very good, so they would be used in their entirety. For other lists, modeling might be used to determine which prospects to contact. A model might be based on appended demographics, when such demographics are available at the household level. When such demographics are not available, neighborhood demographics might be used instead in a different set of models.

The *echo effect* (also called the halo effect) is a challenge in building data mining models for acquisition. Prospects may be reached by one channel but respond through another. A company sends a group of prospects an e-mail message. Instead of clicking on the link in the e-mail, some respondents might call. Prospects may receive an advertising message or direct mail, yet respond through the website. Or an advertising campaign may encourage responses through several different channels at the same time. Figure 2-4 shows an example of the echo effect, as shown by the correlation between two channels, inbound calls, and direct mail.

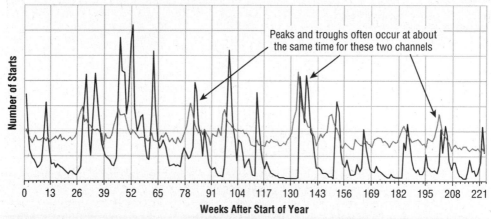

Figure 2-4: The echo effect may artificially under- or overestimate the performance of channels, because customers inspired by one channel may be attributed to another.

Customer Activation

The activation process may be as simple as a customer filling out a registration form on a website. Or, it might involve a more lengthy approval process, such as a credit check. Or, it could be even more onerous, as in the example of life insurance companies who require an underwriting exam before setting rates. In general, activation is an operational process, more focused on business needs than analytic needs.

As an operational process, customer activation may seem to have little to do with data mining. Activation provides a view of new customers at the point when they start. This perspective is very important, and as a data source, it needs to be preserved. Both the initial conditions and subsequent changes are of interest.

TIP Customer activation provides the initial conditions of the customer relationship. Such initial conditions are often useful predictors of long-term customer behavior.

The process of activation is often depicted as a funnel as shown in Figure 2-5, although a stack of strainers might be a more apt metaphor. Everything poured into the top of a funnel eventually comes out the bottom; the same is not true of prospects.

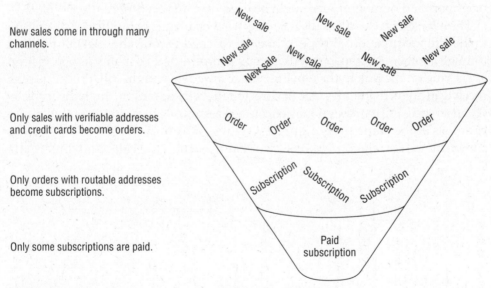

New sales come in through many channels.

Only sales with verifiable addresses and credit cards become orders.

Only orders with routable addresses become subscriptions.

Only some subscriptions are paid.

Figure 2-5: The customer activation process funnel eliminates responders at each step of the activation process.

The figure illustrates the activation process for home-delivery subscribers of a newspaper. It has the following steps:

1. *The Sale.* A prospect shows interest in getting a subscription, by providing address and payment information, either on the Web, on a call, or on a mail-in response card.

2 *The Order*. An account is created, which includes a preliminary verification on the address and payment information.

3. *The Subscription*. The paper is actually physically delivered, requiring further verification of the address and special delivery instructions.

4. *The Paid Subscription*. The customer pays for the paper.

Each of these steps loses some customers, perhaps only a few percent, or perhaps more. For instance, credit cards may be invalid, have improper expiration dates, or not match the delivery address. The customer may live outside the delivery region. The deliverers may not understand special delivery instructions. The address may be in an apartment building that does not allow access. Most of these are operational considerations (the exception is whether or not the customer pays), and they illustrate the kinds of operational concerns and processes involved with customer activation.

Data mining can play a role in understanding whether or not customers are moving through the process the way they should be — or what characteristics cause a customer to fail during the activation stage. These results can help improve operational processes. They can also provide guidance during acquisition, by highlighting strategies that bring in sales that are not converted to paid subscriptions.

For Web-related businesses, customer activation is usually, although not always, an automatic process that takes little time. When it works well, there is no problem. Despite the brief duration of the activation phase, it is a critical part of the customer acquisition process. When it fails, potentially valuable customers are kept away.

Customer Relationship Management

The primary goal of customer relationship management is to increase the customer's value. This usually entails the following activities:

Up-selling. Having the customer buy premium products and services.

Cross-selling. Broadening the customer relationship, such as having customers buy CDs, plane tickets, and cars, in addition to books.

Usage stimulation. Ensuring that the customer comes back for more; for example, by ensuring that customers see more ads or use their credit card for more purchases.

Customer value calculation. Assigning a future expected value to each customer.

A danger for companies that offer many products and services is failing to get the right message across. Customers do not necessarily want choice; customers may want simplicity. Making customers find the one thing that interests them in a barrage of marketing communication does a poor job of getting the message across. For this reason, it is useful to focus messages to each customer on a small number of products that are likely to be of interest. Of course, each customer has a different potential set. Data mining plays a key role in finding these affinities.

Data mining can also play a role in understanding the operational side of the business. Chapter 21 contains a case study of how a large satellite TV provider combined structured and unstructured call center data to spot a performance problem with one of its operational systems. Calls on certain topics, as determined by mining the comment text, were taking too long to resolve. The problem was not with the service representatives, but with an unresponsive system used to resolve a particular family of problems.

Perhaps the single most important part of customer relationship management is retaining customers. This is one of the areas where predictive modeling is applied most often. There are two approaches for looking at customer retention. The first is to compare customers who left after a short time with customers who had long tenures. The second approach is survival analysis (see Chapter 10), which models customer tenure directly.

Winback

Even after customers have left, there is still the possibility that they can be lured back. Winback tries to do just that, by providing valuable former customers with incentives, products, and pricing promotions.

Winback tends to depend more on operational strategies than on data analysis, but data mining may play a role in determining why customers left, particularly when customer service complaints and other behavioral data can be incorporated into model sets. Chapter 21 has a case study on identifying customers who leave a media company due to a boycott. Clearly, the winback strategy for these customers is different from the winback strategy for other customers.

Some companies have specialized "save teams." Customers cannot leave without talking to a person who is trained in trying to retain them. In addition to saving customers, save teams also do a good job of tracking the reasons why customers leave — information that can be very valuable to future customer retention efforts.

Trying to lure back disgruntled customers is quite hard. The more important effort is trying to keep them in the first place with competitive products, attractive offers, and useful services.

Data Mining Applications for Customer Acquisition

For most businesses, relatively few of Earth's seven billion or so people are actually prospects. Most can be excluded based on geography, age, ability to pay, language, or need for the product or service. A bank offering home equity lines of credit would naturally restrict offers of this type to homeowners who reside in jurisdictions where the bank is licensed to operate. A company selling backyard swing sets would like to reach households with children at addresses that seem likely to have backyards. A magazine targets people who read the appropriate language and will be of interest to its advertisers.

Data mining can play many roles in prospecting. The most important of these are:

- Identifying good prospects
- Choosing a communication channel for reaching prospects
- Picking appropriate messages for different groups of prospects

Although all of these are important, the first — identifying good prospects — is the most widely implemented.

Identifying Good Prospects

The simplest definition of a good prospect — and the one used by many companies — is someone who might at least express interest in becoming a customer. More sophisticated definitions are more choosey. Truly good prospects are not only *interested* in becoming customers; they can afford to become customers, they will be profitable to have as customers, they are unlikely to defraud the company and likely to pay their bills, and if treated well, they will be loyal customers and recommend others. No matter how simple or sophisticated the definition of a prospect, the first task is finding them.

Targeting is important whether the message is to be conveyed through advertising or through more direct channels such as mailings, telephone calls, or e-mail. Even messages on billboards are targeted to some degree; billboards for airlines and rental car companies tend to be found next to highways that lead to airports where people who use these services are likely to be among those driving by.

To apply data mining, first define what it means to be a good prospect and then find rules that allow people with those characteristics to be targeted. For many companies, the first step toward using data mining to identify good prospects is building a response model. Later in this chapter is an extended discussion of response models, the various ways they are employed, and what they can and cannot do.

Choosing a Communication Channel

Prospecting requires communication. Broadly speaking, companies intentionally communicate with prospects in several ways. One way is through public relations, which refers to encouraging media to cover stories about the company and spreading positive messages by word of mouth. Although highly effective for some companies (such as Facebook, Google, and eBay), public relations are not directed marketing messages. Even here, data mining can help, as explained in the section on sentiment analysis in Chapter 21.

Of more interest, from a data mining perspective, are advertising and direct marketing. Advertising can mean anything from matchbook covers to ad words, sponsored links on commercial websites to television spots during major sporting events to product placements in movies. In this context, advertising targets groups of people based on common traits; however, many advertising media do not make it possible to customize messages to individuals.

Picking Appropriate Messages

Even when selling the same basic product or service, different messages are appropriate for different people. A classic example is the trade-off between price and convenience. Some people are very price sensitive, and willing to shop in warehouses, make their phone calls late at night, and always change planes to get a better deal. Others will pay a premium for the most convenient service. A message based on price will not only fail to motivate the convenience seekers, it runs the risk of steering them toward less profitable products when they would be happy to pay more.

A Data Mining Example: Choosing the Right Place to Advertise

One way of targeting prospects is to look for people who resemble current customers. Through surveys, one nationwide publication determined that its readers have the following characteristics:

- 59 percent of readers are college educated.
- 46 percent have professional or executive occupations.
- 21 percent have household income in excess of $75,000/year.
- 7 percent have household income in excess of $100,000/year.

Understanding this profile helps the publication in two ways: First, by targeting prospects who match the profile, it can increase the rate of response to its own promotional efforts. Second, this well-educated, high-income readership can be used to sell advertising space in the publication to companies wanting to reach such an audience.

Because the theme of this section is targeting prospects, let's look at how the publication used the profile to sharpen the focus of its prospecting efforts. The basic idea is simple. When the publication wants to advertise on radio, it should look for stations whose listeners match the profile. When it wants to place billboards, it should do so in neighborhoods that match the profile. When it wants to do outbound telemarketing, it should call people who match the profile. The data mining challenge was to come up with a good definition of what it means to match the profile.

Who Fits the Profile?

One way of determining whether a customer fits a profile is to measure the similarity — also called distance — between a customer and the profile. The data consists of survey results that represent a snapshot of subscribers at a particular time. What sort of measure makes sense with this data? What should be done about the fact that the profile is expressed in terms of percentages (58 percent are college educated; 7 percent make over $100,000), whereas an individual either is or is not college educated and either does or does not make more than $100,000?

Consider two survey participants. Amy is college educated, earns $80,000/year, and is a professional. Bob is a high-school graduate earning $50,000/year. Which one is a better match to the readership profile? The answer depends on how the comparison is made. Table 2-1 shows one way to develop a score using only the profile and a simple distance metric.

Table 2-1: Calculating Fitness Scores for Individuals by Comparing Them along Each Demographic Measure

	READER-SHIP	YES SCORE	NO SCORE	AMY	BOB	AMY SCORE	BOB SCORE
College educated	58%	0.58	0.42	YES	NO	0.58	0.42
Prof or exec	46%	0.46	0.54	YES	NO	0.46	0.54
Income >$75K	21%	0.21	0.79	YES	NO	0.21	0.79
Income >$100K	7%	0.07	0.93	NO	NO	0.93	0.93
Total						2.18	2.68

This table calculates a score based on the proportion of the audience that agrees with each characteristic. For instance, because 58 percent of the readership is college educated, Amy gets a score of 0.58 for this characteristic. Bob, who did not graduate from college, gets a score of 0.42 because the other 42 percent of the readership presumably did not graduate from college. This is continued for each characteristic, and the scores are added together. Amy ends with a score of 2.18 and Bob with the higher score of 2.68. His higher score reflects the fact that he is more similar to the profile of current readers than is Amy.

The problem with this approach is that while Bob looks more like the profile than Amy does, Amy looks more like the audience the publication really targets — namely, college-educated, higher-income individuals. The success of this targeting is evident from a comparison of the readership profile with the demographic characteristics of the U.S. population as a whole.

Compared to the overall population, the readership is better educated, more professional, and better paid. In Table 2-2, the "Index" columns compare the readership's characteristics to the entire population by dividing the percent of the readership that has a particular attribute by the percent of the population that has it. The readership is almost three times more likely to be college educated than the population as a whole. Similarly, they are only about half as likely not to be college educated. By using the indexes as scores for each characteristic, Amy gets a score of 8.42 (2.86 + 2.40 + 2.21 + 0.95) versus Bob with a score of only 3.02 (0.53 + 0.67 + 0.87 + 0.95). The scores based on indexes correspond much better with the publication's target audience. The new scores make more sense because they now incorporate the additional information about how the target audience differs from the U.S. population as a whole.

Table 2-2: Calculating Scores by Taking the Proportions in the Population into Account

	YES			NO		
	READERSHIP	**U.S. POP.**	**INDEX**	**READERSHIP**	**U.S. POP.**	**INDEX**
College educated	58%	20.3%	2.86	42%	79.7%	0.53
Professional or executive	46%	19.2%	2.40	54%	80.8%	0.67
Income >$75K	21%	9.5%	2.21	79%	90.5%	0.87
Income >$100K	7%	2.4%	2.92	93%	97.6%	0.95

DATA BY CENSUS TRACT

The U.S. government is constitutionally mandated to carry out an enumeration of the population every 10 years. The primary purpose of the census is to allocate seats in the House of Representatives to each state. In the process of satisfying this mandate, the census also provides a wealth of information about the American population.

Even in non-census years, the U.S. Census Bureau (www.census.gov) surveys the American population using questionnaires containing detailed questions about income, occupation, commuting habits, spending patterns, and more. The responses to these questionnaires provide the basis for demographic profiles.

The Census Bureau does not release information about individuals. Instead, it aggregates the information by small geographic areas. The most commonly used is the *census tract*, consisting of about 4,000 individuals on average. Although census tracts do vary in size, they are much more consistent in population than other geographic units, such as counties and zip codes.

The census does have smaller geographic units, *blocks* and *block groups*; to protect the privacy of residents, some data is not made available below the level of census tracts. From these units, it is possible to aggregate information by county, state, metropolitan statistical area (MSA), legislative districts, and so on. The following figure shows some census tracts in the center of Manhattan:

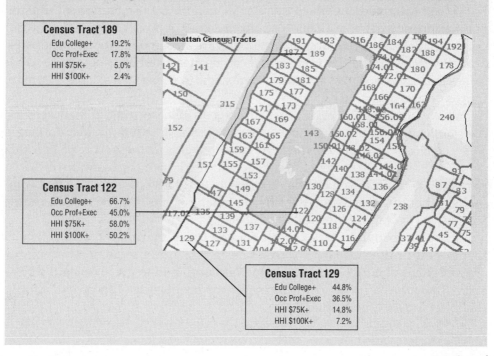

Continued

DATA BY CENSUS TRACT *(continued)*

One philosophy of marketing is based on the old proverb "birds of a feather flock together." People with similar interests and tastes live in similar areas (whether voluntarily or because of historical patterns of discrimination). According to this philosophy, marketing to people where you already have customers and in similar areas is a good idea. Census information can be valuable, both for understanding where concentrations of customers are located and for determining the profile of similar areas.

TIP When comparing customer profiles, keeping in mind that the profile of the population as a whole is important. For this reason, using indexes is often better than using raw values.

Measuring Fitness for Groups of Readers

The idea behind index-based scores can be extended to larger groups of people. This is important because the particular characteristics used for measuring the population may not be available for each customer or prospect. Fortunately, and not by accident, the preceding characteristics are all demographic characteristics available through the U.S. Census and can be measured by geographical divisions such as census tract, zip code, county, and state (see the sidebar, "Data by Census Tract").

The goal is to assign each census tract a score according to its fitness for the publication. For instance, if a census tract has an adult population that is 58 percent college educated, then everyone in it gets a fitness score of 1 for this characteristic. If 100 percent are college educated, then the score is still 1 — a perfect fit is the best you can do. If, however, only 5.8 percent graduated from college, then the fitness score for this characteristic is 0.1. The overall fitness score is the average of the individual scores.

Figure 2-6 provides an example for the three Manhattan census tracts mentioned in the sidebar. Each tract has a different proportion of the four characteristics being considered, which is combined to get an overall fitness score for each tract. The score represents the proportion of the population in that tract that fits the profile.

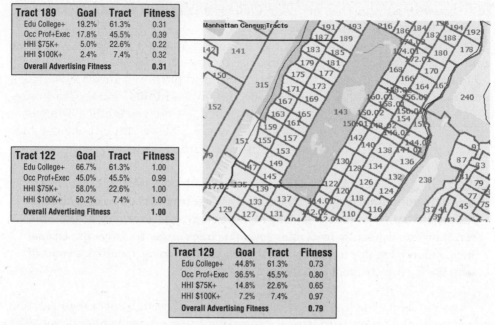

Tract 189	Goal	Tract	Fitness
Edu College+	19.2%	61.3%	0.31
Occ Prof+Exec	17.8%	45.5%	0.39
HHI $75K+	5.0%	22.6%	0.22
HHI $100K+	2.4%	7.4%	0.32
Overall Advertising Fitness			**0.31**

Tract 122	Goal	Tract	Fitness
Edu College+	66.7%	61.3%	1.00
Occ Prof+Exec	45.0%	45.5%	0.99
HHI $75K+	58.0%	22.6%	1.00
HHI $100K+	50.2%	7.4%	1.00
Overall Advertising Fitness			**1.00**

Tract 129	Goal	Tract	Fitness
Edu College+	44.8%	61.3%	0.73
Occ Prof+Exec	36.5%	45.5%	0.80
HHI $75K+	14.8%	22.6%	0.65
HHI $100K+	7.2%	7.4%	0.97
Overall Advertising Fitness			**0.79**

Figure 2-6: Example of calculating readership fitness for three census tracts in Manhattan.

Data Mining to Improve Direct Marketing Campaigns

Advertising can be used to reach prospects about whom nothing is known as individuals. Direct marketing requires at least a tiny bit of additional information such as a name and address or a phone number or e-mail address. Where there is more information, there are more opportunities for data mining. At the most basic level, data mining can be used to improve targeting by selecting which people to contact.

The first level of targeting does not require data mining, only data. In the United States, quite a bit of data is available about the population. In many countries, companies compile and sell household-level data on all sorts of things including income, number of children, education level, and even hobbies. Some of this data is collected from public records. Home purchases, marriages, births, and deaths are matters of public record that can be gathered from county courthouses and registries of deeds. Other data is gathered from product registration forms. Some is imputed using models.

The rules governing the use of this data for marketing purposes vary from country to country. In some, data can be sold by address, but not by name. In others data may be used only for certain approved purposes. In some countries, data may be used with few restrictions, but only a limited number of households are covered. In the United States, some data, such as medical records, is completely off limits. Some data, such as credit history, can only be used for certain approved purposes. Much of the rest is unrestricted.

WARNING   The United States is unusual in both the extent of commercially available household data and the relatively few restrictions on its use. Although household data is available in many countries, the rules governing its use differ. There are especially strict rules governing transborder transfers of personal data. Before planning to use household data for marketing, familiarize yourself with the legal restrictions on making use of it.

Household-level data can be used directly for a first rough cut of segmentation based on such things as income, car ownership, or presence of children. The problem is that even after the obvious filters have been applied, the remaining pool can be very large relative to the number of prospects likely to respond. Thus, a principal application of data mining is targeting — finding the prospects most likely to actually respond to an offer.

Response Modeling

Direct marketing campaigns typically have response rates measured in the low single digits. Response models are used to improve response rates by identifying prospects who are more likely to respond to a direct solicitation. The most useful response models provide an actual estimate of the likelihood of response, but this is not a strict requirement. Any model that allows prospects to be ranked by likelihood of response is sufficient. Given a ranked list, direct marketers can increase the percentage of responders reached by campaigns by mailing or calling people near the top of the list.

The following sections describe several ways that model scores can be used to improve direct marketing. This discussion is independent of the data mining techniques used to generate the scores. Many of the data mining techniques in this book can and have been applied to response modeling.

According to the Direct Marketing Association, an industry group, a typical mailing of 100,000 pieces costs about $100,000 dollars, although the price can vary considerably depending on the complexity of the mailing. Of that, some of the costs, such as developing the creative content, preparing the artwork, and initial setup for printing, are independent of the size of the mailing. The rest of the cost varies directly with the number of pieces mailed. Mailing lists of known mail order responders or active magazine subscribers can be purchased on a price-per-thousand-names basis. Mail shop production costs and postage are charged on a similar basis. The larger the mailing, the less important the fixed costs become. For ease of calculation, the examples in this chapter assume that the cost to reach one person with a direct mail campaign is one dollar. This is not an unreasonable estimate, although simple mailings cost less and fancy mailings cost more.

Optimizing Response for a Fixed Budget

The simplest way to make use of model scores is to use them to assign ranks. After prospects have been ranked by a propensity-to-respond score, the prospect list can be sorted so that those most likely to respond are at the top of the list and those least likely to respond are at the bottom. Many modeling techniques can be used to generate response scores, including regression models, decision trees, and neural networks.

Sorting a list makes sense whenever there is neither time nor budget to reach all prospects. If some people must be left out, leave out the ones who are least likely to respond. Not all businesses feel the need to leave out prospects. A local cable company may consider every household in its town to be a prospect and it may have the capacity to contact all households several times a year. When the marketing plan calls for making offers to every prospect, there is not much need for response modeling! However, data mining may still be useful for selecting the proper messages and to predict how prospects are likely to behave as customers.

A more likely scenario is that the marketing budget does not allow the same level of engagement with every prospect. Consider a company with one million names on its prospect list and $300,000 to spend on a marketing campaign that has a cost of one dollar per contact. This company, the Simplifying Assumptions Corporation (or SAC for short), can maximize the number of responses it gets for its $300,000 expenditure by scoring the prospect list with a response model and sending its offer to the prospects with the top 300,000 scores, as illustrated in Figure 2-7.

The upper, curved line plots the *concentration*, the percentage of all responders captured as more and more of the prospects are included in the campaign. The straight diagonal line is there for comparison. It represents what happens with no model so the concentration does not vary as a function of *penetration*, the percentage of prospects contacted. Mailing to 30 percent of the prospects chosen at random would find 30 percent of the responders. With the model, mailing to the top 30 percent of prospects finds 65 percent of the responders. The ratio of concentration to penetration is the lift. The difference between these two lines is the *benefit*. Benefit and lift are discussed in a sidebar.

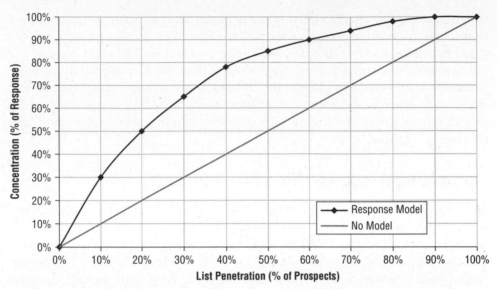

Figure 2-7: A cumulative gains or concentration chart shows the benefit of using a model.

The model pictured here has lift of 2.17 at the third decile. Using the model, SAC will get twice as many responders for its expenditure of $300,000 than it would get by randomly contacting 30 percent of its prospects.

BENEFIT AND LIFT

Cumulative gains charts, such as the one shown in Figure 2-7, are usually discussed in terms of lift. Lift measures the relationship of concentration to penetration. If 10% of responders are in the population, but 20% are in a group picked by a model, the lift is 2. Lift is a useful way of comparing the performance of two models at a given depth in the prospect list. However, it fails to capture another concept that seems intuitively important when looking at the chart — namely, how far apart are the lines, and at what penetration are they farthest apart?

The statistician Will Potts gives the name *benefit* to the difference between concentration and penetration. Using his nomenclature, the point where this difference is maximized is the *point of maximum benefit.* Note that the point of maximum benefit does not correspond to the point of highest lift. Typically, lift is maximized at the left edge of the concentration chart where the concentration is highest and the slope of the curve is steepest.

The maximum benefit is proportional to the maximum distance between the cumulative distribution functions of the probabilities in each class.

The model score that cuts the prospect list at the penetration where the benefit is greatest is also the score that maximizes the Kolmogorov-Smirnov (KS) statistic. The KS test is popular among some statisticians, especially in the financial services industry. It was developed as a test of whether two distributions are different. Splitting the list at the point of maximum benefit results in a "good list" and a "bad list" whose distributions of responders are maximally separate from each other. In this case, the "good list" has a maximum proportion of responders and the "bad list" has a minimum proportion.

The maximum benefit point on the concentration curve corresponds to the maximum perpendicular distance between the corresponding ROC curve and the no-model line.

The ROC curve, described more fully in Chapter 5, resembles the more familiar concentration or cumulative gains chart, so it is not surprising that there is a relationship between them. The ROC curve shows the trade-off between two types of misclassification error. The maximum benefit point on the cumulative gains chart corresponds to a point on the ROC curve where the separation between the classes is maximized.

The maximum benefit point corresponds to the decision rule that maximizes the unweighted average of sensitivity and specificity.

As used in the medical world, *sensitivity* measures the likelihood that a diagnosis based on the test is correct. It is the proportion of true positives among people who get a positive result on a test. In other words, it is the true positives divided by the sum of the true positives and false positives. *Specificity* is the proportion of true negatives among people who get a negative result on the test. A good test should be both sensitive and specific. The maximum benefit point is the cutoff that maximizes the average of these two measures.

The maximum benefit point corresponds to a decision rule that minimizes the expected loss assuming the misclassification costs are inversely proportional to the prevalence of the target classes.

One way of evaluating classification rules is to assign a cost to each type of misclassification and compare rules based on that cost. Whether they represent responders, defaulters, fraudsters, or people with a particular disease, the rare cases are generally the most interesting so missing one of them is more costly than misclassifying one of the common cases. Under that assumption, the maximum benefit picks a good classification rule.

Optimizing Campaign Profitability

There is no doubt that doubling the response rate to a campaign is a desirable outcome, but how much is it actually worth? Is the campaign even profitable? Although lift is a useful way of comparing models, it does not answer these important questions. To address profitability, more information is needed. In particular, calculating profitability requires information on revenues as well as costs. Let's add a few more details to the SAC example.

The Simplifying Assumptions Corporation sells a single product for a single price. The price of the product is $100. The total cost to SAC to manufacture, warehouse, and distribute the product is $55. As already mentioned, it costs $1 to reach a prospect. There is now enough information to calculate the value of a response. The gross value of each response is $100. The net value of each response takes into account the costs associated with the response ($55 for the cost of goods and $1 for the contact) to achieve net revenue of $44 per response. This information is summarized in Table 2-3.

Table 2-3: Profit/Loss Matrix for the Simplifying Assumptions Corporation

MAILED	RESPONDED	
	YES	NO
YES	$44	−$1
NO	$0	$0

This table says that if a prospect is contacted and responds, the company makes $44. If a prospect is contacted, but fails to respond, the company loses $1. In this simplified example, there is neither cost nor benefit in choosing not to contact a prospect. A more sophisticated analysis might take into account the fact that there is an opportunity cost to not contacting prospects who would have responded, that even non-responders may become better prospects as a result of the contact through increased brand awareness, and that responders may have a higher lifetime value than is indicated by the single purchase.

This simple profit and loss matrix can be used to translate the response to a campaign into a profit figure. Ignoring campaign overhead fixed costs, if one prospect responds for every 44 who fail to respond, the campaign breaks even. If the response rate is better than that, the campaign is profitable.

WARNING   If the cost of a failed contact is set too low, the profit and loss matrix suggests contacting everyone. This may not be a good idea for other reasons. It could lead to prospects being bombarded with inappropriate offers.

A more sophisticated analysis of campaign profitability takes account of the startup cost for the campaign, the underlying prevalence of responders in the population, and the cutoff penetration of people contacted. Recall that SAC had a budget of $300,000. Assume that the underlying prevalence of responders in population is 1 percent. The budget is enough to contact 300,000 prospects, or 30 percent of the prospect pool. At a depth of 30 percent, the model provides lift of about 2, so SAC can expect twice as many responders as it would have without the model. In this case, twice as many means 2 percent instead of 1 percent, yielding 6,000 (2% × 300,000) responders, each of whom is worth $44 in net revenue. Under these assumptions, SAC grosses $600,000 and nets $264,000 from responders. Meanwhile, 98 percent of prospects or 294,000 do not respond. Each of these costs a dollar, so SAC loses $30,000 on the campaign.

Table 2-4 shows the data used to generate the cumulative gains chart in Figure 2-7. It suggests that the campaign could be made profitable by spending less money to contact fewer prospects while getting a better response rate. Mailing to only 10,000 prospects, or the top 10 percent of the prospect list, achieves a lift of 3. This turns the underlying response rates of 1 percent into a response rate of 3 percent. In this scenario, 3,000 people respond, yielding revenue of $132,000. Now 97,000 people fail to respond and each of them costs one dollar. The resulting profit is $35,000. Better still, SAC has $200,000 left in the marketing budget to use on another campaign or to improve the offer made in this one, perhaps increasing response still more.

Table 2-4: Lift and Cumulative Gains by Decile

PENETRATION	GAINS	CUMULATIVE GAINS	LIFT
0%	0%	0%	0.000
10%	30%	30%	3.000
20%	20%	50%	2.500
30%	15%	65%	2.167
40%	13%	78%	1.950
50%	7%	85%	1.700
60%	5%	90%	1.500
70%	4%	94%	1.343
80%	4%	96%	1.225
90%	2%	100%	1.111
100%	0%	100%	1.000

A smaller, better-targeted campaign can be more profitable than a larger, more expensive one. Lift increases as the list gets smaller, so is smaller always better? The answer is no because the absolute revenue decreases as the number of responders decreases. As an extreme example, assume the model can generate lift of 100 by finding a group with 100 percent response rate when the underlying response rate is 1 percent. That sounds fantastic, but if only 10 people are in the group, it is still only worth $440. Also, a more realistic example would include some up-front fixed costs. Figure 2-8 shows what happens with the assumption that the campaign has a fixed cost of $20,000 in addition to the cost of $1 per contact, revenue of $44 per response, and an underlying response rate of 1 percent. The campaign is only profitable for a small range of file penetrations around 10 percent.

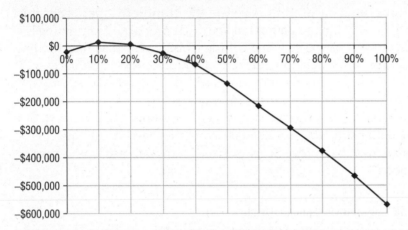

Figure 2-8: Campaign profitability as a function of penetration.

Using the model to optimize the profitability of a campaign seems more attractive than simply using it to pick whom to include on a mailing or call list of predetermined size, but the approach is not without pitfalls. For one thing, the results are dependent on the campaign cost, the response rate, and the revenue per responder, none of which are known prior to running the campaign. In real life, these can only be estimated. A small variation in any one of these can turn the campaign in the earlier example completely unprofitable or make it profitable over a much larger range of deciles.

Figure 2-9 shows what would happen to this campaign if the assumptions on cost, response rate, and revenue were all off by 20 percent. Under the pessimistic scenario, the best that can be achieved is a loss of $20,000. Under the optimistic scenario, the campaign achieves maximum profitability of $161,696 at 40 percent penetration. Estimates of cost tend to be fairly accurate because they are based on postage rates, printing charges, and other factors that can be determined in advance. Estimates of response rates and revenues are usually little more than guesses.

Optimizing a campaign for profitability sounds appealing; it is unlikely to be useful without conducting an actual test campaign. Modeling campaign profitability in advance is primarily what-if analysis to determine likely profitability bounds based on various assumptions. Calculating the profitability of a campaign after it has run is more useful. To do this effectively, customers with a full range of response scores must be included in the campaign — even customers from lower deciles.

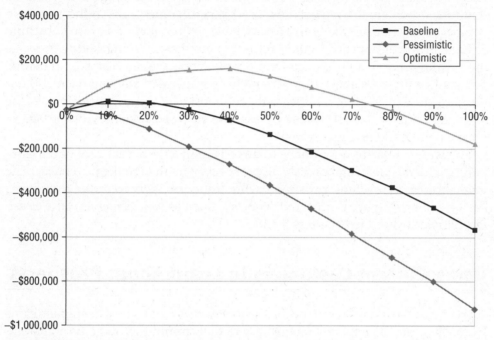

Figure 2-9: A 20 percent variation in response rate, cost, and revenue per responder has a large effect on the profitability of a campaign.

WARNING The profitability of a campaign depends on so many factors that can only be estimated in advance, the only reliable way to do it is to use an actual market test.

Reaching the People Most Influenced by the Message

A subtle simplifying assumption is that the marketing offer inspires the response. Another possibility exists, however: The model could simply be identifying people who are likely to buy the product with or without the offer.

TIP To test whether both a model and the campaign it supports are effective, track the relationship of response rate to model score among prospects in a holdout group who are not part of the campaign as well as among prospects who are included in the campaign.

The goal of a marketing campaign is to change behavior. In this regard, reaching a prospect who is going to purchase anyway is little more useful than reaching a prospect who will not purchase despite having received the offer. A group identified as likely responders may also be less likely to be influenced by a marketing message. Their membership in the target group means that they are likely to have been exposed to similar messages in the past from competitors. They are likely to already have the product or a close substitute or to be firmly entrenched in their refusal to purchase it. A marketing message may make more of a difference with people who have not heard it all before. Segments with the highest scores might have responded anyway, even without the marketing investment. This leads to the almost paradoxical conclusion that the segments with the highest scores in a response model may not provide the biggest return on a marketing investment.

The way out of this dilemma is to directly model the actual goal of the campaign, which is not simply reaching prospects who then make purchases. The goal should be reaching prospects who are more likely to make purchases because of having been contacted. This is known as *incremental response modeling*, a topic covered in Chapters 5 and 7.

Using Current Customers to Learn About Prospects

A good way to find good prospects is to look where today's best customers came from. That means having some of way of determining who the best customers are today. It also means keeping a record of how current customers were acquired and what they looked like at the time of acquisition.

The danger of relying on current customers to learn where to look for prospects is that current customers reflect past marketing decisions. Studying current customers will not suggest looking for new prospects anyplace that hasn't already been tried. Nevertheless, the performance of current customers is a great way to evaluate the existing acquisition channels.

For prospecting purposes, knowing what current customers looked like back when they were prospects themselves is important. Ideally you should:

- Start tracking customers before they become customers.
- Gather information from new customers at the time they are acquired.
- Model the relationship between acquisition-time data and future outcomes of interest.

The following sections provide some elaboration.

Start Tracking Customers Before They Become "Customers"

Start recording information about prospects even before they become customers. Websites issue a cookie when a visitor is seen for the first time and start an anonymous profile that remembers what the visitor did on that website. When the visitor returns (using the same browser on the same computer), the cookie is recognized and the profile is updated. When the visitor eventually becomes a customer or registered user, the activity that led up to that transition becomes part of the customer record.

Tracking responses and responders is good practice in the offline world as well. The first critical piece of information to record is the fact that the prospect responded — or did not respond. Data describing who responded and who did not is a necessary ingredient of future response models. Whenever possible, the response data should also include the marketing action that stimulated the response, the channel through which the response was captured, the timing of the marketing message, and when the response came in.

Determining which of many marketing messages stimulated the response can be tricky. In some cases, it may not even be possible. To make the job easier, response forms and catalogs include identifying codes. Website visits capture the referring link. Even advertising campaigns can be distinguished by using different telephone numbers, post office boxes, Web addresses, and as a last resort, asking the responder.

Gather Information from New Customers

When a prospect first becomes a customer, there is a golden opportunity to gather more information. Before the transformation from prospect to customer, any data about prospects tends to be geographic and demographic. Purchased lists are unlikely to provide anything beyond name, contact information, and list source. Use the address to infer other things about prospects based on characteristics of their neighborhoods. Name and address together can be used to purchase household-level information about prospects from providers of marketing data. This sort of data is useful for targeting broad, general segments such as "young mothers" or "urban teenagers" but is not detailed enough to form the basis of an individualized customer relationship.

TIP Demographic information at the geographic level (zip codes, census tracts, and so on) is very powerful. However, such information does not provide information about an individual customer or household; it provides information about his or her neighborhood.

Among the most useful fields that can be collected for future data mining are the initial purchase date, initial acquisition channel, offer responded to, initial product, initial credit score, time to respond, and geographic location. The authors have found these fields to be predictive of a wide range of outcomes of interest, such as expected duration of the relationship, bad debt, and additional purchases. These initial values should be maintained, rather than being over-written with new values as the customer relationship develops.

Acquisition-Time Variables Can Predict Future Outcomes

By recording everything that was known about a customer at the time of acquisition and then tracking customers over time, businesses can use data mining to relate acquisition-time variables to future outcomes such as customer longevity, customer value, and default risk. This information can then be used to guide marketing efforts by focusing on the channels and messages that produce the best results. For example, you can use the survival analysis techniques described in Chapter 10 to establish the average customer lifetime for each channel. Often, some channels yield customers that last twice as long as the customers from others. Assuming that a customer's value per month can be estimated, this translates into an actual dollar figure for how much more valuable a typical channel A customer is than a typical channel B customer — a figure that is as valuable as the cost-per-response measures often used to rate channels.

Data Mining Applications for Customer Relationship Management

Customer relationship management naturally focuses on established customers. Happily, established customers are the richest source of data for mining. Best of all, the data generated by established customers reflects their actual individual behavior. Does the customer pay bills on time? Check or credit card or PayPal? When was the last purchase? What product was purchased? How much did it cost? How many times has the customer called customer service? How many times has the customer been contacted? What shipping method does the customer use most often? How many times has the customer returned a purchase? This kind of behavioral data can be used to evaluate customers' potential value, assess the risk that they will end the relationship, assess the risk that they will stop paying their bills, and anticipate their future needs.

Matching Campaigns to Customers

Response model scores are even more useful with existing customers than prospects for customizing the mix of marketing messages directed to existing customers. Marketing does not stop once customers have been acquired. There are cross-sell campaigns, up-sell campaigns, usage stimulation campaigns, loyalty programs, retention campaigns, and so on. You can think of these campaigns as competing for access to customers.

When each campaign is considered in isolation, and all customers are given response scores for every campaign, what typically happens is that a similar group of customers gets high scores for many of the campaigns. Some customers are just more responsive than others, a fact that is reflected in the model scores. This approach leads to poor customer relationship management. The high-scoring group is bombarded with messages and becomes irritated and unresponsive. Meanwhile, other customers never hear from the company and so are not encouraged to expand their relationships.

An alternative is to send a limited number of messages to each customer, using the scores to decide which messages are most appropriate for each one. Even a customer with low scores for every offer has higher scores for some than others. *Mastering Data Mining* (Wiley, 1999) describes how this system has been used to personalize a banking website by highlighting the products and services most likely to be of interest to customers based on their banking behavior. Figure 2-10 shows how this works.

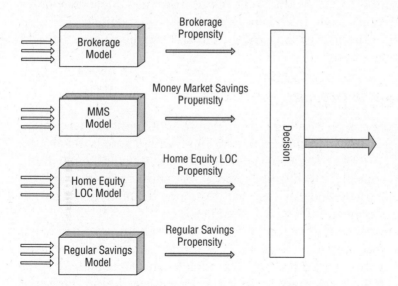

Figure 2-10: Comparing scores from multiple models to decide which offers will be shown to customers.

Each customer is given a propensity score for each product. The propensity score is an estimate of the probability that the customer would respond to an offer for the particular product. Part of the scoring logic is that customers who already have a product have propensity scores of zero. In the decision box, the propensity scores are multiplied by the average first-year profit associated with each product to get an expected dollar value. The customer is offered the product with the highest expected values.

eBay provides another example. The online marketplace uses a decision engine to decide what to show people who arrive at the site by way of a Google search. A landing page is created on the fly based on the search string the user entered into the search engine and on the user's stored profile in the eBay system. The landing page typically consists of a mix of links to eBay's own sellers and advertising links placed on the page by an outside advertising service.

eBay receives a small payment when arriving customers click on an advertising link, and a larger one when they actually buy something from a marketplace seller. Customers who frequently make actual purchases are shown only links to eBay sellers. Customers who frequently browse without buying see more advertising links. For these customers, the expected value of an advertising click is higher than the expected value of a link to a seller.

Reducing Exposure to Credit Risk

Learning to avoid bad customers (and noticing when good customers are about to turn bad) is as important as holding on to good customers. Most companies whose business exposes them to consumer credit risk do credit screening of customers as part of the acquisition process, but risk modeling does not end after the customer has been acquired.

Predicting Who Will Default

Assessing the credit risk on existing customers is a problem for any business that provides a service that customers pay for in arrears. There is always the chance that some customers will receive the service and then fail to pay for it. Not paying debt is one obvious example; newspaper subscriptions, telephone service, gas and electricity, and cable service are among the many services that are usually paid for only after they have been used.

Of course, customers who fail to pay for long enough are eventually cut off. By that time they may owe large sums of money that must be written off. With early warning from a predictive model, a company can take steps to protect itself. These steps might include limiting access to the service or decreasing the length of time between a payment being late and the service being cut off.

Involuntary churn, as termination of services for nonpayment is sometimes called, can be modeled in multiple ways. Often, involuntary churn is considered as a binary outcome, in which case techniques such as logistic regression and decision trees are appropriate. Chapter 10 shows how this problem can also be viewed as a survival analysis problem, in effect changing the question from

"Will the customer fail to pay next month?" to "How long will it be until half the customers have been lost to involuntary churn?"

One of the big differences between voluntary churn and involuntary churn is that involuntary churn often involves complicated business processes, as bills go through different stages of being late (these are often called Dunning levels, named for a researcher at IBM who originally developed automated techniques for dealing with late payers). The best approach is often to model each step in the business process.

Improving Collections

When customers have stopped paying, data mining can aid in collections. Models are used to forecast the amount that can be collected and, in some cases, to help choose the collection strategy. Collections is basically a type of sales. The company tries to sell its delinquent customers on the idea of paying its bills instead of some other bill. As with any sales campaign, some prospective payers will be more receptive to one type of message and some to another.

Determining Customer Value

Data mining plays an important role in customer value calculations, although such calculations also require getting financial definitions right. A simple definition of customer value is the total revenue due to the customer minus the total cost of maintaining the customer over some period of time. But how much revenue should be attributed to a customer? Is it what he or she has spent in total to date? What he or she spent this month or is expected to spend over the next year? How should indirect revenues such as advertising revenue and list rental be allocated to customers?

Costs are even more problematic. Businesses have all sorts of costs that may be allocated to customers in peculiar ways. Is it fair to blame customers for costs over which they have no control? Two Web customers order the exact same merchandise and both are promised free delivery. The one that lives farther from the warehouse may cost more in shipping, but is she really a less valuable customer? What if the next order ships from a different location? Mobile phone service providers are faced with a similar problem, with the ubiquitous uniform nationwide rate plans. The providers' costs are far from uniform when they do not own the entire network. Some of the calls travel over the company's own network. Others travel over the networks of competitors who charge high rates. Can the company increase customer value by trying to discourage customers from making calls when visiting states where the provider's costs are high?

After all of these problems have been sorted out, and a company has agreed on a definition of *retrospective* customer value, data mining comes into play in order to estimate *prospective* customer value. This comes down to estimating the revenue a customer will bring in per unit time and then estimating the customer's remaining lifetime. The second of these problems is the subject of Chapter 10.

Cross-selling, Up-selling, and Making Recommendations

With existing customers, a major focus of customer relationship management is increasing customer profitability through cross-selling and up-selling. Data mining is used for figuring out what to offer to whom and when to offer it.

Finding the Right Time for an Offer

Charles Schwab, the investment company, discovered that customers generally open accounts with a few thousand dollars even if they have considerably more stashed away in savings and investment accounts. Naturally, Schwab would like to attract the rest of the money as well. By analyzing historical data, analysts discovered that customers who transferred large balances into investment accounts usually did so during the first few months after they opened their first account. After a few months, there was little return on trying to get customers to move in large balances. The window was closed. As a result, Schwab shifted its strategy from sending a constant stream of solicitations throughout the customer lifecycle to concentrated efforts during the first few months.

Making Recommendations

One approach to cross-selling makes use of association rules, the subject of Chapter 15. Association rules are used to find groups of products that usually sell together or tend to be purchased by the same person over time. Customers who have purchased some, but not all of the members of such a group are good prospects for the missing elements. This approach works for retail products where many such clusters can be found. Clever application of the same ideas is also effective in other areas such as financial services where there are fewer products.

Retention

Customer attrition is an important issue for any company, and it is especially important in mature industries where the initial period of exponential growth has been left behind. Not surprisingly, attrition (or, to look on the bright side, retention) is a major application of data mining.

Recognizing Attrition

One of the first challenges in modeling attrition is deciding what it is and recognizing when it has occurred. This is harder in some industries than in others. At one extreme are businesses that deal in anonymous cash transactions. When a once-loyal customer deserts his regular coffee bar for another down the block, the barista who knew the customer's order by heart may notice, but the fact will not be recorded in any corporate database. Even in cases where the customer is identified by name, telling the difference between a customer who has churned and one who just hasn't been around for a while may be hard. If a loyal Ford customer who buys a new F150 pickup every five years hasn't bought one for six years, has the customer defected to another brand?

Attrition is a bit easier to spot when a monthly billing relationship exists, as with credit cards. Even there, attrition might be silent. A customer may stop using the credit card, but not cancel it. Attrition is easiest to define in subscription-based businesses, and partly for that reason, attrition modeling is most popular in these businesses. Long-distance companies, mobile phone service providers, insurance companies, cable companies, financial services companies, Internet service providers, newspapers, magazines, and some retailers all share a subscription model where customers have a formal, contractual relationship that must be explicitly ended.

Why Attrition Matters

Lost customers must be replaced by new customers, and new customers are expensive to acquire. Often, new customers generate less revenue in the near term than established customers. This is especially true in mature industries where the market is fairly saturated — anyone likely to want the product or service probably already has it from somewhere, so the main source of new customers is people leaving a competitor.

Figure 2-11 illustrates that as the market becomes saturated and the response rate to acquisition campaigns goes down, the cost of acquiring new customers goes up. The chart shows how much each new customer costs for a direct mail acquisition campaign, given that the mailing costs $1, and it includes an offer of $20 in some form, such as a coupon or a reduced interest rate on a credit card. When the response rate to the acquisition campaign is high, such as 5 percent, the cost of a new customer is $40. (It costs $100 to reach 100 people, five of whom respond at a cost of $20 dollars each. So, acquiring five new customers costs $200 dollars.) As the response rate drops, the cost increases rapidly. By the time the response rate drops to 1 percent, each new customer costs $120. At some point, it makes sense to spend that money to hold on to existing customers rather than to attract new ones.

Retention campaigns can be effective, but also expensive. A mobile phone company might offer an expensive new phone to customers who renew a contract. A credit card company might lower the interest rate. The problem with these offers is that any customer who is made the offer will accept it. Who wouldn't want a free phone or a lower interest rate? Many of the people accepting the offer would have remained customers anyway. The motivation for building attrition models is to figure out who is most at risk for attrition so as to make the retention offers to high-value customers who might leave without the extra incentive.

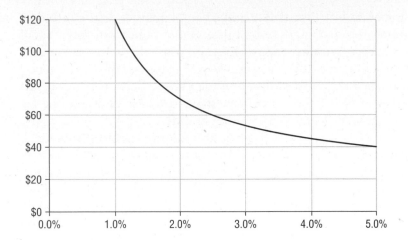

Figure 2-11: As the response rate to an acquisition campaign goes down, the cost per customer acquired goes up.

Different Kinds of Attrition

The preceding discussion of why attrition matters focuses on the voluntary sort. Customers, of their own free will, decide to take their business elsewhere. This type of attrition, known as *voluntary attrition*, is actually only one of three possibilities. The other two are *involuntary attrition* and *expected attrition*.

Involuntary attrition, also known as *forced attrition*, occurs when the company, rather than the customer, terminates the relationship — most commonly due to unpaid bills. *Expected attrition* occurs when the customer is no longer in the target market for a product. Babies get teeth and no longer need baby food. Families move away and switch cable providers.

It is important not to confuse the different types of attrition, but easy to do so. Consider two mobile phone customers in identical financial circumstances. Due to some misfortune, neither can afford the mobile phone service any more. Both call up to cancel. One reaches a customer service agent and is recorded as leaving voluntarily. The other hangs up after ten minutes on hold and continues to use the phone without paying the bill. The second customer is forced to leave. The underlying problem — lack of money — is the same for both customers, so it is likely that they will both get similar scores. The model cannot predict the difference in hold times experienced by the two subscribers.

Companies that mistake forced attrition for voluntary attrition lose twice — once when they spend money trying to retain customers who later go bad and again in increased write-offs.

Inaccurate predictions of forced attrition can also be dangerous. Because the treatment given to customers who are not likely to pay their bills tends to be nasty — phone service is suspended, late fees are increased, and collection letters are sent more quickly. These remedies may alienate otherwise good customers and increase the chance that they will leave voluntarily.

From a data mining point of view, addressing both voluntary and involuntary attrition together is better because all customers are at risk for both kinds to varying degrees.

> **TIP** When modeling attrition, it is a good idea to model all types. Until they succumb to one or the other, subscribers are at risk for both involuntary and voluntary churn. Customers with high scores for one risk may (or may not) have high scores for the other as well.

Different Kinds of Attrition Model

There are two basic approaches to modeling attrition. The first treats attrition as a binary outcome and predicts which customers will leave and which will stay. The second tries to estimate the customers' remaining lifetime.

Predicting Who Will Leave

To model attrition as a binary outcome, picking some time horizon is necessary. If the question is, "Who will leave tomorrow?" the answer is hardly anyone. If the question is, "Who will leave in the next hundred years?" the answer, in most businesses, is nearly everyone. Binary outcome attrition models usually have a fairly short time horizon such as 60 or 90 days or one year. Of course, the horizon cannot be too short or there will be no time to act on the model's predictions.

Such models can be built with any of the usual tools for classification including logistic regression, decision trees, and neural networks. Historical data describing a customer population at one time is combined with a flag showing whether the customers were still active at some later time. The modeling task is to discriminate between those who left and those who stayed.

Such models typically produce scores that rank customers by their likelihood of leaving. The most natural score is simply the probability that the customer will leave within the time horizon used for the model. Those with voluntary attrition scores above a certain threshold can be included in a retention program. Those with involuntary attrition scores above a certain threshold can be placed on a watch list.

Typically, the predictors of attrition turn out to be a mixture of things known about the customer at acquisition time, such as the acquisition channel and initial credit class; things that occurred during the customer relationship such as problems with service, late payments, and unexpectedly high or low bills; and customer demographics. The first class of attrition drivers provides information on how to lower future attrition by acquiring fewer attrition-prone customers. The second class of attrition drivers provides insight into how to reduce the risk for customers who are already present.

Predicting How Long Customers Will Stay

The second approach to attrition modeling is survival analysis, explained in Chapter 10. The basic idea is to calculate for each customer (or for each group of customers that share the same values for model input variables such as geography, credit class, and acquisition channel) the probability that having made it as far as today, he or she will leave before tomorrow. For any one tenure, this *hazard probability*, as it is called, is quite small, but it is higher for some tenures than for others. The chance that a customer survives to reach some more distant future date can be calculated from the intervening hazards.

Beyond the Customer Lifecycle

Data mining is naturally suited to the customer lifecycle. However, not all data mining applications are directly tied to the lifecycle. For instance, forecasting is generally a critical business process. You an use data mining to forecast customer numbers and future attrition rates as well as for customer segmentation, or even discovering unexpected customer types or behaviors.

Chapter 11 has a case study on distinguishing customer complaints from other kinds of customer comments. This is an example of applying text mining to customer relationship management. Not all applications of data mining deal with customer data. Chapter 21 contains examples of text mining, including one about assigning keywords to news stories; the keywords help readers find the right stories. Chapter 12 describes a data mining project at the *Boston Globe* that was focused on whole towns rather than individual subscribers. Towns were clustered according to demographic similarity. These demographic clusters were then combined with geographic proximity to create regions for customized versions of the newspaper.

Data mining has many applications. Because customers are common to all businesses, customer-centric applications are the most common ones. The techniques described in this book have been used for customer relationship management, and beyond.

Lessons Learned

In most of the book, the focus on customer-centric applications is implicit in the choice of examples used to illustrate the techniques. In this chapter, that focus is more explicit. Customer relationships follow a natural lifecycle that begins with prospecting and customer acquisition, moves on to activation, and continues with an extended period of managing relationships with established customers. Part of customer relationship management is holding on to these established customers through retention efforts, and trying to win back customers who have been lost.

All phases of the customer relationship generate data that you can use for mining. During the acquisition phase, data mining supports both advertising and direct marketing to identify the right audience, choose the best communication channels, and pick the most appropriate messages. Prospective customers can be compared to a profile of the intended audience and given a fitness score. Should information on individual prospects not be available, you can use the same method to assign fitness scores to geographic neighborhoods using data of the type available from the U.S. Census Bureau, Statistics Canada, and similar official sources in many countries.

A common application of data mining in direct modeling is response modeling. A response model scores prospects on their likelihood to respond to a direct marketing campaign. This information can be used to improve the response rate of a campaign, but is not, by itself, enough to determine campaign profitability. Estimating campaign profitability requires reliance on estimates of the underlying response rate to a future campaign, estimates of average order sizes associated with the response, and cost estimates for fulfillment and for the campaign itself. A more customer-centric use of response scores is to choose the best campaign for each customer from among a number of competing campaigns. This approach avoids the usual problem of independent, score-based campaigns, which tend to pick the same people every time.

Distinguishing between the ability of a model to recognize people who are interested in a product or service and its ability to recognize people who are moved to make a purchase based on a particular campaign or offer is important. Incremental response analysis offers a way to identify the market segments where a campaign will have the greatest impact.

Companies can use information about current customers to identify likely prospects by finding predictors of desired outcomes in the information that was known about current customers before they became customers. This sort of analysis is valuable for selecting acquisition channels and contact strategies as well as for screening prospect lists. Companies can increase the value of their customer data by beginning to track customers from their first response, even before they become customers, and gathering and storing additional information when customers are acquired.

After customers have been acquired, the focus shifts to customer relationship management. The data available for active customers is richer than that available for prospects and, because it is behavioral in nature rather than simply geographic and demographic, it is more predictive. Data mining can identify additional products and services that should be offered to customers based on their current usage patterns. It can also suggest the best time to make a cross-sell or up-sell offer.

One of the goals of a customer relationship management program is to retain valuable customers. Data mining can help identify which customers are the most valuable and evaluate the risk of voluntary or involuntary attrition associated with each customer. Armed with this information, companies can target retention offers at customers who are both valuable and at risk, and take steps to protect themselves from customers who are likely to default. When attrition modeling is framed as, "When will a customer leave?" then the models can be used for estimated customer value.

Data mining is a valuable tool throughout the customer lifecycle. The next chapter moves from how data mining helps the business to the challenges of implementing data mining in the business environment.

CHAPTER 3

The Data Mining Process

Chapter 1 describes the virtuous cycle of data mining as a business process that divides data mining into four stages:

1. Identifying the problem
2. Transforming data into information
3. Taking action
4. Measuring the outcome

This chapter shifts the emphasis to data mining as a technical process, moving from identifying business problems to translating business problems into data mining problems. The second stage, transforming data into information, is expanded into several topics including hypothesis testing, model building, and pattern discovery. The ideas and best practices introduced in this chapter are elaborated further in the rest of the book. The purpose of this chapter is to bring the different styles of data mining together in one place.

The best way to avoid breaking the virtuous cycle of data mining is to understand the ways it is likely to fail and take preventive measures. Over the years, the authors have encountered many ways for data mining projects to go wrong. This chapter begins with a discussion of some of these pitfalls. The rest of the chapter is about the data mining process. Later chapters cover the aspects of data mining methodology that are specific to the particular styles of data mining — directed data mining and undirected data mining. This chapter focuses on what these approaches have in common.

The three main styles of data mining are introduced, beginning with the simplest approach — testing hypotheses typically by using ad hoc queries — and working up to more sophisticated activities such as building models that can be used for scoring, and finding patterns using undirected data mining techniques. The theme of the chapter is getting from a clear statement of the business goal to a clear understanding of the data mining tasks required to achieve the goal and the data mining techniques appropriate to the task.

What Can Go Wrong?

Data mining is a way of learning from the past in order to make better decisions in the future. The best practices described in this chapter are designed to avoid two undesirable outcomes of the learning process:

- Learning things that aren't true.
- Learning things that are true, but not useful.

Ancient mariners learned to avoid the rocks of Scylla and the whirlpool of Charybdis that protect the narrow straits between Sicily and the Italian mainland. Like the ancient sailors who learned to avoid these threats, data miners need to know how to avoid common dangers.

Learning Things That Aren't True

Learning things that aren't true is more dangerous than learning things that are useless because important business decisions may be made based on incorrect information. Data mining results often seem reliable because they are based on actual data processed in a seemingly scientific manner. This appearance of reliability can be deceiving. The data may be incorrect or not relevant to the question at hand. The patterns discovered may reflect past business decisions or nothing at all. Data transformations such as summarization may have destroyed or hidden important information. The following sections discuss some of the more common problems that can lead to false conclusions.

WARNING The most careful and painstaking analysis, using the most sophisticated techniques, yields incorrect results when the data analyzed is incorrect or simply not relevant. In information technology circles, a popular aphorism is, "garbage in, garbage out."

Patterns May Not Represent Any Underlying Rule

It is often said that figures don't lie, but liars do figure. When it comes to finding patterns in data, figures don't have to actually lie in order to suggest things that aren't true. So many ways to construct patterns exist that any random set of data points reveals one if examined long enough. Human beings depend so heavily on patterns in our lives that we tend to see them even when they are not there. We look up at the nighttime sky and see not a random arrangement of stars, but the Big Dipper, or the Southern Cross, or Orion's Belt. Some even see astrological patterns and portents that can be used to predict the future. The widespread acceptance of outlandish conspiracy theories is further evidence of the human need to find patterns.

Presumably, the reason that humans have evolved such an affinity for patterns is that patterns often do reflect some underlying truth about the way the world works. The phases of the moon, the progression of the seasons, the constant alternation of night and day, even the regular appearance of a favorite TV show at the same time on the same day of the week are useful because they are stable and therefore predictive. We can use these patterns to decide when it is safe to plant tomatoes, when to eat breakfast, and how to program the DVR. Other patterns clearly do not have any predictive power. If a fair coin comes up heads five times in a row, there is still a 50–50 chance that it will come up tails on the sixth toss.

The challenge for data miners is to figure out which patterns are useful and which are not. Consider the following patterns, all of which have been cited in articles in the popular press as if they had predictive value:

- The party that does not hold the presidency picks up seats in Congress during off-year elections.

- When the American League wins the World Series, Republicans take the White House.

- When the Washington Redskins win their last home game, the incumbent party keeps the White House.

- In U.S. presidential contests, the taller man usually wins.

The first pattern (the one involving off-year elections) is explainable in purely political terms. Every four years, just over half of the American voters get all excited and vote for their candidate for president. A few months later, the candidate takes over, and the disappointment begins — politicians simply cannot keep all the promises that their base expects. Two years later, in the Congressional elections, a backlash occurs, usually caused by disappointed supporters who do not turn out to vote. Because this pattern has an underlying explanation, it seems likely to continue into the future, implying that it has predictive value.

The next two alleged predictors, the ones involving sporting events, seem just as clearly to have no predictive value. No matter how many times Republicans and the American League may have shared victories in the past (and the authors have not researched this point), there is no reason to expect the association to continue in the future.

What about candidates' heights? Since 1948 when Truman (who was short, but taller than Dewey) was elected, the election in which Carter beat Ford and the one in which Bush beat Kerry are the only ones where the shorter candidate won more popular votes. The 2000 election that pitted 6'1" Gore against the 6'0" Bush still fits the pattern, if one assumes that the pattern relates to winning the popular vote rather than the electoral vote. In 2008, the basketball-playing Obama out-polled the shorter McCain. Height does not seem to have anything to do with the job of being president. However, our language exhibits "heightism": we look *up* to people as a sign of respect, and look *down* on people to show disdain. Height is associated with better childhood nutrition, which in turn leads to increased intelligence and other indicators of social success. As this chapter explains, the right way to decide whether a rule is stable and predictive is to compare its performance on multiple samples selected at random from the same population. In the case of presidential height, the authors leave this as an exercise for the reader. As is often the case, the hardest part of the task is collecting the data — before the age of Google, determining the heights of unsuccessful presidential candidates from previous centuries was not easy!

The technical term for finding patterns that fail to generalize is *overfitting*. Overfitting leads to unstable models that work one day, but not the next, on one data set but not on another. Building stable models is the primary goal of the data mining methodology.

The Model Set May Not Reflect the Relevant Population

The *model set* is the data used to create a data mining model, and it necessarily describes what happened in the past. The model can only be as good as the data used to create it. For inferences to be valid, the model set must reflect the population that the model is meant to describe, classify, or score. A sample that does not properly reflect the population being scored or the overall population is *biased*.

A biased model set can lead to learning things that are not true. Unless the biases are taken into account, the resulting model is also biased. Biases can be hard to avoid. Consider:

- Customers are not like prospects.
- Survey responders are not like non-responders.
- People who read e-mail are not like people who do not read e-mail.

- People who register on a website are not like people who do not register.

- After an acquisition, customers from the acquired company are not necessarily like customers from the acquirer.

- Records with no missing values reflect a different population from records with missing values.

Consider the first point. Customers are not like prospects because they represent people who responded positively to whatever messages, offers, and promotions were made to attract customers in the past. A study of current customers is likely to suggest more of the same. If past campaigns have gone after wealthy, urban consumers, then any comparison of current customers with the general population would likely show that customers tend to be wealthy and urban. Such a model may miss opportunities in middle-income suburbs.

TIP Careful attention to selecting and sampling data for the model set is crucial to successful data mining.

The consequences of using a biased sample can be worse than simply a missed marketing opportunity. In the United States, there is a history of "redlining," the illegal practice of refusing to write loans or insurance policies in certain neighborhoods (usually low-income or minority neighborhoods). A search for patterns in the historical data from a company that had a history of redlining would reveal that people in certain neighborhoods are unlikely to be customers at all. If future marketing efforts were based on that finding, data mining would help perpetuate illegal and unethical practices.

Data May Be at the Wrong Level of Detail

In more than one industry, the authors have been told that usage often goes down in the month before a customer leaves. Upon closer examination, this may turn out to be an example of learning something that is not true. Figure 3-1 shows the monthly minutes of use for a group of cellular telephone subscribers who are recorded as stopping in month nine. For seven months, the subscribers use about 100 minutes per month. In the eighth month, their usage declines to about half that. And in the following month, there is no usage at all, because the subscribers have stopped. This suggests that a marketing effort triggered by a decline in usage might be able to save these customers.

These subscribers appear to fit a pattern where a month with decreased usage precedes abandonment of the service. Appearances are deceiving. These customers have no usage in month nine because the actual stop date is in month eight. On average, the stop date would be halfway through the month. These customers continue to use the service at a constant rate until they stop, presumably because on that day, the customers begin using a competing service. The putative period of declining usage does not actually exist and so certainly does not provide a window of opportunity for retaining the customer. What appears to be a leading indicator is actually a trailing one.

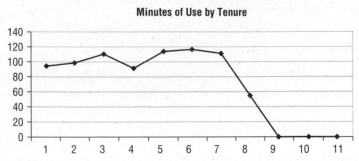

Figure 3-1: Does declining usage in month 8 predict attrition in month 9?

Figure 3-2 shows another example of confusion caused by aggregation. Sales appear to be down in October compared to August and September. The picture comes from a business that has sales activity only on days when the financial markets are open. Because of the way that weekends and holidays fell in 2003, October had fewer trading days than August and September. That fact alone accounts for the entire drop-off in sales.

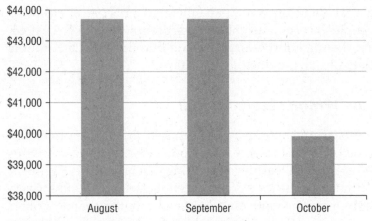

Figure 3-2: Did sales really drop off in October?

In the previous examples, aggregation leads to confusion. Failure to aggregate to the appropriate level can also lead to confusion. One member of a household might have a checking account with a low balance and little activity while another member of the same household has multiple large accounts. Treating the small account holder as a less-than-valuable customer might put the relationship with the entire household at risk. In this case, a total balance figure may be more important than the balance in any one account.

TIP When summarizing data, choose a level of aggregation that does not hide important patterns within a single period. A business with strong week-to-week changes should not report activity summarized monthly.

Learning Things That Are True, but Not Useful

Although not as dangerous as learning things that aren't true, learning things that aren't useful is more common. This can happen in several ways.

Learning Things That Are Already Known (or Should Be Known)

Data mining should provide new information. Many of the strongest patterns in data represent things that are already known. People over retirement age tend not to respond to offers for retirement savings plans. People living outside home delivery zones do not become newspaper subscribers. Even though they may respond to subscription offers, service never starts. People who do not own cars do not purchase car insurance.

Data mining can also discover patterns that should have been known to be true. In one interesting example, the authors were working on a project analyzing purchase patterns in grocery store data. When the first set of data arrived, we set out to find products that are purchased together. The first combinations were "eggs and meat," "eggs and milk," and "eggs and soda." The rules continued in the same vein — eggs were rushing off the shelves with just about every product in the store. At first, this seemed like a potential problem in the data. Then, one of our colleagues noted that the data came from the week before Easter. And, indeed, when people go grocery shopping before Easter, they often buy eggs to dye or hide for the Easter holiday.

The strongest patterns often reflect business rules. If data mining "discovers" that people who have anonymous call blocking also have caller ID, the reason is perhaps because anonymous call blocking is only sold as part of a bundle of services that also includes caller ID. If data mining "discovers" that maintenance agreements are sold with large appliances (as Sears once found), that is because maintenance agreements are almost always sold after the appliance. Not only are these patterns uninteresting, their strength may obscure less obvious but more actionable patterns.

Learning things that are already known does serve one useful purpose. It demonstrates that, on a technical level, the data mining techniques are working and the data is reasonably accurate. This can be comforting, even if not helpful. When data mining techniques are powerful enough to discover things that are known to be true, there is reason to believe that they can discover more useful patterns as well.

Learning Things That Can't Be Used

Data mining can uncover relationships that are both true and previously unknown, but still hard to make use of. Sometimes the problem is regulatory. A customer's wireless calling patterns may suggest an affinity for certain land-line long-distance packages, but a company that provides both services may not be allowed to take advantage of the fact due to legal restrictions. Similarly, a customer's credit history may be predictive of future insurance claims, but regulators may prohibit making underwriting decisions based on such information. Or, in what is becoming a more prevalent example, a person's genetic material may suggest propensity for certain diseases — a characteristic that insurance companies in the United States and most European countries are barred from using.

Other times, data mining reveals that important outcomes are outside the company's control. A product may be more appropriate for some climates than others, but it is hard to change the weather. Mobile phone service may be worse in some regions for reasons of topography, but that is also hard to change.

> **TIP** A study of customer attrition may show that a strong predictor of customers leaving is the way they were acquired. It is too late to go back and change that for existing customers, but that does not make the information useless. Future attrition can be reduced by changing the mix of acquisition channels to favor those that bring in longer-lasting customers.

Data miners must take care to steer clear of the Scylla of learning things that aren't true and the Charybdis of not learning anything useful. The methodologies laid out in Chapter 5 and Chapter 12 are designed to ensure that data mining efforts lead to stable models that successfully address business problems.

Data Mining Styles

Chapter 1 says that data mining involves the "exploration and analysis of large quantities of data to produce meaningful results." That is a broad enough definition to cover many different approaches. These come in three main styles:

- Hypothesis testing
- Directed data mining
- Undirected data mining

In hypothesis testing, the goal is to use data to answer questions or gain understanding. In directed data mining, the goal is to construct a model that explains or predicts one or more particular target variables. In undirected data mining, the goal is to find overall patterns that are not tied to a particular target. During the course of a data mining project, you may spend time working in any or all of these styles depending on the nature of the problem and your familiarity with the data.

Although the three styles of data mining have some technical differences, they also have much in common. Many of the topics discussed in Chapter 5 in the context of directed data mining are also important for hypothesis testing and finding patterns. In fact, the first three steps of the directed data mining methodology — translating a business problem into a data mining problem, selecting appropriate data, and getting to know the data — could just as well be covered in this chapter.

Hypothesis Testing

Hypothesis testing is a part of almost all data mining endeavors. Data miners often bounce back and forth between approaches, first thinking up possible explanations for observed behavior (often with the help of business experts) and letting those hypotheses dictate the data to be analyzed, and then letting the data suggest new hypotheses to test.

A *hypothesis* is a proposed explanation whose validity can be tested by analyzing data. Such data may simply be collected by observation or generated through an experiment, such as a test marketing campaign. Hypothesis testing sometimes reveals that the assumptions that have been guiding a company's actions are incorrect. For example, a company's advertising is based on a number of hypotheses about the target market for a product or service and the nature of the responses. It is worth testing whether these hypotheses are borne out by actual responses.

Depending on the hypotheses, this may mean interpreting a single value returned from a simple query, plowing through a collection of association rules generated by market basket analysis, determining the significance of a correlation found by a regression model, or designing a controlled experiment. In all cases, careful critical thinking is necessary to be sure that the result is not biased in unexpected ways. Proper evaluation of data mining results requires both analytical and business knowledge. Where these are not present in the same person, making good use of the new information requires cross-functional cooperation.

By its nature, hypothesis testing is ad hoc, but the process has some identifiable steps, the first and most important of which is generating good hypotheses to test. Next comes finding or generating data to confirm or disprove the hypotheses.

Generating Hypotheses

The key to generating hypotheses is getting diverse input from throughout the organization and, where appropriate, outside it as well. Outsiders may question things that insiders take for granted — perhaps providing valuable insight. Often, all that is needed to start the ideas flowing is a clear statement of the problem itself — especially if it is something that has not previously been recognized as a problem.

More often than one might suppose, problems go unrecognized because they are not captured by the metrics used to evaluate performance. If a company has always measured its sales force on the number of new sales made each month, the salespeople may never have given much thought to the question of how long new customers remain active or how much they spend over the course of their relationship. When asked the right questions, however, the sales force may have insights into customer behavior that marketing, with its greater distance from the customer, has missed.

The goal is to come up with ideas that are both testable and actionable. Consider the following hypotheses:

- Most customers who accept a retention offer would stay anyway.
- Families with high-school age children are more likely than others to respond to a home equity line offer.
- Customers who buy more distinct product types have higher overall spending.

All of these propositions might or might not be true, and in each case, knowing the answer suggests some concrete action. If the first hypothesis is true, stop spending money to retain customers who are not at risk of leaving or find a better way of targeting retention offers to customers who really are going to leave. If the second hypothesis is true, continue the current marketing focus on this group. If the third hypothesis is correct, encourage salespeople to do more cross selling.

Testing Hypotheses Using Existing Data

It is often possible to test a new hypothesis by looking for evidence in existing historical data. For example, a manufacturer of medical devices sold to hospitals had the hypothesis that customers who bought products in multiple categories tended to spend more. As a first step, they looked at average sales by number of distinct products and produced the chart shown in Figure 3-3.

The chart clearly shows that customers who buy many kinds of product generate substantially more revenue per customer, but it does not show to what extent cross-selling drives additional revenue. Larger institutions naturally spend more, and perhaps they are also more likely to need products from multiple categories. Perhaps high revenue and multiple product categories are both driven by customer size — something not in the company's control. That, too, is a testable hypothesis: Group customers by size and type and look for a relationship between distinct products and revenue within each group.

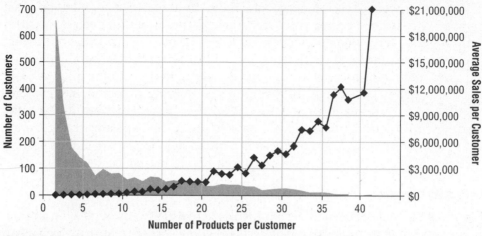

Figure 3-3: Customers who buy more product types spend more money.

Testing long-held beliefs can be harder because historical data reflects whatever assumptions have been made in the past. If families with high-school children have always been targeted for a particular product, this fact will be reflected in higher adoption rates for those families. This does not prove that they are the most responsive segment; some other group, such as small business owners, might have responded even more. In such cases, conducting a controlled experiment is advisable.

Small changes in what and how data is collected can greatly increase its value for analysis. For example, use different web addresses or call-in numbers in different ads and keep track of how each response comes in.

> **TIP** Each time a company solicits a response from its customers, whether through advertising or a more direct form of communication, it has an opportunity to gather information. Slight changes in the design of the communication, such as including a way to identify the channel when a prospect responds, can greatly increase the value of the data collected.

Hypothesis Testing and Experimentation

Although many hypotheses can be tested against historical data, many cannot. Take the hypothesis that the people who accepted a retention offer would have stayed with or without the added enticement. Historical data describes who received the offer, who accepted the offer, and who ended up staying, but unless the campaign was set up as a proper experiment with a control group, it does not answer the question about what would have happened if the offer had not been made. This question cannot be answered by comparing retention for those who received the offer and those who did not because the two groups almost certainly differ in systematic ways.

If the offer went to customers considered to be at high risk for attrition, then people who did not get the offer may have better retention even if the offer really saved a large number of customers. On the other hand, if the offer went to customers considered particularly valuable, they may have better retention than non-recipients for reasons that have nothing to do with the offer. A valid test of the program's effectiveness requires comparing two groups of customers that are similar in every way except for the thing being tested. Data like that may not occur naturally, so you have to design an experiment to generate it. Experimental design and analysis is a broad field in statistics. This section covers some key points about specifics common to marketing tests.

Test and Control

The most basic experimental design involves creating two groups. One, known as the *test group* or *treatment group*, receives some sort of treatment such as an e-mail or phone call. The other group, known as the *control group*, does not receive the treatment. The two groups are picked to be as similar as possible — the same average age, the same average income, the same distribution of men and women, the same distribution of customer tenure, and so on. That may sound painstaking, but it is not. Basically, choose an overall group, and then randomly divide it into the test and control group. As long as the test and control groups are large enough, the laws of probability ensure that the groups are similar to each other (and to the whole population). If you want ensure that the groups are representative for certain key traits (say sex and tenure), then sort the population by these fields and take every nth record for the control group.

After the experiment, any significant difference between the groups can confidently be attributed to the treatment. Chapter 4 explains the concept of statistical significance and how to test for it.

A/B Tests

An A/B test compares two (or possibly more) treatments. Customers are randomly assigned to group A or group B. The two groups receive different treatments such as different advertising messages, web page layouts, prices, or payment options. Analytically oriented companies routinely run A/B tests to determine the effect of even seemingly minor changes because small changes can have large and unanticipated effects.

One online retailing company found that adding a box where customers could enter a discount coupon code reduced the proportion of customers who made purchases by a significant 6.5 percent. Most shoppers did not have coupons and apparently the invitation to supply a discount code caused people without one to think they were getting a bad deal. Perhaps such shoppers were encouraged to search for a coupon on Google, possibly finding a better price in the process.

A/B testing is usually associated with direct marketing and web-based retailing because in these environments controlling which customers get which messages is relatively simple. A/B testing is also useful for less directed kinds of advertising such as billboards, radio, and television. The trick is to run different campaigns in similar markets. Such tests are called *paired tests*, because they depend on pairs of different markets (or store locations or whatever) to be as similar as possible for testing purposes. One half of the pair gets the treatment and the other half is the control. Chapter 9 discusses paired tests in more detail.

Champion/Challenger Tests

A common form of A/B testing compares a new treatment, the *challenger*, with the existing treatment, the *champion*. This idea is often applied to data mining models used to score customers. The new model should not be adopted until it is shown to be better than the old one.

Amazon.com is particularly adept at this form of A/B testing. Everything on its website — from the placement of product reviews and product descriptions to the number of user comments and keywords — has been tested against the "champion" best layout. In Amazon's live environment, visitors to the website are chosen randomly for the test group to see a modified layout. After a few hours or days, enough data has been gathered to suggest whether the tested modifications to the layout produce higher or lower sales than the champion. If improvements are significant, the test becomes the new champion.

Case Study in Hypothesis Testing: Measuring the Wrong Thing

This is a story about a company that makes recommendation software for retailing websites. Its clients, the retailers, leave some blank areas on particular web pages, such as the product pages, the shopping cart, and check-out pages. The recommendation software provides product recommendations to fill in the blanks when customers are shopping at the site. When a customer purchases the recommended item, the software company makes a commission. The goal, of course, is to increase the overall sales on the site, which benefits the retailers and encourages them to keep using the recommendation software.

The software company had a conundrum: According to all its metrics, its recommendations were improving year after year. More customers were clicking on and purchasing the recommended items. However, retailers complained that revenues were not rising as much as expected. In some head-to-head tests, the sophisticated recommendation software was not doing as well as simple general rules developed by clients.

This is not a well-formed problem for directed data mining. What is the target variable? It is also not a good candidate for undirected pattern finding; the pattern is all too clear. It is a perfect fit for hypothesis testing. The data miner's job was to brainstorm about what might be going wrong and then test the resulting hypotheses.

The software company approached Data Miners (the consulting company founded by the authors) to help make sense of this conundrum. We received data from an A/B test that had yielded disappointing results. In an A/B test, half the shoppers were randomly selected to receive recommendations from the company while the other half received competing recommendations from the retailer. This data included an order line table with details about each item such as its price, product category, and, in cases where the shopper had clicked on a recommendation for the product, a click ID. For each click, a clicks table showed which of several recommendation algorithms had generated the recommendation, and what item the shopper had been looking at when the recommendation was made.

Using simple SQL queries, we found that customers on our client's side of the test indeed clicked on more recommendations and, on both sides of the test, customers who clicked were more likely to make a purchase. More purchases should mean more money. And more money should mean the retailers are happy.

How could the A side — our client's side — lose given these metrics? The first clue was that the average price of items clicked was lower on the A side than the B side. Our first hypothesis was that A was recommending a different mix of products than B, but that was easily disproven. We kept trying out other hypotheses until we found two that, together, explained what was happening:

- The A side's recommendations yielded more substitutions and fewer cross-sells.
- Many of the A side's recommendations were down-sells.

Cross-sells are when consumers buy recommended products *in addition* to products they are already considering, resulting in a larger total purchase. A substitution is when consumers buy recommended products *instead* of the original ones. A cross-sell is more valuable to the retailer because it increases the amount the customer spends. However, our client's commission was only based on whether or not the end consumer purchased its recommendation. The retailer designed its recommendations to generate cross-sells. Where it did recommend substitutions, the recommended product was nearly always something pricier — up-selling. By comparison, our client's recommendations were down-sells on average.

Our conclusion was that our client had been measuring the wrong thing. Its recommendations "improved" over time in the sense of attracting more clicks, but clicks are not useful by themselves. The easiest way to attract clicks is to show shoppers cheaper substitutes for the items they are looking at. This behavior generated commissions for our client, but (inadvertently) at the expense of the retailer who ended up selling a cheaper item and paying a commission for the privilege! We recommended that the software company change its commission structure so it would be rewarded for incremental revenue rather than clicks: a valuable result from data mining using hypothesis testing.

Directed Data Mining

Directed data mining is another style of data mining. Directed data mining focuses on one or more variables that are targets, and the historical data contains examples of all the target values. In other words, directed data mining does not look for just any pattern in the data, but for patterns that explain the target values. A very typical example is retention modeling. The historical data contains examples of customers who are active and others who have stopped. The goal of directed data mining is to find patterns that differentiate between factors that cause customers to leave and customers to stay.

In statistics, the term *predictive modeling* is often used for directed data mining. In the authors' opinion, this is a bit of a misnomer, because although predictive modeling is definitely one aspect of directed data mining, it has other aspects, as well. Chapter 5 differentiates between predictive modeling and profile modeling, based on the temporal relationship between the target variable and the inputs. Predictive modeling is specifically when the target comes from a timeframe later than the inputs; profile modeling is specifically when the target and inputs come from the same timeframe.

Undirected Data Mining

Undirected data mining is a style of data mining that does not use a target variable, at least not explicitly. In directed data mining, different variables play different roles. Target variables are the objects of study; the rest of the variables are used to explain or predict the values of the targets. In undirected data mining, there are no special roles. The goal is to find overall patterns. After patterns have been detected, it is the responsibility of a person to interpret them and decide whether they are useful.

The term *undirected* may actually be a bit misleading. Although no target variable is used, business goals must still be addressed. The business goals addressed by undirected data mining may sound just as directed as any other goals; "Find examples of fraud," is an example of a business goal that might call for either directed or undirected data mining depending on whether training data contains identified fraudulent transactions. A directed approach would search for new records that are similar to cases known to be fraudulent. An undirected approach would look for new records that are unusual.

Increasing average order size is another example of a business goal that could be addressed using undirected data mining. Association rules, an undirected data mining technique, reveal patterns about which items are frequently sold together. This information could be used to increase order sizes through improved cross-selling.

Sometimes, the business goals themselves may be a bit vague and the data mining effort is a way to refine them. For example, a company might have a goal of developing specialized services for different customer segments without having a clear idea of how customers should be segmented. Clustering, an undirected data mining technique, could be used to discover customer segments. Studying the segments might yield insight into what segment members have in common, which in turn might suggest common needs that a new product could address.

Goals, Tasks, and Techniques

A data mining consultant the authors know says that he lives in fear of clients reading a magazine article that mentions some particular data mining technique by name. When a vice president of marketing starts asking about neural networks versus support vector machines, it is probably time to reset the conversation. Data mining always starts with a business goal, and the first job of the data miner is to get a good understanding of that goal. This step requires good communication between people in upper management who set the goals and the analysts responsible for translating those goals into data mining tasks. The next job is to restate the business goal in terms of data mining tasks, and only then are particular data mining techniques selected.

Data Mining Business Goals

The data mining applications in the previous chapter provide several good examples of business goals:

- Choose the best places to advertise.
- Find the best locations for branches or stores.
- Acquire more profitable customers.
- Decrease exposure to risk of default.
- Improve customer retention.
- Detect fraudulent claims.

The rest of this book also contains many examples of data mining being used in the real world to solve real problems. Not all business goals lend themselves to data mining directly; sometimes they need to be turned into data mining business goals. For data mining to be successful, the business goal should be well-defined and directed towards particular efforts that are amenable to analysis using available data. A data mining business goal can usually be expressed in terms of something measurable such as incremental revenue, response rate, order size, or wait time.

Achieving any of these goals requires more than just data mining, of course, but data mining has an important role to play. The first step is to design a high-level approach to the problem. To acquire more profitable customers, you might start by learning what drives profitability for existing customers and then recruit new customers with the right characteristics. Decreasing exposure to credit risk might mean predicting which of the customers currently in good standing are likely to go bad and preemptively decrease their credit lines. Improving customer retention might focus on improving the experience of existing customers or on recruiting new customers with longer expected tenures. The high-level approach suggests particular modeling tasks.

Data Mining Tasks

Data mining tasks are technical activities that can be described independently of any particular business goal. If a business goal is well-suited to data mining, it can usually be phrased in terms of the following tasks:

- Preparing data for mining
- Exploratory data analysis
- Binary response modeling (also called binary classification)
- Classification of discrete values and predictions
- Estimation of numeric values
- Finding clusters and associations
- Applying a model to new data

Data mining projects typically involve several of these tasks. Take the example of deciding which customers to include in a direct marketing campaign. Exploratory data analysis suggests which variables are important for characterizing customer response. These variables could then be used to find clusters of similar customers. A customer's cluster assignment could be an important explanatory variable in a binary response model. And, of course, the whole point of creating the model is to apply it to new data representing prospective customers to score them for propensity to respond to the campaign.

Preparing Data for Mining

Preparing data for mining is the subject of Chapters 18 through 20. The amount of effort required depends on the nature of the data sources and the requirements of particular data mining techniques. Some data preparation is nearly always required and it is not unusual for data preparation to be the most time-consuming part of a data mining project. Some data preparation is required to fix problems with the source data, but much of it is designed to enhance the information content of the data. Better data means better models.

Typically, data from a variety of sources must be combined to form a customer signature with one record per customer and a large number of fields to capture everything of interest about them. Because the source data is usually not at the customer level, building the customer signature requires many transformations. Transactions must be summarized in useful ways. Trends in time series might be captured as slopes or differences. For data mining techniques that work only on numbers, categorical data must somehow be represented numerically. Some data mining techniques cannot handle missing values, so missing values must somehow be dealt with; the same goes for outliers. When some outcomes are rare, using stratified sampling to balance the data may be necessary. When variables are measured on different scales, standardizing them may also be necessary.

Data preparation may involve creating new variables by combining existing variables in creative ways. It may also involve reducing the number of variables using principal components and other techniques.

Exploratory Data Analysis

Exploratory data analysis is not a major focus of this book, but that is not because we think it is unimportant. In fact, one of the authors (Gordon) has written a book that is largely devoted to this data mining task: *Data Analysis Using SQL and Excel*. The product of exploratory data analysis may be a report or a collection of graphs that describe something of interest. Exploratory data analysis can also be used for adding new measures and variables in the data.

Profiling is a familiar approach to many problems, and it need not involve any sophisticated data mining algorithms at all. Profiles are often based on demographic variables, such as geographic location, sex, and age. Because advertising is sold according to these same variables, demographic profiles can turn directly into media strategies. Simple profiles are used to set insurance premiums. A 17-year-old male pays more for car insurance than a 60-year-old female. Similarly, the application form for a simple term life insurance policy asks about age, sex, and smoking — and not much more.

Powerful though it is, profiling has serious limitations. One is the inability to distinguish cause and effect. As long as the profiling is based on familiar demographic variables, this is not noticeable. If men buy more beer than women, we do not have to wonder whether beer drinking might be the cause of maleness. We can safely assume that the link is from men to beer and not vice versa.

With behavioral data, the direction of causality is not always so clear. Consider a couple of examples from real data mining projects:

- People who have purchased certificates of deposit (CDs) have little or no money in their savings accounts.

- Customers who use voice mail make a lot of short calls to their own number.

Not keeping money in a savings account is a common behavior of CD holders, just as being male is a common feature of beer drinkers. Beer companies seek out males to market their product, so should banks seek out people with no money in savings in order to sell them certificates of deposit? Probably not! Presumably, the CD holders have no money in their savings accounts because they used that money to buy CDs. A more common reason for not having money in a savings account is not having any money, and people with no money are not good prospects for investment accounts. Similarly, the voice mail users call their own number so much because in this particular system that is one way to check voice mail. The pattern is useless for finding prospective users.

Binary Response Modeling (Binary Classification)

Many business goals boil down to separating two categories from each other — the good from the bad, the sheep from the goats, or (at the risk of being sexist and ageist) the men from the boys. In a direct marketing campaign, the good respond and the bad do not. When credit is extended, the good pay what is owed and the bad default. When claims are submitted, the good are valid and the bad are fraudulent. There are techniques, such as logistic regression, that are specialized for these sorts of yes or no models.

Depending on the application, a response model score can be the class label itself or an estimate of the probability of being in the class of interest. A credit card company wanting to sell advertising space in its billing envelopes to a ski boot manufacturer might build a classification model that put all of its cardholders into one of two classes, skier or non skier. More typically, it would assign each cardholder a propensity-to-ski score. Anyone with a score greater than or equal to some threshold is classified as a skier, and anyone with a lower score is considered not to be a skier.

The estimation approach has the great advantage that the individual records can be rank ordered according to the estimate. To see the importance of this, imagine that the ski boot company has budgeted for a mailing of 500,000 pieces. If the classification approach is used and 1.5 million skiers are identified, then it might simply place the ad in the bills of 500,000 people selected at random from that pool. If, on the other hand, each cardholder has a propensity-to-ski score, it can contact the 500,000 most likely candidates.

Classification

Classification, one of the most common data mining tasks, seems to be a human imperative. To understand and communicate about the world, we are constantly classifying, categorizing, and grading. We divide living things into phyla, species, and genera; matter into elements; dogs into breeds; people into races; steaks and maple syrup into USDA grades.

Classification consists of assigning a newly presented object to one of a set of predefined classes. The classification task is characterized by a well-defined definition of the classes, and a model set consisting of preclassified examples. The task is to build a model of some kind that can be applied to unclassified data in order to classify it.

Examples of classification tasks that have been addressed using the techniques described in this book include:

- Classifying credit applicants as low, medium, or high risk
- Choosing content to be displayed on a Web page
- Determining which phone numbers correspond to fax machines, which to voice lines, and which are shared
- Spotting fraudulent insurance claims
- Assigning industry codes and job designations on the basis of free-text job descriptions

In all of these examples, there are a limited number of classes, and the task is to assign any record into one or another of them.

Estimation

Classification deals with discrete outcomes: yes or no; measles, rubella, or chicken pox. Estimation deals with continuously valued outcomes. Given some input data, estimation comes up with a value for some unknown continuous variable such as income, order size, or credit card balance.

Examples of estimation tasks include:

- Estimating a family's total household income
- Estimating the lifetime value of a customer
- Estimating the value at risk if a customer defaults
- Estimating the probability that someone will respond to a balance transfer solicitation
- Estimating the size of the balance to be transferred

The product of the estimates created in the last two bullet points is the expected value of the balance transfer offer. If the expected value is less than the cost of making the offer, the solicitation should not be made.

Finding Clusters, Associations, and Affinity Groups

Determining what things go together in a shopping cart at the supermarket, and finding groups of shoppers with similar buying habits are both examples of undirected data mining. Products that tend to sell together are called *affinity groups* and customers with similar behaviors comprise *market segments.* Retailers can use affinity grouping to plan the arrangement of items on store shelves or in a catalog so that items often purchased together will be seen at the same time. Marketing people can design products and services to appeal to particular segments.

Affinity grouping is one simple approach to generating rules from data. If two items, say cat food and kitty litter, occur together frequently enough, you can think of how to use this information in marketing campaigns. It also brings up another issue: What are customers not buying that they should? A customer who buys lots of kitty litter should also be buying cat food — where are they getting it?

Clustering is the task of segmenting a heterogeneous population into a number of more homogeneous subgroups or clusters. What distinguishes clustering from classification is that clustering does not rely on predefined classes. In classification, each record is assigned a predefined class on the basis of a model developed through training on preclassified examples.

In clustering, there are no predefined classes and no examples. The records are grouped together on the basis of self-similarity. It is up to the user to determine what meaning, if any, to attach to the resulting clusters. Clusters of symptoms might indicate different diseases. Clusters of customer attributes might indicate different market segments.

Clustering is often a prelude to some other form of data mining or modeling. For example, clustering might be the first step in a market segmentation effort: Instead of trying to come up with a one-size-fits-all rule for "what kind of promotion do customers respond to best," first divide the customer base into clusters or people with similar buying habits, and then ask what kind of promotion works best for each cluster. Chapters 13 and 14 cover techniques for cluster detection in detail.

Applying a Model to New Data

Many of the tasks listed earlier usually involve applying a model to new data. This is not true of exploratory data analysis, and it may or may not be true of clustering, but for binary response modeling, classification, and estimation, the data used to create the model contains known values of the target variable. One reason for applying a model to data where the target value is already known is to evaluate the model. After the model has been deployed, its purpose is to score new data where the probability of response, class, or value to be estimated is unknown.

Applying a model to new data is called *scoring*. The data to be scored must contain all the input variables required by the model along with a unique identifier for each row. The result of scoring is a new table with at least two columns — the identifier and the score.

Data Mining Techniques

The title of this book starts with "Data Mining Techniques," and most of the chapters describe individual techniques.

In many cases, data mining is accomplished by building models. In one sense of the word, a model is an explanation or description of how something works that reflects reality well enough that it can be used to make inferences about the real world. Without realizing it, human beings use models all the time. When you see two restaurants and decide that the one with white tablecloths and real flowers on each table is more expensive than the one with Formica tables and plastic flowers, you are making an inference based on a model you carry in your head based on your past experience. When you set out to walk to one of the restaurants, you again consult a mental model of the town.

In a more technical sense of the word, a model is something that uses data to classify things, make predictions, estimate values, or to produce some other useful result. As shown in Figure 3-4, pretty much anything that can be applied to data to produce a score of some kind fits the definition of a model.

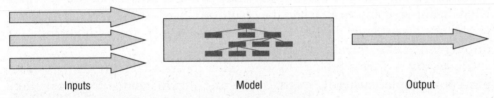

Inputs   Model   Output

Figure 3-4: Models take an input and produce an output.

A data mining model serves two purposes. The first purpose is to produce scores that you can use to guide decisions. The second is to provide insight into the relationship between the explanatory variables used to build the model and the target. Depending on the application, one or the other of these purposes may be more important than the other.

Data mining techniques fall into two categories: They can be either directed or undirected, which means respectively whether techniques themselves require or do not require target variables. Directed and undirected techniques should not be confused with directed and undirected data mining, because both types of techniques can be used for both types of data mining.

Formulating Data Mining Problems: From Goals to Tasks to Techniques

Business goals, data mining tasks, and data mining techniques form a kind of staircase from the general to specific and from non-technical to technical. Formulating a data mining problem involves descending this staircase one step at a time; going first from business goals to data mining tasks and then from data mining tasks to data mining techniques. Typically, each step requires the involvement of different staff with different skill sets. Setting and prioritizing goals is the responsibility of upper management. Translating these goals into data mining tasks and using data mining techniques to accomplish them is the role of data miners. Gathering the requisite data and transforming it into a suitable form for mining often requires cooperation with database administrators and other members of the information technology group.

Choosing the Best Places to Advertise

A company is trying to reach new profitable customers. Where should it look? Google AdWords? A reality TV show about cooking? A magazine? If so, which one? *Architectural Digest*? *People en Español*? *Rolling Stone*?

Many factors affect the decision, including overall cost, cost per impression, and cost per conversion. Data mining can provide input to the decision by matching the demographics of the advertising vehicle to the demographics of the best customers. Behavioral data for the profitable customers does not help, because advertising is based only on demographic data.

One possible approach is:

1. Profile existing profitable customers using demographic and geographic characteristics such as age, sex, occupation, marital status, and neighborhood characteristics. Use this profile to define the prototypical profitable customer.

2. Define the audience of each potential advertising vehicle using the same variables used to profile profitable customers.

3. Estimate the distance from each advertising channel to the prototypical profitable customer. This distance is the advertising channel's similarity score; as in golf, smaller is better.

4. Advertise in the venues with the lowest scores.

This is an example of a similarity model, which is covered in Chapter 6.

Determining the Best Product to Offer a Customer

What is the best next offer to make to a customer? This question is an example of cross-selling that occurs in many industries.

There are several possible approaches to this problem, depending, among other things, on the number of products to choose from. If the number of products is manageably small, a good approach is to build a separate model for each product so every customer can be given as many scores as there are products, as shown in Figure 3-5. A customer's best offer is the product for which he or she has the highest score (possibly excluding products the customer already has).

1. For each product, build a binary response model to estimate the propensity of customers for the product.

2. Set the propensity score to 0 for customers who already have a product.

3. Using the propensity scores, design a decision procedure that assigns the best product to each customer, based on something like the highest propensity or the highest expected profit.

Natural choices for Step 1 include decision trees, neural networks, and logistic regression.

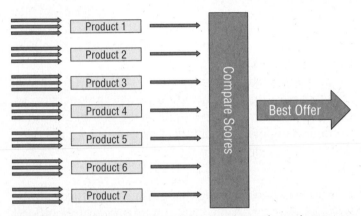

Figure 3-5: Individual propensity scores for each product are compared to determine the best offer.

A binary response model is not the only method for developing propensity scores. Another method is to cluster the data using input variables and see which products predominate in each cluster. The proportion of the cluster with a given product can be assigned as the propensity score. This method would use k-means clustering or another clustering technique.

Finding the Best Locations for Branches or Stores

What are the best locations for new stores? In this scenario, performance data for existing stores is available along with data about the catchment area — the natural market area from which each store draws its customers. The idea is to find the combination of explanatory variables that predicts good performance for a store.

The following modeling tasks are one approach to addressing this problem:

1. Build a model to estimate some store performance metric based on the available explanatory variables for the catchment area.

2. Apply the model to candidate locations so the highest scoring locations can be selected.

This is basically an estimation model, which can use a variety of techniques, such as neural networks, regression, or MBR.

An alternative approach is to classify the stores as good or bad, and then build a model that predicts these groups. Often, a good way to approach this is using the *excluded middle* approach: The profitability of each store is divided into thirds — high, medium, and low. Remove the "medium" stores and build a model to separate the high from the low (a case study in Chapter 15 takes this approach for finding the factors that distinguish stores in Hispanic areas from those in non-Hispanic areas):

1. Classify existing stores as good or bad and build a model that can distinguish between the two classes.

2. Apply the model to candidate locations so the good one can be selected.

Likely explanatory variables include the population within driving distance, the number of competitors within driving distance, and demographic factors. This is a profiling model because the goal is to link current performance with current conditions. The modeling techniques are those used for classification, such as logistic regression, decision trees, and MBR.

Segmenting Customers on Future Profitability

A method for defining profitability has been established, such as the total revenue or net revenue generated by customers over the course of one year. The goal is to segment customers today based on their anticipated profitability over the next year.

There are many ways to approach profitability calculations. This approach removes some of the more difficult areas, such as predicting how long a customer will remain a customer (and hence deciding on future discount rates), and how to attribute network effects to the customers.

For this approach, turn the clock back one year and take a snapshot of each customer who was active on that date. Then, measure the total revenue during the following year. This is the model:

1. Prepare the data for modeling by turning the clock back one year and taking a snapshot of each customer who was active on that date. Then, measure the total revenue during the following year. This creates a prediction model set.

2. Use this model set to estimate how much someone will be worth in the next year.

3. Segment the anticipated revenue into thirds, to get high, medium, and low anticipated revenue.

Step 2 requires building an estimation model, using a technique such as neural networks, MBR, or regression.

A slight variation on this approach would be to classify the customers in the model set as high, medium, or low generators of revenue in the upcoming year. This would use a classification model, which might use decision trees (with a three-way target) or three logistic regression models (one for each of the three groups).

Decreasing Exposure to Risk of Default

The goal of this business problem is to detect warning signs for default while there is still time to take steps to decrease exposure. One detection method uses a binary response model, with a target of "default." The model set is a snapshot of all customers at a given point in time (for example, the first of the year) and a flag that indicates whether or not they default in the three months after the snapshot date. New customers can then be scored with the binary response model to predict their probability of default. Perhaps customers with high levels of default should have their credit lines lowered.

Such a binary response model could be built using a variety of techniques, such as logistic regression, decision trees, or neural networks. Undirected techniques, such as clustering, could even be used. Build clusters on the input variables, and then measure the ability of the clusters to separate the target values. This is an example of using an undirected technique for a directed model.

Another approach combines the probability of default with the amount of default. This two-stage model estimates how much a customer would owe after defaulting. The model set for this consists only of customers who have defaulted, with the target being the amount owed. This model would be used to calculate the expected value of the loss, which is the probability of default multiplied by the estimated amount owed. The estimate of the amount owed could be built using MBR, neural networks, regression, or possibly decision trees.

Yet another approach would be to treat this as a time-to-event problem, estimating when a customer is likely to default. In this case, the model set consists of all customers, with their start date, end date, and whether or not the customer defaulted. The model would estimate the amount of time until a customer defaults. When scoring new customers, if the estimated time to default is in the near future, then actions would be taken to mitigate the default. This type of model would typically be built using survival analysis.

Improving Customer Retention

There are many different ways to improve customer retention:

- Find customers most at risk of leaving and encourage them to stay.
- Quantify the value of improving operations, so customers will stick around.
- Determine which methods of acquiring customers bring in better customers.
- Determine which customers are unprofitable, and let them leave.

This section only discusses the first of these.

The task list for determining who will stay is similar to the task list for any binary response model. Build a model set that consists of customers who stay and go, and let the model find the patterns that distinguish between them. This provides a model score that you can then use for a retention effort.

This type of binary response model can be built using many techniques, such as decision trees, neural networks, logistic regression, and MBR. An alternative approach would be to estimate the remaining customer tenure using survival analysis, and apply the retention message to those customers most likely to leave in the near future.

Sometimes the most important output from a model is not the scores it produces, but the understanding that comes from examining the model itself. The model may be able to explain whether customers are primarily leaving due to service disruptions, price sensitivity, or other causes. However, this requires using a technique that can explain its results. Decision trees and logistic regression are the best of the bunch for explicability.

Detecting Fraudulent Claims

The translation of this goal into modeling tasks depends on whether examples of known fraud are available. If so, this is a directed data mining task:

1. Build a profiling model that is capable of distinguishing fraudulent claims from legitimate ones.

2. Use the model to score all claims that come in. Mark claims that score higher than some threshold for additional scrutiny before approval.

Decision trees and logistic regression are likely techniques for building the profiling model in Step 1.

Sometimes, fraud is suspected, but it is not clear which transactions are fraudulent. This situation calls for undirected data mining:

1. Form clusters of similar claims. Most claims will probably fall into a few large clusters representing different types of legitimate claim.

2. Examine the smaller clusters to see what makes them special.

The claims in the smaller clusters may also be perfectly legitimate. All that the clustering exercise shows is that they are unusual. Some unusual claims turn out to be fraudulent, so all are worth further scrutiny.

ONE GOAL, TWO TASKS: WINNING A DATA MINING CONTEST

Every year, contestants from academia and industry test their data mining skills in a contest held in conjunction with the annual KDD (Knowledge Discovery and Data Mining) conference. One year, it was clear that what separated winners from losers was not the algorithms they used or the software they employed, but how they translated the business problem into data mining tasks.

The business problem was to maximize donations to a non-profit charity. The data was a historical database of contributions.

Exploring the data revealed the first insight: the more often someone contributed, the less money they contributed each time. Expecting the best donors to be those who respond most frequently is quite reasonable.

In this case, though, people seem to plan their charitable giving on a yearly basis. They might donate a lump sum all at once, or space their contributions over time. More checks does not always mean more money. This suggests that the decision to make a donation is separate from the decision of how large a donation to make. The two decisions are quite likely influenced by different factors. Perhaps people of all income levels are more likely to donate to a veterans' organization if they themselves have served in the military. After they have decided to contribute, income level may have an influence on the sizes of the donations.

These insights led to the winning approach, which was to model response and contribution size separately. The response model is built on a training set that contains both contributors and non-contributors. This is a binary outcome classification task.

The contribution size model is built on a training set consisting only of contributors. This is an estimation task. The following figure shows the two models and how their results are combined to produce an expected response value for each prospect.

The three winning entries all took this approach of combining models. The majority of contestants, on the other hand, built a single model with *amount contributed* as the target. These models treated the entire problem as an estimation task with a lack of response represented as a contribution of zero dollars.

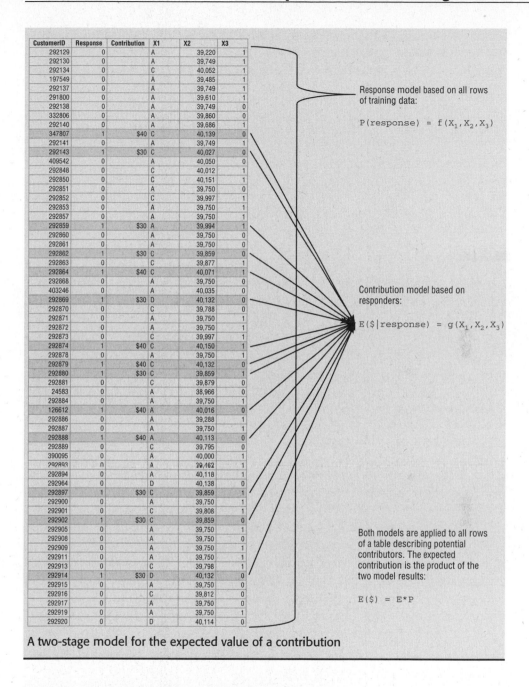

CustomerID	Response	Contribution	X1	X2	X3
292129	0		A	39,220	1
292130	0		A	39,749	1
292134	0		C	40,052	1
197549	0		A	39,485	1
292137	0		A	39,749	1
291800	0		A	39,610	1
292138	0		A	39,749	0
332806	0		A	39,860	0
292140	0		A	39,686	1
347807	1	$40	C	40,139	0
292141	0		A	39,749	1
292143	1	$30	C	40,027	0
409542	0		A	40,050	0
292848	0		C	40,012	1
292850	0		C	40,151	1
292851	0		A	39,750	0
292852	0		C	39,997	1
292853	0		A	39,750	1
292857	0		A	39,750	1
292859	1	$30	A	39,994	1
292860	0		A	39,750	0
292861	0		A	39,750	0
292862	1	$30	C	39,859	0
292863	0		C	39,877	1
292864	1	$40	C	40,071	1
292868	0		A	39,750	0
403246	0		A	40,035	0
292869	1	$30	D	40,132	0
292870	0		C	39,788	0
292871	0		A	39,750	1
292872	0		A	39,750	1
292873	0		C	39,997	1
292874	1	$40	C	40,150	1
292878	0		A	39,750	1
292879	1	$40	C	40,132	0
292880	1	$30	C	39,859	1
292881	0		C	39,879	0
24583	0		A	38,966	0
292884	0		A	39,750	1
126612	1	$40	A	40,016	0
292886	0		A	39,288	1
292887	0		A	39,750	1
292888	1	$40	A	40,113	0
292889	0		C	39,795	0
390095	0		A	40,000	1
292893	0		A	39,462	1
292894	0		A	40,118	1
292964	0		D	40,138	0
292897	1	$30	C	39,859	1
292900	0		A	39,750	1
292901	0		C	39,808	1
292902	1	$30	C	39,859	0
292905	0		A	39,750	1
292908	0		A	39,750	0
292909	0		A	39,750	1
292911	0		A	39,750	0
292913	0		C	39,798	1
292914	1	$30	D	40,132	0
292915	0		A	39,750	0
292916	0		C	39,812	0
292917	0		A	39,750	0
292919	0		A	39,750	1
292920	0		D	40,114	0

Response model based on all rows of training data:

$$P(\text{response}) = f(X_1, X_2, X_3)$$

Contribution model based on responders:

$$E(\$|\text{response}) = g(X_1, X_2, X_3)$$

Both models are applied to all rows of a table describing potential contributors. The expected contribution is the product of the two model results:

$$E(\$) = E * P$$

A two-stage model for the expected value of a contribution

What Techniques for Which Tasks?

You can use all the data mining techniques described in this book in creative ways for applications outside the ones with which they are most often associated. Each major family of techniques has a chapter (or even more than one chapter). The individual technique chapters include examples of how to apply the techniques for various purposes. Still, some techniques are better suited to some tasks. When choosing a technique, ask yourself these questions:

- Is there a target or targets?
- What is the target data like?
- What is the input data like?
- How important is ease of use?
- How important is explicability?

The answers to these questions narrow the choice of techniques.

Is There a Target or Targets?

All directed data mining techniques, including regression, decision trees, and neural networks, require training with known values for the target variables. When the data does not contain such a target, one of the undirected techniques such as clustering or exploratory data analysis is needed.

What Is the Target Data Like?

When the target is numeric and can take on a wide range of values, a technique that produces continuous values is appropriate. Linear regression models can produce any value from negative infinity to infinity, as can neural networks. When the task is to estimate the value of a continuous target, these are natural choices. Regression trees and table lookup models can all be used to estimate numeric values also, but they produce a relatively small number of discrete values. Memory-based reasoning is another choice for numeric targets that can produce a wide range of values, but never outside the range of the original data.

When the target is a binary response or categorical variable, techniques that produce a probability of being in each class are called for. Decision trees are a very natural fit for these kinds of problems, as are logistic regression and neural networks. Depending on other aspects of the problem, and on the nature of the inputs, other techniques such as similarity models, memory-based reasoning, and naïve Bayesian models may be good choices.

What Is the Input Data Like?

Regression models, neural networks, and many other techniques perform mathematical operations on the input values and so cannot process categorical data or missing values. It is of course possible to recode categorical data or replace categorical fields with numeric fields that capture important features of the categories. It is also possible to input missing values. These operations can be time-consuming and inaccurate, however. As the number of categorical fields and fields with missing values goes up, so does the appeal of decision trees, table lookup models, and naïve Bayesian models, all of which can easily handle categorical fields and missing values. When the inputs are numeric and do not contain missing values, regression models and neural networks may be able to make use of more of the information in the data.

How Important Is Ease of Use?

Some techniques require much more data preparation than others. For example, neural networks require all inputs to be numeric and within a small range of values. They are also sensitive to outliers and unable to process missing values. Others, such as decision trees, are much more forgiving and require less data preparation, but may not do as good a job. There is often a trade-off between power, accuracy, and ease of use. As an extreme example, genetic algorithms require so much work on the part of the miner that they are rarely used if an alternative approach is available.

Since the first edition of this book appeared back in the 1990s, data mining software tools have made great strides in the ease-of-use area. The best ones provide user interfaces that support best practices and make even complex techniques such as neural networks relatively user-friendly.

How Important Is Model Explicability?

For some problems, getting the right answer fast is paramount. A modern, no-envelope-required automatic teller machine must be able to recognize hand-written amounts accurately in order to accept checks for deposit. Although it would certainly be fascinating to learn how the algorithm differentiates American "7s" from European "1s", there is no urgent need to do so. In the brief interval between when a credit card is swiped and the approval code is transmitted, the transaction is scored for likelihood to be fraudulent. Getting this decision right is important. Approving a fraudulent transaction has an immediate and obvious cost; rejecting a legitimate transaction annoys a valuable customer. In both these examples, getting the right answer is clearly more important than having a clear explanation of how the decision was made.

At the other extreme, some decisions — whether to grant or deny credit, for example — may be subject to regulatory review. Explaining that credit was denied because the applicant had too many open lines and too great a ratio of debt to income is fine. Saying, "The model identified the applicant as high risk, but we have no idea why," is unacceptable.

Different techniques offer different trade-offs between accuracy and explicability. Decision trees arguably offer the best explanations because each leaf has a precise description in the form of a rule. Although this means that the score for any given record can be explained, it does not mean that a large, complex tree is easy to understand as a whole. The trade-off is that decision trees may not make use of as much of a variable's inherent information as other techniques that make use of the value directly instead of simply comparing it to a splitting value.

With a bit of attention to data preparation, regression models also shed a lot of light on what contributes to a score. When explanatory variables have been standardized, the relative magnitude of the model coefficients show how much each one contributes to the score. In a regression, every small change in the value of an explanatory variable has an effect on the score. In that sense, the regression model makes more use of the information provided by the explanatory variables than do decision trees.

Neural networks are quite flexible and are capable of modeling quite complex functions very accurately, but are essentially inexplicable. Each of these techniques provides a different trade-off between best scores and best explanations. Knowing the strengths and weaknesses, you must decide on the techniques that are most appropriate for your application.

Table 3-1 shows which techniques are typically used for which tasks. As the table makes clear, pretty much any of the directed techniques can be used for classification, prediction, and estimation problems. The final choice is driven by the extent to which the model should be able to tell a story in addition to producing scores, and by characteristics of the data to be mined.

Table 3-1: What Techniques for Which Tasks?

TASK	BEST FIT	ALSO CONSIDER
Classification and prediction	Decision trees, logistic regression, neural networks	Similarity models, table look-up models, nearest neighbor models, naïve Bayesian models
Estimation	Linear regression, neural networks	Regression trees, nearest neighbor models
Binary response	Logistic regression, decision trees	Similarity models, table look-up models, nearest neighbor models, naïve Bayesian models
Finding clusters and patterns	Any of the clustering algorithms	Association rules

Lessons Learned

The data mining process can fail in many ways. Failure can take several forms, including simply failing to answer the questions you set out to answer, as well as "discovering" things you already know. An especially pernicious form of failure is learning things that aren't true. This can happen in many ways: when the data used for mining is not representative; or when it contains accidental patterns that fail to generalize; or when it has been summarized in a way that destroys information; or when it mixes information from time periods that should be kept separate.

There are three styles of data mining. Exploratory data mining produces insights or answers questions rather than producing models used for scoring. Exploratory data mining often involves coming up with hypotheses that can be proven or disproven using data. Exploratory data mining is very important; however, it is not the subject of the advanced techniques in this book.

Directed data mining is used when the historical data contains examples of what is being looked for. For an attrition model, this assumes that the historical data contains examples of customers who have and have not stopped. For a customer value model, this assumes that it is possible to estimate customer value using the historical data. The target (or targets) of the model are these variables. The "explanatory" variables in the model are the inputs.

Undirected data mining does not use a target variable. It is like throwing the data at the computer and seeing where it lands. Making sense of undirected data mining requires understanding and interpreting the results. Without a target, there is no way for the computer to judge whether or not the results are good.

You can use all three data mining styles separately or in combination to accomplish a wide range of business goals. The data mining process starts with a business goal. The data mining process involves translating the business goal into one or more data mining tasks. After the tasks have been defined, the nature of the task, the type of data available, the way that results will be delivered, and the trade-off between model accuracy and model explicability all influence the choice of data mining technique.

Whichever technique you choose, and regardless of the data mining style, using data mining effectively requires some knowledge of statistics, the subject of the next chapter.

Statistics 101: What You Should Know About Data

For statisticians (and economists too), the term *data mining* once had a pejorative meaning. Instead of "to find useful patterns in large volumes of data," data mining had the connotation of searching for data to fit preconceived ideas. This definition is much like what politicians do around election time — search for data to show the success of their deeds. It is certainly not what the authors mean by data mining!

This chapter is intended to bridge some of the gaps between traditional statistics and data mining. The two disciplines are very similar. Statisticians and data miners commonly use many of the same techniques, and statistical software vendors now include many of the techniques described throughout this book in their software packages. Data miners should have a foundation of knowledge in statistics.

A fact that will perhaps surprise some readers is that statistics developed as a discipline distinct from mathematics over the past century and a half to help scientists make sense of observations and design experiments that yield the reproducible and accurate results associated with the scientific method. Because statistics is intimately tied to scientific understanding of the world, applying it to the scientific understanding of business is natural.

For almost all of this period, the issue was not too much data, but too little. Scientists had to figure out how to understand the world using data collected by hand in notebooks. These quantities were sometimes mistakenly recorded, illegible due to fading and smudged ink, difficult to copy, and painful to manipulate (especially by the standards of modern spreadsheets). Early statisticians were practical people who invented techniques to handle whatever problem was at hand. Quite a few of the techniques mentioned in this book date back to the 1950s and 1960s when computers first appeared at universities — and statistics departments were some of the first groups to take advantage of those newfangled machines.

What is remarkable and a testament to the founders of modern statistics is that techniques developed long ago on tiny amounts of data in a world of hand calculations have survived and still prove their utility. These techniques have proven their worth not only in the original domains but also in virtually all areas where data is collected, from agriculture to psychology to astronomy and even to business.

Perhaps the greatest statistician of the twentieth century was R. A. Fisher, considered by many to be the father of modern statistics. In the 1920s, long before the invention of modern computers, he devised methods for designing and analyzing experiments. For two years, while living on a farm outside London, he collected various measurements of crop yields along with potential explanatory variables — amount of rain and sun and fertilizer, for instance. To understand what has an effect on crop yields, he invented new techniques (such as *analysis of variance* — ANOVA) and performed perhaps a million calculations on the data he collected. Although twenty-first-century computer chips easily handle many millions of calculations in a second, each of Fisher's calculations required pulling a lever on a manual calculating machine. Results emerged slowly over weeks and months, along with sore hands and calluses. (In fact, he did not do the calculations himself; many of his "calculators" were women studying statistics.)

The advent of computing power has clearly simplified some aspects of analysis, although its bigger effect is the wealth of available data. The goal in data mining is no longer to extract every last iota of possible information from each rare datum. The goal is instead to make sense of quantities of data so large that they are beyond the ability of human brains to comprehend in their raw format.

The purpose of this chapter is to present some key ideas from statistics that have proven to be useful tools for data mining. This chapter is intended to be neither a thorough nor a comprehensive introduction to statistics; rather, it is an introduction to a handful of useful statistical techniques and ideas. These tools are shown by demonstration, rather than through mathematical proof.

The chapter starts with an introduction to what is probably the most important aspect of applied statistics — a skeptical attitude. It then discusses looking at data through a statistician's eye, introducing important concepts and terminology along the way. Examples of this skepticism are sprinkled through the chapter, especially in the discussion of confidence intervals and the chi-square test. One example, using the chi-square test to understand geography and channel, is an unusual application of the ideas presented in the chapter. Another case study applies the ideas to A/B tests, as a way to determine the best recommendations to make to online customers. The chapter ends with a brief discussion of some of the differences between data miners and statisticians — differences that are more a matter of degree than of substance.

Occam's Razor

William of Occam was a Franciscan monk born in a small English town in 1280 — not only before modern statistics was invented, but also before the Renaissance and the printing press. (The English village, now spelled Ockham, is about 25 miles southwest of London.) William of Occam was an influential philosopher, theologian, and professor who expounded many ideas about many things, including church politics. As a monk, he was an ascetic who took his vow of poverty very seriously. He was also a fervent advocate of the power of reason, denying the existence of universal truths and espousing a modern philosophy that was quite different from the views of most of his contemporaries living in the Middle Ages.

What does William of Occam have to do with data mining? His name has become associated with a very simple idea. He himself explained it in Latin (the language of learning, even among the English, at the time), *"Entia non sunt multiplicanda praeter necessitatem."* In more familiar English, one would say "The simpler explanation is the preferable one" or, more colloquially, "Keep it simple, stupid." Any explanation should strive to reduce the number of causes to the bare minimum sufficient for explaining the phenomenon. This line of reasoning is referred to as Occam's razor and is his gift to data analysis.

The story of William of Occam has an interesting ending. Perhaps because of his focus on the power of reason, he also believed that the powers of the church should be separate from the powers of the state — that the church should be confined to religious matters. This resulted in his opposition to the meddling of Pope John XXII in politics and eventually to his own excommunication. He died in Munich during an outbreak of the plague in 1349, leaving a legacy of clear and critical thinking for future generations.

Skepticism and Simpson's Paradox

The flip side of Occam's razor is that explanations should not be oversimplified. Oversimplification is as bad as overcomplication, when it impedes one's ability to understand what is really happening. As an example, oversimplification can occur when looking at summary statistics, because underlying factors — that affect the summaries — may be hidden.

One of the authors has family in Minnesota and Iowa. There is a joke in Minnesota that goes something like, "Did you hear about the guy who moved from Minnesota to Iowa and raised the average IQ of both states?" The first reaction is that this is impossible. After all, the combined population of the two states remains the same, as does the average IQ of the combined population, regardless of who moves back and forth. How could the average of each state be lower before the move and higher afterwards?

More careful thought reveals how the joke can be true. If the average IQ in Iowa is less than the average IQ in Minnesota, then someone who lives in Minnesota with a higher IQ than the Iowa average but lower than the Minnesota average can move to the adjoining state, raising the average IQ of both states. This type of paradox has a name — Simpson's paradox (named after the statistician Edward Simpson, not the fictional character Homer Simpson).

Simpson's paradox occurs when underlying factors are hidden by summary statistics. In the case of the joke, the average IQs of the two states change, but so does their population. The weighted average remains the same, even though the averages for each group increase. Statisticians have a name for such phenomena; variables that affect the outcome but are not seen in the data are examples of *unobserved heterogeneity*.

A case study later in this chapter was inspired by a version of Simpson's paradox. The metrics used to judge a recommendation engine showed that it was successful; that is, all the metrics except the final bottom-line result.

The Null Hypothesis

Occam's razor is very important for data mining and statistics, although statistics expresses the idea a bit differently. The *null hypothesis* is the assumption that differences among observations are due simply to chance. To give an example, consider a presidential poll that gives Candidate A 45 percent and Candidate B 47 percent. The goal, of course, is to estimate the preference for each candidate in the general population (or perhaps more importantly among people who are going to vote). Because this data is from a poll, there are several sources of error. The values are only approximate estimates of the popularity of each candidate among the larger population. The layperson is inclined to ask, "Is one candidate more popular than the other?" The statistician phrases the question slightly differently, "What is the probability that the two candidates are equally popular, given the difference in their polling numbers?"

Although the two questions are very similar, the statistician's has a bit of an attitude. This attitude is that the difference observed in the polling numbers may have no significance at all, an attitude inspired by the null hypothesis. Just to be clear, there is an observed difference of 2 percent based on the poll. However, the observed polling numbers may be explained by the particular sample of people included in the polling population. Another poll using the exact same methodology might have a difference of 2 percent in the other direction, or a difference of 0 percent, or some other value. All may be reasonably likely results. Of course, if the preferences differed by 20 percent, then sampling variation is much less likely to be the cause. Such a large difference would greatly improve the confidence that one candidate is more popular than the other among the larger population, and greatly reduce the probability of the null hypothesis being true.

> **TIP** The simplest explanation is usually the best one — even (or especially) if it does not prove the hypothesis you want to prove.

This skeptical attitude is very valuable for both statisticians and data miners. Our goal as data miners is to demonstrate results that work, and to discount the null hypothesis. One difference between data miners and statisticians is the volume of data that data miners work with. This is often sufficiently large that worrying about the mechanics of calculating the probability of something being due to sample variation is unnecessary.

P-Values

The null hypothesis is not merely an approach to analysis; it can also be quantified. The *p-value* is the probability of observing a difference as large as the observed difference given that the null hypothesis is true. Remember, when the null hypothesis is true, nothing interesting is really happening, because differences are due to chance (strictly speaking, sampling variation). Much of statistics is devoted to determining bounds for the p-value under different circumstances.

For the previous example of the presidential poll, assume that the p-value is calculated to be 60 percent (more on how this is done later in this chapter). Such a p-value means that when support for the two candidates is in fact equal, then 60 percent of the time a poll of this type will find a difference of at least 2 percent. This is a large value, which provides little evidence to reject the null hypothesis. There is little support for the notion that the two candidates differ in popularity.

Suppose the p-value is 5 percent, instead. This is a relatively small number. It means that if the two candidates have equal popularity, then only 5 percent of the time would a difference as large as 2 percent show up in the poll. In this case, there is little support for the null hypothesis. A common way to phrase this is that you are at least 95 percent *confident* that the null hypothesis is false, hence 95 percent confident that the candidates differ in popularity, with Candidate B doing better than Candidate A. This rephrasing is not strictly accurate, as explained in the sidebar "A Common Misunderstanding."

Confidence, sometimes called the *q-value*, is the flip side of the p-value. Generally, the goal is to aim for a confidence level of at least 90 percent, if not 95 percent or more (meaning that the corresponding p-value is less than 10 percent, or 5 percent, respectively).

A COMMON MISUNDERSTANDING

The definition of the p-value is often shortened to "the probability that the null hypothesis is true." This shorthand is not technically correct, but it does reflect how the value gets used in practice. The p-value really measures the probability of observing a value at least as unlikely as the observed value, given that the null hypothesis is true. As a consequence, when the p-value is small, little evidence exists that the null hypothesis is true, but how little?

There are two scenarios for any test:

▪ The null hypothesis is actually true.

▪ The null hypothesis is actually false.

For any given test, you do not know which of these is true, or the probabilities of one versus the other. The definition of the p-value makes no claim in the second case, only in the first case. When the null hypothesis is actually true, then the p-value measures how often rejecting it is incorrect based on a particular observation. It does not measure how often the null hypothesis is itself true or false. This is a subtle but important distinction.

With respect to the question, "How often is the null hypothesis true?" the p-value is overly conservative, but you cannot say by how much. Why is it overly conservative? Go back to the two cases. The p-value provides a measure in the first case of being wrong when rejecting the null hypothesis. In the second case, rejecting the null hypothesis is never wrong. In the real world, the null hypothesis is sometimes true and sometimes false; however, you just do not know the probability in any given situation.

In other words, when rejecting the null hypothesis, you are wrong between never (in the second case) and the p-value (the first case). The actual probability of being correct in rejecting the statement, "The null hypothesis is true," is therefore between zero and the p-value.

These ideas — the null hypothesis, p-value, and confidence — are three basic ideas in statistics. The next section carries these ideas further and introduces the statistical concept of distributions, with particular attention to the normal distribution.

Looking At and Measuring Data

A *statistic* refers to a measure taken on a sample of data. Statistics is the study of these measures and the samples they are measured on. This section describes various different methods for exploring data.

Categorical Values

Much of the data used in data mining is categorical, rather than numeric. Categorical data shows up to describe products, channels, regions, and other aspects of businesses. This section discusses ways of looking at and analyzing categorical fields.

Histograms

The most basic descriptive statistic for categorical variables is the number of times different values occur. Figure 4-1 shows a *histogram* of stop reason codes during a period of time. A histogram shows how often each value occurs in the data and can have either absolute quantities (204 times) or percentage (14.6 percent). Often, too many values exist to show in a single histogram, such as in this case where dozens of additional codes are grouped into the "other" category.

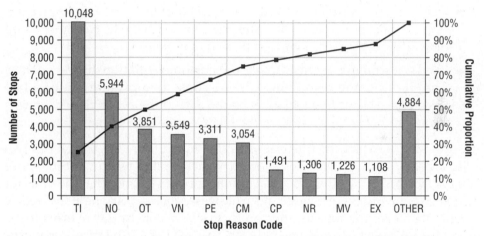

Figure 4-1: This example shows both a histogram (as a vertical bar chart) and cumulative proportion (as a line) on the same chart for stop reasons associated with a particular marketing effort.

In addition to the values for each category, this histogram also shows the cumulative proportion of stops, whose scale is shown on the left side. Through the cumulative histogram, you can see that the top three codes account for about 50 percent of stops, and the top 10, almost 90 percent. As an aesthetic note, the grid lines intersect both the left and right scales at reasonable points on the scale, making it easier to read the values on both vertical axes.

> **TIP** When making charts that have two vertical axes, use grid lines and make the grid lines match the ticks on both axes (this may require playing with the maximum values and tick mark intervals on one or both axes).

Time Series

Histograms are quite useful and easily made with a spreadsheet such as Excel or any statistics package. However, histograms describe a single moment. Data mining is often concerned with what is happening over time. A key question is whether the frequency of values is constant or changing over time.

Answering this question uses a rudimentary form of time series analysis. The first step is deciding on an appropriate time frame for the data; this includes choosing not only the units of time, but also when to start counting from. Some different time frames are the beginning of a customer relationship, when a customer requests a stop, the actual stop date, and so on. Different fields may have different time frames. For example:

- Fields describing the beginning of a customer relationship — such as original product, original channel, or original market — should be looked at by the customer's original start date.

- Fields describing the end of a customer relationship — such as last product, stop reason, or stop channel — should be looked at by the customer's stop date or the customer's tenure at that point in time.

- Fields describing events during the customer relationship — such as product upgrade or downgrade, response to a promotion, or a late payment — should be looked at by the date of the event, the customer's tenure at that point in time, or the relative time since some other event.

The next step is to plot the time series as shown in Figure 4-2, which has two series for stops by stop date. One shows a particular stop type over time (price increase stops) and the other, the total number of stops. Notice that the units for the time axis are in days. Although much business reporting is done at the weekly and monthly level, the authors often prefer to look at data by day in order to see important patterns that might emerge at a fine level of granularity — patterns that might be obscured by summarization.

This chart shows some interesting patterns. One is a weekly pattern in the overall stops, which is evident because of the four or five spikes during each month (additional work is needed to confirm that the peaks are, indeed, exactly one week apart). A big change also occurs between the first four months, which have higher stops, and the subsequent dates. The lighter line, for price increase–related stops, has a very large jump at the end of January. The cause, of course, was an increase in price that went into effect at that time.

TIP When looking at field values over time, look at the data by day to get a feel for the data at the most granular level.

A time series chart has a wealth of information. For example, fitting a line to the data makes it possible to see and quantify long-term trends, as shown in Figure 4-2. Be careful when doing this, because of seasonality. Partial years might introduce inadvertent trends, so try to include entire years when using a best-fit line. The likely correlation between the number of stops and the number of customers suggests that a better measure would be the stop rate, rather than the raw number of stops.

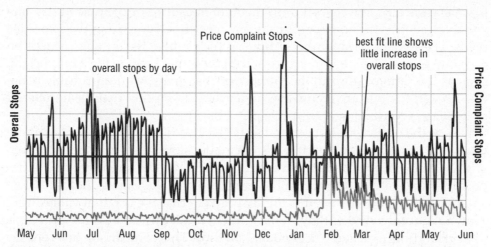

Figure 4-2: This chart shows two time series plotted with different vertical scales. The dark line is for overall stops; the light line for pricing related stops shows the impact of a change in pricing strategy at the end of January.

Standardized Values (Z-Scores)

A time series chart provides useful information. However, it does not give an idea as to whether the changes over time are expected or unexpected. For this, let's borrow some tools from statistics.

One way of looking at a time series is as a bunch of samples of all the data, with a small sample on each day. Remember the null hypothesis: The statistician wants to be a skeptic and ask the question: "Is it possible that the differences seen on each day are strictly due to chance?" The p-value answers this question; recall it is the probability that the observed variation among values would be seen if each day were just a random sample.

Statisticians have been studying this fundamental question for more than a century. Fortunately, they have also devised some techniques for answering it. This is a question about *sample variation*. Each day represents a sample of stops from all the stops that occurred during the period. The variation in stops observed on different days might simply be due to an expected variation in taking random samples.

A basic theorem in statistics, called the *central limit theorem*, says the following:

> *As more and more random samples are taken from a population, the distribution of the averages of the samples (or any similar statistic) follows the normal distribution. As the number of samples grows, the average of the average values of the samples comes closer and closer to the average of the entire population.*

The central limit theorem is actually a very complex idea whose proof is quite interesting to those with an affinity for advanced mathematics. More importantly for everyone else, the central limit theorem is useful. In the case of discrete variables, such as the number of customers who stop on each day, the same idea holds. The statistic used for this example is the count of the number of stops on each day, as shown earlier in Figure 4-2. (Strictly speaking, using a proportion, such as the ratio of stops to the number of customers, would probably make this clearer; the two are equivalent under the assumption that the number of customers is constant over the period.)

How is the central limit theorem used? The idea is easy. If the samples (daily totals) are indeed randomly drawn from all the stops, then the values on each day will follow a normal distribution. As mathematicians might say, the contra-positive is true as well. That is, if the distribution of the values does *not* follow a normal distribution, then it is highly unlikely that the original values were drawn randomly. And, if they weren't drawn randomly, some other process is at work, indicating a likely dependency on time. This comparison does not say what the dependency is, just that a dependency is likely to exist.

The normal distribution is described by two parameters: the average and the standard deviation. The standard deviation measures the extent to which values tend to cluster around the average and is explained more fully later in the chapter; for now, using a function such as STDEV() in Excel or STDDEV() in SQL is sufficient. For the time series, the standard deviation is the standard deviation of the daily counts. Assuming that the values for each day are taken randomly from the stops for the entire period, the set of counts should follow a normal distribution. If they don't, then something besides chance is affecting the values. In this case, the simplest explanation, differences due to sampling, is insufficient to explain the variation in the number of stops from day to day.

Because of their relation to the normal distribution, standard deviations are quite useful. One way to incorporate them directly into data analysis is to convert values in a particular variable into the number of standard deviations from the average. This process, called *standardizing* values, is quite simple for a time series:

1. Calculate the average value for all days.
2. Calculate the standard deviation for all days.
3. For each value, subtract the average and divide by the standard deviation to get the number of standard deviations from the average.

Standardized values, also called *z-scores*, make observing information pertinent to the null hypothesis easier. One property of standardized values is that the sum is always zero.

When the null hypothesis is true, the standardized values should follow the normal distribution (with an average of 0 and a standard deviation of 1). In this case, the standardized value should take on negative values and positive values with about equal frequency. Also, when standardized, about two-thirds (68.4 percent) of the values should be between –1 and 1. A bit more than 95 percent of the values should be between –2 and 2. Values more than 3 or less than –3 should be very, very rare — probably not visible in the data. Of course, "should" here means that the values follow the normal distribution and the null hypothesis need not be rejected (that is, that sample variation is sufficient to explain time-related effects). When the null hypothesis does not hold, it is often apparent from the standardized values. The sidebar, "A Question of Terminology," talks a bit more about distributions, normal and otherwise.

Figure 4-3 shows the standardized values for the data in Figure 4-2. The first thing to notice is that the shape of each standardized curve is very similar to the shape of the original data; what has changed is the scale on the vertical dimension. In the previous figure, overall stops were much larger than pricing stops, so the two were shown using different scales. In this figure, though, the curve for the standardized pricing stops towers over the standardized overall stops in February, even though both are on the same scale.

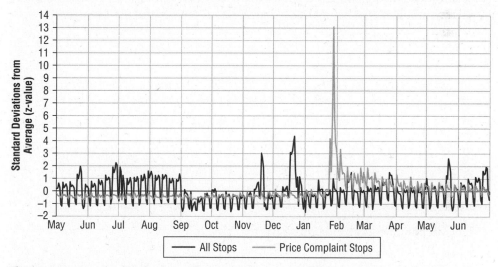

Figure 4-3: Standardized values allow you to compare different groups on the same chart using the same scale; this chart shows overall stops and price increase–related stops.

The overall stops in Figure 4-3 are normal, with the following caveats. A large peak occurs at the end of December, which probably needs to be explained because the value is more than four standard deviations away from the average. Also, there is a strong weekly pattern. To average out the intraweek variation, construct the chart using weekly stops instead of daily stops. Finally, the first four months of stops are consistently on the high side.

A QUESTION OF TERMINOLOGY

A very important idea in statistics is the idea of a *distribution*. For a categorical variable, a distribution is a lot like a histogram — it tells how often a given value occurs as a probability between 0 and 1. For instance, a uniform distribution says that all values are equally represented. An example of a uniform distribution would occur in a business where customers pay by credit card and equal numbers of customers pay with American Express, MasterCard, and Visa.

The normal distribution, which plays a very special role in statistics, is an example of a distribution for a continuous variable. The following figure shows the normal (sometimes called Gaussian or bell-shaped) distribution with an average of 0 and a standard deviation of 1. The way to read this curve is to look at areas between two points. For a value that follows the normal distribution, the probability that the value falls between two values — for example, between 0 and 1 — is the area under the curve. For the values of 0 and 1, the probability is 34.1 percent, meaning that 34.1 percent of the time a variable that follows a normal distribution will take on a value within one standard deviation above the average. Because the curve is symmetric, there is an additional 34.1 percent probability of being one standard deviation below the average, and hence 68.2 percent probability of being within one standard deviation of the average.

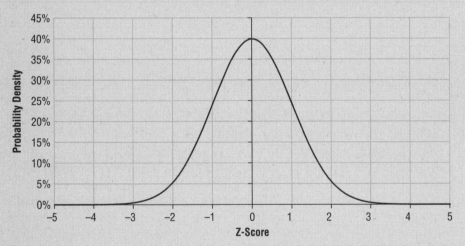

The probability density function for the normal distribution looks like the familiar bell-shaped curve.

The preceding figure shows a picture of a bell-shaped curve and calls it the normal distribution. Actually, the correct terminology is *density function* (or *probability density function*). Although this terminology derives from advanced mathematical probability theory, it makes sense. The density function gives a flavor for how "dense" a variable is for different values. You use a density function by measuring the area under the curve between two points, rather than by reading the individual values themselves. In the case of the normal distribution, the values are densest around 0 and less dense as you move away.

The following figure shows the curve that is more properly called the normal distribution. This form, where the curve starts at 0 on the left and rises to 1 on the right, is also called a *cumulative distribution function*. Mathematically, the distribution function for a value *X* is defined as the probability that the variable takes on a value less than or equal to *X*. Because of the "less than or equal to" characteristic, this function always starts near 0, climbs upward, and ends up close to 1. In general, the density function provides more visual clues about what is going on with a distribution. Because density functions provide more information, they are often referred to as distributions, although that is technically inaccurate.

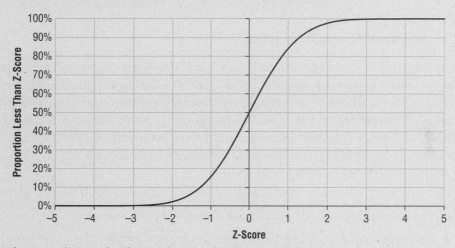

The (cumulative) distribution function for the normal distribution has an S-shape.

Finally, there is one very important point about understanding distributions. People tend to look at the "bulge" in the distribution, coming to the conclusion that a distribution that has a big hump "looks" like a normal distribution. In fact, what makes a distribution normal is what happens in the tails of the distribution as the values get further from the center. The normal distribution has very well-defined tails, and it is extremely unlikely to observe values more than three or four standard deviations from the average.

The lighter line showing the pricing-related stops clearly does not follow the normal distribution. Many more values are negative than positive. The peak is more than 13 — which is way, way too high for a normal distribution. The negative peaks, on the other hand, are never less than –2, so the distribution is highly asymmetric in terms of positive and negative values. The sum of the standardized value is 0, so a few large positive values often result in many small negative ones.

This example uses z-scores to look at values over time to see whether they look like random samples whose variation could be explained as a by-product of sampling itself. Days when the z-score is relatively high or low are suspicious.

Some other factor might be affecting the stops. The high peak in pricing stops can be explained by a change in pricing — a price increase, in fact. This effect is quite evident in the daily z-score.

The z-score is useful for other reasons as well. It is one way of taking several variables and converting them to similar ranges using the same units. That is, different columns, such as amount spent, interest rate, tenure, and so on can all be converted from dollars, percents, and days into a common unit — standard deviations from the average. This can be useful for several data mining techniques, such as clustering and neural networks. Other uses of z-scores are covered in Chapter 19, which covers data transformations.

From Z-Scores to Probabilities

Assuming that a set of standardized values follows the normal distribution allows you to calculate the probability that any given value would have occurred by chance. Actually, there is about a zero percent probability of any particular value exactly occurring. So, the p-value measures the probability that something as far as or farther from the average would have occurred (assuming the null hypothesis). Probabilities are defined on ranges of z-scores as the area under the normal curve between two points.

Calculating something farther from the average might mean one of two things:

- The probability of being more than z standard deviations from the average
- The probability of being z standard deviations greater than the average (or separately z standard deviations less than the average)

The first is called a two-tailed test and the second is called a one-tailed test. Figure 4-4 perhaps makes the terminology a bit clearer. The two-tailed probability is always twice as large as the one-tailed probability for z-scores. The two tests measure different things. The two-tailed tests measure the probability of observing a difference this large between A and B (under the null hypothesis). The one-tailed test measures the probability of observing such a difference *and A is the winner*. The two-tailed p-value is more pessimistic than the one-tailed one, in the sense that it is more likely to assume that the null hypothesis is true. If the one-tailed says the probability of the null hypothesis is 10 percent, then the two-tailed says it is 20 percent.

The two-tailed p-value can be calculated conveniently in Excel, using the function called NORMSDIST(), which calculates the cumulative normal distribution. Using this function, the two-tailed p-value is 2 * NORMSDIST(-ABS(z)). For a value of 2, the result is 4.6 percent, indicating a 4.6 percent chance of observing a value more than two standard deviations from the average — plus or minus. Or, put another way, there is a 95.4 percent confidence that a value falling outside two standard deviations is due to something besides chance. For a precise 95 percent confidence, a bound of 1.96 can be used instead of 2. For 99 percent confidence, the limit is 2.58. The following shows the limits on the z-score for some common confidence levels:

- 90% confidence → z-score > 1.64
- 95% confidence → z-score > 1.96
- 99% confidence → z-score > 2.58
- 99.5% confidence → z-score > 2.81
- 99.9% confidence → z-score > 3.29
- 99.99% confidence → z-score > 3.89

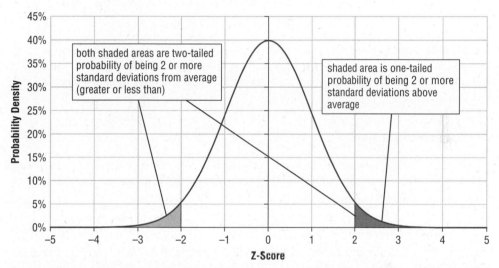

Figure 4-4: The tail of the normal distribution answers the question: "What is the probability of getting a value of *z* or greater?"

Confidence is the opposite of the p-value. When confidence is close to 100 percent, the value is unlikely to be due to chance; when it is close to 0 the value is likely to be due to chance. The signed confidence adds information about whether the value is too low or too high. When the observed value is less than the average, the signed confidence is negative.

Figure 4-5 shows the signed confidence for the data shown in Figures 4-2 and 4-3, using the two-tailed probability. The shape of the signed confidence is different from the earlier shapes. The confidence of the stop count bounces around, usually remaining within reasonable bounds — that is, the confidence does not hover around 0. The pricing-related stops show a very distinct pattern, being too low for a long time, then peaking and descending. The signed confidence levels are bounded by 100 percent and –100 percent. In this chart, the extreme values are near 100 percent or –100 percent, and telling the difference between 99.9 percent and 99.99999 percent is difficult. To distinguish values near the extremes, the z-scores in Figure 4-3 are better than the signed confidence.

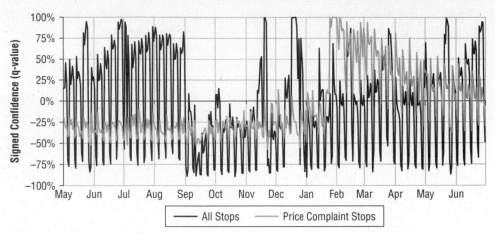

Figure 4-5: Based on the same data from Figures 4-2 and 4-3, this chart shows the signed confidence (q-values) of the observed value based on the average and standard deviation. This sign is positive when the observed value is too high, negative when it is too low.

Cross-Tabulations

Time series are an example of cross-tabulation — looking at the values of two or more variables at one time. For time series, the second variable is the time or date when something occurred.

Table 4-1 shows an example used later in this chapter. The cross-tabulation shows the number of new customers from counties in southeastern New York State by three channels: telemarketing, direct mail, and other. This table shows both the raw counts and the relative frequencies.

Table 4-1: Cross-tabulation of Starts by County and Channel

COUNTY	COUNTS				FREQUENCIES			
	TM	DM	OTHER	TOTAL	TM	DM	OTHER	TOTAL
Bronx	3,212	413	2,936	**6,561**	2.5%	0.3%	2.3%	5.1%
Kings	9,773	1,393	11,025	**22,191**	7.7%	1.1%	8.6%	17.4%
Nassau	3,135	1,573	10,367	**15,075**	2.5%	1.2%	8.1%	11.8%
New York	7,194	2,867	28,965	**39,026**	5.6%	2.2%	22.7%	30.6%
Queens	6,266	1,380	10,954	**18,600**	4.9%	1.1%	8.6%	14.6%
Richmond	784	277	1,772	**2,833**	0.6%	0.2%	1.4%	2.2%
Suffolk	2,911	1,042	7,159	**11,112**	2.3%	0.8%	5.6%	8.7%
Westchester	2,711	1,230	8,271	**12,212**	2.1%	1.0%	6.5%	9.6%
Total	**35,986**	**10,175**	**81,449**	**127,610**	28.2%	8.0%	63.8%	100.0%

Visualizing cross-tabulations is challenging because there is a lot of data to present, and some people do not easily interpret complicated pictures. Figure 4-6 shows a three-dimensional column chart for the counts shown in the table. This chart shows that the "OTHER" channel is quite high for Manhattan (New York County).

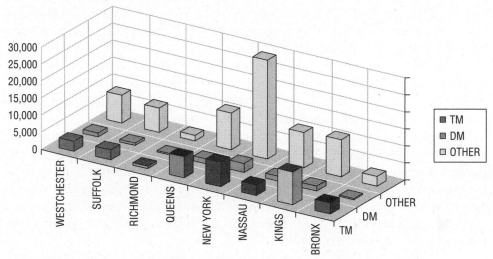

Figure 4-6: A surface plot provides a visual interface for cross-tabulated data.

Numeric Variables

Statistics was originally developed to understand the data collected by scientists, most of which took the form of numeric measurements. In data mining, not all variables are numeric, because of a wealth of descriptive data as well. This section talks about such data from the perspective of descriptive statistics.

Statistical Measures for Continuous Variables

The most basic statistical measures describe a set of data with just a single value. The most commonly used statistic is the arithmetic average value, which statisticians call the *mean*. Some other important values are:

- **Range.** The range is the difference between the smallest and largest observation in the sample. The range is often looked at along with the minimum and maximum values themselves.

- **Average.** The sum of all the values divided by the number of values.

- **Median.** The median value is the one that splits the observations into two equally sized groups, one having values smaller than the median and the other having values larger than the median.

- **Mode.** This is the value that occurs most often.

The median can be used in some situations where calculating the average is impossible, such as when incomes are reported in ranges of $10,000 dollars with a final category "over $100,000" (the Census provides several informative demographic variables in this manner). The number of observations is known for each range, but not the actual values within the range. In addition, the median is less affected by a few observations that are out of line with the others. For instance, if Bill Gates or Carlos Slim Helú moves onto your block, the average net worth of the neighborhood will dramatically increase. However, the median net worth may not change at all.

In addition, various ways of characterizing the range are useful. The range itself is defined by the minimum and maximum value. Looking at percentile information, such as the 25th and 75th percentile, is often valuable for understanding the limits of the middle half of the values as well.

Figure 4-7 shows a chart where the range and average are displayed for order amount by day. This chart uses a logarithmic (log) scale for the vertical axis, because the minimum order is less than $10 and the maximum is more than $1,000. In fact, the daily minimum is consistently around $10, the daily average around $70, and the daily maximum around $1,000. As with categorical variables, it is valuable to use a time chart for continuous values to see when unexpected things are happening.

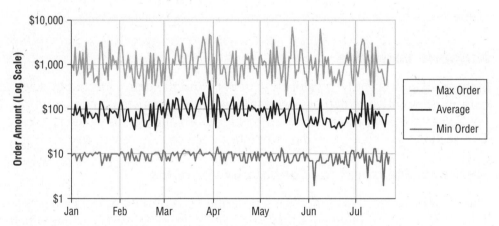

Figure 4-7: A time chart can also be used for continuous values; this one shows the range and average for order amounts each day.

Interesting Properties of the Average and Median

The definition of the average as the sum of all values divided by the number of values is a common definition familiar to most readers. Averages have another property which is also quite interesting, and probably more unfamiliar. The average value is the value that minimizes the sum of the squares of the differences from all other points. For a set of numbers, these definitions are equivalent. However, for computational purposes, computing the sum is much easier than figuring out the value from the other property.

The median has a similar definition. It is the value that minimizes the sum of the absolute differences from all other values. In practice, calculating the median is more computationally difficult than calculating the average, because you basically need to sort the list rather than just summing the values.

Why are these properties important? For more complicated data than just numbers, the common definitions can't be applied. How do you "sum up" points on a scatter plot? How do you "sort" them to find the middle value? In fact, these ideas become quite important in Chapter 13 when describing the various flavors of k-means clustering.

In fact, you don't need to do this. To find the average of a set of points, you can apply the second definition — and it turns out that taking the average along each dimension is the right thing to do. To calculate the median, you can apply the second definition, although the calculations are a bit more cumbersome.

Variance and Standard Deviation

Variance is a measure of the dispersion of data values. Another way of saying this is that variance measures how closely the values cluster around their average. A low variance means that the values stay near the average; a high variance means the opposite. Range is not a good measure of dispersion because it takes only two values into account — the extremes. Removing one extreme can, sometimes, dramatically change the range (indicating an outlier in the data). The variance, on the other hand, takes every value into account. The difference between a given observation and the average of the sample is called its *deviation*. The variance is defined as the average of the squares of the deviations.

Standard deviation, the square root of the variance, is the most frequently used measure of dispersion. It is more convenient than variance because it is expressed in the same units as the values themselves rather than in terms of those units squared. The z-score, introduced earlier, is an observation's distance from the average measured in standard deviations; the calculation makes sense because the data value, the average, and the standard deviation are all measured in the same units. The z-score allows different variables, measured in different units, to be converted to the same unit — distance from the average measured in standard deviations. Assuming the normal distribution, the z-score can be converted to a probability or confidence value.

A Couple More Statistical Ideas

The *Pearson correlation* coefficient (often the "Pearson" is dropped) measures the extent to which a change in one variable is related to a change in another. Correlation, which is called *r*, ranges from –1 to 1. A correlation of 0 means that two variables are not related at all. A correlation of 1 is perfect correlation, meaning that as the first variable changes, the second is guaranteed to change in the same direction, though not necessarily by the same amount. A correlation of –1 simply means that the two variables are totally correlated, except as one goes up the other goes down.

Another measure of correlation is the R^2 value, which is the correlation squared. R^2 goes from 0 (no relationship) to 1 (complete relationship). For instance, the radius and the circumference of a circle are perfectly correlated, although the latter has larger values than the former. A negative correlation means that the two variables move in opposite directions. For example, altitude is negatively correlated with air pressure.

Regression is the process of using the value of one of a pair of variables in order to predict the value of the second. The most common form of regression is ordinary least squares linear regression, so called because it attempts to fit a straight line through the observed X and Y pairs in a sample. After the line has been established, it can be used to predict a value for Y given any X and for X given any Y. Chapter 6 covers the topic of regression in more detail.

Measuring Response

This section looks at statistical ideas in the context of a marketing campaign. The champion-challenger approach to marketing tries out different ideas against business as usual. For instance, assume that a company sends out a million billing inserts each month to entice existing customers to do something. They have settled on one approach to the bill inserts, which is the *champion* offer. Another offer is a *challenger* to this offer. Their approach to comparing these is:

- Send the champion offer to 900,000 customers.
- Send the challenger offer to 100,000 customers, chosen randomly.
- Determine which is better.

The question is how do you tell when one offer is better than the other? This section introduces the idea of the confidence interval to understand this approach in more detail.

Standard Error of a Proportion

The approach to answering this question uses the idea of a confidence interval. The challenger offer, in the preceding scenario, is sent to a random subset of customers. Based on the response in this subset, what is the expected response for this offer for the entire population?

Assume that 50,000 people in the original population would have responded to the challenger offer if they had received it. Then about 5,000 would be expected to respond in the 10 percent of the population that received it. If exactly this number did respond, then the sample response rate and the population response rate would both be 5.0 percent.

On the other hand, it is possible (though highly, highly unlikely) that all 50,000 responders are in the sample that receives the challenger offer; this would yield a response rate of 50 percent. It is also possible (and is also highly, highly unlikely) that none of the 50,000 are in the sample chosen, for a response rate of 0 percent. In any sample of one-tenth the population, the observed response rate might be as low as 0 percent or as high as 50 percent. These are the extreme values, of course; the actual value is much more likely to be close to 5 percent. "How close?," is the question.

Many different samples can be pulled from the population, with widely varying response rates. Now flip the situation around and say that the sample has 5,000 responders. What does this tell you about the entire population? Once again, it is possible that these are all the responders in the population, so the low-end estimate is 0.5 percent. On the other hand, it is also possible that everyone else was a responder and the sample was very, very unlucky. The high end would then be 90.5 percent.

That is, there is a 100 percent confidence that the actual response rate on the population is between 0.5 percent and 90.5 percent. Having a high confidence is good; however, the range is too broad to be useful. One should be willing to settle for a lower confidence level. Often, 95 or 99 percent confidence is quite sufficient for marketing purposes.

The distribution for the response values follows something called the binomial distribution. Happily, the binomial distribution is very similar to the normal distribution whenever the population is larger than a few hundred people. In Figure 4-8, the jagged line is the binomial distribution and the smooth line is the corresponding normal distribution; they are practically identical.

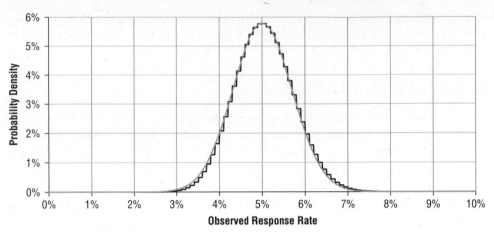

Figure 4-8: Statistics has proven that actual response rate on a population is very close to a normal distribution whose average is the measured response on a sample and whose standard deviation is the standard error of proportion (SEP).

The challenge is to determine the corresponding normal distribution given that a sample with a size of 100,000 has a response rate of 5 percent. As mentioned earlier, the normal distribution has two parameters: the average and standard deviation. The average is the observed average (5 percent) in the sample. To calculate the standard deviation, a formula is needed, and statisticians have figured out the relationship between the standard deviation of a proportion on the one hand (strictly speaking, this is the standard error but the two are similar enough for this discussion) and the average value and sample size on the other. This is called the standard error of a proportion (SEP) and has the formula:

$$SEP = \sqrt{\left(\frac{p * (1 - p)}{N}\right)}$$

In this formula, p is the average value and N is the size of the population. So, the corresponding normal distribution has a standard deviation equal to the square root of the product of the observed response times one minus the observed response divided by the total number of samples.

As discussed earlier in this chapter, about 68 percent of data following a normal distribution lies within one standard deviation of the average value. For the sample size of 100,000, the formula SQRT(5% * 95% / 100,000) is about 0.07 percent, indicating 68 percent confidence that the actual response is between 4.93 percent and 5.07 percent. A bit more than 95 percent is within two standard deviations; so the range of 4.86 percent and 5.14 percent is just over 95 percent confident. So, a 5 percent response rate for the challenger offer implies 95 percent confidence that the response rate on the whole population would have been between 4.86 percent and 5.14 percent. Note that this conclusion depends very much on the fact that people who got the challenger offer were selected randomly from the entire population.

Comparing Results Using Confidence Bounds

The previous section discussed confidence intervals as applied to the response rate of one group who received the challenger offer. In a champion-challenger test, there are actually two response rates, one for the champion and one for the challenger. Are these response rates different? Notice that the observed rates could be different (say 5.000 percent and 5.001 percent), and yet so close that they are effectively the same. One way to compare results is to look at the confidence interval for each response rate and see whether they overlap. If the intervals do not overlap, then the difference in response rates is *statistically significant*.

This example investigates a range of response rates from 4.5 percent to 5.5 percent for the champion model. In practice, a single response rate would be known. However, investigating a range shows what happens as the rate varies from much lower (4.5 percent) to the same (5.0 percent) to much larger (5.5 percent).

The 95 percent confidence bounds is 1.96 standard deviations from the average, so the lower value is the average minus this 1.96 standard deviations, and the upper is the average plus 1.96 standard deviations. Table 4-2 shows the lower and upper bounds for a range of response rates for the champion model going from 4.5 percent to 5.5 percent.

Table 4-2: The 95 Percent Confidence Interval Bounds for the Champion Group for Different Response Rates

RESPONSE	SIZE	SEP	95% CONF	95% CONF * SEP	LOWER	UPPER
4.5%	900,000	0.0219%	1.96	0.0219%*1.96=0.0429%	4.46%	4.54%
4.6%	900,000	0.0221%	1.96	0.0221%*1.96=0.0433%	4.56%	4.64%
4.7%	900,000	0.0223%	1.96	0.0223%*1.96=0.0437%	4.66%	4.74%
4.8%	900,000	0.0225%	1.96	0.0225%*1.96=0.0441%	4.76%	4.84%
4.9%	900,000	0.0228%	1.96	0.0228%*1.96=0.0447%	4.86%	4.94%
5.0%	900,000	0.0230%	1.96	0.0230%*1.96=0.0451%	4.95%	5.05%
5.1%	900,000	0.0232%	1.96	0.0232%*1.96=0.0455%	5.05%	5.15%
5.2%	900,000	0.0234%	1.96	0.0234%*1.96=0.0459%	5.15%	5.25%
5.3%	900,000	0.0236%	1.96	0.0236%*1.96=0.0463%	5.25%	5.35%
5.4%	900,000	0.0238%	1.96	0.0238%*1.96=0.0466%	5.35%	5.45%
5.5%	900,000	0.0240%	1.96	0.0240%*1.96=0.0470%	5.45%	5.55%

Response rates vary from 4.5% to 5.5%. The bounds for the 95% confidence level are calculated using 1.96 standard deviations from the average.

You can determine whether the confidence bounds overlap based on these response rates. The 95 percent confidence bounds for the challenger model vary from about 4.86 percent to 5.14 percent. These bounds overlap the confidence bounds for the champion model when its response rates are 4.9 percent, 5.0 percent, or 5.1 percent. For instance, the confidence interval for a response rate of 4.9 percent goes from 4.86 percent to 4.94 percent; this overlaps 4.86 percent–5.14 percent. Using the overlapping bounds method, these are considered statistically equivalent.

Comparing Results Using Difference of Proportions

The overlapping bounds method is easy but its results are a bit pessimistic. Even when the confidence intervals overlap, the observed *difference* between the values may be significant with some given level of confidence. This suggests another approach, which is to ask whether the difference between the response rates is statistically different from zero. Specifically, the question is: Does the confidence interval for the difference of the values include zero?

Just as a formula exists for the standard error of a proportion, a formula exists for the standard error of the difference of proportions (SEDP):

$$SEDP = \sqrt{\left(\frac{p_1 * (1 - p_1)}{N_1} + \frac{p_2 * (1 - p_2)}{N_2} \right)}$$

This formula is a lot like the formula for the standard error of a proportion, except the part in the square root is repeated for each group. Table 4-3 shows this formula applied to the champion-challenger problem with response rates varying between 4.5 percent and 5.5 percent for the champion group.

Based on the difference of proportions, three response rates on the champion have confidences under 95 percent (that is, the p-value exceeds 5 percent). If the challenger response rate is 5.0 percent and the champion is 5.1 percent, then the difference in response rates might be due to chance. However, if the champion has a response rate of 5.2 percent, then the likelihood of the difference being due to chance falls to under 1 percent. These results are very similar to the overlapping confidence intervals approach.

WARNING Confidence intervals only measure the likelihood that sampling affects the result. Many other factors may need to be taken into consideration to determine whether two offers are significantly different.

Table 4-3: Z-scores and P-values for Difference Between Champion and Challenger Response Rates, with 900,000 contacts for Champion and 100,000 for Challenger

RESPONSE			DIFFERENCE OF PROPORTIONS		
CHAMPION	CHALLENGER	DIFFERENCE	SEDP	Z-VALUE	P-VALUE
5.0%	4.5%	0.5%	0.07%	6.9	0.0%
5.0%	4.6%	0.4%	0.07%	5.5	0.0%
5.0%	4.7%	0.3%	0.07%	4.1	0.0%
5.0%	4.8%	0.2%	0.07%	2.8	0.6%
5.0%	4.9%	0.1%	0.07%	1.4	16.8%
5.0%	5.0%	0.0%	0.07%	0.0	100.0%
5.0%	5.1%	-0.1%	0.07%	-1.4	16.9%
5.0%	5.2%	-0.2%	0.07%	-2.7	0.6%
5.0%	5.3%	-0.3%	0.07%	-4.1	0.0%
5.0%	5.4%	-0.4%	0.07%	-5.5	0.0%
5.0%	5.5%	-0.5%	0.07%	-6.9	0.0%

Size of Sample

The formulas for the standard error of a proportion and for the standard error of a difference of proportions both include the sample size. An inverse relationship exists between the sample size and the size of the confidence interval: the more data, the narrower the confidence interval. So, to have more confidence in results, use larger samples.

Table 4-4 shows the confidence interval for different sizes of the challenger group, assuming the challenger response rate is observed to be 5 percent. For very small sizes, the confidence interval is very wide, often too wide to be useful. The normal distribution is an approximation for estimating the actual response rate; with small sample sizes, the estimates are not very good. Statistics has several methods for handling such small sample sizes. However, these are generally not of much interest to data miners because data mining samples are much larger.

Table 4-4: The 95 Percent Confidence Interval for Difference Sizes of the Challenger Group

RESPONSE	SIZE	SEP	95% CONF	LOWER	UPPER	WIDTH
5.0%	1,000	0.6892%	1.96	3.65%	6.35%	2.70%
5.0%	5,000	0.3082%	1.96	4.40%	5.60%	1.21%
5.0%	10,000	0.2179%	1.96	4.57%	5.43%	0.85%
5.0%	20,000	0.1541%	1.96	4.70%	5.30%	0.60%
5.0%	40,000	0.1090%	1.96	4.79%	5.21%	0.43%
5.0%	60,000	0.0890%	1.96	4.83%	5.17%	0.35%
5.0%	80,000	0.0771%	1.96	4.85%	5.15%	0.30%
5.0%	100,000	0.0689%	1.96	4.86%	5.14%	0.27%
5.0%	120,000	0.0629%	1.96	4.88%	5.12%	0.25%
5.0%	140,000	0.0582%	1.96	4.89%	5.11%	0.23%
5.0%	160,000	0.0545%	1.96	4.89%	5.11%	0.21%
5.0%	180,000	0.0514%	1.96	4.90%	5.10%	0.20%
5.0%	200,000	0.0487%	1.96	4.90%	5.10%	0.19%
5.0%	500,000	0.0308%	1.96	4.94%	5.06%	0.12%
5.0%	1,000,000	0.0218%	1.96	4.96%	5.04%	0.09%

What the Confidence Interval Really Means

The confidence interval is a measure of only one thing, the dispersion of the sample estimate with respect to the overall population estimate. Assuming that everything else remains the same, it measures the amount of inaccuracy introduced by the process of sampling. The confidence interval also rests on the assumption that the sampling process itself is random — that is, that any of the one million customers could have been offered the challenger with an equal likelihood. Random means random. The following examples are not random:

- Use customers in California for the challenger and everyone else for the champion.

- Use the 5 percent lowest and 5 percent highest value customers for the challenger, and everyone else for the champion.

- Use the 10 percent most recent customers for the challenger, and everyone else for the champion.

- Use the customers with telephone numbers for the telemarketing campaign; everyone else for the direct mail campaign.

All of these are biased ways of splitting the population into groups, and it is quite possible that the criterion for the split (California, customer value, customer tenure, presence of a phone number) are correlated with the outcome of the marketing test. The previous results all assume no such systematic bias. When there is systematic bias, the formulas for the confidence intervals are not correct.

Bias creeps in in many different ways. For instance, consider a champion model that predicts the likelihood of customers responding to the champion offer. If this model were used to select recipients, then the challenger sample would no longer be a random sample. It would consist of the leftover customers from the champion model, introducing another form of bias.

Or, perhaps the challenger model is only available to customers in certain markets or with certain products. This introduces other forms of bias. In such cases, similar constraints should be used to select recipients for the champion offer. Another form of bias might come from the method of response. The challenger may only accept responses via telephone, but the champion may accept them by telephone or on the Web. In such a case, the challenger response may be dampened because of the lack of a Web channel. Or, there might need to be special training for the inbound telephone service reps to handle the challenger offer. Having a smaller, specially trained group for the challenge offer might increase wait times, another form of bias.

The confidence interval is simply a statement about statistics and dispersion. It does not address all the other forms of bias that might affect results, and these forms of bias are often more damaging than sample variation. The next section talks about setting up a test and control experiment in marketing, diving into these issues in more detail.

Size of Test and Control for an Experiment

The champion-challenger model is an example of a two-way test, where a new method (the challenger) is compared to business-as-usual activity (the champion). This section talks about ensuring that the test and control are large enough to make an informed determination of which, if either, is better. The previous section explained how to calculate the confidence interval for the sample response rate. This section turns this logic inside out. Instead of starting with the size of the groups, instead consider sizes from the perspective of test design. This requires knowing several things:

- Estimated response rate p for one of the groups
- Difference in response rates d that the test should be able to detect with the specified confidence (acuity of the test)
- Confidence interval (say 95 percent)

These three factors provide enough information to determine the size of the samples needed for the test and control. For instance, suppose that the business as usual has a response rate of 5 percent (p) and the goal is to measure with 95 percent confidence a difference of 0.2 percent (d). This means that if the response of the test group is greater than 5.2 percent, then the experiment can detect the difference with a 95 percent confidence level.

For a problem of this type, the first step is to determine the value of SEDP. What is the standard error associated with a 0.2 percent difference at a 95 percent confidence level? A confidence of 95 percent corresponds to 1.96 standard deviations from the average. The calculation is simple: 1.96 times the standard error is 0.2, meaning that the standard error is 0.102 percent. More generally, the process is to convert the p-value (95 percent) to a z-score (which can be done using the Excel function NORMSINV()) and then divide the desired confidence by this value.

The next step is to plug these values into the formula for SEDP. For this, assume that the test and control are the same size:

$$\frac{0.2\%}{1.96} = \sqrt{\left(\frac{p * (1-p)}{N} + \frac{(p+d) * (1-p-d)}{N}\right)}$$

Plugging in the values just described (p is 5% and d is 0.2%) results in:

$$0.102\% = \sqrt{\left(\frac{5\% * 95\%}{N} + \frac{5.2\% * (94.8\%)}{N}\right)} = \sqrt{\left(\frac{0.0963}{N}\right)}$$

$$N = \frac{((5\%*95\%) + (5.2\%*94.8\%))}{(0.00102)^2}$$

$$= \frac{0.096796}{(0.00102)^2} = 92{,}963$$

So, having equal-sized groups of 92,963 provides sufficient acuity for measuring a 0.2 percent difference in response rates with 95 percent confidence. Of course, this does not guarantee that the results will differ by at least 0.2 percent. It merely says that with control and test groups of at least this size, a difference in response rates of 0.2 percent should be measurable and statistically significant.

The size of the test and control groups affects how the results can be interpreted. However, this effect can be determined in advance, before the test. Determine the acuity of the test and control groups before running marketing tests to be sure that the test can produce useful results.

TIP Before running a marketing test, determine the acuity of the test by calculating the difference in response rates that can be measured with a high confidence (such as 95 percent).

Multiple Comparisons

The discussion has so far used examples with only one comparison, such as the difference between two presidential candidates or between a test and control group. Often, there are multiple tests at the same time. For instance, there might be three different challenger messages to determine whether one of these produces better results than the business-as-usual message. Handling multiple tests affects the underlying statistics, so understanding what happens is important.

The Confidence Level with Multiple Comparisons

Consider two groups that have been tested. You are told that the difference between the responses in the two groups is 95 percent certain to be due to factors other than sampling variation. A reasonable conclusion is that the two groups are different. In a well-designed test, the most likely reason would the difference in message, offer, or treatment.

Now consider the same situation, except that you are now told that there were actually 20 groups tested, and you were shown only the pair with the greatest difference. Now you might reach a very different conclusion. If 20 groups are tested, you should expect one of them to exceed the 95 percent confidence bound due only to chance, because 95 percent means 19 times out of 20. You can no longer conclude that the difference is due to the testing parameters. Instead, because it is likely that the difference is due to sampling variation, this is the simplest explanation.

The calculation of the confidence level is based on only one comparison. With multiple comparisons, the confidence as calculated previously is not quite sufficient.

Bonferroni's Correction

Fortunately, there is a simple way to fix this problem, developed by the Italian mathematician Carlo Bonferroni. Consider the following conclusions with two challengers, instead of one:

- Champion is better than Challenger X with a confidence of 95%.
- Champion is better than Challenger Y with a confidence of 95%.

Bonferroni calculated the probability that both of these are true. Another way to look at it is to determine the probability that one or the other is false, which is actually easier to calculate. The probability that the first is false is 5 percent, as is the probability of the second being false. The probability that either is false is the sum, 10 percent, minus the probability that both are false at the same time (0.25 percent). So, the probability that both statements are true is about 90 percent (actually 90.25 percent).

Looking at this from the p-value perspective says that the p-value of both statements together (10 percent) is approximated by the sum of the p-values of the two statements separately. This is not a coincidence. Using this estimate, to get a 95 percent confidence for two tests, each would have to be 97.5 percent confident (which corresponds to 2.24 standard deviations from the average).

In fact, a reasonable estimate of the p-value of any number of statements is the sum of the p-values of each one. If there were eight test results with a 95 percent confidence, then the expectation is that all eight would be in their ranges 60 percent at any given time (because 8 * 5% is a p-value of 40%).

Bonferroni applied this observation in reverse. If there are eight tests and the goal is an overall 95 percent confidence, then the bound for the p-value must be 5% / 8 = 0.625%. That is, each observation must be at least 99.375 percent confident, corresponding to a z-score of 2.734. The Bonferroni correction is to divide the desired bound for the p-value by the number of comparisons being made, in order to get a confidence of $1 - p$ for all comparisons together.

Chi-Square Test

The difference of proportions method is a very powerful method for estimating the effectiveness of campaigns and for other similar situations. However, another statistical test can also be used. This test, the chi-square test, is designed specifically for multiple tests having at least two discrete outcomes (such as response and non-response).

The appeal of the chi-square test is that it readily adapts to multiple test groups and multiple outcomes, as long as the different groups are distinct from each other. In fact, this is about the only important rule when using the chi-square test. As described in Chapter 7, the chi-square test is also the basis for an important type of decision tree.

Expected Values

The place to start with chi-square is to lay data out in a table, as in Table 4-5. This is an example of a simple 2×2 table, which represents a champion-challenger test with two outcomes, say response and non-response. This table also shows the total values for each column and row; that is, the total number of responders and non-responders (each column) and the total number in the test and control groups (each row). The response rate column is added for reference; it is not part of the calculation.

Table 4-5: The Champion-Challenger Data Laid Out for the Chi-Square Test

GROUP	RESPONDERS	NON-RESPONDERS	TOTAL	RESPONSE RATE
Champion	43,200	856,800	900,000	4.80%
Challenger	5,000	95,000	100,000	5.00%
Total	48,200	951,800	1,000,000	4.82%

What if the data were broken up among these groups in a completely unbiased way? That is, what if there really were no differences between the columns and rows in the table? This is a completely reasonable question. The goal is to calculate the expected values in each cell. The expected value assumes that the response rate is the same for both groups and the overall response rate remains the same.

To calculate the expected values, multiply the overall response rate by the sizes of each group to get the expected champion responders and the expected challenger responders. Do the same calculation for the non-responders (using 1 minus the response rate). Table 4-6 shows the expected values for each of the four cells.

Table 4-6: Calculating the Expected Values and Deviations from Expected for the Data in Table 4-5

	ACTUAL RESPONSE			EXPECTED RESPONSE		DEVIATION	
	YES	NO	TOTAL	YES	NO	YES	NO
Champion	43,200	856,800	900,000	43,380	856,620	−180	180
Challenger	5,000	95,000	100,000	4,820	95,180	180	−180
Total	48,200	951,800	1,000,000	48,200	951,800		
Overall Proportion	4.82%	95.18%					

The expected value shows how the data would break up if there were no difference between the champion and challenger. Notice that the expected value is measured in the same units as each cell, typically a customer count, so it actually has a meaning. Also, the sum of the expected values is the same as the sum of all the cells in the original table. The sums of the rows and the sums of the columns are also the same as in the original table.

The table also includes the deviation, which is the difference between the observed value and the expected value. In this case, the deviations all have the same value, but with different signs. This is because the original data has two rows and two columns. Later in the chapter you see examples using larger tables where the deviations are different. However, the deviations in each row and each column always cancel out, so the sum of the deviations in each row and each column is always 0.

Chi-Square Value

The deviation is a good tool for looking at values. However, it does not provide information as to whether the deviation is expected or not expected. Doing this requires another tool from statistics, namely the chi-square distribution developed by the English statistician Karl Pearson in 1900.

The chi-square value for each cell is simply the calculation:

$$\text{Chi-square}(x) = \frac{(x - \text{expected}(x))^2}{\text{expected}(x)}$$

The chi-square value for the entire table is the sum of the chi-square values of all the cells in the table. Notice that the chi-square value is always 0 or positive. Also, when the values in the table match the expected value, then the overall chi-square is 0. This is the smallest possible chi-square value. As the deviations from the expected values get larger in magnitude, the chi-square value also gets larger.

Unfortunately, chi-square values do not follow a normal distribution. This is actually obvious, because the value is always positive, and the normal distribution is symmetric, having both positive and negative values. The good news is that chi-square values follow another distribution, which is also well understood. The chi-square distribution depends not only on the value itself but also on the size of the table. Figure 4-9 shows the density functions for several chi-square distributions.

What the chi-square really depends on is the degrees of freedom, which is easier to calculate than to explain. The number of degrees of freedom of a table is calculated by subtracting 1 from the number of rows and the number of columns and multiplying them together. The 2 × 2 table in the previous example has 1 degree of freedom. A 5 × 7 table would have 24 (4 * 6) degrees of freedom. The sidebar "Degrees of Freedom" explains the concept in a bit more detail.

DEGREES OF FREEDOM

The idea behind the degrees of freedom is how many different variables are needed to describe the table of expected values. This is a measure of how constrained the data is in the table.

If the table has r rows and c columns, then there are $r * c$ cells in the table. With no constraints on the table, this is the number of variables that would be needed to describe it. However, the calculation of the expected values has imposed some constraints. In particular, the sum of the values in each row is the same for the expected values as for the original table. That is, if one value were missing, you could recalculate it by taking the constraint into account. The unknown value would be the total sum of the row minus the sum of the values that are present. This suggests that the degrees of freedom is $r * c - r$. The same situation exists for the columns, yielding an estimate of $r * c - r - c$.

However, there is one additional constraint. The sum of all the row sums and the sum of all the column sums must be the same. It turns out that the constraints have been overcounted by one. The degrees of freedom are really $r * c - r - c + 1$. Another way of writing this is $(r - 1) * (c - 1)$.

WARNING   The chi-square test does not work when the expected value in any cell is less than 5 (and more is better). Although not an issue for large data mining problems, it can be an issue when analyzing results from a small test.

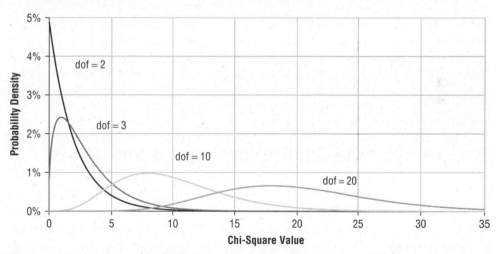

Figure 4-9: The chi-square distribution depends on the degrees of freedom. In general, though, it starts low, peaks early, and gradually descends.

The process for using the chi-square test is:

1. Set up the results as a contingency table.

2. Calculate the expected values.

3. Calculate the deviations from the expected values.

4. Calculate the chi-square (square the deviations and divide by the expected).

5. Sum for an overall chi-square value for the table.

6. Calculate the probability that a chi-square value as large as the observed value would occur when the null hypothesis is true (in Excel, you can use the CHIDIST() function).

The result is the probability that the distribution of values in the table would occur under the null hypothesis (that champion and challenger produce the same results). As Occam's razor suggests, the simplest explanation is that the various factors have no influence on the results; that observed differences from expected values are entirely within the range of expectation. Low chi-square values support the null hypothesis; high values support the opposite, that the factors do make a difference.

Comparison of Chi-Square to Difference of Proportions

Chi-square and difference of proportions can be applied to the same problems. Although the results are not exactly the same, they are similar enough for comfort. Table 4-4 earlier in the chapter shows the likelihood of champion and challenger results being the same using the difference of proportions method for a range of champion response rates. Table 4-7 repeats this using the chi-square calculation instead of the difference of proportions. The results from the chi-square test are very similar to the results from the difference of proportions — a remarkable result considering how different the two methods are.

An Example: Chi-Square for Regions and Starts

A large consumer-oriented company has been running acquisition campaigns in the New York City area. The purpose of this analysis is to look at its acquisition channels to try to gain an understanding of different parts of the market area. For the purposes of this analysis, three channels are of interest:

- **Telemarketing.** Customers who are acquired through outbound telemarketing calls.

- **Direct mail.** Customers who are acquired through direct mail pieces.

- **Other.** Customers who come in through other means.

Table 4-7: Chi-Square Calculation for Difference of Proportions Example in Table 4-4

CHALLENGER		CHAMPION			CHALLENGER EXP.		CHAMPION EXP.	
RESP	NON-RESP	RESP	NON-RESP	OVERALL RESP	RESP	NON-RESP	RESP	NON-RESP
5,000	95,000	40,500	859,500	4.55%	4,550	95,450	40,950	859,050
5,000	95,000	41,400	858,600	4.64%	4,640	95,360	41,760	858,240
5,000	95,000	42,300	857,700	4.73%	4,730	95,270	42,570	857,430
5,000	95,000	43,200	856,800	4.82%	4,820	95,180	43,380	856,620
5,000	95,000	44,100	855,900	4.91%	4,910	95,090	44,190	855,810
5,000	95,000	45,000	855,000	5.00%	5,000	95,000	45,000	855,000
5,000	95,000	45,900	854,100	5.09%	5,090	94,910	45,810	854,190
5,000	95,000	46,800	853,200	5.18%	5,180	94,820	46,620	853,380
5,000	95,000	47,700	852,300	5.27%	5,270	94,730	47,430	852,570
5,000	95,000	48,600	851,400	5.36%	5,360	94,640	48,240	851,760
5,000	95,000	49,500	850,500	5.45%	5,450	94,550	49,050	850,950

CHALLENGER		CHALLENGER CHI-SQUARE		CHAMPION CHI-SQUARE		CHI-SQUARE		DIFF. PROP.
RESP	NON-RESP	RESP	NON RESP	RESP	NON RESP	VALUE	P-VALUE	P-VALUE
5,000	95,000	44.51	2.12	4.95	0.24	51.81	0.00%	0.00%
5,000	95,000	27.93	1.36	3.10	0.15	32.54	0.00%	0.00%
5,000	95,000	15.41	0.77	1.71	0.09	17.97	0.00%	0.00%
5,000	95,000	6.72	0.34	0.75	0.04	7.85	0.51%	0.58%
5,000	95,000	1.65	0.09	0.18	0.01	1.93	16.50%	16.83%
5,000	95,000	0.00	0.00	0.00	0.00	0.00	100.00%	100.00%
5,000	95,000	1.59	0.09	0.18	0.01	1.86	17.23%	16. 91%
5,000	95,000	6.25	0.34	0.69	0.04	7.33	0.68%	0.60%
5,000	95,000	13.83	0.77	1.54	0.09	16.23	0.01%	0.00%
5,000	95,000	24.18	1.37	2.69	0.15	28.39	0.00%	0.00%
5,000	95,000	37.16	2.14	4.13	0.24	43.66	0.00%	0.00%

The area of interest consists of eight counties in New York State. Five of these counties are the boroughs of New York City, two others (Nassau and Suffolk counties) are on Long Island, and one (Westchester) lies just north of the city. This data was shown earlier in Table 4-1. The purpose of this analysis is to determine whether the breakdown of starts by channel and county is due to chance or whether some other factors might be at work.

This problem is particularly suitable for chi-square because the data can be laid out in rows and columns, with no customer being counted in more than one cell. Table 4-8 shows the deviation, expected values, and chi-square values for each combination in the table. Notice that the chi-square values are often quite large in this example. The overall chi-square score for the table is 7,200, which is very large; the probability that the overall score is due to chance is basically zero. That is, the variation among starts by channel and by region is not due to sample variation. Other factors are at work.

Table 4-8: Chi-Square Calculation for Counties and Channels Example

COUNTY	EXPECTED			DEVIATION			CHI-SQUARE		
	TM	DM	OTHER	TM	DM	OTHER	TM	DM	OTHER
Bronx	1,850.2	523.1	4,187.7	1,362	−110	−1,252	1,002.3	23.2	374.1
Kings	6,257.9	1,769.4	14,163.7	3,515	−376	−3,139	1,974.5	80.1	695.6
Nassau	4,251.1	1,202.0	9,621.8	−1,116	371	745	293.0	114.5	57.7
New York	11,005.3	3,111.7	24,908.9	−3,811	−245	4,056	1,319.9	19.2	660.5
Queens	5,245.2	1,483.1	11,871.7	1,021	−103	−918	198.7	7.2	70.9
Richmond	798.9	225.9	1,808.2	−15	51	−36	0.3	11.6	0.7
Suffolk	3,133.6	886.0	7,092.4	−223	156	67	15.8	27.5	0.6
Westchester	3,443.8	973.7	7,794.5	−733	256	477	155.9	67.4	29.1

The next step is to determine which of the values are too high and too low and with what probability. Converting each chi-square value in each cell into a probability, using the degrees of freedom for the table, is tempting. The table is 8×3, so it has 14 degrees of freedom. However, this approach is not correct. The chi-square result is for the entire table; inverting the individual scores to get a probability does not necessarily produce valid probabilities at the cell level (although the results are directionally correct).

An alternative approach proves more accurate. The idea is to compare each cell to everything else. The result is a table that has two columns and two rows, as shown in Table 4-9. One column is the column of the original cell; the other column is everything else. One row is the row of the original cell; the other row is everything else.

Table 4-9: Chi-Square Calculation for Bronx and TM

COUNTY	EXPECTED		DEVIATION		CHI-SQUARE	
	TM	NOT_TM	TM	NOT_TM	TM	NOT_TM
Bronx	1,850.2	4,710.8	1,361.8	−1,361.8	1,002.3	393.7
Not Bronx	34,135.8	86,913.2	−1,361.8	1,361.8	54.3	21.3

The result is a set of chi-square values for the Bronx-TM combination, in a table with 1 degree of freedom. This process can be repeated to estimate the effect of each combination of variables. The result is a table that has a set of p-values that a given cell in the original table is caused by chance, as shown in Table 4-10.

Table 4-10: Estimated P-Value for Each Combination of County and Channel, without Correcting for Number of Comparisons

COUNTY	TM	DM	OTHER
Bronx	0.00%	0.00%	0.00%
Kings	0.00%	0.00%	0.00%
Nassau	0.00%	0.00%	0.00%
New York	0.00%	0.00%	0.00%
Queens	0.00%	0.74%	0.00%
Richmond	59.79%	0.07%	39.45%
Suffolk	0.01%	0.00%	42.91%
Westchester	0.00%	0.00%	0.00%

A second correction must still be made because many comparisons are taking place at the same time. Bonferroni's adjustment takes care of this by multiplying each p-value by the number of comparisons — which is the number of cells in the table. For final presentation purposes, convert the p-values to their opposite, the confidence, and multiply by the sign of the deviation to get a signed confidence. Figure 4-10 illustrates the result.

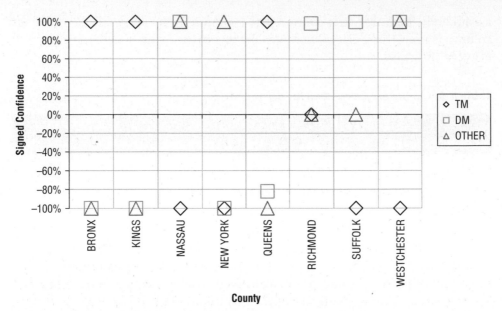

Figure 4-10: This chart shows the signed confidence values for each county and region combination; the preponderance of values near 100% and −100% indicate that observed differences are statistically significant.

The result is interesting. Almost all the values are near 100 percent or −100 percent, meaning that statistically significant differences exist among the counties. In fact, telemarketing (the diamond) and direct mail (the square) are almost always at opposite ends. A direct inverse relationship exists between the two. Direct mail response is high and telemarketing is low in three counties — Manhattan, Nassau, and Suffolk. Many wealthy areas are in these counties, possibly suggesting that wealthy customers are more likely to respond to direct mail than telemarketing. Of course, this could also mean that direct mail campaigns are directed to these areas, and telemarketing to other areas, so the geography was determined by the business operations, rather than the responders. To determine which of these possibilities is correct requires knowing who was contacted as well as who responded.

Case Study: Comparing Two Recommendation Systems with an A/B Test

This case study involves MyBuys, a company that serves up recommendations on the websites of its clients, who are online retailers. On a website that incorporates recommendations from MyBuys, every product page contains recommendations for other products that might also interest the shopper. MyBuys generates recommendations automatically using software that analyzes website behavior and shopping carts.

There are three different types of recommendations. A recommendation might be a *cross sell* — something that the shopper might want to buy in addition to the main item on the product page. It might be an *up sell* — a higher-end version of the main product on the page. A recommendation can also be a *substitution*, an alternative product that is no more expensive, but that might have a better chance of ending up in the shopping cart and being paid for. In all cases, the goal is to get the shopper to spend more money. Figure 4-11 shows the product page for a particular skirt that features four recommendations. Three are cross sells for tops and boots that might go with the skirt. One suggests a different skirt in a similar style.

Figure 4-11: This screen shot shows an example of a site using MyBuys recommendations.

MyBuys did not invent the idea of using recommendations to increase order sizes; online retailers typically do that. MyBuys needs to prove to its prospective clients that the recommendations it delivers are better than the ones the retailers are already using.

MyBuys can (and does) describe the sophisticated profiles built for each shopper and the patented algorithms used to generate recommendations based on those profiles. Its most persuasive sales tool is an A/B test: its challenger against the client's champion, which is typically a system based on rules developed by the client's own merchandisers who are quite knowledgeable about the products and customers.

What constitutes a convincing win? This case study looks at several different ways of analyzing the results from the test. This case highlights the challenges in choosing a metric, as well as the ways to determine which side, if either, is doing better.

First Metric: Participating Sessions

Shoppers have an opportunity to click on recommendations on nearly every page. After a shopper has clicked on any recommendation, the session is called *participating*, because the shopper has shown interest in a recommendation. This understanding of shopper behavior suggests four types of sessions:

- Sessions exposed to MyBuys recommendations that have attracted a click
- Sessions exposed to MyBuys recommendations that have not attracted a click
- Sessions exposed to client recommendations that have attracted a click
- Sessions exposed to client recommendations that have not attracted a click

Participating sessions (the first and third) are known to produce more revenue than non-participating sessions. In most A/B comparisons, the MyBuys recommendation system results in more participating sessions.

Is participating sessions (or more directly, number of clicks) a good metric? Perhaps surprisingly, the answer is no. There are two reasons. One is Simpson's paradox. Even though participating sessions always do better on both sides of an A/B test, the side with more participating sessions can actually produce less revenue if the relationship between revenue and clicks also differs between the two sides. This could happen if, for example, one side specialized in high-value cross-sell recommendations that are less likely to be accepted, but more valuable when they are, and the other side specializes in recommendations for minor upgrades that are often accepted, but worth little.

The second reason that counting clicks is not a good metric is that clicks, in and of themselves, are not valuable. If the goal were to collect clicks, it would be easy to win by recommending fabulous items at ridiculously low prices. But that would be losing sight of the business goal, which is to increase revenue.

Second Metric: Daily Revenue Per Session

The next metric considered was daily revenue per session, regardless of whether shoppers clicked on the recommendations or not. What this means is the average revenue for shoppers on either side of the A/B test — for all shoppers, not just purchasers. Using average dollars per session rather than the total revenue works even when the sizes of the "A" and "B" sides are different.

Figure 4-12 shows the daily revenue standardized over the entire population (so the same average and standard deviation is used for both sides of the tests). This chart also shows the 95 percent confidence bounds, so seeing when a particular day's pattern exceeds thresholds is easy. Using standardized values with such boundaries quickly shows outliers and unusual behavior. However, neither side seems to be consistently doing better than the other, at least by visual inspection of the chart.

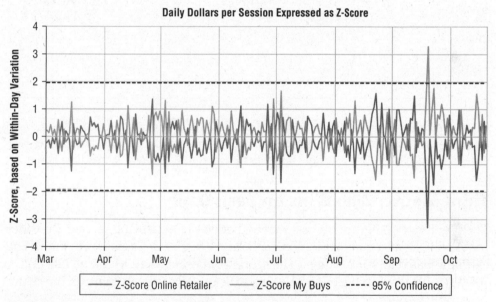

Figure 4-12: The daily revenue for both sides of the A/B tests is usually within the 95% confidence bounds and does not obviously favor one side of the test over the other.

TIP A control chart that shows daily fluctuations conveys more information when confidence bounds are included on the chart.

The chart is highly symmetric because the average and standard deviation are calculated separately for each day, for all sessions on that day. There are only two types of sessions (one for the "A" side and one for the "B" side), so one will tend to be above the overall average and the other below it. Figure 4-13 illustrates similar data for a shorter time-period, but with the vertical axis being the total dollar value of all orders each day. Notice that the first version of the chart takes into account all the inter-day variation; the second version gives a better feel for what happens from one day to the next in terms of dollar volume.

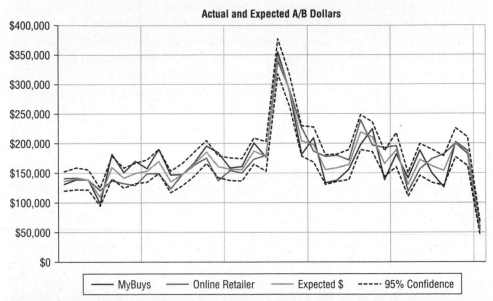

Figure 4-13: Using dollar amounts provides more information about what is happening over time, in terms of sales. The data here is similar to Figure 4-12, but for a shorter time frame.

Third Metric: Who Wins on Each Day?

The previous two figures suggest yet another way of measuring success. Consider the A/B tests as a competition on each day: Which side wins more often? The example has data for 233 days. The score for these days is: MyBuys, 126; client, 107. MyBuys is winning, but is this a significant effect? Or, is it within the realm of sample variation?

This type of question goes far back into history to the 1600s, to the work of the mathematician Jacob Bernoulli, one of several prominent mathematicians in the Bernoulli family. Before there was data mining, there was statistics. Before statistics, probability. Before probability, gambling. Jacob Bernoulli studied games of chance in the 1600s. In doing so, he invented the binomial distribution, which was mentioned earlier in this chapter. This distribution can answer questions such as: "How often will a fair coin land on heads seven or more times in ten coin tosses?"

The particular mathematics are beyond the scope of this book. However, the exact same ideas can be applied — centuries later — to an A/B test run on 233 days to ask: "How often would one side win 126 or more times, assuming there is no difference between the two sides?" The "or more" is generally added because any particular value of wins is highly unlikely; instead the question becomes one about doing "at least as well as 126 wins."

What is the probability that one side wins at least 126 times, assuming no difference between the two sides? The calculation can be done in Excel, using the formula 1-BINOMDIST(126,233,0.5,1). The answer is, about 9.5 percent.

This means that 90.5 percent of the time, in a run of 233 days, neither side wins 126 times. So the MyBuys win record is a bit unusual, but such an outcome is expected about 10 percent of the time. The traditional (although admittedly arbitrary) cutoff for statistical significance is 5%, so, although suggestive, the results are not conclusive. Running the test for more days could resolve this issue, but 233 days is already almost eight months.

Fourth Metric: Average Revenue Per Session

Yet another measure is perhaps the simplest. Instead of breaking out the A/B test by day, just consider the average revenue per session:

- The overall average for 45,213 sessions is $6.01.
- The average for the 22,640 sessions on the MyBuys side of the test is $6.52.
- The average for the 22,573 sessions using the client approach is $5.51.

These numbers suggest that the recommendation software is doing better, with an improvement of $1.01. However, "suggest" is quite different from statistical significance.

Earlier, this chapter introduced the notion of standard error of a proportion to determine whether two proportions are the same or different. The same idea applies to averages, where the notion of standard error of a mean (SEM) has a simple formula:

$$\text{SEM} = \frac{\text{standard deviation}}{\sqrt{\text{sample size}}}$$

In this case, the standard deviation is calculated as 158 and the sample size is 45,213, resulting in a standard error of 0.734. The difference of $1.01 is then 1.36 standard errors above the average. This is a largish number, but statistical significance is usually at the 5% threshold, which implies a value larger than 1.96.

Comparing averages, once again, produces a suggestive result in favor of MyBuys, but not a result that is statistically significant.

Fifth Metric: Incremental Revenue Per Customer

All the measures so far have hinted that the automatic recommendations do a better job than the client's recommendations. However, none are conclusive. After pondering this problem and discussing the issues with the marketing group at MyBuys, the authors realized that a shortcoming exists in all these methods: They focus on sessions rather than customers.

What if a shopper sees a recommendation, then ponders it, and comes back *later* and makes the purchase? None of the metrics discussed so far benefit from this effect, because they measure only what happens in the session containing the particular recommendation.

Instead of looking at sessions on a daily basis, a better approach is to put customers in two groups: the "A" group that sees the MyBuys recommendations and the "B" group that sees the client's. These groups can then be tracked over time. In particular, the total customer revenue can be measured over time for both groups. Does one group have more revenue per customer than the other group?

TIP Metrics focused on the customer often come closer to what the business needs. However, gathering the appropriate data at the customer level may be harder.

Implementing this test required changing the testing methodology. Instead of sessions being assigned to a particular group (A or B) at the beginning of a visit, shoppers are assigned to a particular group and remain in that group for the duration of the test.

This method has several advantages over the other approaches. One is its focus on incremental revenue per customer which, ultimately, is what any retailer wants to improve. If the recommendations encourage customers to return to the site, then this customer-focused metric captures that improvement.

Another is that it allows for the tests to accumulate data over longer periods of time. The test can start, and each day's information accumulates until the numbers are significant. This accumulation typically occurs much more quickly than the "which side won on a particular day" method.

A third advantage is that the results from the tests are impressive and understandable, because they are measured in dollars. Using a 28-day period for testing, the MyBuys recommendations generated more than 15 percent more revenue than the client recommendations. This result had a confidence of more than 99 percent. Furthermore, this metric is more closely aligned with what the retailers want to do, demonstrating the value of the MyBuys recommendation system much more clearly than other metrics.

Data Mining and Statistics

Many data mining techniques were invented by statisticians or have now been integrated into statistical software; they are now extensions of standard statistics. Although data miners and statisticians use similar techniques to solve similar problems, the data mining approach differs from the standard statistical approach in several areas:

- Data miners tend to ignore measurement error in raw data.
- Data miners assume the availability of more than enough data and processing power.
- Data mining assumes dependency on time everywhere.
- Designing experiments in the business world can be hard.
- Data is truncated and censored.

These are differences of approach and emphasis, rather than fundamental differences. As such, they shed some light on how the business problems addressed by data miners differ from the scientific problems that spurred the development of statistics.

No Measurement Error in Basic Data

Statistics originally derived from measuring scientific quantities, such as the width of skulls or the brightness of stars. These measurements are quantitative and the precise measured value depends on extraneous factors such as the type of measuring device and the ambient temperature. In particular, two people taking the same measurement at the same time are going to produce slightly different results. The results might differ by 5 percent or 0.05 percent, but the results are very likely to differ. Traditionally, statistics looks at observed measurements as falling into a confidence interval.

On the other hand, the amount of money a customer paid last January is quite well understood — down to the last penny. The definition of customer may be a little bit fuzzy; the definition of January may be fuzzy (consider 5-4-4 accounting cycles). However, after these are defined, the amount of the payment is precise. There is no measurement error.

There are other sources of error in business data. Of particular concern is operational error, which can cause systematic bias in the data being collected. For instance, clock skew may mean that two events that seem to happen in one sequence may have actually occurred in the opposite order (this is a particular problem when time zone information gets dropped from date and time stamps). A database record may have a Tuesday update date, when it really was updated on Monday, because the updating process runs just after midnight. Such forms of bias are systematic, and potentially represent spurious patterns that might be picked up by data mining algorithms.

One major difference between business data and scientific data is that the latter has many numeric values and the former has many categorical values. Even monetary amounts are discrete — two values can differ only by multiples of pennies (or some similar amount) — even though the values might be represented by real numbers.

A Lot of Data

Traditionally, statistics has been applied to smallish data sets (at most a few thousand rows) with few columns (fewer than a dozen). The goal has been to squeeze as much information as possible out of the data. This is still important in problems where collecting data is expensive or arduous — such as market research, crash testing cars, or testing the chemical composition of Martian soil.

Business data, on the other hand, is very voluminous. The challenge is understanding *anything* about what is happening, rather than *every possible thing*. Fortunately, enough computing power is now available to handle the large volumes of data.

Sampling theory is an important part of statistics. The discipline explains how results on a subset of data (a *sample*) relate to the whole. This is very important when planning to do a poll, because asking everyone a question is not possible; rather, pollsters ask a very small sample in order to derive overall opinion. However, sampling is much less important when all the data is available along with the computing power to process it. Usually, using all the data available produces better results than using a small subset.

There are a few cases when this is not necessarily true. There might simply be too much data. Instead of building models on tens of millions of customers, build models on hundreds of thousands — at least to learn how to build better models. Another reason is to get an intentionally *unrepresentative* sample. Such a sample, for instance, might have an equal number of responders and non-responders, although the original data had different proportions, because many data mining algorithms work better on a balanced sample. However, using more data rather than sampling down and using less is generally better, unless you have a good reason for sampling down.

Time Dependency Pops Up Everywhere

Almost all data used in data mining has a time dependency associated with it. Customers' reactions to marketing efforts change over time. Prospects' reactions to competitive offers change over time. A marketing campaign run this year is rarely going to produce the same results as the same campaign run last year. You should expect the results to change.

On the other hand, scientific experiments should yield similar results regardless of when the experiment takes place. The laws of science are considered immutable; they do not change over time. By contrast, the business climate changes daily. Statistics often considers repeated observations to be independent observations. That is, one observation does not influence another. Data mining, on the other hand, must often consider the time component of the data.

Experimentation Is Hard

Data mining has to work within the constraints of existing business practices. This can make it difficult to set up experiments, for several reasons:

- Businesses may not be willing to invest in efforts that reduce short-term gain for long-term learning.
- Business processes may interfere with well-designed experimental methodologies.
- Factors that may affect the outcome of the experiment may not be obvious.
- Timing plays a critical role and may render results useless.

Of these, the first two are the most difficult. The first simply says that tests do not get done. Or, they are done so poorly that the results are useless. The second poses the problem that a seemingly well-designed experiment may not be executed correctly. There are always hitches when planning a test; sometimes these hitches make reading the results impossible.

Data Is Censored and Truncated

The data used for data mining is often incomplete in one of two special ways. *Censored* values are incomplete because whatever is being measured is not complete. One example is customer tenure. The final tenure of active customers is greater than the current tenure; however, which customers are going to stop tomorrow and which are going to stop 10 years from now? The actual tenure is greater than the observed value and cannot be known until the customer actually stops at some unknown point in the future.

Figure 4-14 shows another situation that illustrates the challenge with censored data. This curve shows sales and inventory for one product at a retailer. Sales are always less than or equal to the available inventory. On the days with the Xs, though, the inventory sold out. What is the demand on these days? The potential sales are greater than or equal to the observed sales — however the full potential is not known.

Truncated data poses another problem in terms of biasing samples. Truncated records are not included in the database, often because they are too old. For instance, when Company A purchases Company B, their systems are merged. Often, data about the active customers from Company B are moved into the data warehouse for Company A. That is, all customers active on a given date are moved over. Customers who had stopped the day before are not moved over (in extreme cases). This is an example of left truncation, and it pops up throughout corporate databases, usually with no warning (unless the documentation is very, very good about saying what is not in the database as well as what is). This can cause confusion when looking at tenures by customer start date — and discovering that all customers who started five years before the merger were mysteriously active for at least five years. This is not due to a miraculous acquisition program. This is because all the ones who stopped earlier were excluded.

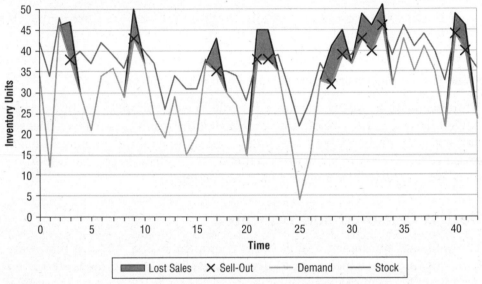

Figure 4-14: A time series of product sales and inventory illustrates the problem of censored data.

Lessons Learned

This chapter covers some basic statistical methods that are useful for analyzing data. When looking at data, it is useful to look at histograms and cumulative histograms to see what values are most common. More important, though, is looking at values over time.

One of the big questions addressed by statistics is whether observed values are expected or not. For this, the number of standard deviations from the average (z-score) can be used to calculate the probability of the value being due to chance, assuming the null hypothesis (the p-value). High p-values mean that the null hypothesis is probably true; that is, nothing interesting is happening. Low p-values are suggestive that other factors may be influencing the results. Converting z-scores to p-values depends on the normal distribution.

Business problems often require analyzing data expressed as proportions. Fortunately, these behave similarly to normal distributions. The formula for the standard error for proportions (SEP) defines a confidence interval on a proportion such as a response rate. The standard error for the difference of proportions (SEDP) helps determine whether two values are similar. This works by defining a confidence interval for the difference between two values.

When designing marketing tests, the SEP and SEDP can be used for sizing test and control groups. In particular, these groups should be large enough to measure differences in response with a high enough confidence. Tests that have more than two groups need to take into account an adjustment, called Bonferroni's correction, when setting the group sizes.

The chi-square test is another statistical method that is often useful. This method directly calculates the estimated values for data laid out in rows and columns. Based on these estimates, the chi-square test can determine whether the results are likely or unlikely. As shown in an example, the chi-square test and SEDP methods produce similar results.

Statisticians and data miners solve similar problems. However, because of historical differences and differences in the nature of the problems, there are some differences in emphasis. Data miners generally have a lot of data with few measurement errors. This data changes over time, and values are sometimes incomplete. The data miner has to be particularly suspicious about bias introduced into the data by business processes.

The rest of the book dives into more detail about modern techniques for building models and understanding data. Many of these techniques have been adopted by statisticians and build on centuries of work in this area. Directed data mining techniques, the subject of the next section of this book, rely heavily on the statistical ideas presented in this chapter. The next chapter starts the discussion on this important class of data mining techniques.

Descriptions and Prediction: Profiling and Predictive Modeling

Chapter 3 introduces data mining in terms of goals, tasks, and techniques. This chapter focuses on the most common type of data mining, directed data mining, and introduces a methodology for descriptive and predictive models. The next six chapters enhance the themes in this chapter by describing specific techniques.

Regardless of the data mining techniques being used, all descriptive models (also called profiling models) and prediction models — the two main types of directed data mining models — have much in common. When using such modeling techniques, the data miner has a goal in mind, and known examples of this goal are available in the model set. The following are all examples of directed data mining:

- Which customers are likely to stop?
- When will customers make their next purchase?
- What is the best next offer for each customer?
- What distinguishes high-end customers from the average customer?

All of these are examples where the historical data contains, respectively, customers who stop, the intervals between purchases, the products different customers purchased, and customers in segments. The goal of the data mining task is usually to find more customers like the good ones in the data.

The chapter starts by explaining what directed data mining models look like. An important part of this discussion is the subject of model stability — models should work not only in the lab but also in the real world. The chapter then continues by explaining the difference between prediction models and profiling models, two approaches that are very similar and only distinguished by characteristics of the model set used in their creation.

The bulk of the chapter is devoted to a methodology for directed data mining. Although the methodology is presented as a simple process, don't be misled. Data mining is an iterative process, and the methodology is really a set of guidelines to stay on track and to build stable, useful models. Before diving into the methodology, though, the chapter first discusses the models themselves.

Directed Data Mining Models

As explained in Chapter 3, data mining is about building models. Directed data mining is about building models for a specific purpose, in this case, to make inferences about the target variable.

Defining the Model Structure and Target

Building a directed data mining model requires understanding and defining the target variable the model is trying to estimate. A very typical example is a binary response model, such as a model to choose customers for a direct mail or e-mail campaign. The model is built using historical examples of customers who have responded to previous similar campaigns. The goal of directed data mining is to find additional similar customers in order to improve the response of the next campaign.

This may seem like a simple example, but diving in a bit deeper reveals additional levels of detail. The goal might not be to simply maximize response. Another reasonable goal is to maximize overall revenue for a given amount spent on the campaign. This, in turn, requires estimating both the expected response and the estimated revenue per responding customer. Figure 5-1 shows such a two-step model that combines the response rate and estimated spend to obtain an expected value. Note that the two models are built using different model sets. The response model is based on historical data of everyone exposed to a campaign and the target is whether or not the individual responded. The estimated spend is built only on those customers who responded, and the target is the amount the individuals spent.

Another reasonable goal, such as maximizing profit rather than revenue for the campaign, might use a two-step model, or might simply use an average customer spend, assuming that all responding customers are created equally.

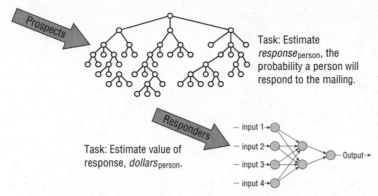

Figure 5-1: This is an example of a two-step model for estimating response amounts. The first model predicts response; the second estimates the amount of the response. The product is the expected response amount.

A binary response model for a campaign might have yet more possible goals:

- Reactivate dormant customers (those who have not made a purchase in a long time).
- Maximize customer value over the next year.
- Minimize "bad debt" (customers who do not pay).
- Increase the number of departments or products used by each customer.

Of course, the campaign can only be optimized to meet one goal — although that goal might combine several subgoals. Diverse goals require diverse modeling approaches. Reactivating dormant customers may require building models on the subset of customers who have not purchased in the previous 18 months. Maximizing customer value over a year may require optimizing models based on more complicated financial calculations. Increasing the breadth of the customer relationship might require building a separate model for each department.

Sometimes the goal is not to determine a subset of customers to receive a specific message; instead, it is to choose one of several "treatments" for each specific customer. This treatment might be the choice of product as determined by a cross-sell model, of marketing message to distinguish between price-sensitive and service-sensitive customers, or of channel of message delivery — that is, which customers should get a telephone call, which customers should get an e-mail message, and which should get the glossy, expensive brochure in the mail.

Figure 5-2 shows the structure of the model when there are a handful of different possibilities. There is a separate model for each possibility, and then a deciding process that determines which model is the best for each customer. The idea is that the models compete for the customers based on some measure of "best" which might be largest revenue, highest profitability, or best response.

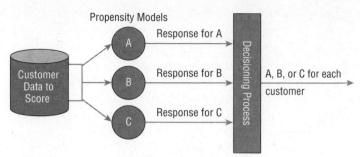

Figure 5-2: A cross-sell model for a handful of options consists of a separate model for each option along with a decision function for choosing the optimal option.

Incremental Response Modeling

A very interesting type of directed model is the *incremental response* or *uplift* model (earlier editions of this book used the term *differential response model*, but this edition uses different terminology because *differential response* has a very specific and unrelated meaning in the child welfare world).

Instead of building models on absolute response, incremental response models estimate the increments in response based on the marketing message. It is particularly applicable to campaigns involving existing customers, although it is sometimes useful for prospecting campaigns. The idea behind incremental response modeling is that the world of customers can be divided into four groups with respect to any marketing campaign:

- *Sure Things* who are going to respond to the offer, regardless of whether they get the message.
- *Persuadables* who are going to respond, but only because they get the offer.
- *Lost Causes* who are not going to respond, regardless of the offer.
- *Sleeping Dogs* who are going to do something nasty like quit, because the campaign reminds them that they do not really want to be customers.

This terminology comes from Portrait Software. Chapter 7 on decision trees has a more detailed case study using its product.

Dividing customers into these four groups is very instructive. The target group for the marketing campaign is the Persuadables. Sure Things are going to respond anyway. Lost Causes are not. Sleeping Dogs are going to do something worse than simply not respond — they are going to leave. Yet another marketing contact is going to push them over the edge and convince them that they no longer want the bother of being a customer, such as when a cable company calls premium customers to encourage them to add more channels — and the result is that some customers downgrade to basic cable.

The basic idea behind incremental response modeling is to develop two models, as shown in Figure 5-3. One model is based on random samples of customers and estimates the background response probability for that data. This is the default estimate of response. The second model is based on previous campaigns, and estimates the response probability based on the campaign. The incremental response is the difference between these scores. Notice that in this formulation, the models themselves can use any appropriate binary response technique.

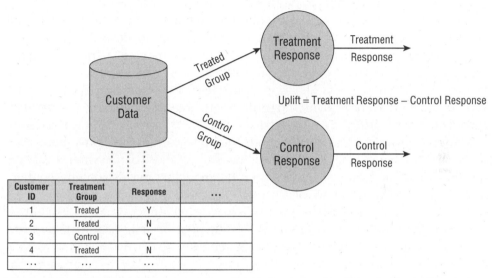

Figure 5-3: An incremental response model can be approximated using two different models — one to estimate the response with no intervention and the other to estimate the response with the intervention.

Portrait Software has an alternative approach. Its software directly attempts to model "persuadability," rather than two separate targets. Chapter 7, which covers decision trees, describes a case study using this approach.

The incremental response score is the difference between two scores. As discussed in Chapter 4, calculating the confidence bounds uses the difference of proportions formula. As a result, the margin of error for the difference is larger than the margin for either model. The important point here is that the sample sizes need to be large for the result to be statistically significant.

TIP Incremental response modeling is a powerful modeling approach when you have a plethora of response data and historical random sample data. The sample sizes must be large, because the incremental response is the difference between two model scores, and hence has a large standard error.

Model Stability

Once upon a time, someone approached the authors at a conference with a story. He worked for a cable company and had built a model to offer premium channels to cable subscribers, a very typical modeling exercise in this industry. His question was simple. Why did the model, which worked so well in the lab, fail to work when he rolled it out? A soufflé that rises in the oven is not so good if it collapses before it hits the table. The problem with his model was that it *overfit* the model set by memorizing the data. Like the soufflé overinflated in the oven, the model was bound to disappoint when moved to another environment.

The goal in modeling is not to produce the best possible model in the lab. The goal of data mining is to do something in the real world, to effect change of some sort. Producing a powerful model in the lab may or may not achieve this goal. There's an old joke about Bill Gates choosing between heaven and hell. Heaven is nice, but when he visits hell, it is a paradise of comfort and bounty, so he chooses hell. When he returns and settles in, the reality is burning and painful. Asked about the difference, Lucifer responds that the first version was a demo.

Models are similar. You don't want the demo version of the model that works in the lab and then crashes and burns in the real world. What you want is *stability*, the ability of a model to work not only on the model set but also on unseen data. Much of the methodology in this chapter is devoted to ensuring stability.

Stability has four big enemies. The first is just getting things wrong — like NASA losing the $125 million Mars orbiter in 1999 because one engineering team used English units and another used metric. Specifically, the thrusters on the rockets expected instructions in newtons, the metric unit for force, but the computers controlling the thrusters produced instructions using pound force. Communication and standards are important. In the data mining world, this type of problem surfaces when the modeling team simply solves the wrong problem. The data may be clean, the analysis exemplary, and yet the solution ends up being useless.

The second problem is *overfitting*. This occurs when the model memorizes the model set instead of recognizing more general patterns. For instance, once upon a time, the authors worked at a company that had a round of layoffs and, by coincidence, everyone named Alex was laid off — three employees in all. A person might find a pattern suggesting that being named "Alex" is a risk factor for being laid off, even though in this situation the Alexes just happened to work in the parts of the company that were scaled back. Human minds recognize patterns, and patterns in first names might stand out. However, such patterns are often spurious, having no applicability to other situations: an example of overfitting.

The third problem is *sample bias*, where the data used to build the model may not accurately reflect the real world. This can occur whenever the model set is not created as a random sample (or stratified random sample) from the original data. For instance, a model built on customers from California might not work, because customers in California might be different in key ways from customers in other places.

Another problem is that the future may not be like the past. Models are built on historical data, but they get applied to other time periods. An implicit assumption is that what happened in the past provides guidance for the future. While it is not a requirement that the future be exactly like the past, models work on the assumption that the past is a prologue to the future.

Time-Frames in the Model Set

Each variable in the model set has a time frame associated with it that describes the period that contributes to the variable. For instance, the total number of purchases is calculated using information from when a customer starts to when the value is calculated. The amount the customer spent in the previous year has a time frame of just one year.

Input variables and target variables both have time frames. The relationship between these is very important. Figure 5-4 shows the two most common situations. The lower half of the figure illustrates that the input variables come from a time frame strictly before the target variable. Any model built on this model set is a prediction model. The alternative, when the input variables and target come from the same time frame, produces profiling models.

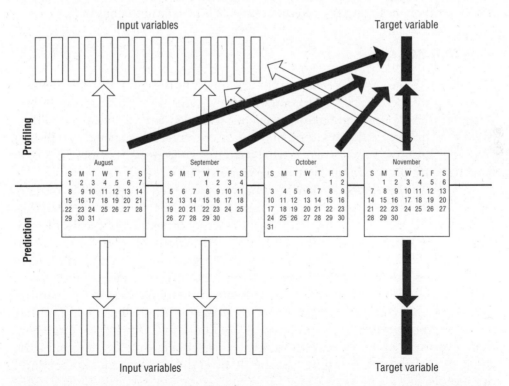

Figure 5-4: Profiling models and prediction models differ only in the temporal relationship of the target variable to the input variables.

Prediction Models

Many data mining problems are framed as prediction problems: Based on past responses, who will respond? Based on past write-offs, who is a bad risk? The best way to approach these problems is for the input variables to come strictly before the target variables, as shown in the lower half of Figure 5-4.

Consider a retailer with a catalog and a website that plans its campaigns in September. The idea is to take a snapshot of customers on September 1st and apply a model to this data to determine which customers should be in the campaign and which marketing treatment they should get. What data should be used to build the model? The same data that will be used for scoring it. So, turn the pages of the calendar back one year, to September 1st of the previous year. Take a snapshot of what the customers look like on that date, and then add in the response to last year's end-of-year marketing efforts. Such an approach guarantees that no "future" information from the inputs pollutes the model's ability to estimate the target.

The challenge with prediction is the amount of work needed to create the model set. Turning the calendar back in time is easier to write about than to implement in a customer-centric, normalized data warehouse. The efforts are worth it, though, because the result is models that are more stable and that do a better job of capturing the causes of important customer behaviors.

Profiling Models

The alternative to prediction is profiling, shown in the top half of Figure 5-4. In a profiling model, the target comes from the same time frame as the inputs. It is a familiar approach to many problems and need not involve any sophisticated data analysis. Surveys, for instance, are one common method to building customer profiles. Surveys reveal what customers and prospects look like, or at least the way survey responders answer questions.

Profiles are often based on demographic variables, such as geographic location, gender, and age. Because advertising is sold according to these same variables, demographic profiles can turn directly into media strategies. Simple profiles are used to set insurance premiums. A 17-year-old male pays more for car insurance than a 60-year-old female. Similarly, the application form for a simple term life insurance policy asks about age, sex, and smoking — and not much more.

Powerful though it is, profiling has serious limitations. One is the inability to distinguish cause and effect. As long as the profiling is based on familiar demographic variables, this limitation is not noticeable. If men buy more beer than women, you do not have to wonder whether beer drinking might be the cause of maleness. It is safe to assume that the link is from men to beer and not vice versa.

WARNING Profiling models find relationships, but they do not specify cause-and-effect. For this reason, profiling models often use customer demographics as inputs and customer behavior as the target, because determining cause-and-effect is more intuitive in this case.

With behavioral data, the direction of causality is not always so clear. Consider some actual examples from real data mining projects:

- People who have certificates of deposit (CDs) have little or no money in their savings accounts.
- Customers who use voice mail make a lot of short calls to their own phone number.
- Customers who pay by automatic withdrawal are almost never late in paying their bills.

Not keeping money in a savings account is a common behavior of CD holders, just as being male is a common feature of beer drinkers. Beer companies seek out males to market their product, so should banks seek out people with no money in savings in order to sell them certificates of deposit? Probably not! Presumably, the CD holders have no money in their savings accounts because they used that money to buy CDs. A more common reason for not having money in a savings account is not having any money, and people with no money are not likely to purchase certificates of deposit.

Similarly, voice mail users call their own number so much because it is one way to check voice mail. The pattern is useless for finding prospective users. And the fact that customers who have automatic payment mechanisms are almost never late does not provide much information about the customers. The payments are automatic.

Directed Data Mining Methodology

The direct data mining methodology has eleven steps:

1. Translate the business problem into a data mining problem.
2. Select appropriate data.
3. Get to know the data.
4. Create a model set.
5. Fix problems with the data.
6. Transform data to bring information to the surface.
7. Build models.

8. Assess models.

9. Deploy models.

10. Assess results.

11. Begin again.

As shown in Figure 5-5, the data mining process is best thought of as a set of nested loops rather than a straight line. The steps do have a natural order, but completely finishing with one before moving on to the next is not necessary or even desirable. Things learned in later steps will cause earlier ones to be revisited.

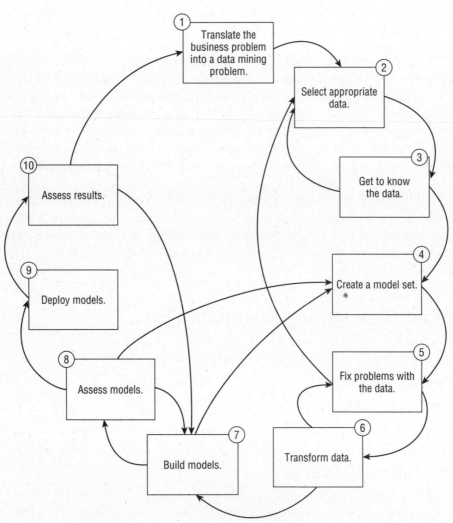

Figure 5-5: Directed data mining is not a linear process.

Step 1: Translate the Business Problem into a Data Mining Problem

A favorite scene from *Alice in Wonderland* is the passage where Alice asks the Cheshire cat for directions:

"Would you tell me, please, which way I ought to go from here?"

"That depends a good deal on where you want to get to," said the Cat.

"I don't much care where — " said Alice.

"Then it doesn't matter which way you go," said the Cat.

" — so long as I get somewhere," Alice added as an explanation.

"Oh, you're sure to do that," said the Cat, "if you only walk long enough."

The Cheshire cat might have added that without some way of recognizing the destination, you can never tell whether you have walked long enough!

The proper destination for a directed data mining project is the solution of a well-defined business problem. Data mining goals for a particular project should not be stated in broad, general terms, such as

- Gaining insight into customer behavior
- Discovering meaningful patterns in data
- Learning something interesting

These are all worthy goals, but even when they have been achieved, they are hard to measure. Projects that are hard to measure are hard to put a value on.

Wherever possible, break the broad, general goals down into more specific ones to facilitate monitoring progress. Gaining insight into customer behavior might turn into concrete goals:

- Identify customers who are unlikely to renew their subscription.
- Design a calling plan that will reduce customer stop rates for home-based business customers.
- Determine which Web transactions are possibly fraudulent.
- List products whose sales are at risk if wine and beer sales are discontinued.
- Forecast the number of customers over the next three years, based on the current marketing strategy.

Directed data mining is often presented as a technical problem of finding a model that explains the relationship of a target variable to a group of input variables. That technical task is indeed central to most data mining efforts, but it should

MISUNDERSTANDING THE BUSINESS PROBLEM: A CAUTIONARY TALE

Data Miners, the consultancy founded by the authors, was once called upon to analyze supermarket loyalty card data on behalf of a large consumer packaged goods manufacturer. To put this story in context, it helps to know a little bit about the supermarket business. In general, a supermarket does not care whether a customer buys Coke or Pepsi (unless one brand happens to be on a special deal that temporarily gives it a better margin), as long as the customer purchases his or her soft drinks at that supermarket. Product manufacturers, who care very much which brands are sold, vie for the opportunity to manage whole categories in the stores. As category managers, they have some control over how their own products and those of their competitors are merchandised, but their goal is to maximize sales of the category, not their own sales.

Our client wanted to demonstrate its ability to utilize loyalty card data to improve category management. The category picked for the demonstration was yogurt because by supermarket standards, yogurt is a fairly high-margin product.

As we understood it, the business goal was to identify yogurt lovers. To create a target variable, we divided loyalty card customers into groups of high, medium, and low yogurt affinity based on their total yogurt purchases over the course of a year and into groups of high, medium, and low users based on the proportion of their shopping dollars spent on yogurt. People who were in the high category by both measures were labeled as yogurt lovers — such people spend a relatively high amount of money on yogurt and a relatively high proportion of their shopping dollar on yogurt.

The transaction data had to undergo many transformations to be turned into a customer signature. Input variables included the proportion of trips and of dollars spent at various different times of day and in various categories, shopping frequency, average order size, and other behavioral variables.

Using this data, we built a profiling model that gave all customers a yogurt lover score. Armed with such a score, coupons could be printed for yogurt when likely yogurt lovers checked out, even when they did not purchase any yogurt on that trip. The model might even identify good prospects who had not yet gotten in touch with their inner yogurt lover, but might if prompted with a coupon.

The model got good lift, and we were pleased with it. The client, however, was disappointed. "But, *who* is the yogurt lover?" asked the client. "Someone who gets a high score from the yogurt lover model" was not considered a good answer. The client was looking for something like, "The yogurt lover is a woman between the ages of X and Y living in a ZIP code where the median home price is between M and N." A description like that could be used for deciding where to buy advertising and how to shape the creative content of ads. Ours, based on shopping behavior rather than demographics, could not.

not be attempted until the target variable has been properly defined and the appropriate input variables identified. These tasks, in turn, depend on a good understanding of the business problem to be addressed. As the story in the sidebar illustrates, failure to properly translate the business problem into a data mining problem leads to one of the dangers you are trying to avoid — learning things that are true, but not useful. You must ask two important questions before beginning the technical work: How will the results be used? And, in what form will the results be delivered? The answer to the first question goes a long way toward answering the second.

How Will Results Be Used?

"How the results will be used?" is perhaps the most important question to ask. Surprisingly often, the initial answer is "we're not sure." An answer is important because, as the cautionary tale in the sidebar illustrates, different intended uses dictate different solutions.

For example, many data mining engagements are designed to improve customer retention. The results of such a study could be used in many different ways:

- Proactively contact high-risk or high-value customers with an offer that rewards them for staying.
- Change the mix of acquisition channels to favor those that bring in the most loyal customers.
- Forecast customer population in future months.
- Alter the product to address defects that are causing customers to defect.

Each of these goals has implications for the data mining process. Contacting existing customers through an outbound telemarketing or direct mail campaign implies that in addition to identifying customers at risk, you want an understanding of *why* they are at risk so an attractive offer can be constructed, and *when* they are at risk so the call is not made too early or too late. Forecasting implies that in addition to identifying which current customers are likely to leave, you need to determine how many new customers will be added and how long they are likely to stay. This latter problem of forecasting new customer starts is typically embedded in business goals and budgets, and is not usually just a predictive modeling problem.

How Will Results Be Delivered?

A directed data mining project may result in several very different types of deliverables. When the primary goal of the project is to gain insight, the deliverable is often a report or presentation filled with charts and graphs. When the project is a one-time proof-of-concept or pilot project, the deliverable may consist of lists of customers who will receive different treatments in a marketing experiment. When the data mining project is part of an ongoing analytic customer relationship management effort, the deliverable is likely to be a computer program or set of programs that can be run on a regular basis to score a defined subset of the customer population along with additional software to manage models and scores over time. The form of the deliverable affects the data mining results. Producing a list of customers for a marketing test is not sufficient when the goal is to dazzle marketing managers.

As another example, a life insurance company was about to embark on a data mining project to predict which customers would be most likely to cancel their policies. Before starting the project, though, the managers asked how the results would be used. This insurance company sold most of its policies through independent agents — agents that sell insurance policies for several different companies. They realized that if they provided the agents with customers who were likely to cancel, the independent agents would simply contact the customers and sell them policies at other companies. Thinking about how the results would be used led to the data mining project being cancelled.

The Role of Domain Experts and Information Technology

As described in Chapter 3, the only way to get good answers to the questions posed earlier is to involve the owners of the business problem in figuring out how data mining results will be used, and analysts, IT staff, and database administrators in figuring out how the results should be delivered. Getting input from a broad spectrum within the organization and, where appropriate, outside it as well, is often useful. The authors suggest getting representatives from the various constituencies within the enterprise together in one place, rather than interviewing them separately. That way, people with different areas of knowledge and expertise have a chance to react to each other's ideas. The goal of all this consultation is a clear statement of the business problem to be addressed. The final statement of the business problem should be as specific as possible. "Identify the 10,000 gold-level customers most likely to defect within the next 60 days" is better than "provide a churn score for all customers."

The role of the data miner in these discussions is to ensure that the final statement of the business problem is one that can be translated into a technical problem. Otherwise, the best data mining efforts in the world may be addressing the wrong business problem.

Step 2: Select Appropriate Data

Data mining requires data. In the best of all possible worlds, the required data would already reside in a corporate data warehouse, cleansed, available, historically accurate, and frequently updated. In fact, just as often it is scattered in a variety of operational systems and data marts in various different formats on computers running different operating systems and accessed through incompatible desktop tools.

The data sources that are useful and available vary, of course, from problem to problem and industry to industry. Some examples of useful data include:

- Warranty claims data (including both fixed-format and free-text fields)
- Point-of-sale data (including ring codes, coupons proffered, discounts applied)
- Credit card charge records
- Medical insurance claims data
- Web log data
- E-commerce server application logs
- Direct mail response records
- Call-center records, including memos written by the call-center reps
- Printing press run records
- Noise level in decibels from microphones placed in communities near an airport
- Telephone call detail records
- Survey response data
- Demographic and lifestyle data
- Economic data
- Hourly weather readings (wind direction, wind strength, precipitation)
- Census data

After formulating the business problem, you should make a wish list of data that would be nice to have. For a study of existing customers, this should include data from the time they were acquired (acquisition channel, acquisition date, original product mix, original credit score, and so on), similar data describing their current status, behavioral data accumulated during their tenure, and demographic data describing the customer and the household. Of course, finding everything on the wish list may not be possible, but starting out with an idea of what you would like to find is better than starting out without one.

Occasionally, a data mining effort starts without a specific business problem. A company becomes aware that it is not getting good value from the data it collects, and sets out to determine whether the data could be made more useful through data mining. The trick to making such a project successful is to turn it into a project designed to solve a specific problem. In this case, a critical success factor is working with domain experts to understand what problems are both useful and feasible to solve with the data.

What Data Is Available?

The first place to look for customer data is in the corporate data warehouse. Data in the warehouse has already been cleaned and verified and brought together from multiple sources. A single data model hopefully ensures that similarly named fields have the same meaning throughout the database and compatible data types. The corporate data warehouse is a historical repository; new data is appended, but historical data is never changed. Because it was designed for decision support, the data warehouse provides detailed data that can be aggregated to the right level for data mining. Chapter 17 goes into more detail about the relationship between data mining and data warehousing.

The only problem is that in many organizations such a data warehouse does not actually exist, or one or more data warehouses exist, but don't live up to the promise. In these cases, data miners must seek data from various departmental databases and from within the bowels of operational systems. These operational systems are designed to perform a certain task such as running websites, processing claims, completing calls, or processing bills. They are designed with the primary goal of processing transactions quickly and accurately. The data is in whatever format best suits that goal and the historical record, if any, is likely to be in a tape archive, perhaps stored deep underground and far way. Getting the data in a form useful for knowledge discovery may require significant organizational maneuvering and programming effort.

In many companies, determining what data is available is surprisingly difficult. Documentation is often missing or out of date. Typically, no one person can provide all the answers. Determining what is available requires looking through data dictionaries, interviewing users and database administrators, examining existing reports, and looking at the data itself.

For some problems, data about prospects is needed as well as data about customers. When such data is needed, external sources and operational systems, such as Web logs, call detail records, call center systems, and sometimes even spreadsheets are often the only recourse.

> **TIP** The surest way to kill a data mining effort is to wait until perfect and clean data is available. Although additional and cleaner data is desirable, data mining must often make do with what is available.

How Much Data Is Enough?

Unfortunately, there is no simple answer to the question of how much data is enough. The answer depends on the particular algorithms employed, the complexity of the data, and the relative frequency of possible outcomes. Statisticians have spent years developing tests for determining the smallest model set that can be used to produce a model. Machine learning researchers have spent much time and energy devising ways to let parts of the training set be reused for validation and testing. All of this work ignores an important point: In the commercial world, statisticians are scarce and data is plentiful.

In any case, where data *is* scarce, data mining is not only less effective, it is less likely to be useful. Data mining is most useful when the sheer volume of data obscures patterns that might be detectable in smaller databases. Therefore, the authors' advice is to use so much data that the questions about what constitutes an adequate sample size simply do not arise. We generally start with tens of thousands if not millions of pre-classified records so that the model set contains many thousands of records.

In data mining, more is better, but with some caveats. The first caveat has to do with the relationship between the size of the model set and its density. *Density* refers to the prevalence of the outcome of interest. When estimating a real number, this means that the full range of the target should be available in the model set, with no particular values highly underrepresented. For a binary response model, the target variable might represent something relatively rare. Prospects responding to a direct mail offer is rare. Credit card holders committing fraud is rare. In any given month, newspaper subscribers canceling their subscriptions is rare. The model set should be balanced with equal numbers of each of the outcomes during the model-building process. A smaller, balanced sample is preferable to a larger one with a very low proportion of rare outcomes.

The second caveat has to do with the data miner's time. When the model set is large enough to build good, stable models, making it larger is counterproductive because everything will take longer to run on the larger dataset. Because data mining is an iterative process, the time spent waiting for results can become very large if each run of a modeling routine takes hours instead of minutes.

How Much History Is Required?

Data mining uses data from the past to make predictions about the future. But how far in the past should the data come from? This is another simple question without a simple answer. The first thing to consider is seasonality. Most businesses display some degree of seasonality. Sales go up in the fourth quarter. Leisure travel goes up in the summer. Health insurance claims go up in the fourth quarter, after deductibles have been paid. There should be enough historical data to capture calendar-related events of this sort.

On the other hand, data from too far in the past may not be as useful for mining because of changing market conditions. This is especially true when some external event such as a change in the regulatory regime has intervened. For many customer-focused applications, two to three years of history is appropriate. However, even in such cases, data about the beginning of the customer relationship often proves very valuable: What was the initial channel? What was the initial offer? How did the customer initially pay?

How Many Variables?

Inexperienced data miners are sometimes in too much of a hurry to throw out variables that seem unlikely to be interesting, keeping only a few carefully chosen variables they expect to be important. The data mining approach calls for letting the data itself reveal what is and is not important.

Often, variables that had previously been ignored turn out to have predictive value when used in combination with other variables. For example, one credit card issuer had never included data on cash advances in its customer profitability models. They discovered through data mining that people who use cash advances only in November and December are highly profitable. Presumably, these people are prudent enough to avoid borrowing money at high interest rates most of the time (a prudence that makes them less likely to default than habitual users of cash advances), but they need some extra cash for the holidays and are willing to pay high interest rates for it.

A final model is usually based on just a few variables. But these few variables are often derived by combining several other variables, and which ones end up being important may not have been obvious at the beginning. Some data mining techniques do work best on smaller numbers of variables; Chapter 20 describes techniques for reducing the number of variables, often by combining many variables into a smaller number.

What Must the Data Contain?

At a minimum, the data must contain examples of all possible outcomes of interest. In directed data mining, where the goal is to predict the value of a particular target variable, the model set must be comprised of pre-classified data. To distinguish people who are likely to default on a loan from people who are not, the model set needs thousands of examples from each class. When a new applicant comes along, his or her application is compared with those of past customers, either directly, as in memory-based reasoning, or indirectly through rules or neural networks derived from the historical data. If the new application "looks like" those of people who defaulted in the past, the new application will be given a low score and hence rejected.

Implicit in this description is the idea that data is available to describe what happened in the past. To learn from our mistakes, we first have to recognize that we have made them. This is not always possible. One company had to give up on an attempt to use directed data mining for building a warranty claims fraud model because, although they suspected that some claims might be fraudulent, they had no idea which ones. Without a model set containing warranty claims clearly marked as fraudulent or legitimate, directed data mining techniques could not be used. (Such a problem is better approached using undirected data mining techniques.) Another company wanted a direct mail response model built, but could only supply data on people who had responded to past campaigns. The company had not kept any information on people who had not responded, so directed data mining techniques could not be used to identify responders.

Step 3: Get to Know the Data

The importance of spending time exploring the data before rushing into building models cannot be emphasized enough. Because of the importance of this topic, Chapters 18 and 19 are devoted to it in detail. Good data miners seem to rely heavily on intuition — somehow being able to guess what a good derived variable to try might be, for instance. The only way to develop intuition for what is going on in an unfamiliar dataset is to immerse yourself in the data. Along the way, you are likely to discover many data quality problems and be inspired to ask many questions that would not otherwise have come up.

Examine Distributions

A good first step is to examine a histogram of each variable in the dataset and think about what it is telling you. Make note of anything that seems surprising. If there is a state code variable, is California the tallest bar? If not, why not? Are some states missing? If so, does it seem plausible that this company does not do business in those states? If a gender variable is in the data, are there similar numbers of men and women? If not, is that unexpected? Pay attention to the range of each variable. Do variables that should be counts or dollar amounts take on negative values? Do the highest and lowest values seem reasonable for that variable? Is the average much different from the median? How many missing values are there? Have the variable counts been consistent over time?

TIP As soon as you get your hands on a data file from a new source, you should profile the data to understand what is going on, including getting counts and summary statistics for each field, counts of the number of distinct values taken on by categorical variables, and where appropriate, cross-tabulations such as sales by product by region. In addition to providing insight into the data, the profiling exercise is likely to raise warning flags about inconsistencies or definitional problems that could destroy the usefulness of later analysis.

Data visualization tools can be very helpful during the initial exploration of a database. Scatter plots, bar charts, geographic maps, and other visualization tools are immensely powerful for seeing what is in the data. This book contains many examples of such charts, showing that they are not only useful for learning about data but also for communicating what is found.

Compare Values with Descriptions

Look at the values of each variable and compare them with the description given for that variable in available documentation. This exercise often reveals that the descriptions are inaccurate or incomplete. In one dataset of grocery purchases, a variable that was labeled as being an item count had many noninteger values. Upon further investigation, it turned out that the field contained an item count for products sold by the item, and a weight for items sold by weight. Another dataset, this one from a retail catalog company, included a field that was described as containing total spending over several quarters. This field was mysteriously capable of predicting the target variable — whether a customer had placed an order from a particular catalog mailing. Everyone who had not placed an order had a zero value in the mystery field. Everyone who had placed an order had a number greater than zero in the field. The authors surmised that the field was misnamed and actually contained the value of the customer's order from the mailing in question. In any case, it certainly did not contain the documented value.

Validate Assumptions

Using simple cross-tabulation and visualization tools such as scatter plots, bar graphs, and maps, validate assumptions about the data. Look at the target variable in relation to various other variables to see such things as response by channel or churn rate by market or income by sex. Where possible, try to match reported summary numbers by reconstructing them directly from the base-level data. For example, if reported monthly churn is two percent, count up the number of customers who cancel one month and see whether it is around two percent of the total.

TIP Trying to re-create reported aggregate numbers from the detail data that supposedly goes into them is an instructive exercise. In trying to explain the discrepancies, you are likely to learn much about the operational processes and business rules behind the reported numbers.

Ask Lots of Questions

Wherever the data does not seem to bear out received wisdom or your own expectations, make a note of it. An important output of the data exploration process is a list of questions for the people who supplied the data. Often these questions will require further research because few users look at data as carefully as data miners do. Examples of the kinds of questions that are likely to come out of the preliminary exploration are

- Why are no auto insurance policies sold in New Jersey or Massachusetts?
- Why were some customers active for 31 days in February, but none were active for more than 28 days in January?
- Why were so many customers born in 1911? Are they really that old?
- Why are there no examples of repeat purchasers?
- What does it mean when the contract begin date is after the contract end date?
- Why are negative numbers in the sale price field?
- How can active customers have a non-null value in the cancellation reason code field?

These are all real questions the authors have had occasion to ask about real data. Sometimes the answers taught us things we hadn't known about the client's industry. At the time, New Jersey and Massachusetts did not allow automobile insurers much flexibility in setting rates, so a company that sees its main competitive advantage as smarter pricing does not want to operate in those markets. Other times we learned about idiosyncrasies of the operational systems, such as the data entry screen that insisted on a birth date even when none was known. As a result, customer service representatives assigned the birthday November 11, 1911 because 11/11/11 is the date you get by typing the "1" key six times (and no other keys work to fill in valid dates as easily). Sometimes we discovered serious problems with the data such as the data for February being misidentified as January. And in the last instance, we learned that the process extracting the data had bugs.

Step 4: Create a Model Set

The model set contains all the data used in the modeling process. Some of the data in the model set is used to find patterns. For several of the techniques, some of the data in the model set is used to verify that the model is stable. The model set is also used to assess the model's performance. Creating a model set requires assembling data from multiple sources to form customer signatures (discussed next) and then preparing the data for analysis.

Assembling Customer Signatures

The model set is a table or collection of tables with one row per item to be studied, and fields for everything known about that item that could be useful for modeling. When the data describes customers, the rows of the model set are often called *customer signatures*. The idea behind the term *customer signature* is that each customer is uniquely identified by the trail of data that he or she leaves, and you can take advantage of the signature to better understand them.

Assembling the customer signatures from relational databases often requires complex queries to join data from many tables and then augmenting the results with data from other sources. Part of the data assembly process is getting all data to be at the correct level of summarization. One row contains all the information about a customer rather than about a transaction or a ZIP code. Chapter 18 covers these issues.

Creating a Balanced Sample

Very often, the directed data mining task involves learning to distinguish between two groups or a small number of groups, such as responders and non-responders, goods and bads, or members of different customer segments. As explained in the sidebar, "Adding More Needles to the Haystack," data mining algorithms do best when these groups have roughly the same number of members. This is unlikely to occur naturally. In fact, the more interesting groups are usually underrepresented.

There are two ways to balance the model set. The first is *stratified sampling* (also called *oversampling*) where the model set is generated by taking equal numbers of records from the different values. The sample rate for each target value is different, hence the name. This method reduces the size of the model set. An alternative method is to add a weighting factor so members of the most popular groups are weighted less than members of the smaller groups. The authors' advice is to set the weight of the least common group to 1 and to set the other weights to less than 1, because these weights work well with the parameters used for decision trees.

TIP When setting the weights for records to balance the model set, set the largest weight value to 1 and the others to less than 1.

ADDING MORE NEEDLES TO THE HAYSTACK

In standard statistical analysis, a common practice is to throw out *outliers* —
observations that are far outside the normal range. In data mining, however,
these outliers may be just what you are looking for. Perhaps they represent
fraud, some sort of error in your business procedures, or some fabulously
profitable niche market. In these cases, you don't necessarily want to throw
out the outliers, you want to get to know and understand them!

   Knowledge discovery algorithms learn by example. Without a sufficient
number of examples of a particular class or pattern of behavior, the data mining
tools are not able to come up with a model for predicting that class or pattern. In
this situation, artificially enriching the model set with examples of the rare event
can improve the chances of effectively modeling that event. When an outcome is
rare, there are two ways to create a balanced sample.

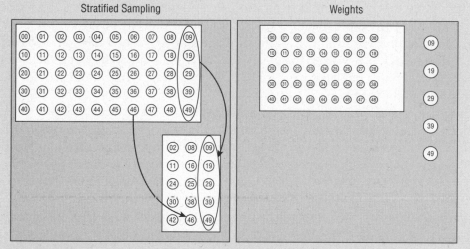

When an outcome is rare, there are two ways to create a balanced sample.

   For example, a bank might want to build a model to determine which customers are likely prospects for a private banking program. These programs
appeal only to the very wealthiest clients, few of whom are represented in
even a fairly large sample of bank customers. To build a model capable of
spotting these fortunate individuals, the model set might have 50 percent
private banking clients even though they represent fewer than 1 percent of all
checking accounts.

   Alternatively, each private banking client might be given a weight of 1
and other customers a weight of 0.01, so the total weight of the exclusive
customers equals the total weight of the rest of the customers (the authors
usually set the maximum weight to 1). Of course, this assumes that the modeling tool can handle weights, and many data mining packages do offer this
functionality.

Including Multiple Timeframes

For models that are intended to be used for a period of time (as opposed to one-time use models such as those for targeting holiday messages), stable models are those that work not only in the lab but on future data, too. This is more likely to happen if the data in the model set includes multiple time frames. Even if the model is to be based on only three months of history, different rows of the model set can use different three-month windows. The idea is to let the model generalize from the past rather than memorize what happened at one particular time in the past.

Building a model on data from a single time period increases the risk of learning things that are not true. One amusing example that the authors once saw was a model built on a single week's worth of point of sale data from a supermarket to find products that sell together. We found that milk and eggs sold together. We found that fresh produce and eggs sold together. We found that soda and eggs sold together. In fact, we found that eggs were very popular products, appearing in almost all the product groups. A keen colleague pointed out that the data came from the week before Easter. And, in fact, eggs sell very well before Easter, appearing in almost everyone's shopping cart, to provide the colorful fodder for Easter egg hunts.

Incorporating multiple time frames in the model set eliminates many of the effects of seasonality. Because seasonal effects are so important, they should be added back into the customer signature explicitly. For instance, holiday shopping patterns are very important. Include an entire year's worth of transaction summaries in the data, and then include variables such as the proportion of a customer's spending during the last holiday season. This might be three months ago or nine months ago, depending on when the model set is created. Chapter 18 discusses creating customer signatures for stable models in more depth.

Creating a Model Set for Prediction

When the model set is going to be used for prediction, you have another aspect of time to worry about. The model set should contain multiple time frames. In addition, any one customer signature should have a gap in time between the predictor variables and the target variable. Time can always be divided into three periods: the past, present, and future. For a prediction, a model uses data from the past to make predictions about the future.

As shown in Figure 5-6, all three of these periods should be represented in the model set. Of course all data comes from the past, so the time periods in the model set are actually the distant past, the not-so-distant past, and the recent past. Predictive models find patterns in the distant past that explain outcomes in the recent past. When the model is deployed, it is then able to use data from the recent past to make predictions about the future.

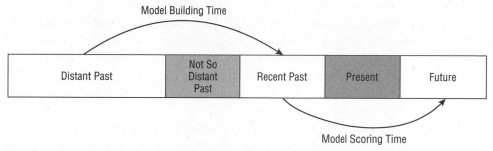

Figure 5-6: Data from the past mimics data from the past, present, and future.

It may not be immediately obvious why some recent data — from the not-so-distant past — is not used in a particular customer signature. The answer is that when you apply the model in the present, no data from the present is available as input. The diagram in Figure 5-7 makes this concept clearer.

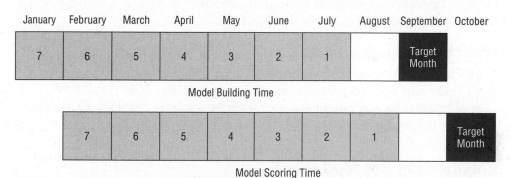

Figure 5-7: Time when the model is built compared to time when the model is used.

If a model were built using data from June (the not-so-distant past) in order to predict July (the recent past), then it could not be used to predict September until August data was available. But when is August data available? Certainly not in August, because it is still being generated. Chances are, not in the first week of September either, because it has to be collected, cleaned, loaded, tested, and approved. The August data may not be available until mid-September or even October, by which point nobody will care about predictions for September. The solution is to skip one month in the model set.

Creating a Model Set for Profiling

The model set for profiling is similar to the model set for prediction, with one exception: the time frame for the target overlaps with the time frame for the inputs.

This seemingly minor difference has a major impact on modeling efforts, because the inputs can "pollute" the patterns related to the target. For instance, in many banks, customers who have investment accounts tend to have very low balances in their savings accounts — because they get better returns in the investment accounts. Does this mean that banks want to target customers with low savings account balances for investment accounts? Probably not; most of these customers have few assets.

One solution to this problem is to very carefully choose the inputs for a profiling model. In this case, which comes from a project the authors worked on, the solution was to combine all account balances into "savings" and "loans." The savings group included all types of savings and investments. This approach worked, as demonstrated by the fact that the ultimate models proved stable, working on customers in different time frames. An even better solution would be to take a snapshot of customers before they open the investment account, and to use that snapshot for modeling. The complication is that the time frame for each customer depends on when that customer opened an account, making the creation of such a model set more difficult.

> **WARNING** When the time frame for the target variable is the same as the time frame for the inputs, then the model is a profiling model, and the inputs may introduce specious patterns that confuse data mining techniques. You need to either be very careful about selecting inputs or rebuild the model set as a prediction model set.

Partitioning the Model Set

After you obtain the pre-classified data from the appropriate time frames, the directed data mining methodology calls for dividing it into three parts. The first part, the *training set*, is used to build the initial model. The second part, the *validation set*, is used to adjust the initial model to make it more general and less tied to the idiosyncrasies of the training set. The third part, the *test set*, is used to gauge the likely effectiveness of the model when applied to unseen data. Three sets are necessary because when data has been used for one step in the process, the information it contains has already become part of the model; therefore, it cannot be used to correct or judge it.

People often find it hard to understand why the training set and validation set are "tainted" after they have been used to build a model. An analogy may help: Imagine yourself back in the fifth grade. The class is taking a spelling test. Suppose that, at the end of the test period, the teacher asks you to estimate your own grade on the quiz by marking the words you got wrong. You will give yourself a very good grade, but your spelling will not improve. If, at the beginning of the period, you thought there should be an "e" at the end of "tomato," nothing will have happened to change your mind when you grade your paper. No new information has entered the system. You need a validation set!

Now, imagine that at the end of the test the teacher allows you to look at the papers of several neighbors before grading your own. If they all agree that "tomato" has no final "e," you may decide to mark your own answer wrong. If the teacher gives the same quiz tomorrow, you will do better. But how much better? If you use the papers of the very same neighbors to evaluate your performance tomorrow, you may still be fooling yourself. If they all agree that "potatoes" has no more need of an "e" than "tomato" and you change your own guess to agree with theirs, then you will overestimate your actual grade on the second quiz as well. That is why the test set should be different from the validation set.

For predictive models, a good idea is for the test set to come from a different time period than the training and validation sets. The proof of a model's stability is in its ability to perform well month after month. A test set from a different time period, called an *out of time* test set, is a good way to verify model stability, although such a test set is not always available.

Step 5: Fix Problems with the Data

All data is dirty. All data has problems. What is or isn't a problem can sometimes vary with the data mining technique. For some techniques, such as decision trees, missing values and outliers do not cause too much trouble. For others, such as regression and neural networks, they cause all sorts of trouble. For that reason, some aspects of fixing problems with data are found in the chapters covering the techniques where the problems cause the most difficulty. The next few sections talk about some of the common problems that should be fixed.

Categorical Variables with Too Many Values

Variables such as ZIP code, county, telephone handset model, and occupation code are all examples that convey useful information, but not in a way that most data mining algorithms can handle. Where a person lives and what he or she does for work are important predictors; however, the variables that describe these attributes take on many, many values. There are so few examples for most of the values that variables such as ZIP code and occupation end up being thrown away (or used incorrectly) along with their valuable information content.

Variables that have many values must be handled in some fashion. One method is to group the values so that many classes that all have approximately the same relationship to the target variable are grouped together. Alternatively, replacing categories with interesting numeric values often produces good models. Replace each ZIP code by its product penetration or median home price or population density or whatever else seems likely to be predictive — and you don't have to choose just one attribute. When building model sets for directed data mining, a powerful transformation is to replace categorical variables with the historical measure of what you are trying to predict. So, historical response rate, historical attrition rate, and historical average customer spend by ZIP code, county, occupation code, or whatever are often more powerful predictors than the original categories themselves.

Numeric Variables with Skewed Distributions and Outliers

Skewed distributions and outliers cause problems for any data mining technique that uses the values arithmetically (by multiplying them by weights and adding them together, for instance). In many cases, discarding records that have outliers solves this problem. In other cases, a better approach is to divide the values into equal sized ranges, such as deciles. Often, the best approach is to transform such variables to reduce the range of values by standardizing the values.

Missing Values

Some data mining algorithms are capable of treating "missing" as a value and incorporating it into the model. Others cannot handle missing values at all. None of the obvious solutions preserve the true distribution of the variable. Throwing out all records with missing values introduces bias because it is unlikely that such records are distributed randomly. Replacing the missing value with some likely value such as the average or the most common value adds spurious information. Replacing the missing value with an unlikely value is even worse because the data mining algorithms do not recognize that –99, say, is an unlikely value for age. The algorithms just go ahead and use it.

A whole branch of statistics is devoted to the problem of imputing missing values. Because values are usually missing because of a business process, imputing values is often not necessary for business data mining problems. Some data mining tools offer missing value imputation, which essentially use data mining techniques to figure out what the value should be. You can also do this manually, by building models to estimate the missing value, and then using that estimate in subsequent models.

However, values are often missing for a good reason. So, a model set designed to use one year of historical data has a problem for customers who started in the last year. They are "missing" values for that period. Or, when you append demographic information onto customers from an outside source, some customers do not match the database, so all the demographic values are missing. In these cases, the best approach is often to build multiple models on different components of the data. Build one model on customers who have been around for more than one year and another for recent customers. Build one model for customers who match the demographic database and another for those who do not. Take advantage of having a lot of data to simplify the modeling process, and eliminate the need for imputing missing values.

TIP When building models, be careful of tools that throw out records with missing values. It is often possible to break the model set into subsets with no missing values, and to build a separate model on each of these.

Values with Meanings That Change over Time

Historical data sometimes suffers a particular problem. The same value in the same field may change its meaning over time. Credit class "A" may always be the best, but the exact range of credit scores that get classed as an "A" may change from time to time. Sometimes the company wants to bring in more customers (regardless of whether they pay) and other times the company wants to reduce its bad debt (thereby only wanting high-credit-quality customers). Dealing with this properly requires a well-designed data warehouse where such changes in meaning are recorded so a new variable can be defined that has a constant meaning over time.

Inconsistent Data Encoding

When information on the same topic is collected from multiple sources, the various sources often represent the same data different ways. If these differences are not caught, they add spurious distinctions that can lead to erroneous conclusions. In one call-detail analysis project, each of the markets studied had a different way of indicating a call to check one's own voice mail. In one market, a call to voice mail from the phone line associated with that mailbox was recorded as having the same origin and destination numbers. In another market, the same situation was represented by the presence of a specific nonexistent number as the call destination. In yet another city, the actual number dialed to reach voice mail was recorded. Understanding apparent differences in voice mail habits by market required putting the data in a common form.

The same data set contained multiple abbreviations for some states and, in some cases; a particular city was counted separately from the rest of the state. If issues like this are not resolved, you may find yourself building a model of calling patterns to California based on data that excludes calls to Los Angeles.

Step 6: Transform Data to Bring Information to the Surface

After you've assembled the data and fixed major data problems, the data must still be prepared for analysis. This involves adding derived fields to bring information to the surface. It may also involve removing outliers, binning numeric variables, grouping classes for categorical variables, applying transformations such as logarithms, turning counts into proportions, and the like. Chapter 19 addresses these issues in more detail.

Step 7: Build Models

The details of building models vary from technique to technique and are described in the chapters devoted to each data mining method. In general terms, this is the step where most of the work of creating a model occurs. In directed data mining, the training set is used to generate an explanation of the dependent or target variable in terms of the independent or input variables. This explanation may take the form of a neural network, a decision tree, a linkage graph, or some other representation of the relationship between the target and the other fields in the database.

Building models is the one step of the data mining process that has been truly automated by modern data mining software. When the authors started working in this field, building models often started by using FTP to get source code from an academic site, getting the program to compile, and then figuring out how to feed the data into it. Happily, actually building models now takes up relatively little of the time in a data mining project, leaving more time for important pursuits such as understanding the business problem, preparing the data, and assessing the models.

Step 8: Assess Models

Assessing models is about determining whether or not the models are working. A model assessment should answer questions such as:

- How accurate is the model?
- How well does the model describe the observed data?
- How much confidence can be placed in the model's predictions?
- How comprehensible is the model?

Of course, the answer to these questions depends on the type of model that was built. Assessment here refers to the technical merits of the model, rather than the "measurement" phase of the virtuous cycle.

Directed models are assessed on their accuracy on previously unseen data. Different data mining tasks call for different ways of assessing performance of the model as a whole and different ways of judging the likelihood that the model yields accurate results for any particular record.

Any model assessment is dependent on context; the same model can look good according to one measure and bad according to another. In the academic field of machine learning — the source of many of the algorithms used for data mining — researchers have a goal of generating models that can be understood in their entirety. An easy-to-understand model is said to have good "mental fit." In the interest of obtaining the best mental fit, these researchers often prefer models that consist of a few simple rules to models that contain many such rules, even when the latter are more accurate. In a business setting, such explicability may not be as important as performance — or may be even more important.

Model assessment can take place at the level of the whole model or at the level of individual predictions. Two models with the same overall accuracy may have quite different levels of variance among the individual predictions. A decision tree, for instance, has an overall classification error rate, but each branch and leaf of the tree also has an error rate as well.

Assessing Binary Response Models and Classifiers

For these types of models, accuracy is measured in terms of the error rate — the percentage of records classified correctly or incorrectly. The classification error rate on the preclassified test set is used as an estimate of the expected error rate when classifying new records. Of course, this procedure is only valid if the test set is representative of the larger population.

The authors' recommended method of establishing the error rate for a model is to measure it on a test dataset taken from the same population as the training and validation sets, but disjointed from them. In the ideal case, such a test set would be from a more recent time period than the data in the model set; however, this is not always possible in practice.

A problem with error rate as an assessment tool is that some errors are worse than others. A familiar example comes from the medical world where a false negative on a test for a serious disease causes the patient to go untreated with possibly life-threatening consequences whereas a false positive only leads to a second (possibly more expensive or more invasive) test. A *confusion matrix* or *correct classification matrix*, shown in Figure 5-8, shows the difference between false positives from false negatives. Some data mining tools allow costs to be associated with each type of misclassification so models can be built to minimize the cost (or maximize the profit) rather than minimize the misclassification rate.

Predicted	Actual	
	YES	**NO**
YES	1,000	200
NO	600	900

Predicted	Actual	
	YES	**NO**
YES	# CORRECT POSITIVE	# FALSE POSITIVE
NO	# FALSE NEGATIVE	# CORRECT NEGATIVE

Figure 5-8: A confusion matrix cross-tabulates predicted outcomes with actual outcomes.

Assessing Binary Response Models Using Lift

Binary response models — where the model is trying to distinguish between two classes or two outcomes — provide some additional methods for assessing their performance. The most common way to compare the performance of such models is to use a ratio called *lift*, which actually measures the change in concentration of a particular class when the model is used to select a group from the general population.

$$\text{lift} = P(\text{class}_t \mid \text{selected group}) / P(\text{class}_t \mid \text{population})$$

An example helps to explain this concept. Suppose that you are building a model to predict who is likely to respond to an e-mail solicitation. As usual, you build the model using a preclassified training set and, if necessary, a preclassified validation set as well. Now you are ready to use the test set to calculate the model's lift.

The classifier scores the records in the test set as either "yes, predicted to respond" or "no, predicted not to respond." Of course, it is not correct every time, but if the model is any good at all, the group of records marked "predicted to respond" contains a higher proportion of actual responders than the test set overall. If the test set contains 5 percent actual responders and the "predicted to respond" group contains 15 percent actual responders, the model provides a lift of 3 (15 divided by 5).

Is the model that produces the highest lift necessarily the best model? Surely a list of people half of whom will respond is preferable to a list where only a quarter will respond, right? Not necessarily — not if the first list has only ten names on it!

Lift itself is a function of the original concentration of the target in the data being scored. The lower the concentration of the target, the higher the potential lift in any model. Lift is also affected by oversampling, as explained in the sidebar "Effect of Oversampling on Lift and Other Measures."

EFFECT OF OVERSAMPLING ON LIFT AND OTHER MEASURES

Oversampling data to produce the model set has an effect on lift and other measures related to the model. The effects are best understood using an example. Assume that the model set is stratified based on a binary target variable, one that takes the values "yes" and "no." The oversampled model set could have any density for the target, but because a balanced sample is typical, assume that it is 50 percent "yes" and 50 percent "no."

A model is built using this data, and some of the records are scored, giving them an 80 percent probability of being "yes." Is this the estimated probability on the original population? No. The answer depends on the prevalence of "yes" in the original population.

Assume that the original population is 10 percent "yes" and 90 percent "no," so the model set is created by taking all the "yes" records and one out of nine of the "no" records. That is, every "yes" in the model set corresponds to one "yes" in the original population, and every "no" corresponds to nine "nos." This correspondence also works for the records with a score of 80 percent. That score is 0.8 "yes" and 0.2 "no" in the model set. The corresponding group in the original population would have 0.8 * 1 "yes" and 0.2 * 9 "no," or 0.8 "yes" for every 1.8 "no." The 80 percent probability in the model set is the same as a 30.8 percent probability (0.8/(0.8+0.2*9)) in the original population.

This calculation also affects lift. Lift is how much better the model does for a set of records than would be expected. If the model finds a group of records such that 80 percent of them are "yes," then on the model set, this group has a lift of 80 percent divided by 50 percent, which is 1.6.

Going back to the original population, things look a bit different. The group that has a "yes" rate of 80 percent on the model set corresponds to a 30.8 percent "yes" rate on the original population. The expected value has decreased. On the other hand, the lift is now 30.8 percent divided by 10 percent, so the expected lift has increased to 3.08 from 1.6. As this example shows, lift is affected by oversampling, as is the expected response rate.

An interesting question is what interesting measures are not affected by oversampling. In fact, there is one. Instead of lift, consider the ratio of "yes" to "no" in the model set (which is simply 1:1). Now consider the ratio of "yes" to "no" in the group with an 80 percent response rate (4:1). And consider the ratio of these ratios, which is four.

Now go back to the original population. It has a ratio of one to nine. The corresponding group no longer has an 80 percent response rate; it has a 30.8 percent response rate (actually 0.8:1.8). The ratio of ratios is four — the same as the ratio on the model set.

So, if you define improvement as the ratio of "yes" to "no" in a subgroup divided by the ratio in the model set, then this ratio is not affected by oversampling. As you will see in a few pages, ROC charts use a similar idea and are similarly unaffected by oversampling.

Assessing Binary Response Model Scores Using Lift Charts

Binary response models can produce scores as well as classifications. In this case, the output of the model is a score for something like probability to respond to an e-mail solicitation, rather than a simple "yes" or "no." Lift charts provide overall information about a model, as well as insight on what model score to use as a cutoff.

Figure 5-9 shows a cumulative gains chart (on the top). The horizontal axis does not contain model scores. Instead, it contains percentages of the test set, chosen by different cutoffs. So, the 10 percent value on the horizontal axis is the model score cutoff corresponding to the top 10 percent of the data.

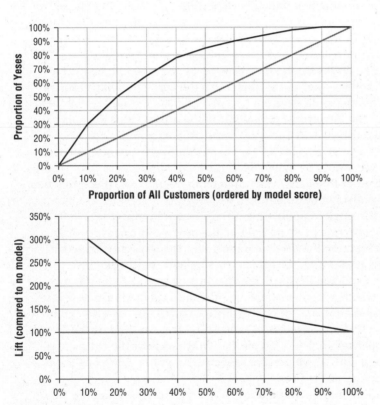

Figure 5-9: The top part of this chart shows the cumulative gains for a binary response model. The lower chart shows the lift (cumulative ratio by decile). A lift chart starts high and descends to 1.

The vertical axis shows the proportion of all responders (yeses) that are in that sample of the data. Cumulative gains charts start at 0 and then increase, preferably bowing upward until they flatten out and end up at one. All cumulative gains charts end up at 1, because when all data is chosen (corresponding to

100 percent on the horizontal axis), all the responders are present (corresponding to 100 percent on the vertical axis).

Figure 5-9 includes a diagonal line, which corresponds to having no model at all. If 10 percent of the test set is chosen randomly (rather than according to a model), then you would expect to get 10 percent of the responders. Instead, using a model, the top 10 percent chosen by the model include 20 percent of the responders. Half the population — using the model — accounts for 70 percent of the responders.

A good cumulative gains chart is one that starts by steeply increasing upward, and then flattening out. However, a curve rises directly to 100 percent and is then totally flat usually indicates a problem. The model is too good, usually meaning that some variable is cheating. Bumps along the way are also not good, where the curve goes up steeply, flattens out, and then goes steeply again. That indicates that the model is overfitting the data.

Charts such as the one in Figure 5-9 are sometimes referred to as lift charts. They do show lift. However, the definition of *lift* is actually the ratio between the curve and the diagonal line — that is, how much better selecting a subset using the model does compared to selecting randomly. The lower part of Figure 5-9 shows an actual lift chart. Notice that an actual lift chart starts high and then descends to the value 1.

Lift is a very handy tool for comparing the performance of two models applied to the same or comparable data. Note that the performance of two models can only be compared using lift when the tests sets have the same density of the outcome.

Assessing Binary Response Model Scores Using Profitability Models

Lift solves the problem of how to compare the performance of models of different kinds, but it is still not powerful enough to answer the most important questions: Is the model worth the time, effort, and money it costs to build it? Will mailing to a segment where lift is 3 result in a profitable campaign?

These kinds of questions cannot be answered without more knowledge of the business context in order to build costs and revenues into the calculation. The information in cumulative gains charts along with a profit-cost matrix can be used to calculate the profitability of different cutoffs. Figure 5-10 shows a profitability model, based on the lift model in Figure 5-9, along with the following assumptions:

- It costs $1 to contact someone.
- If someone responds, the value is worth $44.
- There is an overhead of $20,000 for the campaign.

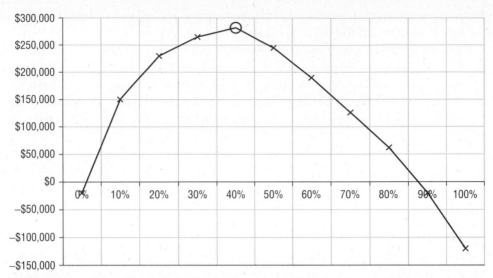

Figure 5-10: A profitability curve translates model results into dollars and cents, making it possible to optimize the model based on financial gain. In this case, maximum profitability occurs when contacting the top 40% of people chosen by the model.

Notice that under these assumptions, choosing no one results in a loss (the overhead for the campaign). And choosing too many people results in a loss (because too many people do not respond). The maximum profit is somewhere in between.

Assessing Binary Response Models Using ROC Charts

The calculation for lift on the test set compares the ratio of responders in the group marked "predicted to respond" with the proportion of responders in the overall test set. A very similar idea is to compare the group marked "predicted to respond" with the group marked "predicted not to respond." This alternative approach is neither better nor worse than lift. The two ideas are very similar, because the ratios contain similar information.

Extending this idea to curves produces what is called an ROC chart that looks a lot like a lift chart. ROC charts have a very particular history and terminology, which is explained in the sidebar "ROC Charts and Their Arcane Terminology." One way to understand ROC charts, as shown in Figure 5-11, is to compare them to lift charts. The vertical axis in a lift chart is the proportion of the desired class ("responders"). The horizontal axis is the entire population. In an ROC chart, the vertical axis is the same, but the horizontal axis is the proportion not in the desired class ("non-responders"). That is, it shows the proportion of yeses that you get at the cost of a certain percentage of nos.

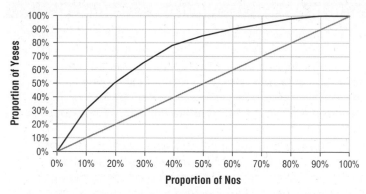

Figure 5-11: An ROC chart looks very similar to a cumulative gains chart, but the horizontal axis is the proportion of false positives, rather than the proportion of the overall population.

Another way of thinking about ROC charts is that the vertical axis shows the true positive rate. This is the proportion of important outcomes that are labeled correctly. The horizontal axis is the false positive rate, the proportion of unimportant outcomes that are mislabeled as being important.

Although ROC charts and lift charts contain very similar information, ROC charts have one advantage: They are independent of the original density of the data. So, an ROC chart for a given model looks the same, regardless of whether the test set is 10 percent, 50 percent, or 90 percent dense in the desired category.

> **TIP** ROC charts have one advantage over cumulative gains charts, because a cumulative gains chart changes shape depending on the density of the desired outcome in the test set. The ROC chart does not change shape.

ROC CHARTS AND THEIR ARCANE TERMINOLOGY

ROC is an acronym that stands for *receiver operating characteristics*. The technical definition of an ROC curve — that it plots the *sensitivity* of the model against *1 – specificity* — probably does not help most people understand the concept.

A bit of history helps in understanding this arcane terminology. These curves originated back in World War II to solve a problem involving radar, which was then first being used in a serious way during wartime. Radar operators were key personnel. Or rather, good radar operators with good equipment were key personnel, because they could determine whether the blips on the radar screen represented enemy craft or something more benign like friendly craft or birds.

The military faced the problem of improving the system to better detect enemy craft. Improvement starts with measurement, and they used ROC curves to assess their radar systems. For them, the vertical axis would be "proportion of

Continued

> **ROC CHARTS AND THEIR ARCANE TERMINOLOGY** *(continued)*
>
> enemy craft identified as enemy craft" and the horizontal axis would be "propor-tion of other things identified as enemy craft." The particular measure for a given system was the area under the ROC curve, which is called *discrimination*.
>
> This helps to explain the name. The "receiver" is the radar system. The "operating" is the ability of the radar system to detect objects. "Characteristics" refers to the ability to differentiate important features, such as enemies from birds.
>
> The terms *sensitivity* and *specificity* are sometimes used in binary response modeling. Sensitivity is how well the models do at identifying the important outcomes (enemy craft). Specificity is how well the models do at identifying other outcomes, so 1 – specificity is the false positive rate. For most people, it is easier to understand the concepts as "true positive rate" and "false positive rate.

Assessing Estimators

For estimation tasks, accuracy is expressed in terms of the difference between the estimated value and the actual value. Both the accuracy of any one estimate and the accuracy of the model as a whole are of interest. A model may be quite accurate for some ranges of input values and less accurate for others. This is particularly true of regression-based models, because they find global patterns in the data. The global patterns are likely to work better for some inputs than for others. Data mining models try to find local patterns in data, mitigating this problem.

The standard way of describing the accuracy of an estimation model is by measuring how far off the estimates are *on average*. But, simply subtracting the estimated value from the true value at each point and taking the average results in a meaningless number. To see why, consider the estimates in Table 5-1.

Table 5-1: Errors cancel each other out (the sum of the error column is zero)

TRUE VALUE	ESTIMATED VALUE	ERROR
127	132	−5
78	76	2
120	122	−2
130	129	1
95	91	4

The average difference between the true values and the estimates is 0; positive differences and negative differences have canceled each other out. The usual way of solving this problem is to sum the squares of the differences rather than the differences themselves. The average of the squared differences is called the *variance*. The estimates in this table have a variance of 10:

$$(-5^2 + 2^2 + -2^2 + 1^2 + 4^2)/5 = (25 + 4 + 4 + 1 + 16)/5 = 50/5 = 10$$

The smaller the variance, the more accurate the estimate.

A drawback to variance as a measure is that it is not expressed in the same units as the estimates themselves. For estimated prices in dollars, knowing how far off the estimates are in dollars rather than *square* dollars is more useful! For that reason, the usual practice is to take the square root of the variance to get a measure called the *standard deviation* or *root mean squared error*. The standard deviation of these estimates is the square root of 10 or about 3.16. To use this book, all you need to know about the standard deviation is that it is a measure of how widely the estimated values vary from the true values, measured in the same units as the original values, and calculated directly from the data.

Assessing Estimators Using Score Rankings

Lift charts and ROC charts are a very effective way of visualizing the performance of binary response models. Score rankings provide a similar mechanism for numeric targets.

The idea behind score ranking charts is to divide the predicted target values into bins, typically deciles. For each decile, the chart shows the average value of the predicted value and the average value of the actual value.

Figure 5-12 shows an example of a score ranking chart. Notice that the predicted averages start high and then descend for subsequent deciles. This is by design, because higher values of the predicted value are in the first deciles.

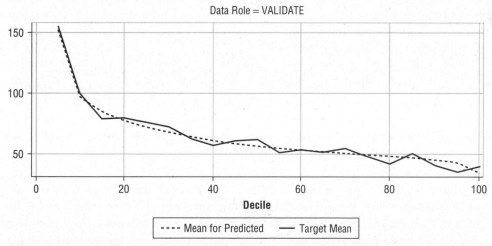

Figure 5-12: This example of a Score Ranking Chart from SAS Enterprise Miner compares the average values of the target variable with the average value of the prediction, by decile (or other grouping).

The actual values should also start high and descend. The closer the actual values are to the predicted values, the more accurate the model. Sometimes, though, the ordering of the predicted values is more important than their actual values. In this case, bumps in the curve, places where the actual values go up and down, are signs of a poor model.

Step 9: Deploy Models

Deploying a model means moving it from the data mining environment to the scoring environment. This process may be easy or hard. In the worst case (and the authors have seen this at more than one company), the model is developed in a special modeling environment using software that runs nowhere else. To deploy the model, a programmer takes a printed description of the model and recodes it in another programming language so it can be run on the scoring platform.

Fortunately, such examples are becoming rarer, as more and more tools produce scoring code in readily transferable formats, such as SAS code, SPSS code, SQL, Java, or C. In addition, PMML (Predictive Modeling Markup Language) is a standard supported by several important data mining vendors. PMML provides a mechanism for moving models and scoring code from one environment to another (more information is available at `www.dmg.org`).

Practical Issues in Deploying Models

Data mining tools now provide score code as part of the model deployment process. This score code may run in a proprietary language such as SAS or SPSS, or in a programming language such as C, Java, or C#. However, deploying the model code itself only solves half the problem because models often use input variables that are not in the original data.

When all data transformations are done in the data mining tool, and the data mining tool emits score code for the data transformations, then the problem is solved. When the transformation code occurs outside the data mining tool, then there can be a problem. Unfortunately, data miners are not always good about keeping a clean, reusable record of the transformations they applied to the data before the model set was created.

The scoring process can be quite challenging, particularly when models are being scored in real time. For instance, a Web application might require model scores every time a customer places an item in a market basket or visits a Web page. Such scoring must take place very quickly, because the process of scoring the customer cannot interfere with the ease of navigating the website.

Optimizing Models for Deployment

As discussed earlier, a profitability chart takes into account the costs and benefits of a model being correct or incorrect. Such a chart shows the actual profitability of a campaign that targets different numbers of people. After all, if developing the model is very expensive, a mass mailing may be more cost effective than a targeted one.

The following are questions to ask to assess the profitability of a model:

- What is the fixed cost of setting up the campaign and the model that supports it?
- What is the cost per recipient of making the offer?
- What is the cost per respondent of fulfilling the offer?
- What is the value of a positive response?

Plugging the answers into a spreadsheet makes it possible to calculate the impact of the model in dollars. The cumulative response chart can then be turned into a cumulative profit chart, which determines where the sorted mailing list should be cut off. If, for example, there are both a high fixed price of setting up the campaign and a fairly high price per recipient of making the offer (as when a wireless company buys loyalty by giving away mobile phones or waiving renewal fees), the company loses money by going after too few prospects because there are not enough respondents to make up for the high fixed costs of the program. On the other hand, if the company makes the offer to too many people, high variable costs begin to hurt.

Of course, the profit model is only as good as its inputs. Although the fixed and variable costs of the campaign are fairly easy to come by, the predicted value of a responder can be harder to estimate. The process of figuring out what a customer is worth is beyond the scope of this book, but having a good estimate helps to measure the true value of a data mining model.

In the end, the most important measure is usually return on investment. Measuring lift on a test set helps choose the right model. Profitability calculations based on lift will help decide how to apply the results of the model. But, measuring these things in the field as well is very important. In a database marketing application, this requires always setting aside control groups and carefully tracking customer response according to various model scores.

Step 10: Assess Results

Assessing the results of a modeling effort usually happens at the financial level: Was the campaign successful? Measuring the actual results — both financially and technically — is very important, so you can learn and do better the next time.

Once upon a time, a large Canadian bank was trying to sell investment accounts to its customers. As with many such companies, the plans included a direct mail campaign to reach likely prospects for the product. The campaign itself was multifaceted and included many other touch points: Customers were exposed to the standard advertising channels; branch personnel were trained to say something like "and would you like to supersize to an investment account?" Even the backs of ATM receipts, the walls of bank branches, and the messages on call waiting were involved. Customers were exposed to the message.

Guess what happened with the direct mail channel? The direct mail group did some sophisticated modeling and found customers likely to open investment accounts. They sent out their direct mail. And, no surprise, the customers with high model scores did, indeed, open more such accounts than customers with low model scores.

Great! However, the direct mail manager allowed a creative test into the mix. This test held back some customers with high model scores from the direct mail. And the results were surprising. Customers with high model scores opened accounts at the same rate, regardless of whether they received the direct mail piece or not; there was no incremental response. The modeling worked, but the particular message was unnecessary. Such a finding is something that only insightful marketing managers really want to know.

Figure 5-13 shows four different test groups for a typical campaign:

- The *test* group has high model scores and receives the message.

- The *modeled holdout* group has high model scores but does not receive the message.

- The *control* group has random or low model scores and receives the message.

- The *holdout* group has random model scores and does not receive the message.

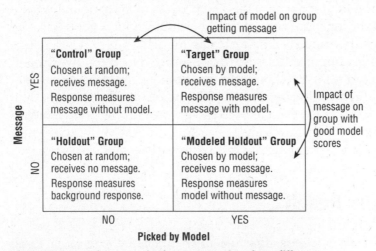

Figure 5-13: When you deploy a campaign, four different treatment groups exist. Comparisons between the groups yield different insights.

When a marketing campaign includes at least three of these groups, then you can measure effectiveness of both the campaign and message.

This example also shows the advantage of incremental response modeling, mentioned earlier in this chapter. Chapter 6, on decision trees, has an example of incremental response modeling in practice.

Step 11: Begin Again

Every data mining project raises more questions than it answers. This is a good thing. It means that new relationships are now visible that were not visible before. The newly discovered relationships suggest new hypotheses to test and the data mining process begins all over again.

Lessons Learned

Directed data mining is searching through historical records to find patterns that explain a particular outcome. The two types of directed data mining models are profiling models and prediction models. These flavors use the same techniques and methodology; they differ only in how the model set is structured.

The solution to a directed data mining problem may involve multiple models that are chained together. So, a cross-sell model may incorporate separate prediction models for each product and a decision rule for choosing the optimal outcome. A response model may be optimized for profitability, so it is really calculating an expected value of the response rather than just the likelihood of response. An even more sophisticated approach is to use incremental response models, where the target is the increase in response rate due to the marketing effort, rather than just the response rate itself.

The primary lesson of this chapter is that data mining is full of traps for the unwary, and following a methodology based on experience can help avoid them. The first hurdle is translating the business problem into a data mining problem. The next challenge is to locate appropriate data that can be transformed into actionable information. After the data has been located, it should be thoroughly explored. The exploration process is likely to reveal problems with the data. It will also help build up the data miner's intuitive understanding of the data. The next step is to create a model set and partition it into training, validation, and test sets.

Data transformations are necessary for two purposes: to fix problems with the data such as missing values and categorical variables that take on too many values, and to bring information to the surface by creating new variables to represent trends and other ratios and combinations. In fact, data transformations are so important that Chapter 19 is devoted to discussing them in greater detail.

After the data has been prepared, building models is a relatively easy process. Each type of model has its own metrics by which it can be assessed, but assessment methods independent of the types of model are also available. Some of the most important of these are the lift and ROC charts, which show how the model has increased the concentration of the desired value of the target variable and the confusion matrix that shows that misclassification error rate for binary response models and the score distribution chart for numeric targets. The next six chapters build on the methodology and dive into directed data mining techniques.

Data Mining Using Classic Statistical Techniques

The notion that data mining and statistics are separate disciplines now seems outdated and even a bit quaint. In fact, all data mining techniques are based on the science of probability and the discipline of statistics. The techniques described in this chapter are just closer to these roots than the techniques described in other chapters.

The chapter begins by describing how even simple, descriptive statistics can be viewed as models. If you can describe what you are looking for, then finding it is easier. This leads to the idea of similarity models — the more something looks like what you are looking for, the higher its score.

Next come table lookup models, which are very popular in the direct marketing industry, and have wide applicability in other fields as well. Naïve Bayesian models are a very useful generalization of table lookup models that allow many more inputs than can usually be accommodated as dimensions of a lookup table.

Much of the chapter is devoted to linear and logistic regression — certainly the most widely used predictive modeling techniques. Regression models are introduced first as a way of formalizing the relationship between two variables that can be seen in a scatter plot. Next comes a discussion of multiple regression, which allows for models with more than a single input, followed by a discussion of logistic regression, which extends the technique to targets with a restricted range such as probability estimates. The chapter ends by discussing fixed effects and hierarchical regression, which allow regression to be applied to individual customers, providing a bridge to more customer-centric data mining techniques.

Similarity Models

A similarity model compares observations to be scored to a prototype. The more similar an observation is to the prototype, the higher its similarity score. Another way of expressing similarity is in terms of distance. The closer an observation is to the prototype, the higher the observation's score. The same mechanism can work for assigning customers to customer segments when each segment has a prototype and customers are assigned to the segment based on the most similar prototype.

A similarity model consists of the prototype and a similarity function. You score it by applying the similarity function to new data.

Similarity and Distance

Chapter 2 has a nice example of a similarity model, based on the fact that readers of a certain publication are wealthier and better educated than the general population. In fact, compared to the U.S. population as a whole, readers are nearly three times as likely to be college educated, and nearly three times as likely to have incomes of more than $100,000. These statistics provide a description of the readership as "well paid and well educated."

To turn a description of the readership into a model that can identify prospective readers requires a precise definition of the ideal reader that can be used to quantify how much a prospect resembles that ideal. Using the average values for current readers as the prototype is one possibility. Another is to ask the advertising sales department to describe the ideal target audience for advertisers. After all, current subscribers may be less than ideal.

TIP Similarity and distance are two ways of talking about the same concept, but the measures go in opposite directions. Two things are similar if they are close to each other according to some distance metric, so when distance is small, similarity is high.

Suppose the ideal reader has 16 years of education and an income of $100,000. How similar to that is a prospect with 14 years of education and an income of $75,000? How about a prospect with 12 years of education and an income of $150,000? Some sort of distance function is needed, and a good choice is the standard Euclidean distance. However, if you try to measure the distance of any prospects from the point ($x = 16$, $y = \$100,000$), income dominates the calculation because its values are much bigger.

This is because income and education are measured on different scales. The solution is to transform both into z-scores, by subtracting the average and dividing by the standard deviation. You can then calculate the Euclidean distance using the z-scores instead of the original values.

The Euclidean distance is only one of many possible distance measures. Other similarity and distance measures are discussed in the chapters on memory-based reasoning (9), clustering (13 and 14), and text mining (21). The important point here is that a statistical description of a prototypical target can be combined with a distance function of some kind to create a model that measures similarity to the prototype. You can use the distance to sort a list of prospects in order of increasing distance from the ideal, or as input to another calculation such as expected revenue or probability of response.

Example: A Similarity Model for Product Penetration

The example in this section is based on a common problem faced by businesses that are contemplating an expansion into new territories. A bank wanting to open new branches, a supermarket planning to build new stores, and an insurance company deciding where to recruit new agents all want to pick good locations. Because they have no performance data for potential sites where they have no business, they use data from current locations to predict what business will be like in the potential new sites.

The authors have used this approach to help choose counties that would be good locations for an insurance company to recruit agents and to pick towns where a regional newspaper could expect to achieve good household penetration.

For consumer-oriented businesses, one approach is to use demographic data from the Census Bureau to describe the best current locations. New locations that are similar to the best locations and dissimilar from the worst locations are good candidates. This approach requires determining the current better and worse locations, typically by looking at the profitability of existing stores.

The Business Problem

Imagine that Hudson and Niagara Stove Company (H&N) is planning to expand from New York across Lake Champlain into the Vermont market where, of course, no product penetration data is available. H&N specializes in selling wood stoves and products to support them. How can H&N use data from its home state to select good locations for dealerships in the new one?

The approach described in this section is to define the ideal locale for H&N's wood-burning products, using available census data. Using this ideal, it can then find towns in Vermont that are similar to the best locations in New York state. Presumably, these towns in Vermont will be good siting choices.

Data Used for Similarity Model

The method is illustrated using publicly available data from the U.S. Census. The rows in the model set are the towns in New York, which are described by many census variables about the town, such as population, area, and proportion of the town that is urban and rural.

The census data is actually much richer than this, including variables that describe ethnicity, age, household composition, industries where people work, and many more attributes. Among the many things that the Census Bureau tracks is the fuel used to heat homes, which includes natural gas, oil, propane, and wood. In this example, imagine that the Census Bureau does not collect this particular item of information. Instead, the proportion of a town using wood for heat represents the product penetration for H&N's line of wood-burning stoves. This variable is the target in the model set.

TIP Although certainly no substitute for a real graphical information system (GIS), scatter plots based on latitude and longitude yield crude but recognizable maps that can be used to illustrate simple geographic patterns.

Figure 6-1 is a crude map of New York, drawn as a scatter plot of the 1,006 towns in the state. Each square is drawn using the latitude and longitude of one of New York's 1,006 towns. Every spot in the state, whether populated or not, belongs to one of these towns. Because the boxes are all the same size, they overlap where towns are small and close together and leave gaps where towns are large and far apart. The dense cluster at the bottom is New York City. The sparse area directly north at the top of the state is the Adirondacks. The boxes are shaded to reflect the percentage of homes using H&N's product.

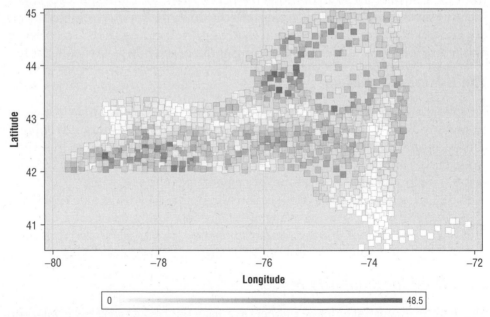

Figure 6-1: This scatter plot is based on the latitude and longitude of towns in New York state; the shading is based on the proportion of the town with wood-burning stoves.

Steps for Building a Similarity Model

Similarity models start with a description of a prototype or ideal to which other things will be compared. The description must be in terms of variables that have significantly different values for candidates that are close to the ideal than for candidates that are far from it.

A good approach for getting the ideal and the distance is to ask three questions:

1. What distinguishes "good" records from "bad" ones?

2. What would the ideal "good" record look like?

3. How should distance from the ideal be measured?

The answers to these three questions provide the information needed to define the model.

Step 1: What Distinguishes High Penetration Towns from Low Penetration Towns?

Which variables vary significantly between high-penetration and low-penetration towns? Knowing that the high-penetration towns all have similar average household sizes or pecentages of high school graduates is no use if these statistics have similar values in low-penetration towns. The real question is not, "What do the high-penetration towns have in common?" it is, "What do the high-penetration towns have in common that sets them apart from the low-penetration towns?"

TIP A similarity model starts with descriptive statistics about the variables. To be useful for modeling, variables must distinguish different values of the target.

Figure 6-2 is a histogram of product penetration. The towns are arranged from left to right in descending order by percentage of wood-burning stoves. In some towns nearly half the homes are heated with wood and other towns have no homes that are heated that way. In Figure 6-3, the towns in the middle third have been removed, leaving only the top third and bottom third. This trick is useful for exploring the differences between the high-penetration and low-penetration towns without getting confused by towns in the middle, which may share characteristics of both groups. The top one-third of towns has an average penetration of 17.6 percent. The bottom third has a much lower average penetration of 1.4 percent.

TIP When characterizing differences based on response rates, average order sizes, or another target variable, you can get a clearer signal by removing cases near the middle in order to compare the extremes.

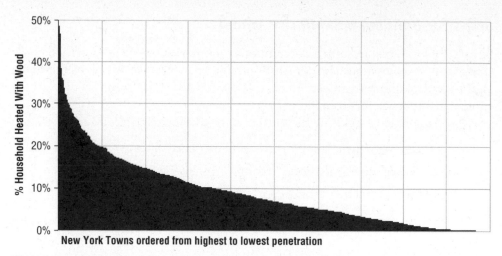

Figure 6-2: The percentage of households in a town heated by wood ranges from near 50 percent to 0.

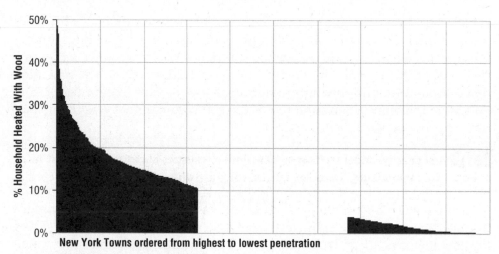

Figure 6-3: Removing towns in the middle of the range sharpens the contrast between high penetration and low penetration.

To select variables to be included in the model, compare the averages of the hundreds of census variables to find ones where there is a large difference between the high-penetration and low-penetration towns. Table 6-1 shows some of the variables that differ significantly across the two groups.

Table 6-1: Variables with significantly different averages in high- and low-penetration towns.

	WORKING IN AGRICULTURE	MULTI-FAMILY HOMES	MEDIAN HOME VALUE
Low Penetration	1.4%	26.3%	$136,296
High Penetration	6.6%	4.7%	$67,902

Step 2: What Would the Ideal Town Look Like?

The variables in the table are good candidates for describing the ideal wood-burning town. Because apartment buildings and other multi-family homes are almost never heated with wood, the ideal town should have no multi-family homes. Based on the comparison between high- and low-penetration towns, saying that the ideal town would have home values near the bottom of the range and percentage working in agriculture near the top makes sense. Based on these considerations, suppose that the ideal town has 10 percent working in agriculture, 0 percent multi-family homes, and a median home value of $60,000.

Step 3: How Far Is Each Town from the Ideal?

Measuring the distance from the ideal requires a distance function. To build one, convert the values from percentages and dollars into z-scores by subtracting the average and dividing by the standard deviation. These are shown in Table 6-2, along with the ideal.

Table 6-2: Averages and standard deviations for the selected variables.

	WORKING IN AGRICULTURE	MULTI-FAMILY HOMES	MEDIAN HOME VALUE
Average	3.9%	14.2%	$95,256
Standard Deviation	3.9%	14.8%	$70,754
Ideal	10.0%	0.0%	$60,000

Using these values, the ideal town has an agriculture z-score of 1.57, a multi-family z-score of -0.95, and a home value z-score of –0.50. As explained in Chapter 4, these z-scores mean that the ideal town has a level of agricultural employment that is more than one-and-a-half standard deviations above the state average, a percentage of multifamily homes that is about one standard deviation below the state average, and home values that are half a standard deviation below the state average.

Using Euclidean distance on the z-scores, each town can be given a score based on its distance from the ideal. The average high penetration town is distance 1.18 away from the ideal. The average low penetration town is distance 3.03 away. These numbers confirm that the proposed ideal does capture the notion of a good town for the product.

The overall state average is distance 1.90 away from the ideal. With a bit of rounding, high-, medium-, and low-penetration towns are at distance 1, 2, and 3 away, which, although a coincidence, provides an elegant description of a town's suitability for wood-burning stoves.

Evaluating the Similarity Model

How well does distance from the ideal correlate with penetration? The Pearson correlation coefficient is −0.57, which corresponds to an R^2 value of 0.32. Overall, the fit is decent but nothing to write home about.

Figure 6-4 provides a more nuanced answer. Distance does a good job of predicting *low* penetration. All towns that are distance 4 or more from the ideal have essentially zero penetration. All towns that are within distance 2 of the ideal have non-zero penetration.

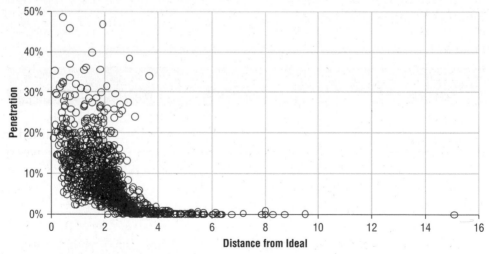

Figure 6-4: As distance from the ideal increases, penetration quickly drops to zero.

The problem is that being close to the ideal does not guarantee *high* penetration. People living in expensive apartments in towns with few agricultural workers are unlikely to heat with wood. People who live in modest, single-family homes in areas where there is a lot of agriculture might or might not heat with wood depending on other factors that are not in the model. Perhaps the degree of forestation, the average price of a cord of wood, or the availability of piped natural gas should be included in a town's description.

In other words, this model does a good job of telling H&N where *not* to build stores. On the other hand, it might not do a great job of differentiating among the top third or half of towns that score well on the model. Fortunately, many other techniques, described in this and upcoming chapters, can help the company build better models.

Part of building the similarity model is choosing variables for measuring distance. The variables chosen for this example are an interesting mix. On the good side, they are definitely correlated with penetration and they do have some explanatory power. On the other hand, they do a better job of predicting low penetration than high penetration.

You can clearly see in Figure 6-4 that the average penetration for distance 0 to 2 is higher than for distance 2 to 4. Using the average penetration for each distance range as a score would turn this into a table lookup model, the subject of the next section.

Table Lookup Models

One simple way to implement a data mining model is as a lookup table. Lookup table models are based on the idea that similar people have similar responses, or more broadly, that things that are similar along multiple known dimensions have similar values for other attributes as well. Scoring a new observation involves two steps. In the first step, the observation is assigned a particular label or key. The key corresponds to a single cell in a lookup table. In the second step, all records that have been assigned to a cell are given the score that was associated with that cell when the model was trained.

The key can be assigned in several ways. Decision tree models, explained in Chapter 7, use a collection of rules to assign observations to particular leaves of the tree. The leaf ID is a key that can be used to look up the score. You can also use the clustering techniques explained in Chapters 13 and 14 to assign labels to observations. These cluster labels can be used as lookup keys.

The first step in building a lookup table is to choose input variables for its dimensions. Each record in the training set is assigned to exactly one cell in the table. The statistics from the training set are used to characterize the cells, with values such as the average value, standard deviation, and the number of training instances that land there. These statistics are used when the model is scored. The score might be the average value of a numeric target, or the proportion belonging to a particular class, or the predominant class in the cell.

Any variables that are not already categorical are partitioned into ranges to create discrete attributes, such as "high," "medium," and "low." Even categorical variables might be grouped, so you might treat the six states in New England as a single region.

If you are thinking of selling your old car, there are websites that can provide an estimate of its value using a simple table lookup model. The interface typically consists of several pull-down menus where you specify the make, model, model year, mileage range, body style, transmission type, engine size, fuel type, and geographic location of the vehicle. These are the dimensions of a lookup table. The site gives the average selling price of cars meeting your description, which is usually a pretty good estimate of what your car is worth on the market.

Choosing Dimensions

Each dimension should be a variable that has some impact on the value of the target. Ideally, the input variables chosen should not be correlated with each other. In practice, it is usually hard to avoid a certain amount of correlation.

The practical effect of correlated variables is that some cells end up with few training examples, a situation that leads to estimates with low confidence. This is not as bad as it sounds, because new observations to be scored should also be sparse in those cells. In the RFM model discussed later, one dimension is total number of purchases, and another dimension is total lifetime spending. These variables are highly correlated because additional purchases generally produce additional revenue. Very few records will fall into the cells for highest number of purchases and lowest revenue or highest revenue and lowest number of purchases.

> **WARNING** Avoid using highly correlated variables as dimensions of the look-up table as it leads to a proliferation of sparse cells. Cells with few training examples produce low-confidence estimates of the target value.

The main limit to the number of dimensions is the number of training records in the cells. There should be dozens, if not hundreds or thousands of training examples in most cells. There is a trade-off between the number of dimensions and the number of partitions along each dimension. With fewer dimensions, you can partition each one more finely.

Some cells might be completely empty if, due to the nature of the problem, there could never be something in that cell. For example, if you have a product dimension and a country dimension, but some products are not sold in some countries, naturally no training examples will exist for the unused combinations. This is acceptable because no customers (or very few, in the age of online shopping) should be in the score set with those combinations. To handle an unanticipated case, the table should include a cell with a default score to be given to any observations that do not match any of the keys. A typical default score is the overall average for a numeric target, or the most common class for a categorical target.

> **TIP** A table lookup model should include a default row to provide a score to any unanticipated examples that do not match any of the expected keys. Typically, the default score is the overall average for a numeric target, or the most common class for a categorical target.

Partitioning the Dimensions

You can often partition categorical dimensions one per category. The only problem with this approach is that some categories can be much larger than others. For a dimension-like state, combining small, similar ones into regions might make sense, or, perhaps, breaking up big ones into smaller districts.

Numeric dimensions are discretized by breaking them in ranges or bins. The bins should have roughly equal numbers of training examples, so terciles or quintiles are convenient choices. Sometimes business rules or other factors suggest particular split points. Following these may be more important than having the same number of records in each bin. A useful split is one that leads to different bins having significantly different values of the target variable. Chapter 19 includes a discussion of supervised binning methods that are designed to ensure this.

There is no requirement for each dimension to be broken into the same number of bins. Each one should be partitioned in a way that makes sense for it. This might be high, medium, and low for one dimension and percentiles for another.

From Training Data to Scores

After you partition the dimensions, measuring the value of the target variable in each cell on the training set is a simple matter. For numeric targets, the average value becomes the score. For categorical targets, there is a score for each class — namely, the proportion of each cell that has each class label. These are estimates, for each class, of the probability that an observation to be scored will be in that class. Often there is one class of particular interest (such as responders or defaulters), in which case only the probability of being in that class is reported as the score.

Handling Sparse and Missing Data by Removing Dimensions

What can be done about cells that do not receive enough data to support the required confidence level for an estimate? One approach, already mentioned, is to reduce the number of splits along each dimension. Another is to reduce the number of dimensions used to define the sparse cells.

For example, one of the authors once wanted to estimate the probability that particular listings would attract clicks on a shopping comparison site, based on characteristics of the listings. One of the inputs to the model was the competitiveness of a listings price measured as a z-score. Price data, in the form of previous listings was available at the UPC level. (UPC stands for Universal Product Code — the lowest level of the product hierarchy.)

The analysis of click attractiveness considered four dimensions based on attributes of the listings:

- Product
- Geography
- Vendor type
- Day of week

For some very popular items, such as popular video game titles and popular models of MP3 players, using all four dimensions made sense. For less popular items, there were not enough listings to support this many dimensions so some were dropped.

For some products, dropping day of week was sufficient. For these products, the comparison would be along three dimensions rather than four:

- Product
- Geography
- Vendor type

For rarer products, listings for all days of the week, regions, and vendor types were combined. For the rarest ones, even the single remaining product dimension was too sparse when viewed at the UPC level. For these products, individual listings were compared to the average price for the entire category rather than the price for a particular brand and model. The idea is to keep removing dimensions and merging cells until each one holds sufficient data.

RFM: A Widely Used Lookup Model

In the direct marketing world, RFM is a familiar acronym for a type of model called Recency, Frequency, and Monetary. The model is named after the three dimensions used for the lookup model that can be used to estimate probability of response and order size.

The logic behind RFM is simple. Customers who have recently made a purchase are more likely to make a purchase in the near future. Customers who have made many purchases in the past are more likely to make another in the near future, and customers who have spent a lot of money in the past are more likely to spend more money in the future.

RFM is not a method that can be applied to prospecting because only existing customers have meaningful recency, frequency, and monetary values. RFM is a technique for harvesting existing customers rather than attracting new ones.

To assign customers to RFM cells, the three RFM variables are turned into quantiles. Recency — the number of days or weeks since the last purchase — is used to assign the R score, typically by dividing the values into three groups (terciles) or five groups (quintiles).

The second variable, frequency, is usually defined as the total number of previous purchases. Customers are given F scores based on their frequency quantile. The last variable is total lifetime spending, which is used to create M scores. Figure 6-5 shows an RFM cube in which each dimension has been partitioned into quintiles.

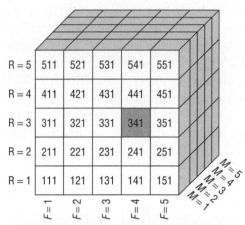

Figure 6-5: Each of the three RFM dimensions has been partitioned into quintiles to form an RFM cube with 125 cells.

Due to correlations between the dimensions — especially F and M — the cells do not receive equal numbers of customers. All that is required is for almost all the data to land in cells that have a sufficient number of records to make an acceptably confident estimate of the target value.

If the target value is order size, the average historical order size in each cell is probably a good prediction, but if the goal is to predict response, a test is called for. Each catalog or marketing offer is different and is made under different market conditions, so response can vary quite a bit from one to the next.

RFM Cell Migration

With every campaign, customers shift RFM cells. Those that respond increase their frequency and monetary numbers and decrease their time since last purchase. The new values often place them in a new cell. Customers who fail to respond may also end up in a new cell as the time increases since their last purchase.

Migrating to a new cell changes the way a customer is treated because it changes expectations for his or her responsiveness. Like any model score, customers' RFM cell assignments should be tracked over time to understand how the customer relationship is evolving.

RFM and the Test-and-Measure Methodology

All data mining methods implicitly assume that the future will be similar to the past. With RFM, the assumption is that particular RFM cells will respond to the next campaign in a similar way they responded to the last one. The next campaign is always going to be different from the last one, if only because market conditions have changed or because some customers who would buy the product have already done so.

RFM is often used in direct marketing contexts, where similar campaigns are run throughout the year. For instance, a cataloguer specializing in gardening has a set of customers interested in this subject. The goal of the catalogs is to sell things to these customers. Although the products may differ from season to season, the campaigns are still pretty similar. For each campaign, all RFM cells are tracked and some are targeted. The targeted cells drive the response to the campaign so everyone in those cells is targeted. The tracked cells provide important information about response for the next campaign, so only a sample of the customers in those cells is used for the campaign.

Every Campaign Is an Experiment

The test and measure methodology is based on the idea of controlled experiments. In a controlled experiment, the idea is to isolate the effects of a treatment — a particular combination of coupons and product positioning statements, for example — from the effects of all the other factors that may influence response or order size or whatever is being measured.

The simplest experimental design involves just two groups, both chosen at random from the population eligible for inclusion in the campaign. Because they are chosen at random, assuming they are of sufficient size, the two groups will have nearly identical distributions for all variables except those manipulated by the experiment. One group, the *treatment group*, is included in the campaign. The other group, the *hold-out group*, is not. Because they are similar in every other way, any difference in response may be assumed to be due to the treatment.

More sophisticated experimental designs incorporate *blocking*. Blocking uses factors known to have a large effect on the target to create cells that are all similar with respect to the blocking factors. In direct marketing response modeling, recency, frequency, and spending are natural blocking factors. Within each block or cell, there is lower variance of the target so the effects of the treatment are amplified.

RFM provides a natural blocking mechanism. Every campaign should include recipients and non-recipients from every RFM cell. This means extending the offer to some people in cells with low expected response rates and withholding the offer from some people in the cells most likely to respond. Including all RFM cells in every campaign is an important part of the test-and-measure methodology.

New Types of Campaigns Should Be Tested Before Being Rolled Out

The test-and-measure methodology is even more important for entirely new campaigns. Before spending millions of dollars on a marketing manager's gut feeling, it is worth finding out what is really likely to happen. Before rolling out a new campaign, you should test it on a carefully constructed sample of customers who receive the proposed offer under conditions that mimic as closely as possible the conditions expected to prevail for the full campaign.

Here, too, the RFM cells come into play. The test campaign uses treatment and control groups that include members of every cell. Response to the test is used to predict response to the full campaign. If a campaign requires a response rate of 2.5 percent to be profitable, then only cells that respond at least that well in the test will be included in the full campaign.

RFM and Incremental Response Modeling

Chapter 5 describes an approach to incremental response modeling based on the difference in scores between two models. Chapter 7 presents an approach to the same problem using decision trees. RFM and other table look-up models provide a method that is simpler than either of those approaches.

Recall that the goal of incremental response modeling is to identify persuadable prospects — the ones who are most affected by the campaign. After the RFM cells have been defined, assign members of each cell to either the test group that receives the marketing message or the hold-out group that does not.

TIP RFM and other cell-based methods are a good way to measure incremental response in addition to overall response by creating a treatment group and a hold-out group in every cell.

The difference in response rates between these two groups determines how well the campaign is doing at finding persuadables. With RFM, this difference can be determined on a cell-by-cell basis. The cells with the largest difference in response rate between test and hold-out are the cells where the campaign has the greatest impact. These may not be the cells with the highest response rates.

Naïve Bayesian Models

Table lookup models are simple and effective, but they have a problem. As the number of inputs goes up, the number of training examples per cell goes down rapidly. Two dimensions with 10 values each is 100 cells, but 3 dimensions partitioned that way yields 1,000 cells, and 4 yields 10,000. Pretty soon, there are not enough training examples to fill them up.

Naïve Bayesian models provide a way out of this dilemma when you are trying to predict a probability. Understanding how requires learning a bit of probability. The basic idea is simple: Each input variable, all by itself, has something to say about whatever it is you are trying to predict. Say the target variable is probability of cancellation, and the explanatory variables are market, acquisition channel, initial credit score, rate plan, phone number type, handset model, and customer age. Each of these variables is predictive. Each can be partitioned into ranges with significantly different cancellation rates. But, for many combinations of these seven variables, too few examples exist to make a good estimate. Think "customers in Wyoming, acquired through direct mail, with credit class C, on rate plan G2, with a Blackberry, who are over 70."

Wouldn't it be nice to take the cancellation rate for Wyoming and somehow combine it with the cancellation rate for the direct mail channel, and the cancellation rate for credit class C, and the cancellation rate for rate plan G2, and the cancellation rate for Blackberry users, and the cancellation rate for customers over 70, in order to estimate the cancellation rate for the combination? That is what naïve Bayesian models do.

Some Ideas from Probability

The Bayesian part of naïve Bayesian models refers to the technique's use of Bayes' law (also called Bayes' rule and Bayes' theorem) which is described in the sidebar "Reverend Bayes and His Law." The naïve part refers to the assumption that the variables used are independent of each other, with respect to the target — more on that later.

Naïve Bayesian models can be explained in fairly simple terms, but the explanation requires precise definitions for several words that are often used interchangeably in other contexts.

Probability, Odds, and Likelihood

In casual speech, the words *probability*, *odds*, and *likelihood* are used interchangeably. In statistics, each word has a specific meaning. The three are closely related and any one of them can be expressed in terms of the others, but they are not synonymous. Statisticians use whichever one is most convenient for a particular calculation. The definitions are as follows:

REVEREND BAYES AND HIS LAW

Bayes' law was derived by Rev. Thomas Bayes, who was born at the beginning of the 18th century to a family of Nonconformists. According to English law at the time, members of non-Anglican churches were officially classified as "Nonconformist"; eventually, he took a ministering position in a Presbyterian church.

Rev. Bayes was quite interested in mathematics, and was a member of the Royal Society, but he may have felt that the study of laws of chance was not a fitting pursuit for a man of religion. His ideas in probability theory were published in 1763, three years after his death, by his friend Richard Price, a Unitarian minister and social activist.

The paper, *An Essay Towards Solving a Problem in the Doctrine of Chances*, appeared in the *Philosophical Transactions of the Royal Society of London* and is available at `www.stat.ucla.edu/history/essay.pdf`. The paper languished for several decades, until found by a French mathematician, Pierre-Simon Laplace, who understood the importance of the ideas and expounded upon them.

Rev. Bayes was interested in *conditional probability*. A conditional probability relates the probability of A given B to the probability of B given A. Consider the two questions:

■ What is the probability that a subscriber who uses a Blackberry fails to renew?

■ What is the probability that a subscriber who fails to renew uses a Blackberry?

How are these two probabilities related to each other?

He found the relationship, which goes by the name Bayes' Law. It is a simple formula:

$$P(A|B) = P(B|A)\frac{P(A)}{P(B)}$$

This formula is read as follows: The probability of A given B is the probability of B given A times the ratio of the probabilities of A and B.

If A refers to stopping, and B refers to having a Blackberry, then the probability of stopping, given a Blackberry, is the probability of having a Blackberry, given a stop, multiplied by the overall probability of stopping, divided by the overall probability of having a Blackberry.

A formula like this is very useful because directly estimating one of the conditional probabilities is often easier than estimating the other. Because of Bayes' law, if one is known, so is the other.

Probability. A number between 0 and 1 indicating the chance of a particular outcome occurring. One way of estimating the probability of an outcome is to calculate the proportion of records having that outcome in a data sample.

Odds. The ratio of the probability of a particular outcome occurring to the probability of it not occurring. If the probability of the event is 0.2, then the probability of the event failing to occur is 0.8, and the odds are one to four. The odds is a number between zero and infinity.

Likelihood. The ratio of two related conditional probabilities — the probability of a particular outcome A, given B, and the probability of outcome A, given not B. An alternative way of expressing the likelihood is as the ratio of two odds — the odds of A given B, and the overall odds of A. The two formulations are equivalent, but one or the other may be easier to calculate in a particular situation.

Refer to these definitions whenever necessary in the following discussion of naïve Bayesian models.

Converting for Convenience

To spare the reader from doing algebra, here are the formulas for going back and forth between probability and odds.

$$odds = \frac{probability}{1 - probability} = -1 + \frac{1}{1 - probability}$$

$$probability = 1 - \frac{1}{1 + odds}$$

Because odds and probability are just two ways of representing the same things, statisticians convert from one to the other as convenient. These formulas will come in handy again later in the chapter, in the section on logistic regression.

The Naïve Bayesian Calculation

The naïve Bayesian formula relates the *odds* of the target event to the *likelihood* of the event for each of any number of attributes. To return to the example of predicting attrition based on market, acquisition channel, initial credit score, rate plan, phone number type, handset model, and customer age, the odds of stopping for an elderly Blackberry user in Wyoming are:

- the overall odds of stopping, multiplied by
- the likelihood of stopping for Blackberry users, multiplied by
- the likelihood of stopping for the Wyoming market

The reason that the calculation is called "naïve" is that multiplying all the likelihoods in this fashion assumes that the inputs are independent of each other. In this example, the assumption is that the likelihood of having a Blackberry does not depend on the market (and the likelihood of being in Wyoming does not depend on the handset type). In practice, having inputs that are truly independent is rare, but the model works pretty well anyway.

One of the most appealing things about the naïve Bayesian model is that if some input values are missing for an observation to be scored, the missing likelihoods simply drop out of the equation. This means that models are free to include inputs (customer age, for example) that are not available for all customers, but are useful when they do happen to be known.

The naïve Bayesian formula calculates the *odds* of stopping, given the *likelihood* of various inputs with respect to stopping. You are probably more interested in the *probability* of stopping. That is why the definitions and conversion formulas have been provided. From the training data, calculating the probability of stopping for people in Wyoming and the probability of stopping for people not in Wyoming is easy. The ratio of the two is the likelihood. After multiplying all the likelihoods, converting the odds thus calculated back to a probability is equally simple.

Comparison with Table Lookup Models

Naïve Bayesian models and table lookup models are closely related for targets that are probabilities. The important difference is how the dimensions are used. In a table lookup model, all the dimensions are used at once to define a cell and then the probability of the target is calculated for each cell. As a result, the lookup models capture interactions among the variables. In a naïve Bayesian model, the likelihoods are calculated separately for each dimension and then combined. The combination of the likelihoods makes an assumption: that the dimensions are independent of each other, with respect to the target.

A table lookup model has nothing to say about combinations of attributes that do not occur with sufficient frequency in the training data. A naïve Bayesian model can make predictions about combinations that have never been seen, but to do so, it has to assume that the effects of the inputs are independent. A table lookup model makes no such assumption, so when there is enough data to support a confident probability estimate, it may do better.

Linear Regression

Regression models are the most commonly used predictive modeling technique. They are available in Excel and in pretty much any other software package that has any claim to supporting analytics. Regression models can be quite sophisticated, but this section starts with the simplest form — the best-fit line. Both the input and target variables must be numeric, and the regression equation describes an arithmetic relationship between them.

This relationship is "best" in the sense that it minimizes the sum of the squares of the vertical distances from the data points to the line. This definition of best is why this form of regression is called ordinary least squares regression, whose history is described in the sidebar "Where Ordinary Least Squares Regression Comes From." Other definitions of the best-fit line are possible. For example, a method called *robust regression* minimizes the sum of the absolute values of the vertical distances rather than the sum of their squares.

WHERE ORDINARY LEAST SQUARES REGRESSION COMES FROM

The most common method for finding the best-fit line in linear regression is called *ordinary least squares*. This method has an interesting history. It was first used by the German mathematician, Carl Friedrich Gauss, to solve a problem in astronomy: Given a handful of somewhat inaccurate observations of the position of a newly discovered planet, what was the best estimate of its actual orbit?

The planet in question is now officially classed as a "dwarf planet," but readers are more likely to have heard of it as the asteroid, Ceres. Its discovery in 1800 caused great excitement among astronomers because they had been looking for a planet between the orbits of Mars and Jupiter ever since the 1760s when the German astronomer, Johan Titius noticed a pattern he felt must be predictive. That pattern, now known as the Titius-Bode law, postulates then-known planets of the solar system were placed at particular positions in accordance with a mathematical rule. In 1766, Titius put it this way:

> *Take notice of the distances of the planets from one another, and recognize that almost all are separated from one another in a proportion which matches their bodily magnitudes. Divide the distance from the Sun to Saturn into 100 parts; then Mercury is separated by four such parts from the Sun, Venus by 4 + 3 = 7 such parts, the Earth by 4 + 6 = 10, Mars by 4 + 12 = 16. But notice that from Mars to Jupiter there comes a deviation from this so exact progression. From Mars there follows a space of 4 + 24 = 28 such parts, but so far no planet was sighted there. But should the Lord Architect have left that space empty? Not at all.*

In 1772, another German astronomer, Johann Bode echoed this sentiment.

> *Now comes a gap in this so orderly progression. After Mars there follows a space of 4 + 24 = 28 parts, in which no planet has yet been seen. Can one believe that the Founder of the universe had left this space empty? Certainly not.*

In the units favored by Titius and Bode, the pattern is that planetary orbits are located at distance $d = 4 + 3*n$ where $n = 0, 1, 2, 4, 8, 16$ … with each new n being twice the one before. The orbits of all planets that were then known fit the pattern pretty well. Mercury is at $n = 0$, Venus is at $n = 1$, Earth is at $n = 2$,

Mars is at $n = 3$, Jupiter is at $n = 5$, and Saturn is at $n = 6$. It is no accident that the formula puts Saturn at distance $4 + 96 = 100$. Saturn was the farthest known planet, so the scale was based on setting the distance from the sun to Saturn at 100.

All that was missing was a planet for $n = 4$. Rather than accept a flaw in the model, or that the Lord Architect/Founder might have used some other formula, astronomers just assumed they had missed a planet. When, in 1781, Sir William Herschel discovered Uranus at $n = 7$, right where the Titius-Bode law said a seventh planet should be, it seemed to confirm its predictive power. Bode and other astronomers intensified the search for the missing fifth planet.

In 1800, the Italian astronomer, Joseph Piazzi found it. In 1800 and early 1801 he made several observations of what is now known as the dwarf planet Ceres. It is at this point that the ordinary least squares method comes into the story. Piazzi found the planet in the winter months in northern Italy, and was only able to get three relatively accurate measurements of its position. In late February, the planet disappeared behind the sun, so it was no longer visible from the earth. The race was on among European astronomers to determine where it would reappear.

Carl Friedrich Gauss, whom some have called the greatest mathematician who ever lived, had just graduated from university and set about solving this problem. A big part of the challenge was the inaccuracy of the observed measurements. When other constraints are included, the three available measurements overfit the data.

Since 1609, when Kepler published the first of his laws of planetary motion, astronomers have understood that a planet's orbit is an ellipse with the sun at one focal point, but with no computers or electronic calculators, most astronomers did not attempt to calculate elliptical orbits.

Gauss calculated an elliptical orbit for Ceres, but there was a problem: With the constraints imposed by physics (such as the sun being at a focus point of the ellipse), two positions completely determine an ellipse, but Piazzi had provided three observations. Gauss invented the idea of finding the ellipse that minimizes the sum of the squares of the distances between the observed points and the points on the ellipse. This idea of using least squares to find the *best fit* to observed data is the basis for ordinary least squares regression and hence of linear regression.

The Best-fit Line

Figure 6-6 is a scatter plot showing the relationship between tenure and revenue for a group of newspaper subscribers. One feature of this scatter plot is worth mentioning. The symbols used are hollow disks. This makes it possible to see areas where the points cluster together, such as in the low tenure, low dollar amount area. This is especially useful when different colors are used to compare different groups of customers.

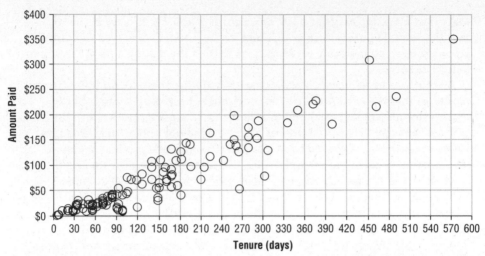

Figure 6-6: The scatter plot shows the relationship between tenure and total amount paid.

The longer customers remain, the more they pay. Visually, the relationship appears linear, which suggests using a line to estimate revenue as a function of tenure. Figure 6-7 shows the best-fit line for these data points.

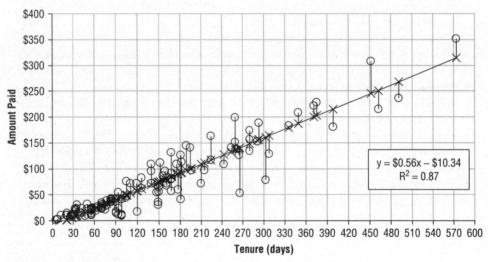

Figure 6-7: The best-fit line minimizes the square of the vertical distance from the observations to the line.

The formula for this line says that to estimate revenue, multiply the tenure by $0.56 and subtract $10.14. So, the estimated revenue for a tenure of 100, is $56 − $10.14 = $45.86.

TIP Scatter plots convey more information when the markers used for the data points are not filled in. Hollow markers do a better job of showing data density.

This line has an important property: Of all possible lines, it is the one where the sum of the squares of the vertical distances from the observed data points to the line is as small as possible. The scatter plot shows the distance from each data point to the line.

This definition of the best-fit line is the ordinary least squares definition invented by Gauss during the hunt for Ceres described in the earlier sidebar. Formulas for Euclidean distance have square roots in them, which is quite difficult in a world without calculators or computers. Gauss may have decided to minimize the sum of the squared distance, rather than the sum of the distance, to simplify the calculations. If so, this was a fortunate choice, because the coefficients for the best-fit line using OLS are easy calculated using relatively simple mathematical operations.

Goodness of Fit

For a given set of data, finding a best-fit line is always possible, but how good is "best"? A typical measure is the difference between the predicted and actual values, which are called the *residuals*. There is also a standard measure, called R^2, for how well a line describes the observed data

Residuals

Figure 6-8 shows the residuals for the newspaper revenue model. An unbiased model should miss high as often as it misses low, so the first thing to look for in the residuals plot is whether the values seem to be about as likely to be above the x-axis as below. This model passes that test for most tenures, although for very low tenures, the residuals are all positive.

A good model should also produce estimates that are close to the true values, so the residuals ought to cluster near the x axis. The newspaper revenue model seems to do fairly well on this measure as well. There are some observations fairly far from the line, but many more close to it.

Finally, there should not be any obvious pattern to the residuals; that would imply a systematic effect not captured by the model. If, for example, the residuals spread out more as the x value gets bigger, it would be a sign that something was wrong. Here, the largest residuals are about in the middle of the tenure range and they are as likely to be positive as negative. The residuals do seem to get a bit larger in magnitude as tenure increases, but the model is still quite good.

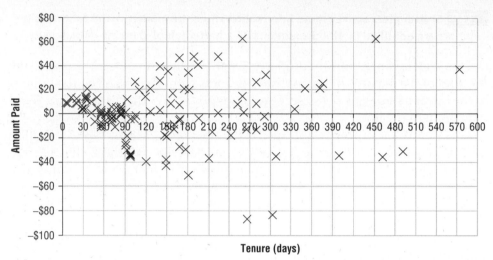

Figure 6-8: There are about as many positive as negative residuals and they do not show any strong patterns.

In the language of statistics, the residuals are considered the *error term* in the regression equation. The equation for the best-fit line was introduced as:

$$Y = \beta_0 + \beta_1 X_1$$

That is correct as far as it goes, but the line itself is not the complete model. A statistician would phrase the model equation as:

$$Y = \beta_0 + \beta_1 X_1 + \varepsilon$$

The error term (usually represented by the Greek letter epsilon) is there as a reminder that X_1 is not a perfect predictor of Y. The error term captures whatever portion of the variation in Y that is not explained by the model.

R^2

Visual inspection of the residuals suggests that the best-fit line is a fairly good representation of the relationship between tenure and revenue. R^2 is a measure that quantifies that subjective statement.

The R^2 value always varies between zero and one for the best-fit line. When the value is near one, the line is doing a very good job of capturing the relationship between the input and the target. When the value is near zero, then the line is doing a lousy job. The R^2 value for the model shown in Figure 6-7 is 0.89, indicating a strong relationship. One way of thinking about R^2 is that it measures the proportion of the variance in the target that is explained by the input. That is, the relationship between tenure and amount paid explains 89% of the relationship seen in the data.

Another way of thinking about R^2 is that it says how much better the model's estimate is than simply always guessing the average value. It's a simple enough definition, but the calculation is a bit more complicated. R^2 compares two lines, the best-fit line and the horizontal line at the average y-value. R^2 is calculated by taking the ratio of two errors and subtracting that ratio from 1. The numerator is the sum of the squares of residuals of the best-fit line. The denominator is the sum of the squares of the residuals of the horizontal line. In other words, R^2 measures how much better the best-fit line is doing than just using the average.

The four charts in Figure 6-9 show four different sets of data with different characteristics. The two on the left have low values of R^2, meaning that the data is quite dispersed and not well described by the best-fit line. The two on the right have high values of R^2, meaning that the data is quite close to the best-fit line.

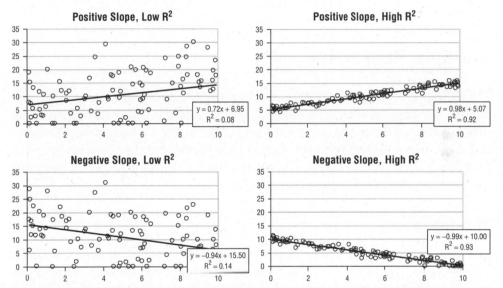

Figure 6-9: R^2 and trend are two ways of characterizing the best-fit line. A high R^2 value implies that the points are very close to the line.

R^2 measures how stable the data is. Will different samples from the same data yield similar models? When the R^2 value is low, then different samples could behave very differently. Or, put another way, a few more observations could dramatically change the coefficients of the model. When the R^2 value is high, this is not likely and the model is more stable.

As explained in Chapter 4, R^2 is the square of Pearson's correlation coefficient which is usually represented by r. Correlation varies from –1 to 1, so R^2 varies from 0 to 1.

Global Effects

Regression equations find global patterns in the data. That is, the coefficients are intended to work for all ranges of input variables. This means that regression models are good at capturing patterns that are always true, but they struggle with local patterns.

For instance, consider the risk by age for purchasers of car insurance. Young drivers have a high level of risk. The risk is much lower as drivers gain experience. For the oldest drivers, the risk increases again. This makes age difficult to use as an input in a regression equation. There is no global pattern here, because the effect of age changes drastically for different age groups.

A skilled modeler can still make use of variables that have different effects in different parts of their ranges by applying appropriate transformations. However, regression equations do not themselves find local patterns. By contrast, many of the data mining techniques discussed in later chapters, such as decision trees, neural networks, and memory-based reasoning, find local patterns as well as global ones.

Multiple Regression

The example used to introduce linear regression used a single input, tenure, to explain the target revenue. This is an oversimplification. Other factors influence revenue such as the market where the subscriber resides; whether the subscriber receives the paper on weekdays, weekends, or both; and the particular promotion to which the subscriber responded. When a regression model has more than one input, it is called *multiple regression*.

The Equation

The general form of a linear regression model (without the error term) is $Y = \beta_0 + \beta_1 X_1 + \beta_2 X_2 + \ldots + \beta_n X_n$. This equation expands the best-fit line equation, by adding more variables and more coefficients for each one.

This is as good a time as any to clear up some differences between the terminology used by statisticians and the perhaps more intuitive terminology used in the rest of this book. The explanatory variables that go into a model — what are generally called "inputs" in data mining circles — are called *independent variables* by statisticians. The independent variables are traditionally named X with subscripts from 1 to the number of independent variables in the model. The target variable is called the *dependent variable*, and is usually named Y. The model coefficients are represented by β (the Greek letter beta) with subscripts to match the independent variables. β_0 is a constant term. For consistency, you can think of it as being the coefficient for X_0, which happens to always have the value 1.

From the statistical point of view, the Xs and Ys are constants and the betas are variables. At first, this seems like a "through-the-looking-glass" view of the world. It does, however, make some sense. The Xs and Ys are observed data, so they are known. The statistical problem is to calculate the betas, because these are not known.

Although extending the geometric interpretation of linear regression to multiple regression is possible by invoking more dimensions — lines become planes become hyper-planes — the analogy becomes less helpful as these high-dimensional figures cannot be drawn or visualized. It is easier to just think of each independent variable contributing something to the estimated value of the dependent variable, with the size and direction of its contribution determined by its coefficient.

The Range of the Target Variable

The equation for a regression is capable of producing any value. As long as there are no restrictions on the X values, there is no restriction on the value of Y. This is easy to visualize using the case of $Y = \beta_0 + \beta_1 X_1$, which is simply a straight line that goes from negative infinity to positive infinity as X_i ranges through different values, but it is true in general.

Many target variables do not have an infinite range. Many are not even continuous. For these cases, statisticians introduce a *link function* that maps the Y values generated by the regression equation to an appropriate range for the target variable. When the target follows a known distribution, a link function can be chosen to produce values with the same average value as the target and a similar distribution. Even when a formal distribution is not known, you can introduce a link function to map estimates to an appropriate range for the target.

A later section of this chapter introduces logistic regression in which a link function is used to map the infinite range of a linear regression to the interval from zero to one, which is appropriate for probability estimates.

Interpreting Coefficients of Linear Regression Equations

A regression model is not only a way of estimating the value of a target variable; it is also a description of the relationship between each input and the target. Each input has a coefficient (its "beta"). The sign of the coefficient says whether the estimated value increases or decreases as the corresponding input increases. When the input values have been standardized, or are naturally on the same scale, the magnitude of the coefficients reflects the relative importance of the input variables.

Figure 6-10 shows the coefficients for a multiple regression model as a bar chart. The taller bars on the left have a larger impact on the model estimate than the shorter bars on the right. The most important variable is one with the tallest bar, which is typically the constant term.

This regression model estimates the percentage of households in towns near Boston that subscribe to the *Boston Globe*, the region's premier newspaper. The tallest bar is the constant β_0 in the regression equation. Its value, about 22 percent, is the baseline estimate for household penetration before information from the input variables is taken into account.

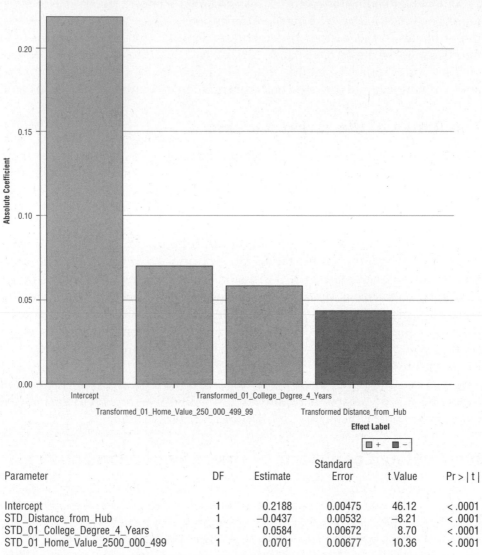

Parameter	DF	Estimate	Standard Error	t Value	Pr > | t |
Intercept	1	0.2188	0.00475	46.12	< .0001
STD_Distance_from_Hub	1	−0.0437	0.00532	−8.21	< .0001
STD_01_College_Degree_4_Years	1	0.0584	0.00672	8.70	< .0001
STD_01_Home_Value_2500_000_499	1	0.0701	0.00677	10.36	< .0001

Figure 6-10: The height of the bars shows the relative importance of the inputs.

The next tallest bar is for the standardized percentage of homes costing between $250,000 and $500,000. The coefficient is positive, meaning that, for any given values of the other inputs, the higher the proportion of relatively expensive homes there are in a town, the higher the proportion of households with a copy of the *Globe* waiting on the front porch in the morning.

Next in importance is the standardized percentage of residents with degrees from four-year colleges. The positive coefficient means that, for any given values of the other inputs, the estimated household penetration goes up with the proportion of college-educated residents.

The final input is standardized distance from the golden dome of the state house on Boston's Beacon Hill. The variable name, *distance from hub*, refers to a nickname for Boston coined by Oliver Wendell Holmes writing in the *Atlantic Monthly* magazine in 1858, where he referred to the Boston State House as "the hub of the solar system." This is the only model input with a negative coefficient. For a given proportion of expensive homes and educated residents, the farther a town is from Boston, the smaller the proportion of its population that subscribes to the *Globe*. Taken together, the model coefficients tell a story. The *Globe*, like the Unitarian church, does best in towns that are wealthy, well-educated, and not too far from Boston.

However, the relationship between *Globe* readership and distance from Boston is more complicated than what is captured in this model — a subject explored in the next section.

Capturing Local Effects with Linear Regression

According to the model in Figure 6-10, all else being equal, household penetration should decrease steadily with distance from Boston. In fact, that is not what happens. Percentagewise, readership is higher in the nearby suburbs than it is in Boston itself. The towns with the highest penetration are about 10 miles from the center of Boston. The global pattern is that penetration decreases with distance, but that disguises a local pattern. In the first ten miles, penetration actually increases with distance.

How can this local knowledge be used to improve the model? At least three possibilities exist:

- Transform the distance variable.
- Replace the distance variable.
- Build separate models for towns close to Boston and towns farther away.

The first possibility is to transform the distance variable so that its relationship to penetration is consistent across the entire range. Because the correlation of distance and penetration changes from positive to negative at about 10 miles, you might try replacing distance with the absolute value of 10-distance. The new variable has decreasing values until the 10-mile mark, and increasing values thereafter.

Another possibility is to replace distance with another input that is better correlated with the target. It turns out that some other variables go up with distance from Boston for a while before going down again. One of these is the median home price. Among towns with home delivery service, median home price is a better predictor of penetration than distance is. The problem with this idea is the model already contains a closely related input — the percentage of homes costing between $250,000 and $500,000.

The third possibility is to create one model for towns close to Boston and another model for towns farther out. These models could both include distance, but the corresponding beta values could be different. A related method is called *piecewise regression*. A piecewise regression model would have one coefficient for distance in the first part of the range and another in the second.

All of these methods are ways of adding domain knowledge about local effects into the regression. Although linear regression is limited to global patterns, by including variables that capture local effects, it is possible to include them in the model as well.

Additional Considerations with Multiple Regression

Having more than one input variable in a regression model brings up several issues that do not come up when there is only a single input.

- Ideally, all inputs should be linearly independent with respect to each other.
- There may be interactions between inputs that should be explicitly included in the model.
- Adding a new input changes the coefficient values for any inputs added previously.

These issues are explored in this section.

Linear Independence

Just as with naïve Bayesian models, inputs to a multiple regression model should be uncorrelated. This means that a change in the value of one input should have no systematic effect on the values of the others. True independence is difficult to achieve. In general, being careful not to include independent variables that are highly correlated with each other is enough. Including such variables often leads to one member of the pair entering the model with a large positive coefficient and the other entering the model with a large negative coefficient. The two variables essentially cancel each other out and the coefficient values shed no light on the true effect of either variable.

Interactions

Even when two variables are completely independent, their effect on the target may not be. The attractiveness of an ice-cream cone may depend on both its price and the weather — especially how hot the day is. These variables may safely be assumed to be independent. (Certainly, the price of ice cream does not determine the temperature; temperature could conceivably affect the price of ice cream, but let us assume it does not.) Despite the independence of these variables, the effect of price may still be affected by temperature. On a very hot day, people may buy ice cream at almost any price, whereas only a really good deal might tempt them when the weather is cold, damp, and drizzly.

Similarly, the effect of a price change on household penetration for the *Boston Globe* may be different at different distances from Boston. These are examples of interactions.

When interactions are considered important, they are often included in the model by adding a new variable that is the product of the standardized values of the variables involved in the interaction.

Adding Variables Can Change the Coefficients of Variables Already in the Model

One natural approach to model development is to start with a very simple model of one input and then gradually increase its complexity by adding additional variables to the mix. If all input variables were completely independent, adding or removing one of them would not change the coefficients of other variables in the model. Alas, input variables are almost never completely independent, so including another variable can change the magnitudes and even the signs of the coefficients of other variables already in the regression.

For example, in the product penetration model for wood-burning stoves discussed earlier in the chapter, a simple regression model with the urban population as its sole input shows that urban population has a strong negative impact — the larger a town's urban population, the lower the product penetration. The regression equation is:

$$penetration = 8.7 - 1.1*STD\_PopUrban$$

Adding the percent of households classified as urban to the model greatly reduces the importance of urban population. The new regression equation is:

$$penetration = 12.5 - 13.5*PercentU + 0.1*STD\_PopUrban$$

In fact, the new variable changes the sign of the coefficient for the urban population.

The actual concept the model needs to capture is rurality. Urban population does an okay job of approximating rurality, because cities have more people than rural areas, but population density captures the concept much better. This is a case where including a new variable may suggest removing one already in the model.

Variable Selection for Multiple Regression

Multiple regression models do not work well with a large number of inputs. Picking the right input variables is the most important part of any modeling effort, which is why Chapter 20 is devoted to this problem. However, regression has some built-in methods for picking the right variables.

TIP Domain knowledge is a powerful variable selection tool. Knowing what ought to be important puts you way ahead.

The place to start is with what you know about the problem and the way the world works — what is sometimes called *domain knowledge*. Retailers know that recency and frequency are important variables for a response model. The *Boston Globe* knows that distance from Boston is important when predicting customer attrition. Wireless analysts know that handset type is often an important predictor for churn.

After you have created a list of candidate variables using domain knowledge and common sense, software for creating regression models can often help pick the best ones to include in a model. The most common methods are *forward selection* and *stepwise selection*. *Backward elimination* may also be used when the number of candidate variables is small.

Forward Selection

Forward selection starts with a set of input variables, some or all of which might end up in the final model. The first step is to create a separate regression model for each input variable; if there are n input variables, then the first step considers n different models with one input variable. The variable whose model scores best on some test becomes the first variable included in the forward selection model.

One way of choosing the best is by choosing the model that has the lowest R^2 value. Another way uses a statistical test called the F-test. Yet another method has a more "data mining" flavor. The best model is the one that has the smallest error on a validation set. This seems more like data mining, because it uses a validation set and makes no assumptions about distributions of input or target values.

After the first variable has been chosen, the process repeats itself. The second time, $n-1$ regression models of two variables are created by adding each of the remaining variables to the model with the variable chosen in the first step. The best of these becomes the basis for the next iteration, which tests multiple regression models of three variables.

This process continues until some stopping criterion is reached. This could be that the maximum desired number of variables has been selected or that no additional variable improves the model by more than some threshold value.

Stepwise Selection

Stepwise selection is just like forward selection, with one exception. In addition to adding a variable at each step, a variable might also be removed. It is possible that a variable that entered the model early on is no longer valuable due to the combined effects of subsequent variables.

Backward Elimination

The backward elimination approach to variable selection begins by creating a multiple regression model using all *n* candidate input variables. Using a statistical test, the worse variable is removed, and the model is refit without it. This process continues until some stopping criterion, such as a minimum number of variables desired, is reached.

Logistic Regression

Linear regression models have a particular form. This is true with any number of input variables, but it is most obvious when you have a single input variable. The regression formula is the equation for a straight line. Among the properties of a straight line is that it goes on forever, continuously in both directions. With the exception of lines parallel to the x-axis, regression models have no minima and maxima. These properties make linear regression models well-suited to estimating continuous quantities that can take on a wide range of values.

The same properties that make linear regression models appropriate for modeling unbounded, continuous targets make them unsuitable for modeling binary outcomes such as yes/no or good/bad. Because binary problems are extremely common, it is not surprising that statisticians have found a way to adapt regression models to the task. The resulting method is called *logistic regression*.

Modeling Binary Outcomes

Modeling a binary outcome does not seem like an estimation task. There are two categories, and the task is to assign each record to one or the other. Surely, this is a classification task? It is.

However, the task can be restated as "What is the probability that this record belongs to class one?" Because probabilities are numbers, the problem is now an estimation task. What happens if you try to model a probability using linear regression?

Estimating Probabilities with Linear Regression

Linear regression was introduced with a model to estimate the amount paid by newspaper subscribers based on their tenure. This example uses the same data to answer a different question: "Has the subscriber ever paid at all?"

Many of the newspaper's subscription sales are made through outbound telemarketing. The call center contacts a list of prospects (selected by a data mining model, of course) and some of them agree to sign up for a subscription. Shortly thereafter they begin receiving the paper, and along with it, their first bill. Some new subscribers never get around to paying the first bill, depriving the newspaper of revenue. After a while, these non-paying subscribers are cut off. Of course, new customers also start who do pay and become good customers in the long term. For the first several weeks, though, there is a relatively high probability that customers will not pay.

The scatter plot shows tenure versus the payment flag. At small tenures, there are payers and non-payers. As tenure increases, the probability of having made a payment goes up. After about 70 days, the probability is at or very close to one. Anyone who has not paid has been dropped from the subscriber rolls by then.

The target can be represented as "0" for customers who never pay and "1" for customers who do, so a best-fit line always exists. That does not mean the best-fit line is a good model. In this case, the best-fit line in Figure 6-11 has an R^2 value of 0.15. Worse, after about 400 days, the probability estimate is greater than 1. It continues increasing indefinitely as tenure goes up. That is the nature of a straight line; it goes on forever with no maximum or minimum.

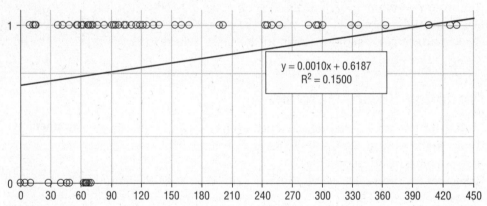

$$y = 0.0010x + 0.6187$$
$$R^2 = 0.1500$$

Figure 6-11: A linear regression model does a poor job of modeling the probability that a subscriber has ever paid.

Bending the Regression Line into Shape

Clearly, a straight line is not a good shape for estimating probabilities. Logistic regression solves that problem by bending the regression line into a more appropriate shape. What is needed is a function that never gets smaller than 0, never gets larger than 1, but takes on every value between. The logistic function fits the bill perfectly.

The Logistic Function

The naïve Bayes model multiplies a bunch of *likelihoods* to estimate *odds*, which are then converted to a *probability*. A similar trick is used to turn linear regression into logistic regression.

The goal is to estimate the probability that a subscriber has paid based on tenure. The first step is to transform that probability, p into odds, by taking the ratio of p over $1-p$. Recall that odds and probability say exactly the same thing, but while probabilities are restricted to the range 0 to 1, odds go from 0 to infinity. That's pretty good and halfway to the range of a line. There is one more step. Taking the log of the odds yields a function that goes from negative infinity to positive infinity, as illustrated in Figure 6-12.

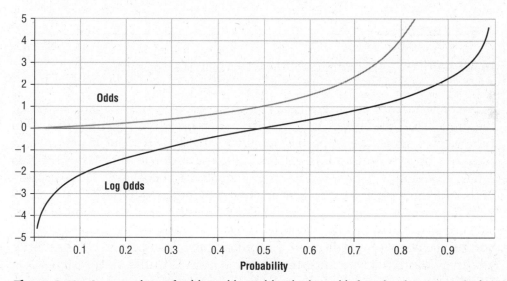

Figure 6-12: A comparison of odds and log odds. The log odds function is symmetrical around 0 and goes from negative infinity to positive infinity.

At this point, the probability has been transformed into a continuous function from negative infinity to positive infinity — just the sort of thing that linear regression is good at estimating! Setting up the log odds as the target variable for the regression looks makes the regression equation look like:

$$\ln\left(\frac{p}{1-p}\right) = \beta_0 + \beta_1 X.$$

Solving for the probability p requires a bit of algebra. The result of which is:

$$p = \frac{1}{1 + e^{-(\beta_0 + \beta_1 x)}}.$$

This is the logistic function. The equation may not be pretty, but the curve it produces certainly is, as shown in Figure 6-13, with β_0 set to zero and β_1 set to one.

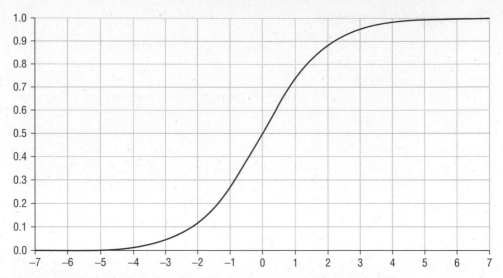

Figure 6-13: The logistic function goes from 0 to 1 just like a probability.

The logistic function itself has a characteristic S shape. The parameters of the model shift the curve left or right and stretch or compress the curve. This function has some nice properties. Around 0, the slope is about 45 percent and the curve approximates a line — from about the region of –1 to 1. Beyond this range, it gradually flattens out, never getting above 1 or below 0. These properties make the logistic a natural curve for expressing probabilities.

In Figure 6-14, the logistic function is used to estimate the probability that a subscriber has paid based on tenure. For early tenures, the estimate is low, but not 0; some people pay right away. The probability of having paid climbs steeply and by about 120 days is indistinguishable from 1. Unlike linear regression, logistic regression provides a good fit to the observed data.

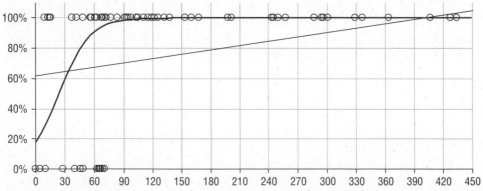

Figure 6-14: Logistic regression does a much better job of estimating the probability that a subscriber has paid.

Although logistic regression looks more "curvy" than a line, the logistic regression also finds global patterns rather than local patterns. To capture local patterns requires explicitly putting in variables to identify these effects.

The ordinary least squares method used to find the best-fit line for linear regression does not work for logistic regression. Instead, a method called *maximum likelihood* is used, which is explained in the sidebar "Fitting Models by the Maximum Likelihood Method."

FITTING MODELS BY THE MAXIMUM LIKELIHOOD METHOD

Fitting any kind of parametric model means using observed data to find parameter values that would calculate target values as similar as possible to the actual target values. This is the reverse of what happens when a model is scored. In scoring, the model is used to produce the best estimate for some value given a certain set of parameter values.

It would be nice if there were a function that, given a proposed parameter value and a set of observations, would return the probability of the parameter's value being correct. Although such a function does not generally exist, there is a useful relationship between the *probability* of observing the target values in the training set given a value for the parameter and the *likelihood* of the parameter having that value — namely, they are proportional. Likelihood is a relative measure of uncertainty, not an absolute measure like probability, but that is sufficient for comparing candidate parameter values.

The actual formula for the likelihood function depends on various assumptions about the data, which in turn depend on the particular parametric model being used.

For some simple probability density functions, finding the maximum point of the likelihood function analytically is possible. However, such cases generally do not arise in data mining problems.

For logistic regression (and several other techniques mentioned in subsequent chapters), the likelihood function has exactly one optimal value. A numerical optimization technique is used to maximize the likelihood, and is guaranteed to find it.

Fixed Effects and Hierarchical Effects

Once upon a time, one of the authors was doing a project in Jackson, Mississippi. Ronnie, one of the people with whom he was working, purchased a home with four bedrooms, two baths, and sitting on acres of land adjoining a state park. The home cost a bit more than $100,000. Even at the time, this price seemed absurdly cheap to the author who lived in New York City where that sum could buy a parking space, but not in a really good neighborhood. It wouldn't pay for enough space to place a comfortable bed, far less the other accoutrements of an apartment.

This story highlights the relative nature of much of the data used in data mining. The friend, Ronnie, was not significantly richer than the author. He simply lived in a place where his money went further.

Hierarchical Effects

The previous story is an example of hierarchical effects. A home worth $200,000 in New York City is quite different from a home worth $200,000 in Jackson, Mississippi. If you are using home value in a model, how can you adjust for this difference?

The answer is by taking the hierarchy into account. In this case, the hierarchy is the geographic hierarchy — which is often the most important hierarchy to consider. The typical way of taking it into account is to adjust for the median or average value in the neighborhood, by calculating an index. So, in 2000 the median home in Manhattan cost about a million dollars. The $200,000 home has an index of 0.2. The median home in Jackson cost about $64,200 so a $200,000 home has an index of more than 3.

What does this index do? It tells you whether the home is worth more or less than its neighbors. To think about this another way, don't consider whether a home is expensive or cheap on a national scale. Compare it to other homes closer by.

Within and Between Effects

When thinking about hierarchical effects, there are, in fact, two types. One is strictly local, which is how individuals compare to their neighbors (which may be geographical or may be defined in some other way). The index just described quantifies this local effect. Such local effects are "within" effects, because they are within a level of the hierarchy.

The second effect is the broader impact of the average. Do areas with low average home values behave differently from areas with high average home values? This is the "between" effect of the variable. The combination of the "within" effect and the "between" effect explains the overall impact of a variable in a model. However, understanding the hierarchy can sometimes prove very valuable.

> **TIP** Hierarchical effects can help you understand whether the value of a variable is important to a model because it is high, or because its neighbors tend to have high values.

You can apply hierarchical models to many more things than home values and cities. Customers may be acquired through different channels. One question is whether the channel makes a difference to long-term behavior (say, how long a customer remains a customer). Another is whether a customer is doing better or worse than other customers acquired the same way.

Fixed Effects

Fixed effects refer to a type of model that might be called multiple regression on steroids. It is particularly useful in situations where a customer has values repeating over time, such as the amount of money billed each month, and the target is related to each observation rather than to the customer. For instance: What factors determine whether or not a customer is likely to be late in paying his or her bill? Or, the very similar question: What is the probability that a given customer will pay the next bill on time?

Each customer has a sequence of bills with a payment history. Assume that the analysis is limited to customers with at least 12 months of history. The sequence might include one or more late payments for the more irresponsible customers, or the sequence might include no late payments, for the conscientious ones.

One way to build a model is to start introducing attributes at the bill level, such as the amount of the bill, how many times the customer has been late previously, and the method of payment for the preceding bill. You could use these types of variables to estimate whether or not a given bill is going to be late.

However, different customers have different propensities for paying on time or paying late. How can the model determine which factors are important at the bill level after taking into account factors at the customer level? This is particularly important because customers who are regularly late would dominate a model built at the bill level, because most examples of lateness come from customers who regularly pay late. When you score customers to determine the probability of their next bill being late, all customers receive a score, whether or not they have ever been late. However, the model itself will be biased toward the most irresponsible customers, because they dominate the late bills in the model set.

One way to fix this is to construct the model set by taking one random bill from each customer; this makes the model set more closely resemble the score set, where each customer appears only once. An alternative is to use fixed effect models.

WARNING When modeling individual transactions for a particular effect, it is easy to introduce bias into the model, because some customers appear more often than others.

The magic of fixed effects models is that they can take into account all features at the customer level to determine unbiased models at the lower level. The approach is to introduce a variable at the customer level to identify each customer. The regression model can then use this as an input to build the model for late payment. This model is then independent of all effects at the customer level, because each customer has been treated individually. The coefficients for such a model do a better job explaining the effects of other variables. Remember, each customer still has multiple bills, so there should be enough data to fit each customer. This approach works even when the number of data points per customer varies (as long as at least a few exist for each of them).

In this example, notice that the model in question is a logistic regression, because the target is binary (does the customer pay late?). You can apply fixed effects modeling to any type of regression.

An alternative to fixed effects is to add a variable to capture each customer's overall propensity to pay late. For example, this could be the proportion of late payments in the model set for each customer. You don't know the probability for each payment, but you do know the probability at the customer level. This can then be incorporated into the model at the customer level.

Fixed effects modeling is particularly popular for *longitudinal* analysis. This is not a study of people in the same time zone. Instead, it refers to studies of individual people over time. The specific term is often used for medical analyses, especially in the phrase "longitudinal patient analysis."

However, the technique can be applied in other cases and even when the hierarchy is not at the customer level. A model to predict spending for shoppers arriving at a retail website might include the referring site as an input variable. Suppose that, on average, shoppers coming from indulgeme.com spend twice as much as those referred by cheapskate.com. Within each group of shoppers, there is a lot of variance. Those from cheapskate.com sometimes make large purchases and those from indulgeme.com sometimes make small ones. Suppose you want to estimate how much shoppers will be worth when they come to the site, so you can choose landing pages based on the amount the customer might spend?

The solution is to include each group's average spending in the model, along with other attributes. This controls for the effects of group membership so you can better model the variation due to other causes.

Lessons Learned

Ideas from probability and statistics are the basis for all data mining techniques. The methods described in this chapter spring directly from traditional statistical techniques.

Given a statistical description of a desired target, similarity measures can be devised to score candidates based on how close they are to a prototype or ideal. One natural similarity measure is Euclidean distance, but many others are possible.

Table lookup models use a different measure of similarity. All observations that fall in the same cell of a table are given the same score. The score is based on the characteristics of training data records that were assigned to that cell. There are many ways to define the cells of a table lookup model, but the simplest and most common is to divide the range of each input into equal-sized groups, such as terciles or quintiles.

Table lookup models suffer from the problem that as the number of inputs goes up, the number of training examples per cell goes down rapidly. When there are many inputs, getting enough data to make confident estimates is hard. One solution is to combine small cells into bigger cells.

Naïve Bayesian models offer another solution by using all the training data for each dimension, and then combining the contributions. The "naïve" in the name refers to the assumption that the input variables are independent, which is often not the case. Nevertheless, naïve Bayesian models often perform quite well.

The most common of all statistical models are regression models. Linear regression models combine all the inputs by multiplying each by a coefficient and then adding up the results. Fitting a regression model means finding the coefficient values that minimize the squared error of the estimates. Linear regression models are quite versatile, but they are not appropriate for all cases. In particular, they are not a good choice for estimating probabilities. Logistic regression models fit the observed data with an S-shaped function instead of a straight line. This produces estimates confined to the range 0 to 1, as is appropriate for a probability.

All regression models find global patterns, meaning that they find patterns for all values of the input variables. In fact, many interesting patterns are local (towns far from Boston behave differently from towns near to Boston in terms of newspaper reading behavior). The next chapter introduces one of the most popular data mining technique, decision trees, which excel at finding local patterns between inputs and the target.

CHAPTER 7

Decision Trees

Decision trees are one of the most powerful directed data mining techniques, because you can use them on such a wide range of problems and they produce models that explain how they work. Decision trees are related to table lookup models. In the simple table lookup model described in Chapter 6, such as RFM cubes, the cells are defined in advance by splitting each dimension into an arbitrary number of evenly spaced partitions. Then, something of interest — a response rate or average order size, for instance — is measured in each cell. New records are scored by determining which cell they belong to.

Decision trees extend this idea in two ways. First, decision trees recursively split data into smaller and smaller cells which are increasingly "pure" in the sense of having similar values of the target. The decision tree algorithm treats each cell independently. To find a new split, the algorithm tests splits based on all available variables. In doing so, decision trees choose the most important variables for the directed data mining task. This means that you can use decision trees for variable selection as well as for building models.

Second, the decision tree uses the target variable to determine how each input should be partitioned. In the end, the decision tree breaks the data into segments, defined by the splitting rules at each step. Taken together, the rules for all the segments form the decision tree model.

A model that can be expressed as a collection of rules is very attractive. Rules are readily expressed in English so that we can understand them. Rules, of the kind that make up a decision tree, can also be expressed in SQL, the database access language, to retrieve or score matching records. As models, decision trees can be used for classification, estimation, and prediction. Decision trees are also useful for data exploration and variable selection even when you plan to use a different technique to create the final model. The variables chosen for inclusion in the tree are also likely to be useful for other data mining techniques.

This chapter opens with an example of a decision tree for a simple prediction task. This example highlights the way decision trees can provide insight into a business problem, and how easy decision trees are to understand. It also illustrates how you can use a tree for selecting variables, making classifications, and estimating real numbers.

The chapter continues with more technical detail on how to create decision trees. In particular, several different criteria for evaluating decision tree splitting rules are introduced and compared. There are many different decision tree algorithms, some bearing names such as CART, CHAID, and C5.0. However, these variants are all based on the same building blocks.

This chapter also presents a discussion of the difference between local and global models using a comparison of decision trees with linear regression models as a case in point. A technical aside compares decision trees with support vector machines, another technique for partitioning classes. Interesting applications of decision trees are scattered throughout the chapter.

What Is a Decision Tree and How Is It Used?

A *decision tree* is a hierarchical collection of rules that describes how to divide a large collection of records into successively smaller groups of records. With each successive division, the members of the resulting segments become more and more similar to one another with respect to the target.

This section presents examples of trees used for various purposes, including gaining insight into a business problem, exploring data (in a directed fashion), making predictions, classifying records, and estimating values.

A Typical Decision Tree

The decision tree in Figure 7-1 was created from a model set describing post-paid phone subscribers; these are subscribers who talk first and pay later. The model set is set up for a predictive model. So, the input variables are recorded for all active customers on a given date, and the target is assigned, based on the customer status 100 days later. The model set is balanced, containing equal numbers of customers who are active 100 days later, who stopped involuntarily (by not paying) and who stopped voluntarily. These three possibilities are represented by the target variable, which takes on one of the three values, **A**, **V**, or **I**.

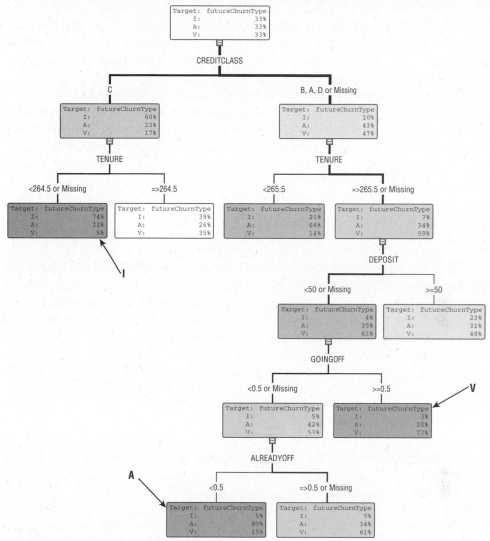

Figure 7-1: A decision tree.

The box at the top of the diagram is the *root node*, which contains all the training data used to grow the tree. In this node, all three classes are represented equally. The root node has two children, and a rule that specifies which records go to which child. The rule at the top of the tree is based on credit class: Credit class "C" goes to the left child and credit classes "A," "B," and "D" go to the right child. The point of the tree is to split these records into nodes dominated by a single class. The nodes that ultimately get used are at the ends of their branches, with no children. These are the *leaves* of the tree.

The path from the root node to a leaf describes a rule for the records in that leaf. In Figure 7-1, nodes with distributions similar to the training data are lightly shaded; nodes with distributions quite different from the training data are darker. The arrows point to three of the darkest leaves. Each of these leaves has a clear majority class.

Decision trees assign scores to new records, simply by letting each record flow through the tree to arrive at its appropriate leaf. For instance, the tree in Figure 7-1 can be used to assign an **A** score, **V** score, and I score to any currently active subscriber. Each leaf has a rule, which is based on the path through the tree. The rules are used to assign subscribers in need of scoring to the appropriate leaf. The proportion of records in each class provides the scores.

Using the Tree to Learn About Churn

In mature markets, nearly all mobile service providers are concerned about *churn*, the industry term for subscribers switching from one provider to another. In markets where telephone penetration is already high, the easiest way to acquire new subscribers is to lure them away from a competitor. The decision tree in Figure 7-1 describes who is doing the churning and which of two variants of churn is more common in particular segments. *Voluntary* churn is when the customer decides to leave. *Involuntary* churn is when the company tells customers to leave, usually because they have not been paying their bills. To create the model set, subscribers active on a particular date were observed and various attributes of each captured in a customer signature.

The first split in the tree is on credit class. Subscribers with credit class C take one path whereas those with any other credit class take another. The credit class is "A," "B," "C," or "D," with "A" meaning excellent credit and "D" the lowest credit rating. The fact that this variable is chosen first means that credit class is the most important variable for splitting the data.

This split drastically changes the distribution of the target in each of the children. Sixty percent of subscribers with credit class "C" experience involuntary churn compared to only 10 percent for all other credit classes. Subsequent splits continue to concentrate the classes. Notice that different variables are used in different parts of the tree. However, any variable can be used anywhere in the tree, and a variable can be used more than once.

In the full tree, most leaves are dominated by a single class. Each node is annotated with the percent of subscribers in each of the three classes. Look first at the leaf marked I. These subscribers are credit class "C" and have tenure of 264 days or less. Seventy-four percent of them were cancelled for non-payment. The rate of voluntary cancellations is quite low because most subscribers are on a one-year contract that includes a hefty cancellation fee. Rather than paying the fee, dissatisfied subscribers whose attitude toward debt repayment has earned them credit class "C" simply walk away.

Now consider the node marked **V**. These subscribers pay no deposit (the smallest deposit is $100) and have been around for at least 265 days. Although they were on contract at the time the inputs were recorded, they were known to be going off contract before the date when the target was recorded. The split on `deposit>=50` is exactly equivalent to a split on `credit class='D'` because everyone with credit class D pays a deposit ranging from $100 to $600, whereas people with credit class "A," "B," or "C" pay no deposit.

Finally, look at the leaf marked **A**. Like those in the node marked **V**, they have no deposit and have been around for more than 265 days. But these subscribers are still on contract and not about to go off contract. Perhaps they signed two-year contracts to start with, or perhaps they were enticed to renew a contract after the first year. In any case, 80% are still active.

Judging by this tree, contracts do a good job of retaining subscribers who are careful with their credit scores, and large deposits do a good job of retaining customers who are not. Both of these groups wait until they can leave voluntarily and without punishment. The worst attrition is among subscribers with credit class "C." They are not forced to pay a deposit, but unlike others who have no deposit, customers with credit class "C" are willing to walk away from a contract. Perhaps these customers should be asked to pay a deposit.

Using the Tree to Learn About Data and Select Variables

The decision tree in Figure 7-1 uses five variables from among the many available in the model set. The decision tree algorithm picked these five because, together, they do a good job of explaining voluntary and involuntary churn. The very first split uses `credit class`, because `credit class` does a better job of separating the target variable classes than any other available field. When faced with dozens or hundreds of unfamiliar variables, you can use a decision tree to direct your attention to a useful subset. In fact, decision trees are often used as a tool for selecting variables for use with another modeling technique. In general, decision trees do a reasonable job of selecting a small number of fairly independent variables, but because each splitting decision is made independently, it is possible for different nodes to choose correlated or even synonymous variables. An example is the inclusion of both `credit class` and `deposit` seen here.

Different choices of target variable create different decision trees containing different variables. For example, using the same data used for the tree in Figure 7-1, but changing the target variable to the binary choice of active or not active (by combining **V** and **I**) changes the tree. The new tree no longer has credit class at the top. Instead, `handset churn rate`, a variable not even in the first tree, rises to the top. This variable is consistent with domain knowledge: Customers who are dissatisfied with their mobile phone (handset) are more likely to leave. One measure of dissatisfaction is the historical rate of churn for handsets. This rate can (and should) be recalculated often because handset preferences change with the speed of fashion. People who have handsets associated with high rates of attrition in the recent past are more likely to leave.

PICKING VARIABLES FOR A HOUSEHOLD PENETRATION MODEL AT THE BOSTON GLOBE

During the data exploration phase of a directed data mining project, decision trees are a useful tool for choosing variables that are likely to be important for predicting particular targets. One of the authors' newspaper clients, the *Boston Globe*, was interested in estimating a town's expected home delivery circulation level based on various demographic and geographic characteristics. Armed with such estimates, it would be possible to spot towns with untapped potential where the actual circulation was lower than the expected circulation. The final model would be a regression equation based on a handful of variables. But which variables? The U.S. Census Bureau makes hundreds of variables available. Before building the regression model, we used decision trees to explore the possibilities.

Although the newspaper was ultimately interested in predicting the actual number of subscribing households in a given city or town, that number does not make a good target for a regression model because towns and cities vary so much in size. Wasting modeling power on discovering that there are more subscribers in large towns than in small ones is not useful. A better target is *penetration* — the proportion of households that subscribe to the paper. This number yields an estimate of the total number of subscribing households simply by multiplying it by the number of households in a town. Factoring out town size yields a target variable with values that range from 0 to somewhat less than 1.

The next step was to figure out which factors, from among the hundreds in the town signature, separate towns with high penetration (the "good" towns) from those with low penetration (the "bad" towns). Our approach was to build a decision tree with a binary good/bad target variable. This involved sorting the towns by home delivery penetration and labeling the top one-third "good" and the bottom one-third "bad." Towns in the middle third — those that are not clearly good or bad — were left out of the training set.

TIP When trying to model the difference between two groups, removing examples that are not clearly in one group or the other can be helpful.

The resulting tree used median home value as the first split. In a region with some of the most expensive housing in the country, towns where the median home value is less than $226,000 dollars are poor prospects for this paper (all census variables are from the 2000 Census). The next split was on one of a family of derived variables comparing the subscriber base in the town to the town population as a whole. Towns where the subscribers are similar to the general population are better, in terms of home delivery penetration, than towns where the subscribers are further from average. Other variables that were important for distinguishing good from bad towns included the average

> years of school completed, the percentage of the population in blue collar occupations, and the percentage of the population in high-status occupations.
>
> Some variables picked by the decision tree were less suitable for the regression model. One example is distance from Boston. The problem is that at first, as one drives out into the suburbs, home penetration goes up with distance from Boston. After a while, however, distance from Boston becomes negatively correlated with penetration as people far from Boston do not care as much about what goes on there. A decision tree easily finds the right distance to split on, but a regression model expects the relationship between distance and penetration to be the same for all distances. Home price is a better predictor because its distribution resembles that of the target variable, increasing in the first few miles and then declining. The decision tree provides guidance about which variables to think about as well as which variables to use.

Using the Tree to Produce Rankings

Decision trees score new records by looking at the input variables in each new record and following the appropriate path to the leaf. For many applications, the ordering of the scores is more important than the actual scores themselves. That is, knowing that Customer A has higher or lower churn than Customer B is more important than having an actual estimate of the churn risk for each customer. Such applications include selecting a fixed number of customers for a specific marketing campaign, such as a retention campaign. If the campaign is being designed for 10,000 customers, the purpose of the model is to find the 10,000 customers most likely to churn; determining the actual churn rate is not important.

Using the Tree to Estimate Class Probabilities

For many purposes, rankings are not sufficient, and probabilities of class membership are needed. The class probabilities are obtained from the leaves. For example, the distribution of classes in the node labeled I in Figure 7-1 comes from applying the rule `credit class='C' and tenure<264.5` to the balanced data at the root node. Saying that any record arriving at node I has probability 0.6 of churning involuntarily in the next 100 days might seem reasonable; however, the distribution of values in the original data is quite different from the distribution in the model set used to build the tree. After six months, 89.30 percent of subscribers are still active, 4.39 percent have left involuntarily, and 6.32 percent have left voluntarily.

Chapter 5 explains one way to convert scores to probability estimates. Another way to estimate the true probabilities is to apply the decision tree rules to the original, unbalanced preclassified data and observe the resulting distribution.

For this particular dataset, selecting all subscribers with `credit class='C'` and `tenure<264.5` yields a sample in which 84.14% are still active, 14.44% have left involuntarily, and 1.42% have left voluntarily. So the correct probability estimate for involuntary churn at this leaf is 14 percent rather than 60 percent. The percentage of involuntary churn in this leaf is well over three times the level in the subscriber population, but even here, "active" is still the most probable outcome by far.

Using the Tree to Classify Records

To use the tree as a classifier, all that is required is to estimate the class probabilities as described earlier and label each leaf with its most probable class. This is a use of decision trees that is often presented as primary in the academic literature. In the marketing world, the class probability estimates are usually more useful than the classification because classifiers quite commonly produce only one outcome. Classifying everyone as nonresponders is not helpful because the point of creating models is to differentiate among records.

A model that puts everyone in the same class is neither surprising nor uncommon in marketing applications where the behaviors of interest (response, fraud, attrition, and so on) tend to be rare. No matter how the segments for a marketing campaign are defined, the most likely outcome in any segment is no response. Fortunately, some segments are more likely to respond than others and that is enough to be useful. A charity does not send you an appeal for donations because they think you will respond; they reach out to you because they think the chance of your responding, while low, is high enough to justify the postage.

Using the Tree to Estimate Numeric Values

A tree used to estimate the value of a numeric target variable (as opposed to the probability of class membership) is referred to as a *regression tree*. The tree is built so that records in any given leaf all have target values close to the average for that leaf — or in the language of statistics, the goal is to minimize the variance of the target values in each leaf. The leaf average is the score assigned to any new record that matches the rule for the leaf.

A regression tree can only generate as many distinct values as there are leaves in the tree. Using a discrete model such as a regression tree to estimate a continuous value may seem odd while using a continuous function to estimate continuous values seems more natural; however, regression trees can be used in other ways, such as selecting the variables for a regression model. Also, regression trees do a good job of breaking up the original data into local segments. Building a different model in each segment using a technique such as regression can also produce effective models. The following section discusses this idea of finding local phenomena in the data.

Decision Trees Are Local Models

The discussion of regression models in the previous chapter points out that regression models are global and, as a consequence, regression models do not do a good job of fitting data that has local characteristics. Trying to fit local phenomena in the input space changes the values of the model everywhere. Decision trees, on the other hand, are local models; they carve the input space into segments and produce a separate estimate for each one.

Figure 7-2 shows a tree that uses only two input variables, `days since last purchase` and `lifetime orders` to predict `order size`, a numeric variable. This tree has 12 leaves and a depth of 4. Figure 7-3 shows the same model as a rectangular box divided into more boxes. Each sub-box represents a leaf in the tree. Notice that the boxes fill the entire rectangle. Just as every record reaches some leaf, every record lands in a box. The shading of the boxes represents the average order size for records landing there; darker boxes have higher average order sizes.

The splits themselves are the vertical and horizontal lines in this box. Each split on `lifetime orders` corresponds to one of the vertical line segments. Each split on `days since last purchase` corresponds to one of the horizontal line segments. The longest vertical line, right down the middle of the figure, is the highest split in the tree.

This example only uses two dimensions, because this is easier to show in a diagram. Introducing another variable would introduce another dimension. Then, the data would be represented as a brick shape (technically, a rectangular polyhedron), and it would be broken up into small bricks, by planes cutting it into pieces.

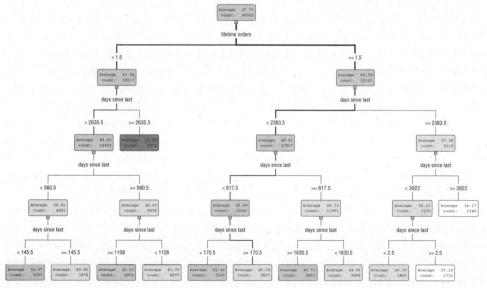

Figure 7-2: A regression tree for average order size as a function of recency and frequency.

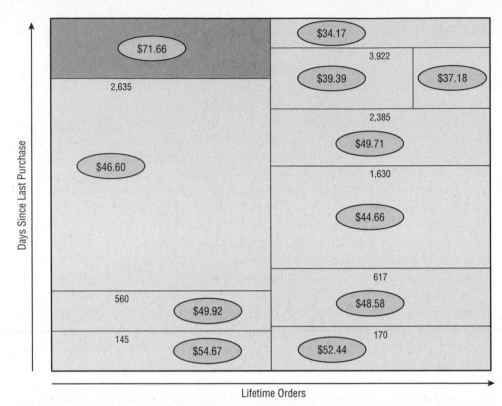

Figure 7-3: The tree puts the records into rectangular boxes.

The box diagram makes it easier to see an interesting pattern that is hard to spot in the tree. For the most part, customers who have made an order recently have larger order sizes. However, a point exists where the correlation between recency and order size changes direction. Over most of the range, average order size increases with recency. In other words, it is inversely correlated with days since last purchase. But surprisingly, the very highest average order size is in the box in the upper-left corner — customers whose sole purchase was more than seven years ago. (As an aside, it seems a bit odd that the company does not purge "customers" who have not made a purchase in seven years from its house file. Perhaps they do purge most such customers, but spare those who have spent more than $50, which could explain why the long-lost customers still on file were all such big spenders.) Whatever its cause, the change in sign of the correlation means that a regression model might not make good use of the recency variable. Regression models assume the relationship between an input and the target is the same everywhere.

Because the decision tree model is local, it is fine for the relationship between recency and order size to be quite different in different leaves. If new customers were to come in and make very large purchases, they would have no effect on the box in the upper left, which only contains customers whose most recent purchase was long ago. Conversely, one could alter the training data to give customers in the upper-left box an average purchase of $100 or even $1,000 without affecting the average order size in any other box. Another strength of the regression tree model is that, because the estimated order sizes associated with each box are averages of actual observed values, they can never be too unreasonable. This is in contrast with a regression model, which may predict negative order sizes or other values outside the range of what has ever been seen.

The traditional tree diagram is a very effective way of representing the actual structure of a decision tree, but for some purposes, box diagrams like the one in Figure 7-3 can be more expressive. A box diagram brings all leaves, no matter how many levels down in the tree, to the surface where they are easy to compare. For example, Figure 7-3 shows at a glance that the top-left corner contains the biggest spenders. One way of thinking about decision trees is that they are a way of drawing boxes around groups of similar records. All the records within a particular box are classified the same way because they all meet the rule defining that box. This differs from global classification methods such as logistic regression, and more recent inventions such as support vector machines, all of which attempt to partition data into classes by drawing a single line or curve or hyperplane through the data space. This is a fundamental distinction: Global models are weak when there are several very different ways for a record to become part of the target class.

In the credit card industry, for instance, there are several ways for customers to be profitable. Some profitable customers, called *revolvers*, have low transaction rates, but keep high revolving balances without defaulting. *Transactors*, on the other hand, pay off their balance in full each month, but are profitable due to the high transaction volume they generate. Yet others, called *convenience users*, have few transactions, but occasionally make a large purchase and take several months to pay it off. Two very dissimilar customers may be equally profitable. A decision tree can find each separate group, label it, and by providing a description of each box, suggest the reason for each group's profitability.

Growing Decision Trees

Although there are many variations on the core decision tree algorithm, all of them share the same basic method for creating the tree: Click on the decision tree icon in your tool of choice or call the appropriate decision tree procedure. But what happens inside? This section dives into more detail, because understanding the detail helps you use decision trees more effectively and makes understanding their results easier.

The decision tree algorithm repeatedly splits the data into smaller and smaller groups in such a way that each new set of nodes has greater purity than its ancestors with respect to the target variable. For the most part, this discussion assumes a binary, categorical target variable, such as responder/ nonresponder. This assumption simplifies the explanations without much loss of generality.

Finding the Initial Split

At the start of the process, there is a model set consisting of preclassified records — that is, the value of the target variable is known for all cases. The goal is to build a tree that uses the values of the input fields to create rules that result in leaves that do a good job of assigning a target value to each record. For a binary target, this value is the probability of membership in each class. Remember that each record in the model set starts with a known target, and this guides the construction of the tree.

The tree starts with all the records in a subset of the model set — the training set — at the root node. The first task is to split the records into children by creating a rule on the input variables. What are the best children? The answer is the ones that are purest in one of the target values, because the goal is to separate the values of the target as much as possible.

To perform the split, the algorithm considers all possible splits on all input variables. For instance, for `days since last purchase`, the tree considers splitting at 100 days, with customers having 0–100 days going into one child and the rest going to the other child. It considers splits at 1 day and at 1,000 days, and at all other distinct values found in the training set. The algorithm evaluates the splits, and chooses the best split value for each variable. The best variable is the one that produces the best split.

The measure used to evaluate a potential split is *purity* of the target variable in the children. Low purity means that the distribution of the target in the children is similar to that of the parent node, whereas high purity means that members of a single class predominate. The best split is the one that increases purity in the children by the greatest amount. A good split also creates nodes of similar size, or at least does not create nodes containing very few records.

These ideas are easy to see visually. Figure 7-4 illustrates some good and bad splits. In this case, the original data consists of nine circles and nine triangles and the goal is to separate these two groups. The first split is a poor one because no increase in purity exists. The initial population contains equal numbers of the two shapes; after the split, so does each child. The second split is also poor, because although purity is increased slightly, the pure node has few members and the purity of the larger child is only marginally better than that of the parent. The final split is a good one because it leads to children of roughly the same size and with much higher purity than the parent. Visualizing purity is perhaps easier than formalizing the concept so it can be calculated by a computer; the next section discusses several different ways to calculate purity, including measures for both categorical and numeric targets.

Splits are evaluated based on how pure the resulting children are in the target variable. This means that the choice of an appropriate splitting criterion depends on the type of the target variable, not on the type of the input variable. Numeric targets have different definitions of purity from categorical and binary targets.

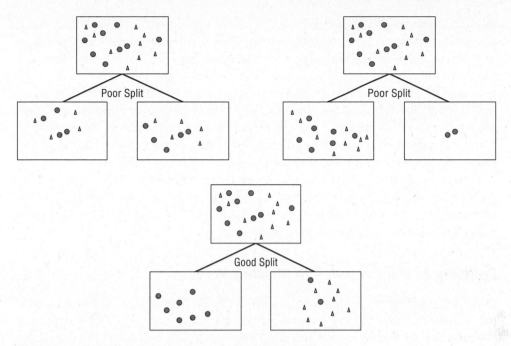

Figure 7-4: A good split increases purity for all the children.

Splitting on a Numeric Input Variable

When searching for a binary split on a numeric input variable, distinct each value that the variable takes on in the training set is treated as a candidate value for the split. Splits on a numeric variable take the form $X<N$. All records where the value of X (the splitting variable) is less than some constant N are sent to one child and all records where the value of X is greater than or equal to N are sent to the other. After each trial split, the increase in purity due to the split is measured. In the interests of efficiency, some implementations of decision trees use a representative sample of the values instead of evaluating every one.

When the decision tree is scored, the only use it makes of numeric inputs is to compare their values with the split points. They are never multiplied by weights or added together as they are in many other types of models. This has the important consequence that decision trees are not sensitive to outliers or skewed distributions of numeric variables.

Splitting on a Categorical Input Variable

The simplest algorithm for splitting on a categorical input variable is to create a new branch for each class that the categorical variable can take on. So, a split on the contract start month would yield twelve children, one for each calendar month. This approach has been used in some software implementations, but it often yields poor results. High branching factors quickly reduce the population of training records available at each child node, making further splitting less likely and less reliable.

A better and more common approach is to group together classes that, taken individually, predict similar outcomes. For a binary target, the simplest approach is to determine the proportion of the target for each value of the input variable. Then, all values that have a smaller proportion of one target value than the parent node go to one child, and the rest go to the other child.

A more sophisticated approach looks at the distributions of the target within each value of the input variable, and combines values whose distributions are very similar. The usual test for whether the distributions differ significantly is the chi-square test explained in Chapter 4.

Splitting in the Presence of Missing Values

One of the nicest things about decision trees is their ability to handle missing values in input fields by using null as an allowable value. This approach is preferable to throwing out records with missing values or trying to impute missing values. Throwing out records is likely to create a biased training set because the records with missing values are probably not a random sample of the population. Replacing missing values with imputed values runs the risk that important information provided by the fact that a value is missing will be ignored in the model.

The authors have seen many cases where the fact that a particular value is null has predictive value. In one such case, the count of non-null values in appended household-level demographic data was predictive of the response to an offer of term life insurance. Apparently, people who leave many traces in Acxiom's household database (by buying houses, getting married, having babies, registering products, subscribing to magazines, and so on) are more likely to be interested in life insurance than those whose lifestyles leave more fields null.

WARNING Decision trees can produce splits based on missing values of an input variable. The fact that a value is null can often have predictive value so do not be hasty to filter out records with missing values or to try to replace them with imputed values.

An alternative approach to missing values, which is part of the CART algorithm and available in several software implementations, keeps several splitting rules for each node. These *surrogate splits* use different fields to produce similar results. When a null value is encountered in the field that yields the best split, the next best rule can be used. The use of surrogate splits is more interesting in theory than in practice because often, when the first variable is missing the surrogates are missing as well. For instance, if the first variable is from census data and describes something about the neighborhood, the surrogates probably also describe the neighborhood. And, if the first variable is missing, it is because the census information is not available for the customer's address, so similar variables are also missing.

Growing the Full Tree

The initial split produces two or more children, each of which is then split in the same manner as the root node. This is called a *recursive* algorithm, because the same splitting method is used on the subsets of data in each child. Once again, all input fields are considered as candidate splitters, even fields already used for splits. Eventually, the tree building stops, for one of three reasons:

- No split can be found that significantly increases the purity of any node's children.
- The number of records per node reaches some preset lower bound.
- The depth of the tree reaches some preset limit. At this point, the full decision tree has been grown.

If a completely deterministic relationship existed between the input variables and the target, this recursive splitting would eventually yield a tree with completely pure leaves. Manufacturing examples of this sort is easy, but they do not occur very often in marketing or CRM applications. Customer behavior data almost never contains clear, deterministic relationships between inputs and outputs. The fact that two customers have the exact same description in terms of the available input variables does not ensure that they will exhibit the same behavior. A decision tree for a catalog response model might include a leaf representing females with age greater than 50, three or more purchases within the last year, and total lifetime spending of more than $145. The customers reaching this leaf will typically be a mix of responders and nonresponders. If the leaf in question is labeled "responder," then the proportion of nonresponders is the *misclassification rate* for this leaf.

One circumstance where deterministic rules *are* likely to be discovered is when patterns in data reflect business rules. The authors had this fact driven home to them while analyzing warranty claims at Caterpillar, a manufacturer of diesel engines. We built a decision tree model to predict which claims would be approved. At the time, the company had a policy of paying certain claims automatically. The results were startling: The decision tree had some leaves that were 100 percent accurate on unseen test data. In other words, the tree had discovered the exact rules used to classify the claims. Of course, discovering known business rules may not be particularly useful; it does, however, underline the effectiveness of decision trees on rule-oriented problems. On this same problem, a neural network also produced good results, but it could not explain the patterns that it found. The decision tree could identify a business rule that explained why the model was doing so well.

Finding the Best Split

Many different criteria may be used to evaluate potential splits. Alternate splitting criteria often lead to trees that look quite different from one another, but have similar performance. That is because there are usually many candidate splits with very similar performance. Different purity measures select different splits, but because all the measures are trying to capture the same idea, the resulting models tend to behave similarly.

Figure 7-5 shows a good split. The parent node contains 9 circles and 9 triangles. The left child contains 7 circles and 1 triangle. The right child contains 8 triangles and 2 circles. Clearly, the purity has increased, but how can the increase be quantified? And how can this split be compared to others? That requires a formal definition of purity, several of which are listed next.

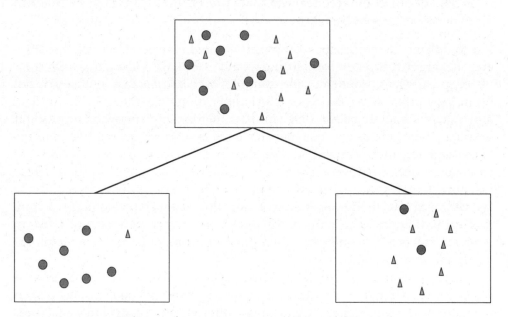

Figure 7-5: A good split on a binary categorical variable increases purity.

Purity measures for evaluating splits for categorical target variables include:

- Gini (also called population diversity)
- Entropy (also called information gain)

- Chi-square test
- Incremental response

When the target variable is numeric, one approach is to bin the value and use one of the preceding measures. However, two measures are in common use for numeric targets:

- Reduction in variance
- F test

Note that the choice of an appropriate purity measure depends on whether the *target* variable is categorical or numeric. The type of the input variable does not matter. The split illustrated in Figure 7-5 could just as easily be provided by a numeric input variable (AGE > 46) or by a categorical variable (STATE is a member of CT, MA, ME, NH, RI, VT).

Gini (Population Diversity) as a Splitting Criterion

One popular splitting criterion is named Gini, after the 20th century Italian statistician and economist, Corrado Gini. This measure, which is also used by biologists and ecologists studying population diversity, gives the probability that two items chosen at random from the same population are in the same class.

As an example, consider an ecosystem that has exactly two animals — wily coyotes and roadrunners. The question is: How pure is this ecosystem? The approach for answering this question is the following: Two ecologists go into the ecosystem and each takes a picture of an animal. Purity is then the probability that these two pictures are of the same type of animal. For a pure population, the probability is 1, because the pictures will always be of that animal. For a population that is half wily coyotes and half roadrunners, the probability is 0.5. This probability is the Gini score.

For the Gini measure, a score of 0.5 means that two classes are represented equally. When a node has only one class, its score is 1. Because purer nodes have higher scores, the goal of decision tree algorithms that use this measure is to maximize the Gini score of the split.

The Gini measure of a node is easy to calculate. It is simply the sum of the squares of the proportions of the classes in the node. For the split shown in Figure 7-5, the parent population has an equal number of circles and triangles. A node with equal numbers of each of two classes has a score of $P(\text{circle})^2 + P(\text{triangle})^2 = 0.5^2 + 0.5^2 = 0.5$, which is expected because the chance of picking the same class twice by random selection with replacement is 1 out of 2. The Gini score for the left child is $0.125^2 + 0.875^2 = 0.781$. The Gini score for the right child is $0.200^2 + 0.800^2 = 0.680$.

To calculate the impact of a split, take the average of the Gini scores of the children, weighted by the size of each child. In this case, 0.444*0.875 + 0.556*0.680 = 0.725.

As shown in Figure 7-6, the Gini score varies between 0.5 and 1. A perfectly pure node has a Gini score of 1. A node that is evenly balanced has a Gini score of 0.5. Sometimes, the score is manipulated so it is in the range from 0 to 1 (doubling the score and subtracting the result from 1). However, such a manipulation makes no difference when comparing different scores to optimize purity.

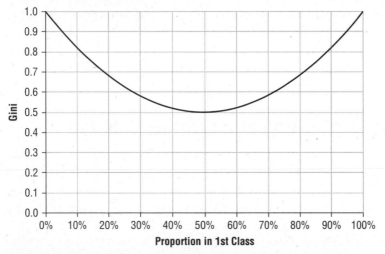

Figure 7-6: For a binary target, the Gini score varies from 0.5 when there is an equal number of each class to 1 when all records are in the same class.

Entropy Reduction or Information Gain as a Splitting Criterion

Information gain uses a clever idea for defining purity, borrowed from the world of machine learning. If a leaf is entirely pure, then the classes in the leaf can be described very easily — there is only one. On the other hand, if a leaf is highly impure, then describing it is much more complicated. Information theory has a measure for this called *entropy*, which measures how disorganized a system is. A comprehensive introduction to information theory is far beyond the scope of this book. For this book's purposes, the intuitive notion is that the number of bits required to describe a particular outcome depends on the number of possible outcomes. You can think of entropy as a measure of the number of yes/no questions it would take to determine the state of the system. If there are 16 possible states, it takes $\log_2(16)$, or four bits, to enumerate them or identify a particular one. Additional information reduces the number of questions needed to determine the state of the system, so information gain means the same thing as entropy reduction. Both terms are used to describe decision tree algorithms.

The entropy of a particular decision tree node can be readily calculated using a formula. The entropy for a node is the sum, for all the target values in the node, of the proportion of records with a particular value multiplied by the base two logarithm of that proportion. (In practice, this sum is usually multiplied by –1 in order to obtain a positive number, because logarithms of probabilities are negative.) Despite the logarithms, this formula is quite similar to the formula for the Gini score; the Gini score multiplies each target value's proportion by itself while the entropy score multiplies each target value's proportion by its logarithm.

As shown in Figure 7-7, an entropy score of 1 means that two classes are represented equally. When a node has only one class, its score is 0. So, purer nodes have lower scores, and the goal is to minimize the entropy score of the split.

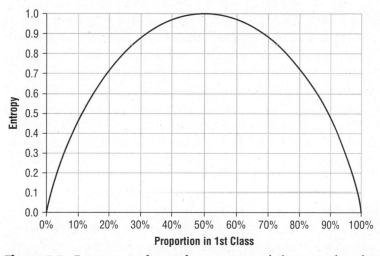

Figure 7-7: Entropy goes from 0 for a pure population to 1 when there is an equal number of each class.

The entropy of a split is calculated in the same way as the Gini score: It is simply the weighted average of the entropies of all the children. When entropy reduction is the splitting criterion, the decision tree algorithm selects the split that reduces entropy by the greatest amount.

For a binary target variable such as the one shown in Figure 7-5, the formula for the entropy of a single node is:

$$-1 * (P(circle)\log_2 P(circle) + P(triangle)\log_2 P(triangle))$$

In this example, for the left child, $P(circle)$ is 7 out of 8 and $P(triangle)$ is 1 out of 8. Plugging these numbers into the entropy formula yields:

$$-1 * (0.875 \log_2(0.875) + 0.125 \log_2(0.125)) = 0.544$$

The first term is for the circles and the second term is for the triangles. For the right child, P(circle) is 2 out of 10 and P(triangle) is 8 out of 10. Plugging these into the entropy formula yields:

$$-1 * (0.200 \log_2(0.200) + 0.800 \log_2(0.800)) = 0.722$$

To calculate the total entropy of the system after the split, multiply the entropy of each node by the proportion of records that reach that node and add them up. In this example, 8 of 18 records are in the left child, and 10 of 18 in the right. The total entropy reduction or information gain due to the split works out to 0.643. This is the figure that would be used to compare this split with other candidates.

Information Gain Ratio

Measures of purity can run into trouble when the splitting methodology allows more than two splits. This was the case for ID3, a decision tree tool developed by Australian researcher J. Ross Quinlan in the 1980s that became part of several commercial data mining software packages. And, it was a particularly severe problem for ID3, because it placed each category into a separate child, resulting in nodes with many children. However, the same problem arises whenever a tree considers splits with different numbers of children. Just by breaking the larger data set into many small subsets, the number of classes represented in each node tends to go down, so each child increases in purity, even for a random split.

Professor Quinlan used entropy for ID3. The decrease in entropy due solely to the number of branches is called the *intrinsic information* of a split. For a random n-way split, the probability of each branch is `1/n`. Therefore, the entropy due solely to splitting from an n-way split is `n * 1/n log (1/n)` or `log(1/n)` (and a similar calculation would apply for Gini). Because of the intrinsic information of many-way splits, decision trees built using the entropy reduction splitting criterion without any correction for the intrinsic information due to the split tend to prefer many splits at a node. Bushy trees with many multiway splits are undesirable because these splits lead to small numbers of records in each node — a recipe for unstable models.

In reaction to this problem, C5.0 and other descendants of ID3 that once used information gain now use the ratio of the total information gain due to a proposed split to the intrinsic information attributable solely to the number of branches created as the criterion for evaluating proposed splits. This test reduces the tendency towards very bushy trees that was a problem in earlier decision tree software packages.

Chi-Square Test as a Splitting Criterion

As described in Chapter 4, the chi-square test is a test of statistical significance developed by the English statistician Karl Pearson in 1900. The chi-square value measures how likely or unlikely a split is. The higher the chi-square value, the less likely the split is due to chance — and not being due to chance means that the split is important.

Calculating the chi-square value relies on a simple formula. For a child node, the chi-square value is the sum of the squares of the differences between the *expected* and *observed* frequencies of each value of the target, divided by the expected frequency. The chi-square value of a split is simply the sum of the chi-square values of all the children — not the weighted average as with Gini and entropy. In common with other significance tests, it is a measure of the probability that an observed difference between samples could occur just by chance. When used to measure the purity of decision tree splits, higher values of chi-square mean that the variation is more significant, and not due merely to chance.

For example, suppose the target variable is a binary flag indicating whether or not customers continued their subscriptions at the end of the introductory offer period and the proposed split is on `acquisition channel`, a categorical variable with three classes: direct mail, outbound call, and e-mail. If the acquisition channel had no effect on renewal rate, the expected number of renewals in each class would be proportional to the number of customers acquired through that channel.

Each proposed split can be evaluated according to the following table:

Table 7-1: Contingency Table for Split Evaluation

	RESPONSE = 0	**RESPONSE = 1**
Left Child	# of 0s on left	# of 1s on left
Right Child	# of 0s on right	# of 1 on right

In a contingency table, such as this, any given record is counted exactly once. The chi-square value measures the probability that the contingency table could be due to chance. The idea is that a split due to chance is not interesting — some other split is more useful. This is measured by looking at the proportions of the target in the children. When they have similar proportions to their parent, then the split is probably due to chance and hence uninteresting. On the other hand, if the distribution of the response in the children differs from that of the parents, a very low probability exists that the split is due to chance and the split is likely to be useful.

Calculating the chi-square value only requires a bit of arithmetic. For each cell in the table, the chi-square test calculates the expected number of 0s and 1s. The chi-square value for each cell is calculated by subtracting the expected value from the observed value, squaring the result, and dividing by the expected number. The overall chi-square is the sum of all the cell chi-square contributions. As described in Chapter 4, the chi-square distribution provides a way to translate this chi-square score to a probability, although this is not necessary when used for decision trees. To measure the purity of a split in a decision tree, the score is sufficient. A high chi-square score means that the proposed split successfully splits the population into subpopulations with significantly different distributions.

Unlike the Gini and entropy measures, the chi-square value does not have a restricted range such as 0 to 1; it grows larger as the amount of data grows. Figure 7-8 graphs the chi-square value for a sample of 100 records, taken from a parent population that has equal numbers in each of two classes, as the number of elements in the first class ranges from 0 to 100.

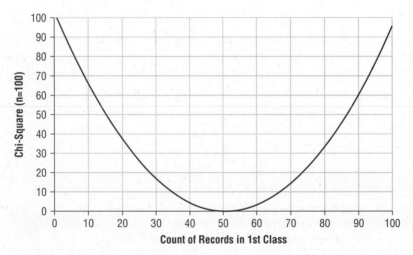

Figure 7-8: Chi-square is 0 when the sample distribution is the same as the population's.

The chi-square test gives its name to CHAID, a well-known decision tree algorithm first published by John A. Hartigan in 1975 and improved upon by Kass in 1980. The full acronym stands for Chi-square Automatic Interaction Detector. CHAID makes use of the chi-square test in several ways — first to merge classes that do not have significantly different effects on the target variable, then to choose a best split, and finally to decide whether it is worth performing any additional splits on a node.

Incremental Response as a Splitting Criterion

The splitting criteria described so far depend only on the target variable. This section discusses a different measure based on the idea of incremental response introduced in Chapter 5. When working with incremental response, there is a test group and a control group as well as responders and non-responders. Incremental response models attempt to isolate *persuadables* — the people most likely to be persuaded by an offer, rather than those who would respond anyway.

Modeling incremental response is different from modeling response. Response can be measured at the level of individuals, but incremental response cannot. A person either responds to an offer or not, but there is no way to measure how someone who was included in a marketing campaign would have behaved had they been left out.

In Chapter 5, the approach is to build two different response models — one for probability of response given treatment (the test group) and one for probability of response given no treatment (the control group). The incremental response is the difference between these two scores. Portrait Software has a clever alternative approach to modeling incremental response. The Portrait Software Uplift Optimizer™ builds a decision tree using the difference in response between the treated group and the control group as the splitting criterion using training records that have both a target variable, such as response or lack of response to an offer, and a field indicating whether the record is from the treatment group or the control group. The best split is the one that maximizes the difference in response between the two groups. The leaves of the resulting tree identify segments that are highly persuadable and segments that are not. There may even be segments that respond better when left untreated. The sidebar describes an application of this approach.

Reduction in Variance as a Splitting Criterion for Numeric Targets

The four previous splitting criteria all apply to categorical targets. When the target variable is numeric, one way to measure a good split is that such a split should reduce the variance of the target variable. Recall that variance is a measure of the extent to which values in a sample stay close to the average value. In a sample with low variance, most values are quite close to the average; in a sample with high variance, many values are quite far from the average.

Although the reduction in variance purity measure is meant for numeric targets, the circles and triangles shown earlier in Figure 7-5 can still be used to illustrate it by considering the circles to be 1 and the triangles to be 0. The average value in the parent node is clearly 0.5. Every one of the 18 observations differs from the mean by 0.5, so the variance is $(18 * 0.5^2) / 18 = 0.25$. After the split, the left child has seven circles and one triangle, so the node mean is 0.875. Seven of the observations differ from the mean value by 0.125 and one observation differs from the mean value by 0.875. In the right child, the two circles and 8 triangles have an average value of 0.2. The eight triangles differ from the average by 0.2 and the two triangles differ from the average by 0.8. So, the variance across both children is $(0.875^2 + 7 * 0.125^2 + 8*0.2^2 + 2*0.8^2) / 18 = 0.138$. The reduction in variance due to the split is $0.25 - 0.138 = 0.112$.

U.S. BANK IMPROVES INCREMENTAL RESPONSE

Headquartered in Minneapolis, U.S. Bank is one of the ten largest banks in the United States with 2,850 branches serving 15.8 million customers. They are true believers in the value of incremental response modeling to capture the true return on marketing dollars; consequently, their product managers' bonuses are based on it.

Back in the 1990s, they did what many of their competitors still do today — they built response models and hoped that high lift for the response model would yield incremental lift as well. Often, it did not. After a campaign, the people most likely to respond were not any *more* likely to respond than they were already. In the years since then, U.S. Bank has tried several approaches to modeling incremental response.

The Difference Model

The first approach taken by U.S. Bank was the one described in Chapter 5. Customers were scored using one model trained on response given inclusion in the campaign and another trained on a control group not included in the campaign. Customers were ranked on the difference between these scores. The difficulty with this approach is that the standard error in the difference of two scores is higher than the standard error of either of the scores alone, and the individual scores may themselves have high standard errors when based on small samples. If constructing good models were the only goal of the campaign, the solution would be to use large, equal-sized treatment and control groups. Unfortunately for modelers, the campaign's primary goal is to reach persuadable customers. Even in an enlightened company such as U.S. Bank, the modelers have to negotiate with marketing managers to get any control group at all for the top deciles and to be allowed to have any members of the lower deciles included in the campaign. As a result, the model for response given no treatment is starved for data in the top deciles and the model for response given treatment is starved for data in the low deciles.

The Matrix Model

U.S. Bank tried a cell-based approach. In cell-based models, customers are placed into segments according to which decile they fall in for each of the variables defining the cells. In a cell-based incremental response model, randomly selected members of each cell are included in a test campaign. The difference in response between those included and those excluded is recorded for each cell, and the cells with the greatest difference in response rate are targeted for the full campaign. U.S. Bank calls this approach the "matrix model." It served as the baseline "champion" for comparison with newer "challenger" models.

One challenge in constructing a cell-based model is deciding which variables should be used to define the cells. U.S. Bank's approach to that problem was essentially a manual decision tree. They tried binning each candidate variable in turn to find the one that produced the greatest difference in response between the treatment group and the control group. The two or three best variables by this measure were used to create the cells.

The Portrait Uplift Optimizer

U.S. Bank eventually settled on a software package that creates decision trees with splits based on incremental lift. They made a head-to-head comparison of the new tool with their home-grown matrix model on a campaign to cross-sell home equity lines of credit to existing customers. It was a bit like John Henry against the steam drill — the matrix model and manual cells were heroic efforts, but in the end they were beaten by modern technology. The Uplift Optimizer from Portrait Software uses a decision tree to choose the best variables based on incremental response. Like any decision tree, it finds the optimal points to split numeric variables rather than using arbitrary boundaries, such as deciles. It deals with the small sample problem, caused by the desire to not miss many persuadables, by using *bagging* and *boosting*. Bagging means combining the votes of several different models trained on the same data. Boosting takes this idea further, by building a second model trained on the examples that were misclassified by the first, and perhaps a third model trained on the mistakes of the second.

The following chart shows the challenger bested the champion, especially on the first three deciles — the ones slated to receive the mailing.

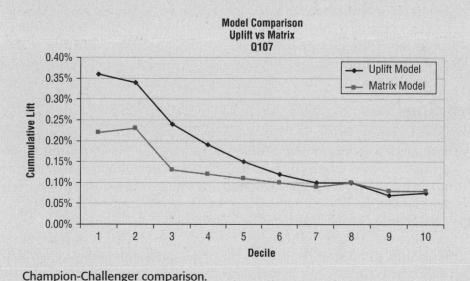

Champion-Challenger comparison.

F Test

Another split criterion that can be used for numeric target variables is the F test, named for another famous Englishman — the statistician, astronomer, and geneticist, Ronald. A. Fisher. Fisher and Pearson reportedly did not get along despite, or perhaps because of, the large overlap in their areas of interest. Fisher's test does for continuous variables what Pearson's chi-square test does for categorical variables. It provides a measure of the probability that samples with different means and variances are actually drawn from the same population.

A well-understood relationship exists between the variance of a sample and the variance of the population from which it was drawn. (In fact, as long as the samples are of reasonable size and randomly drawn from the population, sample variance is a good estimate of population variance; very small samples — with fewer than 30 or so observations — usually have higher variance than their corresponding populations.) The F test looks at the relationship between two estimates of the population variance — one derived by pooling all the samples and calculating the variance of the combined sample, and one derived from the between-sample variance calculated as the variance of the sample means. If the various samples are randomly drawn from the same population, these two estimates should agree closely.

The F score is the ratio of the two estimates. It is calculated by dividing the between-sample estimate by the pooled sample estimate. The larger the score, the less likely it is that the samples are all randomly drawn from the same population. In the decision tree context, a large F score indicates that a proposed split has successfully split the population into subpopulations with significantly different distributions.

Pruning

The basic algorithm for decision trees keeps growing the tree by splitting nodes as long as new splits create children that increase purity. Such a tree has been optimized for the training set, so eliminating any leaves would only increase the error rate of the tree on the training set. Does this imply that the full tree also does the best job on new data? Certainly not!

A decision tree algorithm makes its best split first, at the root node where there is a large number of records. As the nodes get smaller, idiosyncrasies of the particular training records at a node come to dominate the process. The smaller the nodes become, the greater the danger of overfitting. One way to avoid overfitting is to set a large minimum leaf size. Another approach is to allow the tree to grow as long as there are splits that appear to be significant on the training data and then eliminate the splits that prove to be unstable by cutting away leaves through a process called *pruning*. Three approaches to pruning are discussed next. These are not the only possible pruning strategies, but the first two covered here are commonly implemented, and the third one ought to be.

The CART Pruning Algorithm

CART (Classification and Regression Trees) is a popular decision tree algorithm first published by Leo Breiman, Jerome Friedman, Richard Olshen, and Charles Stone in 1984. The CART algorithm grows binary trees and continues splitting as long as new splits can be found that increase purity. As illustrated in Figure 7-9, inside a complex tree are many simpler subtrees, each of which represents a different trade-off between model complexity and accuracy. The CART algorithm identifies a set of such subtrees as candidate models. These candidate subtrees are applied to the validation set, and the tree with the lowest validation set misclassification rate (or average squared error for a numeric target) is selected as the final model.

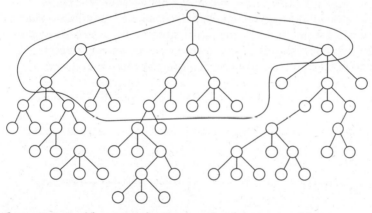

Figure 7-9: Inside a complex tree are simpler, more stable trees.

Creating Candidate Subtrees

The CART algorithm identifies candidate subtrees through a process of repeated pruning. The goal is to prune first those branches providing the least additional predictive power per leaf. To identify these least useful branches, CART relies on a concept called the *adjusted error rate*. This is a measure that increases each node's misclassification rate or mean squared error on the training set by imposing a complexity penalty based on the number of leaves in the tree. The adjusted error is used to identify weak branches (those whose error is not low enough to overcome the penalty) and mark them for pruning.

The formula for the adjusted error rate is:

$$AE(T) = E(T) + \alpha leaf\_count(T)$$

Where α is an adjustment factor that is increased in gradual steps to create new subtrees. When α is 0, the adjusted error rate equals the error rate. The algorithm continues to find trees by adjusting α and pruning back one node at a time, creating a sequence of trees, α_1, α_2, and so on, each with fewer and fewer leaves. The process ends when the tree has been pruned all the way down to the root node. Each of the resulting subtrees (sometimes called the *alphas*) is a candidate to be the final model. Notice that all the candidates contain the root node and the largest candidate is the entire tree.

COMPARING MISCLASSIFICATION RATES ON TRAINING AND VALIDATION SETS

The error rate on the validation set should be larger than the error rate on the training set, because the training set was used to build the rules in the model. A large difference in the misclassification error rate, however, is a symptom of an unstable model. This difference can show up in several ways as shown by the following three graphs. The graphs represent the percent of records correctly classified by the candidate models in a decision tree. Candidate sub-trees with fewer nodes are on the left; those with more nodes are on the right.

As expected, the first chart shows the candidate trees performing better and better on the training set as the trees have more and more nodes — the training process stops when the performance no longer improves. On the validation set, however, the candidate trees reach a peak and then the performance starts to decline as the trees get larger. The optimal tree is the one that works best on the validation set, and the choice is easy because the peak is well-defined.

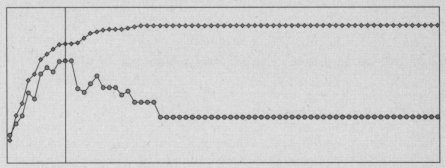

This chart shows a clear inflection point in the graph of the percent correctly classified in the validation set.

Sometimes, though, there is no clear demarcation point. That is, the performance of the candidate models on the validation set never quite reaches a maximum as the trees get larger. In this case, the pruning algorithm chooses the entire tree (the largest possible subtree), as shown.

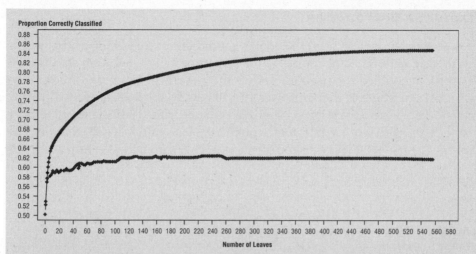

In this chart, the percent correctly classified in the validation set levels off early and remains far below the percent correctly classified in the training set.

The final example is perhaps the most interesting, because the results on the validation set become unstable as the candidate trees become larger. The cause of the instability is that the leaves are too small. In this tree, there is an example of a leaf that has three records from the training set and all three have a target value of 1 — a perfect leaf. However, in the validation set, the one record that falls there has the value 0. The leaf is 100 percent wrong. As the tree grows more complex, more of these too-small leaves are included, resulting in the instability shown:

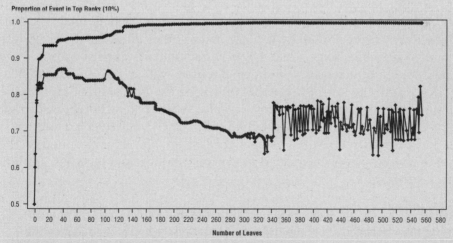

In this chart, the percent correctly classified on the validation set decreases with the complexity of the tree and eventually becomes chaotic.

The last two figures are examples of unstable models. The simplest way to avoid instability of this sort is to ensure that leaves are not allowed to become too small.

Picking the Best Subtree

The next step is to select, from the pool of candidate subtrees, the one that works best on new data. That, of course, is the purpose of the validation set. Each of the candidate subtrees is used to classify the records or estimate values in the validation set. The tree that performs this task with the lowest overall error is declared the winner. The winning subtree has been pruned sufficiently to remove the effects of overtraining, but not so much as to lose valuable information. The graph in Figure 7-10 illustrates the effect of pruning on classification accuracy.

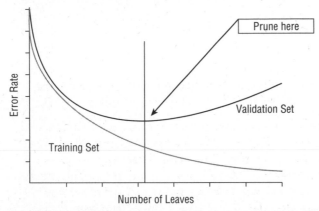

Figure 7-10: Pruning chooses the tree whose miscalculation rate is minimized on the validation set.

The winning subtree is selected on the basis of its overall error when applied to the validation set. But, while one expects that the selected subtree will continue to be the best model when applied to other datasets, the error rate that caused it to be selected may slightly overstate its effectiveness. There may be many subtrees that all perform about as well as the one selected. To a certain extent, the one of these that delivered the lowest error rate on the validation set may simply have "gotten lucky" with that particular collection of records. For that reason, as explained in Chapter 5, the selected subtree is applied to a third preclassified dataset, the test set. The error obtained on the test set is used to predict expected performance of the model when applied to unclassified data.

> **WARNING**   Do not evaluate the performance of a model by its lift or error rate on the validation set or the training set. Both have had a hand in creating the model and so overstate the model's accuracy. Instead, measure the model's accuracy on a test set drawn from the same population as the training and validation sets, but not used in any way to create the model.

Because this pruning algorithm is based solely on the misclassification rate, without taking the probability of each classification into account, it replaces any subtree whose leaves all make the same classification with a common parent that also makes that classification. In applications where the goal is to select a small proportion of the records (the top 1 percent or 10 percent, for example), this pruning algorithm may hurt the performance of the tree, because it may remove leaves that contain a very high proportion of the target class.

WARNING Pruning sometimes removes leaves that should be kept or fails to remove leaves that should be trimmed. The CART pruning algorithm removes children that result in the same classification even when one child is much purer than the other. For some applications, such as when good lift in the highest decile is more important than the overall error rate, retaining such splits to preserve the rule associated with the purer child is preferable. Other pruning algorithms leave some nodes where the distribution of the target differs significantly from the training set to the validation set. It is therefore sometimes advisable to prune by hand.

Pessimistic Pruning: The C5.0 Pruning Algorithm

C5.0 is a more recent version of the decision-tree algorithm that J. Ross Quinlan has been evolving and refining for many years. An earlier version, ID3, published in 1986, was very influential in the field of machine learning and its successors are used in several commercial data mining products.

The trees grown by C5.0 are similar to those grown by CART (although unlike CART, C5.0 makes multiway splits on categorical variables). Like CART, the C5.0 algorithm first grows an overfit tree and then prunes it back to create a more stable model. The pruning strategy is quite different because C5.0 does not make use of a validation set to choose from among candidate subtrees. The same data used to grow the tree is also used to decide how the tree should be pruned. This may reflect the algorithm's origins in the academic world, where in the past, university researchers had a hard time getting their hands on substantial quantities of real data to use for training sets. Consequently, they spent much time and effort trying to coax the last few drops of information from their impoverished datasets — a problem that data miners in the business world do not face.

C5.0 prunes the tree by measuring each node's error on the training data and assuming that the error on unseen data would be substantially worse. The algorithm treats the data as if it resulted from a series of trials, each of which can have one of two possible results. (Heads or tails is the usual example.) As it happens, mathematicians have been studying this particular situation since at least 1713, the year that Jacob Bernoulli's famous binomial formula was posthumously published. So, well-known formulas exist for determining what it means to have observed E occurrences of some event, such as the number of errors, in N trials.

In particular, a formula exists which, for a given confidence level and size of a node, gives the confidence interval — the range of expected numbers of errors. C5.0 assumes that the observed number of errors on the training data is the low end of this range; it then calculates the corresponding number of errors at the high end of the range. When the high-end estimate of the error at a node is less than the estimate for the error of its children, the children are pruned.

Stability-Based Pruning

The pruning algorithms used by CART and C5.0 (and indeed by all the commercial decision tree tools that the authors have used) have a problem. They fail to prune some nodes that are clearly unstable. The split highlighted in Figure 7-11 is a good example. The numbers on the left side of each node show what is happening on the training set. The numbers on the right side of each node show what is happening on the validation set. This particular tree is meant to identify churners. When only the training data is taken into consideration, the highlighted branch seems to do very well; the concentration of churners rises from 58.0 percent to 70.9 percent. Unfortunately, when the very same rule is applied to the validation set, the concentration of churners actually *decreases* from 56.6 percent to 52 percent.

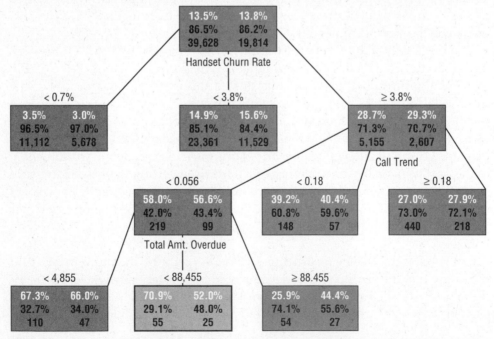

Figure 7-11: An unstable split produces very different distributions on the training and validation sets.

Stable models make consistent predictions on previously unseen records. Any rule that cannot achieve that goal should be eliminated from the model. Many data mining tools allow the user to prune a decision tree manually. This facility is useful, but the authors look forward to data mining software that provides automatic stability-based pruning as an option. Such software would need to have a less subjective criterion for rejecting a split than "the distribution of the validation set results looks different from the distribution of the training set results." A test of statistical significance, such as the chi-square test would be used. The split would be pruned when the confidence level is less than some user-defined threshold, so only splits that are, say, 95 percent confident on the validation set would remain.

> **WARNING** Small nodes cause big problems. A common cause of unstable decision tree models is allowing nodes with too few records. Most decision tree tools allow the user to set a minimum node size. As a general rule, nodes that receive fewer than about 100 training set records are likely to be unstable.

Extracting Rules from Trees

When a decision tree is used primarily to generate scores, one can easily forget that a decision tree is actually a collection of rules. If one of the purposes of the data mining effort is to gain understanding of the problem domain, reducing the huge tangle of rules in a decision tree to a smaller, more comprehensible collection can be useful.

Other situations exist where the desired output is a set of rules. In *Mastering Data Mining* (Wiley 2000), the authors describe the application of decision trees to an industrial process improvement problem, namely the prevention of a certain type of printing defect. In that case, the end product of the data mining project was a small collection of simple rules that could be posted on the wall next to each press.

When a decision tree is used for producing scores, having a large number of leaves is advantageous because each leaf generates a different score. When the object is to generate rules, fewer rules may be better. Fortunately, it is often possible to collapse a complex tree into a smaller set of rules.

As a first step, any subtree where all leaves have the same label can be replaced by its parent node without changing the way anything is classified. C5.0 includes a rule generator that goes further; it is willing to sacrifice some classification accuracy to reduce the number of rules. It does so by removing clauses, then comparing the predicted error rate of the new, briefer rule to that of the original using the same pessimistic error rate assumption described earlier in the pessimistic pruning section. Often, the rules for several different leaves generalize to the same rule, so this process results in fewer rules than the decision tree had leaves.

In the decision tree, every record ends up at exactly one leaf, so every record has a definitive classification. After the rule-generalization process, however, there may be rules that are not mutually exclusive and records that are not covered by any rule. Simply picking one rule when more than one is applicable can solve the first problem. The second problem requires the introduction of a default class assigned to any record not covered by any of the rules. Typically, the most frequently occurring class is chosen as the default.

After it has created a set of generalized rules, C5.0 groups the rules for each class and eliminates those that do not contribute much to the overall accuracy of the rule set. The end result is a small number of hopefully easy-to-understand rules.

Decision Tree Variations

Oak, ash, maple, birch, pine, spruce — real trees come in many varieties and so do decision trees. In addition to named algorithms such as CART, CHAID, and C5.0, there are countless other ways of combining split evaluation criteria, pruning strategies, and other algorithmic choices. This section introduces a few of the many variations.

Multiway Splits

So far, all the trees in the chapter have nodes with exactly two children. In such trees, each node represents a yes-or-no question, whose answer determines by which of two paths a record proceeds to the next level of the tree. Because any multiway split can be expressed as a series of binary splits, there is no real need for trees with higher branching factors. Nevertheless, many data mining tools are capable of producing trees with more than two branches. For example, some decision tree algorithms split on categorical variables by creating a branch for each class, leading to trees with differing numbers of branches at different nodes. Figure 7-12 shows a tree that includes a five-way split on `tenure` and both two-way and three-way splits on `credit class`. This tree was built on the same data and the same table as used earlier in Figure 7-1. The tree with two-way splits performed better than the tree with five-way splits when applied to a test data set. This is probably because after the five-way split on tenure, no further splits were found for most tenure ranges.

WARNING   No relationship exists between the number of branches allowed at a node and the number of classes in the target variable. A binary tree (that is, one with two-way splits) can be used to classify records into any number of categories, and a tree with multiway splits can be used to classify a binary target variable.

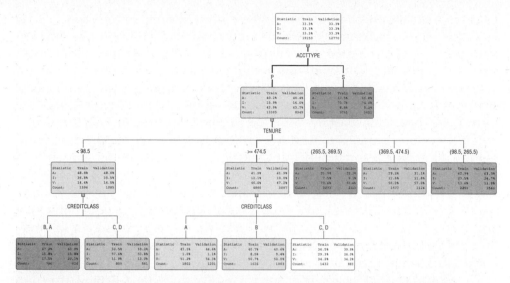

Figure 7-12: This tree with multiway splits does not perform as well as the binary tree in Figure 7-1.

Splitting on More Than One Field at a Time

Most decision tree algorithms test a single variable to perform each split. This approach can be problematic for several reasons, not least of which is that it can lead to trees with more nodes than necessary. Extra nodes are cause for concern because only the training records that arrive at a given node are available for inducing the subtree below it. The fewer training examples per node, the less stable the resulting model.

Suppose that you are interested in a condition for which both age and gender are important indicators. If the root node split is on age, then each child node contains only about half the women. If the initial split is on gender, then each child node contains only about half the old folks.

Several algorithms have been developed to allow multiple attributes to be used in combination to form the splitter. One technique forms Boolean conjunctions of features to reduce the complexity of the tree. After finding the feature that forms the best split, the algorithm looks for the feature which, when combined with the feature chosen first, does the best job of improving the split. Features continue to be added as long as they cause a statistically significant improvement in the resulting split.

Creating Nonrectangular Boxes

Classification problems are sometimes presented in geometric terms. This way of thinking is especially natural for datasets having continuous variables for all fields. In this interpretation, each record is a point in a multidimensional space. Each field represents the position of the record along one axis of the space. Decision trees are a way of carving the space into regions, each of which can be labeled with a class. Any new record that falls into one of the regions is classified accordingly.

Traditional decision trees, which test the value of a single field at each node, can only form rectangular regions. In a two-dimensional space, a test of the form Y less than some constant forms a region bounded by a line perpendicular to the Y axis and parallel to the X axis. Different values for the constant cause the line to move up and down, but the line remains horizontal. Similarly, in a space of higher dimensionality, a test on a single field defines a hyperplane that is perpendicular to the axis represented by the field used in the test and parallel to all the other axes. In a two-dimensional space, with only horizontal and vertical lines to work with, the resulting regions are rectangular. In three-dimensional space, the corresponding shapes are rectangular solids, and in any multidimensional space, they are hyper-rectangles.

The problem is that some things don't fit neatly into rectangular boxes. Figure 7-13 illustrates the problem: The two regions are really divided by a diagonal line; it takes a deep tree to generate enough rectangles to approximate it adequately.

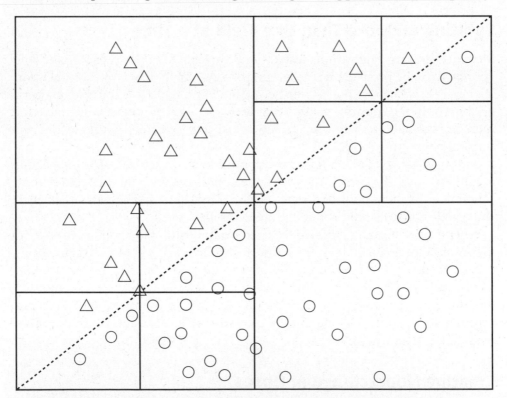

Figure 7-13: The upper-left and lower-right quadrants are easily classified, whereas the other two quadrants must be carved into many small boxes to approximate the boundary between regions.

   In this case, the true solution can be found easily by allowing linear combinations of the attributes to be considered. Some software packages attempt to tilt the hyperplanes by basing their splits on a weighted sum of the values of the fields. A variety of hill-climbing approaches exist for optimizing the weights. This process of searching for a hyperplane that separates two classes is shared with another data mining technique that has generated a lot of excitement in academic circles, *support vector machines*. Although support vector machines have been around since 1995, they have been slow to catch on with practitioners in the business world. The sidebar provides a brief introduction.

SUPPORT VECTOR MACHINES

Support vector machines are a geometric method of separating two classes (responders and nonresponders, for example) by finding the best hyperplane that puts one class above it and the other below. In the very unlikely case that the two classes happen to be entirely separable by a line, this is easy. The following figure shows such a case in three dimensions. A hyperplane that separates the classes is called a *decision surface*. The figure shows a two-dimensional decision surface separating points in three dimensions.

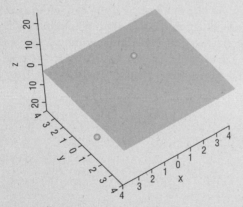

A two-dimensional plane separating points in three dimensional space.

The decision surface has one fewer dimensions than the data it separates. The split at a decision tree node is an example of the simplest case. Because decision trees split on only one field at a time, the decision "surface" is a single point. Every value on one side of the point goes one way, and every value on the other side goes the other way.

   The next figure shows two classes (represented by the noughts and crosses of tic-tac-toe) on a two-dimensional plane. The line separating them is the optimal decision surface. It is optimal because it maximizes the distance from the decision surface to the boundaries of the two classes. The boundary lines are called *supporting hyperplanes* and the data points on these boundaries

Continued

SUPPORT VECTOR MACHINES *(continued)*

are the *support vectors* that give the technique its name. The distance from one supporting hyperplane to the other is called the *margin*. The support vector machine algorithm finds the decision surface that maximizes the margin.

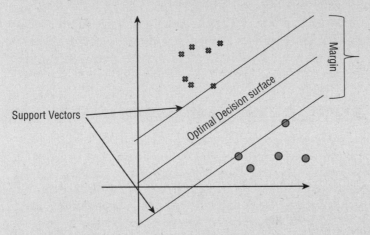

A one-dimensional line separating points on a two-dimensional plane.

The data points shown in the figure above were carefully chosen to make the idea seem easy. Real-life data is unlikely to be so kind. The following figure shows a more usual and difficult situation in two dimensions. Here, even though visually a clear boundary exists between the classes, there is obviously no straight line that can separate the points on this two-dimensional plane.

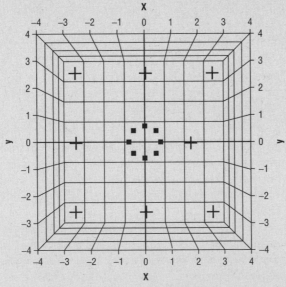

On the plane, boundary between the two classes is not a straight line.

The central insight of support vector machines is to think of the observed two-dimensional data as a projection onto the two-dimensional plane of points that really exist in three dimensions. Suppose you could come up with a transformation on the input variables from two dimensions to three that caused all the crosses to float up above the noughts. Finding a decision surface to separate the classes along the new z axis would then be easy. Such a function is called a *kernel function*. In the following figure, a kernel function has been applied that maps every point (x,y) to (x²,y²,xy). After this transformation, finding a decision surface is easy. The hard part is choosing the kernel function and coming up with the right parameters for it. This is an optimization task much like finding the right weights for a neural network.

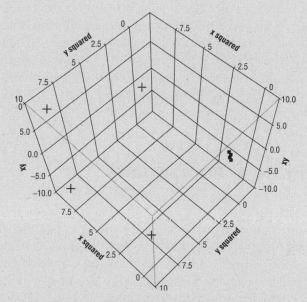

After application of the kernel function, the two classes are easily separated.

Assessing the Quality of a Decision Tree

The effectiveness of a decision tree, taken as a whole, is determined by applying it to the test set — a collection of records not used to build the tree — and observing the percentage classified correctly by a classification tree, or a measure such as the average squared error for a regression tree. This provides an error measure for the tree as a whole, but it is also important to pay attention to the quality of the individual branches of the tree.

At each node, you can measure:

- The number of records entering the node
- The proportion of records in each class or the average value of the target variable
- How those records would be scored if this were a leaf node
- The percentage of records classified correctly or the average squared error
- The difference in distribution between the training set and the test set

Each path through the tree represents a rule, and some rules are better than others.

In the discussion so far, error has been the sole measure for evaluating the fitness of rules and subtrees. In many applications, however, the costs of misclassification vary from class to class. Certainly, in a medical diagnosis, a false negative can be more harmful than a false positive; a scary Pap smear result that, on further investigation, proves to have been a false positive, is much preferable to an undetected cancer. A cost function multiplies the probability of misclassification by a weight indicating the cost of that misclassification. Several tools allow the use of such a cost function instead of a purity measure for building decision trees.

When Are Decision Trees Appropriate?

There is often a trade-off between model accuracy and model transparency. In some applications, the accuracy of a classification or prediction is the only thing that matters; if a direct mail firm obtains a model that can accurately predict which members of a prospect pool are most likely to respond to a certain solicitation, the firm may not care how or why the model works. In other situations, the ability to explain the reason for a decision is crucial. In insurance underwriting, for example, there are legal prohibitions against discrimination based on certain variables. An insurance company could find itself in the position of having to demonstrate to a regulator or court of law that it has not used illegal discriminatory practices in granting or denying coverage. Similarly, hearing that an application for credit has been denied on the basis of a computer-generated rule (such as income below some threshold and number of existing revolving accounts greater than some other threshold) is more acceptable to both the loan officer and the credit applicant than hearing that the application has been rejected for unexplained reasons.

Decision trees have been used in some very imaginative ways. The final case study in this chapter describes how decision trees were used to simulate the operation of an industrial coffee roasting plant. The case study is based on discussions with Marc Goodman and on his 1995 doctoral dissertation. The simulation can be run to project the values of all variables into the future, to be sure that the roasting process stays within acceptable bounds to ensure quality. One of the most interesting things about the case study is that a simulator requires building a separate model for the next value of each input, so variables are both inputs and targets, albeit for different models.

Case Study: Process Control in a Coffee Roasting Plant

Nestlé, one of the largest food and beverages companies in the world, uses a number of continuous-feed coffee roasters to produce a variety of coffee products. Each of these products has a "recipe" that specifies target values for a plethora of roaster variables such as the temperature of the air at various exhaust points, the speed of various fans, the rate that gas is burned, the amount of water introduced to quench the beans, and the positions of various flaps and valves. There are a lot of ways for things to go wrong when roasting coffee, ranging from a roast coming out too light in color to a costly and damaging roaster fire. A bad batch of roasted coffee wastes the beans and incurs a cost; damage to equipment is even more expensive.

To help operators keep the roaster running properly, data is collected from about 60 sensors. Every 30 seconds, this data, along with control information, is written to a log and made available to operators in the form of graphs. The project described here took place at a Nestlé research laboratory in York, England. Nestlé built a coffee roaster simulation based on the sensor logs.

Goals for the Simulator

Nestlé saw several ways that a coffee roaster simulator could improve its processes:

- By using the simulator to try out new recipes, a large number of new recipes could be evaluated without interrupting production. Furthermore, recipes that might lead to roaster fires or other damage could be eliminated in advance.

- The simulator could be used to train new operators and expose them to routine problems and their solutions. Using the simulator, operators could try out different approaches to resolving a problem.

- The simulator could track the operation of the actual roaster and project it several minutes into the future. When the simulation ran into a problem, an alert could be generated while the operators still had time to avert trouble.

Fortunately, Nestlé was already collecting data at half-minute intervals, which could be used to build the simulator.

Building a Roaster Simulation

A model set of 34,000 cases was created from the historical log data. Each case consisted of a set of measurements on the roaster along with the same measurements 30 seconds later. Notice that the same data might be used as targets for one case, and then, for the next case, might be the inputs (where the targets come 30 seconds later).

This training set is more complicated than the training sets we have been working with, because multiple targets exist — all the measurements 30 seconds later. The solution is to build a separate model for each measurement. Each model takes the input from the earlier part of the case, and the target from the later period, as shown in Figure 7-14:

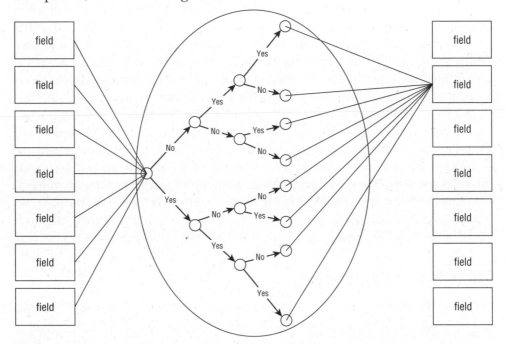

Figure 7-14: A decision tree uses values from one snapshot to create the next snapshot in time.

The entire set of models was trained, resulting in a set of models that takes the input measurements for the roaster and produces estimates of what happens 30 seconds later.

Evaluation of the Roaster Simulation

The simulation was then evaluated using a test set of around 40,000 additional cases that had not been part of the training set. For each case in the test set, the simulator generated projected snapshots 60 steps into the future (that is, 30 minutes into the future). At each step the projected values of all variables were compared against the actual values. As expected, the size of the error increases with time. For example, the error rate for product temperature turned out to be 2/3°C per minute of projection, but even 30 minutes into the future the simulator was considerably better than random guessing.

The roaster simulator turned out to be more accurate than all but the most experienced operators at projecting trends, and even the most experienced operators were able to do a better job with the aid of the simulator. Operators enjoyed using the simulator and reported that it gave them new insight into corrective actions.

Lessons Learned

Decision-tree methods have wide applicability for data exploration, classification, and selecting important variables. They can also be used for estimating continuous values although they are rarely the first choice because decision trees generate "lumpy" estimates — all records reaching the same leaf are assigned the same estimated value. They are a good choice when the data mining task is classification of records or prediction of discrete outcomes. Use decision trees when your goal is to assign each record to one of a few broad categories.

Decision trees are also a natural choice when the goal is to generate understandable and explainable rules. The ability of decision trees to generate rules that can be translated into comprehensible natural language or SQL is one of the greatest strengths of the technique. Even in complex decision trees, following any one path through the tree to a particular leaf is generally fairly easy, so the explanation for any particular classification or prediction is relatively straightforward.

Decision trees are grown using a recursive algorithm that evaluates all values of all inputs to find the split that causes the greatest increase in purity in the children. The same thing happens again inside each child. The process continues until no more splits can be found or some other limit is reached. The tree is then pruned to remove unstable branches. Several tests are used as splitting criteria, including the chi-square test for categorical targets and the F test for numeric targets.

Decision trees require less data preparation than many other techniques because they are equally adept at handling continuous and categorical variables. Categorical variables, which pose problems for neural networks and statistical techniques, are split by forming groups of classes. Continuous variables are split by dividing their range of values. Because decision trees do not make use of the actual values of numeric variables, they are not sensitive to outliers and skewed distributions. Missing values, which cannot be handled by many data mining techniques, cause no problems for decision trees and may even appear in splitting rules.

This robustness comes at the cost of throwing away some of the information that is available in the training data, so a well-tuned neural network or regression model often makes better use of the same fields than a decision tree. For that reason, decision trees are often used to pick a good set of variables to be used as inputs to another modeling technique. Time-oriented data does require a lot of data preparation. Time series data must be enhanced so that trends and sequential patterns are made visible.

Decision trees reveal so much about the data to which they are applied that the authors often make use of them in the early phases of a data mining project even when the final models are to be created using some other technique.

CHAPTER 8

Artificial Neural Networks

Neural networks — the "artificial" is usually dropped — are a class of powerful, flexible, general-purpose techniques readily applied to prediction, estimation, and classification problems. Applications include detecting fraudulent credit card transactions, modeling financial time series, recognizing handwritten numbers and letters, and estimating real estate values.

The first artificial neural networks were conscious attempts to simulate the workings of biological neural networks using digital computers. In addition to biologists interested in the workings of the nervous system, early artificial intelligence researchers saw neural networks as a way to endow computers with the ability to learn. The human brain makes generalizing from experience possible for people; computers, on the other hand, usually excel at following explicit instructions over and over. The appeal of neural networks is that they bridge this gap by modeling, on a digital computer, the neural connections in human brains. When used in well-defined domains, their ability to generalize and learn from data mimics, in some sense, the human ability to learn from experience.

Because of this history, neural networks researchers originally used terminology from biology and machine learning that was quite dissimilar to the terminology used in statistical modeling; it took some time before neural networks were recognized as a useful modeling method by statisticians. In the past twenty years, the development of neural networks as a modeling tool has diverged from the effort to understand and simulate biological neural networks.

This chapter starts with a brief review of the history of artificial neural networks and the biological model that motivated their invention. It then leaves biology behind to describe what goes on inside a single artificial neuron. Next, without going into the details of how a neural network is constructed and trained, it shows how very simple neural networks called *perceptrons* can solve some very simple problems. After demonstrating that neural networks can solve these "toy" problems, the chapter introduces an early case history of using neural networks for real estate appraisal to show how neural networks are applied to practical business problems. The real estate appraisal example helps to explain technical details of how neural networks are trained using *back propagation* and other optimization techniques. The chapter covers two of the most important types of neural network. The first type, *multilayer perceptrons*, is made up of units that are somewhat analogous to biological neurons. The second type, *radial basis function networks*, has a similar topology, but the individual units are quite different.

The chapter ends with a look at some of the practical issues that arise when using neural networks, including data preparation needs and the vexing question of whether neural network models can be explained. Neural networks are best approached as black boxes with internal workings as mysterious as the workings of our brains. Like the responses of the Oracle at Delphi revered by the ancient Greeks, the answers produced by neural networks are often correct, but without an explanation. The results have business value — in many cases, being right is more important than understanding why.

A Bit of History

The original work on the functioning of neurons — biological neurons — took place in the 1930s and 1940s, before digital computers even existed. In 1943, Warren McCulloch, a neurophysiologist at Yale University, and Walter Pitts, a logician, postulated a simple model to explain how biological neurons work and published it in a paper called "A Logical Calculus of the Ideas Immanent in Nervous Activity." Although their focus was on understanding the anatomy of the brain, it turned out that this model provided inspiration for the field of artificial intelligence and would eventually provide a new approach to solving certain problems outside the realm of neurobiology.

In the 1950s, when digital computers first became available, computer scientists implemented models called perceptrons based on the work of McCulloch and Pitts. An example of a problem solved by these early networks was how to balance a broom standing upright on a moving cart by controlling the motions of the cart back and forth. As the broom starts falling to the left, the cart learns to move to the left to keep the broom upright. Although there were some limited successes with perceptrons in the laboratory, the results were disappointing as a general method for solving problems.

One reason for the limited usefulness of early neural networks is that most powerful computers of that era had less computing power than a typical microwave oven. Another reason was that these simple networks had theoretical deficiencies, as shown by Seymour Papert and Marvin Minsky, two professors at the Massachusetts Institute of Technology. In their book, *Perceptrons*, published in 1969, they showed that as classifiers, single-layer perceptrons only work when the classes are linearly separable. See the sidebar "What a Single-Layer Perceptron Can and Cannot Do" for more discussion.

Although they themselves did not say so, the deficiencies that Papert and Minsky demonstrated in simple perceptrons were widely assumed to apply to the more general class of neural network models as well. This mistaken belief contributed to a drastic decline in funding for the study of neural networks during the 1970s. Research did not stop completely, however. In 1974, Paul Werbos developed a learning method called *backpropagation of error* for his Harvard Ph.D. thesis. This training method, combined with the realization that multi-layer perceptrons could surmount many of the shortcomings of the single-layer variety, sparked a renaissance in neural network research in the 1980s, led by John Hopfield of the California Institute of Technology. This led to the widespread adoption of neural networks well beyond the campuses of these famous universities. Also in the early 1980s, Teuvo Kohonen developed self-organizing maps, a type of neural network used for automatic cluster detection. Chapter 14 describes self-organizing maps.

At the same time that researchers in artificial intelligence were developing neural networks as a model of biological activity, statisticians were taking advantage of computers to extend the capabilities of statistical methods. By the mid-1990s, the two strands of research merged, although that required overcoming some cultural barriers.

The Biological Model

The basic idea behind a neural network, whether natural or artificial, is that very complex behavior can arise from relatively simple units if enough of them are acting in concert. It is worth learning just a little bit about biological neural networks in order to understand the analogies between artificial neural nets and the naturally occurring ones that inspired them.

WHAT A SINGLE-LAYER PERCEPTRON CAN AND CANNOT DO

One of the most damning results regarding single-layer perceptrons is that they cannot implement XOR, a function dearly beloved by computer scientists. The XOR function takes two Boolean inputs (TRUE or FALSE), and returns TRUE when exactly one of the inputs is TRUE. Following the usual practice in computer science, in these examples, TRUE is represented by 1, and FALSE is represented by 0. Having a numeric representation for inputs to a perceptron is important because the inputs are multiplied by weights and added together.

The following figure shows the function tables for three logical functions: AND, OR, and XOR. The first two can be represented by the simplest imaginable neural network, a single-layer perceptron. Each network is actually just a single neuron that combines two inputs by summing them. Each input is either a 1 or a 0. In the biological model, the sum is compared to a threshold value to decide whether the neuron will fire, meaning that the logical comparison of the inputs is TRUE, or not fire, meaning that the logical comparison of the inputs is FALSE. In the digital model, there is always an output. It is either 1 for TRUE or 0 for FALSE. The two formulations are equivalent.

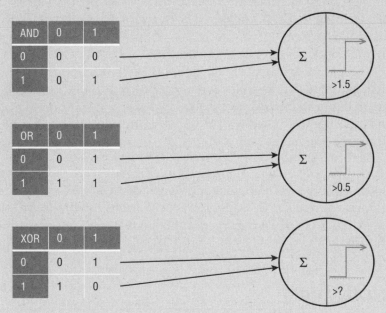

The XOR function cannot be implemented by a single-layer perceptron.

For logical AND, a threshold of 1.5 works because the sum of two Boolean inputs, represented by 1 and 0, has a sum greater than 1.5 only when both inputs are 1. For logical OR, a threshold of 0.5 works because the sum of two Boolean inputs is always greater than 0.5 unless both inputs are 0.

There is no threshold for the sum of two Boolean inputs that correctly implements XOR because the neuron should fire when the sum is 1, but not when it is 0 or 2.

The solution is to use three nodes in two layers. The first layer consists of two neurons, one neuron to compute the OR value and another to compute the AND value. The second layer combines these two outputs to compute XOR. The trick is to have the combining node put a negative weight on the input coming from the AND node. That way, it is easy to choose a threshold such that the output neuron never fires if AND is TRUE, but may or may not fire when AND is FALSE, depending on whether OR is TRUE.

The following figure shows a two-layer perceptron that implements the XOR function. Here the weights are shown. All are set to 1 for the first layer, but for the second layer, the input coming from the AND node is set to –1. When AND is TRUE, the weighted sum of the two inputs to the XOR node can never be greater than 0. When AND is FALSE, the weighted sum will be 1 when OR is TRUE and 0 when OR is FALSE — exactly the right results for XOR. In conclusion, although single-layer perceptrons are unable to represent a large class of fairly simple functions, adding a second layer solves the problem.

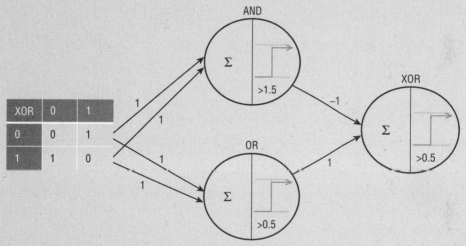

The XOR function is easily implemented by a two-layer perceptron.

The Biological Neuron

A neuron is a single cell that is specialized for communicating with other, similar cells. Figure 8-1 is a simplified schematic view of a neuron. Neurons communicate with other neurons using both chemical and electrical signals. The chemical communication is accomplished using neurotransmitters, some of which stimulate, and some of which inhibit, activity in the receiving neuron. Chemical signals pass from neuron to neuron across small synaptic gaps between adjoining cells. The electrical communication is more direct; the electrical synapses directly connect the axon of one neuron to one of many dendrites of another.

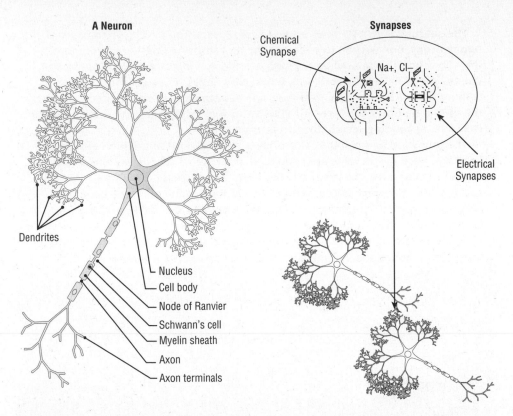

Figure 8-1: A neuron combines input signals from many other neurons to produce an output signal.

A typical neuron in a human brain receives inputs from between 1,000 and 10,000 upstream neurons through the electrical and chemical synapses at its dendrites. These signals, some of which increase and some of which decrease the excitement level of the cell, are relayed to the cell body where they are combined. When the resulting degree of stimulation is greater than the cell's activation threshold, the neuron "fires." That is, it sends an electric signal, through its axon, to its downstream neighbors.

The Biological Input Layer

The input layer of the biological neural network consists of specialized neurons that receive their inputs directly from the environment, rather than from upstream neurons. Examples include the receptor cells of the retina, which are sensitive to light of various wavelengths; the receptor cells of the tongue and nose, which are sensitive to the presence of particular molecules; and the audio receptors of the inner ear, which are sensitive to vibrations of various frequencies. These receptor cells fire when the particular stimuli they have evolved to detect are present. This is how information enters the biological neural network for processing.

The Biological Output Layer

The axons of most neurons relay their signal to other neurons, but some neurons are connected to cells of other types — muscle cells for instance. Muscles react to these signals from the nervous system by contracting. This output layer allows the neural network to cause the body in which it is embedded to turn to get a closer look at something, increase the volume on the radio or, for that matter, breathe in or breathe out.

Neural Networks and Artificial Intelligence

Biological neural networks perform many feats that would clearly be useful to emulate in a robot or intelligent machine. One such feat is to combine information from many specialized systems that are dedicated to recognizing particular patterns. There are neurons within the visual system of a frog that fire in response to fly-like movements, and others that fire in response to things about the size of a fly. These signals are among the inputs to neurons that fire when both fly-like size and fly-like movement is present, causing the frog to stick out its sticky tongue to catch the fly.

Another remarkable feat performed by biological neural networks is learning from experience. A cat is not born knowing the sound that a can of cat food makes when opened, but with its 300,000,000-neuron network, it soon learns. People, with our 100,000,000,000-neuron networks, can learn to speak, read, write, compose music, and ride bicycles. If we want computers to be able to do the same, why not use a similar solution?

Well, lots of reasons, actually. One is that the artificial neural networks developed up to now are far smaller and far simpler than those found in the brain of a person or cat. Even an ant has 10,000 neurons, and ants can do many things that computers are not yet good at. You can construct an artificial neural network with as many neurons as an ant has, but you cannot yet train it to find dropped crumbs and relay their location to other neural nets.

For the rest of this chapter, the early ambitions associated with the biological view of neural networks are replaced by a considerably less ambitious goal: to create data mining models that are more flexible than standard regression models and thus able to capture some relationships better than they can.

Artificial Neural Networks

The place to start understanding neural network models is with the basic unit, the artificial neuron. This is where both the biological analogy and the close relationship to regression models are clearest.

The Artificial Neuron

An artificial neuron takes its inputs and produces an output, as shown in Figure 8-2. The overall behavior is called the node's *activation function*. The activation function is generally split into two parts. The *combination function* combines the inputs into a single value, which is then passed to the *transfer function* to produce an output. As shown in Figure 8-2, each input has its own weight.

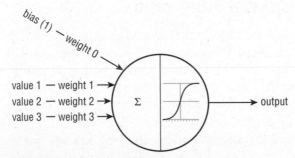

Figure 8-2: The output of the unit is typically a nonlinear combination of its inputs.

Combination Function

The combination function typically uses a set of weights assigned to each of the inputs. As discussed later in this chapter, the process of training the network is the process of assigning the best values to the weights.

A typical combination function is the weighted sum, where each input is multiplied by its weight and these products are added together. The weighted sum is the default in most data mining tools. However, other possibilities exist, such as the maximum of the weighted inputs. Radial basis functions (discussed later) have yet another combination function.

Transfer Function

The choice of transfer function determines how closely the artificial neuron mimics the behavior of a biological neuron, which exhibits all-or-nothing responses for its inputs. To mimic the biological process, a step function, which has the value 1 when the weighted sum of the inputs is above some threshold, and 0 otherwise, is appropriate. To estimate a continuous value, a continuous transfer function is better. Figure 8-3 illustrates several transfer functions: the step, linear, logistic, and hyperbolic tangent functions.

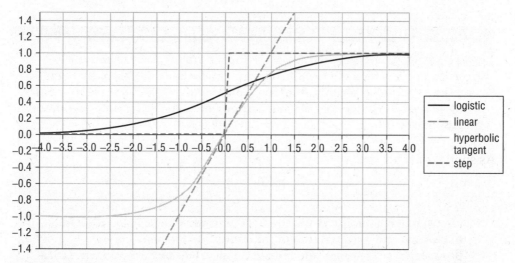

Figure 8-3: Four common transfer functions are the step, linear, logistic, and hyperbolic tangent functions.

With a linear transfer function, the unit does exactly what a linear regression equation does: multiplies the inputs by some coefficients (the weights) and adds them up. An additional input called the *bias* supplies the constant term. A neural network consisting only of units with linear transfer functions and weighted sum combination function represents a linear combination of linear regression models.

The logistic and hyperbolic tangent functions are both *sigmoid* (S-shaped) functions. The major difference between them is the range of their outputs, between 0 and 1 for the logistic and between –1 and 1 for the hyperbolic tangent. As the magnitude of the weighted sum gets larger, these transfer functions gradually saturate (to 0 and 1 in the case of the logistic; to –1 and 1 in the case of the hyperbolic tangent). This behavior corresponds to a gradual movement from a linear model of the input to a nonlinear model.

With a sigmoid transfer function, when the combined values are within some middle range, small changes can have relatively large effects on the output. Conversely, large changes in the inputs have little effect on the output, when the combined inputs are far from the middle range. This property, where sometimes small changes matter and sometimes they do not, is an example of *nonlinear behavior*. Although these functions are not linear, they are almost linear in some regions. Statisticians appreciate linear systems, and almost-linear systems are almost as well appreciated. The power and complexity of neural networks arise from nonlinear behavior, which in turn arises from the particular activation functions used by the constituent neural units. There is also a relationship between the activation function and the range of input values, as discussed in the sidebar, "Sigmoid Functions and Ranges for Input Values."

SIGMOID FUNCTIONS AND RANGES FOR INPUT VALUES

The sigmoid activation functions are S-shaped curves that fall within bounds. For instance, the logistic function produces values between 0 and 1, and the hyperbolic tangent (tanh) function produces values between –1 and 1 for all possible outputs of the summation function. The formulas for these functions are:

$$\text{logistic}(x) = \frac{1}{(1 + e^{-x})}$$

$$\tanh(x) = \frac{e^{2x} - 1}{e^{2x} + 1}$$

When used in a neural network, the x is the result of the combination function, typically the weighted sum of the inputs into the unit.

Because these functions are defined for all values of x, why do we recommend that the inputs to a network be in a small range? The reason has to do with the behavior of these functions near 0. In this range, they behave in an almost linear way. That is, small changes in x result in small changes in the output; changing x by half as much results in about half the effect on the output. The relationship is not exact, but it is a close approximation.

For training purposes, starting out in this quasi-linear area is a good idea. As the neural network trains, nodes may find linear relationships in the data. These nodes adjust their weights so the resulting value falls in this linear range. Other nodes may find nonlinear relationships. Their adjusted weights are likely to fall in a larger range.

Requiring that all inputs have similar ranges also prevents one set of inputs, such as the price of a house — a big number in the hundreds of thousands — from dominating other inputs, such as the number of bedrooms. After all, the combination function is a weighted sum of the inputs, and when some values are very large, they will dominate the weighted sum. When x is large, small adjustments to the weights on the inputs have almost no effect on the output of the unit, making it difficult to train. That is, the sigmoid function can take advantage of the difference between one and two bedrooms, but a house that costs $50,000 and one that costs $1,000,000 would be hard for it to distinguish, and it can take many generations of training the network for the weights associated with this feature to adjust. Keeping the inputs relatively small enables adjustments to the weights to have a bigger impact. This aid to training is the strongest reason for insisting that inputs stay in a small range. Hence, inputs to a neural network should usually be standardized.

The Multi-Layer Perceptron

Figure 8-4 shows the structure of a typical neural network model. It has an input layer, where data enters the network; and a second layer, known as the *hidden layer*, comprised of artificial neurons, each of which receives multiple inputs from the input layer. The artificial neurons summarize their inputs and pass the results to the output layer where they are combined again. Networks with this architecture are called *multi-layer perceptrons* (*MLPs*).

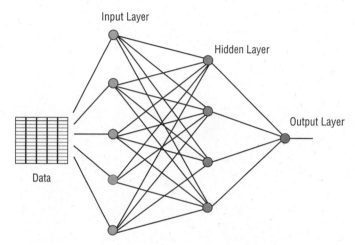

Figure 8-4: A multi-layer perceptron with a single hidden layer.

The input layer is a reminder that the inputs to the network must have similar input ranges, which is usually achieved by standardizing all the inputs. If the ranges are not in a similar range, then one of the inputs will dominate initially (probably the one with the largest values), and the neural network will have to spend many training cycles "learning" that the weights should be small.

> **TIP** Unless the input data is already well behaved, with values close to zero, standardizing the training data for neural networks is a good idea.

The hidden layer contains the non-linear activation functions, of which the hyperbolic tangent is often preferred because it spans both positive and negative values.

The transfer function for the output layer depends on the target for the neural network. For a continuous target, a linear combination is used. For a binary target, a logistic function is used, so the network behaves like a logistic regression producing a probability estimate. In other cases, more exotic transfer functions might be chosen.

A Network Example

The neural network shown in Figure 8-5 represents a model for estimating real estate values. The topology, or structure, of this network is typical of networks used for prediction and classification. The units are organized into three layers. The layer on the left is connected to the inputs and called the *input layer*. In this example, the input layer standardizes the values.

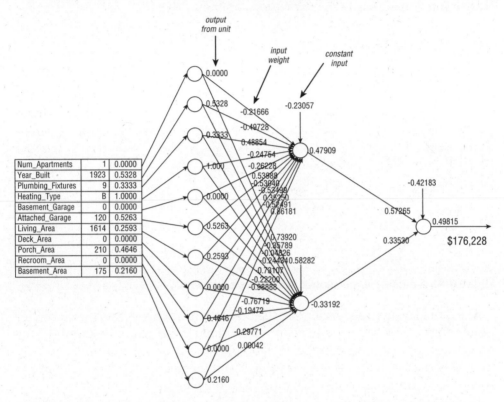

Figure 8-5: The real estate training example shown here provides the input into a neural network and illustrates that a network is filled with seemingly meaningless weights.

The hidden layer is connected neither to the inputs nor to the output of the network. Each unit in the hidden layer is typically fully connected to all the units in the input layer. Because this network contains standard units, the units in the hidden layer calculate their output by multiplying the value of each input by its corresponding weight, adding these up, and applying the transfer function. A neural network can have any number of hidden layers, but in general, one hidden layer is sufficient. The wider the layer (that is, the more units it contains) the greater the capacity of the network to recognize patterns. This greater capacity has a drawback, though, because the neural network can memorize "patterns of one" in the training examples. *You want the network to generalize on the training set, not to memorize it.* To achieve this, the hidden layer should not be too wide.

WARNING   The risk of overfitting increases with the number of hidden-layer nodes. A small number of hidden nodes with non-linear transfer functions are sufficient to create very flexible models.

Notice that the units in Figure 8-5 each have an additional input coming down from the top. This is the constant input, sometimes called a bias, and is always set to 1. Like other inputs, it has a weight and is included in the combination function. The bias is like the intercept in a regression equation; it acts as a global offset that helps the network better capture patterns. The training phase adjusts the weights on constant inputs just as it does on the other weights in the network.

The last unit on the right is the output layer because it is connected to the output of the neural network. It is also fully connected to all the units in the hidden layer. Most of the time, neural networks are used to calculate a single value, so there is only one unit in the output layer. In this example, the network produces a value of $176,228, which is quite close to the actual value of $171,000. The output layer uses a simple linear transfer function, so the output is a weighted linear combination of the hidden-layer outputs.

Network Topologies

It is possible for the output layer to have more than one unit. For instance, a department store chain wants to predict the likelihood that customers will be purchasing products from various departments, such as women's apparel, furniture, and entertainment. The stores want to use this information to plan promotions and direct target mailings.

To make this prediction, they might set up the neural network shown in Figure 8-6. This network has three outputs, one for each department. The outputs are a propensity for the customer described in the inputs to make his or her next purchase from the associated department.

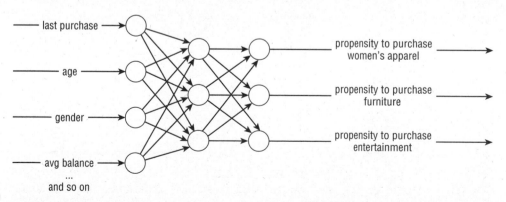

Figure 8-6: This network has more than one output and is used to estimate the probability that customers will make a purchase in each of three departments.

After feeding the inputs for a customer into the network, the network calculates three values. Given all these outputs, how can the department store determine the right promotion or promotions to offer the customer? Some common methods used when working with multiple model outputs:

- Take the department corresponding to the output with the maximum value.
- Take departments corresponding to the outputs with the top three values.
- Take all departments corresponding to the outputs that exceed some threshold value.
- Take all departments corresponding to units that are some percentage of the unit with the maximum value.

All of these possibilities work well and have their strengths and weaknesses in different situations. There is no one right answer that always works. In practice, you want to try several of these possibilities on the test set to determine which works best in a particular situation.

In the department store example, a customer could reasonably have a high propensity to purchase in all three departments. In other classification problems, such as recognizing letters of the alphabet, there is only one right answer. In these cases, a class is only assigned when one output has probability above an acceptance threshold and all other outputs have probability below a rejection threshold. When there are two or more "winners," no classification can be made.

Figure 8-7 illustrates several variations on the basic neural network architecture.

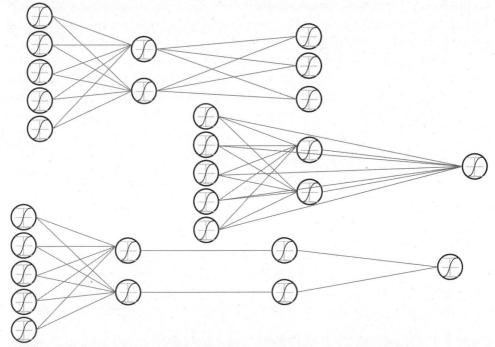

Figure 8-7: There are many variations on the basic neural network architecture.

The top network features multiple outputs. The middle network includes connections directly from the inputs to the target layer, as well as the hidden layer. These connections are called *direct connections*. The bottom network contains more than one hidden layer. All of these networks are examples of feed-forward neural networks. The name arises from the fact that the data starts at inputs and feeds forward to the output — without any loops.

A Sample Application: Real Estate Appraisal

Neural networks have the ability to learn by example, which is analogous to the way that human experts learn from experience. The following example applies neural networks to solve a problem familiar to most readers — real estate appraisal.

The appraiser or real estate agent is a good example of a human expert in a well-defined domain. Houses are described by a fixed set of standard features taken into account by the expert and turned into an appraised value. In 1992, researchers at IBM recognized this as a good problem for neural networks. This application, which was described by Joseph Bigus in his book, *Data Mining with Neural Networks*, is the earliest truly commercial application of neural networks that the authors are aware of.

A neural network takes specific inputs — in this case the information from the housing sheet — and turns them into a specific output — an appraised value for the house. The list of inputs is well defined because of two factors: extensive use of the multiple listing service (MLS) to share information about the housing market among different real estate agents and standardization of housing descriptions for mortgages sold on secondary markets. The desired output is well defined as well — a specific dollar amount. In addition, a wealth of experience exists in the form of previous sales for teaching the network how to value a house.

Why would you want to automate such appraisals? Clearly, automated appraisals could help real estate agents better match prospective buyers to prospective homes, improving the productivity of even inexperienced agents. Another use would be to set up Web pages where prospective buyers could describe the homes that they wanted — and get immediate feedback on how much their dream homes cost.

Perhaps an unexpected application is in the secondary mortgage market. Good, consistent appraisals are critical to assessing the risk of individual loans and loan portfolios, because one major factor affecting default is the proportion of the value of the property at risk. If the loan value is more than 100 percent of the market value, the risk of default goes up considerably. After the loan has been made, how can the market value be calculated? For this purpose, Freddie Mac, the Federal Home Loan Mortgage Corporation, developed a product called Loan Prospector that does these appraisals automatically for homes throughout the United States. Loan Prospector was originally based on neural network technology developed by a San Diego company, HNC, which has since been merged into Fair Isaac.

Back to the example. This neural network mimics an appraiser who estimates the market value of a house based on features of the property. She knows that houses in one part of town are worth more than those in other areas. Additional bedrooms, a larger garage, the style of the house, and the size of the lot are other factors that figure into her mental calculation. She does not apply some set formula, but balances her experience and knowledge of the sales prices of similar homes. Her knowledge about housing prices is not static. She is aware of recent sale prices for homes throughout the region and can recognize trends in prices over time — fine-tuning her calculation to fit the latest data.

TIP Neural networks are good for prediction and estimation problems. A good problem has the following four characteristics:

■ *The inputs are well understood.* You have a good idea of which features of the data are important, but not necessarily how to combine them.

■ *The output is well understood.* You know what you are trying to model.

■ *Experience is available.* You have plenty of examples where both the inputs and the output are known. These known cases are used to train the network.

■ *A black box model is acceptable.* Interpreting the model or explaining how particular scores were arrived at is not necessary.

The first step in setting up a neural network to calculate estimated housing values is determining a set of features that affect the sales price. Some possible common features are shown in Table 8-1. In practice, these features work for homes in a single geographical area. To extend the appraisal example to handle homes in many neighborhoods, the input data might include ZIP code information, neighborhood demographics, and other neighborhood quality-of-life indicators, such as ratings of schools and proximity to transportation. To simplify the example, these additional features are not included here.

Table 8-1: Common Features Describing a House

FEATURE	DESCRIPTION	RANGE OF VALUES
Num_Apartments	Number of dwelling units	Integer: 1–3
Year_Built	Year built	Integer: 1850–1986
Plumbing_Fixtures	Number of plumbing fixtures	Integer: 5–17
Heating_Type	Heating system type	Coded as A or B
Basement_Garage	Basement garage (number of cars)	Integer: 0–2
Attached_Garage	Attached frame garage area (in square feet)	Integer: 0–228

FEATURE	DESCRIPTION	RANGE OF VALUES
Living_Area	Total living area (square feet)	Integer: 714–4185
Deck_Area	Deck / open porch area (square feet)	Integer: 0–738
Porch_Area	Enclosed porch area (square feet)	Integer: 0–452
Recroom_Area	Recreation room area (square feet)	Integer: 0–672
Basement_Area	Finished basement area (square feet)	Integer: 0–810

Training the network builds a model that can then be used to estimate the target value for unknown examples. Training presents known examples (data from previous sales) to the network so that it can learn how to calculate the sales price. The training examples need two more additional features: the sales price of the home and the sales date. The sales price is needed as the target variable. The date is used to separate the examples into training, validation, and test sets. Table 8-2 shows an example from the training set. In addition, the date is used to calculate the number of months in the past when the sale was made, so the network can learn about changes over time.

Table 8-2: Sample Record from Training Set with Values Scaled to Range –1 to 1

FEATURE	RANGE OF VALUES	ORIGINAL VALUE	SCALED VALUE
Months_Ago	0–23	4	–0.6522
Num_Apartments	1-3	1	–1.0000
Year_Built	1850–1986	1923	+0.0730
Plumbing_Fixtures	5–17	9	–0.3077
Heating_Type	Coded as A or B	B	+1.0000
Basement_Garage	0–2	0	–1.0000
Attached_Garage	0–228	120	+0.0524
Living_Area	714–4185	1,614	–0.4813
Deck_Area	0–738	0	–1.0000
Porch_Area	0–452	210	–0.0706
Recroom_Area	0–672	0	–1.0000
Basement_Area	0–810	175	–0.5672

The process of training the network is actually the process of adjusting weights inside it to arrive at the best combination of weights for making the desired predictions. The network starts with a random set of weights, so it initially performs very poorly. However, by reprocessing the training set over and over and adjusting the internal weights each time to reduce the overall error, the network gradually does a better and better job of approximating the target values in the training set. When the approximations no longer improve, the network stops training. The training process is explained in the following section of this chapter.

This process of adjusting weights is sensitive to the representation of the data going in. For instance, consider a field in the data that measures lot size. If lot size is measured in acres, then the values might reasonably go from about 1/8 to 1 acre. If measured in square feet, the same values would be 5,445 square feet to 43,560 square feet. Neural networks work best when their inputs are small-ish numbers. For instance, when an input variable takes on very large values relative to other inputs, then this variable dominates the calculation of the target. The neural network wastes valuable iterations by reducing the weights on this input to lessen its effect on the output. That is, the first "pattern" that the network will find is that the lot size variable has much larger values than other variables. Because this is not particularly interesting, using the lot size as measured in acres rather than square feet would be better. In general, it is a good idea to standardize all numeric inputs to a neural network, although inputs that take on a small range of values (say from zero to one) do not really need to be standardized.

The only categorical variable in this data, *Heating_Type*, only takes on two values, A and B, so the solution is to create an indicator variable, which takes on the value of 0 (when the value is "A") and 1 (when the value is "B"). This can also be standardized, so one value is negative and the other positive. Chapters 18 and 19 discuss such transformations of categorical variables in detail.

With these simple techniques, it is possible to transform all the fields for the sample house record shown earlier (see Table 8-2) into values more suitable for training a neural network. Training is the process of iterating through the training set to adjust the weights in the neural network. Each iteration is sometimes called a *generation*.

After the network has been trained, the performance of each generation must be measured on the validation set to select the generation of weights that minimizes error on data not used for training. As with other modeling approaches, neural networks can learn patterns that exist only in the training set, resulting in overfitting. To find the best network for unseen data, the training process remembers each set of weights calculated during each generation. The final network comes from the generation that works best on the validation set, rather than the one that works best on the training set.

When the model's performance on the validation set is satisfactory, the neural network model is ready for use. It has learned from the training examples and figured out how to calculate the sales price from all the inputs. The model takes descriptive information about a house, suitably mapped, and produces an output, which is the neural network's estimate of the home's value.

Training Neural Networks

Training a neural network means using the training data to adjust the network weights so that the model does a good job of estimating target values for records that are not part of the training data. In some ways, this is similar to finding the coefficients for the best-fit line in a regression model. However, a single best-fit line exists for a particular set of training observations, and there is a simple, deterministic method for calculating its coefficients; there is no equivalent method for calculating the best set of weights for a neural network. This is an example of an optimization problem. The goal is to find a set of weights that minimizes an error function such as the average squared error.

Historically, the first successful training method for neural networks was back propagation. In addition to its historical importance, it also happens to be one of the easier methods to understand.

How Does a Neural Network Learn Using Back Propagation?

At the heart of back propagation are the following three steps:

1. The network gets a training example and, using the existing weights in the network, it calculates the output or outputs.

2. Back propagation then calculates the error by taking the difference between the calculated result and the actual target value.

3. The error is fed back through the network and the weights are adjusted to minimize the error — hence the name *back* propagation because the errors are sent back through the network.

The back propagation algorithm measures the overall error of the network by comparing the value produced for each training example to the actual value. It then adjusts the weights of the output layer to reduce, but not eliminate, the error. However, the algorithm has not finished. It then assigns the blame to nodes in the previous layer and adjusts the weights connecting those nodes, further reducing overall error. The specific mechanism for assigning blame is not important. Suffice it to say that back propagation uses a complicated mathematical procedure that requires taking partial derivatives of the activation function.

Given the error, how does a unit adjust its weights? It estimates whether changing the weight on each input would increase or decrease the error. The unit then adjusts each weight to reduce, but not eliminate, the error. The adjustments for each example in the training set slowly nudge the weights toward more optimal values. Remember, the goal is to generalize and identify patterns in the input, not to memorize the training set. Adjusting the weights is like a leisurely walk, not a sprint. After being shown enough training examples during enough generations, the weights on the network no longer change significantly and the error no longer decreases. This is the point where training stops; the network has learned to recognize patterns in the input.

This technique for adjusting the weights is called the *generalized delta* rule, which has two important parameters. The first is *momentum*, which refers to the tendency of the weights inside each unit to change the "direction" they are heading in. That is, each weight remembers whether it has been getting bigger or smaller, and momentum tries to keep it going in the same direction. A network with high momentum responds slowly to new training examples that want to reverse the weights. If momentum is low, then the weights are allowed to oscillate more freely.

The *learning rate* controls how quickly the weights change. The best approach for the learning rate is to start big and decrease it slowly as the network is being trained. Initially, the weights are random, so large oscillations are useful to get in the vicinity of the best weights. However, as the network gets closer to the optimal solution, the learning rate should decrease so the network can fine-tune to the most optimal weights.

Researchers have invented hundreds of other techniques for training neural networks (see the sidebar "Training as Optimization"). Each of these approaches has its advantages and disadvantages. In all cases, they are looking for a technique that trains networks quickly to arrive at an optimal solution. Some neural network packages offer multiple training methods, allowing users to experiment with the best solution for their problems.

Pruning a Neural Network

One of the dangers with any of the training techniques is falling into something called a *local optimum*. This happens when the network produces okay results for the training set and adjusting the weights no longer improves the performance of the network. However, there is some other combination of weights — significantly different from those in the network — that yields a much better solution. This is analogous to trying to climb to the top of a mountain by choosing the steepest path at every turn and finding that you have only climbed to the top of a nearby hill. A tension exists between finding the local best solution and the global best solution.

Another danger is overfitting. As the network is fed the same training examples multiple times, it begins to recognize them, and the error on the training examples approaches zero. When this happens, training has found an optimal set of weights for predicting the target values in the training data. An overfit model does not generalize well. Training should have been stopped before this point, but when? The answer is provided by the validation set in a manner analogous to the pruning of a decision tree.

During training, the weights are recorded after each cycle through the training set. Each set of weights represents a different candidate model. These models are applied to the validation set and the model with the lowest error on the validation data is chosen as the final model.

Figure 8-8 is a screenshot of a graph produced by SAS Enterprise Miner illustrating the results of pruning a neural network model. The graph plots the average squared error for a neural network model over the course of twenty generations of training. By iteration 20, the error (measured as average squared error — ASE) on the training data has declined to nearly zero. The vertical bar shows the iteration where error was minimized on the validation data. After the seventh iteration, further training was memorizing noise in the training data, rather than improving the model.

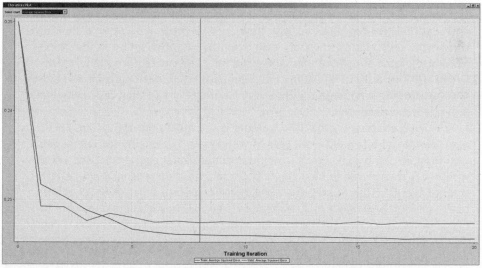

Figure 8-8: After twenty training iterations, error on the training data is nearly zero, but error on the validation data reached its lowest value after just seven iterations.

TRAINING AS OPTIMIZATION

The first practical algorithm for training networks, backpropagation is an inefficient way to train networks. Training a neural network is an optimization problem, and there are several different approaches.

Finding optimal weights is a hard problem for several reasons. One is that the network contains many connections, so there are many, many different weights to consider. For a network that has 28 weights (say, seven inputs and three hidden nodes in the hidden layer), trying every combination of just two values for each weight requires testing 2^{28} combinations of values — or more than 250 million combinations. Trying out all combinations of 10 values for each weight would be prohibitively expensive, even using the largest grid computers.

A second problem is one of symmetry. In general, there is no single best value. In fact, with neural networks that have more than one unit in the hidden layer, there are always multiple optima — because the weights on one hidden unit could be entirely swapped with the weights on another. This problem of having multiple optima complicates finding the best solution. Even worse, the optima are not like the tops of a hill. Instead, they are like ridges, so there is no single value. This further complicates finding the best value.

One approach to finding optima is called hill climbing. Start with a random set of weights. Then, consider taking a single step in each direction by making a small change in each of the weights. Choose whichever small step does the best job of reducing the error and repeat the process. This is like finding the highest point somewhere by only taking steps uphill. In many cases, you end up on top of a small hill instead of a tall mountain.

One variation on hill climbing is to start with big steps and gradually reduce the step size (a giant will do a better job of finding the top of the nearest mountain than an ant). A related algorithm, called *simulated annealing*, injects a bit of randomness in the hill climbing. The randomness is based on physical theories having to do with how crystals form when liquids cool into solids (the crystalline formation is an example of optimization in the physical world). Both simulated annealing and hill climbing require many, many iterations — and these iterations are expensive computationally because they require running a network on the entire training set and then repeating again and again for each step.

A more statistical approach to training is the quickprop algorithm. This algorithm tests a few different sets of weights and then guesses where the optimum is, using some ideas from multidimensional geometry. Each set of weights is considered to be a single point in a multidimensional space. After trying several different sets, the algorithm fits a multidimensional parabola to the points. A parabola is a U-shaped curve that has a single minimum (or maximum). Quickprop then continues with a new set of weights in this region. This process still needs to be repeated; however, quickprop produces better values more quickly than back propagation.

> Many other examples of training algorithms are available, with names like conjugate-gradient and Levenberg–Marquardt. These differ in the details of the search for optimal weights. None is guaranteed to produce the best result. All do converge on a solution, and the solution is usually very good — just not guaranteed to be the best possible.

Radial Basis Function Networks

Radial basis function (RBF) networks are another variety of neural networks. They differ from multi-layer perceptrons (MLPs) in two important ways. One is that the interpretation relies more on geometry than on biology. Another is that the training method is different, because in addition to optimizing the weights used to combine the outputs of the RBF nodes, the nodes themselves have parameters that can be optimized.

Overview of RBF Networks

The diagram like the one in Figure 8-4 that represents a multi-layer perceptron can also be reused to represent a radial basis function (RBF) network, but this time, the nodes in the hidden layer are described in terms of geometry rather than biology. As with other forms of neural network, the data processed by an RBF network is always numeric, so it is possible to interpret any input record as a point in space. In an RBF network, the hidden layer nodes are also points in the same space. Each one has an address that is specified by a vector with as many elements as there are input variables.

Instead of a combination function and a transfer function, RBF nodes contain a distance function and a transfer function. The distance function is the standard Euclidean one — the square root of the sum of the squared differences along each dimension. The node's output is a non-linear function of how close the input is; the closer the input, the stronger the output. The "radial" in the name of radial basis functions refers to the fact that all inputs that are the same distance from an RBF node's position produce the same output. In two dimensions, these points form a circle; in three dimensions, a sphere, and so on.

The RBF nodes are in the hidden layer and also have transfer functions. Instead of the S-shaped transfer functions commonly used in MLP networks, these are bell-shaped functions called Gaussians. Gaussians are the generalization in many dimensions of the familiar normal curve.

Unlike a multi-layer perceptron, an RBF network does not have any weights associated with the connections between the input layer and the hidden layer.

Instead of weights, this layer has the RBF node's position, width, and height. Weights are associated with the connections between the hidden layer and the output layer. As with an MLP, these weights are optimized when the RBF network is trained. The output layer nodes of an RBF network are the same as those in an MLP. They contain a combination function — usually a weighted sum of the inputs — and a transfer function that is often linear or logistic.

As more inputs are added into the network, the behavior of the network gets more complicated. Figure 8-9 shows what happens in three dimensions. Each Gaussian is centered at the location of its node in the hidden layer. The height and width of the Gaussians can be fixed, or they can be trainable parameters like the weights.

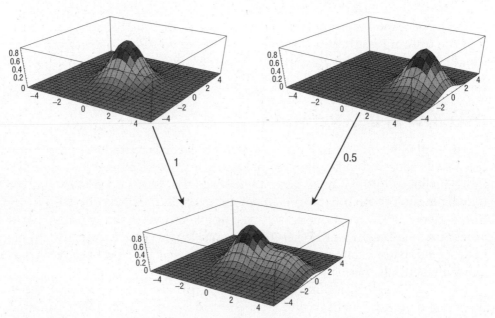

Figure 8-9: Two Gaussian surfaces are added to produce the output surface.

The transfer function in the output layer of an RBF network is usually linear, with trainable weights associated with the outputs from the RBF layer. In Figure 8-9, the output of two radial basis functions with equal heights and widths, but different centers, are combined using weights of 1 and 0.5 to create an output surface.

Choosing the Locations of the Radial Basis Functions

The output of each radial basis node is a function of how close it is to an input record, so clearly, the placement of the nodes is important. One strategy, illustrated in Figure 8-10, is to choose locations that cover the space evenly, making no assumptions about patterns in the input data.

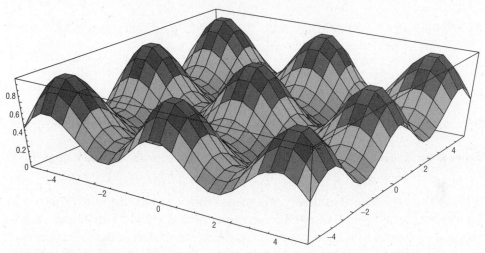

Figure 8-10: Radial basis functions can be placed in a grid to provide even coverage of the input space.

Another approach is to start by detecting clusters in the input data so that the radial basis functions can be located at cluster centers. The idea is to give the radial basis function network a head start by ensuring that there is a radial basis function that will respond strongly to members of each segment of the input data.

Universal Approximators

Neural networks derive much of their power from their ability to find local patterns in data. Figures 8-9 and 8-11 show how radial basis functions can be combined to form complex curves and surfaces. An arbitrarily complex RBF network can approximate any function, given enough RBF nodes in the network.

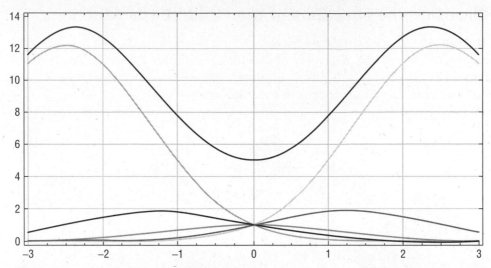

Figure 8-11: Several bell-shaped curves are added to produce a sinusoidal output curve.

Figure 8-12 shows that multi-layer perceptrons are as versatile as RBF networks. Each chart plots the sum of two hidden layer nodes, each of which has a single variable input and a bias. Adjusting the weights associated with the inputs leads to the gentle wave in the top chart, or the two-step functions in the bottom chart, or countless other continuous curves.

The activation function for the nodes in an MLP network starts low and then goes high, with a linear area in the middle. For an RBF network, the activation function starts low, goes high, and then goes low again (the peak is the location parameter for each RBF node). Both these types of activation functions are quite capable of finding local phenomenon inside data. An example of a local phenomenon would be a well-defined group of customers that behaves a certain way.

This property makes both RBFs and MLPs examples of *universal approximators*. A universal approximator is a theoretical concept that says that as a neural network gets more complicated, it can fit any function. Decision trees have the same property. Just imagine the decision tree getting more and more refined with smaller leaves until there is only one point in each leaf. This theoretical property does not mean that a neural network will produce a perfect model.

It does mean that both MLPs and RBFs are theoretically able to produce better models than regression alone.

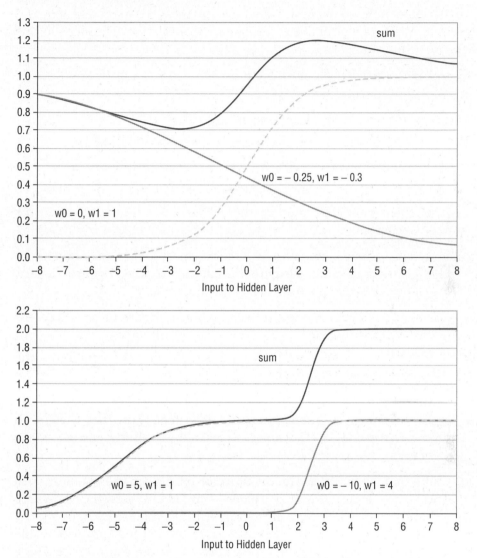

Figure 8-12: Varying the weights in an MLP with two hidden layer nodes leads to a variety of output curves.

Neural Networks in Practice

The real estate valuation example illustrates the most common use of neural networks: building a model for classification or prediction. The steps in this process are as follows:

1. Identify the input and output features.
2. Standardize the inputs.
3. Set up a network with an appropriate topology.
4. Train the network on a representative set of training examples.
5. Use the validation set to choose the set of weights that minimizes the error.
6. Evaluate the network using the test set to see how well it performs.
7. Apply the model generated by the network to predict outcomes for unknown inputs.

Fortunately, data mining software now performs most of these steps automatically. Although an intimate knowledge of the internal workings is not necessary, there are some keys to using neural networks successfully:

- As with all predictive modeling tools, the most important issue is choosing the right training set.

- The second is representing the data in such a way as to maximize the ability of the network to recognize patterns in it.

- The third is interpreting results produced by the network.

- Finally, understanding some specific details about how they work, such as network topology and parameters controlling training, can help make better performing networks.

One of the dangers with any model used for prediction or classification is that the model becomes stale as it gets older — and neural network models are no exception to this rule. For the appraisal example, the neural network has learned about historical patterns that allow it to predict the appraised value from descriptions of houses based on the contents of the training set. There is no guarantee that current market conditions match those of last week, last month, or six months ago, or whenever the training set was made. New homes are bought and sold every day, creating and responding to market forces that are not present in the training set. A rise or drop in interest rates, or an increase in inflation, may rapidly change appraisal values. The problem of keeping a neural network model up to date is made more difficult by two factors:

- The model does not readily express itself in the form of rules, so it may not be obvious when it has grown stale.

▪ When neural networks degrade, they tend to degrade gracefully, making the reduction in performance less obvious.

In short, the model gradually expires and it is not always clear exactly when to update it.

The solution is to incorporate more recent data into the neural network. One way is to take the same neural network back to training mode and start training it on new values. This approach works well when the network is only in need of a bit of tweaking, such as when the network is fairly accurate, but you think you can improve its accuracy even more by giving it more recent examples. Another approach is to start over again by adding new examples to the training set (perhaps removing older examples) and training an entirely new network, perhaps even with a different topology. This is appropriate when market conditions may have changed drastically and the patterns found in the original training set are no longer applicable.

The virtuous cycle of data mining described in Chapter 1 puts a premium on measuring the results from data mining activities. These measurements help in understanding how susceptible a given model is to aging and when a neural network model should be retrained.

WARNING A neural network is only as good as the training set used to generate it. The model is static and must be explicitly updated by adding more recent examples to the training set and retraining the network (or training a new network) to keep it up-to-date and useful.

Choosing the Training Set

The training set consists of records whose prediction or classification values are already known. Choosing a good training set is critical for all data mining modeling. A poor training set dooms the network, regardless of any other work that goes into creating it. Fortunately, there are only a few things to consider when choosing a good one.

Coverage of Values for All Features

The most important of these considerations is that the training set needs to cover the full range of values for all features that the network might encounter, including the output. In the real estate appraisal example, this means including inexpensive houses and expensive houses, big houses and little houses, and houses with and without garages. The training set should contain many examples of each class for categorical inputs and values from throughout the range of numeric inputs. The goal is a training set that captures the distributions of all inputs.

Number of Features

The number of input features affects neural networks in two ways. One is that the more features used as inputs into the network, the larger the network needs to be, increasing the risk of overfitting and increasing the size of the training set. Another is that the more features, the longer is takes the network to converge to a set of weights. Plus, with too many features, the weights are less likely to be optimal. Chapter 20 covers the topics of variable selection and variable reduction extensively.

Size of Training Set

The more features the network has, the more training examples are needed to get a good coverage of patterns in the data. Unfortunately, there is no simple rule to express the relationship between the number of features and the size of the training set. However, thousands of rows is a good start. The authors have worked with neural networks that have only six or seven inputs, but whose training set contained hundreds of thousands of rows. In general, the more training examples, the better. The downside of a really large training set is that it takes the neural network longer to train.

Number and Range of Outputs

In general, good coverage of the inputs results in good coverage of the outputs. It is worth checking that the training examples produce outputs across the whole expected range. In addition, if the network has more than one node in the output layer, the training examples should generate the full expected range of outputs from each one.

> **TIP** The training set for a neural network has to be large enough to cover all the values taken on by all the features. You should have at least dozens, if not hundreds or thousands, of examples for each input value.

Rules of Thumb for Using MLPs

Even with sophisticated neural network packages, getting the best results from a neural network takes some effort. This section covers some heuristics for setting up a network to obtain good results.

Probably the biggest decision is the number of units in the hidden layer. The more units, the more patterns the network can recognize. This would argue for a very large hidden layer. However, there is a drawback. The network might end up memorizing the training set instead of generalizing from it. In this case, more is not better. Fortunately, you can detect ths type of overfitting quite easily.

If the network performs very well on the training set, but does much worse on the validation set, then it has memorized the training set. Some neural network software packages automate this process by selecting the model that minimizes error on the validation set.

How large should the hidden layer be? The real answer is that no one knows. It depends on the data, the patterns being detected, and the type of network. Because overfitting is a concern, having more hidden layer nodes than input nodes is not advisable. Begin by experimenting with one, two, and three nodes in the hidden layer. Even a small number of hidden layer nodes produce flexible, non-linear models.

When using a network for classification, one approach is to start with one hidden layer node per class in hopes that each one will specialize in a particular class.

Another decision is the size of the training set. The training set must be sufficiently large to cover the ranges of inputs available for each feature. In addition, you want several training examples for each weight in the network. For an MLP network with s input units, h hidden units, and 1 output, there are $h * (s + 1) + h + 1$ weights in the network (each hidden layer node has a weight for each connection to the input layer, an additional weight for the bias, and then a connection to the output layer and its bias). For instance, if there are 15 input features and 10 units in the hidden network, then the network has 171 weights. You should have many examples for each weight. Requiring 100 examples per weight says that the training set should have at least 17,100 rows. And that assumes that 100 examples per weight is sufficient, which it might or might not be.

When using back propagation, the learning rate and momentum parameters are very important for getting good results. Initially, the learning should be set high to make large adjustments to the weights. As the training proceeds, the learning rate should decrease to fine-tune the network. The momentum parameter allows the network to move toward a solution more rapidly, preventing oscillation around less useful weights.

Preparing the Data

Preparing the input data is often the most complicated part of using a neural network. Chapters 18 through 20 are devoted to data preparation issues. Data preparation looms larger with neural networks than with many other techniques because neural networks do more with their inputs. When a decision tree rule divides salaries into "less than $68,000" and "greater than or equal to $68,000" a salary of $70,000 and a salary of seven million are treated the same way. A neural network that multiplies input values by weights, sums them, and then applies some non-linear function might be greatly affected by the difference.

Of particular importance with neural networks is getting all the inputs to be numeric and in a small range. This means finding good numeric representations for categorical data. When there are only a few categories, using indicator variables is a good approach. When there are many categories, a better approach is to find a natural ordering of the categories, or replace the categories with numeric attributes that vary by category. It also means making sure that numeric inputs are mostly close to zero, in the near-linear portion of the transfer function. Standardization is the recommended approach.

Because neural networks are so sensitive to data issues, they reward extra attention to data transformations that embody some of the data miner's knowledge of the problem domain. The following sidebar "Thermometer Codes" describes one such transformation.

THERMOMETER CODES

Here is an interesting transformation that may be appropriate when change in one part of a variable's range is more important than change in another portion of the range: For many marketing applications, for example, there is a large difference between no children and one child. It may also make a difference whether there is one child or two children, but it probably makes no difference whether there are four or five. In the following table, the number of children is transformed from a count into *thermometer codes*:

0	→	0 0 0 0	= 0/16 = 0.0000
1	→	1 0 0 0	= 8/16 = 0.5000
2	→	1 1 0 0	= 12/16 = 0.7500
3	→	1 1 1 0	= 14/16 = 0.8750

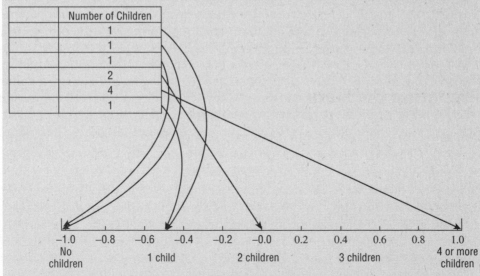

When codes have an inherent order, they can be mapped onto the unit interval.

The name arises because the sequence of 1s starts on one side and rises to some value, like the mercury in a thermometer; this sequence is then interpreted as the binary representation of an integer between 0 and 15. Dividing the entries by 16 puts them in the range of 0 to 0.9375 — a suitable range for inputs to a neural network. Using a thermometer code, the number of children variable is mapped as follows: 0 (for 0 children), 0.5 (for one child), 0.75 (for two children), 0.875 (for three children), and so on.

Thermometer codes are one way of including prior information into the coding scheme. They keep certain codes values close together because you have a sense that these code values should be close. This type of knowledge can improve the results from a neural network — don't make it discover what you already know. Feel free to map values onto the unit interval so that codes close to each other match your intuitive notions of how close they should be.

Interpreting the Output from a Neural Network

The transfer function used in the output layer changes the interpretation of the output value. A linear transfer function can produce estimates in any range, so when the target variable is an untransformed numeric quantity, the output of the network is directly interpretable as an estimated value for the target. A logistic transfer function can directly estimate a probability, so when the target variable is binary with two outcomes represented as 0 and 1, the output of the network is directly interpretable as an estimate of the probability that the input record belongs to the category represented by 1.

Some cases are not so simple. If the target variable was put through some transformation before the neural net was trained, the inverse transformation must be applied to the network output to get an estimate in the proper units. The distribution of the output values reflects the distribution of the target in the training data. So, if "churn" is given a value of 1 and "no-churn" a value of –1, then output values near 1 represent churn, and those near –1 represent no churn. The average value produced by the network during training will be close to the average value in the training set. If the original training set has 50 percent churn, then the average output value will be close to 0.0. Values higher than 0.0 are more like churn; those less than 0.0, are less like churn. These output values can be turned into probability estimates by scoring a validation set and measuring the proportion of each class for different ranges of the output value.

In Figure 8-13, the tickmarks are spaced 0.2 apart. For output scores between –0.4 and 0.4, two examples are in category A and two in category B, so a score in that range suggests a 50 percent probability for either class. The validation examples with scores above 0.4 are all B, and the validation examples with scores below –0.4 are all A.

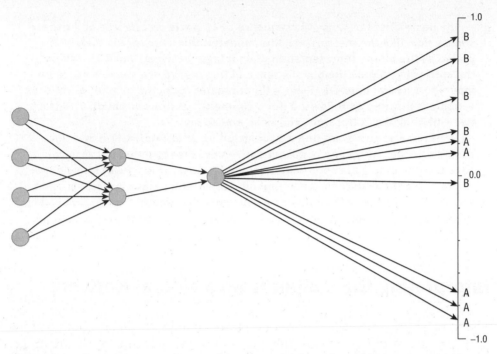

Figure 8-13: Running a neural network on examples from the validation set can help determine how to interpret results.

Of course, 10 examples is not enough to come up with good probability estimates; the figure merely illustrates the idea.

TIP Because neural networks produce continuous values, the output from a network can be difficult to interpret for categorical results (used in classification). The best way to calibrate the output is to run the network over a validation set, entirely separate from the training set, and to use the results from the validation set to calibrate the output of the network to categories. In many cases, the network can have a separate output for each category; that is, a *propensity* for that category. Even with separate outputs, the validation set is still needed to calibrate the outputs.

This approach can easily be extended to more than two categories when these are ordinal by calculating the proportion of each category in each range of output scores. For multiple categories that are not ordinal, a natural ordering can often be found based on some numeric attribute of the category. Alternatively, create a network with multiple outputs, one for each category. Each output represents the strength of evidence that its category is the correct one. An input can be assigned the label with the highest output value, with confidence based on some function of the relative strengths of the outputs. This approach is particularly valuable when the outcomes are not exclusive. For example, a shopper may make purchases in several departments.

Neural Networks for Time Series

In many business problems, the data naturally falls into a time series. Examples of such series are the closing price of IBM stock, the daily value of the Euro to U.S. dollar exchange rate, a forecast of the number of customers who will be active on any given date in the future, or the amount of shampoo a manufacturer needs to produce. For financial time series, someone who is able to predict the next value, or even whether the series is heading up or down, has a tremendous advantage over other investors.

Time Series Modeling

In time series modeling, something of interest is measured at different points in time. The previous chapter gave the example of measures in a factory that roasts coffee. Other examples abound, such as the value of the stock market, how may widgets get made every week, and the number of new customers who start.

One way to model time series is by assuming that there is a relationship between the value at a given time t and the values at earlier times t-1, t-2, t-3, and so on for as many lags as required. The time series with 10 days of history, shown in Table 8-3, can easily be converted to the representation shown in Table 8-4, which includes the lagged observations for the closing price

Table 8-3: Time Series

DATA ELEMENT	DAY-OF-WEEK	CLOSING PRICE
1	1	$40.25
2	2	$41.00
3	3	$39.25
4	4	$39.75
5	5	$40.50
6	1	$40.50
7	2	$40.75
8	3	$41.25
9	4	$42.00
10	5	$41.50

Table 8-4: Time Series with Time Lag

DATA ELEMENT	DAY-OF-WEEK	CLOSING PRICE	PREVIOUS CLOSING PRICE	PREVIOUS-1 CLOSING PRICE
1	1	$40.25		
2	2	$41.00	$40.25	
3	3	$39.25	$41.00	$40.25
4	4	$39.75	$39.25	$41.00
5	5	$40.50	$39.75	$39.25
6	1	$40.50	$40.50	$39.75
7	2	$40.75	$40.50	$40.50
8	3	$41.25	$40.75	$40.50
9	4	$42.00	$41.25	$40.75
10	5	$41.50	$42.00	$41.25

Notice that the time-series data is not limited to data from just a single time series. It can take multiple inputs. For instance, to predict the value of the Euro to U.S. dollar exchange rate, other time-series information might be included, such as the volume of the previous day's transactions, the U.S. dollar to Japanese yen exchange rate, the closing value of the stock exchange, and the day of the week. In addition, non–time-series data, such as the reported inflation rate in the countries over the period of time under investigation, might also be candidate features.

The number of lags in the training data controls the length of the patterns that the network can recognize. For instance, keeping 10 historical lags for a network predicting the closing price of a favorite stock will allow the network to recognize patterns that occur within two-week time periods (because exchange rates are set only on weekdays). Relying on such a network to predict the value three months in the future may not be a good idea — unless you discover that it works in practice. For that matter, predicting market prices with neural networks may not be a good idea in the first place!

A Neural Network Time Series Example

Chapter 7 includes a case study in which a decision tree with lagged inputs is used to predict a time series of instrument readings in a coffee roasting plant. Neural networks are actually a more usual choice for that sort of application. Neural networks have been used to forecast time series data including airline passenger load factors, daily retail sales, and foreign exchange rates.

The example presented here comes from Dr. Sven Crone of the Lancaster Centre for Forecasting.

Beiersdorf, a global manufacturer of branded consumer goods including the Nivea line of skin care products needs to make product-level forecasts for hundreds of products in dozens of markets. These forecasts are used for planning worldwide production and logistics.

Dr. Crone compared a neural network–based approach with the company's baseline approach, which used more traditional time series techniques. The advantage of neural networks is that a single neural network architecture is capable of modeling time series having different trend and seasonality characteristics. The traditional methods required tweaking models to capture patterns specific to each product or region. For instance, some products may sell more in the summer than the winter. Some products may sell more during back-to-school time. Some countries may have important holidays in January or April, and others in November and December, and others may have holidays that change from year to year. Maintaining and customizing thousands of separate models is a major problem for a global company.

Dr. Crone designed an experiment to see whether neural networks could be used for this purpose. He used a sample of 286 time series that varied in length from 12 to 55 months. The neural network was trained on the beginning of the time series (say the initial 8 to 40 time periods). The results were then compared on the remaining time periods.

The neural network forecast was compared against seven others, including the one in current use. The forecasts were compared on two measures: the Mean Absolute Percentage Error (MAPE), which is a standard measure of forecast accuracy, and another measure, preferred by Beiersdorf, that takes into account cost as well as the absolute error in the forecast of units sold in the final month of the forecast. The winning model was an ensemble model that averaged the estimates of 10 different neural nets. However, all the neural networks did well, and all required much less human intervention than the standard methods in use.

Can Neural Network Models Be Explained?

Neural networks are opaque. Even knowing all the weights on all the nodes throughout the network does not give much insight into why the network produces the results that it produces. This lack of understanding has some philosophical appeal — after all, we do not understand how human consciousness arises from the neurons in our brains. As a practical matter, though, opaqueness impairs our ability to understand the results produced by a network.

If only we could ask it to tell us how it is making its decision in the form of rules. Eventually, research into rule extraction from networks may bring good results. Until then, users of neural networks willingly sacrifice explicability for the predictive accuracy that neural networks can deliver.

Sensitivity Analysis

A technique called *sensitivity analysis* can be used to get an idea of how opaque models work. Sensitivity analysis does not provide explicit rules, but it does indicate the relative importance of the inputs to the result of the network. Sensitivity analysis uses the test set to determine how sensitive the output of the network is to each input. The following are the basic steps:

1. Find the average value for each input. For standardized inputs, the average value is zero.

2. Measure the output of the network when all inputs are at their average value.

3. Measure the output of the network when each input is modified, one at a time, to range through different values.

For some inputs, the output of the network changes as the input changes. The network is not *sensitive* to these inputs (at least when all other inputs are at their average value). Other inputs have a large effect on the output of the network. The network is *sensitive* to these inputs. The amount of change in the output measures the sensitivity of the network for each input. Using these measures for all the inputs creates a relative measure of the importance of each feature.

The problem with sensitivity analysis is that, given the complex, non-linear interactions inside a neural network, it is entirely possible that an input that seems to do nothing when other inputs are held to their average values becomes very important when some other input is at an extreme value.

WARNING Sensitivity analysis may explain what inputs are important for a neural network. On the other hand, the benefit of neural networks is that they find local patterns — and such patterns may easily be missed by sensitivity analysis.

Using Rules to Describe the Scores

Another method for trying to gain insight into the workings of a neural network model is to use the scores produced by the neural net as the target variable for a regression tree. The inputs to the tree model are the same as those used for the neural network model. This produces leaves containing records that are close to the average score for that leaf along with rules describing each leaf. Unfortunately, although this provides a description of high-scoring and low-scoring segments, it does not actually explain how the scores were arrived at.

When being able to provide an explanation for why someone got a particular score is important, neural networks are simply not the right tool. In one case, the authors built several attrition models for a mobile telephone service provider using various modeling techniques. A neural network model provided the best lift, but provided no insight into what should be done to retain a customer who was scored as highly likely to leave. A decision tree model that did not do quite as well at spotting the quitters provided rules that made it clear whether a high score was due to the customer being on an inappropriate rate plan, or having an unpopular handset, or living in a high-attrition area. The decision tree model was preferred.

Lessons Learned

Neural networks are a versatile data mining technique. Across a large number of industries and a large number of applications, neural networks have proven themselves over and over again in complicated domains, such as analyzing time series and detecting fraud, which are not easily amenable to other techniques.

The inspiration for artificial neural networks is a biological model of how brains work. Although predating digital computers, the basic ideas have proven powerful. In biology, neurons fire after their inputs reach a certain threshold. This model can be implemented on a computer as well. The field has really taken off since the 1980s, when statisticians started to use them and understand them better.

A neural network consists of artificial neurons connected together. Each neuron mimics its biological counterpart, taking various inputs, combining them, and producing an output. Because digital neurons process numbers, the activation function characterizes the neuron. In most cases, this function takes the weighted sum of its inputs and applies an S-shaped function to it. The result is a node that sometimes behaves in a linear fashion, and sometimes behaves in a nonlinear fashion — an improvement over standard statistical techniques.

The most common network for predictive modeling is the multi-layer perceptron. Radial basis function networks are also popular.

Neural networks require careful attention to data preparation. They are most easily trained when input fields have been mapped to a small range close to zero. This is a guideline to help train the network. Neural networks still work when a small amount of data falls outside the range.

Neural networks do have several drawbacks. One is that they work best when there are only a handful of input variables, and the technique itself does not help choose which variables to use, so variable selection is an issue. Also, when training a network, there is no guarantee that the resulting set of weights is optimal. To increase confidence in the result, build several networks and take the best one.

Perhaps the biggest problem is that a neural network cannot explain what it is doing. Decision trees are popular because they can provide a list of rules. There is no way to get an accurate set of rules from a neural network. In some sense, a neural network is explained by its weights, and a very complicated mathematical formula. Unfortunately, making sense of this is beyond our human powers of comprehension. Overall neural networks are very powerful and can produce good models; they just can't tell us how they do it.

Nearest Neighbor Approaches: Memory-Based Reasoning and Collaborative Filtering

You hear someone speak and immediately guess that she is from Australia. Why? Because her accent reminds you of other Australians you have met. Or you try a new restaurant expecting to like it because a friend with good taste recommended it. Both of these are examples of decisions based on experience. When faced with new situations, people are guided by memories of similar situations that they have experienced in the past. That is the basis for the data mining techniques introduced in this chapter.

Nearest-neighbor techniques are based on the concept of similarity. Memory-based reasoning (MBR) results are based on analogous situations in the past — much like deciding that a new friend is Australian based on past examples of Australian accents. Collaborative filtering (also called *social information filtering*) adds more information, using not just the similarities among neighbors, but also their preferences. The restaurant recommendation is an example of collaborative filtering.

Central to all these techniques is the idea of *similarity*. What really makes situations in the past similar to a new situation? Along with finding the similar records, there is the challenge of combining the information from the neighbors. These are the two key concepts for nearest-neighbor approaches.

This chapter begins with an introduction to MBR and an explanation of how it works. Because measures of distance and similarity are important to nearest-neighbor techniques, there is a section on distance metrics, including a discussion of the meaning of distance for data types, such as free text, that have no obvious geometric interpretation. The ideas of MBR are illustrated through two case studies, showing how MBR and MBR-like ideas have been applied in very diverse areas. Yet another case study, involving text mining, appears in Chapter 21. The chapter then looks at collaborative filtering, a popular approach to making recommendations, especially on the Web. Collaborative filtering is also based on nearest neighbors, but with a slight twist — instead of grouping restaurants or movies into neighborhoods, it groups the people recommending them.

Memory-Based Reasoning

The human ability to reason from experience depends on the ability to recognize appropriate examples from the past. A doctor diagnosing diseases, a claims analyst flagging fraudulent insurance claims, and a mushroom hunter spotting morels all follow a similar process. Each first identifies similar cases from experience and then applies knowledge of those examples to the problem at hand. This is the essence of memory-based reasoning. A database of known records is searched to find preclassified records similar to a new record. These *neighbors* are used for classification and estimation.

Applications of MBR span many areas:

Fraud detection. When new cases of fraud are similar to known cases of fraud (or quite dissimilar from known cases of not-fraud), MBR can find and flag them for further investigation.

Customer response prediction. The next customers likely to respond to an offer are probably similar to previous customers who have responded. MBR can easily identify the next likely customers.

Medical treatments. The most effective treatment for a given patient is probably the treatment that resulted in the best outcomes for similar patients. MBR can find the treatment that produces the best outcome.

Classifying responses. Free-text responses, such as those on the U.S. Census form for occupation and industry or complaints coming from customers, need to be classified into a fixed set of codes. MBR can process the free-text and assign the codes.

One of the strengths of MBR is its ability to use data "as is." Unlike other data mining techniques, it does not care about the format of the records. It only cares about the existence of two operations: a *distance function* capable of calculating a distance between any two records and a *combination function* capable of combining results from several neighbors to arrive at an answer. These functions can be defined for many kinds of records, including records with complex or unusual data types such as geographic locations, images, audio files, and free text — types of data that are usually difficult to handle with other analysis techniques. One case study in this chapter describes using MBR for medical diagnosis, an example that takes advantage of ideas from image processing to determine whether a mammogram is normal or abnormal. Another case study borrows from the field of acoustic engineering, using ideas from MBR to describe how a popular mobile app, Shazam, manages to identify songs from snippets captured on mobile phones.

Another strength of MBR is its ability to adapt. Merely incorporating new data into the historical database causes MBR to learn about new categories and new definitions of old ones. MBR also produces good results without a long period devoted to training or to massaging incoming data into the right format. For instance, in the example of Shazam's recognizing songs, new songs are added into the database on a daily basis — and the application just works.

These advantages come at a cost. MBR tends to be a resource hog because a large amount of historical data must be readily available for finding neighbors. Classifying new records can require processing all the historical records to find the most similar neighbors — a more time-consuming process than applying an already-trained neural network or an already-built decision tree. There is also the challenge of finding good distance and combination functions, which often requires a bit of trial and error and intuition.

Look-Alike Models

Look-alike models are the simplest type of MBR model, because they use only one neighbor. The model itself consists of two things:

- A training set with known target values
- A similarity measure

The combination function is easy — whatever the value is at the neighbor. Look-alike models and similarity models (introduced in Chapter 6) are almost the same thing; the difference is that similarity models use the distance as the target, and look-alike models use target information from the nearest neighbor.

Training and Scoring a Look-Alike Model

The process of scoring a look-alike model is easy. For any unknown record, a look-alike model finds the most similar record in the training set, and then simply uses the target value from that record.

What is the process of training a look-alike model? It is almost as easy as scoring it. The training data simply needs to be stored somewhere, such as in a database. And, the similarity measure needs to be defined.

Sometimes, defining the similarity measure is quite easy. For instance, if all the inputs are numeric in the training set, then the records can be treated as points in space, and Euclidean distance is a good measure of similarity (standardizing the values is a good idea in this case). Euclidean distance between a new record and a record in the training set is simply the process of taking the square root of the sum of the squares of the difference between the values in the new record and the record in the training set. Later in this chapter, the case study on identifying songs describes a much more complicated similarity measure for a look-alike model.

Look-Alike Models and Paired Tests

Look-alike models are related to what statisticians call *paired tests*. Consider a nationwide retailer that wants to test something new — say a new product, new pricing, a new store layout, or whatever. How might it do this testing? The problem is that even if it makes the change and sees sales increase, the retailer cannot be sure the change is responsible; sales might have increased anyway. How can the retailer increase the confidence that the sales increase is due to its conscious efforts?

The solution is the paired test. The idea is to find pairs of stores that are as similar as possible to each other. The stores have similar demographics in their local neighborhoods; they have similar sizes and formats. The sales for the stores have similar responses to past campaigns. After pairs of stores have been identified, the retailer can apply the treatment to one half of each pair. The comparison between the two stores in a pair gives a much better idea of whether or not the treatment has an effect. If sales go up by the same amount in both stores, then the treatment is probably not the cause. On the other hand, if the treated store has a significant increase in sales compared to the untreated one, there is a good chance that the treatment is causing the increase.

A paired test is very similar to look-alike models, because both involve the idea of distance (or equivalently, similarity), and both use results in the nearest neighbor for analysis.

Example: Using MBR to Estimate Rents in Tuxedo, New York

The next simplest case after the look-alike model (which looks at one nearest neighbor) is combining information from the two nearest neighbors. This example illustrates how MBR works by estimating the cost of renting an apartment in the town of Tuxedo by combining data on rents in two *similar* towns.

The first step is to identify the neighbors, and the second is to combine the information from them. Figure 9-1 illustrates the first of these steps by using a scatter plot of towns in New York State. The dimensions on the scatter plot are not geographic; they are the population (on a log scale) and the median home value. Just the scatter plot itself is interesting. Brooklyn and Queens, for instance, are close neighbors in the chart, both geographically and on this scatter plot, because they have similar populations and similar median home values. They are quite distant from Manhattan, because Manhattan's home prices are in a class by themselves.

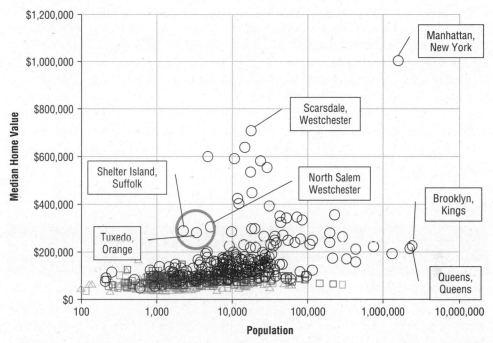

Figure 9-1: Based on 2000 census population and home value, the town of Tuxedo in Orange County has Shelter Island and North Salem as its two nearest neighbors.

TIP Neighborhoods can be found in many dimensions. The choice of dimensions determines which records are close to one another. For some purposes, geographic proximity might be important. For other purposes home price or average lot size or population density might be more important. The choice of dimensions and the choice of a distance metric are crucial to any nearest-neighbor approach.

The goal of the MBR example is to make predictions about the town of Tuxedo in Orange County, New York, by looking at its neighbors — not its *geographic* neighbors in the Ramapo Mountains between the Hudson and Delaware Rivers, but rather its neighbors based on descriptive variables. On the scatter plot, Tuxedo's nearest neighbor is Shelter Island, which is really an island near the tip of Long Island's North Fork. Tuxedo's second-closest neighbor is North Salem, a town in Westchester County near the Connecticut border. These towns fall at about the middle of a list sorted by population and near the top of one sorted by home value. Although they are many miles apart, along these two dimensions, Shelter Island and North Salem are very similar to Tuxedo.

The next step after identifying the neighbors is to combine information from the neighbors to infer something about the unknown record. For this example, the goal is to estimate the cost of renting a house in Tuxedo. There is more than one reasonable way to combine data from the neighbors. Table 9-1 shows what the 2000 Census reports about rents in the two towns selected as neighbors. For each town, the Census provides two types of information about rents. One is the median rent in the town. The second is the proportion of households paying rent in each of several price bands. The challenge is to figure out how best to use this data to characterize rents in the neighbors and then how to combine information from the neighbors to come up with an estimate that characterizes rents in Tuxedo in the same way. (And, of course, the Census Bureau provides this information about Tuxedo, but this example ignores that information.)

Table 9-1: The Neighbors

TOWN	POP.	RENTING HOUSE- HOLDS	MEDIAN RENT	RENT <$500	RENT $750	RENT $1000	RENT $1,500	RENT >$1,500	NON- CASH
Shelter Island	2,228	160	$804	3.1%	34.6%	31.4%	10.7%	3.1%	17.0%
North Salem	5,173	244	$1,150	3.0%	10.2%	21.6%	30.9%	24.2%	10.2%
Tuxedo	3,334	349	$907	4.6%	27.2%	29.6%	23.8%	3.8%	14.8%

Although Tuxedo's nearest neighbors, the towns of North Salem and Shelter Island, have similar median rents, the distributions of rents in the two towns are quite different. On Shelter Island, a plurality of homes, 34.6 percent, rent in the $500 to $750 range. In the town of North Salem, the largest number of homes, 30.9 percent, rent in the $1,000 to $1,500 range. Furthermore, while only 3.1 percent of homes on Shelter Island rent for more than $1,500, 24.2 percent of homes in North Salem do. On the other hand, at $804, the *median* rent on Shelter Island is above the $750 ceiling of the most common range, while the median rent in North Salem, $1,150, is below the floor of the most common range for that town. If the *average* rent were available, it too would be a good candidate for characterizing the rents in the various towns.

The average rent can be estimated from the percents in the rent ranges, by estimating the average within each range. The midpoint is a reasonable average; however, an estimate is needed for the two extremes. Using the values of $400 for the under-$500 crowd and $1,750 for the over-$1,500 crowd results in the following estimated averages:

▪ Shelter Island, $691.40

▪ North Salem, $1,074.50

Notice that the averages differ much more than the medians, probably because the distribution of rents is quite different in each town.

The next question is how to combine the averages. Here are four possibilities:

▪ The average ($882.95)

▪ Average weighted by number of renting households ($922.78)

▪ Average weighted by distance

▪ Average weighted by both distance and number of renting households

(There is no estimate for the last two, because the exact distances have not been calculated.)

Another way is to take the average of the two median rents, resulting in an estimate of $977 for Tuxedo. The weighted average has a value of $1,012.97. More exotic approaches, such as taking the midpoint of the most common range might also be appropriate in some circumstances.

The median rent in Tuxedo is $907. Taking the unweighted estimated average from the two neighbors underestimates the value. The weighted average slightly overestimates the average. The two ways of combining the median are also overestimates. It is hard to say which is better. The moral is that there is not always an obvious "best" combination function.

Challenges of MBR

In the simple example in the previous section, the training set consists of all towns in New York, each described by a handful of numeric fields such as population, number of renting households, and median rent. Distance is determined by placement on a scatter plot with axes scaled to appropriate ranges, and the number of neighbors arbitrarily set to two. The combination function is some sort of average of the values at the neighbors.

All these choices are useful for a simple demonstration, although they may not be the best choices in practice. In general, using MBR involves several choices:

▪ Choosing an appropriate set of training records

▪ Choosing the most efficient way to represent the training records

▪ Choosing the distance function, the combination function, and the number of neighbors

Let's look at each of these in turn.

Choosing a Balanced Set of Historical Records

The training set needs to provide good coverage of the population so that the nearest neighbors of an unknown record are useful for predictive purposes. A random sample may not provide sufficient coverage for all target values. Some categories are much more frequent than others and the more frequent categories dominate the random sample.

> **TIP** When selecting the training set for MBR, be sure that each target category has roughly the same number of records supporting it. As a general rule, several dozen records for each category are a minimum to get adequate support; hundreds or thousands of examples are not unusual.

MBR is similar to other techniques that prefer a balanced training set. Heart disease is more common than liver cancer, normal mammograms are more common than abnormal mammograms, responders are less common than non-responders, and so on. To achieve balance, the training set should, if possible, contain roughly equal numbers of records representing the different categories.

Representing the Training Data

The performance of MBR in making predictions depends on how the training set is represented. The scatter plot approach illustrated in Figure 9-1 works for explaining the ideas with two or three variables and a small number of records, but it does not scale well.

Exhaustive Comparisons

The simplest method for finding the nearest neighbors requires calculating the distance from an unknown case to all the records in the training set, and then choosing the records that have the smallest distance. As the number of records grows, the time needed to find the neighbors for a new record grows just as quickly. This is especially true if the records are stored in a relational database (Chapter 17 describes relational databases in more detail). In this case, the query looks something like:

```
SELECT distance(),rec.category
FROM historical_records rec
ORDER BY 1 ASCENDING;
```

The notation `distance()` fills in for whatever the particular distance function happens to be. In this case, the database is probably going to sort all the historical records to get the handful needed for the nearest neighbors, requiring a full-table scan followed by a sort — an expensive couple of operations for scoring a single record. It is possible to eliminate the sort by walking through the table while updating another table of the records with the smallest distances, inserting and deleting records as appropriate.

The performance of relational databases is pretty good nowadays. The challenge with scoring data for MBR is that each record getting scored needs to be compared against every case in the database. Scoring a single new record does not take much time, even when there are millions of historical records. However, scoring many new records can have poor performance.

R-Tree

An alternative to a full table scan is a specialized type of index that is not generally available in relational databases. This index is called an *R-Tree*. Although the technical details are beyond the scope of this book, a typical use of R-Trees is familiar to most readers. Consider the problem of using a geographic map — particularly for zooming out and panning to neighboring locations (and trying to keep track of what is on the map while this is going on). R-Trees were invented to speed up such operations, by building two-dimensional index structures. In databases, the traditional indexes are one-dimensional; there is no way to put longitude and latitude into a single index, so the index "knows" which locations are close to each other in whatever direction. A traditional index only knows when the latitudes are close, or when the longitudes are close (although some databases do have special extensions to support R-Trees, particularly to support geographic data types).

An R-Tree keeps track of neighbors in any direction (and there might be more than two dimensions) by placing a grid over the points. The grid divides the data into boxes. The R-Tree knows two things about each box: which data points are in the box and where its neighbors are. Such a structure is quite efficient for maps. A user sees a map, which really consists of one or more boxes of the R-Tree. As the user pans and zooms out, each operation requires finding more boxes that are next to what is on the map. This is much more efficient than searching through all the geographic data to find this information.

The same idea works for MBR. Instead of scanning through all the records to find a neighbor, an R-Tree index on the training set makes finding neighbors more efficient. SAS's Enterprise Miner employs such an approach in its implementation of MBR. However, most data mining tools do not offer MBR functionality at all.

Reducing the Training Set Size

Another way to make MBR more efficient is to reduce the number of records in the training set. Figure 9-2 shows a scatter plot for categorical data, with a well-defined boundary between the two categories. The points above the line are all diamonds and those below the line are all circles. Although this graph has forty points in it, most of the points are redundant. That is, they are not really necessary for classification purposes.

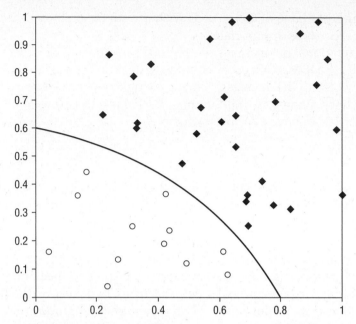

Figure 9-2: Perhaps the cleanest training set for MBR is one that divides neatly into two disjoint sets.

Figure 9-3 shows that only eight points in it are needed to get essentially the same classification results using MBR. Given that the size of the training set has such a large influence on the performance of MBR, being able to reduce the size is a significant performance boost.

How can this reduced set of records be found? The most practical method is to look for clusters containing records all in a single category. The centers of the clusters are candidates for a reduced set. However, better candidates might be records that are on the edges of the clusters (as in the example in the previous two figures). This works well when the different categories are quite separate. However, when the categories overlap and are not so well-defined, using clusters to reduce the size of the training set can cause MBR to produce poor results. Finding an optimal set of "support records" has been an area of research, and is related to the idea of support vector machines discussed in Chapter 7 and to Voronoi maps in Chapter 13. When such an optimal set can be found, the historical records can sometimes be reduced to the level where they fit inside a spreadsheet, making the application of MBR to new records quite efficient.

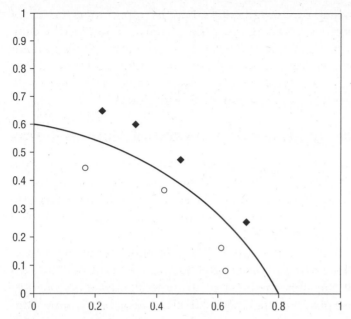

Figure 9-3: This smaller set of points returns the same results as in Figure 9-2 using MBR.

Determining the Distance Function, Combination Function, and Number of Neighbors

The distance function, combination function, and number of neighbors are the key ingredients in using MBR. The same set of historical records can prove very useful or not at all useful for predictive purposes, depending on these criteria. Before discussing these issues in detail, take a look at a detailed case study.

Case Study: Using MBR for Classifying Anomalies in Mammograms

This example of MBR is based on work by Dr. Georgia Tourassi at Duke University Medical Center. Her specialty is radiology, and, in particular, understanding whether a particular mammogram contains anomalies that pose a danger to the patient.

One of the challenges in working on automated diagnostic systems are doctors themselves: They tend to be skeptical of automated methods. Some of this skepticism is based on their education, which is rich in case-by-case examples, teaching them to rely on their own judgment. Perhaps as important is the risk of malpractice, when the doctor's interpretation differs from an automated system. As you will see, the beauty of Dr. Tourassi's system is that it informs the radiologist, and makes suggestions, but it always shows the evidence to back up the suggestion. It serves more as a knowledgeable assistant than as a know-it-all, perhaps explaining why she gives it the name "Bosom Buddy."

The Business Problem: Identifying Abnormal Mammograms

Women potentially at risk for breast cancer periodically go through radiological tests called mammograms. These tests produce images of the breast tissue, which radiologists inspect for abnormalities. Happily, most abnormalities do not threaten the patient's health. The purpose of the exam, though, is to screen the patient for potentially dangerous tumors and cancers.

Clearly, an automated assistant for diagnosis is a benefit. For one thing, different radiologists have different strengths, in terms of finding different types of abnormalities or any abnormality at all. In general, the net is cast wide, meaning that a high false positive rate is acceptable, because the mammogram is followed up by more tests, such as a biopsy of any suspected mass. A false negative is much more serious, because missing an abnormality can result in adverse health consequences that go untreated.

Applying MBR to the Problem

A radiologist learns how to read mammograms by studying thousands of them, before he or she ever sees any patients. Some systems for finding anomalies might try to identify features in the mammograms and develop rules. Instead, the MBR approach essentially takes many preclassified mammograms and, for a new mammogram, finds the ones that are closest.

Figure 9-4 shows the basic idea. The knowledge base contains several thousand mammograms. Dr. Tourassi faced the problem of measuring how close different images are. She investigated several different measures, settling on a measure called *mutual information*. As the sidebar "Mutual Information for Comparing Images" explains, this is a measure for answering the question: "When you have one mammogram, how much more information do you need to obtain the other?" The idea is that two identical mammograms require no additional information, so their mutual information similarity is maximized (the resulting distance between them is zero). If there is no relationship at all between the pixels in the images, then the images are not similar.

Mutual information requires a complex calculation to measure the distance between two mammograms. So, Bosom Buddy first finds candidate images using simpler techniques to define the neighborhood. It then calculates the mutual information measure between the original image and each of these candidates, returning the closest candidates back to the radiologist.

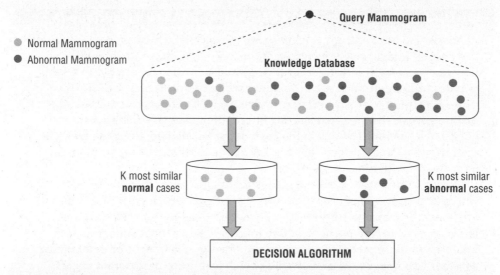

Figure 9-4: The basic idea for automated diagnosis of mammogram abnormalities using MBR finds similar normal and abnormal cases in the knowledge base, and then decides which to present to the physician. (Courtesy of Dr. Tourassi)

MUTUAL INFORMATION FOR COMPARING IMAGES

Mutual information is a measure that dives into the world of probability and information theory to determine how close two sets of variables are. For images, the basic idea is to look at the mutual information of two images on a pixel-by-pixel basis. This requires that the images be aligned and sized in the same way, and have similar lighting. Fortunately, mammograms are taken in a constrained environment, so they generally meet these requirements.

The definition of mutual information can be stated as: Given one image, how much information is needed to construct the second image? If the two images are the same, then no additional information is needed, and the mutual information is very high. If half the second image is identical to the first, and the other half relatively random, then the mutual information is in the middle range. One way to think of mutual information is that it extends the idea of correlation to situations more complex than simple numbers.

The calculation of mutual information is much more complicated than its definition. The idea is to treat each image as if it were a long sequence of pixels, and then to calculate the mutual information based on the pixel representation. The concept is closely related to the information theoretic notion of entropy — the same entropy introduced in Chapter 7 on decision trees. An image has an entropy associated with it, which is a measure of the "disorder" of the pixels comprising the image. An image that is all black has zero entropy, because there is no disorder in the sequence of pixels. An image of random pixels has high entropy.

Continued

MUTUAL INFORMATION FOR COMPARING IMAGES *(continued)*

An extension of entropy is *conditional entropy*, which measures the entropy in a second image, given the information in the first image. Mutual information can be defined directly from entropy and conditional entropy. The mathematics of the definition are beyond the scope of this book. However, the concept is quite useful in a variety of domains. The concept of mutual information gets used when transmitting information using a coding scheme in a noisy environment. The bits in the code might get flipped along the way. The right original code is essentially the valid code that has the highest mutual information with the observed bits.

Mutual information is advantageous for image processing, because it works at the level of pixels without trying to figure out, a priori, features in the image. The example here is as a similarity measure for MBR. However, it is also used to find portions of two images that are most similar to each other — something that is very useful for aligning two images or determining whether two images are of the same object, just taken at different angles.

One interesting question about this system is why the neighborhood is, in essence, calculated twice, once for the normal cases and once for the abnormal cases. This is a solution to the problem of balancing the model set. In the real world, almost all mammograms are normal, so that is not a good training set. In fact, there may be more ways for a mammogram to be abnormal than normal, so the proportion of abnormal cases in the knowledge base might be much more than the proportion of normal cases. And, as time goes by, more abnormal cases may be added than normal cases. By selecting each neighborhood individually, and then doing further analysis, Bosom Body remains more stable, because adding more of one type of case still allows the other type to be considered.

TIP With MBR, one way to work with an unbalanced training set is to find the nearest neighbors with each class label, then process the neighbors afterwards to determine which are really the best.

The Total Solution

Figure 9-5 shows what the system looks like in practice. On the left of the screen is a new mammogram. On the right are the most similar examples from the database, with their classifications of normal or abnormal. The system suggests an outcome, using a color coding scheme (that does not show up in black and white), both for the new mammogram and for those from the knowledge base.

One advantage of this system is that the nearest neighbors are available for further analysis. The radiologist can agree or disagree with the similarity measure, and — because the nearest neighbors are visible — has the information to make a more informed decision.

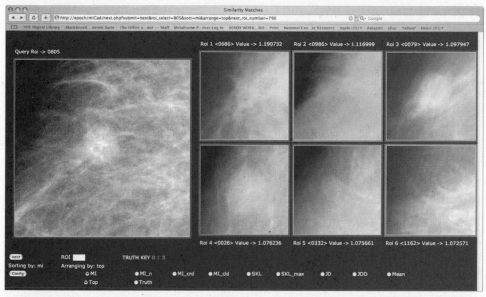

Figure 9-5: Similarity matches for a mammogram suggest whether or not the mammogram is normal or abnormal — and provide nearby examples for further investigation.

Measuring Distance and Similarity

Suppose you are going to travel to a small town and you want to know the weather. If you have a newspaper that lists weather reports for major cities, what you might do is find the weather for cities near the small town. You might look at the closest city and just take its weather, or do some sort of combination of the forecasts for, say, the three closest cities. This is an example of using MBR to find the weather forecast. The distance function being used is the geographic distance between the two locations. Web services and phone apps that provide a weather forecast for any ZIP code supplied by a user do something similar.

What Is a Distance Function?

Distance is the way the MBR measures similarity, and distance has a strict mathematical definition. A true distance metric, where the distance from point A to point B is denoted by d(A,B), has four key properties:

- **Well-defined.** The distance between two points is always defined and is a non-negative real number, $d(A,B) \geq 0$.
- **Identity.** The distance from one point to itself is always zero, so $d(A,A) = 0$.

- **Commutativity.** Direction does not make a difference, so the distance from A to B is the same as the distance from B to A: d(A,B) = d(B,A). This property precludes one-way roads, for instance.

- **Triangle inequality.** Visiting an intermediate point C on the way from A to B never shortens the distance, so d(A,B) ≥ d(A,C) + d(C,B).

What makes these properties useful? The fact that distance is well-defined implies that every record has a neighbor somewhere in the database — and MBR needs neighbors in order to work. The identity property makes distance conform to the intuitive idea that the most similar record to a given record is the original record itself. Commutativity and the triangle inequality make the nearest neighbors local and well-behaved. Adding a new record into the database does bring an existing record any closer. Similarity is a matter reserved for just two records at a time.

However, for the purposes of MBR, the mathematical definition of distance is overkill. MBR simply needs a measure for determining the closest records in the database, and some of the conditions can be relaxed. For instance, the distance function does not need to be *commutative*; that is, the distance from A to B may not be the same as the distance from B to A. This is analogous to measuring road distance in a city where many of the streets are one-way. The distance between two locations driving in a car might be quite different, because of the one-way streets.

Even when the distance measure follows all the mathematical rules, the set of nearest neighbors can have some peculiar properties. For instance, the nearest neighbor to a record B may be A, but A may have many neighbors closer than B, as shown in Figure 9-6. This situation does not pose a problem for MBR.

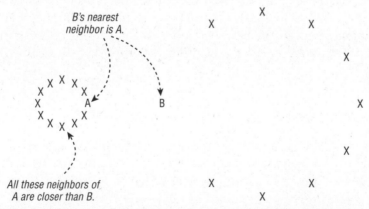

Figure 9-6: B's nearest neighbor is A, but A has many neighbors closer than B.

Building a Distance Function One Field at a Time

Understanding distance as a geometric concept is easy, but how can distance be defined for records consisting of many different fields of different types? The answer is: one field at a time. Consider some sample records such as those shown in Table 9-2.

Table 9-2: Five Customers in a Marketing Database

RECNUM	GENDER	AGE	SALARY
1	Female	27	$ 19,000
2	Male	51	$ 64,000
3	Male	52	$105,000
4	Female	33	$ 55,000
5	Male	45	$ 45,000

Figure 9-7 illustrates a scatter plot in three dimensions. The records are a bit complicated, with two numeric fields and one categorical. This example shows how to define field distance functions for each field, then combine them into a single record distance function that gives a distance between two records.

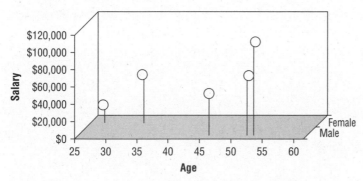

Figure 9-7: This scatter plot shows the five records from Table 9-2 in three dimensions — age, salary, and gender — and suggests that standard distance is a good metric for nearest neighbors.

The four most common distance functions for numeric fields are:

■ Absolute value of the difference: $|A{-}B|$
■ Square of the difference: $(A{-}B)^2$

- Normalized absolute value: |A–B|/(maximum difference)
- Absolute value of the difference of standardized values: |(A – average)/(standard deviation) – (B – average)/(standard deviation)| *which is equivalent to* |(A – B)/(standard deviation)|

Of these, the last two are more useful than the first two, because they remove bias based on the size of the numeric value. The normalized absolute value is always between 0 and 1. Because ages are much smaller than the salaries, the normalized absolute value is a good choice when both of them are in the data — so neither field will dominate the record distance function (difference of standardized values is also a good choice). For the ages, the distance matrix looks like Table 9-3.

Table 9-3: Distance Matrix Based on Ages of Customers

	27	51	52	33	45
27	0.00	0.96	1.00	0.24	0.72
51	0.96	0.00	0.04	0.72	0.24
52	1.00	0.04	0.00	0.76	0.28
33	0.24	0.72	0.76	0.00	0.48
45	0.72	0.24	0.28	0.48	0.00

Gender is an example of categorical data. The simplest distance function is the "identical to" function, which is 0 when the genders are the same and 1 otherwise:

d_{gender}(female, female): = 0

d_{gender}(female, male): = 1

d_{gender}(female, female): = 1

d_{gender}(male, male): = 0

So far, so simple. Now three field distance functions need to merge into a single record distance function. The two common ways to do this are:

- Manhattan distance or summation: $d_{sum}(A,B) = d_{gender}(A,B) + d_{age}(A,B) + d_{salary}(A,B)$
- Euclidean distance: $d_{Euclid}(A,B) = sqrt(d_{gender}(A,B)^2 + d_{age}(A,B)^2 + d_{salary}(A,B)^2)$

Table 9-4 shows the nearest neighbors for each of the points using the three functions.

Table 9-4: Set of Nearest Neighbors for Three Distance Functions, Ordered Nearest to Farthest

	D_{SUM}	D_{NORM}	D_{EUCLID}
1	1,4,5,2,3	1,4,5,2,3	1,4,5,2,3
2	2,5,3,4,1	2,5,3,4,1	2,5,3,4,1
3	3,2,5,4,1	3,2,5,4,1	3,2,5,4,1
4	4,1,5,2,3	4,1,5,2,3	4,1,5,2,3
5	5,2,3,4,1	5,2,3,4,1	5,2,3,4,1

In this case, the sets of nearest neighbors are exactly the same regardless of how the component distances are combined. This is a coincidence, caused by the fact that the five records fall into two well-defined clusters. One of the clusters is lower-paid, younger females and the other is better-paid, older males. These clusters imply that if two records are close to each other relative to one field, then they are close on all fields, so the way the distances on each field are combined is not important. This is not a very common situation, because records do not usually cluster quite so cleanly.

Consider what happens when a new record (Table 9-5) is used for the comparison. This new record is not in either of the clusters. Table 9-6 shows her respective distances from the training set with the list of her neighbors, from nearest to farthest.

Table 9-5: New Customer

RECNUM	GENDER	AGE	SALARY
New	Female	45	$100,000

Table 9-6: Set of Nearest Neighbors for New Customer

	1	2	3	4	5	NEIGHBORS
d_{sum}	1.662	1.659	1.338	1.003	1.640	4,3,5,2,1
d_{Euclid}	0.781	1.052	1.251	0.494	1.000	4,1,5,2,3

Now the set of neighbors depends on how the record distance function combines the field distance functions. In fact, the second-nearest neighbor using the summation function is the farthest neighbor using the Euclidean and vice versa. Compared to the summation metric, the Euclidean metric tends to favor neighbors where all the fields are relatively close. It punishes Record 3 because the genders are different and are maximally far apart (a distance of 1.00). Correspondingly, it favors Record 1 because the genders are the same.

The summation and Euclidean functions can also incorporate weights so each field contributes a different amount to the record distance function. MBR usually produces good results when all the weights are equal to 1. However, sometimes weights can be used to incorporate a priori knowledge, such as a particular field suspected of having a large effect on the classification.

Distance Functions for Other Data Types

A five-digit American ZIP code is often represented as a simple number. Do any of the default distance functions for numeric fields make any sense? No. The difference between two randomly chosen ZIP codes has no meaning. Well, almost no meaning — a ZIP code does encode location information. The first three digits represent a postal zone — for instance, all ZIP codes in Manhattan start with "100," "101," or "102."

Furthermore, there is a general pattern of ZIP codes increasing from east to west. Codes that start with 0 are in New England and Puerto Rico; those beginning with 9 are on the West Coast. This suggests a distance function that approximates geographic distance by looking at the high-order digits of the ZIP code.

- $d_{ZIP}(A,B) = 0.0$ if the ZIP codes are identical

- $d_{ZIP}(A,B) = 0.1$ if the first three digits are identical (for example, "20008" and "20015")

- $d_{ZIP}(A,B) = 0.5$ if the first digits are identical (for example, "95050" and "98125")

- $d_{ZIP}(A,B) = 1.0$ if the first digits are not identical (for example, "02138" and "94704")

Of course, if geographic distance were truly of interest, a better approach would be to look up the latitude and longitude of each ZIP code in a table and calculate the distances that way (this information is available for the United States from www.census.gov). For many purposes, however, geographic proximity is not nearly as important as some other measure of similarity. The ZIP codes 10011 and 10031 are both in Manhattan, but from a marketing point of view, they don't have much else in common. One is an upscale downtown neighborhood and the other is a working class Harlem neighborhood. On the other hand 02138 and 94704 are on opposite coasts, but are likely to respond similarly to direct mail from a political action committee, because they are for Cambridge, Massachusetts, and Berkeley, California, respectively.

To capture the demographic characteristics of a ZIP code, replacing the ZIP code with descriptive information from the census is better than using the ZIP code by itself. The Census Bureau provides information such as the median household income, proportion of households with children, and commuting distance. Replacing ZIP codes with such descriptors allows MBR to consider as neighbors two ZIP codes that are similar along these dimensions.

When a Distance Metric Already Exists

In some situations a distance metric already exists, but it is difficult to spot. These situations generally arise in one of two forms. Sometimes, a function already exists that provides a distance measure that can be adapted for use in MBR. Chapter 21 has an example of classifying news stories, which is based on a distance metric that already existed to support a text retrieval application that could retrieve stories similar to one already found.

Other times, there are fields that do not appear to capture distance, but can be pressed into service. An example of such a hidden distance field is solicitation history. Two customers who were chosen for a particular solicitation in the past are "close," even though the reasons why they were chosen may no longer be available; two who were not chosen, are close, but not as close; and one that was chosen and one that was not are far apart. The advantage of this metric is that it can incorporate previous decisions, even if the basis for the decisions is no longer available. On the other hand, it does not work well for customers who were not around during the original solicitation, so some sort of neutral weighting must be applied to them.

Considering whether the original customers responded to the solicitation can extend this function further, resulting in a solicitation metric like:

- $d_{solicitation}(A, B) = 0$, when A and B both responded to the solicitation
- $d_{solicitation}(A, B) = 0.1$, when A and B were both chosen but neither responded
- $d_{solicitation}(A, B) = 0.2$, when neither A nor B was chosen, but both were available in the data
- $d_{solicitation}(A, B) = 0.3$, when A and B were both chosen, but only one responded
- $d_{solicitation}(A, B) = 0.3$, when one or both were not considered
- $d_{solicitation}(A, B) = 1.0$, when one was chosen and the other was not

The particular values are not sacrosanct; they are only meant as a guide for measuring similarity and showing how previous information and response histories can be incorporated into a distance function.

The Combination Function: Asking the Neighbors for Advice

The distance function is used to determine which records comprise the neighborhood. This section presents different ways to combine data gathered from those neighbors to make a prediction. The first example in this chapter estimated the median rent in the town of Tuxedo by taking an average of the median rents in similar towns. In that example, averaging was the combination function. This section explores other methods of canvassing the neighborhood.

The Simplest Approach: One Neighbor

The simplest approach for MBR is to use only one neighbor. This is the approach taken by the look-alike model. Simply find the closest neighbor and choose the value on the neighbor. This method works for both categorical and numeric targets.

The Basic Approach for Categorical Targets: Democracy

One common combination function is for the k nearest neighbors to vote on an answer — "democracy" in data mining. When MBR is used for classification, each neighbor casts its vote for its own class. The proportion of votes for each class is an estimate of the probability that the new record belongs to the corresponding class. When the task is to assign a single class, it is simply the one with the most votes. When the target has only two categories, an odd number of neighbors should be polled to avoid ties. As a general rule, use $c+1$ neighbors when there are c categories to ensure that at least one class has a plurality.

In Table 9-7, the five test cases presented earlier have been augmented with a flag that signals whether the customer has become inactive.

Table 9-7: Customers with Attrition History

RECNUM	GENDER	AGE	SALARY	INACTIVE
1	Female	27	$19,000	no
2	Male	51	$64,000	yes
3	Male	52	$105,000	yes
4	Female	33	$55,000	yes
5	Male	45	$45,000	no
New	Female	45	$100,000	?

For this example, three of the customers have become inactive and two have not, an almost balanced training set. For illustrative purposes, try to determine whether the new record is active or inactive by using different values of k for two distance functions: the Euclidean distance and the summation distance (Table 9-8).

Table 9-8: Using MBR to Determine Whether the New Customer Will Become Inactive

	NEIGHBORS	NEIGHBOR ATTRITION	K = 1	K = 2	K = 3	K = 4	K = 5
d_{sum}	4,3,5,2,1	Y,Y,N,Y,N	yes	yes	yes	yes	yes
d_{Euclid}	4,1,5,2,3	Y,N,N,Y,Y	yes	?	no	?	yes

The question marks indicate that no prediction has been made due to a tie among the neighbors. Notice that different values of k do affect the classification. This suggests using the percentage of neighbors in agreement to estimate the level of confidence in the prediction (Table 9-9).

Table 9-9: Attrition Prediction with Confidence

	K = 1	K = 2	K = 3	K = 4	K = 5
d_{sum}	yes, 100%	yes, 100%	yes, 67%	yes, 75%	yes, 60%
d_{Euclid}	yes, 100%	yes, 50%	no, 67%	yes, 50%	yes, 60%

The confidence level works just as well with more than two categories. However, with more categories, there is a greater chance that no single category will have a majority vote. One of the key assumptions about MBR (and data mining in general) is that the training set provides sufficient information for predictive purposes. If the neighborhoods of new cases consistently produce no obvious choice of classification, then the data simply may not contain the necessary information and the choice of dimensions and possibly of the training set needs to be reevaluated. Measuring the effectiveness of MBR on the test set determines whether the training set has a sufficient number of examples.

WARNING MBR is only as good as the training set it uses. To measure whether the training set is effective, measure the results of its predictions on the test set using two, three, and four neighbors. If the results are inconclusive or inaccurate, then the training set may not be large enough or the dimensions and distance metrics chosen may not be appropriate.

Weighted Voting for Categorical Targets

Weighted voting is similar to voting in the previous section except that the neighbors are not all created equal — it's more like shareholder democracy than one-person, one-vote. The size of the vote is proportional to the similarity of each neighbor, so closer neighbors have stronger votes than neighbors farther away do. To prevent problems when the distance might be 0, adding 1 to the distance before taking the inverse is common. Adding 1 also makes all the votes between 0 and 1.

Table 9-10 applies weighted voting to the previous example. The "yes, customer will become inactive" vote is the first; the "no, this is a good customer" vote is second.

Table 9-10: Attrition Prediction with Weighted Voting

	K = 1	K = 2	K = 3	K = 4	K = 5
d_{sum}	**0.749** to 0	**1.441** to 0	**1.441** to 0.647	**2.085** to 0.647	**2.085** to 1.290
d_{Euclid}	**0.669** to 0	**0.669** to 0.562	0.669 to **1.062**	**1.157** to 1062	**1.601** to 1.062

Weighted voting has introduced enough variation to prevent ties. The confidence level can now be calculated as the ratio of winning votes to total votes (see Table 9-11).

Table 9-11: Confidence with Weighted Voting

	1	2	3	4	5
d_{sum}	yes, 100%	yes, 100%	yes, 69%	yes, 76%	yes, 62%
d_{Euclid}	yes, 100%	yes, 54%	no, 61%	yes, 52%	yes, 60%

In this case, weighting the votes has only a small effect on the results and the confidence. The effect of weighting is largest when some neighbors are considerably farther away than others.

Numeric Targets

As with the example for rents in Tuxedo, you can also use MBR for numeric targets. The typical combination function is the average of the values in the neighbor (as in the example) or an average weighted by the similarity of the neighbors (the inverse of one plus distance).

MBR has both strengths and shortcomings for predicting numeric variables. One strength is that the resulting predictions are always reasonable, in the sense that they fall in the right range. This is because the resulting prediction is based on the actual values at the neighbors. Remember, regressions and neural networks can produce impossible results because the predictions range from negative infinity to positive infinity, and the range of reasonable values may not be so extreme. Another strength is that MBR produces many different values. Remember, decision trees always produce reasonable values, but decision trees produce too few distinct values — only one distinct value per leaf in a tree.

TIP MBR is a powerful technique for predicting numeric values. The technique produces reasonable values with many distinct values.

The biggest negative is that the range of predicted values is narrower than the range in the knowledge base. This is due to the averaging combination function, which smoothes out the maximum and minimum values.

One tweak to MBR that fixes this last problem is to combine it with regression. The idea is to calculate a local regression based on the neighbors. When doing such a regression, the variables for the regression are typically chosen first, and they may or may not be the same as the MBR dimensions. A group of neighbors is identified — typically at least ten neighbors — and the regression coefficients calculated just for the neighbors. This model can then be applied to the new data point being predicted. One problem with this method is that the resulting predictions might be discontinuous — that is, a very small change in an input value might change the nearest neighbors, and that might, in turn, have a big impact on the result.

This technique is closely related to a statistical technique based on local regression, called LOESS (locally estimated scatter plot smoothing), which was originally developed in the late 1970s and 1980s. As its name implies, the original application was to smooth scatter plots. Moreover, the original application insists that the predictions be continuous throughout the space. Local regression using MBR has no such requirement. LOESS and similar methods produce continuous predictions, unlike the local regression method, where moving a point just a little bit might change the neighbors and hence the final prediction.

Case Study: Shazam — Finding Nearest Neighbors for Audio Files

Arthur C. Clark once observed that any sufficiently advanced technology is indistinguishable from magic. The idea that a mobile device could listen to a song and identify it would have seemed quite far-fetched even in the 1990s. And yet, that is what Shazam and similar mobile applications do. Just let Shazam use your mobile device to listen to a song. After about half a minute of listening,

Shazam identifies the song, providing the name, artist, and so on. And, on some devices, you have a link to purchase the song online. Wow! This is magic. Or is it just advanced technology?

Of course, Shazam is not magic; it is just one of hundreds of thousands of mobile phone applications. This description of the algorithm is based on discussions with and papers by Avery Wang, the inventor of the algorithm. As the inventor, he tends to focus on the lower-level details, particularly the acoustic science and implementation to enhance performance (which are both quite impressive). However, the algorithm can also be understood in terms of MBR, particularly look-alike models, with the definition of distance being the most interesting aspect.

Building cool apps for mobile phones is not the only use for automatically identifying songs. Another use is listening to broadcast programming to find out which songs are being played — and then to determine whether or not the appropriate royalties are being paid. Shazam is not the only company that offers song identification apps, but it was the first one to do so.

Why This Feat Is Challenging

Recognizing songs through a mobile device is very challenging. For one thing, people do not usually listen to music in acoustic sound rooms, which eliminate outside sounds and offer no echoes or distortions. Not at all. People are more likely to be listening to music in a car, in a club, on the radio, or with friends, and always in an environment that has ambient noise, ranging from a car engine to background talking to random city sounds, sirens, children screaming, and so on.

Mobile phones do not offer best-of-breed microphones for picking up the sound. Mobile microphones are fine for picking up voice, but they are not designed for picking up all the nuances of music. To compound this problem, mobile phones then compress the sound and send it over noisy networks. All of these steps affect acoustic acuity. These problems are compounded by the fact that a general-purpose solution must work across a wide range of mobile phone models and transmission technologies.

Another challenge is that the snippet being matched can start at any point in the song. Shazam does not have the luxury of requiring that all songs start at the beginning. So, in addition to finding the match, Shazam must also determine where the matched snippet begins in the actual song.

For all these reasons, doing a direct comparison of two audio files is not going to work. Even if it were feasible, such comparisons would be very computationally expensive when matching one song requires comparing it to millions of known songs.

The Audio Signature

The first step in doing the match is representing songs and snippets of songs in the computer. This requires a bit of knowledge about how songs are composed of frequencies.

Figure 9-8 is a picture of a song in the frequency domain, called a spectrogram. The vertical axis has the possible frequencies that might be in the music. The horizontal axis is time. In this example, the frequencies are sampled every half second, and the strongest frequencies are darker in this chart. A spectrogram uniquely identifies any song. In fact, two spectrograms for a song are likely to differ, because of the factors just described. Background noise, compression, equipment acuity, all of these have some effect on the spectrogram.

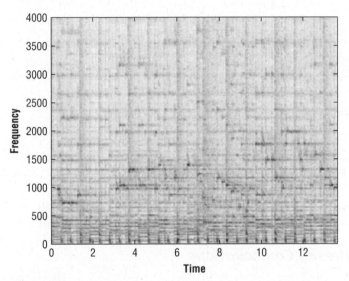

Figure 9-8: A spectrogram is a picture of a song in the frequency domain, with frequencies sampled every half second.

Figure 9-9 shows an alternative representation of the audio signature. The constellation plot simply contains the peaks in the spectrogram. By including only the peaks, the constellation plot solves many of the problems involving the quality of the sound, because background noise and compression have much less effect on the peaks in the spectrogram than in the other areas.

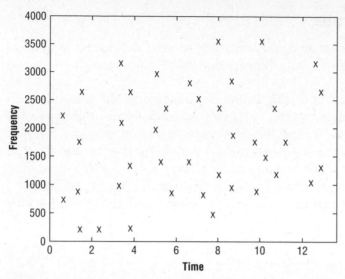

Figure 9-9: A constellation is a picture of the peaks of frequencies for a song in the frequency domain.

Measuring Similarity

Each song is defined by a unique constellation that maps out the peaks in the frequency domain. The problem of identifying a song becomes the problem of finding the nearest neighbors for the constellation of the new song in the database of known songs. This section discusses several different methods for finding the most similar songs.

Simple Distance Between Constellations

A constellation makes a pretty picture. However, it is essentially a list of the peaks, where each peak has three values:

- Time into song (X-coordinate)
- Frequency (Y-coordinate)
- Strength

For the purpose of identifying songs, it turns out the first two are sufficient for characterizing the song. So, a naïve similarity metric is the number of peaks that two songs have in common. Actually, a good variation on this metric is the number of peaks the two songs have in common, divided by the total number of distinct peaks.

This might work for two complete songs, or even for a complete song and another song starting at the beginning. However, it does not work for a snippet of a song, because the time into the snippet is different from the time into the song, so the anchors would never match (the X-coordinates would always be different).

Time Slice Similarity

The problem with the simple metric is that it does not take into account the fact that a snippet might not start at the beginning of the song. A variation is to look at the time slices (remember, the frequencies are sampled every second), and to ask how many, and which, time slices match.

Two time slices match if the peaks match. This can be relaxed, as for the simple metric, by counting the number of matching peaks divided by the number of peaks. If more than, say, 90% of the peaks match between two time slices, then the time slices match.

At first glance, it might seem that the number of matching time slices is a good measure of similarity. However, it is still insufficient, because similarity of random time slices is not enough. Instead, they need to be in time sequence, representing consecutive seconds of overlap between the snippet and the song. The similarity metric is the longest sequence of matching time slices, where the sequence requires that the time slices be sequential both in the snippet and in the song. In other words, the similarity metric is the number of seconds of overlap between the two song files.

The problem with this metric is simply one of calculation. All peaks in the time slices for the song need to be compared to all peaks in the time slices for the snippet — and this is a large number of time slices that need to be compared to each other for a single song, much more for the millions of songs in the comparison database.

Anchor Point Distance

The solution that Shazam came up with (and patented) involves the creation of anchor points in the constellation, and then comparing the anchor points instead of time slices. An anchor point is a peak in the constellation chart. This peak is then paired with other peaks that occur after it time-wise and within a particular range of frequencies, as illustrated in Figure 9-10.

For each pair, an anchor has the following information:

- The difference in time between the peak and the anchor
- The difference in frequency between the peak and the anchor
- The time and frequency of the anchor itself

Notice that the information is now relative instead of absolute. Instead of having the actual time of the paired peak, the time difference and frequency difference are included.

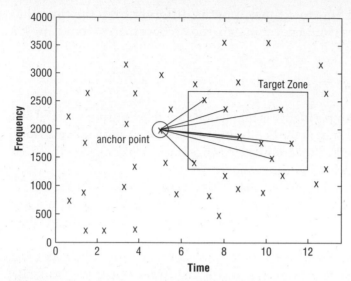

Figure 9-10: An anchor point is defined only by the set of peaks within a particular range of frequencies and times after the point in question.

The next step is to match the anchors between the song and the snippet. Now, two anchors match if enough of the paired peaks match, similar to matching the time slices in the previous section. Of course, some anchors match randomly. However, as Figure 9-11 shows, there is a pattern for overlapping matches. The matches that start at 41 seconds indicate an overlap. Anchors at 41 seconds in the song match the snippet at 0 seconds. There are no matches for three seconds, and then the anchors at 45 seconds match the snippet at 4 seconds, at 46 seconds match at 5 seconds, and so on. This figure captures a picture of the overlap.

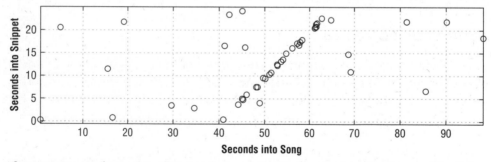

Figure 9-11: Anchor points that match are plotted in the absolute timeframe of both the song and the snippet. The vertical line starting at 41 seconds indicates that the snippet is matching that portion of the song.

Shazam Implementation

Shazam matches a snippet to a song by identifying the number of seconds of consecutive overlap, using MBR-like ideas. The overall approach is to:

1. Convert the snippet into a constellation of peaks

2. Turn the constellation into anchor points

3. Create the anchor-peak pairs

4. Identify matching anchor points between the song and the snippet

5. Determine the longest consecutive sequence of overlap between the snippet and each song

6. Return the song with the longest overlap

Much of the cleverness of Shazam's system involves making the comparisons as efficient as possible. Their system stores millions of songs, in a grid computing environment, and is able to compare a snippet to the entire database in a very short time, a short enough time for someone with a mobile app to click listen and to have the song identified long before the song ends.

Collaborative Filtering: A Nearest-Neighbor Approach to Making Recommendations

Neither of the authors considers himself a country music fan, but one of them is the proud owner of an autographed copy of an early Dixie Chicks CD. The Chicks, who did not yet have a major record label, were performing in a local bar one day and some friends who knew them from Texas made a very enthusiastic recommendation. The performance was truly memorable, featuring Martie Erwin's impeccable Bluegrass fiddle, her sister Emily on a bewildering variety of other instruments (most, but not all, with strings), and the seductive vocals of Laura Lynch (who also played a stand-up electric bass). At the break, the band sold and autographed a self-produced CD that the author still likes better than the one that later won them a Grammy. What does this have to do with nearest neighbor techniques? Well, it is a human example of collaborative filtering. A recommendation from trusted friends will cause one to try something one otherwise might not try.

Collaborative filtering is a variant of memory-based reasoning particularly well suited to the application of providing personalized recommendations. A collaborative filtering system starts with a history of people's preferences. The distance function determines similarity based on overlap of preferences — people who like the same thing are near to each other. In addition, votes are weighted by distances, so the votes of closer neighbors count more for the recommendation. In other words, it is a technique for finding music, books, wine, blogs, vacation spots, or anything else that fits into the existing preferences of a particular person by using the judgments of a peer group selected for its similar tastes. This approach is also called *social information filtering*.

Collaborative filtering automates the process of using word-of-mouth to decide whether people would like something. Knowing that lots of people liked something is not enough. *Who* liked it is also important. Everyone values some recommendations more highly than others. The recommendation of a close friend whose past recommendations have been right on target may be enough to get you to go see a new movie even if it is in a genre you generally dislike. On the other hand, an enthusiastic recommendation from a friend who thinks *Ace Ventura: Pet Detective* is the funniest movie ever made might serve to warn you off one you might otherwise have gone to see.

Preparing recommendations for a new customer using an automated collaborative filtering system has three steps:

1. Building a customer profile by getting the new customer to rate a selection of items such as movies, songs, or restaurants.

2. Comparing the new customer's profile with the profiles of other customers using some measure of similarity.

3. Using some combination of the ratings of customers with similar profiles to predict the rating that the new customer would give to items he or she has not yet rated.

The following sections examine each of these steps in a bit more detail.

Building Profiles

One challenge with collaborative filtering is that there are often far more items to be rated than any one person is likely to have experienced or be willing to rate. That is, profiles are usually sparse, meaning that there is little overlap among the users' preferences for making recommendations. Think of a user profile as a vector with one element per item in the universe of items to be rated. Each element of the vector represents the profile owner's rating for the corresponding item on a scale of –5 to 5, with 0 indicating neutrality and null values for no opinion.

If thousands or tens of thousands of elements are in the vector and each customer decides which ones to rate, any two customers' profiles are likely to end up with few overlaps. On the other hand, forcing customers to rate a particular subset may miss interesting information because ratings of more obscure items may say more about the customer than ratings of common ones. A fondness for the Beatles is less revealing than a fondness for Mose Allison.

A reasonable approach is to have new customers rate a list of the 20 or so most frequently rated items (a list that might change over time) and then allow them to rate as many additional items as they please.

Comparing Profiles

After a customer profile has been built, the next step is to measure its distance from other profiles. The most obvious approach would be to treat the profile vectors as geometric points and calculate the Euclidean distance between them, but many other distance measures have been tried. Some give higher weight to agreement when users give a positive rating especially when most users give negative ratings to most items. Still others apply statistical correlation tests to the ratings vectors.

Making Predictions

The final step is to use some combination of nearby profiles to come up with estimated ratings for the items that the customer has not rated. One approach is to take a weighted average where the weight is inversely proportional to the distance. The example shown in Figure 9-12 illustrates estimating the rating that Nathaniel would give to *Planet of the Apes* based on the opinions of his neighbors, Simon and Amelia.

Simon, who is distance 2 away, gave that movie a rating of –1. Amelia, who is distance 4 away, gave that movie a rating of –4. No one else's profile is close enough to Nathaniel's to be included in the vote. Because Amelia is twice as far away as Simon, her vote counts only half as much as his. The estimate for Nathaniel's rating is weighted by the distance:

$$\left(\tfrac{1}{2}\,(-1) + \tfrac{1}{4}\,(-4)\right) / \left(\tfrac{1}{2} + \tfrac{1}{4}\right) = -1.5 / 0.75 = -2.$$

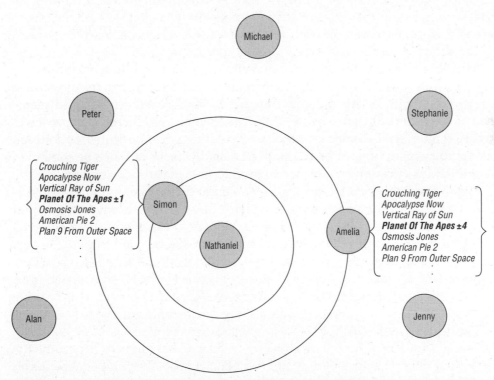

Figure 9-12: The predicted rating for *Planet of the Apes* is –2.66.

A good collaborative filtering system gives its users a chance to comment on the predictions and adjust the profile accordingly. In this example, if Nathaniel rents the video of *Planet of the Apes* despite the prediction that he will not like it, he can then enter an actual rating of his own. If it turns out that he really likes the movie and gives it a rating of 4, his new profile will be in a slightly different neighborhood and Simon's and Amelia's opinions will count less for Nathaniel's next recommendation.

Lessons Learned

Memory-based reasoning is a powerful data mining technique that can be used to solve a wide variety of data mining problems involving both categorical and numeric targets. Unlike other directed data mining techniques that use a training set of preclassified data to create a model and then discard the training set, the training set, with a few rules, essentially *is* the model for MBR.

Choosing the right training set is perhaps the most important step in MBR. The training set should include sufficient numbers of examples of all possible classifications. This may mean enriching it by including a disproportionate number of instances for rare classifications in order to create a balanced training set with roughly the same number of instances for all categories. A training set that includes only instances of bad customers will predict that all customers are bad. In general, the size of the training set should have at least thousands, if not hundreds of thousands or millions, of examples.

MBR is a *k*-nearest neighbors approach. Determining which neighbors are near requires a distance function. There are many approaches for measuring the distance between two records. The careful choice of an appropriate distance function is a critical step in using MBR. The chapter introduced an approach to creating an overall distance function by building a distance function for each field and normalizing it. The normalized field distances can then be combined in a Euclidean fashion or summed to produce a Manhattan distance.

When the Euclidean method is used, a large difference in any one field is enough to cause two records to be considered far apart. The Manhattan method is more forgiving — a large difference on one field can more easily be offset by close values on other fields. A validation set can be used to pick the best distance function for a given model set by applying all candidates to see which produces better results. Sometimes, the right choice of neighbors depends on modifying the distance function to favor some fields over others. This is easily accomplished by incorporating weights into the distance function.

The next question is the number of neighbors to choose. Once again, investigating different numbers of neighbors using the validation set can help determine the optimal number. There is no right number of neighbors. The number depends on the distribution of the data and is highly dependent on the problem being solved.

The basic combination function, weighted voting, does a good job for categorical data, using weights inversely proportional to distance. The analogous operation for estimating numeric values is a weighted average.

One good application for memory-based reasoning is making recommendations. Collaborative filtering is an approach to making recommendations that works by grouping people with similar tastes together using a distance function that can compare two lists of user-supplied ratings. Recommendations for a new person are calculated using a weighted average of the ratings of his or her nearest neighbors.

CHAPTER 10

Knowing When to Worry: Using Survival Analysis to Understand Customers

Hazards. Survival. The very terms conjure up scary images, whether a shimmering blue, ball-eating golf hazard or something a bit more frightful from a Stephen King novel, a hatchet movie, or some reality television show. Perhaps such dire associations explain why these techniques have not been traditionally associated with marketing.

If so, this is a shame. Survival analysis, which is also called time-to-event analysis, is nothing to worry about. It's exactly the opposite: Survival analysis is very valuable for understanding customers. Although the roots and terminology come from medical research and failure analysis in manufacturing, the concepts are tailor-made for marketing. Survival tells you *when* to start worrying about customers doing something important, such as stopping or making another purchase. It identifies which factors are most correlated with the event. Hazards and survival curves also provide snapshots of customers and their life cycles, answering questions such as, "How much should we worry that this customer is going to leave in the near future?" or "This customer has not made a purchase recently; is it time to start worrying that the customer will not return?"

Survival analysis takes advantage of the most important facet of customer behavior: tenure. How long customers have been around provides a wealth of information, especially when tied to particular business problems. How long customers will remain customers in the future is a mystery, but a mystery that past customer behavior can help illuminate. Almost every business recognizes the value of customer loyalty. As described later in this chapter, a guiding principle of loyalty — that the longer customers stay around, the less likely they are to stop at any particular point in time — is really a statement about hazard probabilities.

The world of marketing is a bit different from the world of medical research, the scientific area where survival analysis predominates. For one thing, the consequences of marketing actions are much less dire: A patient may die from poor treatment, whereas the consequences in marketing are merely measured in dollars and cents. Another important difference is the volume of data. The largest medical studies have a few tens of thousands of participants, and many draw conclusions from just a few hundred. In the manufacturing world, where survival analysis is an important component of failure analysis, determining the mean time between failure (MTBF) or mean time to failure (MTTF) — manufacturing lingo for how soon an expensive piece of machinery breaks down — often uses no more than a few dozen examples of failure.

In the world of customers, tens of thousands of examples is a typical lower limit, because customer databases often contain data on hundreds of thousands or millions of customers and former customers. Much of the statistical background of survival analysis is focused on extracting every last bit of information out of a few hundred data points. In data mining applications, the volumes of data are so large that statistical concerns about confidence and accuracy are replaced by concerns about managing large volumes of data.

The importance of survival analysis is that it provides a way of understanding time to events, such as:

- When a customer is likely to leave
- The next time a customer is likely to migrate to a new customer segment
- The next time a customer is likely to broaden or narrow the customer relationship
- The factors that increase or decrease likely customer tenure
- The quantitative effect of various factors on customer tenure

These insights into customers feed directly into the marketing process. They make it possible to understand how long different groups of customers are likely to be around — and hence how profitable these segments are likely to be. They make it possible to forecast numbers of customers, taking into account both new acquisitions and the decline of the current base. Survival analysis also makes it possible to determine which factors, both those at the beginning of customers' relationships as well as later experiences, have the biggest effect on customers' staying around the longest. The analysis can also be applied to things other than the end of the customer tenure, making it possible to determine when another event — such as a customer returning to a website — is no longer likely to occur.

A BRIEF HISTORY OF SURVIVAL ANALYSIS

Of all the techniques discussed in this book, survival analysis is perhaps the oldest. Its history dates back to the early years of the Royal Society, a group founded in London centuries ago. Almost everything that we understand today to be science, including the scientific method and peer review, dates back to a group of scientists and philosophers who, in 1660, created the Royal Society. In 1665, it started publication of *Philosophical Transactions*, the first journal devoted exclusively to science.

In 1693, a few decades after its founding, Edmund Halley — surely better known for the famous comet — presented a paper called *An Estimate of the Degrees of the Mortality of Mankind Drawn from Curious Tables of the Births and Funerals at the City of Breslaw; with an Attempt to Ascertain the Price of Annuities upon Lives*. Phew, that is quite a mouthful. The title of the paper incorporates many of the modern notions of data mining. (You can find the original paper online at `www.pierre-marteau.com/c/boehne/halley.html`; Pierre Marteau is a website devoted to publishing works from the 17th, 18th, and 19th centuries online.)

What Halley called "the degrees of mortality" are what are now known as hazard probabilities. The "Curious Tables" are birth and death records. Such records were not particularly common at the time, because governments did not require registration of such events. In Breslau (the more common spelling of the city's name, which is now called Wroclaw), these records were maintained by churches. Halley's paper was inspired by the availability of data.

Why did he have to venture to the city of Breslau, more than 800 miles from London? This distance was made all the more difficult without airplanes, trains, automobiles, or even credit cards. Halley was not the first person to attempt to "ascertain the price of annuities" using birth and death records. Earlier work used data gathered in London. The problem was this: Many more deaths occurred in London than births. One interpretation might be that London is somehow bad for one's health. The more enlightened (and accurate) interpretation is that the end of the 1600s was the very beginning of the industrial revolution, and London was growing quickly, attracting migrants from more distant places. Presumably, not so many people moved into and out of Breslau.

Finally, why was Halley interested in this topic? He wanted to price life insurance and pensions. Overall, Halley's paper is an inspiration for data miners. He went out and found the available data that he needed. He used advanced technology for his analyses (the slide rule was also invented in the 1600s). He had a well-defined business purpose.

The methods presented in the paper are life table methods that have been in use by actuaries for several centuries. Times have changed. However, the methods themselves are still appealing because they let the data speak. They make few assumptions, and the ones they do make are transparent.

A good place to start with survival is visualizing survival curves. The discussion then moves on to hazard probabilities, the building blocks of survival. Hazard probabilities are in turn combined to create survival curves. The chapter ends with a discussion of Cox Proportional Hazard Regression. Along the way, the chapter provides particular applications of survival in the business context.

Customer Survival

Survival is a good way to measure customer retention, a concept familiar to most businesses that are concerned about their customers. Survival curves also provide a well-grounded framework for understanding customer retention, including important measures such as customer half-life and average truncated tenure.

What Survival Curves Reveal

A *survival curve* shows the proportion of customers that are expected to survive up to a particular point in tenure, based on the historical information of how long customers have survived in the past. The curve always starts at 100 percent and then descends; a survival curve may flatten out, but it never increases. The curve may descend all the way to zero, but typically does not, indicating that some customers with long tenures remain active. Stopping is a one-time event. After a customer has stopped, the customer cannot come back.

Figure 10-1 compares the survival of two groups of customers over a period of ten years. The points on the curve show the proportion of customers who are expected to survive for one year, for two years, and so on. The picture clearly shows that one group is better than the other. How can this difference be quantified?

The simplest measure is the survival value at particular points in time. After ten years, for instance, 24 percent of the regular customers are still around, and only about a third of them even make it to 5 years. Premium customers do much better. More than half make it to 5 years, and 42 percent have a customer lifetime of at least 10 years.

Another way to compare different groups is by asking how long it takes for half the customers to leave — the customer half-life (the statistical term is the *median customer lifetime*). The half-life is a useful measure because the few customers who have very long or very short lifetimes do not affect it. In general, medians are not sensitive to a few outliers.

Figure 10-2 illustrates how to find the customer half-life using a survival curve. This is the point where exactly 50 percent of the customers remain, which is where the 50 percent horizontal gridline intersects the survival curve.

The customer half-life for the two groups shows a much starker difference than the ten-year survival — the premium customers have a median lifetime of close to seven years, whereas the regular customers have a median a bit less than two years.

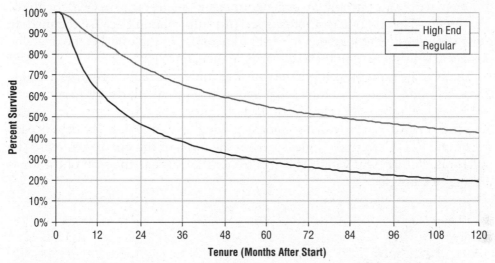

Figure 10-1: Survival curves show that high-end customers stay around longer.

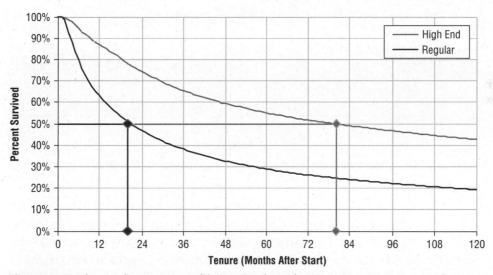

Figure 10-2: The median customer lifetime is where the retention curve crosses the 50 percent point.

Finding the Average Tenure from a Survival Curve

The customer half-life is useful for comparisons and easy to calculate. It does not, however, answer an important question: "How much, on average, are customers worth during this period of time?" Answering this question requires having an average customer worth per time and an average survival for all the customers. The median cannot provide this information because the median only describes what happens to the one customer in the middle; the one who leaves when exactly half the original customers have left.

The average remaining lifetime is the area under the retention curve. Finding the area under the curve may seem daunting — particularly for readers who may have memories of calculus. In fact, the process is quite easy. Figure 10-3 shows a survival curve with a rectangle holding up each point. The base of each rectangle has a length of 1, measured in the units of the horizontal axis. The height is the survival value. The area under the curve is the sum of the areas of these rectangles.

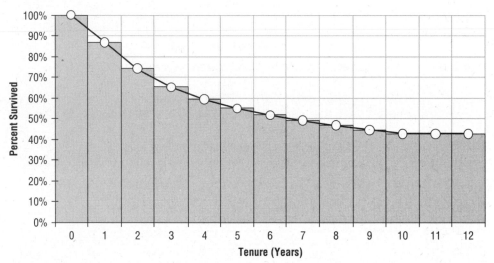

Figure 10-3: Circumscribing each point with a rectangle makes it clear how to approximate the area under the survival curve.

The area of a rectangle is base times height, which is 1 multiplied by the survival value. The sum of all the rectangles, then, is just the sum of all the survival values in the curve — an easy calculation in a spreadsheet. *Voilà*, an easy way to calculate the area and quite an interesting observation as well: The sum of the survival values (as percentages) is the average customer lifetime. Notice also that each rectangle has a width of one time unit, in whatever the units are of the horizontal axis. So, the units of the average are also in the units of the horizontal axis.

TIP The area under the survival curve is the average customer lifetime for the period of time in the curve. For instance, for a survival curve that has two years of data, the area under the curve represents the two-year average tenure.

This simple observation explains how to obtain an estimate of the average customer lifetime. There is one small clarification. The average is really an average for the period of time under the survival curve. Consider the pair of survival curves in the previous figure. These survival curves were for ten years, so the area under them is an estimate of the *average customer lifetime during the first 10 years of the customer relationship.* For customers who are still active at ten years, there is no way of knowing whether they will all leave at ten years plus one day; or if they will all stick around for another century. For this reason, determining the real average is not possible until all customers have left.

This value, called *truncated mean lifetime* by statisticians, is very useful. As shown in Figure 10-4, the better customers have an average 10-year lifetime of 6.1 years; the other group has an average of 3.7 years. If, on average, a customer is worth, say, $1,000 per year, then the premium customers are worth $6,100 – $3,700 = $2,400 more than the regular customers during the 10 years after they start, or about $240 per year. This $240 might represent the return on a retention program designed specifically for the premium customers, or it might give an upper limit of how much to budget for such retention programs.

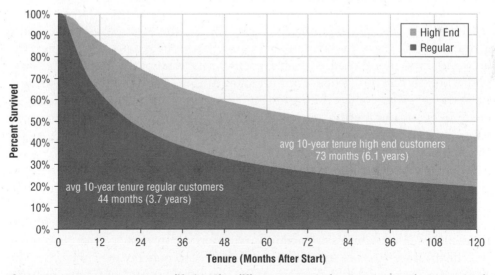

Figure 10-4: Average customer lifetime for different groups of customers can be compared using the areas under the survival curve.

Customer Retention Using Survival

How long do customers stay around? This seemingly simple question becomes more complicated when applied to the real world. Understanding customer survival requires two pieces of information:

- When each customer starts
- When each customer stops

The difference between these two values is the customer *tenure*. Any reasonable database that purports to be about customers should have this data readily accessible. There are two challenges. The first is deciding on the business definition of a start and a stop. The second is technical: finding start and stop dates in available data may be less obvious than it first appears.

For subscription and account-based businesses, start and stop dates are well understood. Customers start magazine subscriptions at a particular point in time and end them when they no longer want to pay for the magazine. Customers sign up for telephone service, a banking account, Internet service, cable service, an insurance policy, or electricity service on a particular date and cancel on another date. In all of these cases, the beginning and end of the relationship is well defined.

Even when the business definition is well understood, translating it to the technical data can be challenging. Consider magazine subscriptions. Do customers start on the date when they sign up for the subscription? Do customers start when the magazine first arrives, which may be several weeks later? Or do they start when the promotional period is over and they start paying?

In making decisions about what data to use, the focus is usually on the economic aspects of the relationship. Costs and/or revenue begin when the account starts being used — that is, on the issue date of the magazine — and end when the account stops. For understanding customers, it is interesting to have the original contact date and time in addition to the first issue date (are customers who sign up on weekdays different from customers who sign up on weekends?), but this is not the beginning of the economic relationship. As for the end of the promotional period, this is really an *initial condition* or *time-zero covariate* on the customer relationship. When the customer signs up, the initial promotional period is known. Survival analysis can take advantage of such initial conditions for refining models.

Many businesses do not have continuous, account-based relationships with their customers. Examples are retailing, web portals, and hotels. Each customer's purchases (or visits) are spread out over time — or may be one-time only. The beginning of the relationship is clear — usually the first purchase or visit. The end is more difficult but is sometimes created through business rules. For instance, a customer who has not made a purchase in the previous 12 months may be considered lapsed.

Looking at Survival as Decay

Although the authors don't generally advocate comparing customers to radioactive materials, the comparison is useful for understanding survival. Think of customers as a lump of uranium that is slowly, radioactively decaying into lead. The "good" customers are the uranium; the ones who have left are the lead. Over time, the amount of uranium left in the lump looks something like the survival curves seen earlier, with the perhaps subtle difference that the timeframe for uranium is measured in billions of years, as opposed to smaller time scales for human activities.

One very useful characteristic of uranium is that scientists have determined how to calculate exactly how much uranium will survive after a certain amount of time. They are able to do this because they have built mathematical models that describe radioactive decay, and these have been verified experimentally.

Radioactive materials have a process of decay described as *exponential* decay. This means that the same proportion of uranium turns into lead during a given amount of time, regardless of how much has already done so. The most common form of uranium has a half-life of about 4.5 billion years. So, about half the lump of uranium has turned into lead after this time. After another 4.5 billion years, half the remaining uranium will decay, leaving only a quarter of the original lump as uranium and three-quarters as lead.

WARNING Exponential decay has many useful properties for predicting beyond the range of observations. Unfortunately, time-to-event problems in business hardly ever exhibit exponential decay.

What makes exponential decay so nice is that the decay fits a nice simple equation that describes how much uranium is around at any given point in time. Wouldn't it be nice to have such an equation for customer survival? It would be very nice, but it is unlikely, as shown in the example in the sidebar "Parametric Approaches Do Not Work for Survival of Customers."

To shed some light on the issue, imagine a world where customers did exhibit exponential decay. For the purposes of discussion, these customers have a half-life of one year. Of 100 customers starting on a particular date, exactly 50 would still be active one year later. After two years, 25 would be active and 75 stopped. Exponential decay would make forecasting the number of customers in the future easy.

The problem with this scenario is that the customers who have been around for one year are behaving just like new customers. Consider a group of 100 customers of various tenures, 50 leave in the following year, regardless of the tenure of the customers at the beginning of the year — exponential decay says that half are going to leave regardless of their initial tenure. That means that customers who have been around for a while are no more loyal then newer customers.

In the real world, it is often the case that customers who have been around for a while are actually *better* customers than new customers. For whatever reason, longer tenured customers have stuck around in the past and are probably a bit less likely than new customers to leave in the future. Exponential decay is a bad approximation, because it assumes the opposite: that the tenure of the customer relationship has no effect on the rate that customers are leaving (an even worse scenario would have longer term customers leaving at consistently higher rates than newer customers — the "familiarity breeds contempt" scenario).

PARAMETRIC APPROACHES DO NOT WORK FOR SURVIVAL OF CUSTOMERS

Trying to fit some known function to a survival curve is tempting. This approach is an example of regression, where a few parameters describe the shape of the survival curve. The power of a parametric approach is that it can be used to estimate survival values in the future, beyond the data used to generate the curves.

A line is the most common shape for a regression function. A line has two parameters, the slope of the line and where it intersects the y-axis. Another common shape is a parabola, which has an additional X^2 term, so a parabola has three parameters. The exponential that describes radioactive decay actually has only one parameter, the half-life.

The following figure shows part of a survival curve for seven out of thirteen years of data. The figure also shows three best-fit curves. The statistical measure of fit is R^2, which varies from 0 to 1. Values over 0.9 are quite good, so by standard statistical measures, all these curves fit very well.

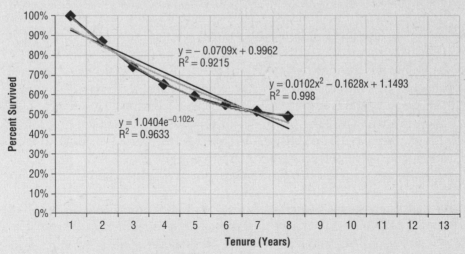

Fitting parametric curves to a survival curve is easy.

The real question, though, is not how well these curves fit the data in the range used to define it, but rather how well do these curves work beyond the original range?

The next figure answers this question. It extrapolates the curves ahead another five years. Quickly, the curves diverge from the actual values, and the difference seems to get larger farther out.

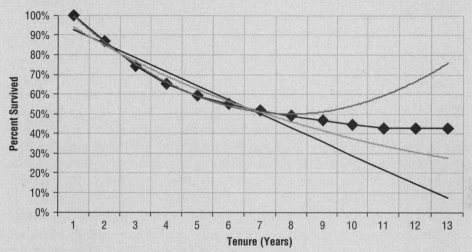

The parametric curves that fit a retention curve do not fit well beyond the range where they are defined.

Of course, this illustration does not prove that a parametric approach does not work in all cases. Perhaps some function is out there that, with the right parameters, would fit the observed survival curve for customers very well and continue working beyond the range used to define the parameters. However, this example does illustrate the challenges of using a parametric approach for approximating survival curves directly, and it is consistent with the author's experience even when using more data points. What looks like a very good fit to the survival curve in one range turns out to diverge pretty quickly outside that range.

Hazard Probabilities

Survival curves are useful, and they are quite simple to understand. This understanding, though, is only in terms of their data. There is no general shape, no parametric form, no grand theory of customer decay. The data is the message.

Hazard probabilities extend this idea. As discussed here, they are an example of a nonparametric statistical approach — letting the data speak instead of finding a special function to speak for it. Empirical hazard probabilities simply let the historical data determine what is likely to happen, without trying to fit data to some preconceived form. They also provide insight into customer survival and provide the foundation for producing survival curves.

The Basic Idea

A hazard probability answers the following question:

> *Assume that a customer has survived for a certain length of time, so the customer's tenure is* t. *What is the probability that the customer leaves before* t+1?

Another way to phrase this is: The hazard probability at tenure *t* is the risk of losing customers between tenure *t* and tenure *t*+1. As with many seemingly simple ideas, the definition of the hazard probability has significant consequences.

To provide an example of hazard probabilities, let's step outside the world of business for a moment and consider life tables, which describe the probability of someone dying at a particular age. Figure 10-5 shows that the mortality rate starts sort of high, around 0.7 percent, indicating that being born is dangerous. Then it goes very low and gradually starts to climb again. Not until someone is about 55 years old does the risk rise as high as it is during the first year. This is a characteristic shape of some hazard functions and is called the *bathtub* shape. Such hazards start high, remain low for a while, and then gradually increase again.

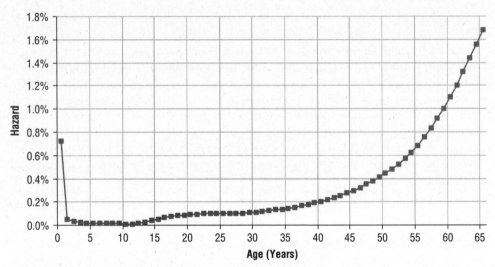

Figure 10-5: The shape of a bathtub-shaped hazard function starts high, plummets, and then gradually increases again.

The same idea can be applied to customer tenure, although customer hazards are more typically calculated by day, week, or month instead of by year. Calculating a hazard for a given tenure *t* requires only two pieces of data. The first is the number of customers who stopped at tenure *t* (or between *t* and

t+1). The second is the *population at risk*, which is the total number of customers who could have stopped during this period. For the empirical hazard calculation, the population at risk consists of all customers whose tenure is greater than or equal to t, including those who stopped at tenure t. The hazard probability is the ratio of these two numbers, and being a probability, it is always between zero and one. Hazard calculations are provided by life table functions in statistical software such as SAS, SPSS, and R. The calculations can also be done in a spreadsheet using data directly from a customer database.

For the calculation to be accurate, every customer included in the population count for a given tenure must have the opportunity to stop at that particular tenure. This has a big influence when looking at subsets of the population. In particular, for the empirical hazard estimates to be accurate, the subset must be defined on initial conditions, rather than on things that occur during the customer lifecycle. Later in this chapter a modification to the approach is described that loosens this restriction.

WARNING To get accurate hazards and survival curves, use groups of customers who are defined only based on initial conditions. In particular, do not define the group based on how or when the members left or on events experienced during the customer life cycle.

When populations are large, you do not need to worry about statistical ideas such as confidence and standard error. However, when the populations are small — as they are in medical research studies or in some business applications — then the confidence interval may become an issue. What this means is that a hazard of 5 percent might really be somewhere between 4 percent and 6 percent. Statistical methods that provide information about standard errors are appropriate when working with smallish populations (say, less than a few thousand). For most applications involving customers this is not an important concern.

Examples of Hazard Functions

The examples that follow are intended to help in understanding hazards and what they say about customers. The first two examples are basic. The third is from real-world data, and it gives a good flavor of how hazards can be used to provide an x-ray of customers' lifecycles.

Constant Hazard

The constant hazard hardly needs a picture to explain it. What it says is that the hazard of customers leaving is exactly the same, no matter how long the customers have been around. This looks like a horizontal line on a graph.

Suppose the hazard probability is being measured by days, and it is a constant 0.1 percent. That is, one customer out of every thousand leaves every day. After a year (365 days), about 30.6 percent of the customers have left. It takes about

692 days for half the customers to leave. It will take another 692 days for half of the remainder to leave, and so on.

The constant hazard means the chance of a customer's leaving does not vary with the length of time the customer has been around. This sounds a lot like the decay of radioactive elements. In fact, a constant hazard probability corresponds to an exponential form for the survival curve. Although constant hazards do appear in physics, they do not happen much in marketing.

Bathtub-Shaped Hazard

The life table for the U.S. population provides an example of the bathtub-shaped hazard function. This is common in the life sciences, although bathtub-shaped curves turn up in other domains. As mentioned earlier, the bathtub hazard initially starts out high, then it goes down and flattens out for a long time, and finally, the hazard probabilities increase again.

One phenomenon that causes this is when customers are on contracts (for instance, for cell phones or ISP services), typically for one year or longer. Early in the contract, customers stop because the service is not appropriate or because they do not pay. During the period of the contract, customers are dissuaded from canceling, either because of the threat of financial penalties or perhaps only because of a feeling of obligation to honor the terms of the initial contract. When the contract is up, customers often rush to leave, and the higher rate continues for a while because customers have been liberated from the contract.

After the contract has expired, there may be other reasons, such as the product or service no longer being competitively priced, that cause customers to stop. Markets change, and customers respond to these changes. As rates drop, customers are more likely to switch to a competitor than to negotiate with their current provider for lower rates.

A Real-World Example

Figure 10-6 shows a real-world example of a hazard function, for a company that sells a subscription-based service (the exact service is unimportant). This hazard function is measuring the probability of a customer stopping a given number of weeks after signing on.

The curve has several interesting characteristics. One is that it starts high. The customers who stop quickly are those who sign on, but are not able to be started for some technical reason such as their credit card not being approved. In some cases, customers did not realize that they had signed on — a problem that the authors encounter most often with outbound telemarketing campaigns.

Next is that the curve has an M-shaped feature with peaks at about nine and twelve weeks. The first of these peaks occurs because of nonpayment. Customers who never pay a bill, or who cancel their credit card charges, are stopped for nonpayment after about two months. Because a significant number of customers leave at this time, the hazard probability spikes up.

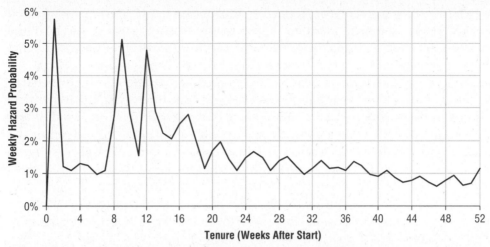

Figure 10-6: A subscription business has customer hazard probabilities that look like this.

The second peak in the "M" coincides with the end of the initial promotion that offers introductory pricing. This promo typically lasts for about three months, and then customers have to start paying full price. Many decide that they no longer really want the service. The possibility is quite strong that many of these customers reappear to take advantage of other promotions at later times, an interesting fact not germane to this discussion on hazards but relevant to the business.

After the first three months, the hazard function has no more really high peaks. There is a small cycle of peaks about every four or five weeks, corresponding to the monthly billing cycle. Customers are more likely to stop just after they receive a bill.

The chart also shows a gentle decline in the hazard probabilities after about six months. This decline is a good thing, because it means that the longer a customer stays around, the less likely the customer is to leave. Another way of saying this is that customers are becoming more loyal the longer they stay with the company.

TIP The long-term decline in the hazard rate is a measure of customer loyalty, because it indicates that the longer someone is a customer, the less likely he or she is to leave.

Censoring

So far, this introduction to hazards has glossed over one of the most important concepts in survival analysis: censoring. Remember the definition of a hazard probability: the number of stops at a given tenure t divided by the population at that time. Clearly, customers who stop before tenure t are not included in the population count.

Stopped customers with smaller tenures are not the only ones who must be excluded from the population at risk. Customers whose tenure is shorter — regardless of whether they are active or stopped — must be excluded from the population at risk. These customers could not stop at tenure *t*, because that would be in the future. Censoring — dropping some customers from some of the hazard calculations — proves to be a very powerful part of survival analysis.

Look at this with a picture. Figure 10-7 shows a set of customers on two charts. The top chart shows what happens on the calendar time scale. Customers are shown as lines, which end in a small circle that is either open or closed. When the circle is filled in, the customer has already left (think "closed account") and their exact tenure is known because the stop date is known. An open circle means that the customer has survived to the analysis date (think "open account"), so the stop date is not yet known. This customer — or in particular, this customer's tenure — is *censored*. The customer's final tenure will be at least the current tenure, but most likely larger. How much larger is unknown, because that customer's exact stop date has not yet happened.

The bottom chart shows the same group of customers, but on the tenure time scale instead of the calendar time scale. Now, all customers start at tenure zero. The customers end at different tenures. In particular, customers can be censored at any tenure.

The Hazard Calculation

Let's walk through the hazard calculation for these customers, paying particular attention to the role of censoring. Both the tenure and the censoring flag are needed for the hazard calculation. Table 10-1 summarizes information for customers in Figure 10-7.

Table 10-1: Tenure Data for Several Customers

CUSTOMER	CENSORED	TENURE
1	Y	12
2	N	6
3	N	6
4	N	3
5	Y	3
6	N	5
7	N	6
8	Y	9

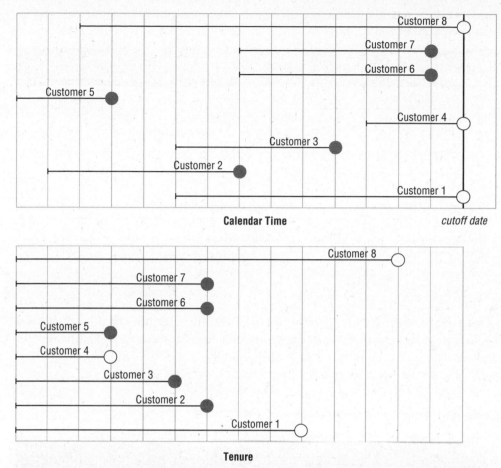

Figure 10-7: The top chart shows a group of customers who all start at different times; some customers are censored because they are still active. The bottom chart shows the same customers on the tenure time scale.

Seeing what is happening during each time period is instructive. At any point in time, a customer might be in one of three states: ACTIVE, meaning that the relationship is still ongoing; STOPPED, meaning that the customer stopped during that time interval; or CENSORED, meaning that the customer is not included in the calculation. Table 10-2 shows what happens to the customers during each time period.

Table 10-2: Tracking Customers over Several Time Periods (A=Active; S=Stopped; blank=Censored)

						TENURE PERIOD							
CUSTOMER	0	1	2	3	4	5	6	7	8	9	10	11	12
1	A	A	A	A	A	A	A	A	A	A	A	A	A
2	A	A	A	A	A	A	S						
3	A	A	A	A	A	A	S						
4	A	A	A	S									
5	A	A	A	A									
6	A	A	A	A	A	S							
7	A	A	A	A	A	A	S						
8	A	A	A	A	A	A	A	A	A	A			

Table 10-3 summarizes what happens in each time period. Notice that the censoring takes place one time unit later than the lifetime. That is, Customer #1 survived to Tenure 5; what happens after that is unknown. The hazard at a given tenure is the number of customers who are STOPPED divided by the total of the customers who are either ACTIVE or STOPPED.

Table 10-3: From Times to Hazards

						TENURE PERIOD							
	0	1	2	3	4	5	6	7	8	9	10	11	12
ACTIVE	8	8	8	7	6	5	2	2	2	2	1	1	1
STOPPED	0	0	0	1	0	1	3	0	0	0	0	0	0
CENSORED	0	0	0	0	2	2	3	6	6	6	7	7	7
HAZARD		0.0%	0.0%	0.0%	12.5%	0.0%	16.7%	60.0%	0.0%	0.0%	0.0%	0.0%	0.0%	0.0%

The hazard probability at tenure 3 is 12.5 percent, because one out of eight customers stop at this tenure. All eight customers survive to tenure 3 and all could have stopped, but only one did. At tenure 4, six customers remain — Customer #4 stopped at tenure 3, and Customer #6 has been censored. None of these six stops at tenure 4, so the hazard is 0.

This calculation shows that the hazard probabilities can be highly erratic — jumping from 0 percent to 60 percent from one day to the next. Typically, hazards do not vary so much. This erratic behavior arises only because this simple example has so few customers. Similarly, showing the state of every customer at every tenure is useful for didactic purposes to demonstrate the calculation on a manageable set of data. In the real world, such an approach is not feasible, because there are likely to be thousands or millions of customers going down the table and hundreds or thousands of days going across.

It is also worth mentioning that this treatment of hazards introduces them as conditional probabilities, which vary between zero and one. This is possible because the hazards are estimated at tenures measured in discrete units, such as days or weeks. In the scientific world, statisticians often work with hazard rates rather than probabilities. The ideas are clearly strongly related, but the mathematics using rates involves daunting integrals, complicated exponential functions, and difficult-to-explain adjustments to this or that factor. For the purposes of this discussion, the simpler hazard probabilities are not only easier to explain, they also solve the problems that arise when working with customer data.

Other Types of Censoring

The previous section introduced censoring in two cases: hazards for customers after they have stopped and hazards for customers who are still active. There are other useful cases as well. To explain other types of censoring, going back to the medical realm is useful.

Imagine that you are a cancer researcher and have found a medicine that cures cancer. You run a study to verify that this fabulous new treatment works. Such studies typically follow a group of patients for several years after the treatment; say, five years. For the purposes of this example, you only want to know whether patients die from cancer during the course of the study (medical researchers have other concerns as well, such as the recurrence of the disease, but that does not concern us in this simplified example).

So you carefully select 100 patients, give them the treatment, and their cancers seem to be cured. You follow them for several years. During this time, seven patients celebrate their newfound health by visiting Iceland. In a horrible tragedy, all seven happen to die in an avalanche caused by a submerged volcano. What is the effectiveness of your treatment on cancer mortality? Just looking at the data, it is tempting to assign a 7 percent mortality rate. However, this mortality is clearly not related to the treatment, so the answer does not feel right.

In fact, the answer is not right. This is an example of *competing risks*. A study participant might live, might die of cancer, or might die as a result of a mountain climbing accident on a distant island nation. The patient might move to Tahiti and drop out of the study. As medical researchers say, such a patient has been "lost to follow-up."

The solution is to censor the patients who exit the study before the event being studied occurs. If patients drop out of the study, then they were healthy to the point in time when they dropped out, and the information acquired during this period can be used to calculate hazards. Afterward there is no way of knowing what happened. They are censored at the point when they exit. If a patient dies of something else, then he or she is censored at the point when death occurs, and the death is not included in the hazard calculation.

TIP The right way to deal with competing risks is to develop different sets of hazards for each risk, where the other risks are censored. Removing customers entirely from the population biases the hazard probabilities.

Competing risks are familiar in the business environment as well. For instance, two types of stops are voluntary stops, when a customer decides to leave, and involuntary stops, when the company decides a customer should leave — often due to unpaid bills

In doing an analysis on voluntary churn, what happens to customers who are forced to discontinue their relationships due to unpaid bills? If such a customer were forced to stop on day 100, then that customer did not stop voluntarily on days 1–99. This information can be used to generate hazards for voluntary stops. However, starting on day 100, the customer is censored. Censoring customers, even when they have stopped for other reasons, is the best approach for analyzing different types of stops.

From Hazards to Survival

This chapter started with a discussion of survival curves. These are most useful when created from hazard probabilities. A related idea, retention curves, is also useful for understanding the advantages of survival. This section compares retention and survival.

Retention

A retention curve provides information about how many customers have been retained for a certain amount of time. One common way of creating a retention curve is to do the following:

- For customers who started one week ago, measure the proportion that are currently active: the 1-week retention.

- For customers who started two weeks ago, measure the proportion that are currently active: the 2-week retention.

- And so on.

Figure 10-8 shows an example of a retention curve based on this approach. The overall shape of this curve is similar to a survival curve. However, the curve itself is quite jagged. It seems odd, for instance, that 10-week retention would be better than 9-week retention, as suggested by this data.

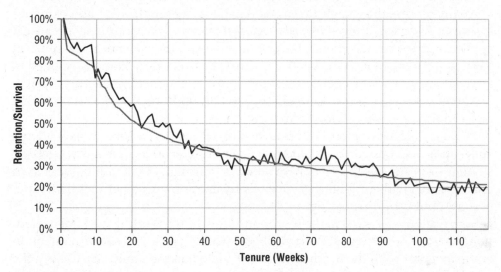

Figure 10-8: A retention curve might be quite jagged, especially in comparison to the survival curve for the same data.

Actually, it is more than odd — it violates common sense. The retention curve might cross the 50 percent threshold more than once, leading to the odd, and inaccurate, conclusion that there is more than one median lifetime. What is happening? Are customers being reincarnated?

These problems are an artifact of the way the curve is created. Customers acquired in any given time period may be better or worse than the customers acquired in other time periods. Perhaps nine weeks ago a special pricing offer brought in bad customers. Customers who started ten weeks ago were the usual mix of good and bad, but those who started nine weeks ago were particularly bad. So, fewer customers remain from the group that started nine weeks ago than remain from the group that started 10 weeks ago, even though the latter group has had an additional week to stop.

The quality of customers might also vary due merely to random variation. After all, in the previous figure, more than 100 time periods are being considered — so, all things being equal, some time periods would be expected to exhibit differences.

A compounding reason is that marketing efforts change over time, attracting different qualities of customers. For instance, customers arriving by different channels often have different retention characteristics, and the mix of customers from different channels is likely to change over time.

Survival

Hazards give the probability that a customer might stop at a particular tenure. Survival gives the probability of a customer surviving up to that tenure. In other words, survival is the cumulative probability that the event has not occurred.

At any tenure, the chance that a customer survives to the next unit of tenure is simply *1 – hazard*, the *conditional survival at tenure t*. It is conditional because it applies only to the customers who have survived up to that tenure. The survival value starts at one (or 100 percent) at tenure 0, because all customers included in analysis survive to the beginning of the analysis. Calculating the full survival for larger tenures requires accumulating all the conditional survivals up to that point in time by multiplying them together.

Because the hazard probability is always between zero and one, the conditional survival is also between zero and one. Hence, survival itself is always getting smaller — because each successive value is multiplied by a number less than one. The survival curve starts at one, gently goes down, sometimes flattening, perhaps, but never increasing.

Survival curves often make more sense for understanding customer retention than the retention curves described earlier. Figure 10-8 shows a retention curve together with the survival curve calculated on the same data. Clearly, the survival curve is smoother, and it slopes downward at all times. The retention curve bounces all over the place. This makes the survival curve a better choice for calculating measures, such as the median customer lifetime and the average customer tenure.

Comparison of Retention and Survival

The differences between the retention curve and the survival curve may, at first, seem non-intuitive. The retention curve is actually pasting together a whole bunch of different pictures of customers from the past, like a photo collage pieced together from a bunch of different photographs to get a panoramic image. In the collage, the picture in each photo is quite clear. However, the boundaries do not necessarily fit together smoothly. Different pictures in the collage look different, because of differences in lighting or perspective — differences that contribute to the aesthetic of the collage.

The same thing happens with retention curves, where customers who start at different points in time have different perspectives. Any given point on the retention curve is close to the actual survival value; however, taken as a whole, it looks jagged. One way to remove the jaggedness is to use a cohort of customers who start at about the same time and measure their retention at different points in time. However, this limits the retention curve to older customers, ignoring information from more recent customers.

TIP Instead of using retention curves, use survival curves. That is, first calculate the hazard probabilities and then work back to calculate the survival curve.

The survival curve, on the other hand, looks at as many customers as possible, not just the ones who started exactly t time periods ago. The survival at any given tenure t uses information from all customers, because all customers are in the population at risk at tenure zero. And survival at any tenure includes the hazard probabilities at all earlier tenures.

Because survival calculations use all the data, the values are more stable than retention calculations. Each point on a retention curve limits customers to having started at a particular point in time. Also, because a survival curve always slopes downward, calculations of customer half-life and average customer tenure are more accurate. By incorporating more information, survival provides a more accurate, smoother picture of customer retention.

For analyzing customers, both hazards and survival provide valuable information about customers. In many ways, survival is the expected value for retention, using all the information provided by all the customers. For instance, in Figure 10-8, retention is higher than survival from about 65 to 90 weeks. A good question is: What was being done correctly during 65 to 90 weeks ago that attracted better customers?

Because survival is cumulative, it can hide patterns at a particular point in time. Hazard probabilities make the specific causes more apparent. Earlier, the discussion on real-world hazards identified events during the customer life cycle that were drivers of hazards. Survival curves do not highlight such events as clearly as hazards do.

The question may also arise about comparing hazards for different groups of customers. Comparing average hazards over a period of time does not make sense. Mathematically, "average hazard" does not make sense. The right approach is to turn the hazards into survival and compare the values on the survival curves.

The description of hazards and survival presented so far differs a bit from how the subject is treated in statistics. The sidebar "A Note about Survival Analysis and Statistics" explains the differences further.

A NOTE ABOUT SURVIVAL ANALYSIS AND STATISTICS

The discussion of survival analysis in this chapter assumes that time is discrete. In particular, things happen on particular days, and the time of day is not important. This is not only reasonable for the problems addressed by data mining, but it is also more intuitive and simplifies the mathematics.

The statistical approach to survival analysis makes the opposite assumption, that time is continuous. Instead of hazard probabilities, statisticians work with hazard rates. The statistical definitions make use of lots of calculus, including differentiation and integration. In fact, the original paper on Cox Proportional Hazards Regression (discussed later in this chapter) starts with two sets of double integrals on the first page — not the type of paper that is readily understood by most business managers.

One difference between a rate and a probability is that the rate can exceed 1 or be negative, whereas a probability never does. Also, a rate seems less intuitive for many survival problems encountered with customers.

The method for calculating hazards in this chapter, called empirical hazard estimation (which is quite related to its close cousin the life-table method), assumes that time is discrete. A very similar method, called Kaplan-Meier, is used for continuous time data. Continuous time data essentially means that no two customers who have stopped have exactly the same tenure, an assumption that is reasonable in the scientific world but not reasonable in the business world. The two techniques produce almost exactly the same results when events occur at discrete times.

An important part of statistical survival analysis is the estimation of hazards using parameterized regression — trying to find the best functional form for the hazards. This is an alternative approach, calculating the hazards directly from the data.

The parameterized approach has the important advantage that it can more easily include covariates in the process. Earlier in this chapter, you saw an example based on such a parameterized model. Unfortunately, the hazard function rarely follows a form that would be familiar to non-statisticians. The discrete hazards, calculated empirically by counting stops, do such a good job of describing the customer life cycle that it would be shocking if a simple function captured that rich complexity.

Proportional Hazards

Sir David Cox is one of the most cited statisticians of the past century; his work comprises numerous books and more than 250 articles. He has received many awards, including a knighthood bestowed on him by Queen Elizabeth in 1985. Much of his research centered on understanding hazard functions, and his work has been particularly important in the world of medical research.

His seminal paper in this area was about determining the effect of initial factors (time-zero covariates) on hazards. By assuming that these initial factors have a uniform proportional effect on hazards, he was able to figure out how to measure this effect for different factors. The purpose of this section is to introduce proportional hazards and to suggest how they are useful for understanding customers. This section starts with some examples of why proportional hazards are useful. It then describes an alternative approach before returning to the Cox model itself.

Examples of Proportional Hazards

Consider the following statement about one risk from smoking: *On average, someone who smokes a pack or more of cigarettes each day lives seven years less than someone who never smoked.* This result is a classic example of proportional hazards. At the time of the study, the researchers knew whether someone was or was not a smoker. Notice the way the results are stated, though. The results do not say how long someone will actually live. The results just give a relative measure of the effect of smoking on lifetime.

Figure 10-9 provides an illustration from the world of marketing. It shows two sets of hazard probabilities, one for customers who joined from a telephone solicitation and the other from direct mail. How someone became a customer is an example of an initial condition. The hazards for the telemarketing customers are higher; looking at the chart, telemarketing customers seem to be a bit less than twice as risky as direct mail customers. The exact proportion varies by tenure, with the ratio being much larger than two around nine weeks.

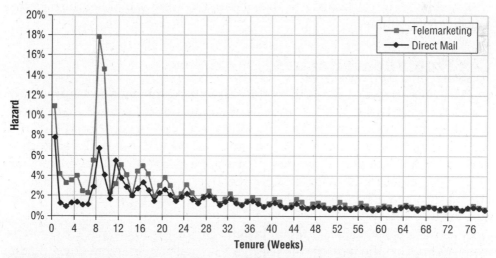

Figure 10-9: These two hazard functions suggest that the risk of attrition is about one and a half times as great for customers acquired through telemarketing versus direct mail, although the ratio does differ somewhat by tenure.

Stratification: Measuring Initial Effects on Survival

Figure 10-9 shows hazard probabilities for two different groups of customers, one that started via outbound telemarketing campaigns and the other via direct mail campaigns. These two curves clearly reveal differences between these channels. Based on these survival curves, the difference between the two groups can be quantified using one-year survival, median survival, or average truncated tenure. This approach to measuring differences among different groups defined by initial conditions is called *stratification* because each group is analyzed independently from other groups. Stratification produces good visualizations and accurate survival values. It is also quite easy, because statistical packages such as SAS and SPSS have options that make it simple to stratify data for this purpose (and the calculations can also easily be done using SQL and Excel).

Stratification solves the problem of understanding initial effects assuming that two conditions are true. The first is that the initial effect must be a categorical variable or a continuous variable that has been binned into discrete chunks.

The second is that each group must be fairly big. When starting with lots and lots of customers and only using one variable that takes on a handful of values, such as channel, this is not a problem. However, there may be multiple variables of interest, such as:

- Acquisition channel
- Original promotion
- Geography

When more than one dimension is included, the number of categories grows very quickly. This means that the data gets spread thinly, making the hazards less and less reliable.

Cox Proportional Hazards

In 1972, Sir David Cox recognized this reliability problem and he proposed a method of analysis, now known as Cox Proportional Hazards Regression, which overcomes these limitations. In essence, Cox proportional hazards regression provides a way to quantify the relative effect of both categorical and continuous covariates, by providing a single proportionality constant for all tenures. Conceptually, it calculates the "average" effect across all tenures. For the two groups in Figure 10-9, the average would be approximately one and a half.

Cox's work is based on a brilliant insight. He focused on the original conditions and not on the hazards themselves. The question is: What effect do the initial conditions have on hazards? His approach to answering this question is worth understanding.

The Basic Idea

Fortunately, the ideas are simpler than the mathematics that implements them. The key idea is the partial likelihood. Assuming that only one customer stops at a given tenure t, the partial likelihood at t is the likelihood that exactly that particular customer stopped.

Imagine that each customer has his or her own hazard function that generates the hazards for any given tenure. Actually, the function is really a function of covariates multiplied by some baseline hazard. The customer's survival can be estimated by calculating the hazards based on the initial covariates and then combining them to obtain the survival. This is the traditional way to think of survival analysis.

Cox looked at the same picture of customers, but he asked a different question. Instead of asking about the survival of a single customer, he asked the question, "What is the likelihood that exactly the one particular group of customers stops at a given tenure and the remaining customers do not?" This question is about a vertical slice through the data, rather than a horizontal slice, as shown in Figure 10-10.

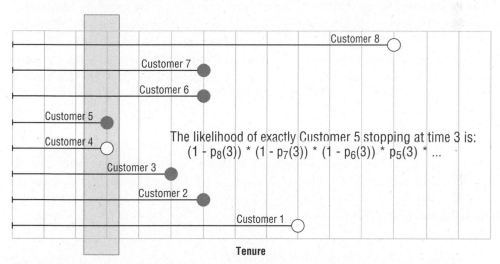

The likelihood of exactly Customer 5 stopping at time 3 is:
$$(1 - p_8(3)) * (1 - p_7(3)) * (1 - p_6(3)) * p_5(3) * \ldots$$

Figure 10-10: Cox's insightful observation that led to proportional hazards modeling is to look at all customers at a given tenure and ask, "What is the likelihood that exactly one set of customers stops when the rest remain active?"

Cox set up a big equation, for all the customers who stop at all tenures. This equation contains complicated expressions of tenure, hazards, and covariates. However, by making an assumption that the covariates affect hazards in the same proportion, regardless of tenure, all the tenure components cancel out. What is left is a complicated mathematical formula containing only the covariates. The hazards themselves have disappeared from the equation.

Cox proportional hazards regression then calculates the coefficients on the covariates that make the observed stops the most likely set of stops. The coefficients, in turn, specify the effect on the hazards. For any particular covariate, proportional hazards produce results along the lines of "an increase in the value of a particular covariate (say, the number of cigarettes smoked per day) increases or decreases the hazard at any tenure by X percent." Another way of looking at this is that when a covariate takes on a particular value, then the ratio of the hazard probability to the baseline hazard value is a constant for all tenures — hence the name "proportional hazards regression."

The underlying method for calculating the effects of the covariates uses a statistical method called maximum likelihood estimation, which is similar to the methods used for solving logistic regressions.

Using Proportional Hazards

Proportional hazards regression calculates the effects of covariates on hazards, but does not calculate the hazards themselves. To do the calculation, you need a set of baseline hazards. Using the overall hazards as the baseline hazards is tempting. However, this is typically not a good idea. Instead, you want the baseline hazards to be the set of hazards when the covariates have a value of zero.

To give an example why, consider a set of customers where half the customers come from direct mail and half come from telemarketing. A variable called "direct mail" takes on a value of 1, for the direct marketing customers, and 0 for the telemarketing ones.

The overall hazard rate for the customers then has an average "direct mail" value of 0.5. However, for the baseline, it is better for the average to be 0, because the effect of the "direct mail" variable is usually specified by going from a value of 0 to 1, rather than 0.5 to 1. Fortunately, most software that does proportional hazards regression, such as the SAS procedure PHREG, calculates the appropriate set of baseline hazards.

Limitations of Proportional Hazards

Cox proportional hazards regression is very powerful and very clever. However, it has its limitations. For all this to work, Cox had to make many assumptions. He designed his approach around continuous time hazards and also made the assumption that only one customer stops at any given time. However, the basic ideas also work discrete time hazards and handle multiple stops at the same time.

WARNING Cox proportional hazards regression ranks and quantifies the effects of initial conditions on the overall hazard function. However, the results are highly dependent on the often dubious assumption that the initial conditions have a constant effect on the hazards regardless of tenure. Use it carefully.

The biggest assumption in the proportional hazards model is the assumption of proportionality. That is, that the effect of the initial conditions on hazards does not have a tenure component. In practice, this is simply not true. It is rarely, if ever, true that initial conditions have such perfect proportionality, even in the scientific world. In the world of customer behavior, this is even less likely. Customers are not a controlled experiment. Things are constantly changing; new programs, pricing, and competition are always arising.

The bad news is that no simple algorithm explains initial conditions, taking into account different effects over time. The good news is that it often does not make a difference. Even with the assumption of proportionality, Cox regression does a good job of determining which covariates have a big impact on the hazards. In other words, it does a good job of explaining what initial conditions are correlated with customers leaving.

Cox's approach was designed only for time-zero covariates, as statisticians call initial values. The approach has been extended to handle events that occur during a customer's lifetime — such as whether they upgrade their product or make a complaint. In the language of statistics, these are time-dependent covariates, meaning that the additional factors can occur at any point during the customer's tenure, not only at the beginning of the relationship. Such factors might be a customer's response to a retention campaign or making complaints. Since Cox's original work, he and other statisticians have extended this technique to include these types of factors.

Survival Analysis in Practice

Survival analysis has proven to be very valuable for understanding customers and quantifying marketing efforts in terms of customer retention. It provides a way of estimating how long it will be until something occurs. This section gives some particular examples of survival analysis in practice.

Handling Different Types of Attrition

Businesses that deal with customers have to deal with customers leaving for a variety of reasons. Earlier, this chapter described hazard probabilities and explained how hazards illustrate aspects of the business that affect the customer life cycle. In particular, peaks in hazards coincided with business processes that forced out customers who were not paying their bills.

Because nonpaying customers are treated differently, removing them entirely from the hazard calculation is tempting. This is the wrong approach. The problem is, which customers to remove is only known *after* the customers have been forced to stop. As mentioned earlier, using knowledge gained at the end of the customer relationship to filter customers for analysis is a bad idea that produces incorrect hazard estimates.

The right approach is to break this into two problems. What are the hazards for voluntary attrition? What are the hazards for forced attrition? Each of these uses all the customers, censoring the customers who leave due to other factors. When calculating the hazards for voluntary attrition, whenever a customer is forced to leave, the customer is included in the analysis until he or she leaves — at that point, the customer is censored. This makes sense. Up to the point when the customer was forced to leave, the customer was at risk for leaving voluntarily.

Having a survival curve for each risk is not sufficient. Instead, the goal is to understand what happens to customers across different tenures in terms of the risks. Figure 10-11, for instance, shows what happens to some mobile phone customers over time. The lower region corresponds to the part under the survival curve, so these are the customers who remain active. The middle region consists of customers who left voluntarily, so there is missed opportunity. The top region consists of customers who were forced to leave, because they did not pay; these customers represent an actual loss.

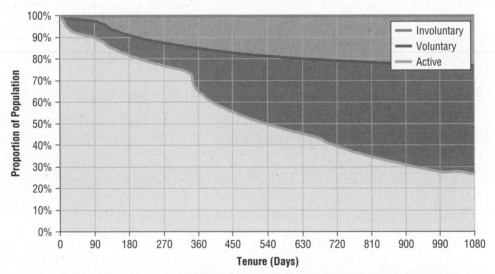

Figure 10-11: Using competing risks, creating a chart that shows the proportion of customers that succumb to each risk at any given tenure is possible.

Another way of looking at this chart is from a financial perspective. The lower region has active customers who have continued to pay money every month. The top region has the customers forced to stop; they paid for a while but then they cost the company money (the amount each such customer owed when he or she left). Finally, the middle region consists of customers who left voluntarily. They represent opportunity to recapture lost revenue — what is the value of reducing such attrition by 5 percent?

Notice that the total sum of these three regions adds up to 100 percent for all tenures. These curves are constructed in two parts. First, the overall survival curve is used to determine the proportion of customers who leave at a given tenure (this is actually the hazard probability). These stops are then partitioned based on the hazards for each competing risk. The chart shows the original survival curve and the cumulative sums of the stops of the different types.

TIP The area under the survival curve represents customers who are still active (have not experienced the event). The area above the curve represents customers who have stopped (experienced the event).

This approach can be extended for other purposes. Once upon a time, the authors were trying to understand different groups of customers at a newspaper — in particular, whether and how survival by acquisition channel was or was not changing over time. Unfortunately, during one of the time periods, a group of readers cancelled their subscriptions in response to a boycott of the newspaper, raising the overall stop levels during that period. Not surprisingly, the hazards went up and survival decreased during this time period.

Is there a way to take into account these particular stops? The answer is "yes," because the company did a good job of recording the reasons why customers stopped. The customers who boycotted the paper were simply censored on the day they stopped — as they say in the medical world, these customers were "lost to follow-up." By censoring, an accurate estimate of the overall hazards without the boycott could be calculated.

When Will a Customer Come Back?

So far, the discussion of survival analysis has focused on the end of the customer relationship. You can use survival analysis for many things besides predicting the probability of bad things happening. For instance, you can use survival analysis to estimate when customers will return after having stopped.

In this case, the hazard is the probability that a customer returns a given number of days after the deactivation. The corresponding survival curve shows the proportion of deactivated customers who remain deactivated. The inverse, one minus the survival curve, is then the cumulative number of customers who have reactivated; this is generally more interesting and is shown in Figure 10-12. Notice that this curve starts at zero percent and gradually rises upwards.

These curves have several interesting features. One is that the initial reactivation rate is very high. In the first week, more than a third of customers reactivate. Business rules explain this phenomenon. A majority of deactivations are due to customers not paying their bills. Many of these customers are just holding out until the last minute — they actually intend to keep their phones; they just don't like paying the bill. However, when the phone stops working, they quickly pay up.

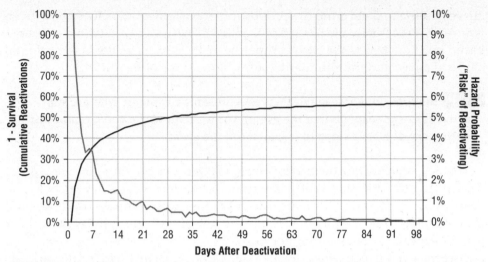

Figure 10-12: This chart shows 1-Survival, the cumulative number of reactivations as well as the "hazard probability" of reactivation.

After 90 days, the hazards are practically zero — customers do not reactivate. Once again, the business processes provide guidance. Telephone numbers are reserved for 90 days after customers leave. Normally, when customers reactivate, they want to keep the same telephone number. After 90 days, the number may have been reassigned, and the customer would have to get a new telephone number.

This discussion has glossed over the question of how new (reactivated) customers were associated with the expired accounts. In this case, the analysis used the telephone numbers in conjunction with the customer's name. This pretty much guaranteed that the match was accurate, because reactivated customers retained their telephone numbers and billing information. This is very conservative but works for finding reactivations. It does not work for finding other types of win-back, such as customers who are willing to cycle through telephone numbers to get introductory discounts.

Another approach is to try to identify individuals over time, even when they are on different accounts. For businesses that collect Social Security numbers or driver's license numbers as a regular part of their business, such identifying numbers can connect accounts together over time. (Be aware that not everyone who is asked to supply this kind of identifying information does so accurately.) Sometimes matching names, addresses, telephone numbers, and/or credit cards is sufficient for matching purposes. More often, this task is outsourced to a company that assigns individual and household IDs, which then provide the information needed to identify which new customers are really former customers who have been won back.

Studying initial covariates adds even more information. In this case, "initial" means whatever is known about the customer at the point of deactivation. This includes not only information such as initial product and promotion, but also customer behavior before deactivating. Are customers who complain a lot more or less likely to reactivate? Customers who roam? Customers who pay their bills late?

This example shows the use of hazards to understand a classic time-to-event question. Other questions of this genre amenable to survival analysis include:

- When customers start on a minimum pricing plan, how long will it be before they upgrade to a premium plan?

- When customers upgrade to a premium plan, how long will it be before they downgrade?

- What is the expected length of time between purchases for customers, given past customer behavior and the fact that different customers have different purchase periods?

One nice aspect of using survival analysis is that it is easy to calculate the effects of different initial conditions — such as the number of times that a customer has visited in the past. Using proportional hazards, it is possible to determine which covariates have the most effect on the desired outcome, including which interventions are most and least likely to work.

Understanding Customer Value

Customer value is a very important concept for businesses, especially subscription-based businesses where customers have well-defined beginnings and ends to their relationships. A full customer value calculation should take into account three things:

- Revenues generated by customers

- Costs associated with customers

- Length of the customer relationship

Although most applicable to subscription-type relationships, you can apply these ideas to other types of relationships as well.

Survival analysis can play a very important role in customer value calculations, because it solves the third piece of the puzzle, the length of the customer relationship. The ideas behind survival analysis can also be applied to understanding the revenues as well.

This section is meant to be an overview of the subject. Full customer value calculations often require much more detail. In particular, the focus is typically on revenues, because these are clearly incremental per customer. On the other hand, accounting for costs can be quite tricky. In addition, customers may offer other benefits, such as referrals, which are not readily accounted for by the simple calculation.

Doing the Basic Calculation

The basic calculation for customer value is focused on revenues and is the product of the following two values:

- The length of time the customer is expected to remain a customer
- The value of the customer per unit time

Survival analysis provides an estimate of the expected remaining tenure for customers. The value per unit time might be a constant value for all customers or a constant value for groups of customers, based on initial conditions.

A survival curve does not give a single estimate of expected tenure. Instead, it provides an estimate of the probability of a customer surviving to any particular tenure. For customer value calculations, a time horizon is needed. This time horizon — typically something like one, two, or five years — provides a time frame for the calculation. The question, "How much is a customer worth?" instead becomes, "How much is a customer worth in the next two years?"

This makes it possible to use the truncated average tenure for the customer value calculation. Remember, for new customers this is the area under the survival curve, which is easily calculated as the cumulative sum of the survival values. For existing customers, use the area under the survival curve assuming the customer has survived up to their current tenure. This is the conditional survival curve, and it is calculated as the survival curve divided by the survival at the current tenure, as shown in Figure 10-13.

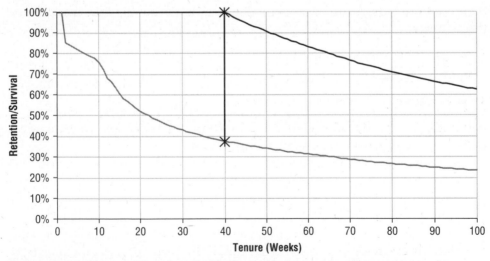

Figure 10-13: The conditional survival is the survival, assuming that a customer has survived to a particular tenure. It is calculated by dividing the survival value by the value at that tenure.

The basic customer value calculation, therefore, is simply the truncated average tenure times an estimate of the value of a customer per unit time. The truncated average tenure is either based on the overall survival curve (for new customers) or on the conditional survival (for existing customers).

Extending the Ideas to the Money Side

You can also apply the ideas behind survival analysis to the financial side of the equation. The simplest way of calculating the average value per unit of time is to take an average, say, of monthly revenue based on initial conditions. However, this does not take into account changes in customer purchasing patterns over time.

Instead, ask the question, "For customers who are active during the nth time unit, what is their average revenue?" For instance, customers who are active for one year would contribute monthly revenue for each of the first twelve months of their tenure. The monthly amounts might differ from month to month, depending on the actual revenue. However, this group of customers would not be included in the average for month thirteen, because they are not active during that month.

The key is that this revenue is only for active customers. It can be combined with the survival curve, in the same way that the active revenue can be.

Including Customer Migration

Often, there are different tiers for the customer relationship. Typically, this would be based on the type of products a customer has. For instance, a banking customer with one or two products might be considered a "new" customer; with three or four, a "growing" customer; and with five or more, a "loyal" customer. Part of the customer value question then becomes, "How long until a customer moves from one group to the next?"

One company divided their subscription customers into three groups. Customers with less than one year of tenure were considered "New"; with one to two years of tenure "Marginal"; and with more than two years "Loyal." In this case, the definition of the customer groups is based solely on tenure, so figuring out the migration pathways using survival analysis is easy.

In other cases, such loyalty may be based on different values of product, such as regular credit card holders versus premium cards (gold, platinum, titanium, black, and so on). From the customer value perspective, each of these different groups has a different value proposition. The full customer value calculation wants to use competing risks to determine when customers are going to keep the same product, upgrade, downgrade, or stop.

Forecasting

Another interesting application of survival analysis is forecasting the number of customers into the future, or equivalently, the number of stops on a given day in the future. In the aggregate, survival does a good job of estimating how many customers will stick around for a given length of time.

Any such forecast has two components. The first is a model of existing customers, which can take into account various covariates during the customer's life cycle. Such a model works by applying one or more survival models to all customers. If a customer has survived for 100 days, then the probability of stopping tomorrow is the hazard at day 100. To calculate the chance of stopping the day after tomorrow, first assume that the customer does not stop tomorrow and then does stop on day 101. This is the conditional survival (one minus the hazard — the probability of not stopping) at day 100 times the hazard for day 101. Applying this to all customer tenures results in a forecast of stops for existing customers in the future.

Figure 10-14 shows such a forecast for stops for one month, developed by survival expert Will Potts. Also shown are the actual values observed during this period. The survival-based forecast proves to be quite close to what is actually happening. This results in the weekly cycle of stops evident in the graph.

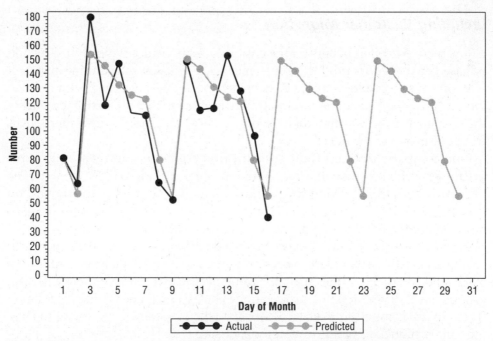

Figure 10-14: You can also use survival analysis for forecasting customer stops.

The second component of a customer-level forecast is a bit more difficult to calculate. This component is the effect of new customers on the forecast, and the difficulty is not technical. The challenge is getting estimates for new starts. Fortunately, budget forecasts often contain new starts, sometimes broken down by product, channel, or geography. Survival models can be refined to take into account these effects. Of course, the forecast is only as accurate as the budget. The upside, though, is that the forecast, based on survival techniques, can be incorporated into the process of managing actual levels against budgeted levels.

The combination of these components — stop forecasts for existing customers and stop forecasts for new customers — produces estimates of customer levels into the future. The authors have worked with clients who have taken these forecasts forward years. Because the models for new customers included the acquisition channel, the forecasting model provides a tool for optimizing the future acquisition channel mix.

Hazards Changing over Time

One of the more difficult issues in survival analysis is whether the hazards themselves are constant or whether they change over time. The assumption in scientific studies is that hazards do not change. The goal of scientific survival analysis is to obtain estimates of the "real" hazard in various situations.

This assumption may or may not be true in marketing. Certainly, working with this assumption, survival analysis has proven its worth with customer data. However, considering the possibility that hazards may be changing over time can also provide interesting insights. In particular, if hazards do change, that gives some insight into whether the market place and customers are getting better or worse over time.

One approach to answering this question is to base hazards on customers who are stopping rather than customers who are starting, especially, say, customers who have stopped in each of the past few years. In other words, were the hazards associated with customers who stopped last year significantly different from the hazards associated with customers who stopped the previous year? Earlier, this chapter warned that calculating hazards for a set of customers chosen by their stop date does not produce accurate hazards. How can we overcome this problem?

There is a way to calculate these hazards. This method uses time windows on the customers to estimate the hazard probability based on stops during the time window. Remember the definition of the empirical hazard probability: the number of customers who stopped at a particular time divided by the number of customers who could have stopped at that time. Up to now, all customers have been included in the calculation. The idea is to restrict the customers only to those who could have stopped during the period in question.

As an example, consider estimating the hazards based on customers who stopped in 2010. Customers who stopped in 2010 were either active on the first day of 2010 or were new customers during the year. In either case, customers only contribute to the population count starting at whatever their tenure was on the first day of 2010 (or 0 for new starts).

Let's consider the calculation of the one-day hazard probability. What is the population of customers who could have stopped with one day of tenure and also have the stop in 2010? Only customers that started between December 31, 2009 and December 30, 2010 could have a one-day stop in 2010. So, the calculation of the one-day hazard uses all stops in 2010 where the tenure was one day as the total for stops. The population at risk consists of customers who started between December 31, 2009 and December 30, 2010. As another example, the 365-day hazard would be based on a population count of customers who started in 2009.

The result is an estimate of the hazards based on stops during a particular period of time. For comparison purposes, survival proves to be more useful than the hazards themselves. Figure 10-15 provides an example, showing that survival is indeed decreasing over the course of several years. The changes in survival are small. However, the calculations are based on hundreds of thousands of customers and do represent a decline in customer quality.

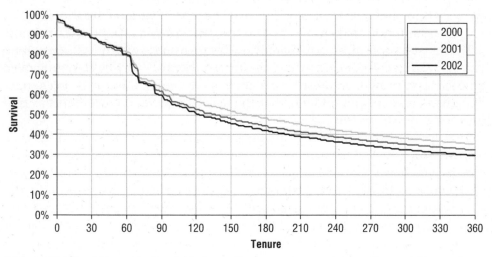

Figure 10-15: A time-window technique allows you to see changes in survival over time.

Lessons Learned

Hazards and survival analysis are designed for understanding customers. This chapter introduced hazards as the conditional probability of a customer leaving at a given tenure defined in discrete time units. This treatment of survival analysis is unorthodox in terms of statistics, which prefers an approach based on continuous rates rather than discrete time probabilities. However, this treatment is more intuitive for analyzing customers.

Hazards are like an x-ray into the customer lifecycle. The related idea of survival, which is the proportion of customers who survive up to a particular point in time, enables comparing different groups of customers and translating results into dollars and cents. When there are enough customers (and usually there are), stratifying the customers by building a separate curve for each group provides a good comparison. Other measures, such as the survival at a particular point in time, the customer half-life, and the average tenure, are useful for understanding customers better.

One of the key concepts in survival analysis is censoring. This means that some customers are dropped from the analysis. The idea of censoring can be extended to understand competing risks, such as voluntary versus forced attrition. Censoring also makes it possible to discard certain outcomes, such as a one-time boycott, without adversely biasing overall results.

One of the most powerful aspects of hazards is the ability to determine which factors, at the onset, are responsible for increasing or decreasing the hazards. In addition to stratifying customers, another technique, Cox Proportional Hazards Regression, has proven its worth since the 1970s and continues to be extended and improved upon.

Survival analysis has many applications beyond measuring the probability of customers leaving. It is often a fundamental component of customer value calculations. It is also used for forecasting customer levels, as well as for predicting other types of events during the customer life cycle. It is a very powerful technique, seemingly designed specifically for understanding customers and their life cycles.

Genetic Algorithms and Swarm Intelligence

Like memory-based reasoning and neural networks, genetic algorithms and swarm intelligence are problem-solving techniques inspired by biological processes. Evolution and natural selection have, over the course of millions of years, resulted in adaptable, specialized species that are highly suited to their environments. Evolution optimizes the fitness of individuals over succeeding generations by propagating the genetic material in the fittest individuals of one generation to the next generation. Among the most successful products of natural evolution are social insects such as ants, bees, and termites. These small, seemingly simple creatures cooperate to solve complex problems, such as finding the most efficient route to a source of food, that seem well beyond the ability of the individual members of the hive or colony. This chapter looks at how to apply insights gained from the study of evolution and social insects to data mining.

Most of the techniques described in this book are widely used in the business world and are easily available as part of commercial data mining packages. The inclusion of the techniques described in this chapter cannot really be justified on those grounds, but the authors feel they are too exciting to ignore, even though it means using some examples that are a bit more academic than the case studies used to illustrate other techniques.

The chapter begins with a brief look at a variety of problem-solving techniques based on the idea of using many simple agents to do something complex. That is the thread that ties together cellular automata, swarm intelligence, and genetic algorithms. These approaches have all been applied successfully to a variety of optimization problems. Optimization may not seem like a data mining task, but it turns out that many data mining problems can be reformulated as optimization problems. All that is required is a way to generate candidate solutions and a way to measure the quality or "fitness" of a potential solution. Many problems can be described in this way; the challenge is encoding the problem in the right fashion.

The chapter uses a very simple optimization problem — finding the maximum of a parabola — to introduce the main elements of genetic algorithms: selection, crossover, and mutation. It then moves on to the traveling salesman problem, a famous and much more difficult optimization problem, to which both genetic algorithms and swarm intelligence have been applied. The traveling salesman problem appears again in Chapter 16 as an example of link analysis.

Swarm intelligence is an approach to problem solving based on the way that complex behavior can emerge from the interactions of many simple individual elements. Like genetic algorithms, swarm intelligence can be used to find solutions to difficult optimization problems.

These techniques are not of purely academic interest. Genetic algorithms have been applied to practical optimization problems in several industries, including complex scheduling problems in clinics and airlines, resource optimization in large factories, classification problems involving free text documents, and financial modeling. Swarm intelligence has been used to improve the routing of packets in communications networks. The chapter closes with a couple of business application examples.

Optimization

Optimization is about finding extreme values — maxima or minima depending on the problem. More precisely, optimization is about finding the conditions that lead to those extreme values. Consider the problem of assigning crews to flights for a large airline. The assignment has many constraints: union contracts, government regulations, and having the crews end each trip at or near their home base. What assignment of crews to flights leads to the maximum utilization of crews subject to these?

What Is an Optimization Problem?

Optimization problems have three features:

- A set of parameters that can be adjusted
- An *objective function* that combines the parameters into a single value
- A set of constraints on the parameters

The goal is to find the parameters that maximize or minimize the objective function, subject to the constraints. Searching through all combinations of parameters that meet the constraints is too cumbersome for even the fastest computers; even for a small number of parameters, the number of combinations is too large to search.

Problems that can be represented as well-behaved, continuous functions (fairly rare in a business context) and have maxima and minima can be found analytically using calculus. The derivative of such a function describes the rate at which it is increasing or decreasing. At a maximum or minimum value, the function is doing neither, so the derivative is zero. You can find an optimum by setting the derivative equal to zero and solving for the parameters. In practice, few functions are differentiable, but calculus also includes ideas for estimating solutions in other cases. The "solver" capability in Excel is based on these ideas.

You can solve another class of optimization problems with *linear programming*. These are problems where the objective function is linear and all the constraints are also linear. These are often resource allocation problems, such as:

> *A company produces widgets in a set of factories. Each factory has a capacity, a cost of production, and a cost for transporting widgets to customers. How many widgets should each factory produce to satisfy customer demand at minimal cost?*

The standard method for solving such problems is called the Simplex method, and it is computationally efficient. Such problems have been solved with thousands of variables.

You can tackle many other problems using hill-climbing algorithms such as Newton's method, gradient descent, and conjugate gradient. These methods start with an approximate solution and iteratively improve upon it using local search.

Yet another approach is called *simulated annealing*. This uses an analogy to a physical process: Some liquids cool and form crystalline patterns as they cool, minimizing certain types of energy across the entire crystal. Scientists studying physical properties are the most common users of simulated annealing.

An Optimization Problem in Ant World

Hilly landscapes are often used as a metaphor for optimization problems. The metaphor is a good one because the optimization task of finding the highest peak or lowest valley is easy to visualize. In this chapter, the hilly landscape is populated with *autonomous agents* that can move about the landscape under their own power. Imagine these agents as ants that have been genetically modified to want to reach the highest possible altitude. Each ant, working on its own, finds the highest point it can. An ant is not happy until it believes it has found the highest point in Ant World — ant nirvana.

Wait — that's not quite fair. The Ant World landscape is continuous and has infinitely many points; an ant could never be sure it has found the highest one. As a kindness, the ants have been engineered to be happier the higher they are. The continuous landscape can be divided into squares. Ants only have to visit the center of each square, and are satisfied when they think they have found the square with the highest center. As the creator of Ant World, you can make the squares as large or as small as you want. After ants have located the highest square, you can subdivide it into many smaller squares and have the ants restart their quests.

By altering the design of the genetically engineered ants, they can be used to explain both swarm intelligence and genetic algorithms. The first idea shared by these two techniques is that many small agents, working independently or cooperatively, can solve complex problems.

E Pluribus Unum

Figure 11-1 is a map of the hilly landscape of an optimization problem in two dimensions. The problem is to find the highest point. It happens to be located near the upper-right corner, at the position labeled (4, 4), but several other points are nearly as high.

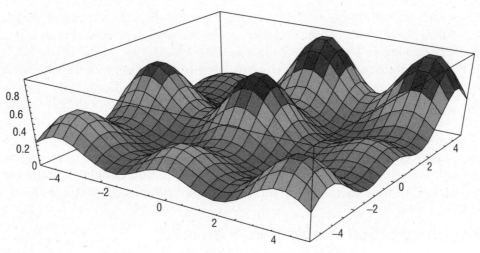

Figure 11-1: The optimization challenge is to find the highest hill.

To be sure of finding the highest square, a single ant, equipped with an altimeter, would have to visit each of the 576 cells of the 24 × 24 grid. It might happen to visit the highest square early in its journey, but it has no way of knowing that none of the squares it has yet to visit is higher. Clearly, the process could be sped up by using more ants. In fact, there are many variations on this idea, generally involving a trade-off between how many ants are needed and how capable each ant must be.

The simplest approach might be termed "brute-force parallelism." Shower the landscape with 576 legless, myopic ants, none of which can see beyond its own square, but each of which can transmit its position and altitude to some central processor that is capable of comparing all the altitudes to find the position of the highest point. In this model, an individual ant has no idea whether its square is the highest; it contributes only a single observation.

A Smarter Ant

Brute-force parallelism is simple, and it works, but as the landscape gets larger — or as more dimensions get added — the bottleneck of having a single combining point could become a problem. One way to improve the situation is to design a more capable ant. For instance, if the ants could communicate with each other and do math, they could cooperate to figure out which one was on the highest square.

Even immobile ants that can only communicate with home base can do better if they can see farther. These superior ants can see a distance of one square in all directions. An ant that sees at least one neighboring cell that is higher than its own does not bother to report back to the central processor. On this map, only nine squares are higher than all neighbors, so the central processor only receives nine messages and only has to compare nine altitudes to find the largest. These new, improved ants are an example of *cellular automata*. A cellular automaton reacts what is going on in neighboring cells, but is not *directly* influenced by what goes on farther afield.

A cellular automaton is indirectly influenced by distant events through a chain of neighbors. This is the mechanism by which a single bird's reaction to a possible predator can cause the whole flock to sound the alarm and change direction even though only the immediate neighbors of the first bird hear its initial alarm. One of the fascinating things about cellular automata is that very complex *emergent behavior* can stem from very simple rules. An excellent example is Conway's Game of Life, which is described in the sidebar. These simple rules can produce orderly structures from random starting positions, self-replicating patterns, and even structures that can perform computations.

Examples in nature are even more impressive. Individual termites do not have to keep a blueprint for a giant termite mound in mind (whatever that might be for a termite); they simply have to respond to the presence of a particular structure by adding to it in a particular way. The same goes for bees cooperating to build a honeycomb, or an entire ant colony taking the shortest path to a food source. These are all examples of *swarm intelligence*.

CONWAY'S GAME OF LIFE

Life is the name of a game invented by British mathematician, John Conway. In 1970, it was introduced to the world in Martin Gardner's "Mathematical Games" column in *Scientific American*. It was an immediate sensation among the kind of people who read *Scientific American* for the games. Actually, the word *game* is a bit of a misnomer because the game has no players, only a creator and an audience, who are often one and the same.

The Game of Life takes place on a large grid of squares like graph paper. Each square is either colored or not, indicating whether the square is "alive" or "dead." What makes the game fascinating is that very simple rules can lead to complex and even beautiful patterns, including some that grow forever, some that move across their simple planar universe leaving a trail of droppings, some that settle into stable crystalline shapes, some that produce offspring, and some that disappear without a trace. All of these behaviors depend solely on the initial pattern laid on a grid by the creator, and the simple rules.

Patterns develop according to the following four rules:

1. Any live cell with fewer than two live neighbors dies.

2. Any live cell with more than three live neighbors dies.

3. Any live cell with exactly two or three live neighbors lives.

4. Any dead cell with exactly three live neighbors becomes a live cell.

Notice that these rules are at the level of a single square and its immediate neighbors. Each cell follows the rules without knowing what is happening in the aggregate. This is the central characteristic of cellular automata.

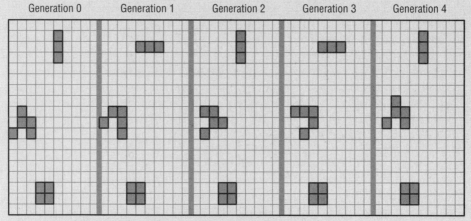

Several generations of the Game of Life from two starting patterns.

The figure shows what happens to three simple starting patterns. The first, called a *blinker*, oscillates between two positions. The second, called a *glider*, moves across the grid forever (until it bumps into another shape; that can be really fun). The third, called a *block*, just sits there.

Back to the ants on the hills. In the cellular automata approach, only nine ants send messages to the central processor, but there is still a requirement for 576 ants. Once again, the solution can be improved by designing a more capable ant; in particular, an ant that can move around and explore the grid. Release a small number of ants at widely scattered points and have them wander around for a while before reporting the location of the highest point they have seen on their journeys.

If different ants follow different rules for deciding where to go next, they will have different probabilities of ending up at a high point in the landscape. Consider some different strategies:

- The ants could only go downhill. Now, this is not reasonable, if the goal is to find the highest point. The ants will end up in valleys, and never on summits. Reject this strategy.

- The ants could only go uphill, taking a step in the steepest direction. This works for certain types of problems, notably landscapes that have a single maximum point, with all other points curving towards it. A landscape that looks like the normal distribution would have this property. In fact, the parameters of a logistic regression also have this property (which is why logistic regressions are readily solvable using maximum likelihood estimation). In a more complex problem, each ant will end up at least as high as the initial points. However, the ants might all get stuck on nearby hills, rather than finding the highest mountain.

- The ants could walk randomly. This gives them the opportunity to bypass nearby hills. However, random walks can take a long time. Other variations are possible, such as ants that start off on stilts taking big steps, and then take progressively smaller and smaller steps.

Genetic algorithms (GAs), the main topic of this chapter, is a variation of the random walk. With GAs, the ants compete against each other. Those that reach high elevations are rewarded with greater opportunities to pass on their genes to the next generation.

Genetic Algorithms

Data mining tasks are usually framed as estimation, classification, or prediction, rather than on optimization, so rephrasing these tasks in terms of optimization is often the first challenge. For instance, a typical data mining problem might be to predict the level of inventory needed for a given item. This can be rephrased as an optimization problem: minimizing the discrepancy between inventory level and demand.

Even for optimization problems, genetic algorithms are only one choice of many techniques. As software to implement them has become more widely available (as add-ins for Excel, for example), their popularity has increased.

A Bit of History

The first work on genetic algorithms dates back to the late 1950s, when biologists and computer scientists worked together to model the mechanisms of evolution on early computers. A bit later, in the early 1960s, Professor John Holland and his colleagues at the University of Michigan applied this work on computerized genetics — chromosomes, genes, alleles, and fitness functions — to optimization problems. In 1967, one of Holland's students, J. D. Bagley, coined the term *genetic algorithms* in his graduate thesis to describe the optimization technique. At the time, many researchers were uncomfortable with genetic algorithms because of their dependence on random choices during the process of evolving a solution; these choices seemed arbitrary and unpredictable. In the 1970s, Professor Holland developed a theoretical foundation for the technique. His theory of schemata gives insight into why genetic algorithms work — and intriguingly suggests why genetics itself creates successful, adaptable creatures such as ourselves.

Starting in the 1980s and continuing into the twenty-first century, the related area of *evolutionary programming* has been an active area of research. Instead of the genomes described in the next section, the building blocks of genetic programming are the instructions that make up a computer program. Multiple versions of a program compete to perform a task and parts of the best solutions are combined to create new ones.

Genetics on Computers

The power of genetic algorithms comes from their foundation in biology, where evolution has proven capable of adapting life to a multitude of environments (see the sidebar "Simple Overview of Genetics"). The language used to describe the data mining technique borrows heavily from the biological model.

A simple example helps illustrate how genetic algorithms work: trying to find the maximum value of a simple function with a single integer parameter p. The function in this example is the parabola defined by $31p - p^2$ where p varies between 0 and 31 (see Figure 11-2). You can solve this trivial optimization problem many ways, including:

■ **Guessing:** The function is clearly 0 when $p = 0$ or $p = 31$ so the right answer is probably about halfway between 0 and 31. Say, about 15 or 16.

- **Calculus:** The derivative of $31p - p^2$ is $31 - 2p$. At a maximum or minimum, the derivative is 0 because the function is not increasing or decreasing. Solving the equation $31 - 2p = 0$ for p yields 15.5. The closest integers are 15 and 16.

- **Exhaustive search:** Only 32 possibilities exist. Trying all of them shows that 15 and 16 yield the highest value, 240.

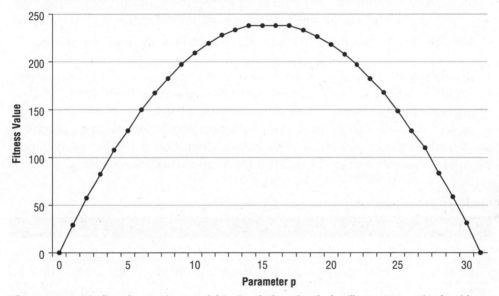

Figure 11-2: Finding the maximum of this simple function helps illustrate genetic algorithms.

How can genetic algorithms be used to solve this simple problem?

The first decision is how to represent candidate solutions. For this problem, the parameter p is expressed as a string of five bits to represent the numbers from 0 to 31; this bit string is the computerized genetic material, called a *genome*. The fitness function peaks at the values 15 and 16, represented as *01111* and *10000*, respectively. This example shows that genetic algorithms are applicable even when there are multiple, dissimilar peaks.

GAs work by evolving successive generations of genomes that get progressively more and more *fit*; that is, the generations have genomes that are better and better solutions to the original problem. As with many optimization techniques on complex problems, GAs are not guaranteed to produce the best value. However, by creating successive generations of solutions that get better and better, they have proven successful in practice.

In nature, evolution arises from the ability of the fittest organisms to survive and reproduce. On a computer, evolution is simulated with the following steps:

1. Identify the genome and fitness function.
2. Create an initial generation of genomes.
3. Modify the initial population by applying the operators of genetic algorithms that mimic the mechanisms of natural selection.
4. Repeat step 3 until the fitness of the population no longer improves.

In this simple example, the genome consists of a single, five-bit bit string representing the parameter p. The fitness function is the parabola. Over the course of generations, the fitness function will be maximized.

Table 11-1 shows that the initial generation consists of ten genomes, randomly produced. The average fitness of the initial generation is 159.0 — pretty good, because the actual maximum is 240, but evolution can improve it.

Table 11-1: Ten Randomly Generated Genomes

COUNT	16	8	4	2	1	P	FITNESS
1	0	1	1	1	0	14	238
1	0	1	0	0	0	8	184
1	1	0	1	1	1	23	184
1	0	1	0	1	0	10	210
1	1	1	0	0	0	24	168
1	1	1	1	1	0	30	30
1	0	0	1	0	0	4	108
1	0	1	1	0	1	13	234
1	1	1	0	0	1	25	150
1	0	0	0	1	1	3	84

The basic algorithm modifies the initial population using the three operators illustrated in Figure 11-3 — selection, crossover, and mutation. The next three sections explain these operators.

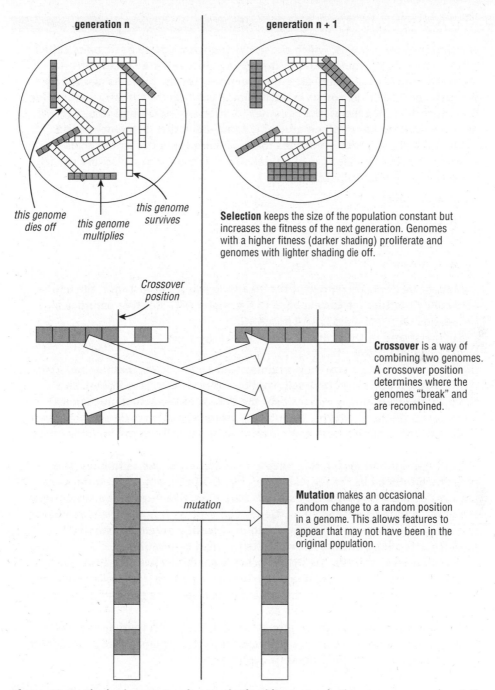

generation n

generation n + 1

this genome dies off

this genome multiplies

this genome survives

Selection keeps the size of the population constant but increases the fitness of the next generation. Genomes with a higher fitness (darker shading) proliferate and genomes with lighter shading die off.

Crossover position

Crossover is a way of combining two genomes. A crossover position determines where the genomes "break" and are recombined.

mutation

Mutation makes an occasional random change to a random position in a genome. This allows features to appear that may not have been in the original population.

Figure 11-3: The basic operators in genetic algorithms are selection, crossover, and mutation.

SIMPLE OVERVIEW OF GENETICS

Life depends on proteins, which consist of sequences of 20 basic units called amino acids. The chromosomes in the nucleus of a cell are strands of DNA (deoxyribonucleic acid) that carry the blueprints for the proteins needed by the cell. The 23 chromosomes in each human cell together are the genome for that individual. In general, the genomes of different individuals in a species are very similar to each other; crucially, some individual differences exist.

The DNA in the genome encodes these blueprints for the amino acids sequences using strands of nucleotides. These nucleotides constitute the four letters of the genetic alphabet:

- A, adenine
- C, cytosine
- G, guanine
- T, thymine

Triplets of nucleotides represent the 20 amino acids. For instance, the amino acid called methionine corresponds to the triplet ATG. Another amino acid, lysine, has two "spellings": AAA and AAG.

So, if a strand of DNA contains the following letters:

ATG AAG ATG CGA

then it decodes into a protein containing four amino acids: methionine, ATG; lysine, AAG; methionine, ATG; followed by arginine, CGA (see figure). This description intentionally glosses over the details of the actual biochemical mechanism that turns the blueprints into proteins, but it provides a high-level outline of the mapping from genetic information in DNA to the building blocks of proteins.

In this simplified model, the process of evolution works as follows. The proteins produced by the representations in the DNA express themselves as features of the living organism, such as blue eyes, five fingers, the structure of the brain, a long trunk, and so on. Genes can express themselves in damaging ways, causing the resulting organism to die. Healthy organisms survive to produce offspring and pass their DNA to the next generation.

In higher-level animals, the DNA is actually combined with the DNA from another survivor during sexual reproduction, using a technique called crossover. Sometimes, mistakes are made in passing genes from one generation to the next — these are mutations.

The combination of all these processes with the pressure of natural selection, over the course of many generations, results in organisms highly adapted to their environment: the process of evolution.

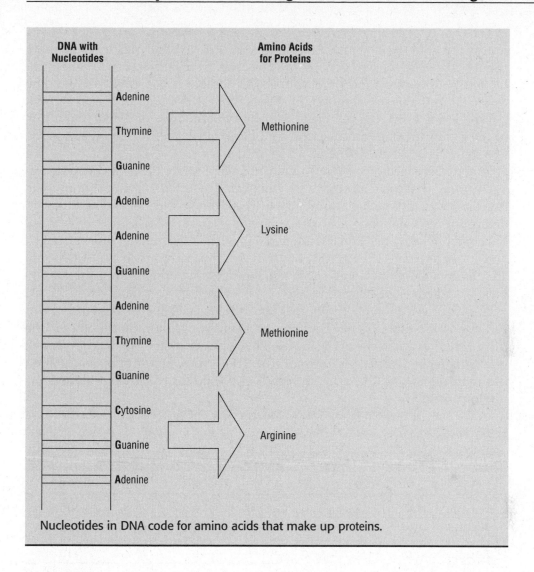

Nucleotides in DNA code for amino acids that make up proteins.

Selection

The selection step is analogous to the process of natural selection where only the fittest individuals in the population survive to pass their genetic material on to the next generation. Unlike natural populations, though, the size of the population remains constant from one generation to the next, so there is no chance of the population becoming extinct (which would clearly not be an optimum solution!).

The chance of a genome surviving to the next generation is proportional to its fitness value — the better the fitness value relative to other genomes, the more copies survive to the next generation. The ratio of the fitness of each genome to the total population fitness determines the number of copies of each genome expected in the next generation. In this example, the total fitness of the initial population is 1,590. The genome *01110* has a fitness value of 238, or about 15% of the total fitness. In contrast, the genome *11110* has a fitness value of 30, or less than 2% of the total fitness.

Survival is based on randomly choosing genomes for the next generation in such a way that the chance of a genome being selected is proportional to its fitness. A series of random numbers between 0 and 1 is generated and used to determine how many copies of each genome survive in the following generation. Each member of generation 0 is allotted a portion of the number line between 0 and 1. In this example, each copy of *01110* gets 15% of the space; *11110* gets only 2%. Because the population size is ten, ten random numbers are generated to pick the members of generation one.

Applying selection to the original ten genomes yields the survivors shown in Table 11-2. Notice that in general this procedure produces more copies of the fitter genomes and fewer of the less fit. The population diversity has decreased; now only eight distinct genomes survive. The average fitness of the population has increased from 159.0 to 192.2. However, the fitness of the best solution has not improved.

Table 11-2: The Population After Selection

COUNT	16	8	4	2	1	P	FITNESS
1	1	0	0	0	0	16	240
1	0	1	0	0	0	8	184
1	1	0	1	1	1	23	184
2	0	1	0	1	0	10	210
1	1	1	0	0	0	24	168
1	0	0	1	0	0	4	108
2	0	1	1	0	1	13	234
1	1	1	0	0	1	25	150

Crossover

The next operator applied to the surviving genomes is crossover. Crossover, which is analogous to sexual reproduction in nature, creates two new genomes from two existing ones by gluing together pieces of each one. *Single-point crossover* is the simplest approach. Single-point crossover starts with two genomes and a random position, the crossover point. The first part of one genome swaps places with the first part of the second. For instance, starting with the two genomes *10110* and *00010* and using a crossover position between the second and third position works as follows:

10 | 1 1 0

00 | 0 1 0

The result of crossover (with the genes from the second genome are underlined) is:

10 | 0 1 0

00 | 1 1 0

The resulting genomes, called children, each have a piece of their genetic code inherited from each of their parents.

Applying crossover to the population proceeds by selecting pairs of genomes and randomly deciding whether they split and swap. The crossover probability is a parameter that can be varied. The value should be high enough to cause many new candidate solutions to be tried, but not so high that promising traits that may be represented by long substrings of the genome are broken up before they can demonstrate their value. A value near 0.5 generally produces good results. In some implementations, all genomes have an equal chance of becoming parents. In other implementations, genomes with higher fitness have a higher probability of being selected for crossover. In nature, high fitness is often advertised with traits such as large antlers, flashy tail feathers, or expensive cars; in a computer program, the fitness value can be read directly to determine a genome's chance of participating.

For pairs selected as parents, a random position is chosen and the children of the original genomes replace them in the next generation. In the earlier example, the two genomes *10110* and *00010* are selected for crossover, and the crossover point is between the second and third genes.

Other popular approaches to crossover include *two-point crossover* which, as the name implies, involves picking two random crossover positions, and *uniform crossover* in which every bit in the genome has some probability (typically 0.5) of being swapped with the corresponding gene from the other parent. And speaking of the other parent, sometimes there are actually multiple other parents. Although the biological model suggests using two parents, nothing restricts the number of parents in a computer program. Some researchers have reported good results using three-way and four-way crossover operations.

As in nature, one has no reason to expect children to be any more or less fit than their parents; just different. The genomes of children include traits inherited from both parents. When a particular combination turns out to have a high fitness value, it is likely to be replicated in future generations. When the solution space is very large, as it would be in a more typical application of genetic algorithms, there is a high probability that the children are different from any genome that has already been tried. Some of these novel offspring will happen to be very fit, and favored by selection. This is how crossover improves the average fitness of the population over time. From the population in Table 11-2, a very fortunate match would be the third row, *10111*, with the seventh row, *01100*, with crossover after the second bit. One of their children is one of the optimal solutions, *01111*. It is important to realize, though, that many other parents are also capable of producing the optimal solutions. After enough generations, they are bound to appear and out-compete all rivals.

In the natural world, the fitness function itself is constantly changing due to environmental changes and the continuing evolution of predators and prey. Traits that were once valuable become less so, and new traits become important. The combination of mortality and sexual reproduction allows a population to evolve gradually over time. In data mining problems, the fitness function is usually fixed, but some impressive academic work has used genetic algorithms to create adaptive systems that respond to changing conditions.

For the parabola maximization problem used in this example, in fact, as selection causes the population to be dominated by the fittest genomes, many of the pairs selected for crossover consist of a *10000* and a *01111*, the two fittest. All children of such a pair are less fit than the parents, and about a quarter of them will be the doomed *11111* and *00000* genomes with 0 fitness that, under the selection rules specified earlier, can never survive to reproduce. If that sounds harsh, the rules can be adjusted so that fitness is never less than some small value. This preserves population diversity that may be useful in future crossovers. For example, the lowly *11111* is likely to have children similar to *01111*, one of the optimal solutions.

The mechanics of crossover depend on the representation of the genome. One of the nice things about using bit strings is that any pattern of bits has a sensible interpretation. Some genomes do not have that characteristic. For example, a genome used to evolve a solution to the traveling salesman problem (described later in the chapter) might consist of the list of cities visited. Because each city can only occur once, crossing over two genomes would yield defective children that are missing some cities and have others twice. Genetic algorithms are tolerant of a few children with zero fitness — two of the thirty-two genomes in the parabola maximization problem have zero fitness, after all — but a population where *most* children are defective is clearly not desirable. The answer is to use a smarter crossover operation, or a different representation of the genome.

Mutation

Children are a lot like their parents. They may represent a novel combination of parental traits, but some changes cannot occur through crossover alone. As a simple example, consider a population of 128-bit genomes in which all members of generation zero share the same value for bit 20. No amount of crossover will ever produce a child with that bit flipped. That is what mutation is for.

Mutation is quite rare in nature where it is the result of miscoded genetic material being passed from a parent to a child. The resulting change in the gene occasionally represents a significant improvement in fitness over the existing population, although more often than not, the results are harmful. Selection and crossover do a good job of searching the space of possible genomes, but they depend on initial conditions and randomness that might conspire to prevent certain valuable combinations from being considered in succeeding generations. Mutation provides a mechanism for avoiding getting stuck at a local optimum, by occasionally tossing a genome into a completely new part of the solution space.

The mutation rate is quite small in nature and is usually kept quite low for genetic algorithms as well — no more than one mutation or so per generation is a reasonable bound. For genomes represented as bit strings, when a mutation occurs, a randomly selected bit changes from a 0 to a 1 or from a 1 to a 0.

The primary *modus operandi* of genetic algorithms is the combination of selection and crossover. When the initial population provides good coverage of the space of possible combinations, succeeding generations move quickly toward the optimal solution by means of selection and crossover. Changes introduced by mutation are likely to be destructive and do not last for more than a generation or two.

Representing the Genome

The previous example illustrates the basic mechanisms for applying genetic algorithms to the optimization of a simple function, $31p - p^2$. Because the goal is to maximize a particular function, the function itself serves as the fitness function. The genomes are quite easy to create, because the function has one parameter — a five-bit integer that varies between 0 and 31. This genome contains a sequence of five binary bits. The choice of representation using binary sequences is not accidental. As explained later in the section on schemata, genetic algorithms work best on binary representations of data — a highly convenient circumstance, since computers themselves work most efficiently on binary data.

Genetic algorithms are different from other data mining and optimization techniques in that they manipulate the patterns of bits in the genomes and do not particularly care about the values represented by the bits — only the fitness function knows what the patterns really mean. One requirement for the fitness function is the ability to transform any genome into a fitness value. This requirement does not seem particularly onerous, because computers are used to working with data in bits. However, some patterns of bits may violate constraints imposed on the problem. When the genome violates such constraints, then the fitness is set to a minimum. That is, testing for constraints in the fitness function incorporates constraints into the solution.

For instance, the parabola example might have a constraint that there should never be more than five "1s" in the solution. This was made implicitly true by using five bits to represent the genome. What if there were eight bits? In this case, the fitness function might look like:

- $31 - p^2$ when p has at most five "1s" in its binary representation
- 0 otherwise

The general rule here is to include a minimum fitness value for any bit patterns that do not make sense or that violate problem constraints. Such patterns may not be in the original population, but they might appear because of crossover and mutation.

> **TIP** The fitness function is defined on the genome. It must be able to return a fitness value for any genome it encounters, including defective genomes that do not make sense according to the constraints of the problem. Defective genomes should receive very low fitness scores so the invalid pattern is not passed on to succeeding generations.

Although convenient for many problems, bit strings are not the only possible representation of a genome. In fact, the other examples of genetic algorithms in this chapter do not use bit strings to represent their genomes. In one example, the genome consists of a list of cities to be visited by a traveling salesman. In another — the case study on identifying complaints that appears later in this chapter — the genome consists of a vector of integer weights.

One of the reasons that bit strings are often preferred has to do with the way substrings that match a particular pattern or *schema* represent whole families of potential solutions. The next section explores this idea.

Schemata: The Building Blocks of Genetic Algorithms

The fact that genetic algorithms work well in practice may be sufficient justification for using them, and the fact that they are modeled on the process that produced, not only ourselves, but all living things, may be reason enough not to be surprised at their power. However, knowing that the technique has a theoretical foundation is still comforting. Professor John Holland developed his theory of schemata processing in the early 1970s to explain why selection, crossover, and mutation work so well in practice.

What Is a Schema?

A *schema*, which comes from the Greek word meaning "form" or "figure," is simply a representation of the patterns present in a binary genome. Schemata (the plural is formed from the Greek root) are represented as sequences of symbols. The *1*s and *0*s (called the *fixed positions*) of genomes are augmented by an asterisk, that matches either a *0* or a *1*. The relationship between a schema and a genome is simple. A genome matches a schema when the fixed positions in the schema match the corresponding positions in the genome.

An example should make this quite clear; the following schema:

10**

matches all the following four genomes because they all have four symbols, beginning with a *1* followed by a *0*:

1000

1001

1011

1010

The schema does not match any other genomes.

The *order* of a schema is the number of fixed positions that it contains. For instance, the order of *1*10111* is 6, of ****1010**1* is 5, and of *0************** is 1. The *defining length* of a schema is the distance between the outermost fixed positions. So, the defining length of *1*10111* is 6 (counting from the left, 7 − 1), of ****1010**1* is 6 (10 − 4) and of *0************** is 0 (1 − 1).

Schemata as Building Blocks

Now, consider fitness functions in terms of schemata. If the genome *000* survives from one generation to the next, then the schema *0*** has also survived, as have **0**, ***0*, **00*, *0*0*, *00**, and *****. The fitness of a particular schema, then, is the average fitness of all the genomes that match the schema in a given population. For instance, the fitness of the schema *0*** is the average fitness of the genomes *000*, *001*, *010*, and *011* because the schema survives when these genomes survive, at least considering only the selection operator.

Consider two schemata from the previous example using the fitness function $31p - p^2$: *10**** and *00****. One genome in the initial population matches *10****, so its fitness is 176. The two genomes matching *00**** have fitness values of 87 and 58. The first schema is fitter than the second. In fact, in the next generation only one genome matches *00**** and two match *10****. The fitter schema has survived and proliferated; the less fit one is disappearing.

A geometric view of schemata is sometimes helpful for understanding them. Consider the eight possible genomes of length three: *000*, *001*, *010*, *011*, *100*, *101*, *110*, and *111*. These lie at the corners of a unit cube, as shown in Figure 11-4. Schemata then correspond to the edges and faces of the cube. The edges are the schemata of order 2 and the faces of order 1. As genetic algorithms are processing different genomes, they are also processing schemata, visualized by these features on a cube. The population covers pieces of the cube trying to find the corners with the best fitness, and the schemata provide information about large regions of the possible solutions. This geometric perspective generalizes to higher dimensions, where the selection, crossover, and mutation operators correspond to cuts through hypercubes in some higher-dimension space that is a bit harder to visualize.

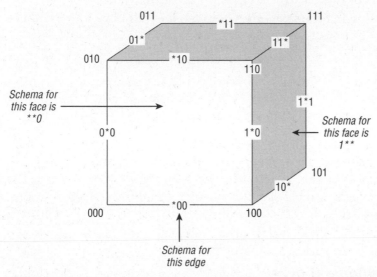

Figure 11-4: A cube is a useful representation of schemata on three bits. The corners represent the genomes, the edges represent the schemata of order 2, the faces, the schemata of order 1, and the entire cube, the schema of order 0.

Consider the schema, *1***1*. This is also quite fit in the original population, with a fitness of 150. One genome matches it in the original population and the same one in the next generation. This schema has survived only because the genome containing it did not cross over with another genome. A crossover would have a 50-50 chance of destroying it. Compare this to *10**** that survived a crossover. The shorter the defining length of a schema, the more likely it will be to survive from one generation to another. So, even longer schemata that are very fit are likely to be replaced by shorter, but fit, cousins. Using more complicated crossover techniques, such as making two cuts, changes the behavior entirely. With more complicated techniques, the defining length is no longer useful, and Holland's results on schemata do not necessarily hold.

Why Fit Schemata Survive

Holland proved these two observations and summed them up in the *Schema Theorem* (also called the Building Block Hypothesis): short, low-order schemata with above-average fitness increase in population from one generation to the next. In other words, short, low-order schemata are the building blocks that genetic algorithms work on. From one generation to the next, the fittest building blocks survive and mix with each other to produce fitter and fitter genomes.

The Schema Theorem explains that genetic algorithms are really searching through the possible schemata to find fit building blocks that survive from one generation to the next. A natural question is how many building blocks are typically being processed? We will spare the reader the details, but Holland showed that the number of schemata being processed by a population of n genomes is proportional to n^3. This means that each generation is really evaluating n^3 different schemata, even though it is only doing work on n different genomes. Holland calls this property *implicit parallelism*. The computational effort for a genetic algorithm is proportional to the size of the population, and in this effort, the algorithm is usefully processing a number of schemata proportional to n^3. The property of implicit parallelism should not be confused with explicit parallelism that is available when running genetic algorithms in a grid computing environment.

The Schema Theorem gives us insight into why genomes work better when there are only two symbols (0s and 1s) in the representation. Finding the best building blocks requires processing as many schemata as possible from one generation to the next. For two symbols, the number of different genomes of a given length is 2^{length} and the number of different schemata is 3^{length}. Roughly, the number of unique schemata being processed by a single genome is about 1.5^{length}. Now, what happens if there are more symbols in the alphabet, say by adding 2 and 3? Now the number of genomes of a given length is 4^{length}, and the number of different schemata is 5^{length} (because the asterisk adds one more symbol). Although there are more schemata, the number of schemata corresponding to a given genome is only 1.25^{length}. As the number of symbols increases, the relative number of schemata decreases. Another way of looking at this is to consider the schema *00. If there are only two letters in the alphabet, then only two genomes process this schema, 000 and 100. If there are four letters, then there are four genomes: 000, 100, 200, and 300. Because genetic algorithms search for the best schemata using a given population size, the additional genomes do not help the search.

Schemata are the building blocks of the solutions, and using only two symbols allows the maximum number of schemata to be represented in a given population size. These estimates are not exact, but they are suggestive. More rigorous treatment confirms the result that an alphabet of two symbols is optimal from the point of view of processing schemata.

Beyond the Simple Algorithm

Researchers have been pushing the bounds on genetic algorithms in several directions. Some of these enhancements are refinements to the basic algorithm; others modify the algorithm to provide a better model of genetic activity in the natural world. This work is often performed under the rubric of machine learning, an area of research that aims to enable computers to learn in ways analogous to humans. Companies are starting to offer solutions that apply these evolutionary techniques to marketing.

The simple genetic algorithm previously described has room for improvement in several areas. The genomes discussed so far consist of only a single strand of genes. Didn't we learn back in high school that DNA consists of two intertwining strands in a helix structure? And what happened to those other concepts buried back in this high-school past, such as recessive and dominant genes? The genetics used so far is based on the simplest chromosomes found in nature, single-stranded, or *haploid* chromosomes. These tend to be found in uncomplicated, single-cell organisms. In more complex organisms, the chromosomes are two-stranded, or *diploid*, as in our own DNA.

The algorithmic characteristics of diploid chromosomes are much the same as haploid chromosomes, because diploid chromosomes can be treated as two chromosomes tied together. The actual algorithm proceeds in much the same way: Selection, crossover, and mutation are the same. The difference is that now there are two versions or *alleles* for each gene instead of one. When they match, there is no problem. When they do not, which does the fitness function use? In the language of genetics, this is asking which of the alleles is *expressed*. For instance, when an allele for blue eyes pairs up with an allele for brown eyes, the brown eyes "win"; that is, they are expressed instead of the blue eyes. (Actually, eye color is a bit more complicated than this simple example, but this is useful for explanatory purposes.) Researchers have solved this problem by including information about dominance in the alleles themselves. The details of this mechanism are beyond the scope of this book.

Why should you care about diploid structures? Geneticists have long wondered why two-stranded chromosomes predominate in nature, when single-stranded ones are simpler. They believe that the two-stranded structure allows an organism to "remember" a gene that was useful in another environment, but has become less useful in the current one.

The Traveling Salesman Problem

A famous example of a difficult optimization problem is the "Traveling Salesman Problem." In this problem, a salesman needs to visit customers in various cities. He plans on flying to one of the cities and, from that starting point, driving to each of the other cities to call on his customers. He drives back to the original city and flies home. The salesman can take many possible routes. What route minimizes the total distance that he travels while still allowing him to visit each city exactly once? Actually, once the salesman has identified the path that connects all the cities, he can fly to any one of them (the one with the cheapest airfare) and travel through the cities, and return home.

The traveling salesman problem is emblematic of a whole class of problems for which there is no known way to efficiently get an optimal solution. The family includes finding the best way to lay out components on a chip, and planning routes for school buses and delivery trucks. Problems that can be restated as variants of the traveling salesman problem come up in logistics, genomics, and the study of crystal formation, as well as other areas.

Exhaustive Search

When the number of cities is very low, calculating the length of every possible path is feasible. When there are four cities, any one of the four can be the starting point. From there, the second leg can be to any of the three remaining cities. After that, there is only a choice of two cities to visit next, and the trip ends at whichever city was saved for last. So, there are 4 * 3 * 2 * 1 = 24 possible trips. In general, if there are n cities on the tour, there are $n!$ (n-factorial) paths. Because factorials get very big, very fast, trying all the possibilities quickly becomes impractical.

Finding the minimum path is an optimization problem. As is often the case with such problems, finding a "pretty good" answer is preferable to waiting forever for the absolute best one. This chapter describes two approaches to this problem, one using genetic algorithms, and one using swarm intelligence. Chapter 16 describes another approach using link analysis.

A Simple Greedy Algorithm

Another approach is the so-called greedy algorithm. This starts by finding the two closest cities. Then another city is added to this path, which is closest to one or the other endpoint. This process continues, until all the cities are visited, and the salesman travels back to the other endpoint.

This is called "greedy" because the shortest segment is added to the path at each step, without considering the consequences. Although this method does find a path through the cities, it is usually not the shortest path. In fact, with a bit more effort, it is usually possible to find better routes.

The Genetic Algorithms Approach

As with the parabola maximization problem, the first decision is how to represent potential solutions as genomes that can be manipulated through selection, crossover, and mutation. Two popular choices are:

- The list of cities itself, in the order visited
- A permutation vector — the indices of the cities visited

As a practical matter, both methods work. The fitness function is the total distance covered by a tour that visits all the cities and returns to the beginning. The goal is to minimize this distance.

Selection proceeds exactly as in the previous example, except that in this case, the goal is to minimize the fitness function, so the chance of getting replicated in the next generation is proportional to the reciprocal of the distance.

Mutation works a little bit differently than in the parabola maximization example. Reaching in and changing the value of a single location in the genome doesn't make sense, because every genome must contain each city exactly once. Any change to just one location is guaranteed to create a defective genome. Therefore, a mutation consists of randomly selecting two locations within the genome and swapping them.

The biggest difference is with crossover. With the binary strings used in the parabola maximization genome, any sequence of bits is valid. That is not true for the traveling salesman genome because every city must be represented exactly once. What this means is that, assuming single-point crossover, for a given genome and crossover point, there is a restricted pool of suitable mates. If the crossover point is after the third city, suitable mates are those that start with the same three cities (in any order). Alternatively, the crossover operation could accept any mate, but replace any cities that would be duplicates with other cities that are not. The first alternative requires a very large population to work. But the second alternative breaks up sequences that may have evolved to be very fit.

The Swarm Intelligence Approach

Swarm intelligence is another approach to solving optimization problems based on the method used by ant colonies to find the best route to a source of food. Marco Dorigo developed this approach as part of his Ph.D. thesis at the Politecnico di Milano in 1992. Others have embellished it since then, but the basic idea stays the same: Find a good tour for the traveling salesman by mimicking ant colonies.

Real Ants

Foraging ants wander around, apparently at random, until one of them finds something good to eat. The lucky ant returns to the nest leaving a *pheromone* trail. Pheremones are chemicals used by ants (and many other living things) to communicate with each other. When a wandering ant comes across a phero-mone trail, it follows the trail with some probability. This probability increases with the strength of the pheromones along the trail. This, in turn, is a function of how many ants have taken the trail and how recently they have done so. It is important that ants don't *always* follow a pheromone trail because some ants should always be out exploring for new food sources. It is also important that the pheromone trails degrade over time so that trails that no longer lead anywhere stop being attractive and so that suboptimal paths can be replaced by better ones.

In one ant experiment that has been replicated several times, two bridges, one long and one short, were set up between an ant colony and a food source. At first, ants are equally likely to take either bridge, but the first ants to arrive back at the nest with news of the food source are the ones that happened to take the short route in both directions. Even though the ants coming back by the long route also deposit pheromones, the initial period when only the short path is marked causes more ants to take that route. The system has positive feedback. If a few more ants go one way, that way becomes more attractive, so even more ants take it in future. Pretty soon, nearly all ants are on the shorter path.

Artificial Ants

To start, ants are distributed randomly to the starting cities. Each ant makes a probabilistic choice of the next city to visit. Its decision is influenced by several factors.

- Each ant has a memory of all the cities it has already been to; only cities not yet visited are considered.

- The attractiveness of a city is inversely correlated with its distance from the current location, so the ant is more likely to visit a nearby city than a distant one.

- A city's attractiveness is positively correlated with the amount of virtual pheromone that has been laid down on the path between it and the current location. More pheromone means that the link has been part of many highly rated tours.

Each ant completes a tour of all the cities and then reinforces all the links it traversed by depositing an amount of pheromone that is inversely related to the length of the tour.

One of the most important parameters is the relative weight given to distance and pheromone strength. Too much weight on distance leads to a greedy algorithm that does not explore a sufficient number of alternatives. Too much weight on pheromones leads to early convergence on suboptimal paths. Other parameters include the number of ants, the rate of decay of the pheromone, and the relationship between tour length and the amount of pheromone deposited.

Getting this approach to work well requires a lot of fiddling with the parameters, but once good values have been found, the artificial ants do a good job of finding a short route among the cities.

Case Study: Using Genetic Algorithms for Resource Optimization

One area where genetic algorithms have proven quite successful is in problems involving scheduling resources subject to a wide range of constraints. These types of problems involve competition for limited resources, while adhering to a complex set of rules that describe relationships. The key to these problems is defining a fitness function that incorporates all the constraints into a single fitness value. These problems are outside the range of what have traditionally been thought of as data mining problems; however, they are interesting and illustrate the power of genetic algorithms.

An example of such a problem is the assignment of 40 medical residents to various duties in an outpatient clinic, as faced by Dr. Ed Ewen at the Medical Center of Delaware. The clinic is open seven days a week, and the residents are assigned to one particular day of the week through an entire year, regardless of their other duties. The best assignment balances several different goals:

- The clinic must have staff at all times.
- The clinic should have a balance of first-, second-, and third-year residents.
- Third-year residents see eight patients per day, second-year residents see six, and first-year residents see four.

So far, this problem is not so complicated.

However, each resident spends four weeks on a rotation in a given part of the hospital, such as the intensive care ward, the oncology unit, or a community hospital. These rotations impose some other constraints:

- Senior residents do not go to the clinic when they are assigned to the medical intensive care rotation, but all other residents do.
- Junior residents do not go to the clinic when they are assigned to the cardiac care rotation, but all other residents do.
- No more than two residents from the intensive care rotation can be assigned to the clinic on the same day.
- No more than three residents from other rotations can be assigned to the clinic on the same day.

As an example of problems that may arise, consider that during one rotation, five residents are assigned to the clinic on a particular day. During the next rotation, the senior is on the medical intensive care rotation and the two juniors are on the cardiac care rotation. Now only two residents are left at the clinic — and this is insufficient for clinic operations.

The genetic algorithms approach recognizes that probably no perfect solution to this problem exists, but that some assignments of residents to days of the week are clearly better than others. Dr. Ewen recognized that he could capture the "goodness" of a schedule using a fitness function. Actually, the function that Dr. Ewen used was an anti-fitness function — the higher the value, the worse the schedule. This function imposed penalties for violating the constraints:

- For each day when the clinic has fewer than three residents, an amount is added — a larger amount the bigger the size of the deficit.

- For each day when no seniors are in the clinic, a small amount is added.

- For each day when fewer than three residents are left on a rotation, a large amount is added to the fitness function.

- And so on.

Setting up a spreadsheet with these functions, Dr. Ewen tried to minimize the functions to get the best assignment. His initial assignments had scores in the range of 130 to 140. After several hours of work, he was able to reduce the score to 72. Pretty good.

However, he had available a genetic algorithms package from the Ward Systems Group (www.wardsystems.com) that plugs into Excel spreadsheets. He started with a population of 100 randomly generated assignments, none of which were very good. After 80 generations, the package lowered the score to 21 — considerably better than he was able to do by hand.

This example gives a good feeling for optimization problems where genetic algorithms are applicable. They differ from most data mining problems because they are more rule-oriented than data-oriented. The key to solving these problems is to incorporate the constraints into a single fitness function to be optimized (either by finding a maximum or a minimum). The resulting fitness function might be highly nonlinear, which makes optimization using other techniques difficult.

TIP Genetic algorithms are a good tool when you have more rules than data in the problem (although they are useful in other areas as well). These types of scheduling problems often involve competition for limited resources subject to complex relationships that describe resources and their users.

Case Study: Evolving a Solution for Classifying Complaints

Direct feedback from customers is a powerful source of information for businesses. When a customer makes a complaint, the company has an opportunity to make a good impression by fixing the problem promptly or, if it is too late for that, by making up for the problem somehow. For some companies, such as product goods manufacturers, complaints provide dates of actual product use — a bit of additional information to add to manufacturing and shipping dates. Customer complaints also hand companies an opportunity to improve processes so that they have fewer dissatisfied customers in the future.

In the author's work building retention models for mobile phone companies, there have been situations where customers who make calls to customer service are more loyal than other customers. Apparently, responding to the expressed needs of customers can make them happier and more loyal, especially when the response is prompt and appropriate.

Yet, at other mobile phone companies, calls to customer service indicate a higher probability of churn, due no doubt to the long wait periods at their call centers. This case study talks about using genetic algorithms to identify complaints so they can be routed to a quick response team.

> **TIP** Sometimes the same input variable can have very different — even opposite — effects at different companies in the same industry in the same country. Testing your assumptions is always a good idea.

Business Context

The custom service department of a major international airline processes many customer comments, which arrive via several channels:

- Email messages
- Telephone calls to the customer service center
- Comment forms on the airline's website
- Response cards included in the in-flight magazine

Different comments have different priorities for responses. Compliments, for example, may result in an automated "thank you for being a loyal customer" type of message. A compliment can be handled today, tomorrow, or the day after — there is usually not so much urgency to responding to good news.

On the other hand, complaints must be acknowledged, and many complaints require follow-up action. The sooner the company responds, the better the chance of keeping a perhaps valuable, but disgruntled, customer. If the complaint indicates a system problem (such as bad food), the airline can work to fix the problem as quickly as possible.

This particular problem, classifying comments as a complaint or compliment, is an example of a message routing problem. Complaints must be routed to the right group quickly to determine how to handle the situation. Compliments can be routed somewhere else, and often have a lower priority.

Airline personnel spend significant amounts of time analyzing customer comments, first sorting them into complaints and other comments, and then routing the complaints to the appropriate group for follow-up. When customers are already upset about lost baggage, canceled flights, rude treatment, or lousy food, a slow or inappropriate response only makes things worse.

This particular airline decided to reduce the time it took to respond to a complaint by automating the initial categorization of comments. Their approach evolved a solution using software from Semcasting, Inc. (www.semcasting.com), a marketing services company in Andover, Massachusetts.

Data

All customer comments end up in a comment database, regardless of the channel they come in by. This database includes both fixed fields describing the comment and the actual text itself. A complete customer comment record has the following fields:

- Date
- Source (email, comment card, telephone contact, letter, other)
- Flight number
- Class of service
- Departure airport
- Destination airport
- Mileage account number
- Organization receiving comment
- Names of involved airline employee(s) if mentioned
- Free-text comments

Some records are missing data for some fields. Comments coming in through the call center are usually filled in correctly, because the call-center reps are trained to fill in all the fields. However, left to themselves, customers may not fill in all the fields when sending a comment card or email message.

The Comment Signature

The first step is creating a comment signature from the pre-classified training data. The comment signature, shown in Figure 11-5, has one row per comment and a large number of columns to capture comment attributes. Before the signature is created, the raw comments are pre-processed to correct spelling errors and to remove *stop words* (words too common to be interesting). The fields of the signature are all derived variables. Some capture global features of the comment such as its length, measured in number of words, and the method (email, transcribed phone call, response card) of submission. Most fields in the comment signature are counts. There is one field for each word or phrase that occurs more than some threshold number of times in the training data as a whole. Because most words do not occur in most comments, there are many zero values.

There are also fields for interaction variables, such as whether both "baggage" and "JFK" are mentioned or whether both "food" and "chicken" are mentioned. Finally, because this is a directed data mining task, there must be a target field. In this case, it is a flag indicating whether or not the message is a complaint. The comment signature is quite wide.

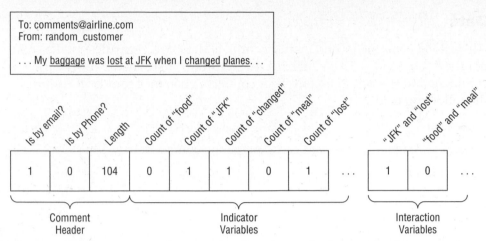

Figure 11-5: The comment signature describes the text in the comment.

The Genomes

Solving a problem with genetic algorithms requires genomes and a fitness function. As shown in Figure 11-6, the genome is a set of weights corresponding to the columns of the signature (along with an additional weight called a bias). Just as in a neural network, these weights start out random and become meaningful through training. Genetic algorithms accomplish the training by having the genomes compete to be selected for the next generation. The competition requires a fitness function to identify winners and losers.

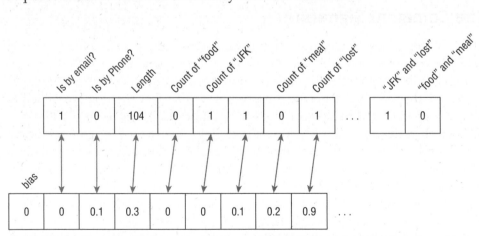

Figure 11-6: The genome has a weight for each field in the comment signature, plus an additional weight called a bias.

The Fitness Function

The fitness function is a bit complicated. Each weight in the genome is multiplied by the corresponding field in the comment signature as shown in Figure 11-6. (The bias weight, which has no corresponding field, is multiplied by one.) The results are summed and compared to a cutoff score. Comments with scores above the threshold are classified as complaints. The predicted classifications are compared with the actual classifications to calculate the percent correctly classified. The percent correctly classified is the fitness score. The evolutionary goal is to maximize it.

The Results

The genetic algorithm software creates a random population of genomes. These genomes generally have most of the weights set to low values, and just a few set to high values. That is, the initial population consists of genomes that are specialized for the simplest features in the comment signature. Although the initial population performed very poorly, its use of selection, crossover, and mutation lead to better and better solutions. After tens of thousands of generations, the final model was able to classify 85 percent of the records correctly — enough to speed up the airline's complaint processing.

Lessons Learned

Genetic algorithms and swarm intelligence are very powerful optimization techniques. Optimization can solve interesting and important problems. In fact, some data mining algorithms, such as neural networks, depend on optimization "under the hood."

The key to the power of genetic algorithms is that they depend on only two things. One is the genome and the other is the fitness function. The fitness function makes sense of the genome by producing a value from what looks like a random set of bits. The genome encodes the problem; often it consists of a set of weights on some equation. Genetic algorithms work on a wide variety of fitness functions, which makes it possible to encode many different types of problems that are not easily handled by other means.

The process of evolution starts with a random population and then applies three transformation steps. The first is selection, which means that more fit genomes survive from one generation to another. This corresponds to natural selection. The second is crossover, where two genomes swap pieces, and is analogous to a similar natural process. The third is mutation, where some values are changed randomly. Mutations are usually quite rare both in nature and in genetic algorithms.

The application of these three processes produces a new generation, whose average fitness should be greater than the original. As more and more generations are created, the population moves to an optimal solution. These processes have a theoretical foundation, based on schemata. This theory explains how genetic algorithms move toward a solution.

Swarm intelligence shares some ideas with genetic algorithms, but instead of a large population of individual genomes competing with one another, the model is the cooperative behavior of ants, bees, termites, and other social insects. The core idea is that complex behavior can emerge from a large collection of simple agents with only local communication.

Genetic algorithms and swarm intelligence have been applied to practical problems, often to resource optimization problems. They can even be used for predictive modeling and classification, as explained in the case study on classifying comments sent to an airline.

Tell Me Something New: Pattern Discovery and Data Mining

Earlier chapters focus on directed data mining techniques. These techniques are particularly good when the purpose of data mining is to answer a specific question, and the historical data contains examples to help find the best answer. In directed data mining, the answer to the question is "phrased" as a target variable, and the various techniques discover patterns to discern the value of the target.

This chapter, along with the next four, move on to what is perhaps the more challenging side of data mining. Undirected and semi-directed data mining are most applicable when you do not know the question, or when the question does not have a simple answer residing in the data. These situations may occur in several different ways:

- The goal may be to discover something new, such as groups of customers that are similar to each other or products that sell together.

- The goal may be ill-defined, so defining the target is more than half the battle. For instance, determining which credit card customers are revolvers (who keep a large balance), transactors (who use the card and pay the balance every month), or convenience users (who charge up for furniture or a vacation and then pay off the balance over time).

- The goal may be well-defined but historical examples may not help. Fraud detection is one example. Another example is customer-centric forecasting, discussed in Chapter 10 on survival analysis.

With undirected data mining, the data miner is part of the toolkit. Two qualities that make a good data miner are creativity and curiosity. Data miners often delve into information, wanting to learn more. Data miners are skeptical, not taking everything at face value. This attitude helps with undirected data mining, because the data miner provides the judgment needed to evaluate results and move forward.

The process of undirected data mining is both quite different and quite similar to the process for directed data mining. The similarities are important. Both work with data and require exploration and understanding of the data and underlying business. Both are improved by incorporating intelligent variables into the data that identify and quantify different aspects of the business. Undirected data mining differs in not having a target variable, and this poses a couple challenges:

- One is that the process of undirected data mining cannot be fully automated, because judgment is involved. As powerful and advanced as computers are today, software is still not available to distinguish between the more useful and the less useful. Humans play a critical role.

- Another challenge is that there is no right or wrong answer, no simple statistical measure such as the percent correct or the R^2 value that summarizes the goodness of the results. Instead, descriptive statistics and visualization are key parts of the process. Undirected data mining techniques, do, of course, have various measures. These measures are more qualitative than the ones associated with directed techniques.

The issues that lead to the partitioning of the model set into training, validation, and test sets are generally unimportant for undirected data mining techniques. Similarly, the distinction between a prediction model set and a profiling model set is irrelevant, because the techniques do not use target variables.

The terminology even poses a challenge — with the words *directed* and *undirected* having two distinct usages, one for the data mining problem and one for the techniques. There is much overlap between the two usages. However, they are not synonymous. Directed techniques can provide key insights, via undirected data mining. Such serendipity occurs when you find something that you were not looking for. Undirected techniques can even be adapted for use on directed problems.

This chapter starts with a comparison of directed and undirected data mining, followed by an example of knowledge discovery using directed data mining techniques. It then continues by discussing different types of undirected data mining, including dealing with ambiguous target variables and forecasting.

Undirected Techniques, Undirected Data Mining

Data mining techniques are traditionally divided into two groups, based on whether or not the technique requires target variables. This section investigates this distinction, including a case study of discovering interesting patterns in data, using that most directed of techniques, decision trees.

Undirected versus Directed Techniques

Directed techniques, which are the subject of the previous seven chapters, use one or more *target* variables that guide the technique as it processes data. The target variables allow the technique to define the best possible model, because there is an unambiguous definition of "best" — the best model is the one that best estimates the value of the target variable. Different measures may lead to different choices of the "best" model. The lift on the top ten percent of the population might imply "best" for one business problem. For another, the goal may be to minimize root mean squared error, or the maximum value of a profitability function.

More abstractly, the target variable is a way of putting domain expertise into the modeling process. The data miner is saying, "this is what is important… take it from here." With this information, directed techniques have enough information to optimize their models and proceed.

Undirected techniques have no such hint. With these techniques, the data miner is instead throwing the data at the computer (well, not literally) and asking the computer to make some sense of it: "Tell me something interesting about this data." Although this may sound like a harder problem, from the technical perspective it is not necessarily hard. If human data miners have a low threshold of what constitutes an interesting pattern, computers have an even lower, quirkier one. What computers find interesting may be perplexing to humans, or painfully obvious. Regardless, using undirected data mining techniques requires even more human understanding than directed techniques.

Undirected versus Directed Data Mining

Just as techniques can be directed or undirected, the style of data mining can also be directed or undirected. Often, the style of data mining matches the type of technique. Using directed techniques for directed data mining and undirected techniques for undirected data mining makes sense. However, this is not a hard and fast rule.

For instance, you can use undirected techniques to find "clusters" of similar records based on, say, demographic characteristics. By mapping behavioral variables over the demographic clusters, you can determine whether and how the demographic clusters differ in terms of customer behavior, customer profitability, or response to a particular campaign.

> **TIP** Building similarity clusters on one type of data (for example, demographic data) and then overlaying another type (such as behavioral data) on the clusters can be a powerful way to find relationships that would otherwise be difficult to spot.

The opposite is also true. Directed techniques such as decision trees provide a lot of information about different groups of records — namely the ones that show up in the same leaf on a tree. Although the tree is generated through a directed technique, the leaves are also examples of clusters. The next section discusses a case study where something interesting was found in the rules lurking in a decision tree.

Case Study: Undirected Data Mining Using Directed Techniques

One of the first projects that came to the authors' consulting company still provides some important lessons. The purpose of the project was to teach a wireless phone company in South Korea how to build certain types of models. This project provided several important lessons, one of which involves discovering unexpected patterns.

As with many mystery books — which are also about discovering unexpected patterns — this story starts with a phone call, a static-filled, bad connection with a person who spoke heavily accented English on the other end. Upon receiving this call, the response was what you might expect: "Sorry, you have a wrong number." Hang up.

Fortunately, Injung Hwang did not give up so easily; he called back because he needed a data mining consultant and was literally willing to call halfway around the world to find one. A few weeks later, one of the authors found himself on an airplane, flying to a foreign land.

The goal of the project was ostensibly to build a churn model; that is, to assign a score to customers to determine who would leave in the near future. However, the real goals were more diverse than that. The purpose of the project was not a single churn model, but transferring knowledge to build a churn modeling system. The client wanted to build an automated system for doing such work, and needed to understand how the data and data mining techniques interacted with each other.

Another goal was more prosaic: to demonstrate the value of the data warehouse. The company had spent millions of dollars building a database with important customer information. After doing so, they learned what many companies learn: Databases don't "do" anything, they just sit around and store data. Well, they do clean and combine and validate data. They also organize, back up, and disambiguate data. However, applications are what actually convert the data into business value. Would data mining be such an application?

The project also had to demonstrate that the database marketing group was technically competent for the challenges at hand. This goal became apparent when the first comment in the first meeting with marketing started with a statement that was roughly translated as, "I don't know why I am wasting my time at another meeting. The last time you built a churn model it didn't work at all." Hmmm, "the last time." This was the first hint of earlier efforts. The rest of the meeting was incredibly valuable, because it provided an opportunity to learn what had gone wrong in the past. Remember: Data miners want to learn more. Understanding what went wrong (and right) on earlier occasions is useful.

> **TIP** Learn from past efforts, even if you didn't do the work. This is the only way to do a better job in the future.

All these goals led to several modeling efforts. These efforts were centered on decision trees (pretty pictures of the trees helped overcome language barriers). Because the goal was to understand the best way to build a tree, many different types of trees with different parameters were tried out. Many different variables were tried out (and in the context of derived variables, this project is discussed again in Chapter 19). The target was the deactivation of a telephone number.

Along the way, one of the decision trees proved very interesting. Figure 12-1 shows the important part of the tree, a handful of leaves from a much larger tree. At first glance, nothing is suspicious about these leaves. Let's go through the path on the left in more detail:

- The split at the top is the number of accounts billed to the same number. This particular part of the tree consists of accounts that are the sole account on their bill, the most common situation.

- The next split is for customers on the CFBAS pricing plan. This pricing plan is the basic family pricing plan, devised for members of a household to get discounts when calling each other.

- The bottom split is for the popularity of the handset, with more popular handsets on the left and less popular handsets on the right.

The difference in churn rates on the bottom is remarkable — 21 percent for the leaf on the left and 60 percent for the leaf on the right.

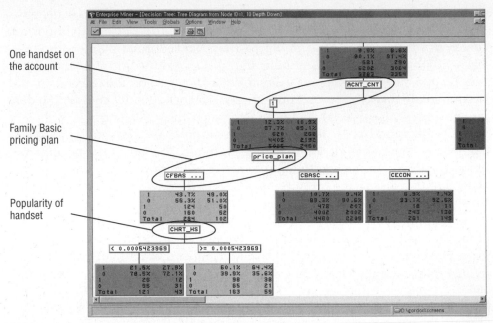

Figure 12-1: This decision tree reveals an interesting pattern, unrelated to the target variable, that is not obvious without knowledge of the business.

The difference in churn rates is striking. However, focusing on the churn rates is directed data mining. The splits themselves are even more intriguing — although the reason may not be immediately obvious. The two leaves at the bottom left contain customers who are using the family plan, even though the customers have only one handset. The family plan is devised for families that have multiple phones billed on one account. Why would customers have the family plan with only one phone? And why would such customers have such high churn rates when the handset is unpopular?

Although decision trees are a directed data mining technique, they can uncover unusual relationships not directly related to the target. The tree itself cannot explain why; the tree cannot even recognize that such a pattern is potentially of interest. Seeing the pattern in the tree and asking questions is an example of undirected data mining.

The customers in these leaves are indeed an interesting segment. At the time this particular phone company provided subsidies on the latest-and-greatest handsets to new customers, but it did not subsidize these handsets for existing ones. There is something of a paradox here. The company would lure in new customers with the promise of the latest and greatest technology. Then, six months or a year later, the policies would specifically deprive these customers of the next generation of handsets by denying them a discount (after all, who wants to pay full price?). Of course, this is only a paradox from the perspective of customers. From the perspective of financing the subsidies, the policy makes a lot of sense.

Some customers learned to outsmart the company's efforts, and these are the customers identified in the decision tree. These customers would start with a handset that is out-of-fashion — horrors! They would sign up for a family plan, and the basic family plan is the least expensive one available. A feature of the family plan is that new phones added to the plan are eligible for the new-customer subsidy. Then, these savvy, fashion-conscious customers would add a new phone and receive the discount. Normally, in this situation, the account would have a new phone with a new number. But, because these customers were on the family plan, they could transfer the old number to the new phone, and put the new number on the old phone. This was allowed, and even encouraged, as a way for Mom or Dad to give their old phone to little Junior.

No children are in this picture, though. The savvy, fashion-conscious customers were doing this only for the discount on the new handset. As soon as possible after receiving the new handset, the customer would turn off the old one. This is the churn captured by this part of the decision tree — clever customers beating the system.

What is Undirected Data Mining?

The previous case study about learning from data and paying attention to unexpected patterns is an example of undirected data mining. Serendipity can occur during even the most directed data mining efforts. In this context, undirected data mining has the following two key pieces:

- Pay attention to interesting patterns.
- Explain and understand the patterns, typically by investigating their causes with the business people.

Finding such unexpected patterns is one example of undirected data mining.

Broadly speaking, undirected data mining has four flavors. The first is exploring data. The second is finding groups of records that are similar to each other. The third is working with data that has no explicit target variables or where the target may be one of the inputs. The fourth is simulation, where the goal is to understand what might happen under different scenarios and the scenarios are not directed by a particular target variable.

Data Exploration

Exploring data is an opportunity to learn about what is in the data. Earlier chapters, particularly Chapter 4, cover various aspects of data exploration. Much of the learning is about the processes that generate the data — essentially data quality issues. This is to be expected. The data that data miners work with usually comes from many different source systems, which might include data warehouses, external sources of data, operational systems, marketing spreadsheets, and so on. One goal of the initial exploration is deciding on a definition for the rows of the customer signature. Chapter 18 discusses the topic of finding the customer in the data, because this is such a common and underappreciated problem.

> **TIP** Data exploration often uncovers data quality issues. You should expect this because data mining looks at data differently from other applications.

What do you want to look for when exploring data? Typically, there are two areas of keen interest. The first is to pay attention to outliers that do not belong in the model set. For instance, retailing data based on loyalty cards often contains examples of customers — or at least loyalty cards — with thousands of dollars of spending per week.

The largest amounts might correspond not to customers at all, but to "store cards." Customers come in without a card, but the cashier wants to give the discount anyway. Customers who spend hundreds or thousands of dollars per week can suggest small businesses, which should perhaps be modeled separately from households. These are examples of outliers. Perhaps the scope of the data used for analysis needs to be refined to find a better set of customers.

The second area is to be open to new patterns in the day. Chapter 1 has a business case from Bank of America about an unexpected correlation among some customers in a particular cluster. An undirected data mining technique, k-means clustering, found a segment where customers had both a high propensity for home equity lines of credit and also had small business accounts. Such a coincidence risks being found and discarded — ignored by highly competent technical people who do not understand the business.

> **WARNING** Technical expertise is not enough to find unexpected patterns. You should understand the business and often the overall culture, as well.

In the right context, on the other hand, such an observation can lead to suspicions, questions, speculation, hypotheses, and verification. In this case, the observation led to the speculation that customers took out home equity lines of credit to start small businesses. The verification was an additional question on a quarterly survey of branch managers (something like "do your customers use home equity lines of credit to start small businesses?"). The results changed the marketing approach for these products, both at Bank of America and eventually at its competitors, as well.

Segmentation and Clustering

The idea that "birds of a feather flock together" is a common theme in the marketing world. The assumption is that you want to find more customers that are like your good customers, and fewer customers who are like your bad customers. This is easy to state, but what exactly does it mean for two customers to be "like" each other? Is geographic similarity sufficient?

Distance Between Records

Earlier chapters introduce the idea of distance as a measure of similarity between records. The next chapter, on k-means clustering, returns to the notion of distance, but without the target variable. The idea is simply to assign each record to a group so that close neighbors tend to be in the same group.

A method for measuring distance between records is key for finding similar records. There is no single correct way to measure distance for the complex records that describe customers. Sometimes you might want to limit the input to demographic variables to find demographic clusters. At other times, you might want to limit the analysis to customer behavior variables to find behavioral clusters.

One of the challenges when dealing with distance between records is the sheer number of columns that are available. Chapter 20 introduces several methods for reducing the number of variables. This is important because many variables say similar things. For instance, many census variables capture the notion of whether the neighborhood is wealthy or poor, including the median family income, average housing cost, type of housing, and proportion of the population earning more than $100,000 per year or less than $10,000 per year. A dataset that has many of these variables and uses a technique based on distance may inadvertently be overweighting "wealth" at the expense of other characteristics.

WARNING When you have a lot of columns in your data, be careful because some concepts, such as "frequent purchasers" or "wealthy households" may be overweighted. That is, many columns might describe the same phenomenon.

Segmentation

Segmentation refers to the business goal of identifying groups of records that are similar to each other. The purpose of segmentation is usually to direct marketing campaigns to different groups of customers. It can also be used for tracking purposes. As the customer relationship evolves, customers migrate between different customer segments.

One method for customer segmentation is simply definition. So, a credit card company may divide its customers into "green," "gold," and "platinum" customers, depending on the color of the credit card they use. Another subscription-based company that the authors have worked with divided their customers into "new," "marginal," and "core" based on the tenure of the customer relationship. "New" refers to customers whose tenure is less than one year; "marginal" between one and two years; and "core" refers to customers who have been around longer than two years.

One data mining technique for segmentation is automatic cluster detection; however, this is not the only choice. Automatic cluster detection does not guarantee that the clusters will be useful. Often, what looks like an undirected data mining problem is really a directed data mining problem.

Directed Segmentation

Once upon a time, a large company approached the authors with a project: Use k-means clustering (described in the next chapter) to find something called "retention segments." The purpose was to find groups of similar customers, and then to discover differences among these groups based on retention characteristics.

Is this undirected data mining? Although the company wanted to use an undirected data mining technique, the data mining problem itself was directed — because the goal was to find differences in retention among the resulting clusters.

Of course, an undirected technique can be used for such purposes. You can create clusters, using a variety of techniques, and then analyze retention differences among the clusters. However, that may not be the best approach.

A better approach is to construct the problem as a directed data mining problem, with tenure as the target variable. A particularly suitable technique for this would be decision trees, but with a very large leaf size to prevent the tree from growing too large. Just a handful of leaves are sufficient for the tree. Each leaf becomes a cluster in its own right. The leaves themselves are guaranteed to differ with respect to retention, because that is the target variable used for creating the tree.

TIP The leaves of a decision tree built on customer signatures — particularly for a tree with just a handful of leaves — are examples of customer segments created using directed data mining.

Target Variable Definition, When the Target Is Not Explicit

Directed data mining techniques focus on well-defined target variables, but sometimes the target variables are not known in advance, at least not explicitly. Instead, the goal is to search for patterns that suggest targets. For instance, by looking at correlations between different variables, rules such as the following might be found:

- When the customer stop date field is empty, then the status is active.
- When the customer does not have a cable bundle, then the customer does not have any premium channels.

These types of patterns are not necessarily interesting, although exceptions to these rules might point to data quality problems. They do illustrate the point that the data mining process can consider different variables as targets, choosing the most appropriate ones in each situation.

The canonical technique in this area is association rules, discussed in Chapter 15 on market basket analysis. Association rules traditionally work only on values within a single column, which are typically the products that are purchased by a customer. Variations on the technique can take more information into account, such as the time sequencing of actions.

A somewhat different situation occurs when you need to define the target in order to develop data mining models. This may occur, for instance, when you try to find profitable customers and discover that the challenge is defining profitability. It can also occur when you have some ideas about different customer groups in the data. The goal is to find these groups in the data. Although this is similar to segmentation, the focus in this section is a bit different: developing definitions for the groups using available data.

The credit card industry, for example, recognizes several different types of customer behavior:

- *Transactors* are customers who make purchases every month and pay off their bills.
- *Revolvers* are customers who make charges every month, but do not pay off the balance.
- *Convenience users* are customers who make large charges, such as for a vacation or to buy furniture, and then pay these off over a few months.

Of the three, transactors are usually the least profitable. Although the card issuer collects a percentage of each transaction, these customers do not generate interest and fee income. Furthermore, American Express has been targeting this group of customers for decades (at least in the United States), siphoning off the wealthier and less risky transactors.

The sidebar "Defining Transactors, Revolvers, and Convenience Users" discusses defining these groups using available billing data. This example shows that segmentation may be directed by ideas, rather than specific variables. Defining these terms is an example of semi-directed data mining. The direction is understood, but the path is not at all clear.

DEFINING TRANSACTORS, REVOLVERS, AND CONVENIENCE USERS

As the text describes, the credit card industry recognizes several different types of customers. These customers vary by how much they charge on the card each month and how much they pay. The following figure illustrates the different types of customers, showing their payments and charges.

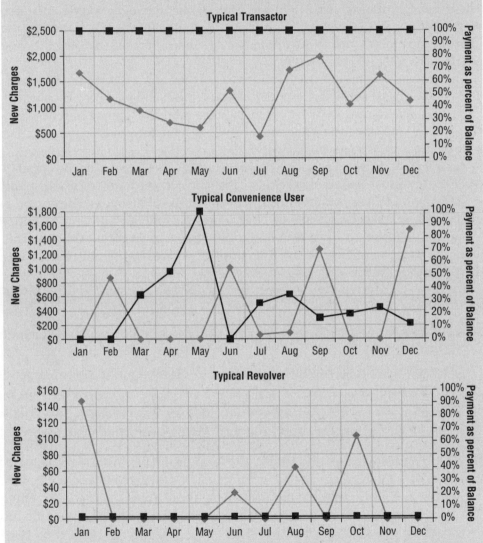

Three different types of credit card customers differ in their payment and usage patterns.

How can these customers be identified in the data?

The idea is to define a measure that describes each of these behavior classes. As an example, consider a transactor, who is defined by two characteristics:

■ Makes charges every month

■ Pays no interest

Let's combine these observations into a measure of "transactor-like" behavior. To start, define a separate measure for each characteristic.

The first dimension is "makes charges every month." Let's add that the more charges a customer has, the more like a transactor the customer is. However, expecting that a customer would spend up to his or her credit line every month is unreasonable (especially because the credit line would then increase). Let's use a threshold of 25 percent. Customers who charge 25 percent of their credit line every month, or more, would rate "high" on the "makes charges every month" dimension. Customers who charge 1 percent would rate low.

To generate this measure, calculate the following ratio each month: the dollar amount of new charges divided by 25 percent of the credit line. If the number exceeds 1, set it to 1. The "makes charges every month" measure is the average value of this ratio over several months, as shown in the following table for the three sample customers:

Charge Measure for Transactors

	Transactor (Limit $2,000)			Convenience User (Limit $2,000)			Revolver (Limit $2,000)		
	Charge	% Of Limit	Measure	Charge	% Of Limit	Measure	Charge	% Of Limit	Measure
Jan	$1,250.44	62.5%	1.00	$1,172.51	58.6%	1.00	$0.00	0.0%	0.00
Feb	$1,546.52	77.3%	1.00	$0.00	0.0%	0.00	$135.95	6.8%	0.27
Mar	$1,661.93	83.1%	1.00	$0.00	0.0%	0.00	$90.28	4.5%	0.18
Apr	$522.87	26.1%	1.00	$47.28	2.4%	0.09	$0.00	0.0%	0.00
May	$1,937.79	96.9%	1.00	$0.00	0.0%	0.00	$25.86	1.3%	0.05
Jun	$863.30	43.2%	1.00	$738.99	36.9%	1.00	$0.00	0.0%	0.00
Jul	$841.93	42.1%	1.00	$0.00	0.0%	0.00	$113.94	5.7%	0.23
Aug	$1,237.68	61.9%	1.00	$53.56	2.7%	0.11	$0.00	0.0%	0.00
Sep	$1,741.01	87.1%	1.00	$60.57	3.0%	0.12	$0.00	0.0%	0.00
Oct	$959.30	48.0%	1.00	$1,086.34	54.3%	1.00	$151.61	7.6%	0.30
Nov	$1,954.05	97.7%	1.00	$0.00	0.0%	0.00	$88.15	4.4%	0.18
Dec	$1,051.92	52.6%	1.00	$0.00	0.0%	0.00	$0.00	0.0%	0.00
Overall			1.00			0.28			0.10

Continued

DEFINING TRANSACTORS, REVOLVERS, AND CONVENIENCE USERS (*continued*)

Notice that the measure does a good job of capturing how much the charging behavior of each type of customer is like a transactor.

The second dimension captures the fact that a transactor pays off his or her balance each month. For this, the measure can just be the percent of the balance paid off (see the following table). For the same three customers:

Payment Measure for Transactors

	Transactor (Limit $2,000)			Convenience User (Limit $2,000)			Revolver (Limit $2,000)		
	Balance	Payment	Measure	Charge	Payment	Measure	Charge	Payment	Measure
Jan	$1,250.44	$1,250.44	1.00	$1,172.51	$0.00	0.00	$1,500.00	$30.00	0.02
Feb	$1,546.52	$1,546.52	1.00	$1,172.51	$300.00	0.26	$1,620.95	$29.70	0.02
Mar	$1,661.93	$1,661.93	1.00	$872.51	$300.00	0.34	$1,696.37	$32.12	0.02
Apr	$522.87	$522.87	1.00	$619.79	$300.00	0.48	$1,680.31	$33.61	0.02
May	$1,937.79	$1,937.79	1.00	$319.79	$300.00	0.94	$1,689.37	$33.27	0.02
Jun	$863.30	$863.30	1.00	$758.77	$19.79	0.03	$1,672.73	$33.45	0.02
Jul	$841.93	$841.93	1.00	$738.99	$300.00	0.41	$1,769.95	$33.12	0.02
Aug	$1,237.68	$1,237.68	1.00	$492.55	$300.00	0.61	$1,753.39	$35.07	0.02
Sep	$1,741.01	$1,741.01	1.00	$253.12	$192.55	0.76	$1,735.85	$34.72	0.02
Oct	$959.30	$959.30	1.00	$1,146.91	$60.57	0.05	$1,870.10	$34.37	0.02
Nov	$1,954.05	$1,954.05	1.00	$1,086.34	$300.00	0.28	$1,941.07	$37.06	0.02
Dec	$1,051.92	$1,051.92	1.00	$786.34	$300.00	0.38	$1,922.54	$38.45	0.02
Overall			1.00			0.38			0.02

Notice that this also does a good job of distinguishing the transactor from the other two customers.

The total "transactor" measure combines the two values, typically by taking the average or using a more exotic combination such as the square root of the sum of the squares.

Defining a convenience user and revolver involve the same ideas as defining a transactor. A convenience user is characterized by having charges in a wide range. In many months, convenience users charge very little; in some months, they charge a lot. They tend to pay more than the minimum, but not the entire balance. A revolver tends to charge very little and to pay the minimum balance, so the measures that define a transactor are also good for a revolver; whereas the transactor has high values, a revolver has values close to zero.

In general, customer segmentation is often "directed" by marketing ideas. The method is:

1. Identify one or more dimensions of customer characteristic that can be measured in the data.

2. Define a measure that captures the essence of each characteristic.

3. Validate the measures against different types of customers.

4. Place the measures on the same scale, either a range such as zero to one or by standardizing them.

5. Combine the different measures into a single measure for the customer segment.

In the end, there is a measure of similarity for each of the customer segments. This may be sufficient, or the best segment may be chosen as the one with the highest similarity score.

Simulation, Forecasting, and Agent-Based Modeling

Perhaps the most advanced form of data analysis is to simulate what might happen. A simulation is an example of undirected data mining, because the solution is not directed to find a particular target. Instead, the simulation characterizes the most likely outcomes across a range of measures. The simulation itself is not taking aim; it just casts the dice to see what happens.

One approach to simulation, often used for time-series forecasting in the financial and econometric world, uses summarized data. The output is defined as some function of the inputs, and the inputs for the simulation are assumed to come from various statistical distributions. Such an approach, called Monte Carlo simulation, produces a distribution for one or more outputs.

Another approach is to simulate what is happening at a finer level of granularity. The survival-based forecasts explained in Chapter 10 are an example. Customer segments are assumed to follow survival curves, and the simulation tracks them into the future. Agent-based modeling takes this one step further, by modeling each customer separately.

Monte Carlo Simulation

Monte Carlo simulation is a technique used to test different scenarios about what might happen in the future. It is particularly popular in the area of risk management, finance, and economics, because the different scenarios represent different possibilities of what could happen. The technique is well-suited to Excel, where the scenarios can be set up and then analyzed, either directly or using various add-ins.

This section shows an example of Monte Carlo simulation in the context of a simple financial model. The purpose is not to explain the details of spreadsheet models. Instead, the purpose is to introduce the concept of top-down simulation in order to understand how it relates to more traditional forms of data mining.

A Simple Financial Spreadsheet Problem

A common problem in the financial side of business is to determine the financial characteristics of some new endeavor. Let's look at a simplified version of the problem. The question is, "Should a subscription-based business invest in a marketing campaign to bring in new customers over the course of the next year?" This is a rather complicated question, even in its simplified form.

The marketing campaign is a significant investment. The campaign in question will last six months, and it is a multichannel approach that might include sports sponsorships, website tie-ins, and billboards, as well as more traditional direct marketing methods.

Assume the campaign has the following parameters:

- The cost is $3,000,000, spread over six months.
- 12,000 customers are expected to start, at a cost per start of $250.
- Each customer has expected net revenue of $30 per month.
- Customers leave at the rate of 5 percent per month.

Figure 12-2 shows the simple spreadsheet model with these assumptions, showing the cumulative revenue and costs for twelve months.

Cost Per Month	$500,000
Number of Months	6
Cost Per New Customer	$250.00
Expected Discount Rate	1.0%
Revenue Per Customer Month	$30
Attrition Rate Per Month	5.0%

	1	2	3	4	5	6	7	8	9	10	11	12
	Jan	Feb	Mar	Apr	May	Jun	Jul	Aug	Sep	Oct	Nov	Dec
Cost	$500,000	$500,000	$500,000	$500,000	$500,000	$500,000	$0	$0	$0	$0	$0	$0
Starts	2,000	2,000	2,000	2,000	2,000	2,000	0	0	0	0	0	0
Attrition Rate	5%	5%	5%	5%	5%	5%	5%	5%	5%	5%	5%	5%
New Customers	1,000.0	1,000.0	1,000.0	1,000.0	1,000.0	1,000.0	0.0	0.0	0.0	0.0	0.0	0.0
Contribution to Base Customers	0.0	1,900.0	3,705.0	5,419.8	7,048.8	8,596.3	10,066.5	9,563.2	9,085.0	8,630.8	8,199.2	7,789.3
Revenue/Customer	$30	$30	$30	$30	$30	$30	$30	$30	$30	$30	$30	$30
Revenue	$30,000	$87,000	$141,150	$192,593	$241,463	$287,890	$301,995	$286,895	$272,551	$258,923	$245,977	$233,678
Cumulative Cost	$500,000	$1,000,000	$1,500,000	$2,000,000	$2,500,000	$3,000,000	$3,000,000	$3,000,000	$3,000,000	$3,000,000	$3,000,000	$3,000,000
Cumulative Revenue	$30,000	$117,000	$258,150	$450,743	$692,205	$980,095	$1,282,090	$1,568,986	$1,841,537	$2,100,460	$2,346,437	$2,580,115
Monthly Discount Rate	1.0%	1.0%	1.0%	1.0%	1.0%	1.0%	1.0%	1.0%	1.0%	1.0%	1.0%	1.0%
Net Discount Rate	1.0%	2.0%	3.0%	3.9%	4.9%	5.9%	6.8%	7.7%	8.6%	9.6%	10.5%	11.4%
Discounted Revenue	$29,700	$85,269	$136,958	$185,004	$229,629	$271,042	$281,479	$264,731	$248,980	$234,165	$220,233	$207,129
Cum Discounted Revenue	$29,700	$114,969	$251,926	$436,930	$666,559	$937,601	$1,219,081	$1,483,812	$1,732,792	$1,966,957	$2,187,190	$2,394,319
Cum Costs	$500,000	$1,000,000	$1,500,000	$2,000,000	$2,500,000	$3,000,000	$3,000,000	$3,000,000	$3,000,000	$3,000,000	$3,000,000	$3,000,000
Net Revenue	–$470,300	–$885,031	–$1,248,074	–$1,563,070	–$1,833,441	–$2,062,399	–$1,780,919	–$1,516,188	–$1,267,208	–$1,033,043	–$812,810	–$605,681

Figure 12-2: This financial spreadsheet model calculates the impact of a marketing campaign for acquiring new customers.

This spreadsheet has six inputs, whose values are input in the shaded cells on the upper-left side:

- Cost per month of the campaign
- Number of months the campaign will last

- Cost per new customer
- Expected discount rate (cost of money) to be applied to future revenues
- Revenue per customer per month
- Attrition rate of the new customers per month

These are the inputs into the spreadsheet.

From these inputs, the spreadsheet calculates several different values of interest. The number of customers is the net customers at any given time produced by the campaign (the new starts minus the new customers who leave). The spreadsheet shows the financial impact of these customers, and the net revenue associated with them (the total revenue minus the campaign cost). A discount rate is applied to future revenues.

For instance, the January number of –$470,300 is the difference between the revenue and the $500,000 cost of the campaign. The revenue is for an estimated 2,000 customers who start in the month. At $30/month, they would be expected to generate $60,000. However, these customers do not all start at the beginning of the month, so the revenue is pro-rated assuming the average customer is around for half the month. The resulting $30,000 is then discounted by 1 percent to get $29,700. The calculations for the various rows are shown in Figure 12-3.

Cost Per Month	500000		
Number of Months	6		
Cost Per New Customer	250		
Expected Discount Rate	0.01		
Revenue Per Customer Month	30		
Attrition Rate Per Month	0.05		
		1	2
		Jan	Feb
Cost	=IF(B$8<=$B$2, $B$1, 0)		= F(C$8<=$B$2, $B$1, 0)
Starts	=B10/$B$3		=C10/$B$3
Attrition Rate	=$B$6		=$B$6
New Customers	=B11/2		=C11/2
Contribution to Base Customers	=IF(ISNUMBER(A14), (A14+A11)*(1–B12), 0)		=IF(ISNUMBER(B14), (B14+B11)*(1–C12), 0)
Revenue/Customer	=$B$5		=$B$5
Revenue	=B15*(B14+B13)		=C15*(C14+C13)
Cumulative Cost	=B10+IF(ISNUMBER(A17), A17, 0)		=C10+IF(ISNUMBER(B17), B17, 0)
Cumulative Revenue	=B16+IF(ISNUMBER(A18), A18, 0)		=C16+IF(ISNUMBER(B18), B18, 0)
Monthly Discount Rate	=$B$4		=$B$4
Net Discount Rate	=1–IF(ISNUMBER(A20), 1–A20, 1)*(1–B19)		=1–IF(ISNUMBER(B20), 1–B20, 1)*(1–C19)
Discounted Revenue	=B16*(1–B20)		=C16*(1–C20)
Cum Discounted Revenue	=IF(ISNUMBER(A22), A22, 0)+B21		=IF(ISNUMBER(B22), B22, 0)+C21
Cum Costs	=IF(ISNUMBER(A23), A23, 0)+B10		=IF(ISNUMBER(B23), B23, 0)+C10
Net Revenue	=B22–B23		=C22–C23

Figure 12-3: The spreadsheet performs the calculations needed for a financial spreadsheet model.

At the end of the year, the cumulative cost is $3,000,000 and the cumulative net revenue is –$605,681. Based on the one-year time horizon, the campaign is a losing proposition. At the end of the year, though, there are more than 7,000 additional customers, and these continue to contribute revenue into the future.

Extending to Longer Periods of Time

Table 12-1 shows the cost and revenue, by year, for the five years after the campaign starts. After two years, it looks as if the revenue generated by the new customers brought in by the campaign outpaces the costs. It would seem that the only question regarding the return-on-investment is the time horizon.

Table 12-1: Various Financial Measures for the Campaign

YEAR	COST	REVENUE	NET REVENUE	NUMBER OF CUSTOMERS
1	$3,000,000	$2,394,319	−$605,681	7,789.3
2	$3,000,000	$4,100,195	$1,100,195	4,209.0
3	$3,000,000	$4,917,253	$1,917,253	2,274.4
4	$3,000,000	$5,308,597	$2,308,597	1,229.0
5	$3,000,000	$5,496,038	$2,496,038	664.1

The revenue reported by this model uses a discount rate to account for the fact that revenue from three years in the future is not worth as much as money today, especially when the costs are incurred today. The discount rate works like inflation. If the discount rate is 1 percent per month, then $100 next month is worth only $99 today. Typical discount rates are in the range of 0.5 percent to 1.5 percent per month, depending on financial conditions such as inflation, the prevailing interest rates that affect the cost of borrowing money, and other factors.

Incorporating What-Ifs

The financial model just described explicitly calculates to the last penny how much the campaign is going to be worth. This is an awful lot of certainty for financial flows going out five years. Chapter 4 introduces the notion of confidence interval. Isn't this a perfect case to know the value, in terms of confidence?

There is no confidence interval when all the inputs are given as constant numbers with no variance. Instead, consider the following slightly more realistic scenario:

- The cost of the campaign varies from $2.7M to $3.3M, uniformly distributed.
- The cost per new customer varies from $220–$280, uniformly distributed.

▪ The monthly discount rate follows a normal distribution with an average of 1 percent and a standard deviation of 0.15 percent (and is then assumed constant for the entire period).

▪ The monthly revenue per customer is estimated to be between $25 and $35 dollars per month, uniformly distributed.

▪ The monthly attrition rate follows a normal distribution, with an average of 5 percent and a standard deviation of 0.2 percent (and then assumed constant for the entire period).

Now these assumptions are no longer suitable for the simple spreadsheet model. Instead, the spreadsheet needs to draw the input values from various distributions, as shown in Figure 12-4. This spreadsheet uses Excel's RAND() function to produce a random number between zero and one. By scaling this number (for the uniform distribution variables) or using NORMINV() for the normal distribution, the spreadsheet can calculate the outcome of a scenario.

Cost Per Month	=IF(C1="uniform",RAND()*(E1-D1)+D1,IF(C1="normal",NORMINV(RAND(),D1,E1)))/B2	uniform	2700000	3300000
Number of Months	6	fixed		
Cost Per New Customer	=IF(C3="uniform",RAND()*(E3-D3)+D3,IF(C3="normal",NORMINV(RAND(),D3,E3)))	uniform	220	280
Expected Discount Rate	=IF(C4="uniform",RAND()*(E4-D4)+D4,IF(C4="normal",NORMINV(RAND(),D4,E4)))	normal	0.01	0.0015
Revenue Per Customer Month	=IF(C5="uniform",RAND()*(E5-D5)+D5,IF(C5="normal",NORMINV(RAND(),D5,E5)))	uniform	25	35
Attrition Rate Per Month	=IF(C6="uniform",RAND()*(E6-D6)+D6,IF(C6="normal",NORMINV(RAND(),D6,E6)))	normal	0.05	0.002

Figure 12-4: This spreadsheet introduces "uncertainty" into the financial model by having the inputs come from various distributions.

The "Monte Carlo" in Monte Carlo Simulation

One scenario does not provide much information. It is one possibility out of an infinite number that could occur. The "Monte Carlo" in "Monte Carlo simulation" stands for rolling the dice over and over again, to try out different scenarios. Of course, the simulation does not actually roll dice. Instead, it uses random numbers.

The idea is that when the numbers are really random, you can run the simulation for, say, a thousand iterations. Each iteration produces a different set of values for the five input variables:

▪ Campaign cost
▪ Cost per new customer
▪ Attrition rate
▪ Revenue per customer
▪ Discount rate

These, in turn, lead to many different results associated with the scenario, including the cumulative discounted revenue, the total cost, and the number of customers.

Finding the confidence intervals is then easy. There is a big table of simulated values. The confidence interval for the two-year net revenue, for instance, would take the two-year net revenue and rank order the values. If there are 1,000 values, then the 95 percent confidence interval is defined by the values with ranks 25 and 975 — the middle 95 percent of the values in the list. For this example, these values range from about −$200,000 to about $1.3 million, as shown in Figure 12-5, which illustrates the cumulative distribution for the two-year net revenue values. The value of the simulation is that it produces not only expected values but also confidence intervals.

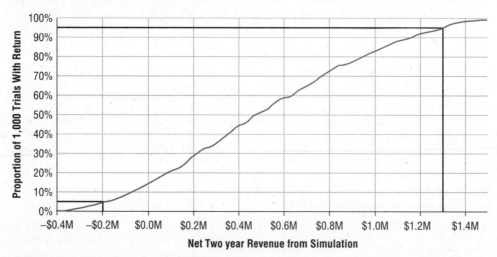

Figure 12-5: This chart shows the distribution of net revenue after two years, along with lines showing the 5 percent and 95 percent confidence range.

Notice that the 95 percent confidence range includes negative numbers. Although the expected value of the campaign is quite large, it is possible that the campaign will lose money, even with a two-year time horizon. Of course, the accuracy of such results is only as good as the assumptions going into the model, and such models are very sensitive to the assumptions.

Simulation and Directed Data Mining

Simulation is not directed data mining, because it only evaluates the inputs, using well-defined (although complex) formulas. On the other hand, simulation can be used in a directed way. The previous scenario is for one campaign. However, a real marketing effort includes many possible campaigns that all compete for budget dollars, and one of the major processes is budget allocation.

Often budget allocation has a specific goal such as "acquire a million net customers this year at the least possible cost." How should the budget be allocated among campaigns to meet this goal? A given campaign has outside inputs, typically the budget amount and the timing, and internal assumptions, such as the ones described earlier. The optimization evaluates different budget allocations based on the goal: minimizing total cost under the constraint that at least a million net new customers are acquired.

The optimization could be accomplished using data mining techniques mentioned in this book, such as genetic algorithms. More commonly, a technique such as hill-climbing (which is discussed in an aside in Chapter 11) would be used.

Customer-Centric Forecasting

The traditional methods for forecasting something like customer counts in the future or the attrition rate often use a high-level approach called ARIMA, which is discussed in the sidebar "Traditional Time Series Modeling Using ARIMA." An alternative approach uses survival-based modeling, as discussed in Chapter 10.

The key idea is to build up the forecast one customer or customer segment at a time, simulating what happens to a customer using survival curves. If a group of 100 customers starts tomorrow, how many of them will remain after one month? After six months? After a year?

The horizontal axis on a survival curve measures tenure, because it represents the tenure of existing customers. When using a survival-based model for forecasting, the horizontal axis no longer represents just tenure. It represents days in the future. The cohort of customers who start tomorrow is expected to follow the survival curve. So, if the survival curve says that 60 percent are still active after one year, the forecast predicts that 60 percent of this cohort of customers will still be active one year later.

Figure 12-6 gives an idea of what this means for two cohorts of new customers. One group of 100 customers starts today. The second group of 50 customers starts in six months. Each of these groups is expected to follow the survival curve. Of course, no single customer is going to be 70 percent active on a given day. Instead, 70 out of 100 customers would be active. The overall forecast is the sum of the forecasts for each cohort.

This is an example of forecasting the contribution of new customer starts. The real challenge is getting the expected numbers of customers starting at any given point of time in the future. However, this is usually part of a well-defined business process to forecast future new customers.

The other piece of the forecasting problem is forecasting existing customers. Figure 12-7 shows the solution to this problem. If there are 100 customers today with a tenure of one year, imagine that these are really 138 customers who started one year ago and follow the survival curve into the future.

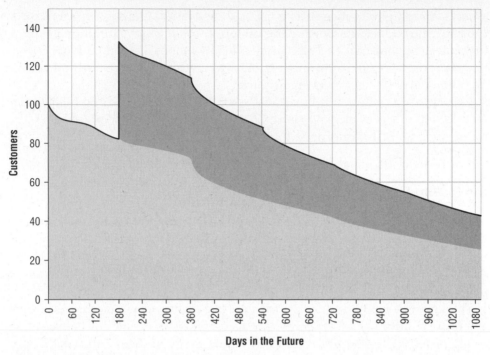

Figure 12-6: Assuming that 100 customers start on the first day of the forecast and 50 more start half a year later, survival curves determine how many customers are expected to still be around on any day in the future.

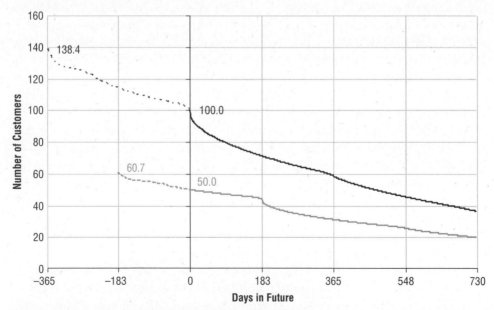

Figure 12-7: For customers who are active today, the survival curve can be retrofitted to the past and then extended into the future.

Survival-based forecasting is an application of survival analysis in an undirected data mining way. The forecast estimates each customer's survival, adding the results together across all customers, and then produces the final result. This process is not "directed" to achieve some particular number. The results simply are what they are.

TRADITIONAL TIME SERIES MODELING USING ARIMA

The standard approach to forecasting time series is called *ARIMA*, which stands for *auto-regressive, integrated, moving average*. This is actually a family of related techniques used for forecasting time series of all kinds. This sidebar introduces the simplest ARIMA model.

Three steps are involved in building a simple ARIMA model:

1. The time series is made "stationary" by removing the overall trend. (This is the "integrated moving average" part of ARIMA.)

2. Any regular, cyclical patterns are removed by expressing the value at time t in terms of the value $t - n$ for various values on n. (This is the "auto-regressive" part of ARIMA.)

3. The remaining variation is modeled in terms of whatever explanatory variables are found to be significant.

Often step 3 is eliminated because trend and seasonality alone are sufficient to describe the time series fairly well. The rest of this section walks through an example. The particular series uses a population of subscribers who are active in May 2000, and then tracks how many of them are active after that point in time.

Eliminating the Trend

The trend is simply the best-fit line, as shown in the following figure, which has the original series and trend on the top and the residuals beneath that.

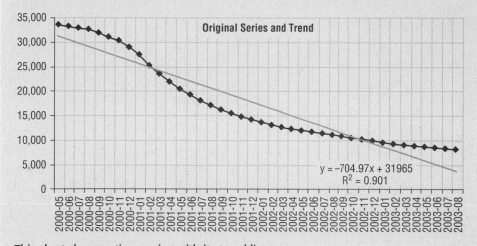

This chart shows a time series with its trend line.

Continued

TRADITIONAL TIME SERIES MODELING USING ARIMA *(continued)*

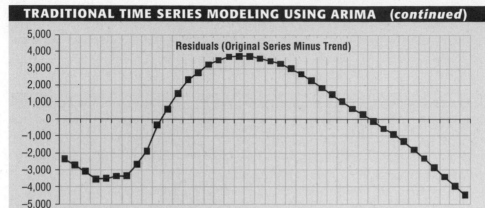

The difference between the data and the trend line is called the *residuals*.

The high R^2 value shows that the best-fit line explains most of the variance in the number of base subscribers over the period. For some purposes, this very simple model may be good enough. Its slope is the rate that customers leave over time. This is the first component of the model: the trend. The next step is to remove the trend to see what else is happening.

An Autoregressive Model on the Residuals

The residuals start low, then go high, then low again. This is certainly not a seasonal pattern linked to the calendar such as "we always miss high in winter and low in summer," but it could conceivably be part of a cyclical pattern with some other period. One way to explore that is to look at the correlation of observations at different lags. This is the auto-regressive part of ARIMA.

The chart shown in the following figure is called a *correlogram* and it is used to measure the correlation of the residual values at various lags.

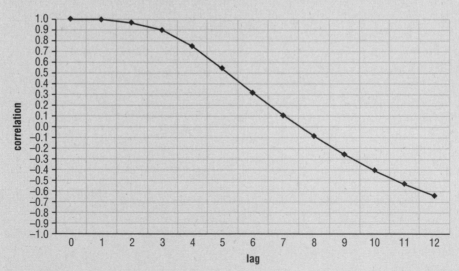

This chart shows a correlogram, which is the correlation coefficient of a time series using different lags.

The correlogram starts with a correlation of 1 for lag 0 because, of course, any observation is perfectly correlated with itself. The correlation at lag 1 is also strong. This is typical of many time series. If yesterday was hotter than average, today is likely to be as well. In fact, weather forecasters have to work quite hard to beat the simple forecast that tomorrow will be just like today. By lag 7, the correlation is close to 0. At lag 12, it has become fairly strongly negative.

Which of the lags show strong enough correlation to warrant inclusion in the model? The lags can be chosen by common sense. There is also a statistical test, called the t-distribution, which is generated by the following formula:

$$t = \frac{r}{\sqrt{(1-r^2)/(N-2)}}$$

This example has 27 months of data for which lags 1 through 12 have been calculated. The correlations at lags 1 and 12 are strong enough to be considered significant. This suggests an auto-recursive model of the form $y_t = \beta_0 + \beta_1 y_{t-1} + \beta_2 y_{t-12}$.

Fitting this model to the observed, de-trended data yields the formula $y_t = -169.56 + 1.02\, y_{t-1} - 0.09 y_{t-12}$. Note that this formula describes the residuals after the trend has been removed. To get the full model, simply subtract this predicted residual from the original linear forecast.

Evaluating the Forecast

The following chart compares the forecast made using the basic ARIMA model just described and the actual data.

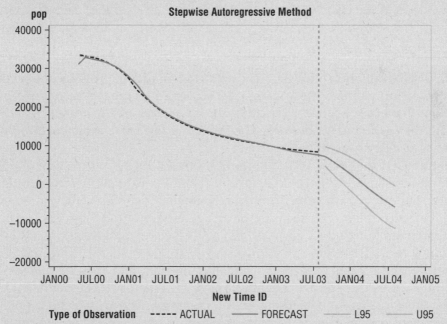

ARIMA forecasts often do well for the period of the forecast, but do less well when extrapolating into the future.

Continued

TRADITIONAL TIME SERIES MODELING USING ARIMA *(continued)*

This model does a good job forecasting the data for the period where there are actual observations. However, it does not do a good job extrapolating into the future — in fact, the forecast population becomes negative fairly quickly.

The time-series approach to forecasting easily captures major, aggregate-level patterns such as trend and seasonality, but not the causes of deviations from these major patterns.

There are many cases where a forecast fails to predict fluctuations that, upon investigation, should have been foreseeable. For example, one mobile phone company was surprised by a sudden spike in deactivations. Meetings were hastily called and managers demanded to know what was going on. Was there a sudden decrease in service quality? Had a competitor announced a particularly attractive offer? Actually, no. One year earlier they had run a very successful acquisition campaign that added many new subscribers on one-year contracts. Those contracts were now expiring and, as expected, many subscribers failed to renew.

The "as expected" is emphasized because the fact that many people cancel their subscriptions at the end of the contract period was well known. The problem was that the forecast did not take this fact into account. The customer-centric approach to forecasting is an alternative approach specifically designed to address two weaknesses of traditional forecasts: the lack of sensitivity to the customer mix and the inability to drill down to diagnose errors and discrepancies.

Agent-Based Modeling

Monte Carlo simulation introduces the notion of simulation from the top-level. The simulation works by assuming a particular set of measures, defined by equations that have dependent variables. These variables are not known directly; instead, they follow distributions. The modeling process simulates different scenarios to determine what happens.

Agent-based modeling is an alternative simulation approach, one that is much more intriguing to the data miner. The idea is to simulate activities from the bottom up rather than from the top down. Customer-centric forecasting is, perhaps, the most basic example of agent-based modeling. The idea is that customers follow their appropriate survival curve, and these are used to generate forecasts.

Agent-based modeling creates a bunch of entities, and then has rules on how the entities interact and change over time. The result is essentially an ecosystem of agents, simulated in computer memory. The ecosystem can then be monitored and measured to learn about what happens. When the agents represent customers, then agent-based models simulate what the customers are doing.

Perhaps the easiest way to describe agent-based modeling is by describing genetic algorithms in this way. Each genome is essentially an agent. The rules for modeling the agents consist of the following:

- The evaluation of the genome to produce a fitness value
- The evolutionary operations of selection, crossover, and mutation

Each agent follows exactly the same rules, but starts with a different genome. At this point, genetic algorithms introduce the notion of "survival of the fittest," which makes the technique a directed data mining technique.

The beauty of agent-based models is that the agents do not have to be identical. Imagine a simulation of customers and prospects. Each agent could represent a single person. Some of these agents would respond more to price-based offers, and others to convenience-based ones. Some would have large networks of friends and acquaintances, which provide a network effect. Some would be technically sophisticated, and others Luddites.

Each agent would be set up independently, but using a set of parameters, carefully designed to respond to other agents and to things that happen in their environment.

For example, consider a set of agents where each agent has a channel propensity and a propensity to respond to a particular offer — a credit card upgrade, a premium cable channel, or something like that. Different channels have different costs, as well as different probabilities of affecting customers' behaviors. The question is, "What is the best way to sequence communications, both to reduce cost and to maximize response?"

An agent-based approach would set up multiple agents, each with its own parameters describing:

- Likelihood to respond within a channel
- Likelihood to want the offer
- Likelihood to be "listening" to the channel
- Time from offer to response

The idea is to create a population and simulate what happens with different types of campaigns.

Methodology for Undirected Data Mining

Chapter 5 describes a methodology for directed data mining as an introduction for six chapters covering a wide variety of directed data mining techniques. This chapter introduces undirected data mining. However, the notion that there is a single methodology is not true for undirected data mining.

There Is No Methodology

Undirected data mining does not have a specific methodolgy for the simple reason that the data and techniques are not sufficient for solving — or sometimes even defining — the data mining problem. For directed data mining, the methodology clearly describes the inputs, the target, the relationships between the two, and the mechanisms for extracting information from the inputs that lead to the target.

Undirected data mining is more about exploration, understanding, and refinement. These are creative endeavors that do not lend themselves to a specific set of steps.

Many of the steps in the directed methodology described in Chapter 5 are still very important, particularly the initial steps of understanding the data, developing derived variables, and understanding the problem domain. Issues such as using a training, validation, and test set and oversampling are generally not relevant for undirected data mining.

Things to Keep in Mind

Undirected data mining techniques come in many flavors. Each technique has its own peculiarities, with respect to organizing the data and getting good results.

For instance, association rules find relationships among products in a shopping basket (or similar problems). Such techniques look through all the items purchased by individual customers, using the information to spot statistically significant patterns. When using association rules, a very important consideration is that customers who purchase more have more associations. Period. This can introduce a form of bias because the results say more about frequent purchasers than occasional purchasers.

Clustering techniques take records and find groups that are self-similar. In this case, the results of clustering are well-defined across a range of disparate techniques — the resulting models simply assign records to clusters. Often the result is what the authors call "solar system clusters." A big cluster is in the middle, corresponding to "typical data," with various smaller clusters "orbiting" around. These smaller clusters may correspond to important segments such as fraudulent claims or unusually active purchasers.

Undirected data mining is fundamentally about working closely with data to understand relationships within it and how they can be used for business objectives. The necessity to understand business objectives means undirected data mining cannot be performed in a vacuum.

A very important way to combine business knowledge and modeling is to include measures in the data as derived variables (covered in Chapter 19). Such measures are important in several different ways. They can prove useful for modeling, by making stronger, more confident models. They can prove useful for understanding the results of models and help to interpret models. They can also be used directly through methods such as simulation that simply ask what will happen under different scenarios.

Lessons Learned

Undirected data mining is a style of data mining quite different from directed data mining. The most important difference is that undirected data mining does not use a specific target variable. Without target variables, there is no way to automatically judge and refine models. Human intervention and understanding is part of the process.

Undirected data mining comprises several different approaches. In some cases, the idea is to "throw the data at the computer" and let the computer spot patterns. In the end, understanding these patterns is the responsibility of the data miner and not the data mining technique. This form of undirected data mining is mostly closely associated with undirected data mining techniques. These techniques, such as automatic cluster detections, association rules, and link analysis, do not take a target variable.

Also encompassed by undirected data mining are techniques such as simulation and agent-based modeling. These methods are based on scenarios. Simulation describes a scenario using descriptive variables; however, the exact value of these variables is not known. Instead, they are assumed to be pulled from estimated distributions.

Agent-based modeling goes one step further. It actually simulates individual customers (or other entities) as they interact with the business and each other, while still subject to external influences. Agent-based modeling is still in its infancy, as computing power is just catching up with the needs for this approach.

The next several chapters cover specific data mining techniques associated with undirected data mining, such as clustering, association rules, and link analysis. All of these share some common traits, especially the need for human beings to interpret the results of the algorithms.

CHAPTER 13

Finding Islands of Similarity: Automatic Cluster Detection

This is the first of two chapters about finding islands of similarity in complex data sets. This chapter focuses on the most general of the automatic clustering techniques, k-means clustering, and focuses on practical applications. The next chapter dives into more detail on several other techniques.

Why is cluster detection useful? The patterns found by data mining are not always immediately forthcoming. Sometimes this is because there are no patterns to be found. Other times, the problem is not the lack of patterns, but the excess. The data may contain so much complex structure that even the best data mining techniques are unable to coax out meaningful patterns. When mining such data for the answer to a specific question, competing explanations might cancel each other out. As with radio reception, too many competing signals add up to noise. Low prices stimulate purchases in one customer segment, but make the product seem less appealing to another. In these situations, cluster detection — an undirected technique — can be of assistance. Cluster detection provides a way to learn about the structure of complex data; to break up the cacophony of competing signals into simpler components.

When human beings try to make sense of complex questions, our natural tendency is to break the subject into smaller pieces, each of which can be explained more simply. What do trees look like? It is a hard question to answer, not because you haven't seen any trees, but because you have seen so many. Not all trees look alike, so you start looking for organizing principles. By narrowing the focus to particular clusters defined by these attributes, the question becomes easier to answer.

When clusters have been defined, finding simple patterns within each cluster is often possible. If you happen to define two clusters based on whether trees have broad leaves or whether they have needles, you will notice certain things that members of each cluster have in common with each other and things (other than the defining foliage type) that differ between the clusters. For example, trees in one cluster change color with the seasons; trees in the other do not. A different choice of cluster defining variables might not yield a color pattern, but might reveal some other useful pattern involving timber value or resistance to infestation by beetles.

This is an example of a very noisy dataset being decomposed into a number of better-behaved clusters. The question is: How can these better behaved groups be found? This is where techniques for automatic cluster detection come in — to help see the forest without getting lost in the trees.

This chapter begins with a discussion of customer segmentation and the role that clustering can play in it. This is followed by several examples of the usefulness of clustering in fields as diverse as banking and clothing design. The examples seem very different, but they all share the central idea of cluster detection — finding groups of records that are close to each other and far from records in other clusters. This notion of closeness or similarity is the same idea used to find nearest neighbors for memory-based reasoning, so all the distance and similarity measures introduced in Chapter 9 can also be used for finding clusters.

K-means clustering, which is among the most popular techniques for cluster detection, is used for the examples in this chapter. The next chapter introduces several more clustering techniques. K-means relies on a geometric interpretation of data as points in space. The distance between two data points depends on their representation, so cluster detection has data preparation requirements similar to those for memory-based reasoning.

Whatever technique is used to find them, clusters must be evaluated and, for many applications, interpreted. Several approaches to cluster evaluation and interpretation are described. Occasionally, cluster interpretation leads to new insights that have business value. One of the case studies in this chapter describes a bank that, inspired by results from clustering, changes the way it markets home equity loans. Another case study shows how automatic cluster detection was used to evaluate and propose changes to the boundaries used to define editorial zones for the *Boston Globe*, a daily newspaper.

Clustering can be a preliminary step for directed data mining. Records that have been scored by a cluster model have a field indicating which cluster they belong to. This can be an important input to predictive models. Clusters or segments are also often useful as a dimension for producing reports and cross-tabulations.

The chapter ends with some variations on the k-means algorithm — soft k-means, k-medians, and k-medoids. It also provides some discussion of data preparation issues that are important for clustering.

Searching for Islands of Simplicity

Automatic cluster detection is a tool for undirected data mining, because the automatic cluster detection techniques find patterns in the data without regard to any target variable. Directed data mining starts out with a preclassified model set. In clustering, the model set is not preclassified, or at least the target variable is not used. Instead, clustering algorithms search for groups of records that are similar to each other and different from other records. It is up to you to determine whether the resulting groups of similar records represent something of interest to the business or something inexplicable and perhaps unimportant. Finding clusters is rarely an end in itself. After clusters have been detected, they may become objects of study, or a reporting dimension in an OLAP cube, or the cluster assignments may become inputs to other models, or clusters may be monitored over time to see when and how customers migrate among them.

Clustering does produce data mining models that can be used to produce scores. A cluster model can produce the same kinds of scores as a decision tree. Just as a single decision tree can produce scores as either a class label indicating the most likely class or a list of probability estimates for each of several classes, a cluster model can make "hard" or "soft" cluster assignments. Hard clustering assigns each record to a single cluster. Soft clustering associates each record with several clusters with varying degrees of strength. What distinguishes clustering from other classification techniques is that the classes are detected automatically instead of being provided in the form of a categorical target.

TIP As with other modeling techniques, clustering algorithms find patterns in the model set that can be expressed as rules or formulas that can, in turn, be applied to other data sets to produce scores. The scores produced by cluster models are cluster assignments, which may be a single cluster label, or estimates of probability of membership in each cluster.

Although clustering is undirected in a technical sense, it is often part of a directed activity in the business sense because clusters are sought for some business purpose. In marketing and customer relationship management, clusters are usually called "segments," and customer segmentation is a popular application of clustering.

Customer Segmentation and Clustering

For a variety of marketing purposes, many companies find that segmenting their customer base into groups that are expected to behave similarly is useful. These customer segments may be used for targeting cross-sell offers, for focusing retention efforts, for customizing messaging, or for a myriad of other purposes. The expectation is that by focusing on groups of similar customers, these efforts will be more effective than a one-size-fits-all approach.

Customer segmentation is a business in its own right. It is possible to append commercially available segment labels to ZIP codes, census tracts, and even individual households. The sidebar "Clustering Americans by Demographics and Behavior" describes one such scheme.

CLUSTERING AMERICANS BY DEMOGRAPHICS AND BEHAVIOR

A company called Claritas (now part of Nielsen) divides the United States population into 66 segments. You can go to the Claritas website to look up which segments predominate in your favorite U.S. ZIP codes.

The segments combine demographic data from the U.S. Census with behavioral data gleaned from multiple sources such as magazine subscriptions, product registrations, automobile registrations, and the like. Each segment is a cell in a matrix defined by social groups with catchy names, such as "Urban Uptown" or "City Centers," and lifestage groups with catchy names, such as "Young Achievers" or "Conservative Classics." The segments, called PRIZM codes, are made available at several levels of a geographic hierarchy, including the individual household, the ZIP+4 (the finest granularity postal code in the U.S., which may be a floor in an apartment building or a small group of houses), and ZIP code (an entire town or village, or a neighborhood in a larger city).

According to Claritas, one author's neighbors belong predominantly to these segments:

29	American Dreams
16	Bohemian Mix
07	Money & Brains
31	Urban Achievers
04	Young Digerati

The other author's neighbors belong to these segments:

29	American Dreams
16	Bohemian Mix
07	Money & Brains
26	The Cosmopolitans
04	Young Digerati

Pretty similar. The only difference is that one has Urban Achievers where the other has Cosmopolitans. Urban Achievers, as described by Claritas, are:

Concentrated in the nation's port cities, Urban Achievers is often the first stop for up-and-coming immigrants from Asia, South America, and Europe. These young singles, couples, and families are typically college-educated and ethnically diverse: about a third are foreign-born, and even more speak a language other than English.

Cosmopolitans are:

Educated, upper-midscale, and ethnically diverse, the Cosmopolitans are urbane couples in America's fast-growing cities. Concentrated in a handful of metros — such as Las Vegas, Miami, and Albuquerque — these households feature older, empty-nesting homeowners. A vibrant social scene surrounds their older homes and apartments, and residents love the nightlife and enjoy leisure-intensive lifestyles.

It is debatable whether segment names like these reveal more than they obscure. A name tends to highlight one or two features of a cluster that may be defined by many more factors. The raw data for the authors' two neighborhoods would reveal that their populations are not really as similar as the cluster names suggest. Another way to characterize a cluster is to look at a typical member and then ask which features of the typical member are most different from the overall population.

Customers are often assigned to segments based on geography, product usage, length of relationship, revenue, demographics, or attitudes expressed to market researchers through surveys. After segments have been defined, products or services can be developed with them in mind. Segments can also be used the same way that RFM cells (from Chapter 6) are used — as a way to test and measure the effects of marketing campaigns and to track customers as they move from segment to segment.

There are several approaches to defining customer segments. This section describes various ways that data mining techniques can be made part of the process.

Similarity Clusters

Chapter 6 describes how you can use similarity models to score customers based on their distance from a prototypical or ideal customer. In that example, newspaper subscribers are compared to the reader profile that the newspaper offers to advertisers. You can use the same approach to assign customers to segments. Each segment is represented by a prototype. Customers are assigned to clusters based on their similarity to the segment prototypes.

In another example, in a case the authors described in an earlier book, *Mastering Data Mining*, a credit card issuer defined three profitable customer segments:

- High-balance revolvers
- High-volume transactors
- Convenience users

High-balance revolvers are profitable because they maintain a high balance and pay interest and finance charges on it every month. High-volume transactors are profitable because they make many transactions and the card issuer receives a percentage of each one. Convenience users are profitable because of their occasional large purchases that take months to be paid off.

The bank created a prototype for each of these segments and then gave cardholders three scores based on their distance from each prototype. Cardholders were assigned to a customer segment based on these scores.

A variation on this approach uses clustering to form the initial segments. The prototype for each segment is the cluster centroid. That is how subscribers were assigned to segments in the following example of cluster-based segmentation of newspaper subscribers.

Tracking Campaigns by Cluster-Based Segments

The authors were once asked to use clustering to build customer segments for a newspaper using k-means clustering. For clients to recommend a particular data mining algorithm is unusual. In this case, the client was intrigued by the notion that naturally occurring clusters of customers might reveal segments that would otherwise be missed. The client was especially interested in finding segments with particularly good customer retention, so the project is an example of using an undirected data mining technique for a directed goal.

The clusters found in this project did have different retention characteristics, as hoped, but when a target variable can be identified, a decision tree produces segments chosen to maximize differences in the target. A better approach for finding retention clusters would be to use retention as a target variable for a decision tree, and then to keep the leaf size quite large so only a few leaves are created. Each leaf is a cluster that comes with a built-in description in the form of a rule.

> **WARNING** It is not usually a good idea for business people to select a data mining technique. Business people should concentrate on properly defining the business problem and let a data mining expert decide how best to attack it.

In any clustering project, one of the first questions is what variables should be used to define the clusters. In this case, previous directed models for the same subscriber base provided guidance. The directed models were built for a variety of purposes, such as predicting voluntary cancellation, failure to pay, and the purchase of ancillary products.

Any variable that had proved to be predictive for one of these models was deemed suitable for clustering. These were a mixture of customer behaviors measured and demographic variables measured at the level of the census tract of the subscriber's address. Following is a list of the demographic variables:

- Tenure in the current subscription period
- Number of previous subscriptions, prior to the current one
- Total tenure over all subscriptions
- Original acquisition channel
- Original offer
- Billing frequency
- Original payment type
- Current payment type
- Subscription change rate
- Complaint rate
- Proportion of vacation days to all days in subscription
- Census income per capita
- Census percent white
- Census percent foreign born
- Census percent single household
- Census percent private school
- Census percent management and professional
- Census percent college educated

A few of the variables require explanation. The ones with names ending in "rate" are based on counts of various kinds of events such as complaints, vacation suspensions, and changes to the subscription. In order to allow comparison between subscribers with different tenures, these counts are expressed as events per year even for subscribers with less than a full year of tenure. So, a subscriber with six months of tenure and two complaints has a complaint rate of four per year.

Of the variables on the list, tenure was considered so important that it was used for an initial segmentation, one for new subscriptions with less than a year of tenure and one for established subscriptions. Within each tenure segment, an automatic cluster detection algorithm was used to find four clusters.

The next step is to try to understand the clusters. Several meetings were held to try to come up with descriptive names for them. These meetings considered the average member of each cluster and the variables whose value in the cluster was most different from the population average. The naming effort was eventually abandoned and the names New A, B, C, and D and Tenured A, B, C, and D were adopted. The problem was that any name short enough to be catchy left out too many factors that were important for defining cluster membership. A name such as "Old and Wealthy" leaves out important information, but "Old, Wealthy, Suburban, Married, with few complaints, and few changes in subscription" is not very catchy.

Despite the difficulty in naming the clusters, the cluster-based segments proved their usefulness the first month they were in use. The newspaper conducted an upgrade campaign trying to persuade people who received only the Sunday paper to subscribe to the daily paper as well. Overall, the campaign was not a success. When telemarketers reached the Sunday subscribers, instead of accepting the upgrade offer, some took the opportunity to cancel their subscriptions completely! When the results were analyzed by segment, however, there turned out to be a couple of segments where the campaign had worked quite well. Rather than giving up on the upgrade campaign, future efforts could concentrate on the segments where it was effective.

TIP Lurking inside failed marketing campaigns may be customer segments where the campaign actually worked. Finding these segments can powerfully improve subsequent campaigns.

Clustering Reveals an Overlooked Market Segment

In the previous story, the clusters proved useful because of the differential response to marketing campaigns. The clusters themselves did not provide much insight. In this story, the principal reward of a clustering effort was the insight a marketing analyst gained by examining the clusters.

Back in the 1990s, Bank of America's National Consumer Assets Group in San Francisco embarked on a data mining program that resulted in increased adoption rates for home equity loans. Before the project, home equity loan marketing targeted two groups: parents of college-age children, and people with high but variable incomes. Marketing materials and outbound call lists reflected this focus.

The data mining effort included both directed data mining in the form of propensity models for various products, including home equity lines, and undirected data mining to explore new ways of segmenting customers. While doing the analysis, fourteen clusters were discovered. Many of these were hard to interpret and the clusters did not prove useful as an overall customer segmentation scheme. The effort to interpret them revealed something interesting.

The analysts at the bank tried to understand the clusters by looking at how the propensity scores varied across them. One cluster stood out because it had a high proportion of customers who either had a home equity line of credit or had a high propensity score for that product. Although the cluster included only about 7 percent of customers, it had more than a quarter of the customers with the highest home equity propensity scores.

Clusters can be characterized by what members have in common and by what separates members from the customer population as a whole. Members of this cluster tended to be middle aged, married home owners with teenage children. In addition to the unusually high density of home equity lines, the cluster was notable because 30 percent of cluster members had both personal and business-oriented banking products under the same tax ID. Because only small, sole proprietorships use the owner's Social Security number as a tax ID, the cluster clearly included many small business owners.

A survey of branch managers confirmed that the small business owners and the home equity line customers were often one and the same. Apparently, people were borrowing against their home equity to fund the startup of a small business. None of the bank's marketing material had been oriented that way. A new campaign based on this idea got dramatically better response than the previous campaign, which had focused on using home equity to pay for college tuition.

Fitting the Troops

Cluster detection has even been applied to the field of clothing design — not for shows in New York, Paris, or Milan, but for the U.S. Army. In the 1990s, the army commissioned a study on how to redesign the sizing of uniforms for female soldiers. The army's goal was to reduce the number of different sizes that have to be kept in inventory, while still providing each soldier with well-fitting uniforms. Maintaining inventory and supply lines is a major expense and logistical problem for any army.

As anyone who has ever shopped for women's clothing is aware, there is already a surfeit of classification systems (odd sizes, even sizes, plus sizes, junior sizes, petite sizes, and so on) for categorizing garments. None of these systems was designed with the needs of the U.S. military in mind. Susan Ashdown and Beatrix Paal, researchers at Cornell University's College of Human Ecology, went back to the basics; they designed a new set of sizes based on the actual shapes of women. All soldiers, when they enter the army, are subject to physical exams that take many measurements of body size. This is the data that Professor Ashdown used for her research.

Unlike the traditional clothing size systems, the one Ashdown and Paal came up with is not an ordered set of graduated sizes where all dimensions increase together. Instead, they came up with sizes that fit particular body types. Each body type corresponds to a cluster of records in a database of body measurements. The database contained more than 100 measurements for each of nearly 3,000 women. The clustering technique employed was the k-means algorithm, described in the next section.

Of course, the army has not changed the method of sizing women's uniforms. Although it is heartening to know that there is a more sensible sizing system for women's clothes, history shows that when the military does things differently than the rest of the world, the "mil spec" versions tend to be considerably more costly than civilian alternatives. There is a multi-trillion dollar fashion industry based on the current sizing system. The inertia of the market precludes making big changes to women's sizing, even to a saner system.

The K-Means Clustering Algorithm

The k-means algorithm is one of the most commonly used clustering algorithms. The "k" in its name refers to the fact that the algorithm looks for a fixed number of clusters. K is specified by the user. The version described here was first published by J. B. MacQueen in 1967, but the idea goes back to the 1950s. For ease of explaining, the technique is illustrated using two-dimensional diagrams. Keep in mind that there are usually more than two input variables. However, limiting the example to two dimensions makes it possible to use simple scatter plots to illustrate the procedure, which works the same way in higher dimensions.

Each record is considered a point in a scatter plot, which in turn implies that all the input variables are numeric. The data can be pictured as clouds on the scatter plot. The goal of the clustering algorithm is to find k points that make good cluster centers. The cluster centers define the clusters: Each record is assigned to the cluster defined by its nearest cluster center.

Clearly, good cluster centers should be in the densest parts of the data cloud. The *best* assignment of cluster centers could be defined as the one that minimizes the sum of the distance from every data point to its nearest cluster center (or perhaps the distance squared). Finding that optimal solution is difficult, and the k-means algorithm does not attempt to do so. Instead, it starts with an initial guess and uses a series of steps to improve upon it.

Two Steps of the K-Means Algorithm

After initial cluster seeds have been chosen, the algorithm alternates between two steps known as the *assignment* step and the *update* step. In Figure 13-1, three initial cluster seeds have been chosen randomly. There are several possible approaches to choosing the cluster seeds, and these are explained in a later section. For this illustration three of the data points have been selected arbitrarily to be cluster seeds.

The next step is to assign each record to its closest cluster seed to form initial clusters, as shown in Figure 13-2. This figure also shows the lines that separate the clusters. The cluster boundaries form a "Y" shape with one cluster on the left, one on the right, and one on the top. Drawing the boundaries between clusters is useful for showing the process geometrically. In practice, though, the algorithm only needs to calculate the distance from each record to each seed to assign all records to the closest seed. The assignment step can be performed without actually determining the cluster boundaries.

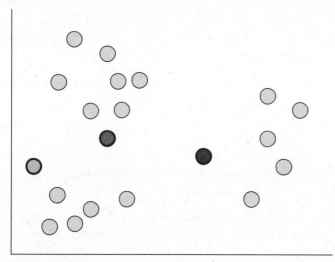

Figure 13-1: Three data points have been chosen as cluster seeds.

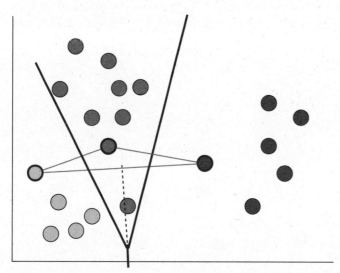

Figure 13-2: The initial clusters are formed by assigning each data point to the closest seed.

In the update step, the *centroid* of each cluster is calculated. The centroid is simply the average position of cluster members in each dimension. Figure 13-3 illustrates the update step.

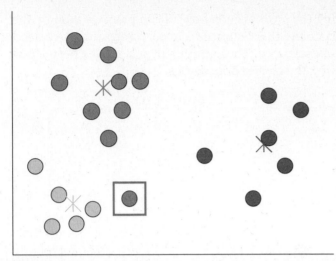

Figure 13-3: In the update step, the cluster centroid is calculated as the average value of the cluster members.

In the assignment step, each data point is assigned to the cluster whose centroid is closest to it. In this example, the highlighted data point is assigned to a new cluster. When the assignment step changes cluster membership, it causes the update step to be executed again. The algorithm continues alternating between update and assignment until no new assignments are made. Although designing pathological datasets in which this process takes exponential time is possible, in practice the algorithm converges quite quickly. Figure 13-4 shows the final clusters after the highlighted record has been reassigned and the new centroids have been calculated.

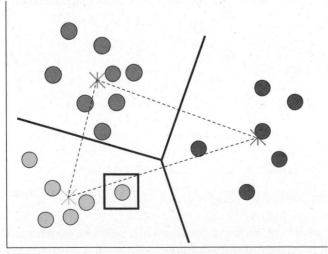

Figure 13-4: The k-means algorithm terminates when no records are reassigned following the latest relocation of the centroids.

Voronoi Diagrams and K-Means Clusters

In the k-means clustering algorithm, the cluster centers can be used to define a *Voronoi diagram*, a diagram whose lines mark the points that are equidistant from the two nearest seeds. The result is that each region on a Voronoi diagram consists of all the points closest to one of the cluster centers, making Voronoi diagrams a good way to visualize the k-means clustering algorithm. One thing that the diagram makes clear is that some clusters are unbounded; clusters that are at the edge of a collection of clusters have no borders in directions where there are no neighbors. See the sidebar for some history and applications of this visualization tool.

Recalling a lesson from high-school geometry makes finding the Voronoi cells easier than it sounds: Given any two points, A and B, all points that are equidistant from A and B fall along a line (called the *perpendicular bisector*) that is perpendicular to the line connecting A and B and halfway between them.

K-means can be defined as successive refinements to a Voronoi diagram. Figure 13-2 shown earlier has light lines connecting the initial seeds; the resulting cluster boundaries are shown with solid lines. Using these lines as guides, it is obvious which records are closest to which seeds. In three dimensions, these boundaries would be planes; in N dimensions they would be hyperplanes of dimension $N - 1$.

After defining the diagram for the initial seeds, the next step in the k-means algorithms is to calculate the average of all the records in a given cell. This average defines a new cluster center. The Voronoi diagram is created based on these new centers. The process continues until the cluster centers no longer move. The result is the same k-means clustering algorithm described in the previous section.

VORONOI DIAGRAMS

Voronoi diagrams are named after Russian mathematician Georgy Voronoi who defined them in 1908. The idea actually goes back much further. The philosopher-mathematician René Descartes used the idea in 1644.

One of the most famous uses of what was not yet called a Voronoi diagram was by the English physician John Snow, who lived from 1813 to 1858. Dr. Snow was an early advocate for the use of anesthetics such as ether and chloroform in surgery. He is also considered a founder of epidemiology because of his work linking a London cholera outbreak of 1854 to a particular water pump on Broad Street in Soho. He drew a map showing that almost all the people who died lived closer to the Broad Street pump than to any other water source.

The illustration for this sidebar was generated using an applet available at `www.cs.cornell.edu/home/chew/Delaunay.html`. The points in the Voronoi diagram pictured here could represent metro stations, in which case the cells indicate each station's natural catchment area.

Continued

VORONOI DIAGRAMS *(continued)*

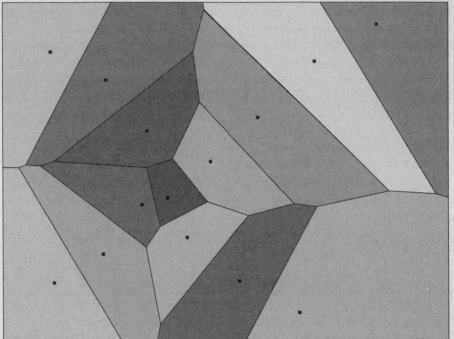

The points in this diagram could represent stations on two metro lines that cross near the center of the map.

Voronoi diagrams facilitate nearest neighbor queries such as the location of the closest metro station, cell phone tower, or Starbucks to a given address. Answering such a question requires determining which Voronoi cell the questioner is in. Fortunately, determining the cell containing a given point requires considerably less computation than calculating the distance from that point to each of the stations, towers, or coffee shops.

Voronoi diagrams are equally useful for finding a spot far away from others. If the points generating the Voronoi diagram represent land mines, or something else to be avoided, the edges of the diagram are paths that give the widest berth to the known dangers. This technique is used by autonomous robots to navigate between obstacles.

The vertexes in the diagram also have an interpretation. Each of the intersecting lines is as far as possible from some pair of points, so the point where two intersect is as far as possible from both pairs. If you want to dump some hazardous waste as far away as possible from drinking water wells, look at the vertices of the Voronoi diagram defined by the wells. Each vertex is the point that is farthest from some group of wells. Find the vertex which is farthest from its closest neighbor, and create your hazardous waste site there.

Choosing the Cluster Seeds

Different choices for the initial cluster seeds can lead to different final clusters. Designing examples where some choices lead to clearly sub-optimal clusters is easy. Figure 13-5 is one example.

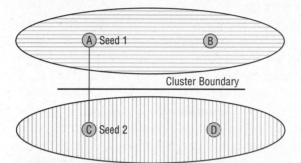

Figure 13-5: With K=2, choosing A and C as the cluster seeds leads to one cluster containing A and B and another containing C and D, which is clearly not the best pair of clusters.

In this diagram, A is closest to C and B is closest to D, but if A and C are chosen as the initial seeds, B is closest to A, and D is closest to C, which leads to the clusters shown.

Because of examples like this, researchers have developed a variety of algorithms for choosing good positions for the initial seeds. As a practical matter, however, if different choices of initial seed positions yield radically different clusters, then the k-means algorithm is not finding stable clusters. This could be because there are no good clusters to be found, or because a different choice for k is needed, or it could be because clusters are present but the k-means algorithm is unable to detect them.

TIP You can try different choices of initial seeds, even for the same value of k. This may result in different clusters, and some may be more useful than others.

Choosing K

How many clusters should you look for? In many cases, the answer to that question is supplied by the business purpose. If the point of customer segmentation is to design different offerings for each segment, k is determined by the number of segments the business can reasonably support. Often, however, the needs of the business do not dictate a precise value for k; there is a range of acceptable values.

When a range of acceptable values exists, the best way to choose is to build clusters using each value of k and then evaluate the resulting clusters. The evaluation may be subjective, "these segments make sense to me," or it may be based on technical criteria such as the ratio of the average intra-cluster distance to the average inter-cluster distance, or the cluster silhouette, a measure of cluster goodness, described later in the chapter.

Mathematical measures of cluster goodness provide some guidance, but the clusters must also be evaluated on a more subjective basis to determine their usefulness for a given application. Consider a deck of playing cards that has four suits, two red and two black. You might look for two clusters in it, and come up with one cluster of the red suits and one cluster of the black suits. Or, you might look for four clusters, and come up with a separate cluster for each suit. And there are other possibilities even for these values. Two clusters might differentiate face cards from number cards. Four clusters might separate red face cards, black face cards, red number cards, and black number cards. Different values of k may lead to very different clusterings that are equally good mathematically speaking. Figure 13-6 shows two ways of clustering a deck of playing cards. Is one better than the other? The answer to that requires human judgment.

Figure 13-6: These examples of clusters of size 2 and 4 in a deck of playing cards illustrate that there is no one correct clustering.

Using K-Means to Detect Outliers

When screening for a very rare defect, there may not be enough data to train a directed data mining model to detect it. One example is testing electric motors at the factory that makes them. Cluster detection methods can be used on a sample containing only good motors to determine the shape of the "usual" cluster or clusters. When a motor comes along that falls outside the usual clusters for any reason, it is suspect. For this to work, "outside" should be defined as beyond some threshold distance from the cluster as measured by single linkage — the distance to the nearest cluster member. The single linkage distance metric takes into account the fact that the "usual" cluster may have a highly irregular shape. Measuring distance to the centroid would not be appropriate because it assumes spherical clusters.

The "outside the usual clusters" approach has been used successfully in medicine to detect the presence of abnormal cells in tissue samples, and in telecommunications to detect calling patterns indicative of fraud.

This method depends on the notion that clusters have a maximum diameter even when its Voronoi diagram does not impose one because it has no neighbors. This maximum may be defined by various attributes of the cluster, such as some function of the average distance from members to the cluster center.

Semi-Directed Clustering

Many applications of automatic cluster detection are directed in the sense that the goal is to discover clusters that have different distributions of one or (more likely) several targets. Unlike a true directed technique, the clustering targets have no direct influence on the clusters discovered. Instead, they are used to profile the clusters as part of the process of evaluating them. Clusters that do not produce the desired variance in the targets are rejected. This rejection of candidate solutions based on the target turns undirected clustering into semi-directed clustering.

Semi-directed clustering is a good option when there is more than one target. (With a single target, decision trees, a fully directed approach, is usually more effective.) This chapter includes a case study from the *Boston Globe* newspaper, which is a good example of semi-directed clustering.

Interpreting Clusters

In marketing applications of clustering, especially customer segmentation, the interpretation of the clusters as meaningful customer segments is quite important. As discussed earlier, giving customer segments catchy names can sometimes be useful to provide a shorthand reminder of key features of the segment. You would typically do this by finding typical members of the segment and brainstorming to come up with names that capture their essence. The same approach works when clustering any kind of data, but it is especially popular among marketing people viewing the clusters as market segments.

There are drawbacks to this idea. One is that the catchy name tends to focus attention on just one or two of the many things that define the cluster. The other is that some clusters just don't seem to lend themselves to catchy names.

Two factors can help when interpreting clusters. The first is what cluster members have in common with each other. The second is what distinguishes each cluster from the others.

WARNING   Customer segments discovered through clustering may not have obvious interpretations of the kind that suggest descriptive names. When understanding segments is an important goal, a more directed approach may be called for.

Characterizing Clusters by Their Centroids

The centroid provides one convenient definition of a cluster's typical member — the one who has the average value in each of the cluster dimensions. Of course, no actual family has 1.86 children and 2.4 cars, so the typical member of a cluster may not exist, but if it did, the typical member would be at the center. K-medoids, a variant of k-means described later, produces clusters with the property that the cluster centers are data points that actually exist in the model set.

The centroids also provide one good way to visualize clusters. The chart in Figure 13-7 is a parallel coordinates plot. The variables used to define the clusters are arranged horizontally. The order is not important. For the clusters shown here, each dimension is a department in a catalog, such as kitchen products and gardening products. The vertical axis is the percent of shoppers in the cluster who have made a purchase in the department. So, everyone in Cluster 2 has made a purchase in Department 22; and everyone in Cluster 3 has made a purchase in Department 23.

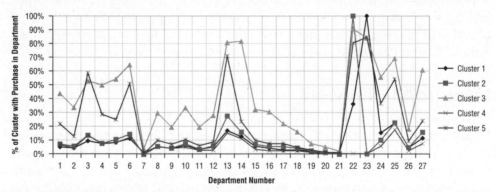

Figure 13-7: This parallel coordinates chart shows five clusters with the percentage of shoppers who have made a purchase in each department.

The vertical axis is on the same scale for all dimensions. Because the clustering process itself works best under these circumstances, that is easy to arrange. In this case the values are percentages, so they range from 0 to 100. Another common approach is to use z-scores, to put all variables on the same scale.

The dimensions for clustering are the 27 departments in the store. An individual shopper has a value of 1 or 0 for each department indicating whether or not he or she has made a purchase in that department. The average value for a cluster is therefore the percentage of shoppers in the cluster who have made a purchase in each department.

Parallel coordinate plots are very handy for seeing where clusters are similar and where they differ. You can clearly see from the chart that some departments are more important than others for distinguishing clusters from each other. For example, Department 7 is equally unpopular in all clusters. Department 23, on the other hand, is very popular with members of Cluster 1, but never visited by members of Cluster 2.

Characterizing Clusters by What Differentiates Them

The parallel dimension plot provides a lot of information about the clusters. However, it does not say which variables are most important for distinguishing one cluster from the others. Some cases are obvious. For instance, Departments 7 and 21 probably do not distinguish any of the clusters, because so few purchases are made in these departments. Which variables are most important for defining which clusters?

A good approach for answering this question is to take the average value of each variable within a particular cluster and compare it to the average of the same variable in the overall population. Represent this difference as a z-score, by dividing the difference by the standard deviation in the overall population. This is a measure of how different the distribution of each variable is in each cluster from the overall population.

In each cluster, order the variables by the magnitude of the z-score. The variables that show the largest difference between the cluster and the rest of the database do a good job of explaining what makes each cluster special. Figure 13-8 shows the results from the Segment Profile node in SAS Enterprise Miner, which essentially takes this approach to determine which variables stand out from the crowd for each cluster.

The two rows of bar charts in Figure 13-8 represent Clusters 2 and 5 from the parallel coordinates chart in Figure 13-7. The bar charts are ordered from the most important variable to the least import. So, for Cluster 2, only two variables are deemed important. Cluster 5 has seven such variables.

The first bar chart on the upper left says that Cluster 2 is most distinguishable from other clusters because of purchases in the Household department. For each customer, the household variable takes on the value 0, indicating no purchase in the department, or 1 indicating a purchase. The solid fill represents the distribution for the cluster; the hollow lines show the overall distribution in the data. The solid fill indicates that everyone in Cluster 2 made a purchase in this department, versus about 40 percent of customers overall.

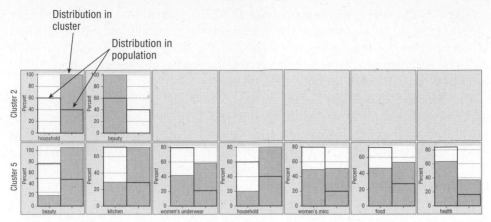

Figure 13-8: This chart compares the distribution of purchasers and non-purchasers in two clusters with the distribution in the overall population.

The situation for the Beauty department is exactly the opposite. What distinguishes Cluster 2 from the overall population is that all customers in this cluster make purchases from Household and none make purchases from Beauty. In the other 25 departments, their behavior is close to average so nothing is shown.

Cluster 5 differs from the population by being more likely than the population as a whole to make purchases in seven departments. There is no department where Cluster 5 makes significantly fewer purchases than average.

Using Decision Trees to Describe Clusters

One way of thinking about decision trees is that they produce directed clusters. Every split in a decision tree increases the purity of its children in terms of the target. The path from the root of the decision tree to one of its leaves is a rule describing that leaf.

When the decision tree's target is a cluster assignment, the result is a set of rules describing the clusters. These rules can be illustrated geometrically, as shown in Figure 13-9. This figure shows both the cluster boundaries discovered by k-means and the leaf boundaries created by a decision tree trained using the same input variables and the k-means cluster assignment as the target.

Quite interestingly, the clusters themselves and the decision trees can both be described geometrically. In fact, this underlines a remarkable similarity in the results from the techniques. There is one important difference, though. The boundaries of the decision tree leaves are always parallel to an axis, because each split on a numeric input is in the form *If X is greater than or equal to n, go left. Otherwise, go right.* Each split is governed by the value of a single X. In contrast, the boundaries of k-means clusters can be at any angle.

A decision tree can do a very good job of explaining the k-means clusters. Several leaves may be needed for a single cluster because the cluster boundaries are at arbitrary angles and the decision tree boundaries are parallel to an axis. Because of the geometric interpretation of the clusters and the associated decision tree, the tree typically does an excellent job of explaining the clusters. Often,there is perfect agreement between the two techniques on a given collection of records to be classified.

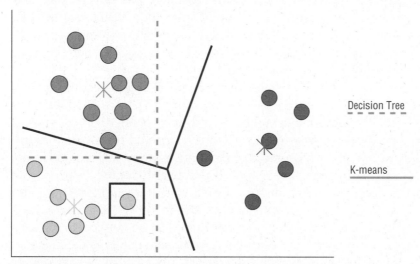

Figure 13-9: The directed clusters found by decision trees have boundaries that are parallel to the axes.

Evaluating Clusters

In general terms, clusters should have members that have a high degree of similarity — or, in geometric terms, that are close to each other — and the clusters themselves should be widely spaced. For many applications, including customer segmentation, clusters should have roughly the same number of members. An exception to this rule is when clustering is used for detecting fraud or other anomalies. There may be a small number of compact, but populous clusters representing the most usual cases and a few less-populous clusters of unusual cases that merit further investigation.

A general-purpose measure that works with any form of cluster detection is to take whatever similarity measure or distance metric is used to form the clusters and use it to compare the average distance between members of a cluster and its centroid to the average distance between cluster centroids. This can be done for each cluster individually and for the entire collection of clusters.

Cluster Measurements and Terminology

Which is bigger: Oklahoma City or New York City? If you answered Oklahoma City, you're right. Oklahoma City covers more than 600 square miles; New York City's five boroughs occupy only 304.8. If you said New York City, you are also right. New York's population of more than 8 million is almost 16 times that of Oklahoma City.

Similarly, depending on context, a small cluster might be one with few members, or one with low variance, or one with a small diameter. A requirement for clusters of similar sizes might refer to the need to create customer segments with similar numbers of members or the need to site warehouses such that they have similar maximum delivery trip lengths.

Because of this potential for confusion, using unambiguous adjectives such as "compact" or "populous" in preference to "small" or "large" is a good idea. For describing how much space a cluster takes up and, and how tight or dispersed it is, the technical terms *cluster diameter* and *cluster variance* have precise definitions.

A cluster's *diameter* is the maximum distance between any two records in the same cluster. Note that, in general, this is not the same as twice the distance from the centroid to the record farthest from the centroid. A cluster's variance is the sum of the squared distance from the centroid of cluster members. A cluster whose members are all close to the centroid has low variance. The square root of the variance also makes a useful measure, because it is in the same units as the distance. Another measure of a cluster's dispersion is its *silhouette*, described in the next section.

Cluster Silhouettes

A cluster's silhouette is a measure of cluster goodness first described by Peter Rousseeuw in 1986. It has some nice properties, but does require a lot of calculation if the clusters have many members. For the benefit of readers who would like to try out the calculations for themselves, Figure 13-10 gives the (x,y) coordinates of the points used in the examples.

To calculate a cluster's silhouette, first calculate the average distance within the cluster. Each cluster member has its own average distance from all other members of the same cluster. The average of these averages is the *dissimilarity* score for the cluster.

Figure 13-11 shows how the dissimilarity score for one record is calculated. Cluster members with low dissimilarity are comfortably within the cluster to which they have been assigned. The average dissimilarity for the cluster is a measure of how compact it is.

Next calculate the dissimilarity of each cluster member from the members of its next nearest cluster. Note that two members of the same cluster may have different neighboring clusters. For points that are close to the boundary between two clusters, the two dissimilarity scores may be nearly equal. Points far from a boundary should be much more similar to other members of their own cluster than they are to members of the neighboring cluster.

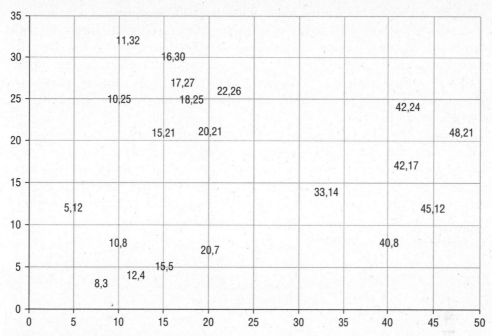

Figure 13-10: The distances used to illustrate the silhouette measure are based on the (x,y) coordinates shown here.

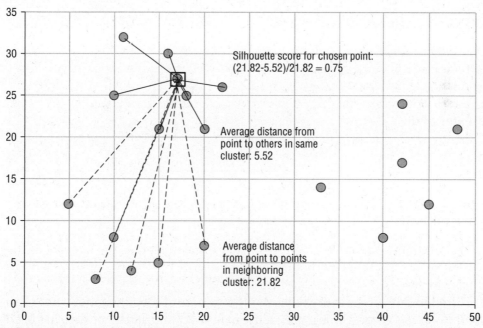

Figure 13-11: The dissimilarity score for a point depends on its distance from members of its own cluster and its distance from members of its neighboring cluster.

Finally, each point is given a score that is the difference between its average dissimilarity with members of its own cluster and its average dissimilarity with members of its neighboring cluster divided by the latter. This is the *silhouette* score. The typical range of the score is from zero when a record is right on the boundary of two clusters to one when it is identical to the other records in its own cluster. Figure 13-12 shows the silhouette scores for the records and clusters from Figure 13-10.

In theory, the silhouette score can go from negative one to one. A negative value means that the record is more similar to the records of its neighboring cluster than to other members of its own cluster. This could potentially happen because the k-means algorithm assigns records based on which cluster centroid they are nearest which, in unusual cases, could be different from the most similar cluster according to the silhouette measure. A cluster's silhouette is the average of these scores.

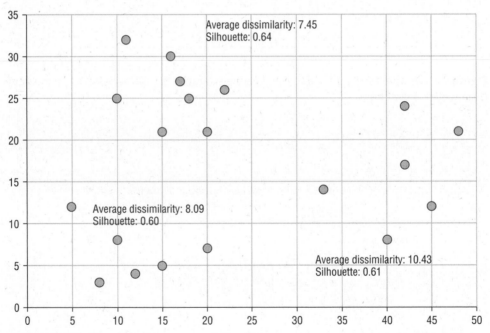

Figure 13-12: The silhouette scores of the cluster members are averaged to obtain the cluster silhouette.

The silhouette score for an entire cluster is calculated as the average of the silhouette scores of its members. This measures the degree of similarity of cluster members.

The silhouette of the entire dataset is the average of the silhouette scores of all the individual records. This is a measure of how appropriately the data has been clustered. What is nice about this measure is that it can be applied at the level of the dataset to determine which clusters are not very good and at the level of a cluster to determine which members do not fit in very well. The silhouette can be used to choose an appropriate value for k in k-means by trying each value of k in the acceptable range and choosing the one that yields the best silhouette. It can also be used to compare clusters produced by different random seeds.

TIP Strong clusters can be identified by their silhouettes.

One way to use silhouettes is to evaluate the strength of clusters. If there are one or two good clusters along with a number of weaker ones, it may be possible to improve results by removing all members of the strong clusters. The strong clusters are worthy of further analysis anyway, and removing their strong pull may allow new clusters to be detected in the records left behind. When doing this, it is important to assign a maximum diameter to the stronger clusters. When scoring, first apply the strong clusters. Then, for records that are not close enough to those, apply the weaker clusters.

Limiting Cluster Diameter for Scoring

Any measurement of a cluster's diameter, variance, or silhouette is actually a measure of a particular set of cluster members. When a new batch of records is scored and given cluster assignments, these measurements can change. If the clusters truly reflect the population from which the new elements are drawn, the cluster measurements should change very little.

What should happen when the cluster model is used to score inappropriate data that includes records far removed from the training data used to create the model? The Voronoi diagram is open at its edges, so all records get assigned to a cluster. As shown in Figure 13-13, even a very distant point is marginally closer to one cluster centroid than all the rest.

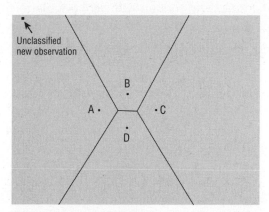

Figure 13-13: Should the new record really be assigned to Cluster A?

The rule that a record should be assigned to the closest cluster allows the clusters to grow literally without bound. Imposing a maximum diameter on all clusters by incorporating it into the cluster model is therefore prudent. Data points that fall outside the maximum diameter of all clusters are classified as unclusterable. This means that reporting systems and other consumers of cluster labels must be prepared to swallow one more case than the actual number of clusters.

WARNING Even points that are very far from any cluster centroid will be assigned to some cluster unless business rules are imposed to require all cluster members to be within some pre-determined distance of the cluster centroid.

Case Study: Clustering Towns

The *Boston Globe* is one of two major dailies serving Boston and the surrounding area of eastern Massachusetts and southern New Hampshire. As with many newspapers, the *Globe* faces declining readership in its core Boston market and strong competition from local papers in the suburban markets where many of its readers have migrated (as well as from other channels such as the Web). In 2003 the *Globe* introduced geographically distinct versions of the paper with specialized editorial content for each of 12 geographically defined zones.

Two days a week, readers are treated to a few pages of local coverage for their area. The editorial zones were drawn up using data available to the *Globe*, common sense, and a map, but no formal statistical analysis. Some constraints on the composition of the editorial zones included:

- The zones had to be geographically contiguous so that the trucks carrying the localized editions from the central printing plant in Boston could take sensible routes.

- The zones had to be reasonably compact and contain sufficient population to justify specialized editorial content.

- The editorial zones had to be closely aligned with the geographic zones used to sell advertising.

Within these constraints, the *Globe* wanted to design editorial zones that would group similar towns together. Sounds sensible, but which towns are similar?

Creating Town Signatures

Before deciding which towns belonged together, there needed to be a way of describing the 200 or so towns that comprise the *Globe*'s home market — a town signature with a column for every feature that might be useful for characterizing a town and comparing it with its neighbors. As it happened, an earlier project to find towns with good prospects for future circulation growth had already defined town signatures. Those signatures, which had been developed for a regression model to predict *Globe* home delivery penetration, turned out to be equally useful for undirected clustering.

This is a fairly common occurrence; after a useful set of descriptive attributes has been collected it can be used for all sorts of things. In another example, a long-distance company developed customer signatures based on call detail data in order to predict fraud and later found that the same variables were useful for distinguishing between business and residential users.

TIP Although the time and effort needed to create a good customer signature can seem daunting, the effort is repaid over time because the same attributes can often be used for many different models. The oft-quoted maxim that 80 percent of the time spent on a data mining project goes into data preparation becomes less true when the data preparation effort can be amortized over several data mining efforts.

The town signatures were derived from several sources, with most of the variables coming from town-level U.S. Census data. The census data provides counts of the number of residents by age, race, ethnic group, occupation, income, home value, average commute time, and many other interesting variables. In addition, the *Globe* had household-level data on its subscribers supplied by an outside data vendor as well as circulation figures for each town and subscriber-level information on discount plans, complaint calls, and type of subscription (daily, Sunday, or both).

The first step in turning this data into a town signature was to aggregate everything to the town level. For example, the subscriber data was aggregated to produce the total number of subscribers and median subscriber household income for each town.

The next step was to transform counts into percentages. Most of the demographic information was in the form of counts. Even things like income, home value, and number of children are reported as counts of the number of people in predefined bins. Transforming all counts into percentages of the town population is an example of normalizing data across towns with widely varying populations. The fact that in the 2000 census data, there were 27,573 people with four-year college degrees residing in Brookline, Massachusetts, is not nearly as interesting as the fact that they represented 47.5 percent of that well-educated town. Even more interesting is the fact that the much larger number of people with similar degrees in Boston proper make up only 19.4 percent of the population there.

Each of the scores of variables in the census data was available for two different years 10 years apart. Historical data is interesting because you can use it to look at trends. Is a town gaining or losing population? School-age population? Hispanic population? Trends like these affect the feel and character of a town so they should be represented in the signature. For certain factors, such as total population, the absolute trend is interesting, so the ratio of the population count in 2000 to the count in 1990 was used. For other factors such as a town's mix of renters and home owners, the change in the proportion of home owners in the population is more interesting, so the ratio of the 2000 home ownership percentage to the percentage in 1990 was used. In all cases, the resulting value is an index that is larger than 1 for anything that has increased over time and less than 1 for anything that has decreased over time.

Finally, to capture important attributes of a town that were not readily discernable from variables already in the signature, additional variables were derived. Both distance and direction from Boston seemed likely to be important in forming town clusters. These are calculated from the latitude and longitude of the gold-domed State House on Boston's Beacon Hill. The distance and direction from the town to Boston could then be calculated from the latitude and longitude.

Creating Clusters

The first attempt to build clusters used signatures that describe the towns in terms of both demographics and geography. Clusters built this way could not be used directly to create editorial zones because of the geographic constraint that editorial zones must comprise contiguous towns. Because towns with similar demographics are not necessarily close to one another, clusters based on the signatures include towns literally all over the map.

Weighting could be used to increase the importance of the geographic variables in cluster formation, but the result would be to cause the nongeographic variables to be ignored completely. Because the goal was to find similarities based mainly on demographic data, the idea of *geographic* clusters was abandoned in favor of *demographic* clusters. The demographic clusters could then be used as one factor in designing editorial zones, along with the geographic constraints.

Determining the Right Number of Clusters

There were business reasons for wanting about a dozen editorial zones. There was no guarantee that a dozen good clusters would be found. This raises the general issue of how to determine the right number of clusters.

The data mining tool used to perform the clustering provided an interesting approach by repeatedly applying k-means clustering. First, decide on a lower bound k for the number of clusters. Build k clusters using the ordinary k-means algorithm. Using a fitness measure (such as the variance, the average distance from the cluster center, or the silhouette measure), determine the worst cluster. Then, using the data only from this cluster, split it to form two clusters. Repeat this process until some upper bound is reached. After each iteration, remember some measure of the overall fitness of the collection of clusters. For this project, the values were two and ten.

The clusters that resulted from each round of splitting were profiled using target variables that were not part of the cluster definitions. The clusters were created based on demographic variables, but evaluated based on customer behavior; in particular, household penetration and average tenure. The cluster tree shown in Figure 13-14 was selected because the four clusters had very different values for these targets.

> **TIP** The variables used to evaluate clusters are generally different from the ones used to create them.

Evaluating the Clusters

The most important fitness measure for clusters is one that is hard to quantify — the usefulness of the clusters for business purposes. In the cluster tree shown in Figure 13-14, the next iteration of the cluster tree algorithm created five clusters by splitting Cluster 2. The resulting clusters 2A and 2B had well-defined differences in demographic terms, but they did not behave differently according to the targets of interest to the *Globe*. Figure 13-14 shows the final cluster tree and lists some statistics about each of the four clusters at the leaves.

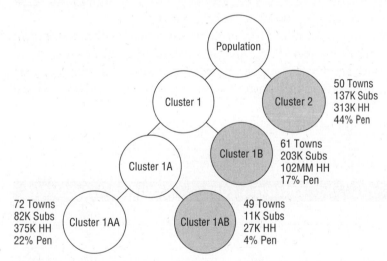

Figure 13-14: A cluster tree divides towns served by the *Boston Globe* into four distinct groups.

Cluster 2 contains 50 towns with 313,000 households, 137,000 of which subscribed to the daily or Sunday *Globe*. This level of home delivery penetration makes Cluster 2 far and away the best cluster. The variables that best distinguish Cluster 2 from the other clusters are home value and education. This cluster has the highest proportion of any cluster of home values in the top two bins; the highest proportion of people with four-year college degrees, the highest average years of education, and the lowest proportion of people in blue-collar jobs.

The next best cluster from the point of view of home delivery penetration is Cluster 1AA, which is distinguished by its ordinariness. Its average values for the most important variables, which in this case are home value and household income, are very close to the overall population averages.

Cluster 1B is characterized by some of the lowest household incomes, the oldest subscribers, and proximity to Boston. Cluster 1AB is most easily characterized by geography even though geographic variables were not used for clustering. These are towns far from Boston. Not surprisingly, home delivery penetration is very low. Cluster 1AB has the lowest home values of any cluster, but incomes are average. You might infer that people in Cluster 1AB have chosen to live far from the city because they want to own homes and real estate is less expensive on the outer fringes of the metro area. Figure 13-15 shows how the demographic clusters are distributed on a map of eastern Massachusetts and southern New Hampshire.

Using Demographic Clusters to Adjust Zone Boundaries

The goal of the clustering project was to validate and improve editorial zones that already existed. Each editorial zone consisted of a set of towns assigned one of the four clusters described earlier. The next step was to manually increase each zone's purity by swapping towns with adjacent zones.

Table 13-1 shows the assignments for ten towns west of Boston, belonging to two zones, the City Zone and West 1. At first glance, the split between the City and West 1 zones seems reasonable. Boston, Brookline, Cambridge, and Somerville are all adjacent to each other. All have universities, and all are connected by the MBTA, the local mass transit system. The other towns are a bit farther out, and are generally accessed by car or bus.

Table 13-1: Towns in the *City* and *West 1* Editorial Zones

TOWN	EDITORIAL ZONE	CLUSTER ASSIGNMENT
Boston	City	1B
Brookline	City	2
Cambridge	City	1B
Somerville	City	1B
Needham	West 1	2
Newton	West 1	2
Waltham	West 1	1B
Watertown	West 1	1B
Wellesley	West 1	2
Weston	West 1	2

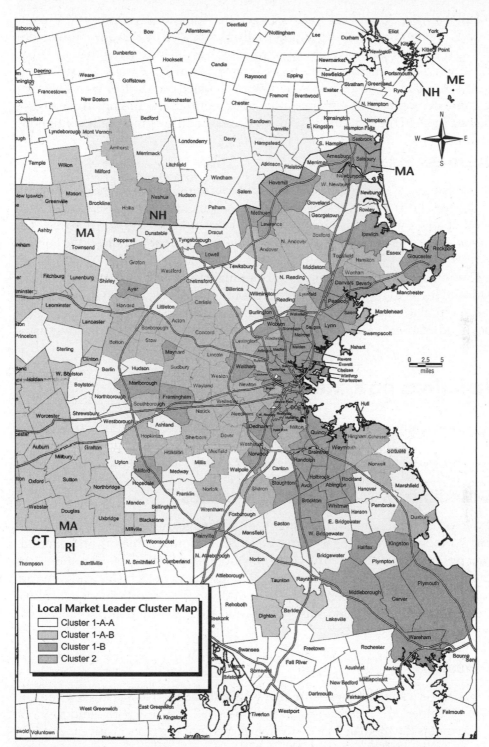

Figure 13-15: The map shows how the demographic clusters are distributed on a map of the *Globe's* coverage area.

However, the cluster assignments suggest that some towns may be in the wrong zone. Although Brookline is geographically surrounded by Boston on three sides, it is also very similar to Newton — a wealthy, leafy suburb more than an urban core town. The demographic cluster assignments hint that Brookline should be in West 1. Similarly, Waltham and Watertown are located even farther west. However, both are demographically more similar to Cambridge and Boston. This suggests placing them in the City zone. The new zones are still geographically contiguous.

Business Success

This clustering is an example of a successful data mining project. The demographic clustering showed that the original zone assignments made sense. On the other hand, it also showed ways in which the zones could be further improved. The *Boston Globe* was sufficiently happy with the results that it allowed the authors to refer to them by name.

Having editorial zones composed of similar towns makes providing sharper editorial focus in its localized content easier for the *Globe*, which should lead to better circulation. More importantly, it allows them to target advertising in the localized editions to similar audiences, which should lead to better advertising sales.

Variations on K-Means

There are many variations on the basic k-means algorithm. One variation has already been discussed, the repeated use of k-means to refine clusters by building a cluster tree. This section discusses other useful variations.

K-Medians, K-Medoids, and K-Modes

Three other closely related variations on k-means are k-medians, k-medoids, and k-modes. Each of these addresses a limitation of k-means and expands the applicability of the technique to new domains. In all these variations, the goal is to minimize the distance between members of a cluster and a central point. Different distance metrics lead to different definitions of centrality. The sidebar "Means, Medians, Modes and their Relationship to Distance" explores this topic.

K-Medians

A median is a statistical measure that is usually defined as the middle value in a list of values. For instance, for the numbers 1, 2, 3, 4, and 5, the middle value is 3 so that is the median. Unlike averages, medians are not sensitive to outliers, so the median of 1, 2, 3, 4, and 999 is still 3.

MEANS, MEDIANS, MODES AND THEIR RELATIONSHIP TO DISTANCE

All the clustering variants described in this chapter attempt to minimize the distance between cluster members and some central point. The location of that central point depends on the function used to measure the distance.

All distance functions follow certain rules:

■ The distance from A to B is always greater than or equal to zero.

■ The distance from A to B is the same as the distance from B to A.

■ The distance from A to itself is zero.

■ The distance from A to B by way of C cannot be less than the distance from A to B without the detour.

Many functions meet these criteria and can be used to measure distance. For simple numerical values, the simplest function is the absolute value of A minus B.

Generalizing this to more dimensions requires figuring out how to combine values along different dimensions. One method is simply to take the sum of the absolute values of distances along each dimension. So, the distance from (3, 0) to (0, 4) is 3 + 4 = 7. This is called the Manhattan distance.

The more familiar Euclidean distance is the square root of the sum of the squares of the differences in each dimension, and it would yield a value of 5 in this case. This introduces a family of distance functions that can be written as $(|\Delta X_1|^d + |\Delta X_2|^d + \cdots + |\Delta X_n|^d)^{1/d}$. When d = 1 this is called the one-norm distance (which is the same as the Manhattan distance). When d = 2, it is called the two-norm distance, or the Euclidean distance. In the context of clustering, dispensing with the outer exponent is alright because minimizing the quantity in parentheses also minimizes its root.

Although clustering usually involves multiple dimensions, the effect of different values of d can be seen in one dimension. For concreteness, consider two points at 2 and 4 on a number line. What point minimizes the distance to these two points? When d = 2, the distance function is Euclidean and the answer is 3, the average of 2 and 4. This is the answer used by k-means.

When d = 1, any value between 2 and 4 works equally well. The closer a point is to 2, the farther it is from 4 and the sum of the two distances is always 2. This is the answer used by k-medians.

When *d* is less than 1, but greater than 0, the distance is minimized at both 2 and 4. This is the answer used by k-modes. In k-modes, the central point is at the most common value. In this example, there are only two points, so either one of them will do. For this to work in more dimensions, *d* must be zero. Any non-zero ΔX_i raised to the power of zero is one, so the distance from one point to another in *n* dimensions is always *n* wherever it is defined. When some $\Delta X_i = 0$, there is a problem because zero to the power of zero is not defined. But, by definition, the distance from a record to itself is 0, which means that for this purpose zero to the power of zero must be treated as zero. With this definition, the zero norm counts the number of non-zero dimensions.

Continued

MEANS, MEDIANS, MODES AND THEIR RELATIONSHIP TO DISTANCE   (*continued*)

The figure graphs the total distance to the points 2 and 4 for a range of values using three different distance functions of the form $|A - B|^d$ with d taking on the values 2, 1, and 0.5.

The relationship between the value of d in the d-norm family of distance functions and three important statistical measures — the mean (which is called average in the rest of the book), median, and mode — sheds light on the relationship between the various clustering methods discussed in this section.

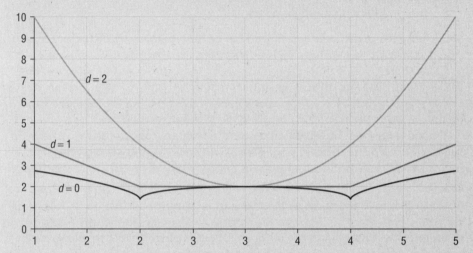

The total distance to the points 2 and 4 is minimized at different points for different values of d using $|A - B|^d$ as the distance function.

Another way of defining the median of a set of numbers exists. It is the value that minimizes the sum of the distances from itself to all members of the set. Unlike the notion of a middle value, this alternative definition works in any number of dimensions, which makes it more useful for the multidimensional data used in data mining.

One variation of the k-means algorithm uses the idea of medians instead of averages. K-medians clustering looks for the set of centroids that minimizes the sum of the distances from cluster members to cluster centroids. Each centroid is the median for the set of records in the cluster. One advantage of k-medians over k-means is that the k-medians algorithm is less sensitive to outliers. The k-means algorithm is sensitive to outliers because a few distant data points can have a large effect on the average but such points have no effect on the median.

The algorithm for k-medians is quite similar to k-means. First, an arbitrary set of cluster centers is chosen. Then, each record is assigned to the nearest cluster. The difference is in the step where the new cluster centroids are calculated. With the k-medians algorithm, the new center is the median along each dimension, rather than the average. The process repeats until the clusters are stable. Medians require more computing power to calculate than an average (essentially, lists have to be sorted rather than summed up for an average), k-medians requires more computing power than k-means.

K-medians clustering is also analogous to the robust regression technique mentioned in Chapter 6. Robust regression finds the line that minimizes the sum of the absolute distance of records from the line, rather than the sum of the squares of the distances (as in ordinary least squares regression). K-medians applies a similar idea to clustering.

As an example of k-medians, pretend that you know where all the coffee drinkers are in a city, and you want to place 100 Starbucks so as to minimize the distance between the coffee drinkers and their nearest Starbucks. The goal of minimizing the distance suggests k-medians, because the minimum is the sum of the absolute values of distances, rather than distances squared. In fact, one major application for k-medians is in the area of siting facilities of one sort or another to minimize such distances. The result is k clusters, each with a facility at its center.

When the choice of cluster centers is limited to the original data points, then the problem is called the facilities location problem. Suppose Starbucks already has 100 sites in a city. It now wants to select six stores where it will bake special coffee cakes and distribute them to the rest of the stores. Which store locations should it use in order to minimize the distance that the coffee cakes need to travel when distributed? The solution to this facilities location problem can be found using k-medians.

K-Medoids

K-means and k-medians are both happy to let centroids fall where they may even when they land somewhere where no actual cluster member could exist. The family with 1.86 children and 2.4 cars comes to mind again. For clustering families, there is no harm in having fractional numbers of children and cars at the centers of clusters. The cluster centers are used as reference points for calculating the distances that determine cluster membership as well as for descriptive purposes, but the cluster center does not have to correspond to an actual record.

For some problems, however, most of the space in which the clusters can form is unusable. For example, the records might describe facilities such as factories, warehouses, and distribution centers that have immovable physical locations. Clustering them involves finding groups of facilities that are close to each other. In such a group, the most central member is called the medoid.

In the k-medoids algorithm, clusters are based on the most representative object, rather than the average. At the start, k objects are chosen at random to be representative objects. These are the cluster seeds. The rest of the objects are then assigned to clusters based on which representative object they are closest to. Next, one by one, cluster members are swapped with the current representative object of their cluster. If the overall variance of the cluster is reduced, there is a new representative object for that cluster. The next round of cluster reassignments is based on the best representative object for each cluster. When things stop changing, the current cluster segments are the cluster medoids.

Because the medoids are actual records, they have actual values for fields not used for clustering. This makes profiling the clusters easy. K-medoids should be used when it is important that cluster centers be actual data points.

The Soft Side of K-Means

Ordinarily, when a hard cluster model is used for scoring, each record is assigned to a cluster based on which centroid it is closest to. To produce soft cluster membership instead, all that is required is a fuzzy membership function. Such a function is actually several functions, one for each cluster centroid.

The authors would like to thank our friend, Dr. Donald Wedding, for introducing us to this approach using the idea of fuzzy membership with k-means clustering. The method starts by creating hard clusters using k-means or any other clustering algorithm that produces cluster centroids.

The fuzzy membership function used by Dr. Wedding was suggested by Dr. James Bezdek. It gives every record a membership score for each of the k clusters based on its distance from that cluster relative to its distance from others. Note that the strength of a records membership in any one cluster depends on its distance from all clusters.

This is best shown by example. Figure 13-16 shows two cluster centroids and a data point to be assigned fuzzy membership in both of them. The record to be scored is distance 3 from Cluster A and distance 2 from Cluster B. By the rules of hard clustering, the record belongs to B, and B alone.

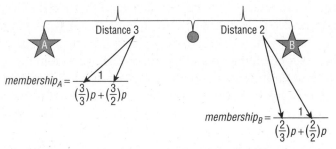

$$membership_A = \frac{1}{\left(\frac{3}{3}\right)p + \left(\frac{3}{2}\right)p}$$

$$membership_B = \frac{1}{\left(\frac{2}{3}\right)p + \left(\frac{2}{2}\right)p}$$

Figure 13-16: The data point shown here is to be assigned fuzzy membership in clusters A and B, which are represented by their centroids.

In this soft variant, the record gets two membership scores, one for each cluster. The scores are calculated by adding up a series of as many fractions as there are clusters and then taking the reciprocal of their sum. To calculate the membership score for this record's membership in Cluster A, the fractions all have the distance to A as the numerator. Each denominator is the distance to a different one of the clusters. There is always a fraction with the value of one because numerator and denominator are the distance to the cluster for which fuzzy membership is being computed.

In this case, the distance to A is 3, so computing fuzzy membership in A involves two fractions with 3 in the numerator. The denominators are 3 and 2 for the distance to A and the distance to B, respectively. Before summing the fractions, each one is raised to a power p, which is a parameter set by the user. If p is 1, the relationship is linear and the membership score for A is the reciprocal of the sum of 3/3 and 3/2, in other words 2/5 or 0.4. Similarly, the membership score for B is the reciprocal of 2/3 + 2/2, which is 3/5 or 0.6.

The parameter p controls the level of fuzziness. As the exponent p gets larger, the fuzzy scores look more and more like the hard clusters. As p goes to zero, the record becomes a member of all clusters equally. A typical value for p is 2. In this example, with $p=2$, the record to be classified gets a membership score for A of about 0.3 and a membership score for B of about 0.7. Table 13-2 shows the fuzzy membership values for this record in both clusters for several different values of p.

Table 13-2: Fuzzy Membership in A and B for Different Values of P

P	MEMBERSHIP IN A	MEMBERSHIP IN B
0	0.50	0.50
1	0.40	0.60
2	0.31	0.69
3	0.23	0.77

Data Preparation for Clustering

The data preparation issues for clustering are similar to those for memory-based reasoning because both rely on the concept of distance. This means that getting everything onto the same scale is especially important. The notions of *scaling* and *weighting* each play important roles in clustering.

Although similar, and often confused with each other, the two notions are not the same. Scaling adjusts the values of variables to take into account the fact that different variables are measured in different units or over different ranges. For instance, household income is measured in tens of thousands of dollars and number of children in single digits. Weighting provides a relative adjustment for a variable, because some variables are more important than others.

Scaling for Consistency

In geometry, all dimensions are equally important. A distance of 1 on the X dimension is the same as a distance of 1 on the Y dimension. It doesn't matter what units X and Y are measured in, as long as they are the same.

Unfortunately, in commercial data mining usually no common scale is available because the different units being used measure quite different things. If variables include plot size, number of children, car ownership, and family income, they cannot all be converted to a common unit. On the other hand, it is misleading that a difference of 20 acres is indistinguishable from a change of $20. As discussed in Chapter 4, the best solution is to convert all the values to z-scores.

TIP Scaling different variables so their values fall roughly into the same range is important. Standardizing the values is a good approach.

Use Weights to Encode Outside Information

Scaling takes care of the problem that changes in one variable appear more significant than changes in another simply because of differences in the magnitudes of the values in the variable. What if you think that two families with the same income have more in common than two families on the same size lot, and you want that to be taken into consideration during clustering? That is where weighting comes in. The purpose of weighting is to encode the information that one variable is more (or less) important than others.

A good place to start is by standardizing all variables so each has a mean of zero and a variance (and standard deviation) of one. That way, all fields contribute equally when the distance between two records is computed.

You can go further. The whole point of automatic cluster detection is to find clusters that make sense to *you*. If, for your purposes, whether people have children is much more important than the number of credit cards they carry, there is no reason not to bias the outcome of the clustering by multiplying the number of children field by a higher weight than the number of credit cards field. After scaling to get rid of bias that is due to the units, use weights to introduce bias based on knowledge of the business context.

Some clustering tools allow the user to attach weights to different dimensions, simplifying the process. Even for tools that don't have such functionality, it is possible to introduce weights by adjusting the scaled values. That is, first scale the values to a common range to eliminate range effects. Then multiply the resulting values by weights to introduce bias based on the business context. Make sure that the tool is not configured to automatically standardize the inputs (which would undo the scaling).

Selecting Variables for Clustering

Before clustering, you must decide which variables will be used to define the clusters. These should be variables that you think ought to be important in defining segments. In semi-directed clustering, the target variables are not usually included among the variables used to define the clusters. Typically, the goal is to understand how targets from one domain, such as customer behavior, are affected by inputs in another domain such as geography or demographics.

There are also technical considerations to keep in mind. When calculating a distance, every dimension is as important as any other and ideally, they should all be linearly independent. Although true independence is hard to achieve, it is important not to include highly correlated variables in the cluster definition. Otherwise, the concept represented by those variables will contribute more than its fair share to the clusters.

Another technical consideration is that finding clusters in two, three, or four dimensions is much easier than in twenty. To be close, records have to have similar values in all dimensions; high-dimensional spaces are very sparse. Chapter 20 discusses variable reduction techniques that you can use to allow a few variables to convey information from many.

Lessons Learned

Automatic cluster detection is an undirected data mining technique that can be used to learn about the structure of complex data. Clustering does not answer any question directly, but studying clusters can lead to valuable insights. One important application of clustering is customer segmentation. Clusters of customers form naturally occurring customer segments of people whose similarities may include similar needs and interests.

Another important application of clustering is breaking complex datasets into simpler clusters to increase the chance of finding patterns that were drowned out in the original data. Automatic cluster detection is a form of modeling. Clusters are detected in training data and the rules governing the clusters are captured in a model, which can be used to score previously unclassified data. Scoring a dataset with a cluster model means assigning a cluster label to each record, or in the case of soft clustering, assigning several scores indicating the probability of membership in various clusters. After cluster labels have been assigned, they often become input to directed data mining models. They may also serve as reporting dimensions.

The k-means cluster detection algorithm creates clusters with boundaries that extend halfway to the neighboring clusters in all directions, even if the neighbor is very far away. In directions where no neighbor exists, a k-means cluster goes on forever. Including a maximum cluster diameter in the cluster scoring model is therefore recommended so distant outliers are declared to be members of no cluster.

Clusters often require interpretation to be useful. The cluster centroid or average cluster member provides one way of thinking about what cluster members have in common. The variables with large z-scores define major differences between a cluster and its neighbors and the population as a whole.

There are various technical measures for evaluating clusters, including cluster variance and silhouettes, but cluster evaluation also requires subjective judgment of usefulness.

The k-means algorithm has a number of variations including soft k-means, k-medians, k-medoids, and k-modes. Each of these extends the usefulness of the technique to new domains.

Clustering is based on distance and similarity so it requires the same sort of data preparation as memory-based reasoning. In addition to standardizing numeric values to put all inputs on a comparable scale, you can use weighting to make sure that variables that are important to the business play a strong part in the definition of the clusters.

K-means and its close relatives are good, general-purpose clustering tools, but there are situations when other cluster detection techniques are more appropriate, as discussed in the next chapter.

CHAPTER 14

Alternative Approaches to Cluster Detection

The previous chapter introduces clustering in the business context, using the most common clustering technique. K-means clustering has much to recommend it. It is powerful and quite scalable, so it can run on very large data sets. It is available in most data mining tools. The ambitious can even manage to implement k-means clustering using SQL.

K-means is not, by any means, the only clustering technique. Because the purpose of clustering is to find interesting patterns, having additional techniques is a benefit. Different clustering techniques give more perspectives on the islands of similarity lurking in the data. Sometimes k-means finds good, useful clusters, but not always. This chapter starts with an explanation of the shortcomings of k-means, showing an example where the clusters it identifies are simply not intuitive.

The first alternative method is called Gaussian mixture models (GMM) or sometimes expectation maximization (EM) clustering. This form of clustering is quite similar to k-means. The most obvious difference is that GMM produces soft clusters rather than hard clusters. With soft clusters, a record can be associated with more than one cluster. However, there are other differences as well, and GMM clusters can be more effective than k-means ones.

The next method, divisive clustering, starts with all the data in one big cluster and then looks for ways to split the data, in a process analogous to the creation of decision trees. The *Boston Globe* case study in the previous chapter uses a variant of divisive clustering, paired with k-means.

Agglomerative clustering (also called hierarchical clustering) does the opposite. It starts with each record in its own cluster, and then combines them together one at a time. The final clustering method covered in this chapter is self-organizing maps, which are the neural network contribution to clustering.

Shortcomings of K-Means

K-means is not guaranteed to produce interesting clusters. Of course, this statement is almost a tautology. No data mining technique is going to produce perfect results all the time, or even the most intuitive results. Generally, though, they do a good job.

In this regard, directed techniques have an advantage over undirected techniques. Directed techniques can always measure their performance with respect to the target variable. Undirected techniques have no such reference point. This places a higher burden on undirected techniques. To phrase this differently, if a neural network produces good estimates of the target, you don't care how the neural network comes up with the answer. For undirected techniques, there is no such thing as good estimates of the target.

> **WARNING** There is no simple measure of "goodness" for a set of clusters. This places a premium on the results seeming reasonable.

Reasonableness

Reasonableness is subjective. Consider the R^2 measure for best-fit lines. This is a measure of how well the line fits the points. And yet, R^2 can be very, very small, even when the line seems like a very, very good fit to the data points, as shown in Figure 14-1.

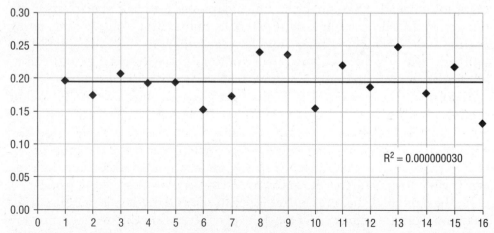

Figure 14-1: The line looks like a pretty good fit, but the R^2 value does not seem to agree. Sometimes measures of goodness do not do such a good job.

Why is R^2 so small in this case? The answer is simple: The best-fit line is completely horizontal, and in this case, the R^2 value is always 0, no matter how close the points are to the line. Admittedly, this is a special case, developed from understanding how the measure works. Nevertheless, it highlights the challenge in measuring "reasonableness," a challenge made even more difficult when you don't have a target variable.

Reasonableness for clustering has to take a different approach. For clustering, the question is whether or not the results are useful, or at least intuitive. The rest of this section discusses an example in two dimensions, which is convenient for visualization purposes.

An Intuitive Example

Figure 14-2 is a scatter plot along two dimensions, which happen to be the third and fourth principal components of data that describes catalog customers. Principal components are derived variables that are linear combinations of input variables; Chapter 20 explains them in more detail.

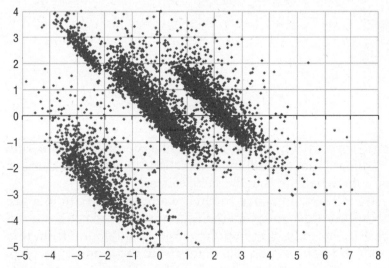

Figure 14-2: How many clusters can you see? There is no right answer.

A casual observer would readily see several clusters in this data. There is one group on the lower left. Then three or so groups are on the upper right. Of course, the clustering is not perfect. The space between these clusters contains some data points. However, a reasonable expectation is that a clustering technique should create something like these clusters. Can k-means recreate what looks obvious to a person?

Figure 14-3 shows an example of k-means clustering, with k set to 2 and randomized initial seeds. The circles in this figure are centered on the cluster centroids and their radius is the average distance of the points in the cluster from the center. The clusters created by k-means are, to be kind, not intuitive. It is striking that for the cluster on the left, the area around the cluster center is basically empty. For both clusters, much of the space in the circle is empty and many of the members are further away. Another reason why these clusters are bad is that the boundary between them is quite dense. All along the vertical line, there are examples from the left and right clusters. Being so close to the boundary, these cluster assignments are not highly confident.

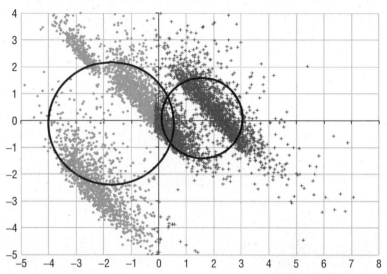

Figure 14-3: Is this really the best way to split the data into two clusters?

The cluster centroids give a hint about what is happening. Imagine that the centroids are balloons that expand in all directions to define the clusters. Everything inside a given balloon is in the same cluster.

Because only two dimensions are in this example, the balloons are represented as circles. Consider any point in the group of records on the lower left. When the balloon is small, all the points in the balloon are from this cluster. As the circle expands, it soon hits points from the group of records, long before it has encountered all the points in the lower one. In other words, the balloon is expanding in a direction that hits the other clusters, because it is expanding equally in all directions. The k-means clusters combine points from both groups because the clusters are circles that grow equally in all directions at the same time.

The initial seeds may be the cause of the poor clustering results. More intuitive clusters could be generated for initial seeds placed close to the centers of the observed clusters. That is, if you know where the clusters are, then you can find them easily. Most random choices have the results shown in the example.

Fixing the Problem by Changing the Scales

Imagine that the points in the scatter plot are on a rubber sheet, rather than on paper. If you could rotate the plot by about 45 degrees, then the separation would be a horizontal line. Then, if you could stretch the figure in the vertical direction (or, equivalently, compress it in the horizontal direction), then the clusters would become more separated.

The points are not on a rubber sheet, but the same idea can be applied using some simple transformations. The idea of rotating the plot and then stretching it is a familiar transformation to mathematicians, who express such transformations as matrices. Fortunately, the details of matrices and linear algebra (the part of mathematics that deals with this subject) are not important for the explanation.

Suffice it to say that the following variables describe a transformation that does exactly what was described two paragraphs ago:

```
Xnew = Yold

Ynew = Xold + 0.5*Yold
```

For the mathematically inclined, this can also be represented by a 2×2 matrix, the cells of which are the coefficients of the equations.

Figure 14-4 shows the results of the transformation. Now, when k-means is applied to the data, the result is two clusters that are much more intuitive. The circles that characterize the clusters are quite separate and a bit smaller. There is no "wall" going right down the center, with lots of points along either side, barely being in one cluster or the other.

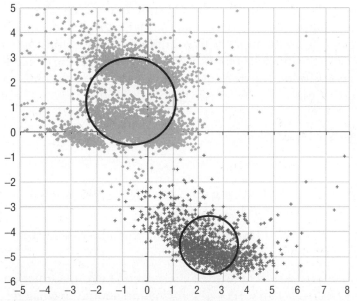

Figure 14-4: Much more intuitive clusters are generated after applying a simple linear transformation.

An interesting thing happens when the cluster results are transferred back to the original data points, as shown in Figure 14-5. The circles in Figure 14-4 are also transformed, resulting in ellipses. These ellipses do a much better job in defining the clusters than the original k-means circles do.

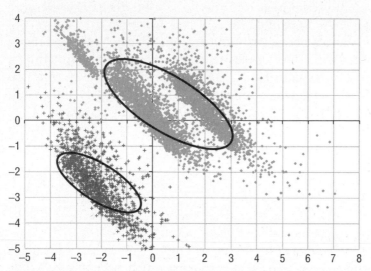

Figure 14-5: Back on the original data points, the clusters are characterized by ellipses rather than circles, and the ellipses are much more intuitive.

In this case, transforming the data worked because the original clusters could easily be seen in the data, although k-means did not spot them. Expanding the gap between the clusters, using linear transformations helps guide k-means so it can produce better clusters. Unfortunately, this cannot really be readily automated, because of a chicken and egg problem: if you know where the clusters are, you can find an appropriate transformation. However, the problem is to find the clusters in the first place.

What This Means in Practice

The preceding example shows two things:

- First, it shows that k-means clustering does not always produce reasonable clusters, even in what looks like a simple case.

- Second, there may be ways to transform the data to make clusters more apparent to the algorithm.

Alas, such transformations are not obvious from the outset. The transformation in the example was successful because it used information about the clusters.

In general, k-means clustering works well when the clusters are well-defined and separate, meaning that a lot of space is between them. Unfortunately, there is no guarantee that the clusters in real-world data are like that. In some ways, you can say that k-means works really well when the clusters are not very hard to find.

So far, the authors have been comfortable characterizing clusters by their centroids, the average values of all points in the cluster. This may not be the best approach. In the earlier examples, k-means produces clusters where the centroids are in the void between two denser regions. The choice makes little practical sense, because no data points are nearby.

Gaussian Mixture Models

Gaussian mixture models (GMM) are the first alternative approach to clustering discussed in this chapter. Although GMMs are in many ways quite similar to k-means clustering, the differences between them are quite important. Gaussian mixture models are also called expectation maximization clustering, after the optimization technique used to calculate the parameters in the model. This discussion starts by explaining them in terms of k-means clustering.

Adding "Gaussians" to K-Means

The "Gaussian" in the name "Gaussian mixture model" refers to the bell-shaped curve that describes the normal distribution as explained in Chapter 4. In one dimension, this is a symmetric curve that starts quite low, reaches a peak at the center values, and then declines again.

Consider the standard k-means clustering model, which produces a set of clusters, each with its own center. One way to think of this is as a set of probability distributions, based on Gaussians, each of which is centered in the middle of the cluster. The probability distributions give the probability of a point anywhere in space belonging to the cluster centered where the Gaussian is centered. Having several Gaussians, each defining a separate cluster, is where the name *Gaussian mixture model* comes from.

Applying the normal distribution to cluster detection brings up two questions:

- The normal distribution is in one dimension — how does it get applied to two or more dimensions?
- The normal distribution is defined by the standard deviation as well as the average — where does that fit in?

These questions are important. The answers lead to the power of GMMs.

Multi-Dimensional Gaussians

The bell-shaped curve defines a probability distribution for a single variable; the prototypical curve has an average of zero and a standard deviation of one.

Let's simply add a second variable and look at what statisticians call the joint probability distribution. The resulting picture is something like a hat or a very symmetric hill, as shown in Figure 14-6.

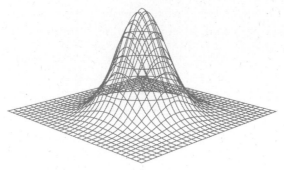

Figure 14-6: The normal distribution can be generalized to two or more dimensions.

With the normal distribution, the area under the curve has a meaning. If you want to know how often the value of the variable is negative, you calculate the area under the normal distribution for all the negative values. Because the curve is symmetric, the area is 50 percent.

In two dimensions, the calculation is no longer just the area under the curve; it is the volume under the curve. If you want to know how often both variables are negative, then you need to calculate the volume under the curve where both values are negative. Sparing the reader the details, the answer is 25 percent.

The same ideas can be extended to more than two dimensions, by adding more variables.

Applying Gaussians to a K-Means Centroid

Consider the centroid of a k-means cluster. Now, consider a normal probability distribution, centered on this point. The distribution also needs a standard deviation. For now, assume that the standard deviation is the same in all directions. What should be the value of the standard deviation for the probability distribution covering the cluster?

There are different ways of answering this question. One way is simply to assign a value, such as one, arbitrarily. A better approach is to use the information in the data. Calculate the variance of the points from the centroid (this is the sum of the squares of the distances), divide by the number of points, and take the square root. This is the typical way of calculating standard deviation.

Consider an alternative way of thinking about the calculation. A given standard deviation assigns a probability to every record. For very small standard deviations — those near zero — the probabilities are high only for records very close to the center. For points just a bit further away, the probability declines quickly. The overall shape is reminiscent of a tall witch's hat. For large standard deviations, the probabilities are a smaller, but they extend over wide areas on all sides of the center.

To rephrase the original question: What standard deviation for the probability distribution maximizes the likelihood that the points fall into the cluster? Here is one method for doing this:

1. Assign a standard deviation to the probability distribution.

2. Assign each record a probability of belonging to the cluster, with that centroid. The probability depends on the standard deviation.

3. Calculate the overall probability of all the records being in the cluster, by multiplying the probabilities for each individual point.

The result is a giant equation, calculated in terms of the standard deviation. Which value of the standard deviation maximizes the likelihood of the points belonging to that cluster?

This form of equation is called a maximum likelihood equation, which was introduced in Chapter 6 as the method for finding the coefficients of a logistic regression. The solution estimates the values of the parameters (in this case, the standard deviation) that maximize the likelihood.

Using Gaussians for K-Means Soft Clustering

In the k-means algorithm, there is not one cluster center — there are several. Essentially the same ideas apply in this case as well. Each cluster has its own probability distribution, described by a Gaussian surface centered on the centroid of the cluster. The standard deviation can be assigned as described in the previous section.

The result is a model that can score all records to produce probabilities of each record being in each cluster. Records closer to a given centroid have a higher probability of belonging to its cluster than points further away. Each record has a separate probability of belonging to each cluster.

This method is one way of turning k-means clusters into soft clusters. Every record has a probability of being in each of the clusters. However, because the sum of all the probabilities can be less than one or greater than one, it does not make sense to treat these sums as probabilities. Instead, the values are likelihoods.

Each record has a likelihood of being in each of the clusters. These likelihoods can be turned into probabilities, using simple arithmetic. The probability of being in cluster X is the likelihood for X divided by the sum of all the likelihoods. The result is similar to the soft clustering approach explained in the previous chapter.

There is one subtle issue. Each record now has two different cluster assignments:

- The hard cluster assignment by k-means
- The soft cluster assignments giving a probability of being in each cluster

For the soft clustering, one cluster has the largest probability — this is the *dominant cluster*. The subtle issue is that this dominant soft cluster may be different from the hard cluster for some records.

To get a stable set of soft clusters, the process repeats itself, using the dominant cluster as the assignment used to determine the center and standard deviation of the probability distribution. Notice that this moves the cluster centroids, although probably not by much, because the members of each cluster have changed only slightly. This process repeats itself until it is stable.

Back to Gaussian Mixture Models

The ideas behind Gaussian mixture models are very similar to applying Gaussians to k-means to generate soft clusters. The difference is that the shapes of the Gaussians are more general, and the final algorithm for calculating the appropriate parameters has a name: expectation maximization.

Different Shapes

A normal distribution has two parameters, an average and a standard deviation. So far, the description of GMM has used two variables, each with an average of zero and a standard deviation of one. If you picture cross-sections of this distribution, parallel to the plane, then the cross-sections are all circles, with the center being where the averages are for each dimension. Recall the earlier example where circles did not do a good job in capturing clusters. Replacing the hard boundaries of k-means with the softer boundaries of probability distributions does not change the basic shape.

However, the standard deviations do not have to be the same in all directions. By changing the standard deviations, the curves become ellipses instead of circles. The general form of the Gaussian allows the ellipses to be tilted at any angle, to have arbitrary aspect ratios, and to be placed anywhere on the plane. The Gaussian is then like a mountain, whose slopes are steeper in one direction than in another, as shown in Figure 14-7.

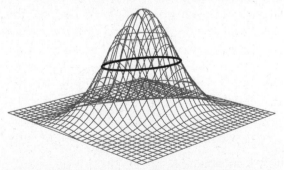

Figure 14-7: The cross-section for the normalized distribution in two dimensions is an ellipse.

The cross-sections define the particular distribution. A canonical measure is the cross-section that defines 90 percent of the distribution (that is, 90 percent of the volume is in the volume under the ellipse). For a given ellipse, exactly one Gaussian curve is characterized in this way.

Instead of thinking about distributions, and their complicated formulas and volumes, thinking about ellipses fitting the clusters is often easier. This is exactly what GMMs do. They are fitting these ellipses to best fit the data points. What does "best fit" mean? It means that the parameters that define the ellipses (that is, the parameters of the distribution) produce best probabilities of membership in the clusters.

The GMM Approach

Like k-means, GMM starts with a fixed number of cluster centers (often generated by first running k-means). In addition, it starts with random parameters to describe the distributions for each cluster. It then continues by calculating the probability that each point is in each cluster.

Using these probabilities, GMM calculates new cluster centers and parameters for the distributions. The method used for k-means is simple: The new cluster center is simply the average value of all the points closer to that center than to any other. For GMM, the calculation is a bit more complicated, using a method called expectation maximization.

Expectation Maximization

The expectation maximization algorithm consists of two appropriately named steps, which are repeated until the values converge.

The *expectation* step calculates the probabilities of each point being in each cluster, given a set of cluster centroids and variance parameters for the clusters. This step works in the same way as using Gaussians for k-means soft clustering.

The result is a set of probabilities for each data point. These are the probabilities of the data point being in the cluster centered at each centroid.

The *maximization* step then recalculates the cluster centroids and distributions, using the assignments from the data points. Basically, each point is weighted by its probability of being in the cluster. The center of the cluster is then the weighted average of all the points. The parameters describing the distribution are also calculated from the data points, using the appropriate statistical formulas.

These steps are similar to the steps in k-means. The "expectation" step in k-means is the assignment of each point to the closest cluster center. The "maximization" step is the moving of the cluster center to the average of the points assigned to it. During the maximization step, the GMM approach changes the shapes of the clusters as well as the locations of their centroids.

This use of multi-dimensional Gaussian distributions is reminiscent of radial basis function neural networks. In fact, Gaussian mixture models are close cousins of RBFs, as explained in the aside, "Gaussian Mixture Models and Radial Basis Function Neural Networks."

GAUSSIAN MIXTURE MODELS AND RADIAL BASIS FUNCTION NEURAL NETWORKS

On the surface, Gaussian mixture models and radial basis function neural networks seem to have little in common. On deeper inspection, though, they have many similarities that help show how each works.

Each node in the hidden layer of an RBF neural network has a Gaussian activation function, with the center specified by the parameters leading into the node. Another set of parameters specifies the variances used to define the function along each dimension. The process of training the RBF neural network is the process of calculating the best values for these parameters. Hmmm, this is very, very similar to how GMMs are set up. In fact, Chapter 8 suggests using clustering as one method for finding the initial locations of the RBF units.

There are two main differences between these techniques. The first is in the output layer of the neural network. GMMs produce a separate probability of membership for every cluster; as a modeling technique, they create multiple scores. A standard RBF network calculates only one value. By simply redefining the output of the network, though, an RBF network can mimic a GMM. The specific mechanism is to take the probability from each node in the hidden layer and divide it by the sum of the probabilities from all other nodes. This needs to be done for each of the probabilities generated by the hidden nodes.

The other main difference is that RBFs are a directed data mining technique. Training an RBF neural network proceeds by optimizing the estimate of the target. GMMs do not have a target. The expectation maximization steps optimize the distribution of the records themselves. There is a duality to this approach. Both are optimizing a complicated function defined on the training set. In one case, the function describes the distribution of the target variable; in the other case, the function describes the distribution of the input variables.

When it comes to finding patterns in data, both RBFs and GMMs take a similar approach. They both define local areas in the data that are closely related — either because the target takes on similar values or because the records themselves cluster together.

Scoring GMMs

The GMM model consists of the cluster centers, along with the formulas that define the Gaussian probability distributions for each of the clusters. These formulas are defined in terms of parameters that have been optimized in the course of training the model. In the end, though, the model is just a collection of rather complicated-looking formulas.

Scoring new records applies these formulas to the data in new records, in the following steps:

1. Calculate the likelihood that the record belongs to each cluster, by applying the appropriate formula for each cluster.

2. Normalize the likelihoods, to obtain probabilities of membership in each cluster (that is, divide each one by the sum of all of them so the total sums up to one).

3. Optionally, assign cluster membership based on the highest probability.

In other words, scoring the data is just a matter of applying the formulas found during training.

Applying GMMs

Chapter 21 has an example of GMM clustering, as applied to clustering customer service comments for DIRECTV, a satellite TV provider.

This type of clustering can also be applied to the problem introduced at the beginning of this chapter, the scatter plot where k-means clustering does not produce good results. To understand this better, compare what happens when the techniques look for four clusters.

Figure 14-8 shows the results for k-means with the setting k = 4. With four clusters, k-means is able to identify the cluster on the lower left, although the upper boundary of this cluster (called Cluster 4) seems arbitrarily cut off. Cluster 2 does not even appear in the diagram, because it consists of only a few outliers. Clusters 1 and 3 are quite awkward, exhibiting a similar problem as in the two-cluster case. The boundaries might make sense according to some abstruse mathematical formula. They don't make particular sense visually.

Figure 14-9 shows what happens when GMM is applied to the same data. All four clusters appear in the data. Cluster 4 is well-defined on the lower left. In addition, the upper two clusters are split much more intuitively (although not perfectly). Sprinkled throughout the scatter plot are examples from Cluster 2, which represent outliers.

This example demonstrates the power of GMM clustering for finding more intuitive results. It is quite interesting that GMM can create a cluster for the outliers, spread throughout the diagram. This is both a blessing and a curse. GMM is quite prone to creating a big cluster in the middle, with outliers surrounding it. It is even more prone to this than k-means. Consider two GMM clusters, both centered at the same location but with different standard deviations. The two probability distributions will intersect in an ellipse (whose exact size and shape is determined by the standard deviations). Everything inside the ellipse is in one cluster. Everything outside is in the other. If the first ellipse is large enough, then it contains almost all the data, and the second ellipse simply contains a few outlying data points.

WARNING GMM clusters are quite sensitive to outliers. The clustering technique can very easily create "solar system" clusters, with a big cluster in the middle and one or more small clusters containing outliers.

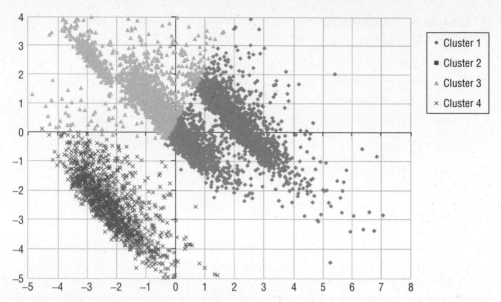

Figure 14-8: Four k-means clusters identify one of the clusters (on the lower left), but do not do a good job on the rest of the data.

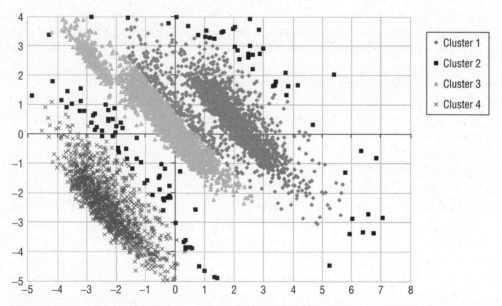

Figure 14-9: Four GMM clusters do a pretty good job of finding the obvious clusters in the data.

Divisive Clustering

Divisive clustering is a top-down approach to clustering. The previous chapter introduces a type of divisive clustering that uses k-means, for the *Boston Globe* case study. The divisive approach starts by using k-means to split the data into two clusters. The larger of these clusters is then split again, and the process repeats until it hits some stop condition. The result is a tree-like structure that defines the clusters.

This section introduces an alternative method for divisive clustering, one more closely related to decision trees.

A Decision Tree–Like Method for Clustering

As discussed in Chapter 7, splitting a decision tree node uses a purity function. In that chapter, the purity function was based on the target variable. This section suggests a variation on the decision tree algorithm: Define a purity function that does not use any target at all. Then, the basic decision tree algorithm can also be used for clustering.

> **TIP** Divisive clustering is very similar to decision trees in that the result is a tree that specifies the clusters. On the other hand, it is quite different, because the definition of purity does not use a target variable.

The idea is to create a purity measure that conforms to "goodness" of clusters. This, in turn, begs the question: What makes a cluster good? As pointed out several times, the answer to this question is subjective judgment. A good cluster is one that is useful for business purposes. Such a definition does not readily translate into a form understandable by computers. A measure of "distinctness" is needed.

When All Fields Are Numeric

There are two traditional ways of measuring purity when all the columns are numeric. These measures assume that the records are points in space.

The first is a measure of tightness. A split is good if the two resulting children are as small as possible in some sense. One way of measuring size is the diameter of the child. The diameter is the distance between the two records that are furthest apart. An alternative way uses the statistical measure of variance in each child. Or, more precisely, the variance of the normalized variables. You don't want variables that take on large values to dominate the variance calculation.

The second way of measuring purity is to measure how far apart the children are. This is usually the minimum distance between points in the two clusters. A split produces two good clusters if the nearest points in the two clusters are as far apart as possible.

The divisive clustering algorithm then continues, the same way that the decision tree algorithm does. There is one caveat. This definition of "goodness" of cluster only works on numeric variables.

Divisive Clustering When All Fields Are Categorical

When all the fields are categorical, a different purity measure is needed because the distance and variance are not defined on categorical values. A natural measure on categorical values is the chi-square value. How can this be applied to divisive clustering?

In an ordinary decision tree, the chi-square value is used to measure the extent to which a proposed split changes the distribution of the target variable. For clustering, there is no target so the chi-square test is applied to all variables. That is, there is a contingency table for each variable, as shown schematically in Table 14-1. The chi-square value can then be calculated based on the contingency table. The overall chi-square value for a split is the sum of the chi-square value for all variables. A good split is one that is "unexpected," so the sum should be as large as possible.

Table 14-1: A Contingency Table for the Chi-Square Calculation for Divisive Clustering on Categorical Variables

VARIABLE A	LEFT CHILD	RIGHT CHILD
Val 1	<count>	<count>
Val 2	<count>	<count>
...		
Val n	<count>	<count>

A General Approach

A general approach for divisive clustering uses an idea based on the chi-square value for categorical variables. Instead of the chi-square value, let's ask the question: how likely is it that the split on a given column is due entirely to chance? You may recognize this as the p-value, which was discussed in Chapter 4. For categorical variables, you can calculate the p-value using the chi-square method. The final step is to look up the p-value corresponding to a given chi-square value.

For numeric variables, the appropriate test uses the standard error of the mean (SEM). After the split, each child has a certain number of records and a certain average value for the numeric variable. By using the SEM, the difference between the averages can be converted into a p-value.

As a result, both categorical and numeric variables can be converted into p-values, which say whether the split is interesting (low p-value) or uninteresting (high p-value) from the perspective of that variable. One way to combine the p-values is by converting them to likelihoods and taking their product, as in the naïve Bayesian approach. Another way is to calculate an "estimated" p-value for all the variables at once, using a formula such as one minus the product of one minus the p-values.

Scoring Divisive Clusters

The divisive clustering model is basically a decision tree, where the goal of the model is to determine the particular leaf where new records are placed. Scoring divisive clusters is the same as scoring decision trees. The split rules at each level determine which child a new record goes into. Then, the record eventually lands at a leaf node, yielding the cluster assignment.

Although the divisive clusters for k-means also create a tree-like structure, they are not scored the same way. In the end, these clusters are k-means clusters. They are scored by determining the closest centroid.

Clusters and Trees

With no change in the purity function, you might say that decision trees provide *directed clustering*; that is, they create clusters of records that are similar with respect to some target variable. Customer segmentation is one possible application of clustering. Often, ordinary decision trees are a better choice for this type of application than the undirected clustering algorithms discussed in this chapter.

If the purpose of the customer segmentation is to find customer segments that are loyal or profitable or likely to respond to some particular offer, it makes sense to use one of those variables (or a proxy) as the target for directed clustering. If, on the other hand, the point of the customer segmentation is to stimulate discussion of new product offerings geared to various naturally occurring clusters of customers, then an undirected approach is more appropriate.

TIP In a sense, decision trees are an example of "directed" clustering, where the purity measure depends on a single variable, the target.

Divisive clustering algorithms create hierarchical clusters. At each level in the hierarchy, clusters are formed by splitting the clusters at that level. A good way of visualizing these clusters is as a tree. Of course, such a tree may look like the decision trees discussed in Chapter 7. But there is a very important difference. Decision trees are built using a target variable in the purity measure. For divisive clustering, no target variable defines the purity measure. Like directed decision trees, though, the trees created through divisive clustering can explain the rules used for the clusters, because these are embedded in the split rules for each node.

Agglomerative (Hierarchical) Clustering

Agglomerative clustering (also known as hierarchical clustering) is a class of techniques quite different from k-means and Gaussian mixture models. The major difference is the results. Agglomerative clustering does not produce a single assignment of clusters to data points. Like divisive clustering, it creates a tree-like structure of clusters, which you can investigate after clustering.

Overview of Agglomerative Clustering Methods

The process of finding agglomerative clusters starts with each record in its own cluster. The clusters gradually merge, forming larger and larger groupings, until all the records have been placed in one large cluster. The entire history is preserved, which makes it possible to choose the level of clustering that works best for a given application.

Toward the beginning of the process, the clusters are very small and very pure — the members of each cluster are few and closely related. Toward the end of the process, the clusters are large and not as well defined.

Scoring agglomerative clusters is a two-step process. First, you determine the number of clusters that you want. The algorithm itself produces a tree-like structure, but does not specify the number of clusters. After you have identified the number of clusters that you want, you then need to assign new data points to them. The scoring process finds the closest original record to the record to be scored. The cluster assigned to that closest record is then used for the new record.

Clustering People by Age: An Example of Agglomerative Clustering

This illustration of agglomerative clustering uses an example in one dimension, to illustrate the process by following the algorithm through several iterations. Also, by using one dimension, you have no need to get bogged down in calculating distances, using squares and square roots. The data consists of the ages of people at a family gathering. The ages are: 1, 3, 5, 8, 9, 11, 12, 13, 37, 43, 45, 49, 51, and 65.

The goal is to cluster the participants using their age, and the metric for the distance between two people is simply the difference in their ages. The metric for the distance between two clusters of people is the difference in age between the oldest member of the younger cluster and the youngest member of the older cluster; that is, the distance between two clusters is defined by the closest records in them.

At the first level, everyone who is one year apart is combined into a single group. Table 14-2 shows the results for the first level. The cluster name shows the ranges of ages of all the original people in the cluster. At this level, the 8- and 9-year-olds are grouped together. Also, the 11-, 12-, and 13-year-olds are grouped together.

Table 14-2: First Level of Hierarchical Clustering, Combining Ages that are One Year Apart

AGE	DISTANCE 1
1	[1]
3	[3]
5	[5]
8	[8-9]
9	[8-9]
11	[11-13]
12	[11-13]
13	[11-13]
37	[37]
43	[43]
45	[45]
49	[49]
51	[51]
65	[65]

This process continues, combining the groups based on the closest ages in the group. After a few levels, three groups appear, as shown in Table 14-3. These three clusters, based on ages, can be given names. The first are the "children," the second are the "parents," and the one outlier is "grandma."

Table 14-3: Clustering of 15 Ages into 3 Clusters

AGE	DISTANCE 1	DISTANCE 2	DISTANCE 3	DISTANCE 4	DISTANCE 7
1	[1]	[1-5]	[1-13]	[1-13]	[1-13]
3	[3]	[1-5]	[1-13]	[1-13]	[1-13]
5	[5]	[1-5]	[1-13]	[1-13]	[1-13]
8	[8-9]	[8-13]	[1-13]	[1-13]	[1-13]
9	[8-9]	[8-13]	[1-13]	[1-13]	[1-13]
11	[11-13]	[8-13]	[1-13]	[1-13]	[1-13]
12	[11-13]	[8-13]	[1-13]	[1-13]	[1-13]
13	[11-13]	[8-13]	[1-13]	[1-13]	[1-13]
37	[37]	[37]	[37]	[37]	[37-51]
43	[43]	[43-45]	[43-45]	[43-51]	[37-51]
45	[45]	[43-45]	[43-45]	[43-51]	[37-51]
49	[49]	[49-51]	[49-51]	[43-51]	[37-51]
51	[51]	[49-51]	[49-51]	[43-51]	[37-51]
65	[65]	[65]	[65]	[65]	[65]

Visualizing the Clusters

An alternative way of visualizing the clusters is shown in Figure 14-10. The original data points are spread along the horizontal dimension, labeled by the age of the individual. The vertical dimension is the distance between the clusters. The tree structure shows the hierarchy of clusters created during the various iterations.

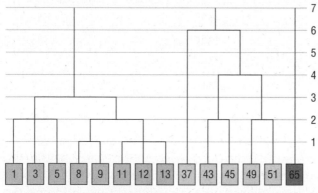

Figure 14-10: This visualization, called a dendogram, shows the clusters created by hierarchical clustering of ages.

Notice that at a distance of seven, there are three clusters. This would not get reduced until the distance of 14, where the cluster with the 51-year-old would merge with "grandma." This suggests that these three clusters are pretty stable, in the sense that they are well-separated from each other.

The result of clustering is a structure, and nothing is sacrosanct about having three clusters. If you have a desire to explore more clusters, then going down in the tree yields more clusters. Conversely, going to higher levels of the tree would eventually distinguish between "children" and "adults." One of the powers of hierarchical clustering is that it produces a tree structure, allowing you to cluster data without choosing the number of clusters in advance.

The tree structure created for agglomerative clusters may look similar to a decision tree. There are two crucial differences. The first has already been discussed: clustering does not use a target variable, whereas directed decision trees do. The other important difference is that a decision tree can explain why a split is being made at each level, because every non-leaf node has a slitting rule. There is also a reason for two clusters to be combined in an agglomerative cluster tree. However, the reason is always the same: These were the closest clusters at this stage in building the clusters.

Combining Nearby Clusters

The distance between two records is easy to calculate. However, as records are combined into clusters, it becomes necessary to calculate the distance between a single record and a cluster of other records, or between two clusters. Three common measures are as follows:

- *Single linkage* is the method used in the example. The distance between two clusters is the distance between their closest members.

- *Complete linkage* is the opposite of single linkage. The distance between two clusters is the distance between their furthest members.

- *Centroid distance* is a compromise. The distance between two clusters is the distance between their centers.

These measures are all similar to the measures for evaluating the distance between clusters, discussed in the previous chapter.

Single linkage is usually a good choice, although there is no hard-and-fast rule. Figure 14-11 shows these three possibilities, using the ages example. For single linkage, the first merging of two clusters (as opposed to original data records) is at a distance of one. For complete linkage, the first merging is at a distance of five. Complete linkage is much more conservative.

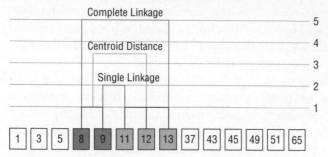

Figure 14-11: Single linkage, complete linkage, and centroid distance are three ways of combining clusters when they contain more than one data record.

An Agglomerative Clustering Algorithm

To describe the agglomerative clustering algorithm, start with the following two assumptions:

- There is a way to combine records in a cluster into a single record, such as by taking the average value.

- There is a way to calculate the distance between any two clusters.

These assumptions essentially treat the records as points in space.

The basic agglomerative clustering algorithm starts by placing each record into its own cluster. Then, the algorithm merges the two clusters that are closest into a larger cluster, and the process repeats itself until only one cluster remains. One important question is how to measure the distance between two clusters, using single linkage, complete linkage, or centroid distance.

Unfortunately, clean definitions of distance are not always available, as the examples in the next section show. Fortunately, the basic algorithm can be tweaked to make it work in more general cases.

One approach is to introduce a *distance matrix* or a *similarity matrix*. This is a table that contains all the pair-wise distances (or equivalently similarity measures) between any two records. Distance and similarity are almost the same thing. When using distance, the goal is to find the smallest distance. When using similarity, the goal is to find the largest similarity.

Table 14-4 shows an example of a distance matrix for the ages data. Notice that this matrix is symmetric along the diagonal. The upper triangle in the table has the same values as the lower triangle. This is because distance (as measured here) is commutative — that is, the distance from A to B is the same as from B to A.

Table 14-4: Distance Matrix for Ages

AGES	1	3	5	8	9	11	12	13	37	43	45	49	51	65
1		2	4	7	8	10	11	12	36	42	44	48	50	64
3	2		2	5	6	8	9	10	34	40	42	46	48	62
5	4	2		3	4	6	7	8	32	38	40	44	46	60
8	7	5	3		1	3	4	5	29	35	37	41	43	57
9	8	6	4	1		2	3	4	28	34	36	40	42	56
11	10	8	6	3	2		1	2	26	32	34	38	40	54
12	11	9	7	4	3	1		1	25	31	33	37	39	53
13	12	10	8	5	4	2	1		24	30	32	36	38	52
37	36	34	32	29	28	26	25	24		6	8	12	14	28
43	42	40	38	35	34	32	31	30	6		2	6	8	22
45	44	42	40	37	36	34	33	32	8	2		4	6	20
49	48	46	44	41	40	38	37	36	12	6	4		2	16
51	50	48	46	43	42	40	39	38	14	8	6	2		14
65	64	62	60	57	56	54	53	52	28	22	20	16	14	

Using the distance matrix, first find the smallest value in the table that is not along the diagonal (because merging a cluster with itself does not further the clustering process). In this example, the smallest value is 1. This example arbitrarily chooses 8 and 9 among the several possibilities where the distance is 1. These two records merge into a single cluster, and the distance matrix is updated, by removing the original two records and adding one for the new cluster. The result is shown in Table 14-5.

What are the new distance values between the new cluster and the other records? This depends on the way that distance is being calculated between clusters. For single linkage, the distance from any other record to the cluster is the minimum of the distances between that record and each record in the cluster. For complete linkage, the distance is the maximum instead. One could imagine an "average" combination as well, but this average would be different from the centroid distance. To integrate the matrix approach with centroid distance requires storing the size of the clusters as well as the distances, and then combining them using weighted averages. In all cases, the distance from the new cluster to itself is zero (or blank, as shown in these distance tables).

Table 14-5: The Distance Matrix for the Ages After Combining 8- and 9-Year-Olds

AGES	1	3	5	8&9	11	12	13	37	43	45	49	51	65
1		2	4	7	10	11	12	36	42	44	9	50	64
3	2		2	5	8	9	10	34	40	42	46	48	62
5	4	2		3	6	7	8	32	38	40	44	46	60
8&9	7	5	3		1	2	3	4	28	34	36	40	42
11	10	8	6	2		1	2	26	32	34	38	40	54
12	11	9	7	3	1		1	25	31	33	37	39	53
13	12	10	8	4	2	1		24	30	32	36	38	52
37	36	34	32	28	26	25	24		6	8	12	14	28
43	42	40	38	34	32	31	30	6		2	6	8	22
45	44	42	40	36	34	33	32	8	2		4	6	20
49	48	46	44	40	38	37	36	12	6	4		2	16
51	50	48	46	42	40	39	38	14	8	6	2		14
65	64	62	60	56	54	53	52	28	22	20	16	14	

After this step, the distance matrix contains at least one fewer row and one fewer column (because the original records were removed). Repeat the merge step $N-1$ times until all records belong to the same large cluster. Each iteration remembers which clusters were merged and the distance between them. This information is used to decide which level of clustering to make use of.

Scoring Agglomerative Clusters

The agglomerative clustering model is a tree-like structure, built from the lowest levels upward. However, typically a subset of the clusters is chosen as the final result. The wrong way to score the clusters is by finding the cluster center that is closest to the record being scored. The advantage of the hierarchical clusters is that they can be of arbitrary shapes, so they cannot be scored like k-means clusters.

The best way to score the clusters is by keeping every training record and its cluster assignment. The distance from a new record being scored to the contents of all the clusters is used to determine which has the minimum distance. The calculation of the minimum distance depends on the type of clustering:

- For single linkage clusters, the closest point in any of the clusters determines the cluster to assign to the new record.

- For complete linkage, the furthest point in any of the clusters that is closest to the new record determines the cluster to assign to the new record.

- For centroid distance, the clusters do behave like k-means; the nearest cluster center determines the cluster to assign.

Single linkage and complete linkage resemble MBR approaches, in that they consider all the training data for the cluster assignments. As with MBR, the number of records needed for scoring can sometimes be reduced to make scoring more efficient.

WARNING   In general, hierarchical clusters need to be scored by considering the distance to every record in the clusters to be scored. Finding the cluster with the nearest center to a given record is not the correct scoring method.

As an example, consider the age clusters identified earlier in this section. If a 20-year-old shows up at the family gathering, to which of the three clusters should that person be assigned?

Because the clusters were identified using single linkage, the method for scoring is to find the closest of the original data points and then to use the cluster assigned to that person. For the 20-year-old, the closest person is the young teenager, and the cluster would be the "children." However, consider what happens with a 58-year-old. This person would enter exactly between the parents and grandma. Even worse, the three clusters were defined at level 7, but if this long-lost cousin had been in the original sample, then the parents and grandma would have been combined at that level.

There is a certain irony here. New data can be scored by using the nearest of the original data points — or, equivalently, by measuring the distance to the final clusters and choosing the one with the smallest distance. However, if the new data points were included in the data used to build the clusters, the clusters might have looked much different.

Limitations of Agglomerative Clustering

Agglomerative clustering has three major, although manageable downsides:

- It can be computationally expensive.
- It can be difficult to visualize the clusters.
- It is quite sensitive to outliers.

These issues are discussed in this section. In the end, agglomerative clustering is a powerful algorithm, but it works best when dozens or, at most, a few hundred records are to be clustered.

> **TIP** Agglomerative clustering works best when you have at most a few hundred records to be clustered. It is usually not the best choice for clustering at the customer level.

Computationally Expensive

Agglomerative clustering requires a lot of data processing. A distance matrix on one million customers would have about one trillion cells. The early stages of the algorithm require searching through all the unclustered records and clusters to find the closest pair. Naïve ways of doing this result in algorithms that do not scale well as the data gets larger.

There are ways to work around this limitation. One way is to take a random sample to reduce the size of the data. Another work-around is to build RD trees, multidimensional indexes explained in Chapter 9 that make finding neighbors efficient.

Difficult to Visualize Clusters

The result of agglomerative clustering is a giant tree. To use the technique to its fullest, you want to visualize this tree. That works with a few dozen records. It does not work with thousands or millions of records.

This difficulty in visualizing the results is another reason why you want to limit the clustering to smaller data sets.

Sensitivity to Outliers

Agglomerative clustering is quite sensitive to outliers. The sensitivity is in the number of clusters that are identified. In general, the technique does a good job of grouping records that are close together into discrete clusters.

The problem is that the records that are not so close to other records end up in their own clusters. As the number of clusters gets smaller, larger clusters merge together, but the outliers are stubborn holdouts. They don't merge until the very end. You may want to choose three or five clusters. Often, this consists of two or four clusters with just a single record and one big cluster with everything else.

Once again, this is a particular problem when more than a few dozen records are being clustered, because you cannot visualize the dendogram very easily. This makes it difficult to spot the outliers and hence to decide on the right number of clusters.

One way around this is to eliminate the outliers during a pre-processing step. To do this, consider the minimum distance from each record to any other record. Require that this meet some threshold value. For instance, you might eliminate the five percent of records whose closest neighbor is relatively far away.

Alternatively, the hierarchical clustering could be used for outlier detection. The outliers are the last singleton (or very small) clusters that get merged in.

Agglomerative Clustering in Practice

Agglomerative clustering is a powerful clustering method that works best with fewer rather than more records. This fact makes clustering at the customer level impractical. Yet, it can be surprisingly useful for customer-centric applications.

Clustering Products by Customer Preferences

Finding groups of products that sell together is most often in the domain of market basket analysis, which is covered in the next chapter. However, it can also be approached using hierarchical clustering. The key is defining the problem correctly.

You have a bunch of records of customer purchasing products. The question you want to answer is: which products fall into naturally occurring groups based on purchase behavior? Such information is particularly powerful for recommendations, to determine the next product to try to sell to a customer; it can also be useful for other purposes such as inventory control. Hierarchical clustering not only places the products into groups, it builds a structure on top of them, so you can determine the size and number of groups most suitable for a particular application.

The first step is to define the distance or similarity between two products. One attempt at defining similarity might simply be the proportion of customers who have purchased both products. However, there is a problem with this definition. Common products are going to rate high on the similarity scale, even if there is no real affinity between them. Rare products are never going seem very similar, even if they always sell together.

Tweaking the measure to take into account how common the products are solves this problem. The tweaked measure is the proportion of customers who have both products divided by the proportion who have either one. So, if all customers who have product A also have product B and vice versa, then the measure would have a value of one. If no customers have both products, then the similarity would be zero.

This measures the affinity of any two products to each other, without punishing rare products. To turn this similarity measure into a distance measure, the value needs to be subtracted from one. This is just one example of a measure. Other possibilities for the distance matrix might take into account how "unusual" it is for the two products to appear together, using a measure such as the chi-square value, or the total amount of money spent on both products.

After you have defined the appropriate distance measure, you can calculate the distance matrix, which in turn can be used for hierarchical clustering. The result is a tree-like structure on the products that shows the most similar products based on customer preferences (which might in turn be based on historical marketing patterns, but that discussion is postponed until the next chapter).

You can use almost exactly the same idea to cluster pages or sections of a website. In this case, the similarity function is the proportion of customers who visited both sections divided by the proportion who visited either one.

Clustering Direct Marketing Campaigns by Customer Response

Direct marketing campaigns are a very important aspect of customer relationship management. To understand campaigns better, clustering them into similarity groups can provide interesting insights. Interesting idea, but how might you do it in practice?

Hierarchical clustering provides both a convenient mechanism for doing the clustering and a useful way of understanding the resulting campaigns. Once again, the key is defining the distance matrix. This is challenging, because different campaigns have different target lists. Few, if any, customers receive all campaigns.

TIP By defining an appropriate similarity measure — such as the number of prospects who responded to two marketing campaigns divided by the number who were targeted by both — almost anything can be clustered using hierarchical clustering.

An appropriate similarity is the number of customers (or prospects) who responded to both campaigns divided by the number who received both campaigns. If two campaigns have no overlap, then you can safely assume that they are far apart. After all, campaign lists are not chosen randomly, so a lack of overlap means that the target groups are quite dissimilar.

Combining Agglomerative Clustering and K-Means

The final example of agglomerative clustering is a hybrid approach with k-means. The two methods of clustering are quite complementary. K-means is scalable, so it works on large quantities of data. Agglomerative clustering does not scale very well, but it does produce very interesting outputs.

Combining them starts with creating lots of k-means clusters — say 100. Agglomerative clustering is then applied to these clusters to create a cluster hierarchy. These clusters can then be analyzed to determine an appropriate smaller number of clusters that combine the k-means clusters.

This method helps to overcome the limitation of k-means where the clusters are, essentially, big circles around the centroids. Instead, lots of smaller clusters end up being combined to create larger clusters, which can have arbitrary shapes.

TIP You can use agglomerative clustering in conjunction with k-means. Use k-means to produce lots of clusters (say, 100), and then use agglomerative clustering to bring them together.

Self-Organizing Maps

Self-organizing maps (SOMs) are a variant of neural networks used for undirected data mining tasks such as cluster detection. The Finnish researcher Dr. Tuevo Kohonen invented self-organizing maps (as described in the aside "Tuevo Kohonen and Self-Organizing Maps"), so they are sometimes called Kohonen networks. Although used originally for images and sounds, these networks can also recognize clusters in data. Although based on similar ideas, SOMs differ from multilayer perceptrons in two respects. They have a different topology and the back propagation method of learning does not apply. They also have a different method for training.

What Is a Self-Organizing Map?

A *self-organizing map* (SOM) is a neural network that can recognize unknown patterns in the data, an example of which is shown in Figure 14-12. Like the networks in Chapter 8, the basic SOM has an input layer and an output layer. Each unit in the input layer is connected to one source, just as in the networks for predictive modeling. Also, like those networks, each unit in the SOM has an independent weight associated with each incoming connection. However, the similarity between SOMs and multi-layer perceptrons ends here.

The output layer consists of many units instead of one or just a handful. Each of the units in the output layer is fully connected to all the units in the input layer. In addition, the output layer is arranged in a grid, as if the units are on the squares of a checkerboard. Even though the units are not connected to each other in this layer, the grid-like structure plays an important role in training an SOM.

How does an SOM recognize patterns? Imagine one of the booths at a carnival where you throw balls at a wall filled with holes. If the ball lands in one of the holes, then you have your choice of prizes. Training an SOM is like being at the booth blindfolded, facing a wall that has no holes — similar to the situation when looking for patterns in large amounts of data and not knowing where to start. Each time you throw the ball, it dents the wall a little bit. Eventually, when enough balls land in the same vicinity, the indentation breaks through the wall, forming a hole. Now, when another ball lands at that location, it goes through the hole, and you get a prize. At the carnival, this is a cheap stuffed animal; with an SOM, it is an identifiable cluster.

TEUVO KOHONEN AND SELF-ORGANIZING MAPS

Self-organizing maps are sometimes called Kohonen networks, after their inventor, the Finnish researcher Teuvo Kohonen. His work in the area of artificial intelligence is so prominent that he is credited with being the most-cited Finnish scientist in academic literature.

Professor Kohonen's work in this area has focused on understanding the mechanisms of neurons in human brains and how similar mechanisms might be applied to computers. In particular, he is fascinated by the brain's associative memory. Associative memory is the ability to relate two different patterns to each other, similar to the way that people "associate" one thing with another.

In the human brain, particular neurons seem to remember or be able to identify particular things in the real world. The layout of the neurons probably looks nothing like the object in question. The part of the brain that recognizes a circle, for instance, could consist of neurons that are all lined up in a straight line.

In Kohonen's networks, two things are going on:

■ The nodes in the output layer are competing against each other, although nodes close to each other cooperate.

■ The weights leading to the nodes can change to better identify patterns.

These have parallels in the structure of human brains.

The name "self-organizing map" refers to the fact that these maps learn automatically from data presented to them. Any set of data can be turned into a two-dimensional map, using this technique. This is an intriguing example of reducing the dimensions in the data. Perhaps more interesting is the comparison to human brains, which do similar things to represent the complexity of the real world.

Of course, the benefit of self-organizing maps is not that they theoretically capture notions of artificial intelligence. The benefit is that they seem to work well in practice. SOMs are easy to train and easy to apply to new data. As with other clustering techniques, the results have to be interpreted. The mimicking of the human brain does not quite extend to understanding when clusters are good or bad.

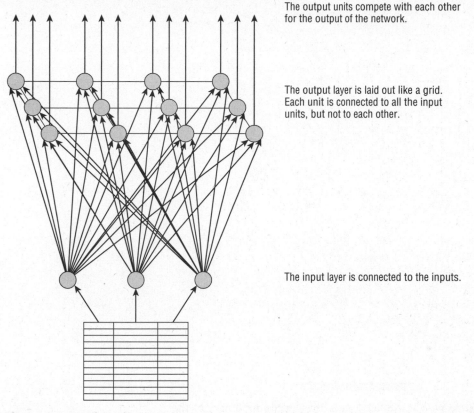

The output units compete with each other for the output of the network.

The output layer is laid out like a grid. Each unit is connected to all the input units, but not to each other.

The input layer is connected to the inputs.

Figure 14-12: The self-organizing map is a special kind of neural network that can be used to detect clusters.

Figure 14-13 shows how this works for a simple SOM. When a member of the training set is presented to the network, the values flow forward through the network to the units in the output layer. The units in the output layer compete with each other, and the one with the highest value "wins." The reward is to adjust the weights leading up to the winning unit to strengthen in the response to the input pattern. This is like making a little dent in the network.

SOMs might be said to associate the winning node with the input pattern. The word "associate" here conjures up the world of human intelligence, and this is not an accident. The idea is that the SOM is creating its own "map" of what constitutes patterns that it "sees" in the records presented to it. The value of SOMs is that sometimes the resulting patterns can, indeed, be quite useful.

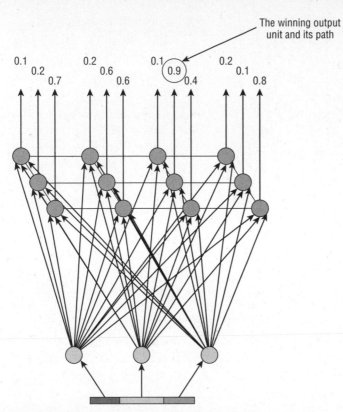

Figure 14-13: An SOM finds the output unit that does the best job of recognizing a particular input.

Training an SOM

Training an SOM is the process of adjusting the weights in the network to produce stable clusters. The process is basically the following:

1. Initialize the network with random weights.
2. Read each row in the training set, adjusting the weights in the network to reinforce the "detector" for each row.
3. Cycle through the training set until the detector for each row no longer changes.

In practice, the complicated activation functions for neural networks are not needed. The detector is the output node with the highest value, and it is the highest value with or without a fancy activation function such as the logistic function. The detector is simply the node that is "nearest" to the inputs.

There is one more aspect to the training of the network. Not only are the weights for the winning unit adjusted in Step 2, but the weights for units in its immediate neighborhood are also adjusted to strengthen their response to the inputs. This adjustment is controlled by a *neighborliness* parameter that specifies the size of the neighborhood and the amount of adjustment.

Neighborliness has several practical effects. One is that the output layer behaves more like a connected fabric, even though the units are not directly connected to each other. Clusters similar to each other should be closer together than more dissimilar clusters. More importantly, though, neighborliness allows for a group of units to represent a single cluster. Without this neighborliness, the network would tend to create random maps of the clusters, based on the initial random seeds. Instead, the output layer is intended to be a "map" of the clusters where nearby clusters are more related than those further apart.

Even with neighborliness, an SOM typically identifies a few large clusters and many smaller ones. That is, the vast majority of clusters consist of less than a few dozen members. Such small clusters are usually not particularly useful. The typical solution is to take all clusters that account for some proportion of the records in the model set; say, 95 percent of them. The remaining records are then placed into their own cluster. Alternatively, the SOM network could go through a second phase, where only the larger clusters are used. The unassigned records would be assigned to the cluster that gets the highest score among the chosen nodes.

Scoring an SOM

The SOM model is a collection of nodes with weights attached. The model itself might be pruned, so only the larger nodes are part of the model. However, this does not affect the scoring mechanism.

After the final network is in place — with the output layer restricted only to the units that identify specific clusters — you can apply it to new instances. An unknown instance is fed into the network and is assigned to the cluster at the output unit with the largest weight. SOMs assign only a single detector to each input record being scored. No need exists to calculate probability assignments for the different nodes.

The network has identified clusters, but you do not know anything about the clusters. To understand the clusters, you need to profile them by looking at average values, characterize them by the variables that most distinguish them, or visualize them in some other way, as explained in Chapter 13.

The original SOMs used two-dimensional grids for the output layer. This was an artifact of earlier research into recognizing features in images composed of a two-dimensional array of pixel values. The output layer can really have any structure — with neighborhoods defined in three dimensions, as a network of hexagons, or laid out in some other fashion.

The Search Continues for Islands of Simplicity

In many ways, clustering is at the heart of data mining. Directed data mining, with a few exceptions, is often based on statistical techniques that have been around for many decades or centuries. These have adapted to the increased data and computer power available in the modern world, but many basic ideas remain the same.

Clustering, on the other hand, is more recent and borne of the availability of lots of data and powerful computers. It is also an area where research continues.

In terms of basic clustering, some companies, such as Google, Amazon, and eBay, are interested in learning more about their business through the data that they collect. The problem for them is a wealth of data, an inundation of bits and bytes.

Hybrid approaches that combine different techniques can be quite useful in this area. The *Boston Globe* case study in the previous chapter combined k-means clustering with divisive clustering. There are other hybrid methods, such as using k-means clustering and then applying hierarchical clustering on the k-means centroids. K-means is commonly used with GMM clustering as a way to obtain initial estimates for the cluster centers.

One approach, which goes by the name *canopy clustering*, is a way of reducing the complexity for very large data sets. The idea is to define a set of "canopies" that cover the data, similar to k-means clustering. However, these canopies overlap, so any given data point is in at least one canopy but likely to be in several. An algorithm such as k-means then runs within the canopies. As it goes through the iterations, the algorithm only considers points that are in the same canopy as the original data point.

The purpose of canopy clustering is to reduce the complexity of the algorithm. One way it does this is by using a simpler distance metric to define the canopies, by focusing on only a few features, and then a more robust measure for the second stage of the technique.

Another interesting area in clustering is *co-clustering*. This involves clustering two dimensions at the same time. For instance, co-clustering attempts to place customers and marketing campaigns into groups, so the customer clusters respond to similar marketing campaigns and the campaign clusters attract similar customers. The techniques used in this area are still more theoretical than applied.

Lessons Learned

Clustering techniques are a family of undirected data mining techniques that find islands of similarity in data. The previous chapter introduced the most common clustering technique, k-means. However, k-means does not always produce good clusters.

An important variant of k-means is Gaussian mixture models (GMM), also called expectation-maximization clustering (EM). This technique identifies clusters using multidimensional probability distributions. In doing so, it can overcome many of the limitations of k-means. On the other hand, it is also quite sensitive to outliers and the initial seeds.

Divisive clustering takes an approach similar to decision trees. The data is repeatedly split, using splitting rules as in a decision tree. The key difference is the measure of similarity. Divisive clustering does not use a target variable for measuring purity. Instead, the purity measure must rely on distributional statistics of the input variables, choosing the best split based on the one that does the best job of separating the children.

Agglomerative or hierarchical clustering is the exact inverse of divisive clustering. It starts with each record in its own cluster, and then combines them together, by merging the most similar first. Its main drawback is that understanding the clusters requires visualizing the dendogram — tree diagram — that describes them. This is challenging, unless there are at most a few hundred data points.

Neural networks also contribute a clustering algorithm. Self-organizing maps adapt neural networks for clustering. In this case, the clustering is basically magic — no tree or nearest neighbor describes the clusters. You have to resort to descriptive statistics to understand what is going on.

Clustering is an ongoing area of research. At one extreme are adaptations of clustering algorithms for the phenomenal amount of data being generated on the Web. At the other extreme are more complicated clustering problems, such as co-clustering, where two different things, such as customers and campaigns, are clustered at the same time, based on information about each other. The next chapter moves from general clustering algorithms to a specific problem in undirected data mining. The fundamental question of market basket analysis is: Which products are purchased together?

Market Basket Analysis and Association Rules

To understand the fundamental ideas of market basket analysis, conjure an image of a shopping cart filled with various products purchased by someone on a quick trip to the supermarket. The basket contains an assortment of items; for example, orange juice, bananas, soft drinks, window cleaner, and detergent. One basket tells you about what one customer purchased at one time. A complete list of purchases made by all customers provides much more information. A loyalty card makes it possible to tie together purchases by a single customer (or household) over time. No wonder that retailers and consumer goods manufacturers are interested in market basket analysis. The contents of those baskets describe the most important part of a retailing business — what merchandise customers are buying and when.

Market basket analysis is much more than just the contents of shopping carts. It is also about how characteristics of customers — such as demographics and geography — affect their purchases. It is also about what customers do not purchase, and why. If customers purchase baking powder, but no flour, what are they baking? If customers purchase a mobile phone, but no case, are you missing an opportunity? It is also about key drivers of purchases; for example, the gourmet mustard that seems to lie on a shelf collecting dust until a customer buys that particular brand of special gourmet mustard in a shopping excursion that includes hundreds of dollars' worth of other products. Would eliminating the mustard (to replace it with a better-selling item) threaten the entire customer relationship?

The data mining technique most closely identified with market basket analysis is *association analysis*, which automatically generates *association rules*. Association analysis is a type of undirected data mining that finds patterns in the data where the target is not specified beforehand. Whether the patterns make sense is left to human interpretation.

Association rules predate the world of loyalty cards and were originally derived from point-of-sale data that describes one transaction consisting of several products. Although their roots are in analyzing point-of-sale transactions, association rules can be applied outside the retail industry to find relationships among other types of "baskets." Some examples of applications are as follows:

- Items purchased on a credit card, such as rental cars and hotel rooms, provide insight into the next product that customers are likely to purchase, as well as profitability and customer segment information.

- Optional services purchased by telecommunications customers (call waiting, call forwarding, DSL, speed call, and so on) help determine how to bundle these services together to maximize revenue.

- Banking products used by retail customers (money market accounts, CDs, investment services, car loans, and so on) identify customers likely to want other products.

- Unusual combinations of insurance claims can be a sign of fraud and can spark further investigation.

- Medical patient histories can give indications of likely complications based on certain combinations of treatments.

With a simple modification, association rules can be used to find sequential associations (purchasing one item leads to purchasing another) and other non-traditional combinations of purchases. Sequential associations are themselves one aspect of *sequential pattern analysis*, an important set of techniques related to market basket analysis.

The chapter starts with an overview of market basket analysis, including more basic analyses of market basket data that do not require association rules. This includes a case study of an ethnic marketing campaign that analyzes the products purchased at stores in different locations. The discussion of association analysis explains how rules are derived and extensions to them. Along the way are examples of using association rules to understand customer complaints and to build better cross-sell models in the insurance industry.

Defining Market Basket Analysis

Market basket analysis does not refer to a single technique; perhaps appropriate to its name, it refers to a set of business problems related to understanding point-of-sale transaction data. The applications of the techniques have been expanded to many different domains. For instance, a more recent application of market basket analysis is for understanding the parts of a website that customers visit. Because the data used for market basket analysis is very specific, this section explains what it looks like.

Four Levels of Market Basket Data

Market basket data is transaction data that typically describes four entities central to the purchasing experience:

- Stores
- Customers
- Orders (also called *transactions*, *purchases*, *baskets,* or in academic papers, *item sets*)
- Items

In a relational database, the data structure for market basket data often looks similar to Figure 15-1.

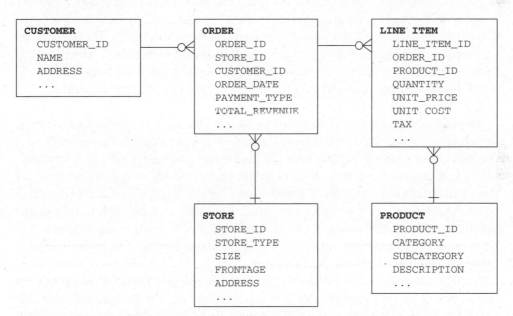

Figure 15-1: A logical data model for transaction-level market basket data has tables for the important entities related to market basket data.

The *order* is the fundamental data structure for market basket data. An order represents a single purchase event by a customer. This might correspond to a customer purchasing a basket of groceries or to the parts of a website visited by a customer during a single session or to all the purchases made by a customer through a catalog (where all purchases over time are combined). Typically, an order includes the total dollar amount of the purchase, additional charges such as taxes and shipping, the number of distinct items, the method of payment, and whatever other data is relevant about the transaction (such as coupon usage and returned merchandise). Sometimes the transaction is given a unique identifier. Sometimes the unique identifier needs to be cobbled together from other data. In one example, the authors needed to combine four fields to get an identifier for purchases in a store — the timestamp when the customer paid, chain ID, store ID, and lane ID.

Individual items in the order are represented separately as *line items*. This data includes the price paid for the item, the number of items, whether tax should be charged, discounts applied, and perhaps the cost (which can be used for calculating margin). The item table also typically has a link to a *product reference table*, which provides more descriptive information about each product. This descriptive information should include the product hierarchy and other static information that might prove valuable for analysis.

The *customer* entity is optional and should be available when a customer can be identified over time. Examples include websites that have registered users and retailers where most customers use loyalty cards. In other cases, finding a customer is not possible, such as for anonymous website browsing and for cash transactions. There are in-between cases, where some transactions can be combined, such as those using the same credit card or same cookie on the browser. Although the customer table may have interesting fields, the most powerful element is the ID itself, because it ties transactions together over time. Chapter 18 discusses the issues of identifying the customer.

Tracking customers over time makes it possible to determine, for instance, which grocery shoppers "bake from scratch" — something of keen interest to the makers of flour as well as prepackaged cake mixes and the makers of aprons and kitchen appliances. Such customers might be identified from the frequency of their purchases of flour, baking powder, and similar ingredients, the proportion of such purchases to the customer's total spending, and the lack of interest in prepackaged mixes and ready-to-eat desserts. Of course, such ingredients may be purchased at different times and in different quantities, making it necessary to tie together multiple transactions over time.

Finally, the *store* entity provides information about where the products are purchased. This type of information is very important for brick-and-mortar retailers, because they can change what happens in different stores. Stores, in turn, have catchment areas that define the neighborhood (and hence demographics) of the natural market area. On the Web, the concept of *store* has less relevance. It might refer to a part of a website or to a customization of the site, leading to the idea that the web experience can be customized for specific customers or groups of customers.

The Foundation of Market Basket Analysis: Basic Measures

Basic measures are the foundation for understanding market basket data, before even starting on fancy techniques. Here are some ideas for basic measures at the level of customer orders:

- Average number of orders per customer
- Change in average number of orders per customer over time
- Average number of unique items per order
- Change in average number of unique items per order over time
- Proportion of customers and average purchase size of customers who purchase the most popular products
- Proportion of customers and average purchase size of customers who purchase the least popular products
- Average order size
- Changes in average order size over time
- Average order size by important dimensions, such as geography, method of payment, time of year, and so on

These measures give broad insight into the business. In some cases, few customers have multiple purchases, so the proportion of orders per customer is close to one, suggesting a business opportunity to increase the number of sales per customer. Or the number of products per order may be close to one, suggesting an opportunity for cross-selling during the sales process. Comparing these measures to each other can be useful.

Figure 15-2 pictures the breadth of the customer relationship (the number of unique items ever purchased) by the depth of the relationship (the number of orders) for customers who purchased more than one item from a small specialty retailer. The size of the bubble represents the number of customers who have that particular breadth and depth in their relationship. The largest bubbles, which represent the bulk of customers, are on the lower left. The bubbles become smaller higher up on the graph and to the right.

The biggest bubble shows that many customers who purchase two products do so at the same time. A surprisingly large bubble also shows that a sizeable number of customers purchase the same product in two orders. Better customers — at least those who returned multiple times — tend to purchase a greater diversity of goods. However, some customers return and purchase the same thing they bought the first time. What products prove so popular that customers buy them over and over? How can the retailer encourage customers to come back and buy more and different products? Market basket analysis cannot answer the latter question directly. It can motivate the question, provide additional information, and provide information about the additional products that good customers do purchase.

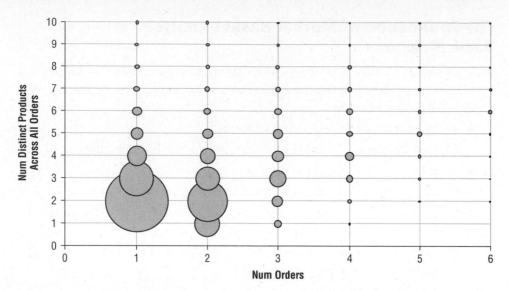

Figure 15-2: This bubble plot shows the breadth of customer relationships by the depth of the relationship.

Order Characteristics

Customer purchases have additional interesting characteristics. For instance, the average order size varies by time and region — and keeping track of these can show changes in the business environment. Such information is often available in reporting systems, because it is easily summarized.

Some information, though, may need to be gleaned from order-level data. Figure 15-3 breaks down transactions by the size of the order and the credit card used for payment — Visa, MasterCard, or American Express — for a retailer. The first thing to notice is that the larger the order, the larger the average purchase amount, regardless of the credit card used. This is reassuring. Also, the use of one credit card type, American Express, is consistently associated with larger orders — an interesting finding about these customers (especially because American Express has traditionally charged merchants higher transaction fees). Furthermore, the difference in order size by card type increases as the number of items purchased increases. For orders with eight or nine items, orders purchased with American Express are more than twice the size of those purchased with Visa.

For web purchases and mail-order transactions, additional information may also be gathered at the point of sale:

- Did the order use gift wrap?
- Is the order going to the same address as the billing address?
- Did the purchaser accept or decline a particular cross-sell offer?

Of course, gathering information at the point of sale and having it available for analysis are two different things. However, gift giving and responsiveness to cross-sell offers are two very useful things to know about customers. Finding patterns with this information requires collecting the information in the first place (at the call center or through the online interface) and then moving it to a data mining environment.

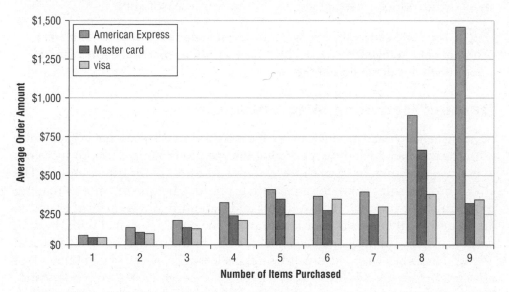

Figure 15-3: This chart shows the average amount spent by credit card type based on the number of items in the order for one particular retailer.

Item (Product) Popularity

What are the most popular items? This question can usually be answered by looking at summary data, which you can generate without having to process transaction-level data. However, knowing the sales of an individual item is only the beginning. Related questions are:

- What is the most common item found in a one-item order?
- What is the most common item found in a multi-item order?
- What is the most common item found among customers who are repeat purchasers?
- For orders that contain an item, how does the average size of the order change when the price of the item changes?
- How has the popularity of particular items changed over time?
- How does the popularity of an item vary regionally?

The first four questions suggest ideas for growing customer relationships. Association analysis can provide answers to these questions, particularly when used with virtual items to represent the size of the order or the number of orders a customer has made.

The last two questions bring up the dimensions of time and geography, which are very important for applications of market basket analysis. Different products have different affinities in different regions — something retailers are very familiar with. Association rules can be used to start to understand these areas by introducing virtual items for region and seasonality.

TIP Time and geography are two of the most important attributes of market basket data in the offline world, because they often point to the exact marketing conditions at the time of the sale.

Tracking Marketing Interventions

Looking at individual products over time is a good way to see what is happening with the product. Including marketing interventions along with product sales over time, as shown in Figure 15-4, conveys the effect of the interventions. The chart shows a sales curve for a particular product, before and after a mailing including that product. Notice that it takes about two weeks for the mail to arrive and for the increased orders to start. The peak associated with the mail drop has a duration of about six weeks. Prior to the mail drop, sales hover at about 50 units per week. Afterward, sales peak at about seven or eight times that amount, before gently sliding down over six or seven weeks. By understanding baseline orders and subtracting these out, such charts make it possible to accurately measure the response to a marketing intervention.

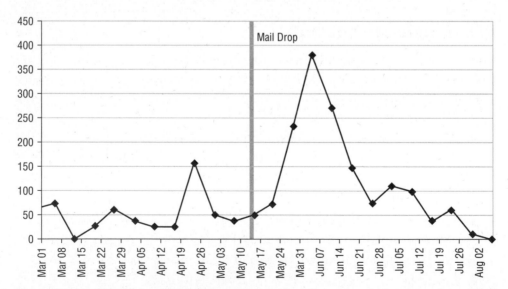

Figure 15-4: Showing marketing interventions and product sales on the same chart makes seeing effects of marketing efforts possible.

Such analysis does not require looking at individual market baskets — daily or weekly summaries of product sales are sufficient. On the other hand, the analysis does require knowing when marketing interventions take place — and sometimes getting such a calendar is the biggest challenge. Another challenge in measuring the effect of a marketing effort is determining whether the additional sales are incremental or are made by customers who would purchase the product anyway at some later time.

TIP Keep a calendar of important marketing events (both positive and negative) that might affect sales.

Analyzing market basket data can answer this question. In addition to looking at the volume of sales before and after an intervention, you can also look at the number of baskets containing the item. When sales increase but the number of customers does not, there is evidence that existing customers are simply stocking up on the item at a lower cost.

A related question is whether discounting results in additional sales of other products (ancillary purchases). Association rules can help answer this question by finding combinations of products that include those being promoted during the period of the promotion. Similarly, you might want to know whether the average size of orders increases or decreases after an intervention. These are examples of questions where more detailed transaction-level data is important.

Case Study: Spanish or English

Data mining usually focuses on customers, and hence on customer-level data. This case study instead uses summarized data that contains no information about individual customers, and this data is used to discern differences in shopping patterns between Hispanics and non-Hispanics at a chain of supermarkets in Texas. Because the demographic characteristics of individual customers are not known, this case study uses the demographic characteristics of the area served by each supermarket instead. Interesting patterns emerge when extrapolating from the stores to learn about the customers.

The Business Problem

The business problem is quite simple: should this chain of supermarkets advertise the same products in Spanish as in English? This chain is located in Texas, which, as the map in Figure 15-5 shows, has areas with very high concentrations of Hispanics. Darker shading indicates a higher concentration of this group, so the counties that border Mexico are at least two-thirds Hispanic. The proportion declines for counties farther from the Mexican border.

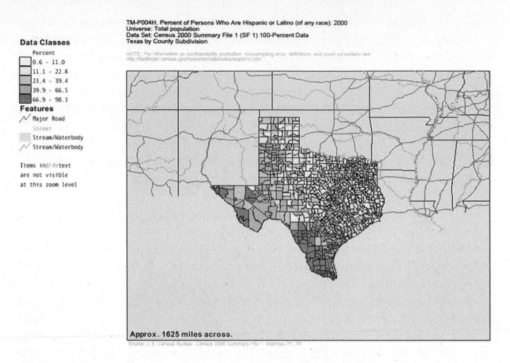

Figure 15-5: The proportion of Hispanics by county in Texas is quite high near the Mexican border, and then declines throughout the rest of the state.

Of course, not all Hispanics speak Spanish as their first language, so the match between the demographic group "Hispanic" and the advertising goal "Spanish-language" is not a perfect match. But it is good enough.

The supermarket chain did not begin this effort with a data mining project. The Spanish-language advertising was already part of its business, and the company did the easy thing: advertise the same items in Spanish as in English. Preliminary analysis at the department level showed that Hispanics and non-Hispanics purchase about the same amount in the meat department, and in the frozen food department, and in the snacks department, and so on. Perhaps out of desperation, the chain launched a data mining project to understand the differences that might distinguish these demographic groups.

The Data

The data for the project was basically a fact table from an online analytic processing system (OLAP), with three dimensions:

- Week of the year
- Product
- Store

Each row in the data described the sales of a single product at a single store for one week. The important measurements on the row included the number of units sold and total revenue for the particular product at the particular store during the particular week.

The data was also augmented with some ethnic variables describing the *catchment area* (also called *micromarket*) of each store. A catchment area is the neighborhood the majority of shoppers come from. Of course, not all shoppers come from the catchment area, and someone can live in the catchment area and never visit the store, but it is a good approximation of the local market. Catchment areas for retailers are defined by third parties such as Experian and IRI. Larger retailers often have the information for each store in the chain.

Ethnic variables in the data described the proportion of each store's neighborhood that was Hispanic and the proportion that was African-American. Actually, the data contained deciles, so "0" means that between 0 percent and 10 percent of the neighborhood is in that ethnic group.

The first analysis revealed a very uninteresting pattern: the higher the African-American decile, the lower the Hispanic decile, and vice versa. Far from saying something profound about ethnic groups in the great state of Texas, this relationship is simply a corollary of the following fact: The proportion of African Americans plus the proportion of Hispanics plus the proportion of others adds up to 1. In general, when one of the groups increases its representation, the others will go down — simply because the sum is 1. As a data miner, you must be careful about such patterns that appear because of the definition of variables.

> **WARNING**   Spurious correlations can arise when variables have relationships among themselves, such as a group of demographic variables that represent proportions whose sum is 1. When one variable increases (or decreases) the others are likely to go in the opposite direction.

Defining "Hispanicity" Preference

The original business question was: "Should Spanish-language advertisements be for the same products as English-language advertisements?" After looking at the available data, the business question was rephrased as: "What are the differences in products sold in stores with a high Hispanic catchment area versus in a low Hispanic catchment area?"

Answering this question is much more feasible with the available data. The idea is to create a *Hispanic preference score* for each product, which is the popularity of the product in stores with highly Hispanic catchment areas minus the popularity in stores whose catchment areas have few Hispanics.

This approach divides stores into three groups:

- Highly Hispanic
- Mixed
- Not very Hispanic

The Hispanic preference score ignores the stores in the middle (so this is sometimes called the *excluded middle* approach). The assumption is that if Hispanics have preferences for or against certain products, then these preferences will show up more clearly by comparing the extremes rather than the stores in the middle.

TIP When looking for patterns about a particular group of customers, using the excluded middle approach can be helpful. The difference in behavior between stores in areas where the group predominates and stores in areas where it is underrepresented may provide insight about the group in question.

The Solution

Figure 15-6 is a scatter plot, showing the Hispanic preference score on the vertical axis and products on the horizontal axis. The size of the marker shows the overall sales of the product. Points above the axis have a positive preference, meaning that highly Hispanic stores purchase more. Points below the axis mean that highly Hispanic stores purchase less. Perhaps the most interesting feature of this chart is that the business users discussed it for more than an hour — even though the products themselves are not labeled (the business users were quite familiar with the numbering system for product codes and quickly deciphered the interesting products).

What makes this chart interesting is the large marker at the top of the chart. This product is much more popular in Hispanic stores than in stores with few Hispanics in their catchment areas. The small markers at the bottom are the opposite, less popular in Hispanic catchment areas. Even without knowing the details, the chart shows that many products are equally popular in Hispanic and non-Hispanic areas — but not all of them. That is what makes the chart valuable.

What are differences in purchasing patterns? It is true that both Hispanics and non-Hispanics purchase meat, for instance. However, non-Hispanics tend to prefer beef and Hispanics have a preference for pork. Similarly, non-Hispanics prefer to snack on potato chips and French fries, whereas Hispanics prefer corn chips as snacks. What does this mean? Ads for Fourth of July picnics should be for hamburgers and potato chips in English, and perhaps for sausages and Doritos corn chips in Spanish.

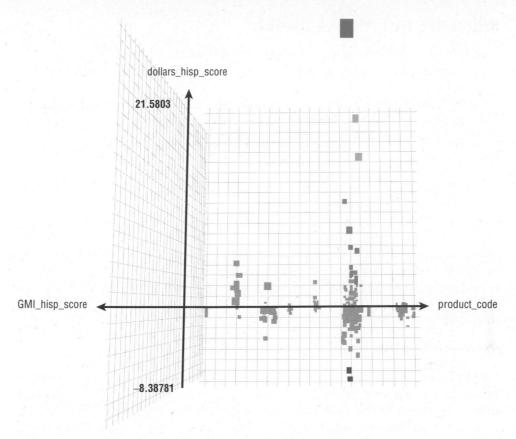

Figure 15-6: This chart shows that one product is both popular (because the cube is big) and has a high preference in Hispanic stores.

Association Analysis

One appeal of association analysis is the clarity of the results, which are in the form of rules about groups of products that appear together in orders. An association rule has an intuitive appeal because it expresses how tangible products and services group together. A rule like, *"if a customer purchases marshmallows and graham crackers, then that customer will also purchase chocolate bars,"* is clear. Even better, it might suggest a specific course of action, such as placing the items close to each other in a grocery store or providing customers with the recipe for that time-honored snack made with the aforementioned ingredients melted over an open flame.

Rules Are Not Always Useful

Although association rules are easy to understand, they are not always useful. The following three rules are examples of real rules generated from real data:

- Wal-Mart customers who purchase Barbie dolls have a 60 percent likelihood of also purchasing one of three types of candy bars.

- Customers who purchase maintenance agreements are very likely to purchase large appliances.

- When a new hardware store opens, one of the most commonly sold items is toilet bowl cleaners.

The first example is quoted in *Forbes* on September 8, 1997. These three examples illustrate the three common types of rules produced by association rules: the *actionable*, the *trivial*, and the *inexplicable*. In addition to these types of rules, the sidebar "A Famous Rule: Beer and Diapers" talks about one other category.

Actionable Rules

Useful rules contain high-quality, actionable information. After the pattern is found, justifying it by telling a story can lead to insights and action. Walmart's discovery about Barbie dolls and chocolate does not suggest that Barbie prefers chocolate bars to other forms of food. Clearly this is not a likely story, because Barbie could not maintain her inhuman figure on a diet of chocolate bars. Instead, imagine Mom going shopping with her two pre-tweens. The purpose: finding a gift for little Susie's friend, Emily, for Emily's upcoming birthday party. A Barbie doll is the perfect gift. At checkout, little Jacob starts crying. He wants something, too — a candy bar fits the bill and is conveniently at eye level for a five-year-old. Or maybe the candy bar is for Mom, because shopping for birthday gifts is exhausting and Mom needs some energy. These scenarios suggest that the candy bar is an impulse purchase added on to that of the Barbie doll.

Whether Wal-Mart can make use of this information is not clear. This rule might suggest more prominent product placement, such as ensuring that customers must walk through candy aisles on their way back from Barbie-land. It might suggest product tie-ins and promotions offering candy bars and dolls together. It might suggest particular ways to advertise the products. It might demonstrate that having candy bars at eye level for five-year-old children is a good idea. Because the rule is easily understood, it suggests plausible causes and possible actions.

A FAMOUS RULE: BEER AND DIAPERS

Perhaps the most talked-about association rule ever "found" is the association between beer and diapers. This is a famous story dating back from the late 1980s or early 1990s, when computers were just getting powerful enough to analyze reasonably large volumes of data. The setting is somewhere in the United States, where a retailer is analyzing point of sale data to find interesting patterns.

Lo and behold, lurking in all the data is the remarkable fact that beer and diapers sell together. This immediately sets marketing minds in motion to explain what is happening. A flash of insight provides the explanation: beer drinkers do not want to interrupt their enjoyment of televised sports, so they buy diapers to reduce trips to the bathroom. No, that's not it! The more likely story is that families with young children are preparing for the weekend — diapers for the kids and beer for Daddy. Daddy probably knows that after he has a few beers, Mommy will change the diapers.

This is a powerful story. Setting aside the analytics, what can a retailer do with this information? There are two competing views. One says to put the beer and diapers close together, so when one is purchased, customers remember to buy the other one. The other says to put them as far apart as possible, so the customer must walk by as many stocked shelves as possible, having the opportunity to buy yet more items. The store could also put higher-margin diapers a bit closer to the beer, although mixing baby products and alcohol might be unseemly in some neighborhoods.

The story is so powerful that the authors have noticed at least five companies using the story — IBM, Tandem (now part of HP), Oracle, Teradata, and SAS. The actual story was debunked on April 6, 1998, in an article in *Forbes* magazine called "Beer-Diaper Syndrome."

The debunked story still has a lesson. Apparently, the sales of beer and diapers were known to be correlated, at least in some stores. The correlations could be seen in inventory curves, which show how much of each item is available in each store by day or by week. For managers working in the stores, the hypothesis is quite obvious: a customer carrying both beer and diapers stands out when he or she finishes paying because these are such bulky items.

While doing a demonstration project for Teradata for a chain of drug stores in Wisconsin, Thomas Blischok, a sales manager, suggested that the demo show something interesting, like "beer and diapers being sold together." With this small hint, analysts were able to find evidence in the data. Actually, the moral of the story is not about the power of association rules to find unexpected patterns. The moral is that hypothesis testing and exploratory data analysis, even using simple query tools, can be very persuasive and actionable. With such tools, you, too, may discover a pattern that becomes data mining legend.

Trivial Rules

Trivial results are already known by anyone at all familiar with the business. The second example ("Customers who purchase maintenance agreements are very likely to purchase large appliances") is an example of a trivial rule. In fact, customers typically purchase maintenance agreements and large appliances at the same time. Why else would someone purchase a maintenance agreement? The two are advertised together, and rarely sold separately (although when sold separately, it is almost always the large appliance sold without the maintenance agreement rather than the other way around). This rule, though, was found after analyzing millions of point-of-sale transactions from Sears, and published at a conference once upon a time.

As a rule, the result is valid and well-supported by the data. It demonstrates the power of the algorithms that find association rules. However, it is a lousy example of data mining. As Chapter 1 emphasizes, the purpose of data mining is to find patterns that are meaningful, and this rule is useless. Similar results abound: people who buy two-by-fours also purchase nails; customers who purchase paint buy paint brushes; oil and oil filters are purchased together, as are hamburgers and hamburger buns, and charcoal and lighter fluid.

A subtler problem falls into the same category. A seemingly interesting result — such as the fact that people who buy cable service from their local telephone service provider almost always buy Internet access as well — may be the result of marketing programs and product bundles. In this case, cable, telephone, and Internet are often bundled together (as the "triple-play option"). The analysis does not produce actionable results; it produces already acted-upon results. Although a danger for any data mining technique, association analysis is particularly susceptible to reproducing the success of previous marketing campaigns because of its dependence on unsummarized point-of-sale data — exactly the same data that defines the success of the campaign. Results from association analysis may simply be measuring the success of previous marketing campaigns.

Trivial rules do have one use, although it is not directly a data mining use. Some rules may be almost 100 percent true. The few cases where these rules do not hold provide a lot of information about data quality. That is, the exceptions to very highly confidence rules point to areas where business operations, data collection, and processing may need to be further refined.

Inexplicable Rules

Inexplicable results seem to have no explanation and do not suggest a course of action. The third pattern ("When a new hardware store opens, one of the most commonly sold items is toilet bowl cleaner") is intriguing, tempting us with a new fact but providing information that does not give insight into consumer behavior or the merchandise or suggest further actions. In this case, a large hardware company discovered the pattern for new store openings, but could not figure out how to profit from it. Many items are on sale during the store openings, but the toilet bowl cleaners stood out. More investigation might give some explanation. One possibility is that new hardware stores often open near new subdivisions, and new home owners need to stock up on toilet bowl cleaner. On the other hand, the result could be just an anomaly from a handful of stores. Whatever the cause, it is doubtful that further analysis of just the market basket data can give a credible explanation.

WARNING **When you're applying market basket analysis, many of the results are often either *trivial* or *inexplicable*. Trivial rules reproduce common knowledge about the business, wasting the effort used to apply sophisticated analysis techniques. Inexplicable rules are flukes in the data and are not actionable.**

Item Sets to Association Rules

Association rules start with transactions containing one or more product or service offerings and some rudimentary information about the transaction. For the purpose of analysis, the products and service offerings are referred to as *items*. Table 15-1 illustrates five transactions from a grocery store. These transactions have been simplified to include only the items purchased. How to use information like the date and time and whether the customer paid with cash or a credit card is discussed later in this chapter.

Table 15-1: Grocery Point-of-Sale Transactions

CUSTOMER	ITEMS
1	Orange juice, soda
2	Milk, orange juice, window cleaner
3	Orange juice, detergent
4	Orange juice, detergent, soda
5	Window cleaner, soda

Each of these transactions gives information about which products are purchased with which other products. This information is shown in a co-occurrence table that tells the number of times that any pair of products was purchased together (see Table 15-2). For instance, the box where the "Soda" row intersects the "OJ" column has a value of "2," indicating that two transactions contain both items. This is easily verified against the original transaction data, where customers 1 and 4 purchased both these items. The values along the diagonal (for instance, the value in the "OJ" column and the "OJ" row) represent the number of transactions containing that item.

Table 15-2: Co-Occurrence of Products

	OJ	WINDOW CLEANER	MILK	SODA	DETERGENT
OJ	4	1	1	2	1
Window Cleaner	1	2	1	1	0
Milk	1	1	1	0	0
Soda	2	1	0	3	1
Detergent	1	0	0	1	2

This co-occurrence table already highlights some simple patterns:

- Orange juice and soda are more likely to be purchased together than any other two items.

- Detergent is never purchased with window cleaner or milk.

- Milk is never purchased with soda or detergent.

These observations are examples of associations. A combination of items is called an *item set*, so the combination of soda and orange juice is an item set that appears in two transactions. In this simple example, it is the only pair of items that appears more than once. Several item sets containing two products, three products, and four products appear in this data.

Item sets are often interesting themselves. In the beer-and-diapers example, for instance, the interesting fact is that the two are purchased together; there is no need to consider rules such as, "If a customer purchases beer, then the customer purchases diapers," or the inverse, "If a customer purchases diapers, then the customer purchases beer." In other cases, the goal is to turn the item set into an association rule, such as, "*If a customer purchases soda, then the customer also purchases orange juice.*"

Such rules are derived from item sets. A single item set has several potential rules. The most interesting are usually the rules that have one product on the right-hand side (after the "then") and zero or more items on the left-hand side (after the "if"). The rule is structured to imply that the presence of the items on the left implies the presence of the item on the right. Let's defer discussion of how to find item sets and rules, and instead ask another question: how good is a particular rule?

How Good Is an Association Rule?

Any given set of transaction data is going to have many possible item sets, and these item sets are going to suggest even more rules. For a few hundred products, the number of combinations quickly climbs into the millions. The association rules technique has to separate the strong from the weak, so from the vast number of possible rules, only the best are chosen. The three traditional methods for measuring the goodness of an association rule are support, confidence, and lift. These measures come from the original work done in this area in the machine learning community. In addition these measures, this section also explains an alternative one, the chi-square test, which is described in Chapter 4, because it often produces a better set of rules.

Support

Support measures the number or proportion of transactions that contain all the items in the rule. Support is typically measured in one of three ways:

- As a count of the number of transactions containing all the items in the rule.
- The count divided by the total number of transactions.
- Less commonly, the count divided by the total number of transactions that have enough items for the rule to apply. This takes into account, for instance, that transactions with only one item are not considered for a rule that contains two or more items.

All rules using the same items — regardless of which items appear after the "then" — have the same support.

In the earlier data, two of the five transactions include both soda and orange juice. These two transactions *support* the rule, "if soda, then orange juice." The support for the rule is two out of five, or 40 percent of all transactions. Because all five transactions have at least two items, the support is still 40 percent, even taking into account the number of items in the rule.

Confidence

Confidence measures how good a rule is at predicting the right-hand side (after the "then" clause of the rule), by comparing how often the right-hand side appears when the condition on the left-hand side (after the "if" clause of the rule) is true. For example, two of the three transactions that contain soda also contain orange juice, implying a high degree of *confidence* in the rule, "if soda, then orange juice." In fact, the confidence is 67 percent.

The inverse rule, *"if orange juice, then soda,"* has a lower confidence. Of the four transactions with orange juice, only two also have soda. Its confidence, then, is 50 percent. Confidence is calculated as the ratio of the number of the transactions supporting the entire rule to the number of transactions supporting the left-hand side of the rule. Another way of saying this is that confidence is the ratio of the number of transactions with all the items to the number of transactions with just the "if" items.

Lift

Confidence tells you how good a rule is at predicting what is on the right-hand side. However, the items on the right-hand side might already be very common, so the rule may not be telling us anything. *Lift* (also called *improvement*) measures the power of the rule by comparing the full rule to randomly guessing the right-hand side. Here, *randomly guessing* means comparing the confidence of the rule to the confidence of the null rule. The null rule has the same item on the right-hand size, but the left-hand side is empty.

Lift is calculated as the ratio of the confidence of the rule to the prevalence of the right-hand side. In the example rule, "if soda, then orange juice," the confidence is 67 percent. However, 80 percent of the transactions contain orange juice, so the rule actually does worse than simply guessing!

Chi-Square Value

The chi-square test produces a useful measure that can be applied to association rules. The chi-square test, as Chapter 4 explains, is used to determine when the cells of a contingency table are produced randomly — or when something more interesting is going on. A *contingency table* is used to compare two dimensions that take on categorical values. The table itself is a record of counts, where each record in the data is counted in exactly one cell of the table (which particular cell depends on the values in the two dimensions). The chi-square value measures the probability that the contingency table could be produced by chance. When the probability is high (and hence, the chi-square value is low), the table is similar to a table produced randomly, so the two dimensions that define the table are probably not interacting with each other. When the probability is low (and hence, the chi-square value is high), the two dimensions are probably interrelated — something is going on.

It may not be immediately obvious, but an association rule has an associated contingency table, as shown in Figure 15-7. The two dimensions are:

- Whether or not the items in the left-hand side of the rule are present in the transaction

- Whether or not the items in the right-hand side of the rule are present in the transaction

The counts of the transactions are in the cells of the table.

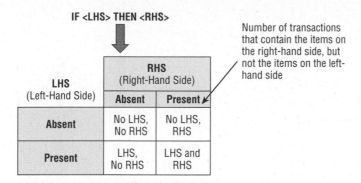

Figure 15-7: An association rule has a corresponding contingency table, where the two dimensions are based on the two sides of the rule. The cells in the table contain counts of the number of transactions that appear or do not appear on either side.

The chi-square value, as calculated from the contingency table, measures the probability that the table is produced by a random splitting of the data. An interesting rule would not split the data randomly, so the higher the chi-square value (and hence, the less likely the split is due to chance), then the better the rule. In practice, the authors have found the chi-square value to be very useful for selecting rules.

Working with the chi-square value does have one caveat. Consider the two rules:

- IF <LHS> THEN <RHS>
- IF <LHS> THEN NOT <RHS>

Both these rules produce the same contingency table, and hence have the same chi-square value. An additional test is needed (lift is a good measure) to determine which is the better rule.

Building Association Rules

This basic process for finding association rules is illustrated in Figure 15-8. Three important concerns when creating association rules are:

- Choosing the right set of items.
- Generating rules by deciphering the counts in the co-occurrence matrix.
- Overcoming the practical limits imposed by thousands or tens of thousands of items.

The next three sections delve into these concerns in more detail.

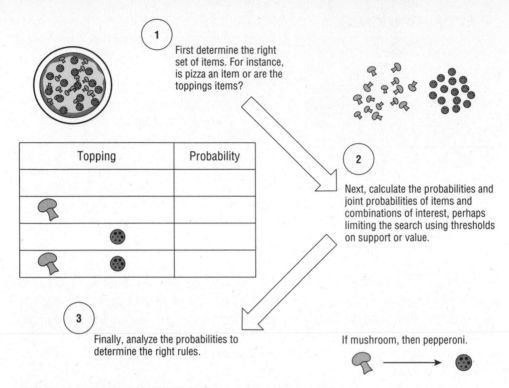

Figure 15-8: Finding association rules has these basic steps.

Choosing the Right Set of Items

Traditionally, the data used for finding association rules is the detailed transaction data captured at the point of sale. Gathering and using this data is a critical part of applying market basket analysis, and the results depend crucially on the items chosen for analysis. As mentioned in the case study on Spanish language marketing, the grocery store chain had already looked at preferences at the department level, and found no interesting patterns, although interesting patterns were found lower down the product hierarchy.

What constitutes a particular item depends on the business need. Within a grocery store where tens of thousands of products are on the shelves, a frozen pizza might be considered an item for analysis purposes — regardless of its toppings (extra cheese, pepperoni, or mushrooms), its crust (extra thick, whole wheat, or white), or its size. So, the purchase of a large whole-wheat vegetarian pizza contains the same "frozen pizza" item as the purchase of a single-serving pepperoni pizza with extra cheese. A sample of such transactions at this summarized level might look like Table 15-3.

Table 15-3: Transactions with More Summarized Items

CUSTOMER	PIZZA	MILK	SUGAR	APPLES	COFFEE
1	X				
2		X	X		
3	X			X	X
4		X			X
5	X		X	X	X

On the other hand, the manager of frozen foods or a chain of pizza restaurants may be very interested in the particular combinations of toppings that are ordered. He or she might decompose a pizza order into constituent parts, with items such as those in Table 15-4.

Table 15-4: Transactions with More Detailed Items

CUSTOMER	EXTRA CHEESE	ONIONS	PEPPERS	MUSHROOMS	OLIVES
1	X	X			X
2			X		
3	X	X		X	
4		X			X
5	X		X	X	X

At some later point in time, the grocery store may become interested in having more detail in its transactions, so the single "frozen pizza" item would no longer be sufficient. Or the pizza restaurants might broaden their menu choices and become less interested in all the different toppings. *The items of interest may vary over time or even at the same time depending on the analysis.* This can pose a problem when trying to use historical data if different levels of detail have been removed or if product hierarchies are no longer available or frequently change.

Choosing the right level of detail is a critical consideration for the analysis. If the transaction data in the grocery store keeps track of every type, brand, and size of frozen pizza — which probably account for several dozen products — then all these items need to map up to the "frozen pizza" item for analysis.

Product Hierarchies Help to Generalize Items

In the real world, items have product codes and stock-keeping unit codes (SKUs) that fall into hierarchical categories, called a *product hierarchy* or *taxonomy*, illustrated in Figure 15-9. What level of the product hierarchy is the right one to use? This brings up issues such as:

- Are large fries and small fries the same product?
- Is the brand of ice cream more relevant than its flavor?
- Which is more important: the size, style, pattern, or designer of clothing?
- Is the energy-saving option on a large appliance indicative of customer behavior?

The number of combinations to consider grows very fast as the number of items used in the analysis increases. This suggests using items from higher levels of the product hierarchy, such as "frozen desserts" instead of "Ben & Jerry's Cherry Garcia" ice cream. On the other hand, the more specific the items are, the more likely the results are to be actionable. Knowing what sells with a particular brand of frozen pizza, for instance, can help in managing the relationship with the manufacturer. One compromise is to use more general

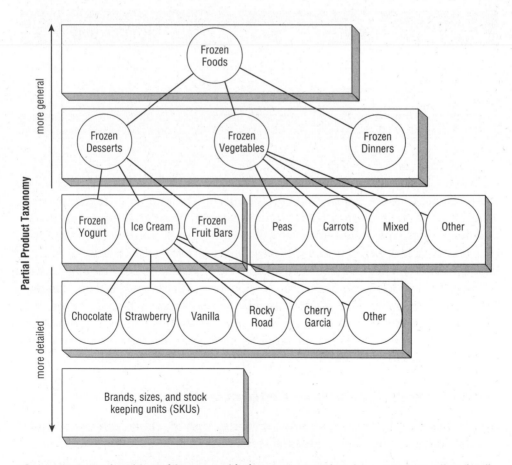

Figure 15-9: Product hierarchies start with the most general and move to increasing detail.

items initially, then to repeat the rule generation to hone in on more specific items. As the analysis focuses on more specific items, use only the subset of transactions containing those items.

The complexity of a rule refers to the number of items it contains. The more different types of items in the transactions, the longer it takes to generate rules of a given complexity. The desired complexity of the rules has an impact on how specific or general the items should be. In some circumstances, customers do not purchase many different items. For instance, customers purchase relatively few items at any one time at a convenience store or through some catalogs, so looking for rules containing four or more items may apply to very few transactions and be a wasted effort. In other cases, such as in supermarkets, the average transaction is larger, so more complex rules are useful.

Moving up the product hierarchy reduces the number of items. Dozens or hundreds of items may be reduced to a single generalized item, often corresponding to a single department or product line. An item like a pint of Ben & Jerry's Cherry Garcia gets generalized to "ice cream" or "frozen foods." Instead of investigating "orange juice," investigate "fruit juices," and so on. Often, the appropriate level of the hierarchy ends up matching a department with a product-line manager; so using categories has the practical effect of finding interdepartmental relationships. Generalized items also help find rules with sufficient support. There will be many more transactions supporting a given rule at higher levels of the taxonomy than at lower levels.

TIP Market basket analysis produces the best results when the items occur in roughly the same number of transactions in the data. This helps prevent rules from being dominated by the most common items. Product hierarchies can help here. Roll up rare items to higher levels in the hierarchy, so they become more frequent. More common items may not have to be rolled up at all.

Just because some items are generalized does not mean that all items need to move up to the same level. The appropriate level depends on the item, on its importance for producing actionable results, and on its frequency in the data. For instance, in a department store, big-ticket items (such as appliances) might stay at a low level in the hierarchy, whereas less expensive items (such as books) might be higher. This hybrid approach is also useful when looking at individual products. Because thousands of products often are in the data, generalize everything other than the product or products of interest.

Virtual Items Go Beyond the Product Hierarchy

The purpose of virtual items is to enable the analysis to take advantage of information that goes beyond the product hierarchy. Virtual items do not appear in the product hierarchy of the original items, because they cross product boundaries. Examples of virtual items might be designer labels, such as Calvin Klein, that appear in both apparel departments and perfumes; low-fat and no-fat products in a grocery store; and energy-saving options on appliances.

Virtual items may even include information about the transactions themselves, such as whether the purchase was made with cash, a credit card, or check, and the day of the week or the time of day the transaction occurred. However, crowding the data with too many virtual items is not a good idea. *Only include virtual items when you have some idea of how they could result in actionable information if found in well-supported, high-confidence association rules.*

There is a danger, though. Virtual items can cause trivial rules. For instance, imagine that there is a virtual item for "diet product" and one for "Coke product"; then a rule might appear like:

If "Coke product" and "diet product," then "diet Coke"

That is, everywhere that "Coke" appears in a basket and "diet product" appears in a basket, then "diet Coke" also appears. Every basket that has Diet Coke satisfies this rule. Although some baskets may have regular Coke and other diet products, the rule will have high lift because it defines Diet Coke. When using virtual items, checking and rechecking the rules to be sure that such trivial rules are not arising is worth your time. One way to avoid creating such rules is to not consider rules when the virtual items come from the same product. With this restriction, only virtual items that appear in different products are included in rules, and such trivial rules are not produced. To implement such a method requires writing your own association rule code, which you can accomplish in SQL as described in *Data Analysis Using SQL and Excel.*

A similar but more subtle danger occurs when the right-hand side of a rule does not include the associated item. So, a rule like:

If "Coke product" and "diet product," then "pretzels"

probably means,

If "diet Coke," then "pretzels"

The danger from having such rules is that they can obscure what is happening.

TIP When applying market basket analysis, you should have a hierarchical taxonomy of the items being considered for analysis. By carefully choosing the levels of the hierarchy, these generalized items should occur about the same number of times in the data, improving the results of the analysis. For specific lifestyle-related choices that provide insight into customer behavior, such as sugar-free items and specific brands, augment the data with virtual items.

Data Quality

The data used for market basket analysis is not necessarily of very high quality. It is gathered directly at the point of customer contact and used mainly for operational purposes such as inventory control. The data is likely to have multiple formats, corrections, incompatible code types, and so on. Much of the explanation of various code values is likely to be buried deep in programming code running in legacy systems and may be difficult to extract. Different stores within a single chain sometimes have different product hierarchies or different ways of handling situations such as discounts.

Here is an example. The authors were once curious about the approximately 80 department codes present in a large set of transaction data. The client assured us that their stores had only 40 departments and provided a nice description of each one. More careful inspection revealed the problem. Some stores had point-of-sale devices provided by IBM and others used devices provided by NCR. The two types of equipment had different ways of representing department codes — hence, two incompatible sets of codes for the 40 departments.

These kinds of problems are typical when analyzing any sort of data. However, they are exacerbated for market basket analysis because this type of analysis depends heavily on the unsummarized point-of-sale transactions.

Anonymous Versus Identified

Market basket analysis has proven useful for mass-market retail, such as super-markets, convenience stores, drug stores, and fast food chains, where many of the purchases have been made with cash. Cash transactions are anonymous, meaning that the store has no knowledge about specific customers because there is no information identifying the customer in the transaction. For anonymous transactions, the only information is the date and time, the location of the store, the cashier, the items purchased, any coupons redeemed, and the amount of change. With market basket analysis, even this limited data can yield interesting and actionable results.

The increasing prevalence of registration on websites, loyalty programs, and purchasing clubs has resulted in more and more identified transactions, providing analysts with more possibilities for information about customers and their behavior over time. Demographic and trending information is available on individuals and households to further augment customer profiles. This additional information can be incorporated into association rule analysis using virtual items.

Generating Rules from All This Data

Calculating the number of times that an item set appears in the transaction data is well and good, but a combination of items is not a rule. Sometimes, just the combination is interesting in itself, as in the Barbie doll and candy bar example. But in other circumstances, finding an underlying rule of the form makes more sense:

if condition, then result

As an example, the rule:

if Barbie doll, then candy bar

is read as, "If a customer purchases a Barbie doll, then the customer is also expected to purchase a candy bar at the same time." The general practice is to consider rules where just one item is on the right-hand side. Table 15-5 shows some summaries of items in transactions. These summaries are useful for showing the calculations needed to turn an item set into rules. In this example, there are only three items, A, B, and C.

Table 15-5: Probabilities of Three Items and Their Combinations

COMBINATION	PROBABILITY
A	45.0%
B	42.5%
C	40.0%
A and B	25.0%
A and C	20.0%
B and C	15.0%
A and B and C	5.0%

Calculating Support

There are three rules with all three items in the rule and one item on the right-hand side:

- If *A* and *B*, then *C*
- If *A* and *C*, then *B*
- If *B* and *C*, then *A*

Because these three rules contain the same items, they have the same support, 5 percent (of all transactions). Only counting transactions that have at least three items (where the rule could apply), these rules have 100 percent support. In this case, counting only transactions where the rule could apply does not make sense.

Calculating Confidence

Confidence is the ratio of the number of transactions with all the items in the rule to the number of transactions with just the items on the left-hand side. The confidence for the three rules is shown in Table 15-6.

Table 15-6: Confidence in Rules

RULE	P(CONDITION)	P(CONDITION AND RESULT)	CONFIDENCE
If A and B, then C	25%	5%	20%
If A and C, then B	20%	5%	25%
If B and C, then A	15%	5%	33%

What is confidence really saying? The rule, *"if B and C, then A,"* has confidence of 33 percent. In other words, when B and C appear in a transaction, there is a 33 percent chance that A also appears in it. That is, one time in three, A occurs with B and C, and the other two times, B and C appear without A.

Calculating Lift

As described earlier, lift is a good measure of how much better the rule is doing. It is the ratio of the density of the target (using the left-hand side of the rule) to the density of the target overall. So the formula is:

$$lift = \frac{\dfrac{p(condition\ and\ result)}{p(condition)}}{p(result)} = \frac{p(condition\ and\ result)}{p(condition)\ p(result)}$$

When lift is greater than 1, then the resulting rule is better at predicting the result than guessing whether the right-hand side of the rule is present based on item frequencies in the data. When lift is less than 1, the rule is doing worse than informed guessing. Table 15-7 shows the lift for the three rules and for the rule with the best lift.

Table 15-7: Lift Measurements for Four Rules

RULE	SUPPORT	CONFIDENCE	P(RESULT)	LIFT
If A and B, then C	5%	20%	40.0%	0.50
If A and C, then B	5%	25%	42.5%	0.59
If B and C, then A	5%	33%	45.0%	0.74
If A, then B	25%	59%	42.5%	1.31

None of the rules with three items shows an improvement over just guessing. The best rule in the data actually only has two items. When "A" is purchased, then "B" is 31 percent more likely to be in the transaction than if "A" is not purchased. In this case, as in many cases, the best rule actually contains fewer items than other rules under consideration.

The Negative Rule

When lift is less than 1, *negating* the result produces a better rule. If the rule:

if A and B, then C

has confidence of 20 percent, then the rule:

if A and B, then NOT C

has confidence of 80 percent. Because C appears in 40 percent of the transactions, it does *not* appear in 60 percent of them. Applying the same lift measure shows that the lift of this new rule is 1.33 (0.80/0.60), better than any of the other rules with three items.

Calculating Chi-Square

The chi-square value is easy to calculate. However, not enough information appears in Table 15-5 to make the calculation, because the chi-square calculation requires counts, rather than percentages. Also, more information is needed about where items do not occur. Table 15-8 shows a summary of the transactions using counts. This data results in the same percentages as Table 15-5.

Table 15-8: Transaction Counts for Data in Table 15-5

GROUPING	COUNT	PROPORTION
A only	100	5%
B only	150	8%
C only	200	10%
AB only	400	20%
AC only	300	15%
BC only	200	10%
ABC only	100	5%
None	550	28%

Consider the rule, "if A and B, then C." To turn this into a contingency table, each transaction needs to be placed into one of the following four categories:

- Not both A and B, and Not C
- Not both A and B, and C
- A and B and Not C
- A and B and C

These groups, in turn, can be sized based on the information in Table 15-8:

- Not both A and B, and Not C: A only, B only, and none
- Not both A and B, and C: C only, AC only, and BC only
- A and B and Not C: AB only
- A and B and C: ABC only

Notice that each of the eight groups is counted exactly once.

This is enough information to calculate the chi-square value, as shown in Table 15-9. The overall chi-square is the sum of the cell chi-square values, which is 111.1. In this case, the splits associated with the rule are significant.

Table 15-9: Chi-Square Calculation for the Rule, "If A and B, then C"

	COUNTS		EXPECTED VALUES		CHI-SQUARE	
	NOT C	**C**	**NOT C**	**C**	**NOT C**	**C**
NOT AB	800	700	900	600	11.1	16.7
AB	400	100	300	200	33.3	50.0

The chi-square value has one catch. The rules, "if A and B, then C" and "if A and B, then not C," produce the same chi-square value. The chi-square calculation has determined that these rules are significant, but which one? Answering that question requires returning to the concept of lift. The lift for the positive rule is 0.5. The rule for the negative rule is 1.33. Both are significant, but the negative rule is useful because it has a lift greater than 1. The rule chosen by the chi-square metric is, "if A and B, then not C."

Overcoming Practical Limits

Generating association rules is a multi-step process. The general algorithm is:

1. Generate counts for single items.
2. Generate the co-occurrence matrix for two items. Use this to find rules with two items.
3. Generate the co-occurrence matrix for three items. Use this to find rules with three items.
4. And so on.

In other words, the process requires counting the frequencies of many item sets.

In the grocery store that sells orange juice, milk, detergent, soda, and window cleaner, the first step calculates the counts for each of these items. During the second step, the following counts are created:

- Orange juice and milk, orange juice and detergent, orange juice and soda, and orange juice and cleaner

- Milk and detergent, milk and soda, milk and cleaner
- Detergent and soda, detergent and cleaner
- Soda and cleaner

This is a total of 10 pairs of items. The third pass takes all combinations of three items and so on. Of course, each of these stages may require a separate pass through the data, or multiple stages can be combined into a single pass by considering different numbers of combinations at the same time.

Although it is not obvious with just five items, increasing the number of items in the combinations requires exponentially more computation, and exponentially growing runtimes — and long, long waits when considering combinations with more than three or four items. The solution is *pruning*. Pruning item sets is a technique for reducing the number of items and combinations of items considered at each step. At each stage, the algorithm throws out a certain number of combinations that do not meet some threshold criterion.

The most common pruning method is called *minimum support pruning*, which requires that a rule have the support of a minimum number of transactions. For instance, if you have one million transactions and the minimum support is 1 percent, then only rules supported by 10,000 transactions are of interest. This makes sense, because the purpose of generating these rules is to pursue some sort of action — such as striking a deal with Mattel (the makers of Barbie dolls) to make a candy bar–eating doll — and the action must affect enough transactions to be worthwhile.

The minimum support constraint has a cascading effect. Consider a rule with four items in it:

if A, B, and C, then D

Using minimum support pruning, this rule has to be true on at least 10,000 transactions in the data. It follows that:

- A must appear in at least 10,000 transactions
- B must appear in at least 10,000 transactions
- C must appear in at least 10,000 transactions
- D must appear in at least 10,000 transactions

In other words, minimum support pruning eliminates items that do not appear in enough transactions. The threshold criterion applies to each step in the algorithm. The minimum threshold also implies that:

- A and B must appear together in at least 10,000 transactions
- A and C must appear together in at least 10,000 transactions
- A and D must appear together in at least 10,000 transactions
- And so on

Each step of the calculation of the co-occurrence table can eliminate combinations of items that do not meet the threshold, reducing its size and the number of combinations to consider during the next pass.

Figure 15-10 shows an example of calculating rules. In this example, choosing a minimum support level of 10 percent would eliminate all the combinations with three items — and their associated rules — from consideration. This is an example where minimum support pruning does not have an effect on the best rule because the best rule has only two items. In the case of pizza, these toppings are all fairly common, so are not pruned individually. If anchovies were included in the analysis — and only 15 pizzas contain them out of the 2,000 — then a minimum support of 10 percent, or even 1 percent, would eliminate anchovies during the first pass.

The best choice for minimum support depends on the data and the situation. Another possibility is to vary the minimum support as the algorithm progresses. For instance, using different levels at different stages, you can find uncommon combinations of common items (by decreasing the support level for successive steps) or relatively common combinations of uncommon items (by increasing the support level).

The Problem of Big Data

A typical fast food restaurant offers several dozen items on its menu, say 100. To use probabilities to generate association rules, counts have to be calculated for each combination of items. The number of combinations of a given size grows exponentially. A combination with three items might be a small fries, cheeseburger, and medium Diet Coke. On a menu with 100 items, how many combinations are there with three different menu items? There are 161,700! (This calculation is based on the binomial formula.) On the other hand, a typical supermarket has at least 10,000 different items in stock, and more typically 20,000 or 30,000.

Calculating the support, confidence, and lift quickly gets out of hand as the number of items in the combinations grows. Such a grocery store has almost 50 million possible combinations of two items and more than 100 billion combinations of three items. Although computers are getting more powerful and processing power cheaper, calculating the counts for this number of combinations is still very time-consuming. Calculating the counts for five or more items is prohibitively expensive. The use of product hierarchies reduces the number of items to a manageable size.

The number of transactions is also very large. In the course of a year, a decent-size chain of supermarkets can generate hundreds of millions of transactions. Each of these transactions consists of one or more items, often several dozen at a time. So, determining whether a particular combination of items is present in a particular transaction may require a bit of effort — multiplied a million-fold for all the transactions.

A pizza restaurant has sold 2000 pizzas, of which:
100 are mushroom only, 150 are pepperoni, 200 are extra cheese.
400 are mushroom and pepperoni, 300 are mushroom and extra cheese, 200 are pepperoni and extra cheese.
100 are mushroom, pepperoni, and extra cheese.
550 have no extra toppings.

We need to calculate the probabilities for all possible combinations of items.

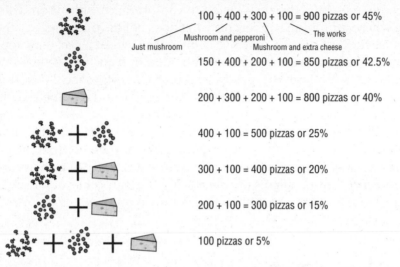

100 + 400 + 300 + 100 = 900 pizzas or 45%

Just mushroom   Mushroom and pepperoni   The works
                 Mushroom and extra cheese

150 + 400 + 200 + 100 = 850 pizzas or 42.5%

200 + 300 + 200 + 100 = 800 pizzas or 40%

400 + 100 = 500 pizzas or 25%

300 + 100 = 400 pizzas or 20%

200 + 100 = 300 pizzas or 15%

100 pizzas or 5%

There are three rules with all three items:

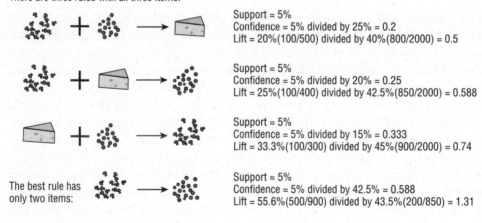

Support = 5%
Confidence = 5% divided by 25% = 0.2
Lift = 20%(100/500) divided by 40%(800/2000) = 0.5

Support = 5%
Confidence = 5% divided by 20% = 0.25
Lift = 25%(100/400) divided by 42.5%(850/2000) = 0.588

Support = 5%
Confidence = 5% divided by 15% = 0.333
Lift = 33.3%(100/300) divided by 45%(900/2000) = 0.74

The best rule has only two items:

Support = 5%
Confidence = 5% divided by 42.5% = 0.588
Lift = 55.6%(500/900) divided by 43.5%(200/850) = 1.31

Figure 15-10: This example shows how to count up the frequencies on pizza sales for market basket analysis.

Extending the Ideas

The basic ideas of association rules can be applied to different areas, such as comparing different stores and making some enhancements to the definition of the rules. These are discussed in this section.

Different Items on the Right- and Left-Hand Sides

The examples for association rules, so far, have assumed that the same items can appear on the left- and right-hand side of the rules, leading to an undirected data mining technique. Association rules can also be used in a more directed fashion by having the left- and right-hand sides have different types of items. A case study describing this technique will clarify this approach.

The case study involves a company that does e-mail marketing. It sends out offers, on behalf of other companies, to e-mail lists. For the purposes of this example, a recipient can take three actions:

- Do nothing, which is by far the most common action.
- Click on the e-mail, indicating interest in the e-mail.
- Complain about the e-mail as unwanted spam.

The first of these actions has no benefit and basically no cost (because e-mail is quite inexpensive to send). The second generates revenue for the company, so it is quite important. The third is a cost, and a big cost. If too many customers complain at a particular ISP (Internet service provider), then the ISP might reject all e-mail offers from the company.

Over time, many people on the company's e-mail list receive multiple e-mails, and each e-mail has an offer-type classification. Its historical data contained numerous examples of customers clicking on email, and many fewer examples of customers complaining. The very first time a customer complains, the customer is removed from all email lists.

How could association rules help this company? Clicks and complaints are different events, even though both are driven by the same content in the email offer. Traditional association rules cannot help in this case. Instead, the solution was to create association rules with *clicks* on the left-hand side and *complaints* on the right-hand side. In particular, the analysis asked the question: what offer types lead to complaints when customers have already clicked on other offers? The resulting rules were of the form:

> *If a customer clicks on offer type A and the customer clicks on offer type B, then the customer is likely to complain on offer type C.*

Figure 15-11 shows some examples of combinations of click offers that lead to complaints on other offers. Two things stand out from this table. The first is that offers of credit reports are associated with complaint clicks, presumably because such offers look a lot like spam. The second is that offers in categories that are quite different from those a customer has clicked on previously are likely to lead to complaints.

Clicks Imply Complaint Rules	Chi-Square
Telecom + Travel ==> Loans	299.0
Telecom + Government Grants ==> Credit Report	299.0
Government Grants + Gifts ==> Credit Report	299.0
Education + College/Scholarship ==> [Uncategorized]	149.0
Debt + Telecom ==> Credit Report	149.0
Debt + Government Grants ==> Credit Report	149.0
Debt + Gifts ==> Credit Report	149.0
Credit Card + Travel ==> Loans	99.0
Credit Card + Government Grants ==> Credit Report	99.0
Entrepreneurial + Credit Report ==> Home Improvement	74.0

Figure 15-11: Some combinations of clicks on e-mail offer types are more likely to lead to complaints on subsequent offers.

Creating these association rules required writing special-purpose code, using the SQL query language. The authors are not familiar with any data mining tools that allow the items on the left-hand side and right-hand side of rules to be different. Also, this example used the chi-square test to find the most important rules. Most data mining tools that implement association rules use support, confidence, and lift for rule selection.

Using Association Rules to Compare Stores

Market basket analysis can be used to make comparisons between locations within a single chain. The rule about toilet bowl cleaner sales in hardware stores is an example where sales at new stores are compared to sales at existing stores. Different stores exhibit different selling patterns for many reasons: regional trends, the effectiveness of management, dissimilar advertising, and varying demographic patterns among their customers, for example. Air conditioners and fans are often purchased during heat waves, but heat waves affect only a limited region. Within smaller areas, demographics of the catchment area can have a large impact; stores in wealthy areas typically exhibit different sales patterns from those in poorer neighborhoods. These are examples where market basket analysis can help to describe the differences and serve as an example of using market basket analysis for directed data mining.

How can association rules be used to make these comparisons? The first step is augmenting the transactions with *virtual items* that specify which group, such as an existing location or a new location, generates the transaction. Virtual items help describe the transaction, although the virtual item is not a product or service. For instance, a sale at an existing hardware store might include the following products:

- A hammer
- A box of nails
- Extra-fine sandpaper

After augmenting the data to specify where it came from, the transaction looks like:

- A hammer
- A box of nails
- Extra-fine sandpaper
- "At existing hardware store"

The virtual item becomes a new item in the transaction for use by association analysis.

TIP Adding virtual transactions into the market basket data enables you to find rules that include store characteristics and customer characteristics.

To compare sales at store openings versus existing stores, the process is:

1. Gather data for a specific period (such as two weeks) from store openings. Augment each of the transactions in this data with a virtual item saying that the transaction is from a store opening.

2. Gather about the same amount of data from existing stores. Here you might use a sample across all existing stores, or you might take all the data from stores in comparable locations. Augment the transactions in this data with a virtual item saying that the transaction is from an existing store.

3. Find association rules.

4. Pay particular attention to association rules containing the virtual items.

Because association rules are undirected data mining, the rules act as starting points for further hypothesis testing. Why does one pattern exist at existing stores and another at new stores? The rule about toilet bowl cleaners and store openings, for instance, suggests looking more closely at toilet bowl cleaner sales in existing stores.

Using this technique, association analysis can be used for many other types of comparisons:

- Sales during promotions versus sales at other times
- Sales in various geographic areas, by county, standard statistical metropolitan area (SSMA), direct marketing area (DMA), or country
- Urban versus suburban sales
- Seasonal differences in sales patterns

Adding virtual items to each basket of goods enables the standard association rule techniques to make these comparisons.

Association Rules and Cross-Selling

Association rules seem, at first sight, to be ideally suited to the problem of cross-selling beyond the world of retailing. A bank, for instance, might have several dozen products (such as checking account, mortgage, auto loan, and so on) and be interested in what sells together. These would seem quite amenable to association analysis.

WARNING   Association rules by themselves often produce poor results for cross-selling in domains such as financial services that have only a few dozen products.

Unfortunately, the results from such analyses can be quite disappointing. One reason is that many financial products are bundled together — products such as a checking account and an overdraft line of credit, or a checking account and a debit card. These rules tend to dominate associations. A more important reason for the disappointment, though, is that association rules skip over a vast repertoire of data describing customers. They only use one set of features — the items purchased in the past. This section discusses an alternative approach for incorporating information from association rules in cross-sell models.

A Typical Cross-Sell Model

Figure 15-12 shows a typical cross-sell model for a company that has, at most, a few dozen products. In this case, the best approach is to develop a separate propensity model for each product. The propensity model for a product estimates the likelihood of a customer purchasing that product. Typically, when the customer already has the product, the propensity is set to 0, so the company does not look stupid, trying to sell customers products that they already have.

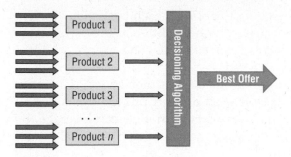

Figure 15-12: A typical cross-sell model builds propensities for each product and then has a decisioning algorithm to choose the best product for each customer.

The propensities for each product are combined using a decisioning algorithm, to allow business users to incorporate other factors into recommendation. The simplest decision is to choose the product with the highest propensity, because this is the product for which the customer has the most affinity. More sophisticated approaches take into account the revenue generated by a product or the net revenue, as well as the propensity. Using this information, each customer can be offered the most profitable product. The decisioning algorithm, in this case, would calculate the expected revenue using the propensity score generated by the product model.

This style of developing product propensity models does not mandate a particular form for each propensity model. Often, logistic regression is the technique of choice. However, decision trees, neural networks, and MBR approaches are also very reasonable choices.

The best way to train these models is to use information known about customers just before they purchase (or do not purchase) each product. Although existing products may play a role in the models, other variables would be likely to dominate the models. One downside to the propensity models is that including associations among products is very difficult.

A More Confident Approach to Product Propensities

As discussed earlier, association rules find associations among products, but other information is difficult to include. Propensity models include lots of rich information, but associations are difficult to include. Perhaps this is a Reese's moment: "you got peanut butter in my chocolate" and "you got chocolate in my peanut butter." By combining the two approaches, something better emerges.

The combination works by augmenting the input data for each product propensity model. One additional variable is added to the data used for each propensity model. Remember, each propensity model is for a specific product. At the same time, you can develop association rules that predict the same product on the right-hand side. Different rules are going to apply to each customer, even for the same product, because different customers have different products for the associations. Of the rules that apply to a given customer, one is more confident than the others, and that is the rule selected.

The confidence for the best rule for each customer is then added as an input variable in the model set used to develop each product propensity model. By including this confidence, the product propensity models can leverage the information from associations, while still using the demographic and behavioral data available about each customer.

Results from Using Confidence

This approach for adding the confidence to product propensity models was developed by a friend of the authors, Frank Travisano, who works for a large insurance company. Although we are not allowed to use results from his endeavors, the resulting propensities were much improved using the confidence value, leading to better cross-sell results.

The biggest challenge in implementing this as a solution is the challenge of scoring the association rules. Finding the rule with the maximum confidence requires scanning through all the rules that a given customer qualifies for to identify the most confident one. Using association rules for this purpose requires special purpose coding.

Sequential Pattern Analysis

Sequential pattern analysis (also called *longitudinal* analysis) adds the element of time to market basket analysis. The analysis considers not only associations among items, but also sequences of items where ordering in time is important. Here are some examples:

- New homeowners purchase shower curtains before purchasing furniture.
- Customers who purchase new lawnmowers are quite likely to purchase a new garden hose in the following six weeks.
- When a customer goes into a bank branch and asks for an account reconciliation, chances are good that he or she will close all his or her accounts within two weeks.

All of these involve actions that occur in a particular order, timewise. All of these — and sequential pattern analysis in general — require identifying a person over time. In particular, sequential pattern analysis does not make sense with anonymous transactions, because these cannot be tied together over time.

WARNING   To consider time-series analyses on your customers, you must have some way of identifying customers. Without a way of tracking individual customers, you cannot analyze their behavior over time.

Finding the Sequences

Sequential pattern analysis starts by looking at what sequences are in the data. The basic data structure for market basket analysis introduced earlier is fine, as long as the order record (or line item) contains a time stamp or some sort of sequential marker.

The example used in this section comes from the world of health care, where such analysis is a very important because of the complexity of medical care. The simple example here looks at particular drugs in a particular market — cholesterol-lowering drugs (technically, the lipid-lowering market).

This results are useful for several reasons. One is that health care providers and pharmaceutical companies can only measure patients' usage by their prescriptions. Most prescriptions are for 30 or 90 days of therapy. So, unlike services such as banking, cable television, and telephone service, customers do not "subscribe" to a therapy; instead, their usage has to be inferred from individual transactions.

Another reason why this is useful is because only a handful of drugs in any market compete against each other. The number of different options is relatively small, making it more feasible to understand the sequencing. Of course, the ideas here go beyond pharmaceutical usage and health care; similar ideas can be applied in many other domains.

Sequential Patterns with Just One Item

In some cases, even one item can be interesting over time. For instance, many pharmaceutical products are for chronic conditions, and should be taken consistently over time. Often, any particular product could be replaced by a competing product.

Consider the situation in the lipid-lowering market, which has been a highly competitive market because lowering cholesterol levels is widely deemed to be beneficial. Pharmaceutical companies want patients to use their product, because such companies want to sell more pills. Health care insurers are interested in these therapies, because patients who control their blood cholesterol levels are at reduced risk for more expensive treatments. And health care providers want to keep patients on the therapy, because it is in the best interest of the patients. A business question that might be asked by any of these is: what sequences of usage patterns do patients exhibit?

Table 15-10 shows an example of prescription sequences over the course of one year for just one product, Lipitor. Each "L" in the sequence represents one prescription filled by a patient. A prescription is typically for 30 or 90 days of therapy. Interestingly, the most common sequence has a length of four, which probably corresponds to four 90-day prescriptions. These patients are on the therapy, happily filling their prescriptions every three months, quite possibly by mail order. The next most common sequence is 12 prescriptions, a similar group of patients that fill their prescriptions once per month.

Table 15-10: Prescription Sequences for One Calendar Year

PURCHASE PATTERN	PRESCRIPTIONS	PATIENTS	PERCENT
LLLL	4	12,099	12.2%
LLLLLLLLLLLL	12	11,910	12.0%
L	1	11,522	11.6%
LLL	3	9,261	9.3%
LLLLLLLLLLL	11	9,042	9.1%
LL	2	8,653	8.7%
LLLLL	5	6,328	6.4%
LLLLLLLLLL	10	6,325	6.4%
LLLLLL	6	6,013	6.1%
LLLLLLLLL	9	5,316	5.4%
LLLLLLL	7	5,147	5.2%
LLLLLLLL	8	4,992	5.0%
OTHER		2,701	2.7%

Such a table can be used to answer questions such as: if a patient has six prescriptions in one year, what is the probability that a patient will have seven? In this data, there are 51,446 patients with six or more prescriptions (all the "OTHER" values are sequences longer than 6). Of these, exactly 6,013 have exactly six. Another way of saying this is that 11.7 percent of the patients stop at six prescriptions, so 88.3 percent continue to have more prescriptions. When doing such analyses, remember that patients with seven, eight, or more prescriptions also have six prescriptions.

This data uses prescriptions for all patients who filled one during the year. Most patients who take cholesterol-lowering drugs do so for long periods of time; some patients would have started during the year. The preceding table cannot be used to answer the question, "What is the probability that a patient will continue to a seventh prescription after his or her sixth prescription?" To answer this question, the data would have to track patients on the tenure timeline, relative to when the patient started therapy, rather than on the calendar timeline. Such an analysis would use ideas from survival analysis.

Sequential Patterns to Visualize Switching Behavior

Homogeneous items are interesting, but switching behavior is usually more interesting. Of course, more additional items means more possible sequences, too many to publish in a small table in a book.

Table 15-11 shows a small subset of possible sequences for the same market. The sequences in this table all start with 11 "Zs," representing 11 Zocor prescriptions. Additional letters represent other products, such as "L" for Lipitor, "V" for Vytorin, "C" for Crestor, and "M" for Mevacor.

Table 15-11: Patients with 11 Zocor Prescriptions

SEQUENCE	LENGTH	PATIENTS	PERCENT
ZZZZZZZZZZZZ	12	8674	44.8%
ZZZZZZZZZZZ	11	7699	39.8%
ZZZZZZZZZZZZZ	13	2063	10.7%
ZZZZZZZZZZZZZZ	14	390	2.0%
ZZZZZZZZZZZV	12	180	0.9%
ZZZZZZZZZZZZZZZ	15	152	0.8%
ZZZZZZZZZZZZZZZZZZ	18	112	0.6%
ZZZZZZZZZZZZZZZZ	16	32	0.2%
ZZZZZZZZZZZCZZ	14	13	0.1%
ZZZZZZZZZZZVV	13	11	0.1%
ZZZZZZZZZZZZC	13	11	0.1%
ZZZZZZZZZZZZLL	14	11	0.1%
ZZZZZZZZZZZZZZZZZZZ	19	11	0.1%
ZZZZZZZZZZZZZZZZZZZZZZ	22	10	0.1%
ZZZZZZZZZZZZZZZZZZZZZZZZZ	25	10	0.1%
ZZZZZZZZZZZZZZZZZ	17	9	0.0%
ZZZZZZZZZZZZZZZZZZZZZZZ	23	9	0.0%
ZZZZZZZZZZZZZZZZZZZZZL	21	8	0.0%
ZZZZZZZZZZZZV	13	7	0.0%
ZZZZZZZZZZZZZZVVZZ	18	7	0.0%
ZZZZZZZZZZZMM	13	6	0.0%
ZZZZZZZZZZZZZZZZLZ	18	4	0.0%
ZZZZZZZZZZZZZZZZZZO	19	4	0.0%

Switching among this group is quite uncommon, which is not surprising because a patient (and his or her doctor) who has 11 prescriptions in a row is probably content with the product. By far, the most common product that such patients switch to is Vytorin. This, too, is not surprising. Vytorin is actually a combination drug, consisting of Zocor and another drug in a single pill (and for some patients, a single copayment means that they save money every month).

These sequences make it possible to quantify the answers to questions such as the following:

- What proportion of patients who have 11 Zocor prescriptions continue to a twelfth?
- What proportion stop at 11 prescriptions?
- What proportion switch to another product?

These questions are actually similar to questions encountered in Chapter 10 on survival analysis. In particular, the last question incorporates the idea of competing risks.

Working with Sequential Patterns

As the number of items increases, the number of potential paths increases dramatically. Unfortunately, not many tools handle such sequences very well, so such analysis often requires custom coding. The earlier examples were developed using programs written in the SAS programming language.

This is just the beginning of what could be accomplished. For instance, stopping a sequence when a customer has had no activity for a period of time might be desirable. A prescription more than three months after the previous one ends, for instance, might start a new "episode of treatment."

These examples are focused on the pharmaceutical industry. However, such paths can occur in many areas. Customers in a bank take a "path" as they acquire and use different bank products. Visitors to a website take paths through the website. Corporate customers take paths as they acquire different hardware products, and so on.

Sequential Association Rules

You can also use the ideas behind association rules for sequential pattern analysis. To handle sequential data, the transaction data must have two additional features:

- A timestamp or sequencing information to determine when transactions occurred relative to each other
- Identifying information, such as account number, household ID, or customer ID that identifies different transactions as belonging to the same customer or household (sometimes called an economic marketing unit)

Building sequential rules is similar to the process of building association rules:

1. All items purchased by a customer are treated as a single order, and each item retains the timestamp indicating its position in the sequence.

2. The process is the same for item sets, groups of items being considered at one time.

3. The item sets contain timestamp (or sequence) information as well as items.

4. To develop the rules, only rules where the items on the left-hand side of the rule appeared before items on the right-hand side are considered.

The result is a set of association rules that can reveal sequential patterns.

Sequential Analysis Using Other Data Mining Techniques

Sequential analysis is related to other data mining techniques. As mentioned earlier in this section, the language for understanding sequences can become similar to the language used for survival analysis. In fact, the two have many similarities. Survival analysis focuses on timing; however, competing risks in combination with repeated events is a type of sequential pattern analysis. Consider a survival analysis of patient therapies. After a patient fills a particular prescription, how long until the next prescription is filled? And will the next prescription be for the same drug or for another one? Even more interesting is the fact that the previous sequence of events — at the time the first prescription is filled — can be incorporated as a covariate.

Sequential pattern analysis also analyzes sequences of customer behavior. The major difference is the definition of time. For survival analysis, time is measured in common units, such as days, weeks, and months. For sequential pattern analysis, the ordering is more important than the particular durations.

From the perspective of statistics, sequential pattern analysis is an example of path analysis. However, path analysis is also often used in the specific context of link analysis for analyzing websites. Regardless of the terminology, there is a relationship between sequential pattern analysis and link analysis, the topic of the next chapter.

Lessons Learned

Market basket data describes what customers purchase. Analyzing this data is complex, and no single technique is powerful enough to provide all the answers. The data itself typically describes the market basket at three different levels. The order is the event of the purchase; the line items are the items in the purchase, and the customer connects orders together over time.

Many important questions about customer behavior can be answered by looking at product sales over time. Which are the best-selling items? Which items that sold well last year are no longer selling well this year? Inventory curves do not require transaction-level data. Perhaps the most important insight they provide is the effect of marketing interventions — did sales go up or down after a particular event?

However, inventory curves are not sufficient for understanding relationships among items in a single basket. One technique that is quite powerful is association analysis. This technique finds products that tend to sell together in groups. Sometimes the groups are sufficient for insight. Other times, the groups are turned into explicit rules — when certain items are present, then you expect to find certain other items in the basket.

There are four measures of association rules. Support tells how often the rule is found in the transaction data. Confidence says how often when the "if" part is true that the "then" part is also true. Lift tells how much better the rule is at predicting the "then" part as compared with having no rule at all. The chi-square measure from statistics can also be adapted to finding the best association rules.

The rules so generated fall into three categories. Useful rules explain a relationship that was perhaps unexpected. Trivial rules explain relationships that are known (or should be known) to exist. And inexplicable rules simply do not make sense. Inexplicable rules often have weak support.

Market basket analysis and association analysis provide ways to analyze item-level detail, where the relationships between items are determined by the baskets they fall into. The ideas can be extended to sequential pattern analysis, which takes into consideration the order in which purchases are made, in addition to their contents. The next chapter turns to link analysis, which generalizes the ideas of "items" linked by "relationships," using the background of an area of mathematics called graph theory.

CHAPTER 16

Link Analysis

Who has friended whom on Facebook? Who calls whom on the telephone? Which physicians prescribe which drugs to which patients? Which pairs of cities generate the most passenger-miles? Which web pages have links that bridge language communities? Who reads which blogs on what topics? These relationships are all visible in data, and they all contain a wealth of information that most data mining techniques are not able to take direct advantage of. In the ever-more-connected world (where, it has been claimed, there are no more than six degrees of separation between any two people on the planet), understanding relationships and connections is critical. Link analysis is the data mining technique that addresses this need.

Link analysis is based on a branch of mathematics called *graph theory*, which represents relationships between different objects as edges in a graph. Link analysis is not a specific modeling technique, so it can be used for both directed and undirected data mining. It is often used for creating new derived variables for use by other modeling techniques. It can also be used for undirected data mining, by exploring the properties of the graphs themselves.

Graph theory is not applicable to all types of data nor can it solve all types of problems. Some areas where it has yielded good results are:

- Identifying authoritative sources of information on the Web by analyzing the links between its pages.

- Analyzing telephone call patterns to find influential customers who can recruit new subscribers from competing networks, and to identify particular market segments such as people working from home.

- Understanding physician referral patterns to gain insight into insurance fraud.

Even where links are explicitly recorded, assembling them into a useful graph can be a data-processing challenge. Links between web pages are encoded in the HTML of the pages themselves. Links between telephones are recorded in call detail records. Neither of these data sources is useful for link analysis without considerable data preparation. In other cases, the links are implicit, and part of the data mining challenge is to recognize them.

The chapter begins with an introduction to graph theory and some of the classic problems in the field. It then moves on to applications in the real world. Two case studies involve mining call graphs extracted from telephone call detail records. One case study finds influential members of social groups; these influencers are in a position to inspire others to adopt new services and may be able to recruit new subscribers from competing networks. The second of these case studies introduces a graph coloring algorithm to identify residential telephone numbers used for fax machines, which in turn are markers for home-based businesses. Finally, the well-known story of Google's rapid rise from a university research project to a dominant force on the Internet is shown to be based at least partly on the benefits of link analysis.

Basic Graph Theory

Graphs are an abstraction developed specifically to represent relationships. They have proven very useful in both mathematics and computer science for developing algorithms that exploit these relationships. Fortunately, graphs are quite intuitive, and a wealth of examples are available that illustrate how to take advantage of them.

What Is a Graph?

A *graph* consists of two distinct parts:

- *Nodes* (sometimes called *vertices*) are the things in the graph that have relationships. These are typically people, organizations, or objects in the real world and often have additional useful properties.

- *Edges* are pairs of nodes connected by a relationship. An edge is represented by the two nodes that it connects, so *AB* represents the edge that connects A and B.

Figure 16-1 illustrates two graphs. The graph on the left has four nodes connected by six edges and has the property that there is an edge between every pair of nodes. Such a graph is said to be *fully connected*. It could represent daily flights between Atlanta, New York, Detroit, and Minneapolis on an airline where these four cities serve as regional hubs. It could represent four people, all of whom know each other, or four mutually related leads for a criminal investigation.

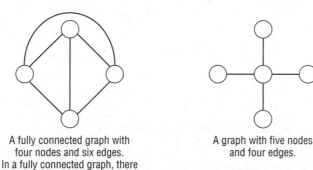

A fully connected graph with
four nodes and six edges.
In a fully connected graph, there
is an edge between every pair
of nodes.

A graph with five nodes
and four edges.

Figure 16-1: The graph on the left is fully connected. The graph on the right has a hub and spokes.

The graph on the right has one node in the center connected to four other nodes. This could represent daily flights connecting Atlanta to Birmingham, Greenville, Charlotte, and Savannah on an airline that serves the Southeast from a hub in Atlanta, or a restaurant frequented by four credit card customers. The graph itself captures the information about what is connected to what. Without any labels, it can describe many different situations. This is the power of abstraction.

In most of the examples in this chapter, the nodes represent one type of object — cities connected by transportation networks, people connected by social network referrals, pages connected by hypertext links, and so on. However, some graphs contain multiple node types to represent connections between entities of different kinds. For instance, doctors can be connected to prescription drugs based on their prescribing habits. In law enforcement, people can be connected to bank accounts, companies, addresses, and so on, in an effort to find the "web" of people associated with a crime.

A few points of terminology about graphs: Because graphs are so useful for visualizing relationships, it is nice when the nodes and edges can be drawn with no intersecting edges. The graphs in Figure 16-2 have this property. They are *planar* graphs, because they can be drawn on a sheet of paper without having any edges intersect. Figure 16-2 shows two graphs that cannot be drawn without having at least two edges cross. There is, in fact, a result in graph theory that says that if a graph is nonplanar, then lurking inside it is a subgraph like one of the two graphs in this figure.

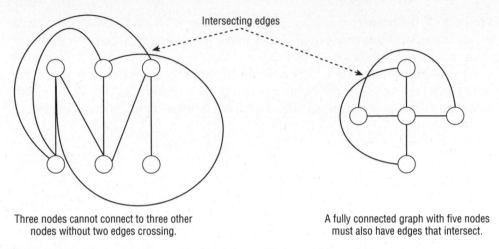

Three nodes cannot connect to three other nodes without two edges crossing.

A fully connected graph with five nodes must also have edges that intersect.

Figure 16-2: Some graphs cannot be drawn without crossing edges.

When a path exists between any two nodes in a graph, the graph is said to be *connected*. The rest of this chapter assumes that all graphs are connected, unless otherwise specified. Many graphs consist of tightly connected islands or clusters, which have only a few bridges to other clusters. For example, most web pages naturally connect to pages written in the same language. Each language forms an island. Chinese and English are the two most common languages for web pages, but a speaker of one can surf for hours without coming across a page in the other. Similar islands exist for Spanish, Japanese, Portuguese, German, Arabic, French, Russian, and Korean web pages.

A *path*, as its name implies, is an ordered sequence of nodes connected by edges. Consider a graph where each node represents a city, and the edges are flights between pairs of cities. On such a graph, a node is a city and an edge is a flight segment — two cities that are connected by a nonstop flight. A path is an itinerary of flight segments that go from one city to another, such as from Greenville, South Carolina to Atlanta, from Atlanta to Chicago, and from Chicago to Peoria.

Directed Graphs

When the edges between nodes are like expressways with the same number of lanes in each direction, the graph is said to be *undirected*. In a *directed* graph, by contrast, the edges are like one-way roads. An edge going from A to B is distinct from an edge going from B to A (and one may exist without the other). A directed edge from A to B is an *outgoing edge* of A and an *incoming edge* of B.

Directed graphs are a powerful way of representing data:

- Flight segments that connect a set of cities
- Hyperlinks between web pages
- Telephone calling patterns
- State transition diagrams
- Recommendations on a social network site

Two types of nodes are of particular interest in directed graphs. All the edges connected to a *source node* are outgoing edges. Because there are no incoming edges, no path exists from any other node in the graph to any of the source nodes. When all the edges on a node are incoming edges, the node is called a *sink node*. The existence of source nodes and sink nodes is an important difference between directed graphs and their undirected cousins.

Weighted Graphs

Figure 16-3 is an example of a *weighted graph,* a type of graph all of whose edges have weights associated with them. In this case, the nodes represent products purchased by customers. The weights represent the *support* for the association, the percentage of market baskets containing both products. This product association graph is an example of an undirected graph, which shows that 22.1 percent of market baskets at this health food grocery contain both bananas and yellow peppers. By itself, this does not explain whether banana sales drive yellow pepper sales or vice versa, or whether something else drives the purchase of all yellow produce.

One common problem in link analysis is finding the shortest path between two nodes. The definition of shortest, though, depends on the weights assigned to the edges. Consider the graph of flights between cities. Does shortest refer to distance? The fewest flight segments? The shortest flight time? Or the least expensive? All these questions are answered the same way using the same graph of flights connecting cities — the only difference is the weights on the edges.

The following three sections describe three classic problems in graph theory that illustrate the power of graphs to represent and solve problems. They are presented to familiarize the reader with graphs by providing examples of key concepts in graph theory and to provide a stronger basis for discussing link analysis.

Seven Bridges of Königsberg

One of the earliest problems in graph theory originated with a simple challenge posed in the eighteenth century by the Swiss mathematician Leonhard Euler. As shown in the simple map in Figure 16-4, Königsberg had two islands in the Pregel River connected to each other and to the rest of the city by a total of seven bridges. The bridges can be reached from either side of the river and from the islands. Figure 16-4 shows a path through the town that crosses over five bridges exactly once.

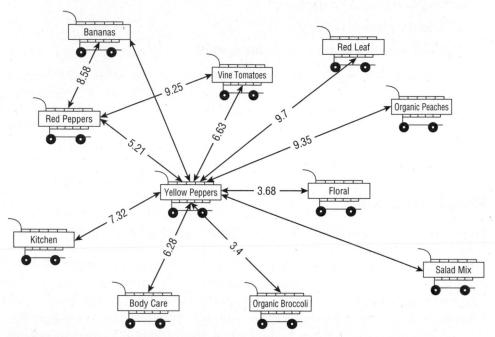

Figure 16-3: This is an example of a weighted graph where the edge weights are the number of transactions containing the items represented by the nodes at either end.

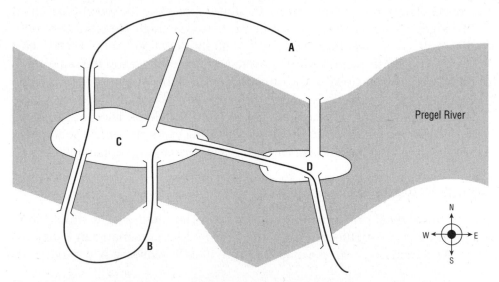

Figure 16-4: The Pregel River in Königsberg has two islands connected by a total of seven bridges, which played an important role in the development of graph theory.

Konigsberg, the capital of East Prussia, was the seat of an important university where Euler taught mathematics. Legend has it that three centuries ago, the students had a drinking game. The idea was to go to a pub, drink a pint of beer, walk over a bridge, and then drink another pint. Could the students do this, traversing each of the bridges exactly once, without getting wet or taking a boat?

Presumably, by trial and error, the students figured out that there was no possible path that covered all seven bridges exactly once. Of course, after drinking five, or six, or seven pints of beer, any given student probably forgot which bridges he had traversed. But that is another story.

Euler, a professor at the university, was intrigued by this problem, and he invented graph theory to understand it. Can someone walk over all seven bridges exactly once, starting from anywhere in the city, without getting wet or using a boat?

To solve this problem, Euler represented the map of Königsberg as the simple graph with four vertices and seven edges shown in Figure 16-5. Some pairs of nodes are connected by more than one edge, indicating that there is more than one bridge between them. Finding a route that traverses all the bridges in Königsberg exactly once is equivalent to finding a path in the graph that visits every edge exactly once. Such a path is called an *Eulerian path* in his honor. A sketch of his proof is provided in the sidebar "When Does an Eulerian Path Exist?"

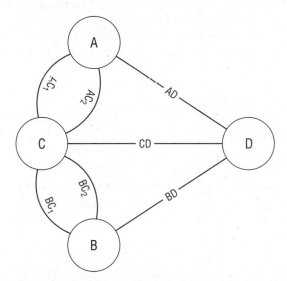

Figure 16-5: This graph represents the layout of Königsberg. The edges are bridges and the nodes are the riverbanks and islands.

As an historical note, the problem has survived longer than the name of the city. In the eighteenth century, Königsberg was a prominent Prussian city on the Baltic Sea nestled between Lithuania and Poland. Now, it is known as Kaliningrad, the westernmost Russian enclave, separated from the rest of Russia by Lithuania and Belarus.

WHEN DOES AN EULERIAN PATH EXIST?

To understand when an Eulerian path exists, you first need to understand the degree of a node. The degree is the number of edges that meet at the node. Euler showed that a path that visits each node exactly once exists only when the degrees on all but at most two nodes are even.

His insight rests on a simple observation about paths in a graph. Consider one path through the bridges:

$$A \rightarrow C \rightarrow B \rightarrow C \rightarrow D$$

The edges are:

$$AC_1 \rightarrow BC_1 \rightarrow BC_2 \rightarrow CD$$

The edges connecting the intermediate nodes in the path come in pairs. That is, for every incoming edge, there is an outgoing edge. For instance, node C has four edges visiting it, and node B has two.

Because the edges come in pairs, each intermediate node has an even number of edges in the path. Because an Eulerian path contains all edges in the graph and visits all the nodes, such a path exists only when all the nodes in the graph (minus the two end nodes) can serve as intermediate nodes for the path. This is another way of saying that the degree of those nodes is even.

Euler also showed that the opposite is true. When all the nodes in a connected graph (save at most two) have even degrees, then an Eulerian path exists. This proof is a bit more complicated, but the idea is simple. To construct an Eulerian path, start at a node (one with an odd degree if any have odd degrees) and move to any other connected node that has an even degree. Remove the edge just traversed from the graph and make it the first edge in the Eulerian path. Now, the problem is to find an Eulerian path starting at the second node in the graph. By keeping track of the degrees of the nodes, it is possible to construct such a path when there are at most two nodes whose degree is odd.

Detecting Cycles in a Graph

An important property of directed graphs is whether the graph contains any paths that start and end at the same node. Such a path is called a *cycle*, implying that the path could repeat itself endlessly: ABCABCABC and so on. If a directed graph contains at least one cycle, it is called *cyclic*.

There is a simple algorithm to detect whether a directed graph has any cycles. If a directed graph has no sink nodes, and it has at least one edge, then any path can be extended arbitrarily. Without any sink nodes, the terminating node of a path is always connected to another node, so the path can be extended by appending that node. Similarly, if the graph has no source nodes, then you can always prepend a node to the beginning of the path. When a path contains more nodes than there are nodes in the graph, you know that the path must visit at least one node twice. Call this node X. The portion of the path between the first X and the second X in the path is a cycle, so the graph is cyclic.

Now consider a graph that has one or more source nodes and one or more sink nodes. Obviously, source nodes and sink nodes cannot be part of a cycle. Removing the source and sink nodes from the graph, along with all their edges, does not affect whether the graph is cyclic. If the resulting graph has no sink nodes or no source nodes, then it contains a cycle, as just shown.

The process of removing sink nodes, source nodes, and their edges is repeated until one of the following occurs:

- No more edges or no more nodes are left. In this case, the graph has no cycles.

- Some edges remain but there are no source or sink nodes. In this case, the graph is cyclic.

If no cycles exist, then the graph is called an *acyclic graph*. These graphs are useful for describing dependencies or one-way relationships between things. For instance, different products belonging to nested hierarchies can be represented by acyclic graphs. The decision trees described in Chapter 7 are another example.

In an acyclic graph, any two nodes have a well-defined precedence relationship with each other. If node A precedes node B in some path that contains both A and B, then A will precede B in all paths containing both A and B (otherwise there would be a cycle). In this case, A is a *predecessor* of B and B is a *successor* of A. If no paths contain both A and B, then A and B are *disjoint*. This strict ordering can be an important property of the nodes and is sometimes useful for link analysis.

The Traveling Salesman Problem Revisited

Chapter 11 introduces the Traveling Salesman Problem and describes approaches to solving it using genetic algorithms and swarm intelligence. As a reminder, the problem is to find a route that minimizes the total distance (or cost, or time) traveled while visiting each of several cities exactly once. The Irish mathematician Sir William Rowan Hamilton formally investigated this problem in the nineteenth century. His study of minimizing energy in physical systems led him to investigate minimizing energy in certain discrete systems that he represented as graphs. In honor of him, a path that visits all nodes in a graph exactly once is called a *Hamiltonian path*.

Graphs are a natural representation of cities connected by roads or flight segments. In the graph representing this problem, the nodes are cities and each edge has a weight corresponding to the distance or travel time between the two cities connected by the edge. Notice that this problem is different from the seven bridges of Königsberg. Finding a path that visits all nodes exactly once is not sufficient; of all possible paths you want the shortest one. All Eulerian paths have exactly the same length, because they contain exactly the same edges. Asking for the shortest Eulerian path does not make sense.

The Traveling Salesman Problem Is Difficult

The traveling salesman problem is difficult to solve. This is not just a subjective statement; there is a formal mathematical reason why it is considered difficult. It would seem that any solution must consider all the possible paths that visit each city exactly once in order to determine the shortest one. The number of paths in a completely connected graph grows very fast — as a factorial. What is true for completely connected graphs is true for graphs in general: The number of possible paths visiting all the nodes grows as an exponential function of the number of nodes (although a few simple graphs exist where this is not true). So, as the number of cities increases, the effort required to find the shortest path grows much more quickly.

This lack of scalability is so important that mathematicians have given it a name: NP, which means that all known algorithms used to solve the problem scale exponentially — not like a polynomial. Such problems are difficult to solve, because all combinations must be considered.

Many practical problems resemble the traveling salesman problem, so algorithms developed for it can be applied to real applications. The goal is to find algorithms that do not require exponential time to find a reasonably good solution.

The Exhaustive Solution

If you would like to experiment with the traveling salesman problem using real maps, you can do so at www.gebweb.net/optimap. This application uses expected trip duration data from Google maps to calculate the optimal path for visiting up to nine addresses. Consider the problem of planning a trip that visits five cities in the San Francisco Bay Area. The five cities are Berkeley, Campbell, Menlo Park, Palo Alto, and San Jose.

The exhaustive solution calculates the length of every possible path through the cities. For the five cities in Figure 16-6, there are 5*4*3*2*1 (120) different paths. The "5" is because the path could start at any city, then it could visit any of the four remaining cities, and so on. The best possible route in this case starts at Campbell, and continues through San Jose, up the east side of the bay to Berkeley, and back down the Peninsula to Palo Alto and Menlo Park.

Figure 16-7 shows the same cities as an abstract graph. The edges show the driving times in between the cities in hours, minutes, and seconds. According to this graph, after converting the trip times into seconds, which is how they are actually reported by the Google API, the optimal trip takes a total of 11,333 seconds (814 + 3,658 + 4,194 + 1,037 + 1,630).

As a simplification, the cities are shown as an undirected graph so the driving times are the same in both directions. Google actually supplies separate estimates for each direction. In the Bay Area, where rush hour goes in all directions, the variance due to time of day is far greater than the variance due to direction of travel when time of day is not taken into account.

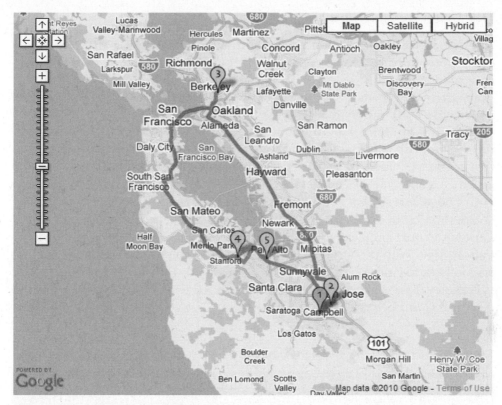

Figure 16-6: This route map, produced by Optimap using data provided by the Google Maps API, shows the best route (measured by driving time) for visiting several cities in the San Francisco Bay Area.

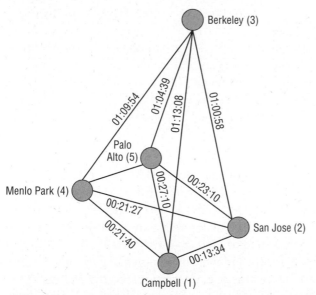

Figure 16-7: This weighted graph shows the expected driving time in hh:mm:ss between selected city pairs.

The Greedy Algorithm

The exhaustive approach always produces the shortest path, but it gets computationally expensive as the number of cities grows. Another approach is the greedy algorithm, which starts the tour by finding the shortest edge in the graph, then lengthens it with the shortest edge available at either end that visits a new city. The resulting path is generally pretty short.

Table 16-1 contains the driving times used in this example. The edge with the shortest trip connects Campbell and San Jose, so the greedy tour starts with that segment, which, by coincidence, is also part of the optimal tour. Next, the greedy algorithm looks for the shortest path that connects a new city to either end. The shortest path out of Campbell is 1,300 seconds to Menlo Park. The shortest path out of San Jose is 1,287, also to Menlo Park. So, San Jose to Menlo Park is the next segment added to the tour. The 1,037 second trip from Menlo Park to Palo Alto is shorter than anything available at the Campbell end, so Menlo Park to Palo Alto is the next segment added. The only city not yet visited is Berkeley. To close the loop, segments are added to connect Berkeley with Palo Alto and Campbell.

Table 16-1: Driving Times Between Addresses in Selected City Pairs

FROM/TO	CAMPBELL (1)	SAN JOSE (2)	BERKELEY (3)	MENLO PARK (4)	PALO ALTO (5)
CAMPBELL (1)	0	814 00:13:34	4,388 01:13:08	1,300 00:21:40	1,630 00:27:10
SAN JOSE (2)	814 00:13:34	0	3,658 01:00:58	1,287 00:21:27	1,390 00:23:10
BERKELEY (3)	4,388 01:13:08	3,658 01:00:58	0	4,194 01:09:54	3,879 01:04:39
MENLO PARK (4)	1,300 00:21:40	1,287 00:21:27	4,194 01:09:54	0	1,037 00:17:17
PALO ALTO (5)	1,630 00:27:10	1,390 00:23:10	3,879 01:04:39	1,037 00:17:17	0

The total estimated travel time for the optimal tour is 11,333 seconds, or 3 hours, 8 minutes, and 53 seconds. The total estimated travel time for the greedy tour is 11,418 (814 + 1,300 + 1,037 + 3,879 + 4,388) seconds, or 3 hours, 10 minutes, and 18 seconds. In this case, the difference of 85 seconds is surely within the margin of error for a trip that is estimated to take well over three hours on California freeways. Although the greedy algorithm may find the optimal path or, as in this example, a nearly optimal path, its results are not guaranteed to be close to the shortest path. It is not hard to design examples where the greedy algorithm picks a path that is much worse than optimal, but most of the time, it works pretty well.

> **TIP** Often, using an algorithm that yields good, but not perfect results is better than trying to arrive at the ideal solution or giving up because there is no guarantee of finding an optimal solution. As Voltaire remarked, *"Le mieux est l'ennemi du bien."* (The best is the enemy of the good.)

Social Network Analysis

Long before there was Facebook, even back before Friendster, sociologists and anthropologists were doing social network analysis. Networks or graphs can be used to represent all kinds of relationships between people such as kinship, commerce (who sells what to whom), and even the transmission of disease (who infected whom). Social network analysis yielded important results in fields from economics to epidemiology, but the work was always hampered by the inability of researchers to see the entire network except in specialized cases such as friendships within a single school or village. An interesting result from one such study is described in the sidebar "Why Your Friends Have More Friends than You Do."

Today, many important connections between people are captured in data. Call detail records can be used to create a graph of who calls whom. A wide variety of web-based services create more explicit social networks. Professional networking sites such as LinkedIn facilitate contacts between job seekers and hiring managers and between would-be collaborators. Dating sites form connections between people looking for mates. Facebook allows parents to learn what their kids are up to, while perhaps reconnecting with long-lost classmates. The primary purpose of these networks is to allow members to interact, but an additional benefit is that researchers can now study large social networks with verifiable data.

Six Degrees of Separation

Results of many earlier social network analysis projects were suspect due to problems capturing complete information. Stanly Milgram's famous small world study, published in 1967, is a case in point. The goal of the study was to determine how many links separate randomly chosen people in the United States. Volunteers recruited in Omaha, Nebraska and Wichita, Kansas were given letters to be sent to recipients in Massachusetts, near Milgram's base at Harvard University. Participants were asked to forward the letter to someone they knew personally who would be likely to know the recipient. Each successive link in the chain was meant to forward the letter again and send a pre-addressed

WHY YOUR FRIENDS HAVE MORE FRIENDS THAN YOU DO

That was the title of a 1991 paper by Scott Feld of the State University of New York at Stony Brook. The paper appeared in the May 1991 issue of *The American Journal of Sociology* and has been cited many times since. It has come to be called *the friendship paradox.*

Professor Feld showed that on average, your friends have more friends than you do. That is, the average number of friends of friends is always greater than the average number of friends of individuals, although the size of the discrepancy depends on the structure of the friendship graph. This finding has sociological and psychological ramifications. If people use the average number of friends that their friends have as a benchmark, most will feel disappointed by having fewer friends than they think they ought to.

Feld points out that this is one of a family of "class size" paradoxes. The original class-size paradox related to college students. College students tend to experience a larger average class size than the average advertised in the literature they received from the admissions department.

How can it be true that your friends have more friends than you do? Is it your annoying habit of bringing up subjects like graph theory and data mining in casual conversation? No, but inspecting a graph can explain the seeming paradox. The following figure is modeled on an illustration from Scott Feld's original paper.

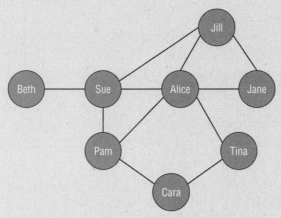

Only Alice has five friends, but because of her, five people have a friend with five friends.

Alice has many friends, so all of these friends have a friend with a lot of friends (namely, Alice). In a typical friendship graph, there are only a few Alices who know lots and lots of people. It is unlikely that you are one of these extremely popular people. On the other hand, you probably know an Alice. And people who know Alice — but are not like her — will tend to have fewer friends than the average of their friends.

postcard to Milgram's group at Harvard. Of the letters that reached their destination, the average length of the chain was slightly less than six. This result was widely reported, and the phrase "six degrees of separation" entered the culture. There was even a Broadway play with that name and a movie adaptation starring Will Smith.

Whether six is really the average path length between randomly chosen Americans is open to question. For one thing, most of the letters never reached their destinations because the chain was broken by some recipient failing to forward the letter. The large number of broken chains may introduce a bias because people who felt they knew someone who was likely to know the final recipient may have been more likely to forward the letter. The original senders were also not chosen randomly. They answered an advertisement that specifically asked for volunteers who considered themselves well connected. The most important flaw, however, was that neither the researchers, nor the participants could actually see the true network. Each participant simply guessed what the best path might be. The true path could be even shorter.

For web-based social networks, the entire graph is available, so calculating the true distance between any two nodes is possible. Search for a person's name on LinkedIn and you will be told that person's distance from you and a list of your connections who could serve as the first link in a path between you and the person you searched for.

What Your Friends Say About You

You can tell a lot about a person by who his or her friends are, including things that users of the network may not intend to share. For example, in a paper published in 2010, three researchers at Facebook show that the geographic locations of a user's Facebook friends are a better predictor of their geographic location than their IP address even though only a small proportion of Facebook users provide a physical address.

Of the roughly 100 million active Facebook users in the United States, about 6 percent have entered a home address. Of these addresses, about 60 percent can be easily parsed and geocoded, yielding several million users with a precisely known location. There is no guarantee that these addresses are correct, but there is little incentive to enter false information because leaving the field blank is easier. Interestingly, the probability of providing an address is much higher for men than women, but it does not vary much by age or geography.

Knowing where users live is important to Facebook because it allows them to provide services and advertising customized for a geographic area. The algorithm for predicting a user's home address involves creating the social graph that connects the user to friends who have known locations. The edges can be weighted by factors such as recency and amount of mutual activity such as exchanging messages or writing on each other's walls. Most people are geographically close to many of their friends.

Geography is not the only thing that can be predicted using social network analysis. Some students at M.I.T. caused a stir by demonstrating, for a class project, that they could correctly predict the sexual orientation and religion of fellow students who had not mentioned these details on their Facebook pages. Interestingly, sexual orientation was easier to predict for men than for women. Gay men have more gay friends than straight men do, but the difference is less pronounced for lesbians.

Finding Childcare Benefits Fraud

The county of Los Angeles in California has the largest population of any county in the United States. With 10 million residents, it is larger than most states and many countries. The county's budget of approximately $23 billion for law enforcement, health, and social services is a tempting target for fraudsters.

Certain crimes that are difficult to detect at the level of individual perpetrators can be detected through link analysis because these crimes involve collusion between clients and service providers. One type of social service provided by the county is subsidized child-care. Some families receive this benefit to enable one or both parents to work. This type of service seems somewhat immune from fraud, because child care providers need to be licensed and the client needs to show proof of a job.

This data is, however, amenable to link analysis. The graph has three types of nodes:

- Child care provider
- Employer
- Client

The connections between these nodes are "provides child-care for" and "is employed by." No direct connections exist between the child care providers and the employers; at least, none are expected.

Social network analysis identified some anomalies. In particular, clients in widely separated parts of the county claimed to work for the same small group of employers and receive child care from the same small group of providers. The home addresses of the clients, the employers, and the providers were surprisingly far apart. Although this might occasionally happen, for most people, it would be a big inconvenience to have child care that is near neither home nor work.

Further analysis showed that non-existent child-care services were being provided to non-existent clients while they went to work at non-existent jobs at non-existent employers. The fraud was being perpetrated by child-care providers who did not actually provide any service and clients who did not actually have any children in care. Participants in the fraud network have many transactions among themselves but few or none with the larger network. The county now saves tens of millions of dollars per year by detecting this kind of activity.

Who Responds to Whom on Dating Sites

People looking for love on online dating sites are not always completely accurate in their self-descriptions. One such site, OkCupid, publishes an amusing blog called oktrends with dating research based on data collected on the site. For example, the reported height of men on the site approximates a normal distribution, but the average is two inches taller than the average for the U.S. population as a whole. The site's data also shows there is good reason to exaggerate one's height. Taller men receive more unsolicited messages.

Messages are an important part of how the site works. Users fill out questionnaires. Based on their responses, the site calculates a match score for other members. The higher the score, the more compatible the potential date. Users can send messages to people who interest them. They may or may not get a response.

One interesting post analyzed response rates by race and sex. The analysis was done separately for gay and straight users. The results discussed here are for straight men and women.

In a survey, overwhelming majorities of all racial groups claimed that race was not an important factor for dating. According to the OkCupid compatibility score, a user's most compatible prospects are distributed across all racial groups. However, the reply rates tell a different story. White men get the most replies of any group and are the least likely to reply to messages they receive. They are especially unlikely to reply to messages from black women. Incidentally, this disinclination to respond to messages from black women is also shared by black men.

The messaging patterns of daters confirm other stereotypes of heterosexual behavior as well. Based on who sends messages to whom, it is clear that women prefer dates around their own age or a little older, whereas men prefer to date younger women. Also the gap between the age of men and the age of the women they are most interested in dating increases with the age of the men. One consequence is that the relative attractiveness of men and women changes with age. Until age 26, women have more suitors than men do. After that age, it is the men who are more pursued. By age 48, men get twice as many messages as women.

If any of the preceding is depressing, remember that an online dating site is a self-selected and highly biased sample. It may not reflect the wider world.

Social Marketing

Social networks are also increasingly being used for marketing purposes. This approach can be very cost-effective and has been used successfully for products ranging from Pabst Blue Ribbon beer to the Ford Fiesta. In 2010, the Fiesta was already a hit in Europe and parts of Asia, but had not yet been introduced to the United States. Ford recruited 100 well-connected bloggers who submitted videos to compete to become part of the "Fiesta Movement." The winners each got a Fiesta imported from Germany. They were given "missions" such as driving the car to music festivals and making videos involving the car. And, of course, they were all expected to tell their friends all about their adventures. The campaign successfully generated a great deal of buzz at a much lower cost than a traditional television-centered introduction.

The social groups have other uses as well. In a country like Australia, with close to 100 percent mobile phone penetration, churn — the industry term for subscribers switching from one service provider to another — is always a concern. The churn rate within a social group is a good predictor of individual churn. If many of your friends are switching to a competitor, there is a good chance that you will switch as well. In fact, at this company, having just one member of a group churn increased the probability of churn for other members of the group by a factor of five!

Mining Call Graphs

Some interesting applications of link analysis in the real world are based on call graphs. Each time a telephone call is made, a call detail record (CDR) records the transaction. In fact, a single call often generates a detail record in several different databases because the data is captured by the originator's telephone company, the recipient's telephone company, and any companies whose networks are involved in routing the call.

The primary purpose of the CDR is to allow someone (usually, the calling party) to be billed for the call, but CDRs are also the building blocks for a call graph. Each call detail record contains information such as:

- The telephone number that originated the call
- The telephone number where the call terminated
- The telephone number of the account to be billed for the call
- The date and time of the call
- The duration of the call
- The day of the week when the call was placed
- The network on which the call originated
- Type of call (voice, SMS, video)
- Megabytes transmitted

In Table 16-2, the data has been narrowed to just three fields: originating number, terminating number, and duration. Figure 16-8 shows these same five records as a call graph. The telephone numbers are the nodes of the graph, and the calls themselves are the edges, weighted by the duration of the calls.

Table 16-2: Five Telephone Calls

ID	ORIGINATING NUMBER	TERMINATING NUMBER	DURATION
1	353-3658	350-5166	00:00:41
2	353-3068	350-5166	00:00:23
3	353-4271	353-3068	00:00:01
4	353-3108	555-1212	00:00:42
5	353-3108	350-6595	00:01:22

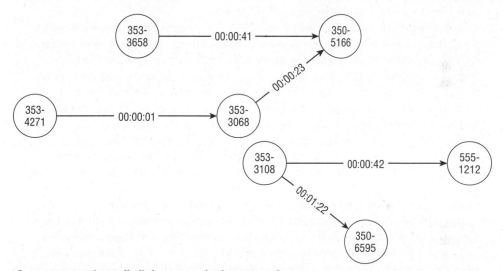

Figure 16-8: Five calls link seven telephone numbers.

Even on this tiny call graph, some features are worth noting. Calls have an origin and a destination, so the graph is directed. Several of the nodes are sinks; they receive calls, but do not make any. With only five calls, no conclusions can be drawn from this, but even in a more realistic sample, some sinks persist. For example, the node labeled 555-1212 is a directory assistance number; people call it to obtain information, but it does not make any outbound calls. Other examples of sinks include voicemail services, the toll-free customer service numbers of businesses of all kinds, and the dial-up numbers for Internet service providers in areas not yet reached by broadband service. Call graphs also include sources — nodes that place outbound calls, but never receive calls. Think of the autodialers used by survey companies and political campaigns. Of course, legal and ethical issues are associated with using such data, as discussed in the sidebar "Legal and Ethical Issues in Call Detail Analysis."

This call graph is acyclic and not connected. As more calls are added, cycles form and bridges are built between the islands. Even in a complete call graph, however, there are clusters of numbers with many calls among members and relatively few links outside the cluster. These clusters represent communities of people and/or businesses. Within a call graph, some nodes are very well-connected within their own cluster, and others are bridges between clusters. All of these features have marketing uses, as the next two case studies show.

LEGAL AND ETHICAL ISSUES IN CALL DETAIL ANALYSIS

As many a red-faced politician has discovered, when and whom you call or text can be a very sensitive subject. Call detail data could easily be used for many purposes that would clearly constitute invasions of privacy. The same is true for data collected by Internet service providers, banks, insurance companies, and even supermarkets, but nothing seems quite as private as our intimate communications with family and friends.

When working with any kind of sensitive information, data miners have an obligation to think about what is legal, what is ethical, and what might offend or upset customers. Many things that are technically possible are illegal, immoral, or simply bad for business. Some cases are clear cut; others less so.

On the clearly taboo side of the line is making use of the *content* of a communication. This is not a big issue for voice calls, because the content is not normally captured, but the content of text messages, email, and other data transmissions is often captured and could be misused. The United States has common carrier laws that protect telecommunications providers from any illegal acts that take place on their networks — and, in turn, prevent the companies from listening in on calls (if they listen in — without a court order — they might then be liable for what happens on the call).

In some countries, taking action based on a specific number dialed is also illegal. The potential usefulness of this information is clear. People who call the sales office of a competitor are clearly at high risk for attrition. People who call a credit counseling service may be at high risk for default. People who call phone sex lines might also be interested in adding an adult video channel to their cable subscription.

Identifying social networks based on who calls whom can be done without using any personally identifiable information. The analysis is really of what numbers call which other numbers, and the numbers themselves can be encrypted. That kind of analysis is clearly permissible. When the phone numbers are tied to individual subscribers, the situation becomes more sensitive. Customers probably don't mind being offered free goodies because they have been identified as "leaders" in their social networks, but they might object to other possible applications.

Governments also take an interest in who calls whom. Link analysis can help an oppressive government keep track of dissenters. It can also help law enforcement agencies protect the public from criminals and terrorists.

Case Study: Tracking Down the Leader of the Pack

The first case comes from a leading telecommunications company in Australia that does extensive social network analysis on its call detail data. The work described here was done by Tim Manns who kindly shared published accounts of his work from a 2009 conference presentation and added additional details in the course of pleasant conversations in a Sydney pub.

The Business Goal

A primary goal of the analysis is to identify key influencers — subscribers who are well-connected and can bring in new subscribers or encourage existing subscribers to adopt new features. The idea is that the opinions of colleagues, friends, and family are far more influential than any messages a company can convey through advertising. By identifying influencers and social relationships within the customer base, the company hopes to target the leaders of social groups and ensure that they are happy. These leaders will then spread the good word within their social circle. Leaders may receive offers to try out new handsets or services to create early buzz.

It works the other way, too. Many social groups include members who are customers of competing telephone service providers. For these customers, only calls made to or received from the company's own customers are captured, but this partial information is often sufficient to identify high-value prospects on these competing networks. The company is not allowed to approach these prospects directly, but it can certainly offer "sign up a friend" rewards to its own subscribers who are part of the same social circle.

The Data Processing Challenge

The billions of rows of call detail data used for the social network analysis are stored in a multi-terabyte data warehouse. The challenge is to convert this data into a form useful for social network analysis. This involves a series of SQL queries, which process the call detail data, locate social groups, and identify leaders within the groups.

To give a general idea of the size of the data, assume that there are eight million mobile customers and on average each makes five calls a day and receives five calls a day. That works out to 80 million call detail records generated each day, or about 560 million every week.

The CDR records are operational records, so the data is not particularly clean. For example, the telephone numbers are not even in a consistent format, because a telephone number can be dialed in multiple ways, such as with or without the country code. A giant SQL case statement converts all numbers to a fully qualified form including the country code and area code.

The call detail data is summarized for each subscriber in two tables, one for inbound calls and one for outbound calls. The summarized data has one row per origin-destination pair (only one of these numbers must be a subscriber, depending on the table). Columns include the total number of voice calls, text messages, picture calls, and video calls, and the number of each of these by time of day, international and domestic, and other factors.

For each recipient, the inbound and output calls are compared to understand the reciprocal nature of the relationship. Which number typically originates the call? What is the difference in average call length between calls originated by one side or the other? The answers to these questions are two of the factors used to identify leaders in a social group.

To reduce the size of the resulting table, and to focus the analysis on ongoing, reciprocal relationships, only number pairs that make more than some threshold number of calls in each direction are retained. This eliminates one-sided relationships such as calls to take-out pizza places or ringtone downloading services.

Finding Social Networks in Call Data

In fact, the numbers themselves form a graph. Finding social groups requires focusing on particular numbers, to find all customers who call the same number, and all numbers (whether customers or not) that call the same customer. What is interesting are groups of numbers that all call each other (or almost all call each other). Such a group is called a *fully connected subgraph*. A fully connected subgraph of numbers is suggestive of a community of interest — a group of people linked by bonds of friendship, business, or a shared passion of some kind.

The data about customers and their calling patterns is used to identify social groups and, in combination with personal data acquired when subscribers sign up, to apply labels identifying likely relationships such as spouse, child, and friend. These labels are useful for a household identification project and also proved to be highly predictive inputs to various up-sell, cross-sell, and attrition models.

An important part of the call graph analysis is measuring the number and percentage of in-network and out-of-network calls made by the mobile customer base, including calls made to fixed line and international services. Customers who make and receive a large number of calls from external networks have friends who are high usage customers of a competitor.

How the Results Are Used for Marketing

The results of social network analysis are used for marketing in two important ways. The first is viral marketing. Within each identified group, customers are given a "leadership" score. Leaders are people who are well-connected (exchange calls and messages with many members of the group) and early adopters of new services. Leaders are offered opportunities to try out new features in the expectation that they will spread the word.

The second application of social network analysis is to entice high-value new customers away from competitors. Although the full value of competitors' customers cannot be calculated directly, non-subscribers with high usage on the company's network are likely to have even higher usage on their own networks. When a group identified by social network analysis includes high-value customers of a competitor, customers who spend a lot of time interacting with the prospect are selected for inclusion in bring-a-friend campaigns. Acquiring these friends not only adds revenue, it also improves profitability by reducing interconnect costs — the payments made to other carriers when calls are routed over their networks.

Estimating Customer Age

In addition to mobile and landline telephone services, the company offers broadband Internet service satellite television subscriptions. The television side of the business includes packages specifically designed for families with children. Can the company use information from the call detail records to make an educated guess as to whether or not a household contains children?

As part of the sign-up process, subscribers are asked their date of birth. This field has missing values for about 5 percent of subscribers, and an additional 5 percent have suspect values. The age, though, is for the person who receives the bill. The 90 percent of customers having a valid age have 1.4 lines per billing account. These additional lines are typically used by other members of the same household, whose ages may or may not be known. In some cases, such as pre-paid accounts, the age of the customer is known, even for minors.

By examining the relationships and ages of known individuals, it is possible to estimate a subscriber's age to within just a few years. It turns out that most people do most of their talking and texting with people close to their own age. A graph plotting number of relationships by difference in age shows that the vast majority of reciprocal relationships are between people within four years of each other in age. There is a small but noticeable bump in communication with an age difference of about 25 to 35 years, presumably due to relationships between parents and children. In the case of multiple lines on a single account held in the name of a 45-year-old subscriber, there is typically one line that has relationships mainly with 40- to 50-year-olds along with one or more that have relationships mainly with 15- to 20-year-olds.

In addition to filling in holes in the company's own customer data, the calling patterns are used to estimate ages for the other party when there is a calling relationship between a subscriber and a non-subscriber. Chances are that the age of the unknown party is within a few years of the average age of the strongest known relationships.

Case Study: Who Is Using Fax Machines from Home?

As noted in the Australian case study, telephone service providers have records of every telephone call that their customers make and receive. This data contains a wealth of information about the behavior of their customers: when they place calls, who calls them, whether they benefit from their calling plan, to name a few. In this case study, which took place in the United States in the 1990s, link analysis was used to analyze the records of local telephone calls to identify which residential customers had a high probability of having fax machines in their home.

Why Finding Fax Machines Is Useful

What is the value of knowing who owns a fax machine? How can a telephone provider act on this information? In this case, the provider had developed a package of services for residential work-at-home customers. Targeting such customers for marketing purposes was a revolutionary concept at the company. Once upon a time, telephone services were tightly regulated; telephone companies lost revenue from work-at-home customers, because these customers could have been paying higher business rates instead of lower residential rates. Far from targeting such customers for marketing campaigns, the companies would deny such customers residential rates — punishing them for behaving like a small business.

The company had several alternatives for defining the target set of customers for the new work-at-home package. The company could effectively use neighborhood demographics, household surveys, estimates of computer ownership by ZIP code and similar data. Although this data improves the definition of a market segment, it is still far from identifying individual customers with particular needs. A team, including one of the authors, suggested that the ability to find residential fax machine usage would improve this marketing effort, because fax machines are often (but not always) used for business purposes. Knowing who uses a fax machine would help target the work-at-home package to a very well-defined market segment, and this segment should have a better response rate than a segment defined by less precise segmentation techniques based on statistical properties.

How Do Fax Machines Behave?

Finding fax machines is based on a simple observation: Fax machines tend to call other fax machines, because they speak the same language. A set of known fax numbers can be expanded based on the calls made to or received from the known numbers. If an unclassified telephone number calls known fax numbers and doesn't hang up quickly, it increases the probability that the unknown number also belongs to a fax machine.

TIP Characterizing expected behavior is a good way to start any directed data mining problem. The better the problem is understood, the better the results are likely to be.

This simple characterization is good for guidance, but it is an oversimplification. A phone line can be used in different ways:

- *Voice*. The line is only used for voice calls.
- *Dedicated fax*. Some fax machines are on dedicated lines, and the line is used only for fax communication.
- *Shared*. Some fax machines share their line with voice calls.

The presumption that fax machines call other fax machines is generally true for machines on dedicated lines, although wrong numbers provide exceptions even to this rule. Any number that calls information (directory assistance services) is presumably used for voice communications, and is therefore a voice line or a shared fax line, but not a dedicated fax line. When a shared line calls an unknown number, there is no way to know if the call is voice or data. These shared lines do represent a marketing opportunity to sell additional lines.

A Graph Coloring Algorithm

Finding the fax machines is an example of a *graph-coloring algorithm*. This type of algorithm walks through a graph and labels nodes with different "colors" based on the characteristics of the node and its neighbors. In this case, the colors are "fax," "shared," "voice," and "unknown" instead of red, green, yellow, and blue. Initially, all the nodes are "unknown" except for the few labeled "fax" from the starting set and the few labeled "voice." As the algorithm proceeds, more and more nodes with the "unknown" label are given more informative labels.

One of the challenges was that incoming calls to a fax machine may sometimes represent a wrong number and give no information about the originating number (actually, if it is a wrong number then it is probably a voice line). The assumption was that such incoming wrong numbers would last a very short time.

The process started with an initial set of fax numbers gathered manually from the *Yellow Pages* based on the annotation "fax." These numbers are only the beginning, the seeds, of the list of fax machine telephone numbers. Although businesses commonly advertise their fax numbers, this is not so common for fax machines at home. The process also included calls to information (such as 411 and 555-1212) as indicators of voice lines.

"Coloring" the Graph to Identify Fax Machines

The sample of telephone records consisted of 3,011,819 telephone calls made over one month by 19,674 households. In the world of telephony, this data sample is very small, but it was sufficient to demonstrate the power of link analysis for this purpose. The analysis was performed using special-purpose code that stored the call detail and allowed a list of fax machines to be expanded efficiently.

Figure 16-9 shows a call graph with 15 numbers and 19 calls. The weights on the edges are the duration of each call in seconds. Nothing is really known about the specific numbers.

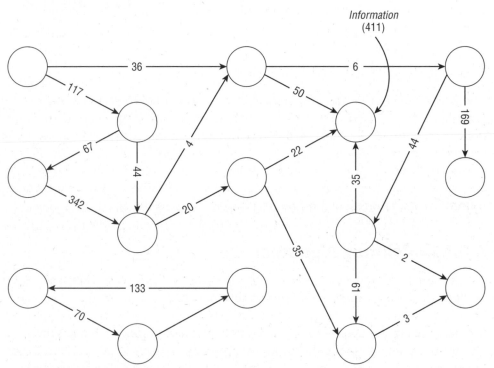

Figure 16-9: A call graph for 15 numbers and 19 calls.

Figure 16-10 shows how the algorithm proceeds. First, the numbers that are known to be fax machines are labeled "F," and the numbers for directory assistance are labeled "I." Any edge for a call that lasted less than 10 seconds has been dropped. The algorithm colors the graph by assigning labels to each node using an iterative procedure:

- Any "voice" node connected to a "fax" node is labeled "shared."
- Any "unknown" node connected mostly to "fax" nodes is labeled "fax."

This procedure continues until all nodes connected to "fax" nodes have a "fax" or "shared" label.

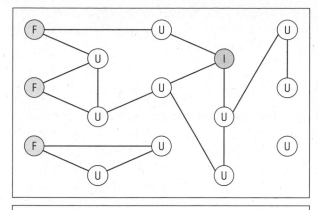

This is the initial call graph with short calls removed and with nodes labeled as "fax," "unknown," and "information."

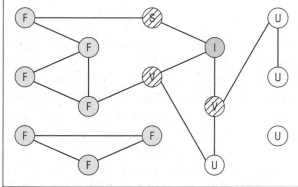

Nodes connected to the initial fax machines are assigned the "fax" label.

Those connected to "information" are assigned the "voice" label.

Those connected to both are "shared."

The rest are "unknown."

Figure 16-10: Applying the graph-coloring algorithm to the call graph shows which numbers are fax numbers and which are shared.

How Google Came to Rule the World

The phenomenal popularity of the Google search engine stems from its ability to help people find reasonably good material on pretty much any subject. This feat is accomplished through link analysis.

The Web is a huge directed graph. The nodes are web pages and the edges are the hyperlinks between them. Special programs called *spiders* or *web crawlers* are continually traversing these links to update maps of the huge directed graph that is the Web. Originally, these spiders indexed the content of web pages for use by purely text-based search engines. Today's crawlers record the Web's global structure as a directed graph that can be used for analysis.

The first generation of search engines analyzed only the nodes of this graph. Text from a query was compared with text from the web pages using techniques similar to those described in Chapter 21. When Google appeared in 1998, it was clearly superior to the incumbent champions such as AltaVista. Google was able to return more relevant results because it made use of the information encoded in the *edges* of the graph as well as the information found in the *nodes*. This approach was soon adopted by all search engines, but not before Google had established a dominant position in the market.

Hubs and Authorities

When an idea's time has come, it often occurs to many people around the same time. Analyzing hypertext links to improve search results is a case in point. In 1998, Sergey Brin and Lawrence Page of Stanford University published a paper, "The Anatomy of a Large-Scale Hypertextual Web Search Engine" in a journal called *Computer Networks and ISDN Systems*, describing what would become the Google search engine. That same year, Professor Jon Kleinberg of Cornell University published a paper, "Authoritative Sources in a Hyperlinked Environment" in the Proceedings of the 9th Annual ACM-SIAM Symposium on Discrete Algorithms, describing an algorithm for identifying authoritative web pages. This section describes Kleinberg's algorithm.

Some websites or magazine articles are more interesting than others even if they are devoted to the same topic. This simple idea is easy to grasp but hard to explain to a computer. So when a search is performed on a topic that many people write about, finding the most interesting or authoritative documents in the huge collection that satisfies the search criteria is difficult.

Professor Kleinberg came up with one widely adopted technique for addressing this problem. His approach takes advantage of the insight that by creating a link from one site to another, a human being is making a judgment about the value of the site being linked to. Each link to another site is effectively a recommendation of that site. Cumulatively, the independent judgments of many website designers who all decide to provide links to the same target confer authority on that target. Furthermore, the reliability of the sites making the link can be judged according to the authoritativeness of the sites they link to. The recommendations of a site with many other good recommendations can be given more weight in determining the authority of another.

At first glance, it might seem that a good method for finding authoritative websites would be to rank them by the number of unrelated sites linking to them. The problem with this technique is that any time the topic is mentioned, even in passing, by a popular site (one with many inbound links), it will be ranked higher than a site that is much more authoritative on the particular subject though less popular in general. The solution is to rank pages, not by the total number of links pointing to them, but by the number of subject-related hubs that point to them. In Kleinberg's terminology, a page that links to many authorities is a *hub*; a page that is linked to by many hubs is an *authority*. (And, under the right circumstances, a page can be both a hub and an authority.) The two concepts can be used together to distinguish between authority and mere popularity.

A search based on link analysis begins with a text-based search that provides an initial pool of pages (often several hundred). The set of documents returned by such a search may not include the documents that a human reader would judge to be the most authoritative sources on the topic because the most authoritative sources are not necessarily the ones that use the words in the search string most frequently. Kleinberg uses the example of a search on the keyword *Harvard*. Most people would agree that www.harvard.edu is one of the most authoritative sites on this topic, but in a purely content-based analysis, it does not stand out among the many tens of millions of web pages containing the word *Harvard*. As a result, it is quite likely that a text-based search will not return the university's own website among its top results. It is very likely, however, that at least a few of the documents returned will contain a link to Harvard's home page.

An essential feature of Kleinberg's algorithm is that it does not simply take the pages returned by the initial text-based search and attempt to rank them; it uses them to construct the much larger pool of documents that point to or are pointed to by any of the documents in the root set. This larger pool contains much more global structure — structure that can be mined to determine which documents are considered to be most authoritative by the wide community of people who created the documents in the pool.

The Details

Kleinberg's algorithm for identifying authoritative sources has three phases:

1. Creating the root set
2. Identifying the candidates
3. Ranking hubs and authorities

In the first phase, a *root set* of pages is formed using a text-based search engine to find pages containing the search string. In the second phase, this root set is expanded to include documents that point to or are pointed to by documents in the root set. This expanded set contains the *candidates*. In the third phase, which is iterative, the candidates are ranked according to their strength as topic hubs, which have links to many authorities, and topic authorities, which have links from many hubs.

Creating the Root Set

The root set of documents is generated using a content-based search. As a first step, *stop words* (common words such as "a," "an," "the," and so on) are removed from the original search string. The remaining search terms may undergo *stemming*. Stemming reduces words to their root form by removing plural forms and other endings due to verb conjugation, noun declension, and so on. Then, the web index is searched for documents containing the terms in the search string. There are many variations on the details of how matches are evaluated, which is one reason why performing the same search on two search engines yields different results.

In any case, some combination of the number of matching terms, the rarity of the terms matched, the number of times the search terms are mentioned in a document, and their proximity to each other is used to give the indexed documents scores that determine their ranks in relation to the query. The top n documents are used to establish the root set. A typical value for n is 200.

Identifying the Candidates

In the second phase, the root set is expanded to create the set of candidates by including pages that the root set links to and a subset of the pages linking to the root set. Locating pages that link to a particular target page is simple if the global structure of the Web is available as a directed graph. The same task can also be accomplished with an index-based text search using the URL of the target page as the search string.

To guard against the possibility of an extremely popular site in the root set bringing in an unmanageable number of pages, only a subset of the pages that link to each page in the root set is used. There is also a parameter d that limits the number of pages that may be brought into the candidate set by any single member of the root set.

If more than d documents link to a particular document in the root set, then an arbitrary subset of d documents is brought into the candidate set. A typical value for d is 50. The candidate set typically ends up containing 1,000 to 5,000 documents.

This basic algorithm can be refined in various ways. One possible refinement, for instance, is to filter out any links from within the same domain, many of which are likely to be purely navigational. Another refinement is to allow a document in the root set to bring in at most m pages from the same site. This is to avoid being fooled by "collusion" between all the pages of a site to, for example, advertise the site of the website designer with a "this site designed by" link on every page.

Ranking Hubs and Authorities

The final phase is to divide the candidate pages into hubs and authorities and rank them according to their strength in those roles. This process also has the effect of grouping together pages that refer to the same meaning of a search term with multiple meanings — for instance, Madonna the rock star versus the *Madonna and Child* in art history, or Jaguar the car versus jaguar the big cat. It also differentiates between authorities on the topic of interest and sites that are simply popular in general. Authoritative pages on the correct topic are not only linked to by many pages, they tend to be linked to by the *same* pages. These hub pages tie the authorities to one another and distinguish them from unrelated but popular pages.

Hubs and authorities have a mutually reinforcing relationship. A strong hub is one that links to many strong authorities; a strong authority is one that is linked to by many strong hubs. The algorithm therefore proceeds iteratively, first adjusting the strength rating of the authorities based on the strengths of the hubs that link to them and then adjusting the strengths of the hubs based on the strength of the authorities to which they link.

For each page, there is a value A that measures its strength as an authority and a value H that measures its strength as a hub. Both these values are initialized to 1 for all pages. Then, the A value for each page is updated by adding up the H values of all the pages that link to it. The A values for all pages are then normalized so that the sum of their squares is equal to 1. The H values are updated in a similar manner. The H value for each page is set to the sum of the A values of the pages it links to, and the new H values are normalized so that the sum of their squares is equal to 1. This process is repeated until an equilibrium set of A and H values is reached. The pages that end up with the highest H values are the strongest hubs; those with the strongest A values are the strongest authorities.

Hubs and Authorities in Practice

The strongest case for the advantage of adding link analysis to text-based searching comes from the market place. Google was the first of the major search engines to make use of link analysis to find hubs and authorities. It quickly surpassed long-entrenched search services such as AltaVista and Yahoo!. The reason was qualitatively better searches.

The authors noticed that something was special about Google back in April of 2001 when we studied the web logs from our company's site, www.data-miners .com. At that time, industry surveys gave Google and AltaVista approximately equal 10 percent shares of the market for web searches, and yet Google accounted for 30 percent of the referrals to our site while AltaVista accounted for only 3 percent. This is apparently because Google was better able to recognize our site as an authority for data mining consulting. It was less confused by the large number of sites that use the phrase "data mining" even though they actually have little to do with the topic.

Lessons Learned

Link analysis is an application of the mathematical field of graph theory. As a data mining technique, link analysis has several strengths:

- It capitalizes on relationships.
- It is useful for visualization.
- It creates derived characteristics that can be used for further mining.

Some data and data mining problems naturally involve links. As the case studies about telephone data show, link analysis is very useful for telecommunications — a telephone call is a link between two people. Opportunities for link analysis are most obvious in fields where the links are explicit such as telephony, transportation, and the Web. The recent explosion of social networking sites has greatly increased opportunities for social network analysis. Link analysis is also appropriate in other areas where the connections do not have such a clear manifestation, such as physician referral patterns, retail sales data, and forensic analysis for crimes.

Links are a very natural way to visualize some types of data. Direct visualization of the links can be a big aid to knowledge discovery. Even when automated patterns are found, visualization of the links helps to better understand what is happening. Link analysis offers an alternative way of looking at data, different from the formats of relational databases and OLAP tools. Links may suggest important patterns in the data, but the significance of the patterns requires a person for interpretation.

Link analysis can lead to new and useful data attributes. Examples include calculating an authority score for a page on the Web and calculating the sphere of influence for a telephone user.

Although link analysis is very powerful when applicable, it is not appropriate for all types of problems. It is not a prediction tool or classification tool like a neural network that takes data in and produces an answer. Many types of data are simply not appropriate for link analysis. Its strongest use is probably in finding specific patterns, such as the types of outgoing calls, which can then be applied to data. These patterns can be turned into new features of the data, for use in conjunction with other directed data mining techniques.

CHAPTER 17

Data Warehousing, OLAP, Analytic Sandboxes, and Data Mining

The final chapters of this book cover the topic of data, a topic that has been present in all the earlier chapters, lurking under the surface of discussions about methodology and techniques. As a bad pun to emphasize the importance of data, one could say that "data" is data mining's first name. This chapter puts data into the larger context of decision support systems. The remaining chapters zoom in for a closer look at methods for transforming data to make records more suitable for data mining, at clever ways for bringing important information to the surface, and at external sources of data.

Since the introduction of computers into data processing centers a few decades ago, just about every operational system in business has been computerized, spewing out large amounts of data along the way, and data mining is one way of making sense out of the deluge of data. Automation has changed how people do business and how we live: online retailing, social networking, automated tellers, adjustable rate mortgages, just-in-time inventory control, credit cards, Google, overnight deliveries, and frequent flier/buyer clubs are a few examples of how computer-based automation has opened new markets and revolutionized existing ones. Automation has also created immense amounts of data at the companies that profit from these activities. Data accumulates, but not information — *and not the right information at the right time.*

Data warehousing is the process of bringing together disparate data from throughout an organization for decision support purposes. A data warehouse serves as a decision-support system of record, making it possible to reconcile diverse reports because they have the same underlying source and definitions. Such a system not only reduces the need to explain conflicting results, it also provides consistent views of the business across different organizational units and time. Data warehouses help managers make more informed decisions, and over time more informed decisions should lead to better bottom-line results. As used here, decision support is an intentionally ambiguous and broad term, covering everything from production reports to sophisticated modeling to online recommendation engines.

Data warehousing is a natural ally of data mining, which has a firm requirement for clean and consistent data in the quest for finding actionable patterns. Much of the effort behind data mining endeavors is in the steps of identifying, acquiring, understanding, and cleansing data. A well-designed corporate data warehouse is a valuable ally. Better yet, if the design of the data warehouse includes support for data mining applications, the warehouse facilitates data mining efforts. The two technologies work together to deliver value. Data mining fulfills some of the promise of data warehousing by converting an essentially inert source of clean and consistent data into actionable information.

The relationship between data and data mining also has a technological component. Apart from the ability of users to run multiple jobs at the same time, most software, including data mining and statistical software, does not readily take advantage of the multiple processors, multiple disks, and large memory available on the fastest servers. Relational database management systems (RDBMS), the heart of most data warehouses, are parallel-enabled and readily take advantage of all of a system's resources for processing a single query. Even more importantly, users do not need to be aware of this fact, because the interface, some variant of SQL, remains the same. A database running on a powerful server can be a powerful asset for processing large amounts of data, such as when creating customer signatures for data mining.

As useful as data warehouses are, such systems are not prerequisite for data mining and data analysis. Statisticians, actuaries, and analysts have been using statistical packages for decades — and achieving good results with their analyses — without the benefit of a well-designed centralized data repository. Such analyses often take place on *analytic sandboxes*, special-purpose systems for analyzing data. Nowadays, statistical work uses data mining tools and statistical software packages; reporting uses OLAP tools and Excel; and ad hoc query analysis takes place on the data warehouse itself. Analytic sandboxes are still useful for pushing the envelope of what can be done, for analyzing the ridiculously large volumes of data generated by web servers or for complex statistical methods to simulate aspects of the business, and for other advanced endeavors.

The perspective of this chapter is that data warehouses are part of the virtuous cycle of data mining. They are a valuable and often critical component in supporting all four phases of the cycle: identifying opportunities, analyzing data, applying information, and measuring results. This chapter is not a how-to guide for building a warehouse — many books are already devoted to that subject, and the authors heartily recommend Ralph Kimball's *The Data Warehouse Lifecycle Toolkit* (Wiley, 2008) and Bill Inmon's *Building the Data Warehouse* (Wiley, 2005).

This chapter starts with a discussion of the different types of data that are available, and then discusses data warehousing requirements from the perspective of data mining. It shows a typical data warehousing architecture and variants on this theme. The chapter explains analytic sandboxes, and how they fit into the decision support picture. A discussion about Online Analytic Processing (OLAP), an alternative approach to the normalized data warehouse, follows. The chapter ends with a discussion on the role of data mining in these environments. As with much that has to do with data mining, however, the place to start is with data.

The Architecture of Data

Many different flavors of information are represented on computers. Different levels of data represent different types of abstraction, as shown in Figure 17-1:

- Operational/Transaction data
- Operational summary data
- Decision-support summary data
- Schema
- Metadata
- Business rules

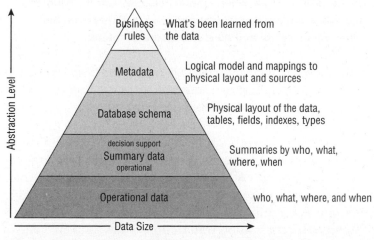

Figure 17-1: A hierarchy of data and its descriptions helps users navigate around a data warehouse. As data gets more abstract, it generally gets less voluminous.

The level of abstraction is an important characteristic of data used in data mining. A well-designed system should allow users to drill down through these levels of abstraction to obtain the base data that supports every summarization and business rule. The lower levels of the pyramid are more voluminous and tend to be the stuff of databases. The upper levels are smaller and tend to be the stuff of spreadsheets and computer code. All these levels are important, because you do not want to analyze the detailed data to merely produce what should already be known.

Transaction Data, the Base Level

Every product purchased by a customer, every bank transaction, every web page visit, every credit card purchase, every flight segment, every delivered package, every telephone call is recorded in at least one operational system. Every time a customer opens an account or clicks on a website or pays a bill or geolocates on a mobile phone, a record of the transaction is stored somewhere, providing information about who, what, where, when, and how much. Such transaction-level data is the raw material for understanding customer behavior. It is the eyes and ears of the enterprise.

Unfortunately, over time operational systems change because of changing business needs. Fields may change their meaning. Important data is rolled off and expunged. Change is constant, in response to the introduction of new products, expanding numbers of customers, acquisitions, reorganizations, and new technology. The fact that operational data changes over time has to be part of any robust data warehousing approach.

> **TIP** Data warehouses need to store data so the information is compatible over time, even when product lines change, when markets change, when customer segments change, and when business organizations change. Otherwise, the data warehouse will have a finite life and quickly become obsolete.

The amount of data gathered from transactional systems can be enormous. A single fast-food restaurant sells hundreds of thousands of meals over the course of a year. A chain of supermarkets can have tens or hundreds of thousands of transactions a day. Big banks process millions of check, credit card, and debit card purchases a day. Large websites have millions of hits each day (in 2009, Google handled more than two billion searches each day). A telephone company has millions of completed calls every hour. A large ad server on the Web keeps track of billions of ad views every day. Even with the price of disk space falling, storing all these transactions requires a significant investment. For reference, remember that a day has 86,400 seconds, so a million transactions a day is an average of about 12 transactions per second all day (and two billion searches amounts to close to 25,000 searches every second!) — with peaks several times higher.

Because of the large data volumes, companies are often reluctant to store transaction-level data in a data warehouse. From the perspective of data mining, this is a shame, because the transactions best describe customer behavior. Analytic sandboxes are an effective alternative for exploring and using transactional data that does not readily fit into the warehouse.

Operational Summary Data

Operational summaries play the same role as transactions; the difference is that operational summaries are derived from transactions. A common example is billing systems, which summarize transactions, usually into monthly bill cycles. These summaries are customer-facing and often result in other transactions, such as bill payments. In some cases, operational summaries may include fields that are summarized to enhance the company's understanding of its customers rather than for operational purposes. For instance, AT&T once used call detail records to calculate a "bizocity" score, measuring the business-like behavior of a telephone number's calling pattern. The records of each call are discarded, but the score is kept up to date.

There is a distinction between operational summary data and transaction data, because summaries are for a period of time and transactions represent events. Consider the amount paid by a subscription customer. In a billing system, amount paid is a summary for the billing period, because it includes all payments during the period. A payment history table instead provides detail on every payment transaction. For most customers, the monthly summary and payment transactions are equivalent. However, two payments might arrive during the same billing period. The more detailed payment information might be useful for insight into customer payment patterns.

Decision-Support Summary Data

Decision-support summary data is the data used for making decisions about the business. The financial data used to run a company provides an example of decision-support summary data; upper levels of management often consider this to be the cleanest information available. Another example is the data warehouses and data marts whose purpose is to provide a decision-support system of record at the customer level.

Generally, it is a bad idea to use the same system for analytic and operational purposes, because operational needs are more important, resulting in a system that is optimized for operations and not decision support. Financial systems are not generally designed for understanding customers, because they are designed for accounting purposes. One of the goals of data warehousing is to provide consistent definitions and layouts so similar reports produce similar results, no matter which business user is producing them or when they are produced.

WARNING Do not expect customer-level data warehouse information to balance exactly against financial systems (although the two systems should be close). Although theoretically possible, such balancing can prove very difficult and distract from the purpose of the data warehouse.

In one sense, summaries destroy information as they aggregate data together. However, summaries can also bring information to the surface. Point-of-sale transactions may capture every can of sardines that goes over the scanner, but only summaries begin to describe the shopper's behavior in terms of her habits — the time of day when she shops, the proportion of her dollars spent on canned foods, whether organic produce complements the sardines, and so on. In this case, the customer summary seems to be creating information or at least bringing it to the surface, making it visible.

Database Schema/Data Models

The structure of data is also important — what data is stored, where it is stored, what is not stored, and so on. The sidebar "What Is a Relational Database?" explains the key ideas behind relational databases, the most common systems for storing large amounts of data.

No matter how the data is stored, there are at least two ways of describing the layout. The *physical data model* describes the layout in the technical detail needed by the underlying software. An example is the `"CREATE TABLE"` statement in SQL. A *logical data model*, on the other hand, describes the data in a way more accessible to end users. The two are not necessarily the same, nor even similar, as shown in Figure 17-2. Note that the term "data model" means something quite different from "data mining model."

WARNING The existence of fields in a database does not mean that the data is actually present. It is important to understand every field used for data mining, and not to assume that a field is populated correctly just because it exists. Skepticism is your ally.

An analogy might help to understand the differences between the physical and logical data models. A logical model for a house is analogous to saying that a house is ranch style, with four bedrooms, three baths, and a two-car garage. The physical model goes into more detail about how it is laid out. The foundation is reinforced concrete, 4 feet deep; the slab is 1,500 square feet; the walls are concrete block; and so on. The details of construction, although useful and complete, may not be so helpful for a family looking for the right home.

Logical Data Model

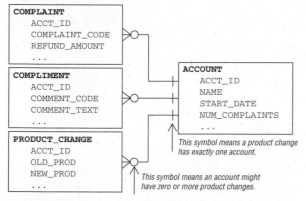

This logical model has four entities for customer generated events and one for accounts.

The logical model is intended to be understood by business users.

Physical Data Model

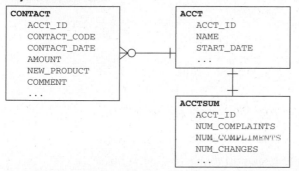

In the physical model, information from three entities is combined into a single CONTACT table, where different types of contacts are distinguished using the CONTACT_TYPE field.

Information about accounts is actually split into two tables, because one is summarized from the CONTACT table.

The physical model also specifies exact types, partitioning, indexes, storage characteristics, degrees of parallel, constraints on values, and many other things not of interest to the business user.

Figure 17-2: The physical and logical data models may not be similar to each other.

WHAT IS A RELATIONAL DATABASE?

One of the most common ways to store data is in a relational database management system (RDBMS). The theoretical foundation of relational databases starts with research by E. F. Codd in the early 1970s on the mathematical properties of a special type of set composed of *tuples* — what you would call rows in tables. His work led to the creation of a relational algebra, consisting of a set of operations that are depicted in the following figure:

Continued

WHAT IS A RELATIONAL DATABASE?   (*continued*)

Before | | After

FILTER (rows)

Filtering removes rows based on the values in one or more columns. The output rows are a subset of the rows in the input table.

SELECT (columns)

Selecting chooses the columns for the output. Each column in the output is in the input, or a function of some of the input columns.

AGGREGATE

Aggregating (group by) summarizes columns based on a common key. All the rows with the same key are summarized into a single output row, by performing aggregation operations on zero or more columns.

JOIN (tables)

Joining combines rows in two tables, usually based on a join condition consisting of a boolean expression involving rows in both tables. Whenever a pair of rows from the two tables match, a new row is created in the output.

Relational databases have four major querying operations.

> In nonscientific terminology, these relational operations are:
>
>> *Filter* a given set of rows based on the values in the rows.
>>
>> *Select* a given set of columns and perform functions on the values of the columns in a single row.
>>
>> *Aggregate* rows together and calculate summary values in the columns.
>>
>> *Join* two tables together by appending rows together based on rows in the table satisfying a match condition.

The relational operations do not include sorting, except for output purposes. These operations specify *what* can be done with tuples, not *how* it gets done. Although relational databases often use sorting for grouping and joining operations, there are non-sort-based algorithms for these operations as well.

SQL, originally developed by IBM in the 1980s, has become the standard language for accessing relational databases and implements these basic operations. Because SQL supports subqueries (that is, using the results of one query as a data source for another query), it can express some very complex data manipulations. Since SQL was first standardized in 1992, SQL has been extended in many ways; some, such as the addition of window functions and grouping sets, have made it even more useful for complex queries and data analysis.

A common way of representing the database structure is to use an entity-relationship (E-R) diagram. The following figure is a simple E-R diagram with five entities and four relationships among them. In this case, each entity corresponds to a separate table with columns corresponding to the attributes of the entity. In addition, columns represent the relationships between tables in the database; such columns are called *keys* (either foreign or primary keys). Explicitly storing keys in the database tables using a consistent naming convention helps users find their way around the database.

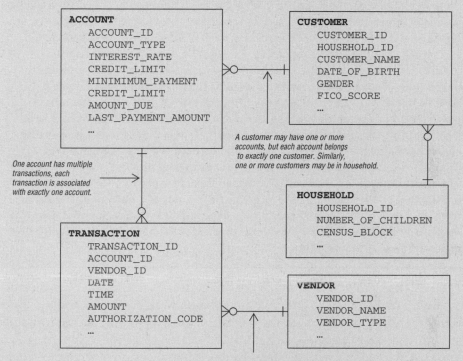

ACCOUNT
ACCOUNT_ID
ACCOUNT_TYPE
INTEREST_RATE
CREDIT_LIMIT
MINIMIMUM_PAYMENT
CREDIT_LIMIT
AMOUNT_DUE
LAST_PAYMENT_AMOUNT
...

CUSTOMER
CUSTOMER_ID
HOUSEHOLD_ID
CUSTOMER_NAME
DATE_OF_BIRTH
GENDER
FICO_SCORE
...

A customer may have one or more accounts, but each account belongs to exactly one customer. Similarly, one or more customers may be in household.

One account has multiple transactions, each transaction is associated with exactly one account.

HOUSEHOLD
HOUSEHOLD_ID
NUMBER_OF_CHILDREN
CENSUS_BLOCK
...

TRANSACTION
TRANSACTION_ID
ACCOUNT_ID
VENDOR_ID
DATE
TIME
AMOUNT
AUTHORIZATION_CODE
...

VENDOR
VENDOR_ID
VENDOR_NAME
VENDOR_TYPE
...

A single transaction has exactly one vendor, but a vendor may have multiple transactions.

An ER diagram can be used to show the tables and fields in a relational database. Each box shows a single table and its columns. The lines between the boxes show relationships, such as 1-many, 1-1, and many-to-many. Because each table corresponds to an entity, this is called a physical model.

Sometimes, the physical model of a database is very complicated. For instance, the TRANSACTION table might actually be split into a separate table for each month of transactions, to facilitate backup and restore processes.

An entity relationship diagram describes the layout of data for a simple credit card database.

Relational databases can be designed so that any given data item appears in exactly one place — with no duplication. Such a database is called *normalized*. Knowing exactly where each data item is located is highly efficient for some purposes, because updating any value requires modifying only one row

Continued

WHAT IS A RELATIONAL DATABASE? *(continued)*

in one table. When a normalized database is well-designed and implemented, there is no redundant data, out-of-date data, or invalid data.

An important idea behind normalization is the creation of reference tables. Each reference table logically corresponds to an entity, and each has a key used for looking up information about the entity. In a normalized database, the "join" operation is used to lookup values in reference tables.

Relational databases are a powerful way of storing and accessing data. However, the focus of their technical implementation is usually to support updating large volumes of data and handling large numbers of transactions. Data mining is interested in combining data together to spot higher-level patterns. Typically, data mining uses many queries, each of which requires several joins, several aggregations, and subqueries — a veritable army of killer queries.

With respect to data mining, relational databases (and SQL) have some limitations. First, they provide little support for time series. This makes it hard to figure out from transaction data such things as the second product purchased, the last three promos a customer responded to, or the most common ordering of a set of events. Another problem is that two operations often eliminate fields inadvertently. When a field contains a missing value (NULL) then it automatically fails any comparison, even "not equals." Also, the default join operation (called an inner join) eliminates rows that do not match, which means that customers may inadvertently be left out of a data pull. The set of functions in SQL is not particularly rich, especially for text data and dates. The result is that every database vendor extends standard SQL to include slightly different sets of functionality.

Data models can also illuminate unusual findings in the data. For instance, the authors once worked with a file of call detail records in the United States that had city and state fields for the destination of every call. The file contained more than 200 state codes — that is a lot of states. What was happening? The city and state fields were never read by operational systems, so their contents were automatically suspicious — data that is not used is not likely to be correct. Instead of the city and state, all location information was derived from ZIP codes. These redundant fields were inaccurate because the state field was written first and the city field, with 14 characters, was written second. Longer city names overwrote the state field next to it. So, "WEST PALM BEACH, FL" ended up putting the "H" in the state field, becoming "WEST PALM BEAC, HL," and "COLORADO SPRINGS, CO" became "COLORADO SPRIN, GS." Understanding the data layout helped us figure out this amusing but admittedly uncommon problem.

Metadata

Metadata goes beyond the data model to let business users know what types of information are stored in the database. This is, in essence, documentation about the system, including information such as:

- The values legally allowed in each field
- A description of the contents of each field (for instance, is the start date the date of the sale or the date of activation?)
- The date when the data was loaded
- An indication of how recently the data has been updated (when after the billing cycle does the billing data land in this system?)
- Mappings to other systems (the status code in table A is the status code field in table B in such-and-such source system)

When available, metadata provides an invaluable service. When not available, this type of information needs to be gleaned, usually from friendly database administrators and analysts — a perhaps inefficient use of everyone's time. For a data warehouse, metadata provides discipline, because changes to the warehouse must be reflected in the metadata to be communicated to users. Overall, a good metadata system helps ensure the success of a data warehouse by making users more aware of and comfortable with the contents. For data miners, metadata provides valuable assistance in tracking down and understanding data.

Business Rules

The highest level of abstraction is business rules. These describe why relationships exist and how they are applied. Some business rules are easy to capture, because they represent the history of the business — what marketing campaigns took place when, what products were available when, and so on. Other types of rules are more difficult to capture and often lie buried deep inside code fragments and old memos. No one may remember why the fraud detection system ignores claims under $500. Presumably there was a good business reason, but the reason, the business rule, may be lost when the rule is embedded in computer code.

Business rules have a close relationship to data mining. Some data mining techniques, such as market basket analysis and decision trees, produce explicit rules. Often, these rules may already be known. A direct mail response model that ends up targeting only wealthy areas may reflect the fact that the historical data used to build the model was focused only on those areas. That is, the model set may only have responders in these areas, because only wealthy people were targeted in the past.

Discovering business rules in the data is both a success and a failure. Finding these rules is a successful demonstration of sophisticated algorithms. However, in data mining, you want actionable patterns and such patterns are not actionable.

A General Architecture for Data Warehousing

The multitiered approach to data warehousing recognizes that data comes in many different forms. It provides a comprehensive system for managing data for decision support. The major components of this architecture (see Figure 17-3) are:

- *Source systems* are where the data comes from.
- Extraction, transformation, and load (ETL) tools move data between different data stores.
- The *central repository* is the main store for the data warehouse.
- The *analytic sandbox* provides an environment for more complex analysis than is possible with SQL queries or data mining tools.
- The *metadata repository* describes what is available and where.
- *Data marts* provide fast, specialized access for end users and applications.
- *Operational feedback* integrates decision support back into the operational systems.
- *End users* are the reason for developing the warehouse in the first place.

One or more of these components exist in virtually every system called a data warehouse. They are the building blocks of decision support throughout an enterprise. The following discussion of these components follows a data-flow approach. The data is like water. It originates in the source systems and flows through the components of the data warehouse ultimately to deliver information and value to end users. These components rest on a technological foundation consisting of hardware, software, and networks; this infrastructure must be sufficiently robust both to meet the needs of end users and to meet growing data and processing requirements.

Source Systems

Data originates in the source systems, typically operational systems and external data feeds. These are designed for operational efficiency, not for decision support, and the data reflects this reality. For instance, transactional data might be rolled off every few months to reduce storage needs. The same information might be represented in multiple ways. For example, one retail point-of-sale source system represented returned merchandise using a "returned item" flag. That is, except when the customer made a new purchase at the same time. In this case, there would be a negative amount in the purchase field. Such anomalies abound in the real world.

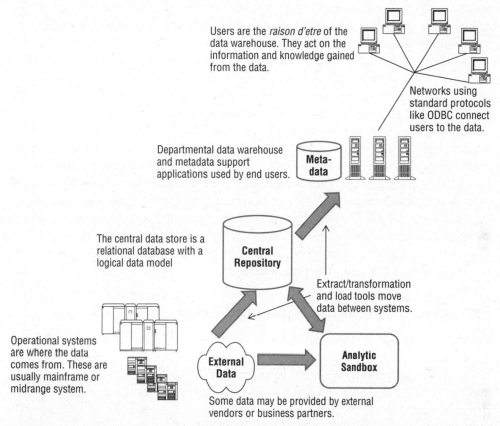

Users are the *raison d'etre* of the data warehouse. They act on the information and knowledge gained from the data.

Networks using standard protocols like ODBC connect users to the data.

Departmental data warehouse and metadata support applications used by end users.

Meta-data

The central data store is a relational database with a logical data model

Central Repository

Extract/transformation and load tools move data between systems.

Operational systems are where the data comes from. These are usually mainframe or midrange system.

External Data

Analytic Sandbox

Some data may be provided by external vendors or business partners.

Figure 17-3: The multitiered approach to data warehousing includes a central repository, data marts, analytic sandboxes, end-user tools, and tools that connect all these pieces together.

Often, information of interest for customer relationship management is not gathered as intended. Here, for instance, are six ways that business customers might be distinguished from consumers in a telephone company:

- Customer type indicator: "B" or "C," for business versus consumer.
- Rate plans: Some are only sold to business customers; others to consumers.
- Acquisition channels: Some channels are reserved for business, others for consumers.
- Number of lines: one or two for consumer, more for business.

- Credit class: Businesses have a different set of credit classes from consumers.
- Model score based on businesslike calling patterns.

Needless to say, these definitions do not always agree. One challenge in data warehousing is arriving at a consistent definition that can be used across the business. The key to achieving this is metadata that documents the precise meaning of each field, so everyone using the data warehouse is speaking the same language.

Gathering data for decision support stresses operational systems because these systems were originally designed for transaction processing. Bringing the data together in a consistent format is almost always the most expensive part of implementing a data warehousing solution.

The source systems offer other challenges as well. They generally run on a wide range of hardware, and much of the software is built in-house or highly customized (or they are outsourced and the raw data may be very difficult to get). They sometimes use complicated and proprietary file structures. Mainframe systems are designed for holding and processing data, not for sharing it. Although systems are becoming more open, getting access to the data is always an issue, especially when different systems support very different parts of the organization. And, systems may be geographically dispersed, further contributing to the difficulty of bringing the data together.

Extraction, Transformation, and Load

Extraction, transformation, and load (ETL) tools solve the problem of gathering data from disparate systems by providing the ability to map and move data from source systems to other environments. Traditionally, data movement and cleansing have been the responsibility of programmers, who wrote special-purpose code as the need arose. Such application-specific code becomes brittle as systems multiply and source systems change.

Although programming may still be necessary, products are now available that solve the bulk of the ETL problems. These tools specify source systems and mappings between different tables and files. They provide the ability to verify data, and spit out error reports when loads do not succeed. The tools also support looking up values in tables (so only known product codes, for instance, are loaded into the data warehouse). The goal of these tools is to describe where data comes from and what happens to it — not to write the step-by-step code for pulling data from one system and putting it into another. Standard procedural languages, such as C++, C#, Java, COBOL, and RPG, focus on each step instead of the bigger picture of what needs to be done. ETL tools often provide a metadata interface, so end users can understand what is happening to "their" data during the loading of the central repository.

This genre of tools is often so good at processing data that the authors are surprised that such tools remain embedded in IT departments and are not more generally used by data miners. *Mastering Data Mining* has a case study from 1998 on using one of these tools from Ab Initio for analyzing hundreds of gigabytes of call detail records — a quantity of data that might still pose a challenge even today.

Central Repository

The central repository is the heart of the data warehouse. It is usually a relational database accessed through some variant of SQL.

One of the advantages of relational databases is their ability to run on powerful, scalable machines by taking advantage of multiple processors and multiple disks (see the sidebar "Background on Parallel Technology"). Most statistical and data mining packages, for instance, can run multiple processing threads at the same time. However, each thread represents one task, running on one processor. More hardware does not make any given task run faster (except when other tasks happen to be interfering with it). Relational databases, on the other hand, can take a single query and, in essence, create multiple threads all running at the same time for that one query. As a result, data-intensive applications on powerful computers often run more quickly when using a relational database than when using non-parallel-enabled software — and data mining is a very data-intensive application.

A key component in the central repository is a logical data model, which describes the structure of the data inside a database in terms familiar to business users. As discussed earlier in this chapter, the logical data model differs from the physical data model. The purpose of the physical data model is to maximize performance and facilitate the work of database administrators (DBAs), such as ensuring security, backing up the database, and so on. The physical data model is an implementation of the logical data model, incorporating compromises and choices along the way to optimize performance and to meet other system objectives.

> **TIP** Data warehousing is a process. Be wary of any large database called a data warehouse that does not have a process in place for updating the system to continuously meet end user needs and evolving business requirements. A data warehouse without a change process will eventually fade into disuse, because users' needs evolve.

When embarking on a data warehousing project, many organizations feel compelled to develop a comprehensive, enterprise-wide data model. These efforts are often surprisingly unsuccessful. The logical data model for the data warehouse does not have to be quite as uncompromising as an enterprise-wide model. For instance, a conflict between product codes in the logical data model for the data warehouse can be (but not necessarily should be) resolved by including both product hierarchies — a decision that takes 10 minutes to make. In an enterprise-wide effort, resolving conflicting product codes can require months of investigations and meetings.

Data warehousing is a process for managing the decision-support system of record. A process is something that can adjust to users' needs as they are clarified and change over time. The central repository itself is going to be a brittle, little-used system without the awareness that as users learn about data and about the business, they are going to want changes and enhancements on the time scale of marketing (days and weeks) rather than on the time scale of IT (months).

BACKGROUND ON PARALLEL TECHNOLOGY

Parallel technology is the key to scalable hardware, and it traditionally comes in two flavors: symmetric multiprocessing systems (SMPs) and massively parallel processing systems (MPPs), both of which are shown in the following figure. An SMP machine is centered on a *bus*, a special very local network present in all computers that connects processing units to memory and disk drives. The bus acts as a central communication device, so SMP systems are sometimes called *shared everything*. Every processing unit can access all the memory and all the disk drives. This form of parallelism is quite popular because an SMP box supports the same applications as uniprocessor boxes — and some applications can take advantage of additional hardware with minimal changes to code. However, SMP technology has its limitations because it places a heavy burden on the central bus, which becomes saturated as the processing load increases. Contention for the central bus is often what limits the performance of SMPs. They tend to work best when they have no more than 10 to 20 processing units.

MPPs, on the other hand, behave like separate computers connected by a very high-speed network, and, in fact, MPP is sometimes referred to as *grid computing*. Each processing unit has its own memory and its own disk storage. Some nodes may be specialized for processing and have minimal disk storage, and others may be specialized for storage and have lots of disk capacity. The bus connecting the processing unit to memory and disk drives never gets saturated, because it is not shared among all processors. However, one drawback is that some memory and some disk drives are now local and some are remote — a distinction that can make MPPs harder to program. Programs designed for one processor can always run on one processor in an MPP — but they require modifications to take advantage of all the hardware. MPPs are truly scalable as long as the network connecting the processors can supply more bandwidth, and faster networks are generally easier to design than faster buses. There are MPP-based computers with thousands of nodes and thousands of disks.

Both SMPs and MPPs have their advantages. Recognizing this, the vendors of these computers are making them more similar to each other. SMP vendors are connecting their SMP computers together in clusters that start to resemble MPP boxes. At the same time, MPP vendors are replacing their single-processing units with SMP units, creating a very similar architecture. Newer technologies, such as solid state disks, ultrafast networks, and cheap memory, are making computers even more powerful with fewer processing bottlenecks. However, regardless of the power of the hardware, software needs to be designed to take advantage of these machines. Fortunately, the largest database vendors have invested years of research into enabling their products to do so.

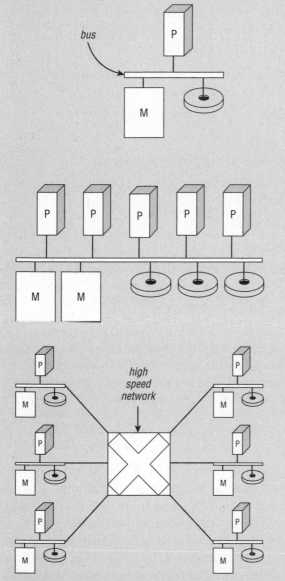

Uniprocessor

A simple computer follows the architecture laid out by Von Neumann. A processing unit communicates to memory and disk over a local bus. (Memory stores both data and the executable program.) The speed of the processor, bus, and memory limits performance and scalability.

SMP

The symmetric multiprocessor (SMP) has a shared-everything architecture. It expands the capabilities of the bus to support multiple processors, more memory, and a larger disk. The capacity of the bus limits performance and scalability. SMP architecture usually max out with fewer than 20 processing units.

MPP

The massively parallel processor (MMP) has a shared-nothing architecture. It introduces a high-speed network (also called a switch that connects independent processor/memory/disk components. MPP architectures are very scalable but fewer software packages can take advantage of all the hardware.

Parallel computers build on the basic Von Neumann uniprocessor architecture. SMP and MPP systems are scalable because more processing units, disk drives, and memory can be added to the system.

Metadata Repository

Metadata should also be considered a component of the data warehouse, although it is often overlooked. The lowest level of metadata is the database schema, the physical layout of the data. When used correctly, though, metadata is much more. It answers questions posed by end users about the availability of data, gives them tools for browsing through the contents of the data warehouse, and gives everyone more confidence in the data. This confidence is the basis for new applications and an expanded user base.

A good metadata system should include the following:

- The annotated logical data model. The annotations should explain the entities and attributes, including valid values.

- Mapping from the logical data model to the source systems.

- The physical schema.

- Mapping from the logical model to the physical schema.

- Common views and formulas for accessing the data. What is useful to one user may be useful to others.

- Information about loads and updates.

- Security and access information.

- Interfaces for end users and developers, so they share the same description of the database.

In any data warehousing environment, each of these pieces of information is available somewhere — in scripts written by the DBA, in e-mail messages, in documentation, in the system tables in the database, and so on. A metadata repository makes this information available to the users in a format they can readily understand. The key is giving users access so they feel comfortable with the data warehouse, with the data it contains, and with knowing how to use it.

Data Marts

Data warehouses do not actually do anything, except store and retrieve clean, consistent data effectively. Applications are needed to realize value, and these often take the form of data marts. A data mart is a specialized system that brings together the data needed for a department or related applications.

Data marts are often associated with reporting systems and slicing-and-dicing pre-summarized data. Such data marts often use OLAP technology, which is discussed later in this chapter. Another important type of data mart is an exploratory environment used for data mining, which is discussed in more detail in the section on analytic sandboxes.

Not all the data in data marts needs to come from the central repository. Often specific applications have an exclusive need for data. The real estate department, for instance, might be using geographic information in combination with data from the central repository. The marketing department might be combining ZIP code demographics with customer data from the central repository. The central repository only needs to contain data that is likely to be shared among different applications, so it is just one data source — usually the dominant one — for data marts.

Operational Feedback

Operational feedback systems integrate data-driven decisions back into the operational systems. For instance, a large bank may develop cross-sell models to determine what product to offer a customer next. This is a result of a data mining system. To be useful this information needs to go back into the operational systems so customers can get a targeted message in their mailbox, at the ATM, on hold at the call center, as banner ads when they log into online banking, and so on. This requires a connection back from the decision-support infrastructure into the operational infrastructure.

Operational feedback offers the capability to complete the virtuous cycle of data mining very quickly. After a feedback system is set up, intervention is only needed for monitoring and improving it — letting computers do what they do best (repetitive tasks) and letting people do what they do best (spot interesting patterns and come up with ideas). One of the advantages of e-businesses is that they can, in theory, provide such feedback to their operational systems in a fully automated way.

Users and Desktop Tools

The users are the final and most important component in any data warehouse. A system that has no users is not worth building. These end users are analysts looking for information, application developers, and business users who act on the information.

Analysts

Analysts want to access as much data as possible to discern patterns and create ad hoc reports. They use special-purpose tools, such as statistics packages, data mining tools, and spreadsheets. Often, analysts are considered to be the primary audience for data warehouses.

Usually, though, just a few technically sophisticated people fall into this category. Although the work that they do is important, justifying a large investment based on increases in their productivity is difficult. The virtuous cycle of data mining comes into play here. A data warehouse brings together data in a cleansed, meaningful format. The purpose, though, is to spur creativity, a very hard concept to measure.

Analysts have very specific demands on a data warehouse:

- The system has to be responsive. Much of the work of analysts is answering urgent questions using ad hoc analysis or ad hoc queries.

- Data needs to be consistent across the database. That is, if a customer started on a particular date, then the first occurrence of a product, channel, and so on should normally be exactly on that date.

- Data needs to be consistent across time. A field that has a particular meaning now should have the same meaning going back in time. At the very least, differences should be well documented or incorporated into slowly changing dimensions.

- Analysts must be able to drill down to the customer level and preferably to the transaction level detail to verify values in the data warehouse and to develop new summaries of customer behavior.

Analysts place a heavy load on data warehouses, and need access to consistent information in a timely manner.

Application Developers

Data warehouses usually support a wide range of applications (in other words, data marts come in many flavors). To develop stable and robust applications, developers have some specific needs from the data warehouse.

First, the applications need to be shielded from changes in the structure of the data warehouse. New tables, new fields, and reorganizing the structure of existing tables should have a minimal impact on existing applications. Special application-specific views on the data help provide this assurance. Open communication and knowledge about what applications use which attributes and entities can prevent development gridlock.

Second, the developers need access to valid field values and to know what the values mean. This is the purpose of the metadata repository, which provides documentation on the structure of the data. By setting up the application to verify data values against expected values in the metadata, developers can circumvent problems that often appear only after applications have rolled out.

The developers also need to provide feedback on the structure of the data warehouse. This is one of the principle means of improving the warehouse, by identifying new data that needs to be included and by fixing problems with data already loaded. Because real business needs drive the development of applications, understanding the needs of developers is important to ensure that a data warehouse contains the data it needs to deliver business value.

The data warehouse is going to change and applications are going to continue to use it. The key to delivering success is controlling and managing the changes. The applications are for the end users. The data warehouse is there to support their data needs — not vice versa.

Business Users

Business users are the ultimate devourers of information derived from the corporate data warehouse. Their needs drive the development of applications, the architecture of the warehouse, the data it contains, and the priorities for implementation.

Many business users only experience the warehouse through printed reports, simple online reports, or spreadsheets — basically the same way they have been gathering information for a long time. Even these users will experience the power of having a data warehouse as reports become more accurate, more consistent, and easier to produce.

More important, though, are the people who use the computers on their desks for more than just e-mail and Facebook and are able to take advantage of direct access to the data warehousing environment. Typically, these users access intermediate data marts to satisfy the vast majority of their information needs using friendly, graphical tools that run in their familiar desktop environment. These tools include off-the-shelf query generators, custom applications, OLAP interfaces, Excel-driven query tools, and report generation tools. On occasion, business users may drill down into the central repository to explore particularly interesting things they find in the data. More often, they will contact an analyst and have him or her do the heavier analytic work or prepare a data extract for Excel.

Business users also have applications built for specific purposes. These applications may even incorporate some of the data mining techniques discussed in previous chapters. For instance, a resource scheduling application might include an engine that optimizes the schedule using genetic algorithms. A sales forecasting application may have built-in survival analysis models. When embedded in an application, the data mining algorithms are usually quite well hidden from the end users, who care more about the results than the algorithms that produced them.

Analytic Sandboxes

Analytic sandboxes are the environment for the ad hoc data transformations, investigations, and analyses that go beyond the capabilities of the data warehouse and the predefined goals of data marts. The term *sandbox* is intended to convey the idea that these are environments where analysts play with data and tools to achieve interesting results.

Why Are Analytic Sandboxes Needed?

Analytics sandboxes serve several purposes. Data warehouses are powerful systems for *publishing* and sharing data. As with publishing books, the data warehousing process cleans and edits the data to be sure that it is consistent and meets standards. However, situations arise where the data in the warehouse may not be sufficient for some reason. These are the situations where analytic sandboxes are important.

Too Much Data

An obvious need for an analytic sandbox arises when the volume of data is simply too large for a relational database. Some data sources grow by tens of millions, hundreds of millions, or even billions of transactions per day, and are often associated with web and telecommunications applications. When the raw data starts measuring in the hundreds of megabytes or gigabytes of data per day — or more — then more advanced tools are often needed for ad hoc analysis.

The data sources feeding an analytic sandbox are still valuable sources for a data warehouse. However, ad hoc analyses that are outside the scope of the warehouse may be needed.

On one project, for instance, the authors were asked to answer a seemingly simple question for a large media company: "How many unique users visit our website in one month?" The website in question had more than a billion page views per month. A page view includes a lot of data, so this corresponds to more than 200GB of raw data per month. The page view contains URIs (which stands for *uniform resource identifier*, but is more commonly known as a web address) for the page being loaded and for the referring page, information about the browser, various cookie IDs, date and time stamps, and so on.

At the website in question, some users identify themselves by logging in. These identified users can be reliably tracked and counted. Users who remain anonymous pose more of a challenge. The idea was to find some metric, such as number of page views per logged-in user, and then use this to determine the total number of users. The actual metric required first *sessionizing* the data, to determine the number of visits to the site, a visit being a contiguous sequence of page views. The key measure was the average number of sessions an identified (logged-in) user has in a month. Dividing the total number of sessions in a month by this average provides an estimate of the number of unique visitors in a month.

The problem was that the data warehouse that stored all the web data did not maintain all the detail needed for this analysis. Answering the question required an analytic sandbox, in this case, one using cloud computing (specifically, Amazon's Elastic Computing Cloud, EC2) and code written using Hadoop, which is discussed later in this section.

The purpose of this example is not to go into the calculation in detail. Instead, when working with large amounts of data, such as the data in web logs, the features extracted for data warehouse data structures may not include all the information needed for a particular analysis. An analytic sandbox provides the infrastructure for answering such questions.

More Advanced Techniques

Analytic sandboxes can support more advanced techniques than supported in a standard data mart or in reporting systems. Often, statistical tools, such as SAS, SPSS, R, and other programming languages are used in this environment, where statisticians write special-purpose code to develop useful methods for analyzing data.

The range of possible techniques is limitless. Some of the more interesting involve simulations described in Chapter 12. A basic type of simulation is the Monte Carlo simulation, named after the famous casino. Consider a situation where a company wants to make a strategic decision on whether it should enter a new line of business. The business model for this decision might involve a number of variables, such as the number of customers the new business would attract and the amount of money the company would need to invest. Another set of inputs into this type of model involve financial measures, such as the cost of money, which in turn depends on the prevailing interest rate and other economic factors.

Of course, the future values of these variables are not actually known. Instead, the values are assumed to follow some statistical distribution, such as a normal distribution with a particular average and standard deviation. Monte Carlo simulation is the process of testing different scenarios, over and over, by pulling the input variables from their appropriate distributions, and then calculating the possible values for the investment.

Monte Carlo simulation is just one example of many. Another computationally intensive approach that requires advanced statistical knowledge is Bayesian models (not to be confused with the naïve Bayesian models introduced in Chapter 6). What these techniques have in common is that they often require advanced statistical knowledge and special-purpose tools.

Complex Data

The third reason why an analytic sandbox might be necessary is for complex data structures that do not fit neatly into a relational data structure. These include text, images, audio, video, social networks, and so on. Relational databases are not optimized for these sorts of content.

LinkedIn is a popular site for professional networking. One feature of the site is "People You May Know." One of the authors was impressed to find his brother at the top of the list. In telling this story to an acquaintance, he was trumped: LinkedIn suggested that the person might know his wife.

The point of this example is that "People You May Know" is not a SQL function, not even in the most advanced database. Although it is based on link analysis, it requires special-purpose code to implement. LinkedIn used an implementation of a methodology called *MapReduce* (discussed in the next section) to create this feature.

Technology to Support Analytic Sandboxes

There are many different types of analytic sandboxes, because there are so many different ways to use them. This section discusses some of the technology that supports them. In some cases, the analytic sandbox can also be the data warehouse — at a certain cost, however. In such cases, the data warehouse would have to be sized to be able to perform both its duties as a data warehouse (delivering quality data to downstream applications and ad hoc query requests) and as a platform for analysis.

Faster Databases

Relational databases have become even more adept at analysis than their inventor, E. F. Codd, envisioned. Partly, this is due to more functionality in the SQL language, such as window functions (sometimes called analytic functions), grouping sets, better scalar functions, and user-defined functions. Another important factor is improvements in performance.

In the past few years, a new breed of database vendor has emerged that complements the traditional vendors such as Teradata, Oracle, IBM, HP, and Microsoft. These databases are based on open-source code, often on a database called PostGres, originally developed at the University of California, Berkeley in the 1980s. What makes PostGres so popular for these new vendors is its open-source license: Although PostGres itself is free and open-source, a vendor can modify the source code and sell the resulting product, something not allowed by all open-source licenses.

The most common feature added to PostGres is parallel processing to make the database scalable; virtually all vendors who use PostGres as a base for their database have this functionality. The first successful company was Netezza (acquired by IBM in 2010), whose product combines a parallel database with a hardware accelerator. XtremeData is another company following the example of a hardware accelerator, whereas companies such as GreenPlum and Aster Data run on generic platforms, without special hardware.

Vertical partitioning refers to storing each column separately from other columns. Such column-oriented databases have the advantage that when one column is used in a query, then the rest of the columns in the same table do not have to be loaded into memory greatly saving time on reading and writing data. Furthermore, compressing each column independently is usually much more efficient than compressing rows (which consists of different types in different columns), providing further performance improvements. Two leading vendors in this area are ParAccel and Vertica.

Yet another feature is in-memory processing, which significantly speeds up the database by storing everything in memory, eschewing slower disk. ParAccel is a leader with this technology.

As time goes by, the good technology offered by different vendors will converge to create faster and faster databases at all vendors. As today's technology becomes standard, new technologies will emerge. The traditional database vendors are not standing still; they are enhancing their databases with similar features to remain competitive.

Improvements in hardware are also speeding up databases, especially the reduced cost of memory and the increased adoption of solid-state disk drives. Both of these are moving in the same direction — obtaining in-memory performance at accessible prices. As time goes by, standard databases will only become stronger in the area of applying SQL for complex ad hoc analyses.

In Database Analytics

Another trend that is becoming popular is putting more advanced analytic functions directly into the database. Because databases are very good at processing data — and powerful databases take advantage of parallel processing — this is a good way to broaden the functionality of SQL, making it possible to use a data mart or data warehouse as an analytic sandbox.

In the mid-1990s, the data mining software package Clementine started offering "in-database" data mining. This allowed the package to take advantage of databases for some model building and scoring work. The first database to support Clementine was produced by a company called Tandem. Moving ahead several years, Clementine is now part of IBM (ISL, the original creator of Clementine, was purchased by SPSS, which IBM purchased) and Tandem is now part of HP (Tandem became Digital became Compaq became HP), and Clementine still supports in-database processing.

Starting in 2002, Oracle Data Mining software started moving all its data mining functionality directly into the database. This speeds the algorithms both because they can access the data directly through the database engine and also because they can take advantage of its parallel capabilities. Since then, Oracle has greatly expanded the data mining functionality of its software.

Because SAS's software is so widespread, SAS's efforts in this area are also very important. Database vendors are implementing certain SAS primitives in the database, and the range of functionality will only grow in the future. This allows SAS's software — which is generally not parallel-enabled — to take advantage of the power of relational databases.

Another step in this direction is offered by companies such as Fuzzy Logix, which extends databases using user-defined functions. Its package offers a range of statistical and data mining routines that can be called directly from SQL. Of course, these functions are not part of the SQL standard.

Statistical Tools

Another reason for an analytic sandbox is to support processing not available in databases or data mining tools. Statistical programming languages — such as SAS, SPSS, R, and S-plus — support a very large variety of statistical routines and data manipulation functions.

As described in the previous section, such processing may take place in the database, taking advantage of parallel processing. More often, such code may access a data warehouse or data mart to retrieve values , process them into new values, and publish the results back into the data warehouse. However, the intermediate processing is independent of the database.

Hadoop/MapReduce

In the early 1960s, a programming language called APL introduced two important ideas. One, called *scalar extension*, was that any function defined on a scalar (a fancy word for a single value) could be applied to the elements of an array of any shape and number of dimensions. For instance, a function could multiply any value by two, and when applied as a scalar extension to an array, would multiply all the values by two. The second idea was the *reduce operator*, so called because it uses a function such as addition or maximum to reduce an array's number of dimensions by one. Plus reduce (spelled +/) applied to a one-dimensional list returns a scalar by adding up the elements of the list. Applied to a two-dimensional table, it returns a one-dimensional list by adding up the rows or columns. Later, these ideas were picked up by other programming languages, including Lisp, where scalar extension is known as map and reduce kept the name used in APL.

Fast forward several decades. Researchers at Google revisited these Lisp primitives and realized that map and reduce could be implemented on MPP systems to process large quantities of data. That realization — and a lot of hard work building the infrastructure to support grid computing, a parallel file system, and code to implement map and reduce — led to the invention of MapReduce. The most common implementation of MapReduce goes by the name of Hadoop, named by the project's founder Dave Cutter (who then worked at Yahoo!), who named it after his son's favorite toy, a stuffed elephant.

Hadoop is an open-source platform that has become increasingly popular for five reasons. First, it works. Second, it is free. Third, it is available on Amazon's Elastic Cloud computing infrastructure. And fourth, if Google, Amazon, and Yahoo! are all involved, then other companies suddenly become interested. Fifth, companies such as Cloudera offer support with training and documentation. Hadoop supports MapReduce, but it also supports other technologies as well.

The technical details of MapReduce and Hadoop are beyond the scope of this book. They are most useful when the volume of data is very, very large. Typical problems involve web logs, which are text files containing information about every web page visited by millions of users. This information includes the referring web page, information about the browser, cookies, date and time stamps, and so on. Placing such data in databases is cumbersome, because even a relatively small site that gets one million page views per day generates more than 100GB of raw data in a year. And the queries to make sense of the data are quite complicated.

MapReduce and Hadoop can approach these tasks efficiently, using grid computing — arrays of processors that provide an MPP approach to processing. The downside is that they generally require programming in order to perform the work. Increasingly, the Hadoop platform is expanding to include higher-level SQL-like languages such as Hive for manipulating data.

Hadoop is not a requirement for using MapReduce. Other implementations are available. For instance, some database vendors include MapReduce functionality in their databases. The example with LinkedIn suggesting "People You May Know" used GreenPlum's implementation of MapReduce inside its database engine.

Where Does OLAP Fit In?

The business world has been generating automated reports to meet business needs for many decades. Figure 17-4 shows a range of common reporting capabilities. Once upon a time, mainframe computers generated reports on green bar paper or green screens. These mainframe reports automated paper-based methods that preceded computers. More modern interfaces have superseded most of these reports.

Producing such reports is often a primary function of IT departments. Even minor changes to the reports require modifying code that can date back decades at some companies. The result is a lag between a user requesting changes and the user seeing the new information that is measured in weeks and months. This is old technology that organizations are generally trying to move away from, except for the lowest-level reports that summarize specific operational systems.

In the middle are off-the-shelf query generation packages that have become popular for accessing data in the past decade. These generate queries in SQL and can talk local or remote data sources using a standard protocol, such as the Open Database Connectivity (ODBC) standard. Such reports might be embedded in a spreadsheet, accessed through the Web, or through some other reporting interface. With a day or so of training, business analysts can usually generate the reports that they need. Of course, the report itself is often running as an SQL query on an already-overburdened database, so response times can be measured in minutes or hours, when the queries are even allowed to run to completion. These response times are much faster than the older report-generation packages, but they still make exploiting the data difficult. The goal is to be able to ask a question and still remember the question when the answer comes back.

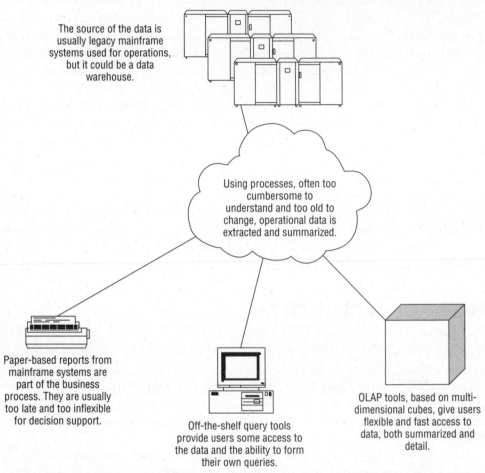

The source of the data is usually legacy mainframe systems used for operations, but it could be a data warehouse.

Using processes, often too cumbersome to understand and too old to change, operational data is extracted and summarized.

Paper-based reports from mainframe systems are part of the business process. They are usually too late and too inflexible for decision support.

Off-the-shelf query tools provide users some access to the data and the ability to form their own queries.

OLAP tools, based on multi-dimensional cubes, give users flexible and fast access to data, both summarized and detail.

Figure 17-4: Reporting requirements on operational systems are typically handled the same way they have been for decades. Is this the best way?

OLAP is a significant improvement over ad hoc query systems, because OLAP systems design the data structure with users and their reporting needs in mind. It starts by defining a set of dimensions (such as month, geography, and product) and storing important measures (such as total sales and total discounts) for each combination of the dimensions. This powerful and efficient representation is called a cube, which is ideally suited for slicing and dicing data. The cube itself is usually stored in a relational database, typically using a star schema. In addition, OLAP tools provide handy analysis functions that are difficult or impossible to express in SQL. If OLAP tools have one downside, it is that business users start to focus only on the dimensions of data represented by the tool. Data mining, on the other hand, is particularly valuable for creative thinking.

Setting up the cube requires analyzing the data and user needs, which is generally done by specialists familiar with the data and the tool, through a process called dimensional modeling. Although designing and loading an OLAP system requires an initial investment, the result provides informative and fast access to users. Response times, after the cube has been built, are almost always measured in seconds, allowing users to explore data and drill down to understand interesting features that they encounter.

TIP Quick response times are important for getting user acceptance of reporting systems. When users have to wait, they may forget the question that they asked. Interactive response times as experienced by users should be in the range of 3–5 seconds.

OLAP is a powerful enhancement to earlier reporting methods. Its power rests on three key features:

- A well-designed OLAP system has a set of relevant dimensions — such as geography, product, and time — understandable to business users. These dimensions often prove important for data mining purposes.
- A well-designed OLAP system has a set of useful measures relevant to the business.
- OLAP systems allow users to slice and dice data, and sometimes to drill down to the customer level.

These capabilities are complementary to data mining, but not a substitute for it. Nevertheless, OLAP is a very important (perhaps even the most important) part of the data warehouse architecture because it has the largest number of users.

What's in a Cube?

A good way to approach OLAP is to think of data as a cube split into subcubes, as shown in Figure 17-5. Although this example uses three dimensions, OLAP can have many more. This example shows a typical retailing cube that has one dimension for time, another for product, and a third for store. Each subcube contains various measures indicating what happened regarding that product in that store on that date, such as:

- Total number of items sold
- Total value of the items
- Total amount of discount on the items
- Inventory cost of the items

The measures are called *facts*. As a general rule, dimensions consist of categorical variables and facts are numeric. As users slice and dice the data, they are aggregating facts from many different subcubes. The dimensions are used to determine exactly which subcubes are used in the query.

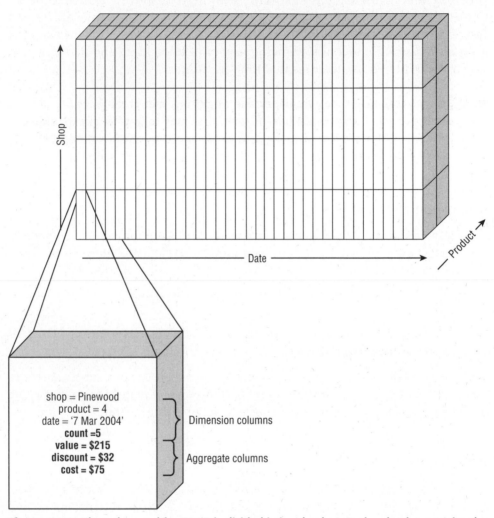

Figure 17-5: The cube used for OLAP is divided into subcubes. Each subcube contains the key for that subcube and summary information for the data falls into that subcube.

Even a simple cube such as the one just described is very powerful. Figure 17-5 shows an example of summarizing data in the cube to answer the question: "On how many days did a particular store not sell a particular product?" Such a question requires using the store and product dimensions to determine which subcubes are used for the query. This question only looks at one fact, the number of items sold, and returns all the dates for which this value is zero. Here are some other questions that can be answered relatively easily:

- What was the total number of items sold in the past year?

- What were the year over year sales, by month, of stores in the Northeast?

- What was the overall margin for each store in November? (Margin being the price paid by the customer minus the inventory cost.)

The ease of getting a report that can answer one of these questions depends on the particular implementation of the reporting interface. However, even for ad hoc reporting, accessing the cube structure can prove much easier than accessing a normalized relational database.

There is one cardinal rule when creating a cube: Any particular item of information should fall into exactly one subcube. When this rule is violated, the cube cannot easily be used to report on the various dimensions. A corollary of this rule is that when an OLAP cube is being loaded, keeping track of any data that has unexpected dimensional values is very important. Every dimension should have an "other" category to guarantee that all data makes it in.

> **TIP** When choosing the dimensions for a cube, be sure that each record lands in exactly one subcube. If you have redundant dimensions — such as one dimension for date and another for day of the week — then the same record will land in two or more subcubes. If this happens, then the summarizations based on the subcubes will no longer be accurate.

Facts

Facts are the measures in each subcube. The most useful facts are *additive*, so they can be combined together across many different subcubes to provide responses to queries at arbitrary levels of summarization. Additive facts can be summarized along any dimension or along several dimensions at one time — which is exactly the purpose of the cube.

Examples of additive facts are:

- Counts

- Counts of variables with a particular value

- Total duration of time (such as spent on a website)

- Total monetary values

The total amount of money spent on a particular product on a particular day is a good example of an additive fact. However, not all facts are additive. Examples include:

- Averages

- Unique counts

- Counts of things shared across different cubes, such as transactions

Averages are an uninteresting example of a nonadditive fact, because an average is a total divided by a count. Because each of these is additive, the average can be derived after combining these facts.

The other examples are more interesting. A common question is how many unique customers did some particular action. Although this number can be stored in a subcube, it is not additive. Consider a retail cube with the date, store, and product dimensions. A single customer may purchase items in more than one store, or purchase more than one item in a store, or make purchases on different days. A field containing the number of unique customers has information about one customer in more than one subcube, violating the cardinal rule of OLAP, so the cube is not going to be able to report on unique customers.

A similar thing happens when trying to count numbers of transactions. The information about the transaction may be stored in several different subcubes, because a single transaction may involve more than one product. So, counts of transactions also violate the cardinal rule. This type of information cannot be gathered at the summary level. On the other hand, counts of transactions can be stored in a separate fact table, using store and time as dimensions, or using store, time, and customer as dimensions.

Another note about facts is that not all numeric data is appropriate as a fact in a cube. For instance, age in years is numeric, but it might be better treated as a dimension rather than a fact. Another example is customer value. Discrete ranges of customer value are useful as dimensions, and in many circumstances more useful than including customer value as a fact.

When designing cubes, there is a temptation to mix facts and dimensions by creating a count or total for a group of related values. For instance:

- Count of active customers of less than one-year tenure, between one and two years, and greater than two years
- Amount credited on weekdays; amount credited on weekends
- Total for each day of the week

Such partial totals suggest the need for another dimension for the cube. The first should have a customer tenure dimension that takes at least three values. The second appeared in a cube where the time dimension was by month. These facts suggest a need for daily summaries, or at least for separating weekdays and weekends along a dimension. The third suggests a need for a date dimension at the granularity of days.

Dimensions and Their Hierarchies

Sometimes, a single column seems appropriate for multiple dimensions. For instance, OLAP is a good tool for visualizing trends over time, such as for sales or financial data. A specific date in this case potentially represents information along several dimensions, as shown in Figure 17-6:

- Day of the week
- Month
- Quarter
- Calendar year

One approach is to represent each of these as a different dimension. In other words, there would be four dimensions, one for the day of the week, one for the month, one for the quarter, and one for the calendar year. The data for January 2004 then would be the subcube where the January dimension intersects the 2004 dimension.

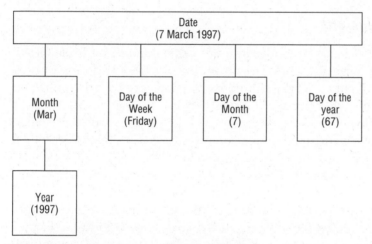

Figure 17-6: Dates have multiple hierarchies.

This is not a good approach. Multidimensional modeling recognizes that time is an important dimension, and that time can have many different attributes. In addition to the attributes described earlier, there are others, such as the week of the year, whether the date is a holiday (which may in turn depend on a particular country), whether the date is a work day, and so on. Such attributes are stored in reference tables, called dimension tables. Dimension tables support changing the attributes of the dimension without changing the underlying fact table.

WARNING   Do not take shortcuts when designing the dimensions for an OLAP system. These are the skeleton of the data mart, and a weak skeleton will not last very long.

Dimension tables contain many different attributes describing each value of the dimension. A detailed geography dimension might be built from ZIP codes and include dozens of summary variables about the ZIP codes. These attributes can be used for filtering ("How many customers are in high-income areas?"). These values are stored in the dimension table rather than the fact table, because they cannot be aggregated correctly. If three stores are in a ZIP code, the ZIP code population fact would get added up three times — multiplying the population by three.

Usually, dimension tables are kept up to date with the most recent values for the dimension. So, a store dimension might include the current set of stores with information about the stores, such as layout, square footage, address, and manager name. However, all of these may change over time. Such dimensions are called *slowly changing dimensions*, and are of particular interest to data mining because data mining wants to reconstruct accurate histories of the business at a given point in the past. Slowly changing dimensions are outside the scope of this book. Interested readers should review Ralph Kimball's books.

Conformed Dimensions

As mentioned earlier, data warehouse systems often contain multiple OLAP cubes. Some of the power of OLAP arises from the practice of sharing dimensions across different cubes. These shared dimensions are called conformed dimensions and are shown in Figure 17-7; they help ensure that business results reported through different systems use the same underlying set of business rules.

A good example of a conformed dimension is the calendar dimension, which keeps track of the attributes of each day. A calendar dimension is so important that it should be a part of every data warehouse. However, different components of the warehouse may need different attributes. For instance, a multinational business might include sets of holidays for different countries, so there might be a flag for "United States Holiday," "United Kingdom Holiday," "France Holiday," and so on, instead of an overall holiday flag. January 1st is a holiday in most countries; however, July 4th is mostly celebrated in the United States.

One of the challenges in building OLAP systems is designing the conformed dimensions so that they are suitable for a wide variety of applications. For some purposes geography might be best described by city and state; for another, by county; for another, by census block group; and for another, by ZIP code. Unfortunately, these four descriptions are not fully compatible, because several small towns can be in a ZIP code, and New York City covers five counties. Multidimensional modeling helps resolve such conflicts.

Star Schema

Cubes are easily stored in relational databases, using a denormalized data structure called the *star schema*, developed by Ralph Kimball, a guru of OLAP. One advantage of the star schema is its use of standard database technology to achieve the power of OLAP.

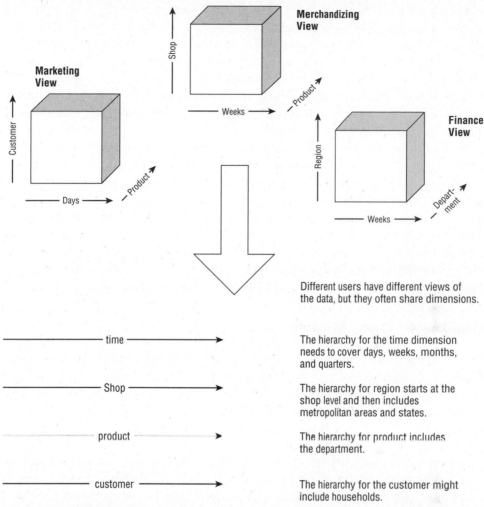

Figure 17-7: Different views of the data often share common dimensions. Finding the common dimensions and their base units is critical to making data warehousing work well across an organization.

A star schema starts with a *central fact table* that corresponds to facts about a business. These can be at the transaction level (for an event cube), although they are more often low-level summaries of transactions. For retail sales, the central fact table might contain daily summaries of sales for each product in each store (shop-SKU-time). For a credit card company, a fact table might contain rows for each transaction by each customer or summaries of spending by product (based on card type and credit limit), customer segment, merchant type, customer geography, and month. For a diesel engine manufacturer interested in repair histories, it might contain each repair made on each engine or a daily summary of repairs at each shop by type of repair.

Each row in the central fact table contains some combination of keys that makes it unique. These keys are called *dimensions*. The central fact table also has other columns that typically contain numeric information specific to each row, such as the amount of the transaction, the number of transactions, and so on. Associated with each dimension are auxiliary tables called *dimension tables*, which contain information specific to the dimensions. For instance, the dimension table for date might specify the day of the week for a particular date, its month, year, and whether it is a holiday.

In diagrams, the dimension tables are connected to the central fact table, resulting in a shape that loosely resembles a star, as shown in Figure 17-8.

In practice, star schemas may not be efficient for answering all users' questions, because the central fact table is so large. In such cases, the OLAP systems introduce summary tables at different levels to facilitate query response. Relational database vendors provide lots of support for star schemas. With a typical architecture, any query on the central fact table would require multiple joins back to the dimension tables. By applying standard indexes, and creatively enhancing indexing technology, relational databases can handle these queries quite well.

OLAP and Data Mining

Data mining is about the successful exploitation of data for decision-support purposes. The virtuous cycle of data mining, described in Chapter 1, reminds us that success depends on more than advanced pattern recognition algorithms. The data mining process needs to provide feedback to people and encourage using information gained from data mining to improve business processes. The data mining process should enable people to provide input, in the form of observations, hypotheses, and hunches about what results are important and how to use those results.

In the larger context of data exploitation, OLAP clearly plays an important role as a means of broadening the audience with access to data. Decisions once made based on experience and educated guesses can now be based on data and patterns in the data. Anomalies and outliers can be identified for further investigation and further modeling, sometimes using the most sophisticated data mining techniques. For instance, a user might discover that a particular item sells better at a particular time during the week through the use of an OLAP tool. This might lead to an investigation using market basket analysis to find other items purchased with that item. Market basket analysis might suggest an explanation for the observed behavior — more information and more opportunities for exploiting the information.

Data mining and OLAP have other synergies. One of the characteristics of decision trees discussed in Chapter 7 is their ability to identify the most informative features in the data relative to a particular outcome. That is, if a decision tree is built to predict attrition, then the upper levels of the tree will have the features that are the most important predictors for attrition. Well, these predictors might be a good choice for dimensions using an OLAP tool. Such analysis helps build better, more useful cubes. Another problem when building cubes is determining how to make continuous dimensions discrete. The nodes of a decision tree can help determine the best breaking point for a continuous value. This information can be fed into the OLAP tool to improve the dimension.

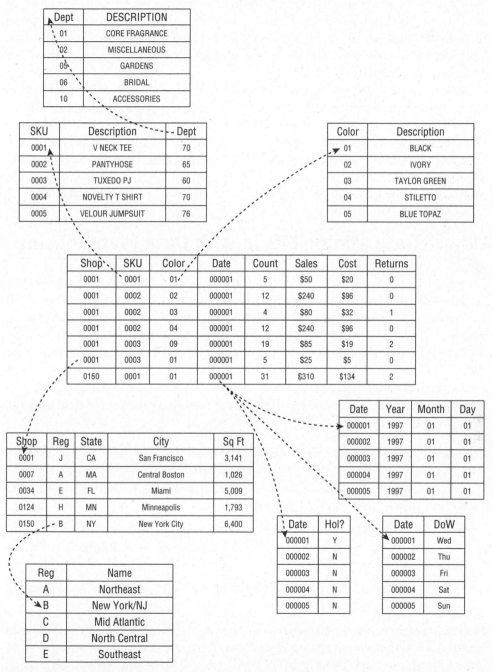

Figure 17-8: A star schema looks more like this. Dimension tables are conceptually nested, with more than one dimension table for a given dimension.

One of the problems with undirected data mining is the difficulty of understanding the results. OLAP to the rescue! Each customer can be assigned his or her cluster, along with other information, such as demographics, purchase history, and so on. This is a good application for a cube. OLAP — with information about the clusters included as a dimension — allows end users to explore the clusters and determining features that distinguish them from each other. The dimensions used for the OLAP cube should include the cluster identifier and other descriptive variables.

As these examples show, OLAP and data mining complement each other. Data mining can help build better cubes by defining appropriate dimensions, and further by determining how to break up continuous values on dimensions. OLAP provides a powerful visualization capability to help users better understand the results of data mining, such as clustering and neural networks. Used together, OLAP and data mining reinforce each other's strengths and provide more opportunities for exploiting data.

Where Data Mining Fits in with Data Warehousing

Data mining plays an important role in the data warehouse environment. The initial value of a data warehouse comes from automating existing processes, such as putting reports online and giving existing applications a clean source of data. The biggest returns are the improved access to data that can spur innovation and creativity — and these come from new ways of looking at and analyzing data. This is the role of data mining — to provide the tools that improve understanding and inspire creativity based on observations in the data.

A good data warehousing environment serves as a catalyst for data mining. The two technologies work together as partners:

- Data mining thrives on large amounts of data and the more detailed the data, the better — data that comes from a data warehouse.

- Data mining thrives on clean and consistent data — capitalizing on the investment in data cleansing tools.

- The data warehouse environment enables hypothesis testing and simplifies efforts to measure the effects of actions taken — enabling the virtuous cycle of data mining.

- Scalable hardware and relational database software can offload the data processing parts of data mining.

However, there is a distinction between the way data mining looks at the world and the way data warehousing does. Normalized data warehouses can store data with time stamps, but it is difficult to do time-related manipulations — such as determining what event happened just before some other event of interest.

OLAP introduces a time dimension. Data mining extends this even further by taking into account the notion of "before" and "after." Data mining learns from data (the "before"), with the purpose of applying these findings to the future (the "after"). For this reason, data mining often puts a heavy load on data warehouses. These are complementary technologies, supporting each other as discussed in the next few sections.

Lots of Data

The traditional approach to data analysis generally starts by reducing the size of the data. The three common ways of doing this are summarizing detailed transactions, taking a subset of the data, and only looking at certain attributes. The reason for reducing the size of the data is to enable analyzing it on the available hardware and software systems (or by hand, in the truly olden days). When properly done, the laws of statistics come into play, allowing you to choose a sample that behaves similarly to the rest of the data.

Data mining, on the other hand, is searching for trends in the data and for valuable anomalies. It is often trying to answer different types of questions from traditional statistical analysis, such as: "What product is this customer most likely to purchase next?" Even if you build a model using a subset of data, you need to deploy the model and score all customers, a process that can be computationally intensive, or score individual customers in real-time (such as on the the Web).

Fortunately, data mining algorithms are often able to take advantage of large amounts of data. When looking for patterns that identify rare events — such as having to write off customers because they failed to pay — having large amounts of data ensures that there is sufficient data for analysis. A subset of the data might be statistically relevant in total, but when you try to decompose it into other segments (by region, by product, by customer segment), there may be too little data to produce statistically meaningful results. Decision trees work very well, even when dozens or hundreds of fields are in each record. Link analysis requires a full complement of the data to create a graph. Neural networks can train on millions of records at a time. And, even though the algorithms often work on summaries of the detailed transactions (especially at the customer level), what gets summarized can change from one run to the next. Prebuilding the summaries and discarding the transaction data locks you into only one view of the business. Often the first result from using such summaries is a request for some variation on them.

Consistent, Clean Data

Data mining algorithms are often applied to gigabytes of data combined from several different sources. Much of the work in looking for actionable information actually takes place when bringing the data together — often 80 percent or more of the time allocated to a data mining project is spent preparing the data — especially when a data warehouse is not available. Subsequent problems, such as matching account numbers, interpreting codes, and assigning accounts to households, further delay analysis. Finding interesting patterns is often an iterative process that requires going back to the data to get additional data elements. Finally, when interesting patterns are found, the process must often be repeated on the most recent data available.

A well-designed and well-built data warehouse helps solve these problems. Data is cleaned once, when it is loaded into the data warehouse. The meaning of fields is well defined and available through the metadata. Incorporating new data into analyses is as easy as finding out what data is available through the metadata and retrieving it from the warehouse. A particular analysis can be reapplied on more recent data, because the warehouse is kept up to date. The end result is that the data is cleaner and more available — and that the analysts can spend more time applying powerful tools and insights instead of moving data and pushing bytes.

Hypothesis Testing and Measurement

The data warehouse (often with the assistance of an analytic sandbox) facilitates two other areas of data mining. Hypothesis testing is the verification of educated guesses about patterns in the data. Do tropical colors really sell better in Florida than elsewhere? Do people really shop during working hours? Are the users of credit cards at restaurants really high-end customers? These questions can be expressed rather easily as queries on the appropriate relational database. Having the data available supports asking such questions and finding out quickly what the answers are.

TIP The ability to test hypotheses and ideas is a very important aspect of data mining. By bringing the data together in one place, data warehouses enable answering in-depth, complicated questions. One caveat is that such queries can be expensive to run, falling into the killer query category.

Measurement is the other area where data warehouses have proven to be very valuable. Often when marketing efforts produce limited feedback on the degree of success achieved, a data warehouse enables you to see the results and to find related effects. Did sales of other products improve? Did customer attrition increase? Did calls to customer service decrease? And so on. Having the data available supports efforts to understand the effects of an action, whether the action was spurred by data mining results or by something else.

Of particular value in terms of measurement is the effect of various marketing actions on the longer-term customer relationship. Often, marketing campaigns are measured in terms of response. Although response is clearly a dimension of interest, it is only one. The longer term behavior of customers is also of interest. Did an acquisition campaign bring in good customers or did the newly acquired customers leave before they even paid? Did an up-sell campaign stick, or did customers return to their previous products? Measurement enables an organization to learn from its mistakes and to build on its successes.

Scalable Hardware and RDBMS Support

The final synergy between data mining and data warehousing is on the systems level. The same scalable hardware and software systems that make storing and querying large databases possible provide a good system for analyzing data. The next chapter talks about building the customer signature. Often, the best place to build the signature is in the central repository or, failing that, in a data mart built off the central repository.

There is also the question of running data mining algorithms in parallel, taking further advantage of the powerful machines. This is often not necessary, because actually building models represents a small part of the time devoted to data mining — preparing the data and understanding the results are much more important. Databases, such as Oracle, Microsoft SQL Server, and the newer generation of PostGres-based databases, are increasingly providing support for data mining algorithms, which enables such algorithms to run in parallel.

Lessons Learned

Data is an integral part of data mining, and data warehousing is a process that can greatly benefit data mining and data analysis efforts. From the perspective of data mining, the most important functionality of data warehouses is the ability to re-create accurate snapshots of history. Another very important facet is support for ad hoc reporting. To learn from data, you need to know what really happened.

A typical data warehousing system contains the following components:

- The source systems provide the input into the data warehouse.

- The extraction, transformation, and load tools clean the data and apply business rules so that new data is compatible with historical data.

- The central repository is a relational database specifically designed to be a decision-support system of record.

- The data marts provide the interface to different varieties of users with different needs.

- One or more analytic sandboxes for handling ad hoc needs, involving larger amounts of data or more sophisticated analyses.

- The metadata repository informs users and developers about what is inside the data warehouse.

One of the challenges in data warehousing is the massive amount of data that must be stored, particularly if the goal is to keep all customer interactions. Fortunately, computers are sufficiently powerful that the question is more about budget than possibility. Relational databases can also take advantage of the most powerful hardware, parallel computers.

Online Analytic Processing (OLAP) is a powerful part of data warehousing. OLAP tools are very good at handling summarized data, allowing users to summarize information along one or several dimensions at one time. Because these systems are optimized for user reporting, they often have interactive response times of less than five seconds.

Any well-designed OLAP system has time as a dimension, in order to see trends over time. Trying to accomplish the same thing on a normalized data warehouse requires very complicated queries that are prone to error. To be most useful, OLAP systems should allow users to drill down to detail data for all reports. This capability ensures that all data is making it into the cubes, as well as giving users the ability to spot important patterns that may not appear in the dimensions.

As pointed out throughout this chapter, OLAP complements rather than replaces data mining. OLAP gives users a better understanding of data and the business. Dimensions developed for OLAP can make data mining results more actionable. However, OLAP does not automatically find patterns in data.

OLAP is a powerful way to distribute information to many end users for advanced reporting needs. It provides the ability to let many more users base their decisions on data, instead of on hunches, educated guesses, and personal experience. OLAP complements undirected data mining techniques such as clustering. OLAP can provide the insight needed to find the business value in the identified clusters. It also provides a good visualization tool to use with other methods, such as decision trees and memory-based reasoning.

Data warehousing and data mining are not the same thing; however, they do complement each other. How data is stored in an organization is just the beginning of the synergies between data mining and data warehousing. The next chapter dives into the complexities of creating customer signatures.

CHAPTER 18

Building Customer Signatures

This chapter is about finding customers in data and building customer signatures to describe them. It is the first of three chapters that deal with various aspects of preparing data for mining. The theme that runs through this chapter is finding customers in data, which means gathering the traces that customers leave when they make purchases, visit websites, contact call centers, pay bills, respond to offers, and interact with the company in other ways. These scattered traces of data must be shaped into a useful customer signature that can be used to train data mining models.

Quite often, the customer signature is the *data* in data mining. As discussed in Chapters 3 and 5, the signature determines whether data mining techniques produce profiling models or predictive models. The signature is the representation of customers that will be used to make decisions about how they are treated — what offers they receive, how their requests are handled by the call center, and how much effort is made to retain them or win them back. In addition to its primary role supporting data mining, the customer signature is a data source for reporting and ad hoc queries.

A customer signature is a representation of a customer as of a particular date. The code that generates the customer signature should be able to create such a representation as of any date for which data exists. It should also be capable of supporting different "as of" dates for different customers and different "as of" dates for model targets and model inputs. The signature also addresses seasonal fluctuations, missing data, and other issues that can make modeling difficult.

Building a customer signature requires dealing with data from a variety of source systems where it may not be stored in a form suitable for mining. Source data may require a certain amount of fixing up, such as mapping multiple names for the same thing to a single identifier, and possibly changing the way missing values are represented. This chapter covers these common data preparation steps.

There is no clear, sharp line between the data preparation step that is the subject of this chapter and the data enhancement steps that are the subject of the next two chapters. For example, building customer signatures requires summarizing transactions. The first motivation for summarizing is to get data at the right level of granularity. But decisions about how to perform the summarization determine how much information is made available for modeling. Because summarizing often involves creating derived variables, it is a topic for the next chapter as well.

Every customer signature design evolves over time, becoming more refined as new ideas are tried out and experience shows which fields are most important. This chapter is about getting the first draft right, including transformations necessitated by the structure of the problem and the requirements of particular data mining techniques. The next chapter takes up the story where this one leaves off. It focuses on refining the signature by creating derived variables to make more information available to data mining techniques. Many of the transformations in this chapter change the data layout by bringing together elements from different source tables, pivoting rows into columns, aggregating transactions, and selectively sampling. Several examples of real customer signature files are provided in technical asides that explain the thinking behind them and the details of how they were constructed. These example signatures were captured fairly early in their evolution; all are from the first data mining project for which they were created.

Finding Customers in Data

All kinds of data, not just customer data, can profitably be mined; however, this book is not only about data mining, but about data mining *for marketing, sales, and customer relationship management*. In that context, customers are the focus. In this chapter, most of the examples of signature tables are *customer* signatures. Customer signatures for data mining have one row for each example of whatever is being studied. If the level of analysis is a town, you need a town signature file; if the level of analysis is a print run, you need a print run signature; and so on.

Sometimes the level of analysis is something other than a customer, even when, ultimately, it is customers who are of interest. Chapter 15 has a case study whose aim is to identify products that are especially appealing to Hispanic shoppers. Because no data was available on the shoppers themselves, the analysis compared sales at stores whose catchment areas had varying levels of Hispanic population. The direct results are about stores, but customers were the real subject of the study.

In this chapter, the level of analysis is assumed to be a customer, so the first task is to decide what is meant by *a customer*. Is it an individual, a household, or a combination of an individual and an account? Is it the person who pays the bill or the person who uses the service?

What Is a Customer?

The question seems simple, but the answer depends on the business goal. Customers play several different roles, and various kinds of marketing and customer relationship management programs engage different subsets of them. Three important roles are the:

- Payer
- Decider
- User

When all the roles are embodied in a single person, he or she is clearly the customer, but often, the roles are divided among multiple people. When a corporate employee travels on company business, the employer may pay for the airline ticket and hotel stay through a corporate account. But who decided which airline to fly and which hotel to stay in? The company may get special discounts from its preferred suppliers and steer all company travel to them. In that case the company is the payer and decider, and the employee is only the user.

Alternatively, employees, influenced by their own loyalty program memberships, may make their own plans and submit them to the corporate travel department. In that case, the employee is the decider and user, and the company is only the payer. Or, the company may expect employees to pay for expenses out of pocket and get reimbursed later while still requiring employees to use the company preferred vendors to qualify for the corporate rate. In that case, employees may appear in the hotel chain's data as both users and payers even though they are not really deciders.

Different customer roles can be difficult to untangle not only in business-to-business relationships but also in business-to-consumer relationships. Families and other households present their own challenges. For example, many services for downloading music and videos require a credit card on file. Because minors do not have credit cards, the payer role is an adult member of the household. In many cases, the payer is not the primary user or decider, but the payer is probably the only person in the household for whom the company has any reliable identity. Chapter 16 includes a story about a company that offers cable television and mobile phone service that used link analysis to estimate the ages of the family members on a family mobile plan to make appropriate offers of television content to the right person in the household. The impact of all this on the customer signature is that different business goals may require different versions of the customer signature with rows corresponding to users, payers, or deciders as appropriate.

Accounts? Customers? Households?

Quite apart from the issue of customer roles, the definition of a customer depends on both the business goal for the analysis and on the level of customer identification achievable with the available data. Because much of the information in a customer signature is summarized from transaction records, a lot depends on what kind of identifying information is captured with each transaction. A number of possibilities exist, among them:

- All transactions are anonymous.
- Some transactions can be tied to a particular credit or debit card, but others cannot; some cards can be tied to particular customers.
- Many transactions can be tied to a cookie; some cookies can be tied to accounts.
- All transactions can be tied to a particular account.
- All transactions can be tied to a particular identified customer.
- All transactions can be tied to a particular customer and household.

The following sections look at the implications of each of these possibilities.

Anonymous Transactions

The cashless society keeps failing to arrive. Until it does, many transactions will continue to be completely anonymous. Indeed, there are systems that allow for anonymous electronic transactions as well. And, in many cases, even when linking some kind of identifying information to a transaction might be possible, the link is not made because there is no operational reason for doing so. When transactions are anonymous, it is only possible to learn as much about a customer as is revealed in a single transaction. An automated couponing system can use the contents of a single purchase transaction to decide which of several coupons to print, for example.

Anonymous transactions along with demographic data for a store's catchment area can be used to study ethnic buying patterns. Collections of anonymous transactions can also be used to create association rules. Association rules are about products, not customers. An association rule says that, in the aggregate, people who buy women's apparel are likely to buy women's shoes as well, but it says nothing about which customers are likely to do either. In short, anonymous transaction data has its uses, but it doesn't contribute much to customer signatures.

Transactions Linked to a Card

Retail transactions can often be linked to a credit or debit card. When a customer chooses to pay using a credit or debit card, the card number is captured and becomes part of the transaction record. All transactions associated with the same card can be linked together for analysis, into what could be called a *card signature*. Some, but not all, card issuers are even willing to supply the identities of the customers behind the account numbers, which makes it possible to append still more information to the card signature. A card signature is not the same as a customer signature because it only captures those transactions for which the customer chooses to use a card. The same customer may, for example, make small purchases with cash, large business-related purchases with one card, and large personal purchases with another. A true customer signature would capture all three types of purchase in one place.

Loyalty cards present similar problems. Customers do not always remember their loyalty cards. Depending on the structure of the loyalty program, customers may only show the loyalty card when they happen to be purchasing something that has a "dollar off when you use the card" promotion in place. Even when the incentive is based on total spending, customers may not always respond to the incentive.

A customer signature based on card users is certainly valuable, but it is important to remember that it only describes those customers who have cards and only captures their behavior on the occasions when they use their cards.

> **TIP** A customer signature based on transactions associated with a particular payment type or channel introduces sample bias at two levels. Customers who use the particular payment type or channel may not be representative of all customers, and the transactions for which they use it may not be representative of all transactions. Consider naming such a signature after the payment type or channel as a reminder that it does not represent all customers.

Transactions Linked to a Cookie

Transactions linked to cookies have all the problems associated with transactions linked to credit cards along with a few more of their own. A cookie does not identify a customer; it identifies a particular browser on a particular computer. The cookie itself is just some information stored in a small text file on the user's commuter so that it persists when the computer is turned off.

When a customer arrives at a website, the web server asks the browser to present its cookie for the site. If the browser doesn't have a cookie, the server gives it a cookie containing a unique identifier to present next time. Typically, the web application stores the cookie in some database table on the server. Ideally, the cookie value links the cookie to a known customer with a rich profile. Failing that, it at least links the current visit to other visits made using the same browser on the same computer, in what could be called a *cookie profile*. Cookies are only semi-permanent. Not only do they typically contain an expiration date, some users make it a point to delete cookies frequently or turn them off entirely.

Linking cookies to customers is a messy business. Some customers register, some never do. Many people in the same house may share one computer. A single customer uses multiple browsers on multiple laptops, net books, and smart phones. Some of these are personal devices; others are in airport lounges, student lounges, at work, and so on. Companies make heroic efforts to link all these cookies to the same customer profile, but no one thinks they get it all right.

In the online ad world, the advertising networks use special tracking cookies that are shared across multiple sites within the network. Often, these cookies can be traced back to a real person whose profile can include appended demographic data as well as the browsing behavior across multiple sites. These rich profiles can greatly improve ad targeting, but many Internet security packages regard tracking cookies as spyware and delete them.

Transactions Linked to an Account

In some industries, every transaction is captured and linked to an account. That is true in banking (with the exception of asking the teller to change a twenty, or buying a roll of quarters for the parking meter), and in post-paid telephony. It is also true of any website that requires users to log in. Companies in these industries can make very good customer/account signatures to describe the way customers use the account. Some can also link multiple accounts to the same customer; others cannot or choose not to.

There are many operational reasons for keeping data on an account level rather than a customer level. One is that the same business may offer products of different types that generate different kinds of data. A credit card is quite different than a car loan and both are different from a mortgage. A bank's having a different system for each is not surprising. Similarly, an insurance company that offers both car insurance and home insurance may treat these products separately. But from a customer relationship management point of view, tying them all together is important. Even if the business problem driving the analysis is all about a single product, the presence of the other products is likely to have an effect. The fact that a customer has a home owner's policy has an effect on attrition risk for other policies from the same company, for instance.

Transactions Linked to a Customer

Having the ability to link transactions to a customer is the best situation. Every transaction is tied to a customer through an account, and all accounts belonging to a customer are linked, so an opportunity exists to construct a customer signature that captures the entire relationship.

Transactions are important because they capture actual customer behavior. Other important sources of data include information collected at the time of account opening, application, or registration, data purchased from external sources such as credit bureaus and household data vendors, and demographic characteristics of the customer's neighborhood based on census data.

When customers are businesses rather than households, demographic data is replaced with *firmographic* data such as industry code, number of employees, and annual revenue. When the analysis concerns prospective customers rather than active customers, behavioral data from transactions is replaced by data describing the responses to previous campaigns.

Designing Signatures

Preparing the signature is one of the more labor-intensive portions of a data mining project. The good news is that after you have a good customer signature, you can use it over and over again to model all sorts of things. Each new task will suggest new elements to add to the signature, but most of the work is in building it the first time.

To be more precise, it is not the actual signature file or table that persists and evolves over time, it is the signature file *design*. Each row of a customer signature is a description of one customer *as of a particular time*. Because customers change over time, so do their signatures. The customer signature design is embodied in a program, script, or query of some kind that allows for parameters such as the "as of" date for the signature to be specified as appropriate. When models are scored, the most recent complete view of the customer is usually best, but for training purposes, a single frozen instance representing customers as of some past date may be used for months at a time. For training, it does not matter who the customers are or whether their descriptions are up to date because the goal is to find general patterns and rules that can be applied to all customers. In fact, updating the training signature would be a distraction. For scoring, on the other hand, the goal is to capture the current state of each individual.

One common scenario is for signatures for scoring to be recreated on a regular basis such as at the end of each billing period. In this scenario, the billing period ends on different days for different customers, but at any given time the customer signature table is a snapshot of all customers as of their last complete billing period. In many environments, customers are scored on a regular basis to update a variety of fields such as a customer value score, an attrition risk score, and propensity scores for various products or services. Updating the customer signature is the first step in the scoring process. The customer signature is also a valuable resource for ad hoc reporting. It may be the only place where customer information from many sources can be found in one place so many questions can be answered without having to resort to complex queries with many joins. Several examples of actual customer signatures are provided in sidebars throughout the chapter.

The design of a customer signature is best approached iteratively, one data source at a time. Start with what is already known about the customer and then add to it. Do not expect to ever complete the task, and do not let the ideal become the enemy of the good. Initial versions of the signature contain data in a form close to the way it is stored in source systems, but over time the signature is likely to be dominated by derived variables that do not exist anywhere in the source systems. It is crucial that the process and code for generating the signature is very well documented and repeatable. Remember that some fields of the signature are destined to become part of models used for scoring. The scoring code must be able to recreate these fields exactly the same way they were created in the customer signature used to train the models. Because any one model usually refers to only a handful of fields, it is tempting to recreate just these few fields as part of the scoring code. This is not recommended because of the danger that multiple definitions of the same field will drift apart over time. The same program should be used to create signatures for training and scoring.

TIP When a model is used to score new data, the fields used by the model must all be created using the same definitions as were used for training the model, albeit with a different "as of" date. Maintaining separate versions of the field definitions in two places — the signature creation code, and the scoring code — is dangerous. A better idea is to use the same program to generate the signatures for both training and scoring.

Although some data mining software packages contain limited facilities for data manipulation, the code for creating the signature is usually written outside of the data mining environment. Depending on the IT infrastructure available and the skill set of the miner, the signature might be constructed as one or more SQL queries, as a program in SAS or SPSS or R, as a PERL script, or using an ETL (Extract/Transform/Load) tool of some kind. In this book, the focus is on what to construct, not how to write the code. Start designing the customer signature by asking a few questions.

SAMPLE CUSTOMER SIGNATURE FOR A FAX-TO-EMAIL SERVICE

The company for which this fax-to-email service signature was built offers a service that allows its subscribers to use a fax number without actually having to deal with the paper jams, busy signals, toner cartridges, and other joys of an actual fax machine. When someone sends the subscriber a fax, it arrives as a PDF attached to an email message. Subscribers can also send documents from their computers as faxes by uploading them to a website. To the recipient, the fax appears to have been sent from the subscriber's fax number.

The primary purpose of this signature is to support attrition modeling. The code to generate the signature can produce the signature at one of two levels — the master account or the individual service profile as described in the following table. The version shown here is for the individual service profile, which corresponds to a single fax number. The service profile usually identifies a single office within a company or, less frequently, an individual or household. Within the same account, there may be service profiles that are very active and others that are hardly ever used. The starting hypothesis is that subscribers who make a lot of use of the service are unlikely to cancel so most analysis is done at the service profile level where the activity occurs.

ID FIELDS

Profile ID	The primary key. Corresponds to a single fax number.
Master Account ID	The account to which this profile belongs.

The signature is in the predictive modeling style. The "as of" date for the fields with names beginning with "Future" is later than the "as of" date for the explanatory variables, which are described in the following table.

FIELDS IN THE TARGET TIMEFRAME

Future Attrition Flag	The target variable.
Future Reason Type	Indicates whether the cancellation was initiated by the subscriber or the company. Because all subscribers supply a bank account or credit card number at sign-up, company-initiated cancellations are rare.

Profile creation time fields are things that were known about the subscriber at the time that the service profile was created. The majority of master accounts have only a single service profile, so for most customers the creation of the profile is the beginning of the relationship. These fields in the following

Continued

SAMPLE CUSTOMER SIGNATURE FOR A FAX-TO-EMAIL SERVICE (*continued*)

table capture things that might be expected to have an influence on usage and longevity. The popularity of faxing varies from country to country and industry to industry. Some referral sources may supply better qualified prospects. Businesses have different fax needs than individuals.

PROFILE CREATION TIME FIELDS	
Referral	The website that referred the subscriber. May be NULL.
Company Indicator	1 if subscriber is a business, 0 otherwise. Nearly always 1.
Country	The country to which the fax number is local.
Reseller	The reseller who acquired the customer. May be NULL if the subscriber was not acquired through that channel.
Search Engine Flag	Did the subscriber arrive at the sign-up page as the result of a search engine query?
Profile Lag	Time between account creation and creation of this profile in days. Distinguishes original profiles from ones added later.
Postal Code	Full ZIP or post code.
Industry Code	From data vendor.
Number of Employees	From data vendor.
Years in Business	From data vendor.
Number Type	The initial fax number type can be a toll-free number or a local number.

A current snapshot field is a picture of the customer as of the date used for the explanatory variables. Some examples are in the following table.

CURRENT SNAPSHOT FIELDS	
Website Login Rate	Logins/months of tenure. Logging in to receive faxes is not necessary. Subscribers log in to send faxes (including batch faxes), update their accounts, view fax history, and so on. Logging in is thought to show greater engagement with the service.
Service Calls	Total all-time service calls since creation of the service profile.

CURRENT SNAPSHOT FIELDS	
Service Call Rate	Service calls/months of tenure.
Master Account Tenure	Time since master profile created in days.
Service Profile Tenure	Time since service profile created in days.
Regional Attrition Rate	Historic attrition rate for the region where the subscriber is located. For Canada, this is the first three characters of the post code. For the U.S. it is the first three digits of the ZIP code.
Months	Number of completed billing cycles.
First Types	Number of distinct transaction types in first month of history.
Last Types	Number of distinct transaction types in most recent month of history.

There are a number of different transaction types, with the most popular being sending a fax and receiving a fax. For each transaction there is a record of how many pages were sent or received and whether the transaction succeeded or failed. Such behavioral fields are in the following table. This section of the signature captures whether use of each transaction type is increasing or decreasing using the slope of the change from the initial month to the most recent complete month. A better measure would be the slope of the best-fit line through all the months of a subscriber's history, but the first and last month calculation is easier. This sort of trade-off is quite typical.

PER TRANSACTION TYPE FIELDS	
First Month Count	Number of transactions of this type in first month of history.
Last Month Count	Number of transactions of this type in last month of history.
First Successful Count	Number of successful transactions of this type in first month of history.
Last Successful Count	Number of successful transactions of this type in last month of history.
First Failed Count	Number of failed transactions of this type in first month of history.
Last Failed Count	Number of failed transactions of this type in last month of history.
First Pages	Number of pages in first month of history.

Continued

SAMPLE CUSTOMER SIGNATURE FOR A FAX-TO-EMAIL SERVICE (*continued*)

PER TRANSACTION TYPE FIELDS	
Last Pages	Number of pages in last month of history.
First Month Dollars	Dollar amount in first month of history.
Last Month Dollars	Dollar amount in last of history.
Transaction Count Difference	Last month – first month.
Successful Difference	Last month – first month.
Failed Difference	Last month – first month.
Pages Difference	Last month – first month.
Dollar Difference	Last month – first month.
Transaction Slope	(Last month – first month) / months.
Successful Slope	(Last month – first month) / months.
Failed Slope	(Last month – first month) / months.
Pages Slope	(Last month – first month) / months.
Dollar Slope	(Last month – first month) / months.

Is a Customer Signature Necessary?

Not all aspects of data mining require a customer signature. A certain amount of exploratory data mining and hypothesis testing can be accomplished by applying ad hoc SQL queries to pre-existing database tables. When the time comes to build models, a signature is usually necessary.

A formal signature, or more precisely, the code to produce it, is what makes model training and scoring a repeatable process. The time invested in designing the signature and writing the code to create it will be repaid in ease of modeling.

What Does a Row Represent?

The first decision when creating a customer signature is the level of granularity. Is it a household, which may include several individuals, each potentially with several accounts? Is it an individual? Is it an account?

Making this decision is not always easy because different business needs result in questions at each level. Often, it makes sense to create multiple versions of the signature at different levels. These may all be SQL views of the same underlying tables. At the bottom level is an account signature where each row represents a unique household-customer-account combination. Next comes a customer-level signature with most of the same fields as the account-level signature, but aggregated to the customer level and with additional fields to summarize the number of accounts, the tenure of the oldest account, the tenure of the newest account, and so forth. Finally, a household signature contains much the same information as the account and customer signatures, but with transactions summarized at the household level and additional data on the makeup of the household. Most of the work goes into creating the account-level signature and if, as is often the case in some industries, nearly all households contain a single customer with a single account, the next levels may never be needed.

Householding

Building signatures at the household level requires some mechanism for deciding which individuals belong together — a process called *householding*. This process is complex and inexact. It involves business rules for matching names, addresses, and other identifying features, all of which may be misspelled, out of date, or inconsistent. It is also worth noting that different householding rules are appropriate for different applications. Should everyone on the same mobile phone family plan be in the same household, even if some members are away at college? For a customer value model, probably yes; for a cross-sell offer, maybe not. A married couple, living together, may share a mortgage, a car, and a satellite dish, but donate money to different political candidates. They are certainly a household for most applications, but political campaigns might want to treat them as individuals. A related issue is de-duplication. The same customer may appear with different email addresses, user IDs, and postal addresses. Commercial packages are available for householding and de-duplication.

WARNING Householding and de-duplication are complex processes that should really be addressed in the source data systems rather than as part of the data mining process. Even when householding has already been performed, the rules used to form households may not be appropriate for every application.

Householding and de-duplication have often already been performed prior to the creation of the customer signature for reasons having nothing to do with modeling. Sending multiple copies of the same mailing to the same household is a waste of money and risks making the sender appear incompetent in the eyes of its customers. When modeling, the risk is that behavior that should be attributed to a single customer is scattered over several partial customers, none of whom bears much resemblance to the actual person or household with whom you are doing business.

SAMPLE CUSTOMER SIGNATURE FOR A SOFTWARE-AS-A-SERVICE VENDOR

This software-as-a-service signature was created for a company that offers software as a service on a subscription basis. This is a business-to-business service, so the rows of the customer signature represent companies. The primary modeling goal was to identify likely prospects for up-selling (increasing the number of licensed seats) and cross-selling (adding licenses for additional products).

The signature is in the predictive modeling style, with upgrades in one quarter predicted by explanatory variables from the previous quarter. The company has a strong seasonal pattern to its sales with the strongest sales in the fourth quarter as salespeople push to hit yearly goals. Because this pattern was well-known, and not an object of study, the signature averages this out by having each customer contribute up to four rows to the signature table, each with a different target quarter. The "as of" date is different for each of the four rows. When the target is from the third quarter, the value of the tenure fields is tenure as of the third quarter, and so on. Customers only contribute rows for quarters for which they were active for the full target quarter and the full quarter preceding it.

The following table shows the variables in the target timeframe. The up-sell target variable is binary with a value of 1 if the customer had more seats at the end of the target quarter than at the end of the previous quarter. The cross-sell variable is also binary, with a value of 1 if the customer holds licenses for more products at the end of the target quarter than at the end of the previous quarter. This design does not follow the recommendation of leaving a gap between the explanatory variables and the target variable because end-of-quarter data is available immediately and the nature of the variables means that leakage of future information is not a problem.

FIELDS IN THE TIMEFRAME OF THE TARGET

Cross-Sell Target	1 if the customer had more products at the end of the target quarter than at the end of the preceding quarter; 0 otherwise.
Products Difference	Number of products at end of target quarter minus number of products at end of preceding quarter.
Up-Sell Target	1 if the customer had more seats at the end of the target quarter than at the end of the preceding quarter.
Seats Difference	Number of seats licensed for the base product as of the end of the target quarter minus the number of seats licensed at the end of the preceding quarter.

One interesting thing about the way this signature is designed is that when an instance of the signature is created, it is for a particular base product, with all the other products as possible cross-sell targets. Only customers with an active subscription for the base product are included. The usage fields refer to usage of the base product.

Some fields are collected when customers are acquired and are not expected to change over time. Such fields are suitable for stratification. The following fields are known at acquisition time:

FIELDS KNOWN AT CUSTOMER ACQUISITION TIME	
User ID	The primary key.
Domain	The customer's Internet domain.
Country	Country where the customer has its legal headquarters.
Language	Language preferred by the customer.
User Segment	One of several customer segments indicating the style of product use expected. Assigned by a salesperson, when known. Often NULL.
Initial Seats	The number of paid seats the customer started with.
Initial Product Count	The number of products the customer was licensed to use as of the initial purchase. Usually 1.
Salesperson ID	Actually a snapshot field rather than an acquisition time field because when a new account manager is assigned, the field is overwritten.
Origin ID	Acquisition channel credited with attracting the customer.
Website	Website credited with referring the customer, if any. Often NULL.
Creative	Advertising message to which the customer responded, if known. Often NULL.

The following fields are explanatory variables that are independent of the as-of date.

EXPLANATORY FIELDS INDEPENDENT OF "AS OF" DATE	
Time To Purchase	The number of days between first recorded visit and making a purchase.
Trial To Purchase	For customers who participated in a free trial, days from start of trial to purchase; NULL otherwise.

The following fields measure tenure in different ways.

EXPLANATORY FIELDS DEPENDENT ON "AS OF" DATE	
First Seen Tenure	Days since customer was first seen on company website.
First Purchase Tenure	Days since customer first made a purchase.

Continued

SAMPLE CUSTOMER SIGNATURE FOR A SOFTWARE-AS-A-SERVICE VENDOR (*continued*)

The following fields are repeated per product for the base product and each of several other products. They represent a current snapshot.

PER-PRODUCT FIELDS

Has Product License	1 if customer has a license for this product; 0 otherwise.
Product Free Trial Flag	1 if the customer has ever participated in a free trial for this product; 0 otherwise.
Past License Flag	1 if customer does not now have a license for this product, but did at some time in the past; 0 otherwise.
Monthly Seats	Number of seats on month-to-month license that can be cancelled at any time without penalty.
Yearly Seats	Number of seats on full-year license.
Total Seats	Sum of the two preceding fields.
Monthly Percentage	Percentage of seats that are on a monthly license.
Free Proportion	Percentage of computers in the domain using a free version of the product meant for personal use by casual users.
Email Contacts	Number of outbound marketing and customer support emails sent to the customer this quarter.
Total Sessions	Total number of times the customer used the product this quarter.
Sessions per Seat	Total sessions divided by the number of seats. This is a measure of how fully utilized the current licenses are so it should be a good predictor of upgrades.

For each product, the company keeps track of how often customers use each of a number of different product features. The feature list is different for each product. These feature usage fields are only included for the base product as shown in the following table:

PER FEATURE FIELDS

Feature Sessions	Number of sessions in which this feature was used.
Feature Proportion	The above divided by the total number of sessions.

For both mailing and modeling, there are also risks involved with householding. From a customer relationship management viewpoint, remember that members of the same household may have very different relationships to the product or service offered and may not want to be treated as part of an undifferentiated whole. This is especially true for services where opinions are expressed. On one bookseller's site, book reviews by any member of a household are attributed to the person with the payer role because that is the only identity the site keeps track of. In another example, Netflix, a video rental service, once announced (for reasons that were not explained) that it would abolish the separate queues maintained by members of a household in favor of one big queue to which everyone in the household could contribute titles. Subscribers raised a fuss and the separate queues were kept. It turns out people like to spend time editing their queue which is, after all, an expression of their personal taste. They did not want to mingle their requests with those of other household members.

Households Change Over Time

Young children who are in the market for lunch boxes decorated with cartoon characters all too soon become part of the market for cell phones, video games, and SAT prep classes. Eventually they leave and start households of their own. Their parents, who moved to the suburbs for the schools may move back to the city. Or perhaps the parents are ready to retire to that place in the country. Or maybe they were just staying together for the kids, and they, too, set up new households.

Because households are not static, householding should be updated periodically in the same way that credit scores, estimated income, and model scores of all kinds should be updated. Ideally, when changes occur, old data should not simply be overwritten. Instead, the change transactions should be recorded so recreating a household as of an earlier date is still possible. The changes themselves can be quite interesting as well. Is a new home in a wealthier or poorer neighborhood?

Changes in the makeup of a household may have dramatic effects on household income, and on the priority the household puts on everything from transportation choices to entertainment choices. Good customer relationship management requires tracking these changes.

Will the Signature Be Used for Predictive Modeling?

A customer signature should be usable for multiple projects, but if any of those projects involve predictive modeling, understanding which fields will be used as targets and which fields will be used as model inputs is important because, as explained in Chapter 5, predictive models require signatures in which the targets are from a different timeframe than the explanatory variables. If the signature will be used for profiling or with undirected techniques, identifying target variables is not necessary at this stage, although often they are known from the start. A good practice is for the script or program that creates the customer signature to accept separate "as of" dates for target fields and input fields. That way, the same code can generate signatures for profiling or predictive modeling as needed.

> **TIP** Use separate parameters to specify the "as of" dates for inputs and targets. That way, the same code can be used to generate signatures for profiling or predictive modeling.

Has a Target Been Defined?

The target variable for a predictive model may or may not already exist in the source data. For a simple direct marketing response model, a field indicating whether or not a customer or prospect responded to an offer should be readily available, but other business goals may not be encapsulated in a single existing variable. For an attrition model, the miner must decide what it means for a customer to have left. When purchases occur at widely separated and irregular intervals, how much time must elapse before a customer is considered lost? There is no right answer to this question, but all interested parties should agree on a definition before modeling begins.

The authors were once asked to build a model that could identify yogurt lovers from loyalty card data. Clearly, yogurt lovers buy more yogurt than other people, but how much more? In consultation with the client, a manufacturer of yogurt and other consumer packaged goods sold in supermarkets, it was decided that a yogurt lover is in the top third of all customers measured by total spending on yogurt and in the top third of all customers measured by percentage of their total spending devoted to yogurt. The second part of the definition was designed to rule out customers who simply buy a lot of everything.

Are There Constraints Imposed by the Particular Data Mining Techniques to be Employed?

The customer signature should be a general portrait of the customer usable for multiple purposes and multiple techniques. That said, if it is known in advance that the signature will be used for training neural networks, it will lead to different design choices than if the signature is expected to support naïve Bayesian models. The former can only accept numeric inputs in a limited range; the latter can only accept categorical inputs.

Though important, these considerations should not dominate the design of the signature. Its job is to capture as much information as possible about the customer. Type conversions and other such issues can be addressed as part of the modeling process. In general, the nature of the data should determine what data mining techniques to use; not the other way around. The needs of particular modeling techniques can be accommodated later by creating new derived variables as needed. On the other hand, information can be represented in multiple ways. When the same person or team is designing the signature and creating the models, there is an opportunity to represent information in a form that is convenient for the intended use.

Which Customers Will Be Included?

If there are multiple customer types, such as business and residential, consider whether they are so different that each type should get its own customer signature. In general, if the two signatures would end up with the same fields, it is easier to just have one. Models for a single type can simply filter on a customer type column. But when different types of customers interact with the company in different ways and generate different kinds of data, giving each customer type its own signature is simpler.

TIP When customers leave, do not throw away the data that describes them. Former customers play an important role in data mining. Comparing former and current customers gives insight into why customers leave and how customer behavior has changed over time.

Another important decision is whether former customers will be included. The best answer is "yes" because some kinds of analysis cannot be done if there is only data for currently active customers. Unfortunately, many companies purge much of what they once know about a customer when the customer leaves. This is a bad idea. You want to keep data about former customers, so you can build signatures in the future. When data for former customers is not available, design the customer signature to support future attrition analysis and survival analysis efforts by ensuring that when today's active customers become inactive, their data remains available.

What Might Be Interesting to Know About Customers?

This is the final question and its answer depends largely on the business goals of the mining process. Bear in mind that many things that might be interesting to know may not be discoverable from the available data. Over the years, the authors have taken part in many attrition modeling projects. At the start of one of these, we asked the client, a mobile phone service provider, whether they had done any surveys of former subscribers to determine the reasons for their departure. They had, and we were given access to the results. Many subscribers cited too many dropped calls as their primary reason for leaving. Unfortunately, no data was available on dropped calls at the customer level. The company kept track of them for network improvement purposes. They could tell us that between 8:00 and 9:00, a particular cell was overloaded, but they could not tell that the overloaded cell was dropping a particular subscriber's call every day during that time. In other words, the information was available to support the network infrastructure, but it wasn't available to support customer relationship management.

At another company, in another country, this information was readily available. Subscribers received a credit on their bills when calls were dropped. As a result, the information was passed from the network switches to the billing system.

Even when some of the wished-for items are unavailable, making a wish list before going ahead with the design of the signature is still worthwhile. This helps prioritize the data sources and, in some cases, you may be able to come up with proxies for some of the fields on the wish list. The sample signatures in the technical asides give a feeling for the kinds of things a signature might contain.

What a Signature Looks Like

Figure 18-1 illustrates some of the various roles that fields in a customer signature can play.

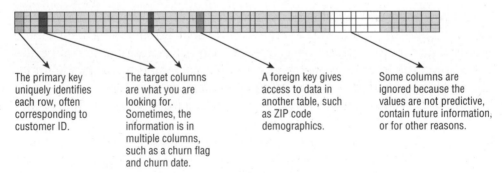

The primary key uniquely identifies each row, often corresponding to customer ID.

The target columns are what you are looking for. Sometimes, the information is in multiple columns, such as a churn flag and churn date.

A foreign key gives access to data in another table, such as ZIP code demographics.

Some columns are ignored because the values are not predictive, contain future information, or for other reasons.

Figure 18-1: The fields of a customer signature have various roles.

Each row is identified by a unique *primary key* that identifies the customer, household, or whatever is described by each row of the signature table. If such a key does not already exist, it should be created. The key should be something that identifies the customer and remains constant even as accounts and household members come and go. For that reason, using an identifier from an item at a lower level of aggregation than the signature row is not a good idea. A signature at the customer level should not be identified by an account number if customers may have multiple accounts. A signature at the household level should not use the identity of one of the household members as the household ID.

WARNING Do not use anything that may not last as long as the customer relationship as the primary key to identify a customer. That includes phone number, email address, and the account number associated with the customer's initial product. Similarly, a household should be identified by an ID that remains constant even as household members leave the nest, die, divorce, and come and go for other reasons. There's nothing wrong with having a phone number signature or an email signature if that is the proper level of analysis for a particular problem. The point is that signature rows should not be identified by a key associated with a lower level of aggregation.

The customer ID may be accompanied by various other fields that provide human-readable customer identifiers to aid reporting. This is useful because the signature may be exported to an analytic sandbox or other environment that lacks the auxiliary tables that would usually be joined in for reporting. Like the primary key, these auxiliary fields are ignored for modeling.

When the signature will be used for training directed models, it should include at least one field with the role of *target*. As discussed previously, target fields used for predictive modeling come from a different timeframe than the explanatory variables. Using a naming convention that clearly identifies such fields so they will not accidentally be used as explanatory variables is a good practice. Alternatively, the signature can be constructed without a target variable, in which case the target will have to be provided later as part of the training process.

A signature is a work in progress and so may contain other fields that should be ignored for modeling. These include *foreign keys* that can be used to join in data from other tables. The eventual goal is a self-contained signature, but initially it may not be clear which of the hundreds of fields available in a ZIP code demographics table or product detail table are likely to be useful enough to earn a permanent place in the signature. There may also be variables that, though not targets themselves, come from the timeframe of the target variable. Such variables may be useful for reporting, but should not be used for modeling. Other variables may be parked in the signature in the hope that they will one day be used in the definitions of derived variables that have yet to be created.

The remaining fields, usually the vast majority, are available as inputs for modeling.

SAMPLE SIGNATURE FOR CATALOG SHOPPERS

This signature for catalog shoppers was developed for a catalog retailer. The primary business goal was to increase the response rate for catalog mailings. The signature also supports modeling order size because that figure is also available in the target timeframe. The signature is in the predictive modeling style, with the target variables in a later timeframe than the explanatory variables. The fields are typical of the data available in a catalog or online retailer's customer file. Most of them document past ordering behavior of the customer.

The Respond and Order Size fields are both in the target timeframe. For any given model, one is used as the target and the other is ignored because it contains information from the target timeframe.

TARGET FIELDS

Respond	1 if customer placed an order from the catalog selected for training; 0 otherwise.
Order Size	Dollar amount of order when the preceding is 1; 0 otherwise. Note that NULL would be a better choice for order size of non-existent orders.

EXPLANATORY FIELDS

Buy Quarters	Count of quarters in which the customer placed at least one order.
Buy Percentage	Quarters with at least one order divided by the customer tenure in quarters.
Payment Methods	Number of different payment methods customer has used.
Catalog Count	Number of catalogs the customer has ever been sent.
Credit Card Only	1 if customer has paid for all orders with a credit card; 0 otherwise.
Check Only	1 if customer has paid for all orders with a check; 0 otherwise.
County ID	The county of the customer's home address for United States customers.
Recency	Days since the customer's last purchase.
Average Order Size	Average dollar amount of past orders.
Total Order Dollars	Dollar value of items ordered over customer's total lifetime.

EXPLANATORY FIELDS	
Recent Dollars	Customer's total spending in previous 24 months.
Net Order Dollars	Dollar value of items ordered over customer's total lifetime minus value of items returned or never received.
Frequency	Count of orders over entire customer tenure.
State	State where home address is located for U.S. customers. Province for Canadian customers. NULL for customers outside of those two countries.
Tenure	Months since customer's first order.
Total Items	Total number of items ordered in customer's lifetime.
Average Price	Average price of items ordered in customer's lifetime.
Items per Order	Average number of items in customer's orders.

The following fields are repeated for each of the twenty or so different departments in the retail catalog.

PER DEPARTMENT FIELDS	
Order Count	Number of orders in this department, lifetime.
Dollars	Total dollars spent in the department, lifetime.

The signature includes two two-year quarterly time series to capture customer spending over time. Unfortunately, most customers have made very few orders. In fact, the most common number of orders is one, with two as a distant second. That is why the signature does not include trend variables which would ordinarily be used to summarize a time series.

TIME SERIES FIELDS	
Order Count	Number of orders this quarter.
Order Dollars	Total spending this quarter.

Process for Creating Signatures

Figure 18-2 illustrates some of the data transformation operations that go into creating a customer signature.

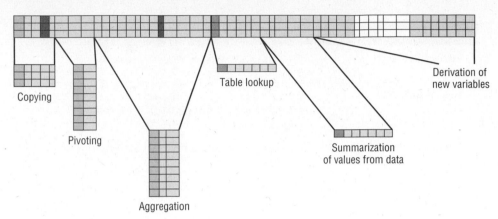

Figure 18-2: Data from most sources must be transformed in various ways before it can be incorporated into the signature.

Typical transformations include aggregating transactions to the appropriate granularity; pivoting monthly snapshots into regular time series; translating calendar dates into ages, tenures, or time before the "as of" date; performing table lookups using various customer attributes as foreign keys; and combining variables in various creative ways to derive new ones. This last transformation is the subject of the following chapter. The rest are covered in this chapter.

Some Data Is Already at the Right Level of Granularity

Some data sources may already contain data stored at the customer or household level that can be copied directly into the signature without transformation. These sources are a good place to begin. Customer level data is likely to include the customer's start date, and, where appropriate, information collected at the start of the relationship such as credit score at application time and date of birth. There may also be a current snapshot of the customer, including the current address, current product, current balances, and the like. Such a snapshot does not provide any history. The current handset model has overwritten any previous ones, as has the current address, current balance, and so on. These historical transitions are important, but they usually must be gleaned from other sources.

Ideally, even a snapshot should use a true customer number that uniquely identifies a single customer for all time, but often it does not. Customers may be identified by account numbers, causing customers with multiple products to have multiple identifiers. Or, customers may be identified by an ID that can be reused for someone else when the current holder releases it. For example, phone companies recycle phone numbers. On any given date, a phone number belongs to only one customer, but over time it may belong to many.

Most of the work that goes into creating a customer signature involves data sources that are not conveniently stored with one row per customer. The next sections describe some of the operations that are likely to be required to get data from source tables of various shapes into the customer signature.

Pivoting a Regular Time Series

Many businesses send out bills on a regular schedule. For an insurance company this may be an annual or semi-annual premium. For a magazine, this is often an annual subscription. For telephone service, internet service, and some types of business software as a service, it is usually a monthly bill. Each row in the billing table includes a customer ID and billing date. The data is "vertical" in the sense that there are multiple rows per customer. It must be rotated into the horizontal format of the customer signature and disentangled from the calendar and billing cycle. Figure 18-3 illustrates the process.

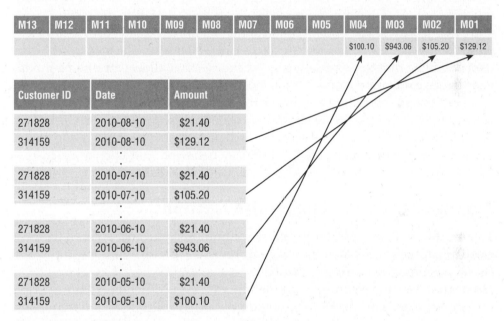

Figure 18-3: Vertical data must be pivoted to insert it into the customer signature

There may be several fields to be pivoted from each row, or there may be several rows per customer per period. For simplicity, this discussion assumes there is a single value because all regular time series get the same treatment. Also for simplicity, the periods are called months although they may be quarters, years, or some other unit.

As discussed in previous chapters, calendar dates are typically less useful for modeling than relative measures of time, such as customer tenure. The date associated with an observation in the source data is not explicitly represented in the signature. Instead, it determines where the pivoted value lands in the customer signature. The customer signature should contain fields named in relation to the "as of" date, which is often the same as the signature creation date (which will be different each time the code that creates the signature is called). If thirteen months of history are kept, the pivoted values land in fields with names like Prior 1, Prior 2…Prior 13. Somewhere, the creation date of the signature should be recorded so that calendar dates can be recreated for reporting purposes. This can be in a field in the signature itself, in which case it will usually have the same value in every row, or in external metadata such as the table name.

Some customers will not have the full thirteen months of history. The missing values should be stored as null rather than zero so that future miners will not have to wonder whether a customer did not yet exist or existed but had zero usage.

The final version of the customer signature may end up without any of the monthly values. They may be replaced by derived variables describing trend and other features. The initial version of the signature should contain sufficient observations to allow these features to be calculated later. The most recent thirteen complete months is usually a good choice. That allows for a same-month year-over-year comparison with the most recent month.

In addition to this rolling window of the most recent months, a snapshot of the customer's initial state, however long ago, should also be kept. The customer's acquisition channel or referral source, initial product, initial credit rating, initial balances and the like can be predictive of later behavior. And, comparing current values with initial values shows how the customer relationship has evolved.

Aggregating Time-Stamped Transactions

Transaction data is typically the most voluminous data and potentially most fruitful source for the customer signature. After all, transactions are where actual customer behavior is captured.

The first decision when aggregating transactions is the choice of time period for aggregation. This depends partly on the expected transaction frequency. Weekly summaries of an activity that only happens every few years would generate very sparse data that would be hard to use for modeling. By the same token, yearly summaries of an activity that occurs daily would miss all sorts of intra-year patterns that might be very important for characterizing customer behavior. The time period should be long enough that most customers have at least one transaction during a period, but short enough that seasonal variation is visible.

For some activities, these goals may be mutually exclusive because transactions at the customer level are too infrequent to reveal seasonal patterns. In that case, using a period short enough so that seasonal patterns can be observed in the aggregate even at the expense of fairly sparse summaries at the customer level is probably best.

Creating a Regular Time Series

Aggregating transactions creates a regular time series that can be pivoted into the customer signature as described earlier. More accurately, it produces many such time series because a single value per period does not provide a rich enough portrait of the customer. Business goals determine which features of the transaction data are most useful, but some typical aggregations are listed here. When there are multiple transaction types such as sends and receives, deposits and withdrawals, cash and credit card, and so forth, these fields are repeated per transaction type:

- Largest transaction
- Smallest transaction
- Average transaction
- Number of transactions
- Most recent transaction
- Earliest transaction

Including summaries broken down by other variables such as location or time of day may also be useful.

When Transactions Are Irregular and Rare

When transactions occur infrequently and at irregular intervals, creating a regular time series means either choosing a very wide aggregation period or accepting many zeroes in the regular series. In this situation, it is worth considering keeping the first transaction and the last n transactions instead of the last n time periods. Insurance claims, major appliance purchases, hospitalizations, and changes in service are examples of events that occur infrequently, but are important for understanding the history of the relationship.

Creating an Overall Transaction Summary

In addition to the time series data, which summarizes the customer's recent history, it is useful to summarize the lifetime transaction history of the customer:

- Time since first transaction
- Time since most recent transaction
- Proportion of transactions at each location
- Proportion of transactions by time of day
- Proportion of transactions by channel
- Largest transaction

- Smallest transaction
- Average transaction

When there are too many locations to have a field for the proportion of transactions at each location, you can still keep the name of the most frequently used location. For some models, these lifetime summaries may be more important than the time series summarizing recent transactions.

SAMPLE SIGNATURE FOR RETAIL BANKING CUSTOMERS

This signature for retail banking customers is an example of a customer signature with no target field. The business goal is to define customer segments with similar habits and needs so that banking products can be designed to meet their needs. The bank in question is in a predominantly Muslim country where one important distinction between segments is expected to be the customer's attitude towards interest, which is an integral part of many bank products, but forbidden under Sharia law. This explains, among others, the field recording religion, which would seem odd in North America or Europe. Some of the fields are present in anticipation of a future survival analysis project. That is also why this signature includes both active and former customers.

Opening a bank account involves being interviewed by a bank officer or filling out application forms. The following fields contain data collected as part of the application process.

FIELDS AS OF OPENING OF FIRST ACCOUNT

Date of Birth	For ease of reporting, actually recorded in two fields — one using the Arabic calendar and one using the western calendar.
Sex	Male or Female. There are separate bank branches to serve each sex.
Religion	Only two categories — Muslim or non-Muslim.
Marital Status	Divorced is not one of the choices.
Number of Children	0 if none; NULL if unknown.
Employment Status	Full time, part time, or not employed.
Employment Start Date	Date when current job started.
Monthly Salary	Best available according to a rule that prioritizes the values in several different source fields. 0 if no income. NULL if not known.
Nationality	Country of citizenship of the account holder.

FIELDS AS OF OPENING OF FIRST ACCOUNT	
Residence Status	Citizen, permanent resident, or temporary resident alien.
City of Residence	Standardized code.
Postal Code	Not directly useful for modeling, but important for creating derived variables based on geography.
Primary Language	Standardized code.
Home Ownership	Own or rent.
Education Level	Categorical variable with codes for various levels from no formal schooling through graduate degree.
Bank Employee Flag	1 if the account holder is an employee of the bank; 0 otherwise.

The fields in the following table present a snapshot of the customer's current relationship with the bank.

RELATIONSHIP SUMMARY FIELDS	
Relationship Tenure	Days since first account opened.
Relationship Active Flag	1 if relationship is still active. 0 if relationship has been terminated. For survival analysis, this field determines whether the relationship tenure field is censored.
Assigned Segment Code	A market segment assigned by bank officer at the time of account opening.
Initial Product Code	First product or, if more than one account is opened on the first day, the one deemed most important.
Initial Product Count	Number of accounts opened on the first day of the relationship.
Count of Active Products	Number of accounts on the "as of" date.
Assets Under Management	Total assets under management with the bank on the "as of" date.
Loans Outstanding	Amount owed on the "as of" date.
Total Deposits	Total deposits on the "as of" date.
Golden Service Flag	1 if customer is a member of the high-value customer program.
Direct Deposit Flag	1 if customer has salary deposited directly into an account at the bank; 0 otherwise.

Continued

SAMPLE SIGNATURE FOR RETAIL BANKING CUSTOMERS (*continued*)

Some fields are repeated to each of the major products offered by the bank. Examples are in the following table. Because most customers have only a few products, many of these fields contain missing values.

PER PRODUCT FIELDS	
Product Flag	1 if customer has ever had the product; 0 otherwise.
Account Open Date	Date when this account was opened.
Account Tenure	The complete tenure if the account has been closed; the censored tenure if the account is still open.
Average Balance Month	Average balance over the previous month.
Average Balance Year	Average balance over the previous year.
Credits per Month	Number of credit card transactions per month averaged over customer lifetime.
Debits per Month	Number of debit card transactions per month averaged over customer lifetime.
Short-Term Trend	Most recent month average balance divided by previous month average balance; NULL if not available.
Long-Term Trend	Most recent month average balance divided by same month last year average balance; NULL if not available.

The final set of fields in the following table attempts to describe customers based on their interactions with the bank.

BEHAVIOR FIELDS	
Saving Ratio	Sum of credits in last 12 months divided by sum of debits in last 12 months.
Conventional Loans	Number of non-Islamic loans originated in the last 12 months.
Islamic Product Count	Count of active Islamic-oriented products.
Risky Product Count	Count of active investment type products. One of the dimensions that the bank hopes will segment customers is appetite for risk.
Passivity Index	Tenure in months divided by number of accounts opened or closed. One of the dimensions that the bank hopes will segment customers is level of activity.

BEHAVIOR FIELDS	
ATM Proportion	Count of ATM transactions in last 12 months divided by total transactions in last 12 months. A measure of how much or how little burden the customer places on bank staff.
Branch Proportion	Count of branch transactions in last 12 months divided by total transactions in last 12 months.
Online Proportion	Count of online transactions in last 12 months divided by total transactions in last 12 months.
Telephone Proportion	Count of telephone transactions in last 12 months divided by total transactions in last 12 months.
Delinquency Rate	Count of late fees divided by number of months available.
Fee Rate	Fee income divided by number of months available.

Dealing with Missing Values

Another choice that must be made when designing the customer signature is what to do with missing values. This is more of an issue with numeric data than with categorical data and more important to some techniques than to others. Before doing anything with missing values, they must be recognized as such in the source data where they have often been cleverly disguised.

Missing Values in Source Data

Missing values may be represented in various ways in source data. Even when data comes directly from a relational database, missing values may or may not be represented using NULL, the SQL value that represents a missing value. When the data has been extracted and stored as comma- or tab-separated values, two delimiters with nothing between them indicates a missing value. Often, however, missing values in categorical data are represented by a special string such as:

- "UNKNWN"
- "N/A"
- "?"
- "."
- Whitespace characters

Missing values in numeric data are often represented as zero or a value such as "999" or "–99," all of which are unfortunate choices.

There is nothing wrong with having a special string to represent missing values in categorical data because one common method of handling missing values is to treat "missing" as its own category. In the customer signature, there should be a single consistent code for missing, even though this may not be the case in the source systems. For example, the "COUNTRY" field in the software as a service sample signature elsewhere in this chapter was taken from a source system that included free text typed in by sales reps. These had to be standardized using rules that, for example, mapped "GB," "England," and "Scotland" to the standard code "UK." When the country was not known, it appeared as blank, "?," and "??," all of which had to be mapped to a standard representation.

Mapping various strings to a standard representation is fairly easy. Figuring out which zeros are real zeros and which stand for missing values can be trickier when zero is a valid value. With luck, there are other fields, such as a customer start date, that can be used to determine whether values should be expected for a given date.

Finally, it is worth looking for missing values disguised as default values. A common cause of this problem is input forms with common defaults pre-filled and drop-down menus with a default choice. People who fail to fill in the fields are given the default value. A human reader can usually spot this problem by noticing unreasonable distributions for the fields in question or by noticing a large number of examples where the default value is present and clearly wrong. One company whose registration page designer was clearly in the U.S., but whose customers were all over the world, had many addresses such as:

200 George St.
Sydney, NSW 2000
UNITED STATES

145 King St. W.
Toronto, ON M5H 1J8
UNITED STATES

No doubt the reader can guess the correct countries for these examples, but that is not the same as being able to write a program to do it. This was a real problem because the company had reason to believe that important measures such as response and attrition varied a lot by country. Simply considering "UNITED STATES" to be equivalent to "missing" would not be acceptable because the U.S. was, in fact, the most common country.

In one case, disguised missing values were revealed by a histogram of customer ages. Nearly a quarter of the customers were in their upper eighties. This seemed unlikely, and upon further investigation, it was not true. This story dates from the closing years of the twentieth century; a large cohort of senior citizens all shared November 11, 1911 as their birthday. Why? Because a business person decided that age was an important thing to know about a customer. So a database designer decided that null values would not be allowed in that column. This led to an input screen design that would not let the operator go on to the next screen until a birth date was filled in. Some customers refuse to reveal their dates of birth. The customer service reps can be pretty smart. They learned that entering 111111 was the quickest way to get to the next screen. This was parsed as November 11, 1911 so that, in effect, became a missing value code.

Unknown or Non-Existent?

A null or missing value can result from either of two quite different situations. The first case is that a value exists, but it is unknown because it has not been captured. Customers really do have dates of birth even if they choose not to reveal them. The second case is that the question simply does not apply. The Spending Six Months Previous field is not defined for customers who have less than six months of tenure. The distinction is important because although imputing the unknown age of a customer might make sense, imputing the non-existent spending of a non-customer does not make sense. For categorical variables, these two situations can be distinguished using different codes such as "Unknown" and "Not Applicable."

What Not to Do

Above all, do no harm. Many common practices for replacing missing variables fail to follow that Hippocratic injunction. Harm can take many forms including biasing the sample, changing the distribution of the variable, and adding noise that makes finding real patterns harder. Some of these problems are mentioned in Chapter 5 as part of the directed data mining methodology. This section goes into more detail.

Don't Throw Records Away

When using a modeling technique that cannot handle missing variables, it is tempting to simply skip over records that contain them — especially if there are relatively few such records. If the missing values were generated randomly so that every record had an equal chance of having one or more of them, skipping records would be fine; the sample size would be reduced, but no bias would be introduced. The problem is that the missing values are not generated at random.

Certain acquisition channels, certain products, certain age groups, certain counties, or certain *something* will be underrepresented when the offending records have been removed.

Even worse, in some signatures, the expectation is that every customer will have missing values. For example, a customer signature for a bank is likely to include product-specific fields for a large number of products. No one customer has all the products, so all rows contain missing values.

Don't Replace with a "Special" Numeric Value

With categorical values, having a category that means "missing" makes sense because, by definition, there is no explicit ordering of the categories. Data mining algorithms may make use of an implicit ordering of categories based on their relationship to the target, and "missing" will take its proper place in that implicit ordering. Numeric values are different; they have a built-in ordering. Representing missing values with a number arbitrarily assigns them a place in that built-in ordering. When the arbitrary value used to represent missing is purposely picked to be unusual, the assignment often says, in effect, "when the value is not known, assume it is smaller (or larger) than any known value." Clearly, that is not a reasonable assumption.

Don't Replace with Average, Median, or Mode

One of the most common approaches is to replace all missing values with a single typical value. This seems seductively sensible: In the absence of any other information, why not assume that the missing value is around average? The clue is in the phrase *in the absence of any other information*. In fact, the non-missing fields in the signature provide a lot of other information about the customer, and that information is likely to conflict with the information provided by the typical value. In other words, replacing missing values with a typical value adds noise by disrupting the relationships that ought to exist between the field with the missing value and other fields in the signature. Table 18-1 illustrates the problem.

In 2005, the median personal income for people over age 25 in the U.S. was $32,140. The average income of the seven rows with known income shown above is $49,720. Replacing the two missing values in the table with either of those values creates a surprisingly well-paid barista and a surprisingly low-paid DBA — neither of whom actually exists. Replacing missing values with a typical value turns unsurprising records that happen to be missing a few values into atypical records with spurious values filled in.

Table 18-1: Customer Occupation and Income

OCCUPATION	AGE	INCOME
Database Administrator	50	$92,000
Flight Attendant	32	$42,240
High School Teacher	45	$64,500
Database Administrator	47	—
Letter Carrier	41	$36,500
Bus Driver	58	$24,000
College Professor	41	$73,300
Barista	22	—
Yoga Instructor	28	$15,500

Things to Consider

So, what *can* you do about missing values? There are several alternatives. The goal is always to preserve the information in the non-missing fields so it can contribute to the model. When this requires replacing the missing values with an imputed value, the imputed values should be chosen so as to do the least harm.

Consider Doing Nothing

Table lookup models, naïve Bayesian models, and decision trees are able to make good use of records containing missing values by treating missing as a category, so one choice that should always be considered is leaving the missing values alone and using one of these techniques.

The fact that a value is missing may even turn out to be an important predictor. The authors once built a decision tree model to estimate probability of response to an offer of term life insurance. One of the strongest predictors was the number of missing values in data appended from a household data vendor; however, this was a negative indicator so fewer missing values meant a higher probability of response. Many of these fields were collected from public records such as marriages, births, and real estate transactions. It turns out that people whose lifestyle leads to a lot of non-missing values by getting married, buying houses, and having children are more likely to be interested in life insurance than people whose lifestyles leave these fields full of missing values.

In another case, households with missing demographic information had higher response rates than other prospects in the database. The reason? The households were matched to census tracts; those that could not be matched to the census geography ended up with missing values. These prospects resided in brand-new subdivisions that did not exist in the previous decennial census. The purchasers of these new homes tended to be relatively wealthy. Apparently, either the newness of these homes or the wealth of their inhabitants caused them to be good prospects.

Consider Multiple Models

Often, a value is missing for a whole class of customers. One common case is when there are multiple tiers of customers such as registered users versus unregistered users, or users of the free version versus users of the pro version. The same situation arises when one company acquires the customers of another, but does not acquire full information about them.

The most common situation is new customers. They lack transactional history. Building separate models for each class of customer makes sense not only because different fields are available, but also because the groups have different needs and motivations. Brand-new telephone subscribers might leave because the service works well at the office but not at home, or because they are surprised by the actual cost when fees for add-on services are taken into account. Long-term subscribers have already passed these hurdles, so their motivations for leaving are more likely to be related to competitive offers or the chance to acquire a coveted new phone.

Consider Imputation

Imputation means replacing missing values with a value that makes sense given the values of the fields that are not missing. In the example from Table 18-1, that would mean filling in appropriate incomes for a 47-year old DBA and a 22-year-old coffee shop worker rather than assigning them each the same typical value. A simple imputation method would be to look up the salaries of all known customers in the same occupation and age range, but pretty much any of the modeling techniques can be used to impute values. The difficulty with this approach is that it requires as many imputation models as there are missing value patterns.

Imputing values for categorical variables is also possible. This is often an attractive alternative to treating "missing" as its own category. One blank that is often left unfilled on registration forms is the Sex or Gender field. This leads to a three-valued variable with categories "M," "F," and "U" for unknown. When the first name is available, the gender can be imputed using data from customers who supplied both a first name and a gender. For each name, calculate the proportion of males and females. This proportion is an empirical estimate of the probability of each assignment. Most names lean strongly one way or the other.

When imputed values are used, that fact should be recorded in another variable. This is not only for documentation; if values are missing for a reason that has bearing on the target, the imputed value flag may turn out to have predictive value.

Imputed Values Should Never Be Surprising

The true value of a variable contains information that is not otherwise available. Two employees with the same job title, seniority, and office location can still have different salaries. (Where that is not true, as in certain government or union positions, there is no point in recording salary because the job code and length of service convey the same information.) With real data, an employee can be surprisingly well paid or surprisingly poorly paid, and that information could have predictive value. The whole point of imputing values when the real values are unknown is to avoid such surprises.

Basically, imputed values are chosen so as not to disturb the information provided by the actual values. In a certain technical sense, imputed values do not add any information because they are a function of other variables that are already known. Like other derived variables, they do make information available in a more convenient form where it is more likely to be useful for modeling and for understanding customer characteristics.

Lessons Learned

The customer signature is the foundation on which many data mining projects are built. It determines whether the models created will be predictive models or profiling models. The fields of the customer signature determine how customers are represented in data. This, in turn, determines how effective and informative data mining models can be.

The rows of a signature table correspond to the unit of analysis — that is, the thing to be studied. In the world of marketing and customer relationship management, that is usually the customer, but it might be some other unit such as a retail outlet or geographic area. Even when it is clear that the object of study is a customer, there are decisions to be made. Is the customer the person who pays the bill? The person who uses the service or product? The person who makes decisions about the account? The answer depends on the particular business problem that data mining is called upon to solve.

Interactions between a company and its customers generate transactions. Transaction summaries of various kinds make up the majority of fields in a typical customer signature design. Transactions are usually aggregated to regular intervals such as weeks, months, quarters, or years, and then pivoted into the customer signature as time series. These time series are not tied to the calendar. Dates are transformed into days before the "as of" date — usually the date that the signature was extracted, but possibly a recreation of some earlier time. When the signature is created to support predictive models, there are two "as of" dates — one for the target and another for the explanatory variables that are inputs to the model.

One problem that arises frequently is fields with missing values. There are many bad ideas in circulation about how to deal with missing values, including rejecting any records that contain a missing value; replacing all missing values with a common value such as the mean, median, or mode; and replacing missing values with a value that is clearly outside the realm of possibility. Values may be missing either because a value exists, but is unknown, or because the field is not applicable to some cases. When a value exists, but is unknown, it can be replaced by an imputed value. Imputed values are the result of models where the missing value is the target and the known values are inputs.

CHAPTER 19

Derived Variables: Making the Data Mean More

The preceding chapter is about getting data to the point where modeling can begin. This chapter is devoted to making models better by improving the quality of the data going into them. For the most part, this is not a matter of obtaining additional data sources; it is about defining new variables that express the information inherent in the data in ways that make the information more useful or more readily available to data mining techniques.

Creating derived variables is one of the most creative parts of the data mining process. If there is an art and science of data mining, creating derived variables is part of the art. Derived variables allow data mining models to incorporate human insights into the modeling process, and allow data mining models to take advantage of important characteristics already known about customers, products, and markets. In fact, the ability to come up with the right set of variables for modeling is one of the most important skills a data miner must have.

Derived variables definitely improve model performance as determined by technical measures such as average squared error, misclassification rate, and lift. Perhaps more importantly, well-chosen derived variables also enhance the ability of models to be understood and interpreted.

However, the variables that work best in one setting may not work in another, seemingly similar setting. Different companies have different drivers in their markets. Some companies compete on convenience and others compete on price. You should expect different derived variables to be important in these different companies. Data miners cannot afford to get lazy and assume that the variables they used the last time are necessarily the best one for the next model.

This chapter starts with a story about modeling customer attrition in the mobile phone industry. The story shows the power and limitation of derived variables, including how:

- Changing market conditions can radically change the predictive power of a variable

- What works well in one market, might not work in another

The chapter then describes standard transformations of a single variable, most of which have been discussed in early chapters — centering, rescaling, standardization, and changes in representation. Single-variable transformations are important, but the most creative transformations involve combinations of variables. After a review of several classic combinations, the chapter provides guidelines for creating your own derived variables. Particular attention is paid to time and geography, two of the most important attributes of customer data.

Handset Churn Rate as a Predictor of Churn

Handsets are a well-known driver of churn in the mobile phone business. *Handset* is the term industry insiders use to refer to the actual device you carry around and use for talking and texting. In many markets, service providers heavily subsidize the price of a new handset for new subscribers, but charge full price to existing subscribers desiring an upgrade. This gives a customer who is dissatisfied with his or her phone an incentive to switch providers to get the new customer discount.

Understanding that handsets are important is not the same as understanding how to include them in a model. There are several problems with just using the handset model number itself in models. One problem is that new handset models come out all the time, and old models are discontinued just as quickly. Any data mining model based on the actual handset model names would quickly go out of date because each month, more and more active handsets would fall into the "other" category. Another problem is that what is cool today will soon seem "so last year." Telephones are not merely communications devices — they are also fashion items, and fashion is fickle.

The first time the authors used handset information in a churn model, it happened to be in South Korea. Although the client believed only 5 or 10 handset models were in use, the data revealed that actually more than 200 were. Having 200 levels of a categorical variable is a lot — too many, in fact. A logistic regression or neural network model would create a separate indicator variable for each type of handset, introducing a lot of model complexity for little purpose.

Only the more recent and more popular models have a sizeable number of active users, so one possibility would be to group all but the most popular handsets into an "OTHER" group. A more sophisticated approach would be to group the variables with respect to the target. All handsets associated with high rates of churn would be placed in the "HIGH" group. Those associated with low rates of churn would be placed in the "LOW" group. Everything else would get labeled "MEDIUM." That is what a decision tree splitting rule would typically do.

Grouping handset models into high, medium, and low churn groups requires calculating the rate of churn associated with each handset, so why not use the rate directly? In fact, this is the approach taken on this project. The model itself was a classical prediction model, as described in Chapter 5. It used four months of history to predict the second month in the future (for the target in June, the inputs would be Jan–Apr, with May data not included in the customer signature). The handset churn rate was calculated using only the data from the input time frame (Jan–Apr, for this example).

The variable worked quite well. In fact, handset churn rate was the single most predictive variable on basically all the models produced. For instance, it was chosen as the top splitter for almost every decision tree built during the project.

Handset churn rate is an example of two variable derivation techniques discussed in this chapter:

- Replacing categorical variables with numeric ones
- Using past values of the target variable

A single categorical variable such as *handset* can provide several useful numeric ones. For instance, this story happened long enough ago that the weight of the phone in grams might have been a factor. As it turned out, though, from the point of view of predicting churn, the most useful thing to know about a phone is how quickly its owners have been leaving recently.

TIP It is not uncommon for variables that are known to be important to go unused because, in their current form, they are difficult to use. Often, the best solution is to create a derived variable that represents the same information in a form better suited to the data mining techniques in use.

There is a second moral to the story. The next time the authors built a churn model, it was for a provider in Canada. Handset churn rate — the variable that had been so predictive in Seoul — was a flop in Toronto. The difference was not due to culture or language but to marketing strategy. The Canadian company offered the same handset discounts to existing customers as it did to new ones, eliminating that particular reason for leaving. The important lesson is not that handset churn rate is a great variable. The important lesson is the importance of finding a way to use the information locked away in hard-to-use variables like handset model.

Single-Variable Transformations

Although making up new transformations is part of the fun of data mining, it is not always necessary. A few transformations are done routinely to increase the amount of usable information in data or to make the information that is already present more visible.

Standardizing Numeric Variables

Chapter 4 introduces standardization as an important transformation for modeling. The subject also comes up in the chapters on clustering, memory-based reasoning, and regression. This section reiterates the importance of standardization for improving the performance and/or interpretability of models.

The main point is to put variables that are measured in incompatible units onto a common scale so that a difference of one along one dimension means the same thing as a difference of one along another dimension. This is especially important for techniques, such as clustering and memory-based reasoning, which depend on the concept of distance.

Even when standardization is not technically necessary, a common scale can make models more meaningful to humans. For instance, when all the inputs to a regression model are on the same scale, the relative size of the beta values has an easy interpretation: Variables with larger coefficients in the regression equation have more effect on the model result. The ultimate regression model performs equally well regardless of whether or not the inputs are standardized, but the standardized inputs make the model easier to understand. The standardization process has two steps and each is useful on its own:

1. The data is centered so the average is zero.
2. The centered value is divided by the standard deviation.

Each of these steps reveals information about a single variable.

Centering

Subtracting the average from each value of a variable yields a derived variable with an average of zero without changing the scale. If the original variable is measured in dollars, the new value is measured in dollars above or below average.

Centering can increase the interpretability because you don't have to know the average order size, for example, to see at a glance whether a particular order is smaller or larger than average and by how much. Centering the data does not actually increase the information available to data mining algorithms because all it does is shift the values by a constant amount. It does make life easier for humans, which is also worthwhile.

Rescaling

Dividing the centered values by the standard deviation yields a derived variable with an average value of 0 and standard deviation equal to 1 — the standardized value (or z-score). No matter what the distribution of the data, this scale is useful because it allows comparison between variables that started out on different scales.

The standard deviation is perfectly well defined for numeric data without regard to distribution. A small standard deviation always means that most values are close to the average and a large standard deviation means that values are more spread out. In the special case when data does happen to be normally distributed, there is an added bonus — knowing a value's distance from the average provides an estimate of its percentile. For example, a value of 3 is greater than 99 percent of values. Although this property is nice, data miners do not usually like to make assumptions about distributions, and calculating percentiles is simple enough.

Turning Numeric Values into Percentiles

Parents love to tell their friends that their babies are in the 95th percentile for length, or weight, or head circumference, or whatever. This is a more effective way of boasting than saying "my baby is 60 cm long" because who (besides pediatricians) knows whether that is big or small for a three-month-old? The absolute measurement does not convey as much information as the fact that this baby is bigger than 95 percent of the "competition." Doctors also find percentiles useful, not because they subscribe to the "bigger is better" fallacy that many parents do, but because a child, whether big or small, who is growing at a normal rate tends to stay near the same percentile. If a baby who was in the 70th percentile at the last checkup is now in the 30th, it may be cause for worry, while a child who has been in the 30th percentile all along is probably doing fine.

Converting numeric values into percentiles has many of the same advantages as standardization. It translates data into a new scale that works for any numeric measure. Instead of the distance from the average, it is the percent of values that are smaller (or in some cases larger). Clearly, these ideas are related: For known distributions, there are tables for converting from one to the other, but percentiles have the advantage of not requiring knowledge of the distribution.

Percentiles spread out skewed distributions. If, due to grade inflation, most students have grades over 90, translating grades to percentiles will reveal that a 91 is not as good as it sounds. This is a transformation to consider whenever relative position seems more important than an absolute measurement. Things such as income and home value, which vary a lot by geography, are likely candidates. Knowing that a family's income is in the top 20 percent for its county may be more useful than knowing the actual amount.

For example, according to the 2000 U.S. Census data, 39110, the richest ZIP code in Mississippi (the poorest state by median household income) had a median income of $73,938. The richest ZIP code in Maryland, 20854, had a median income of $140,222 — nearly twice as high. As might be expected, the Maryland ZIP code also has a higher percentage of college-educated residents, but only by a factor of 1.4. In fact, more than half the population in both places has a college degree. In contrast, in the Maryland ZIP code whose median income is closest to that of the richest one in Mississippi, only about 31 percent have college degrees. To the extent that education can be used as a proxy for social class, wealthy Mississippians have more in common with their even wealthier counterparts in Maryland than they do with Marylanders with the same nominal income.

Turning Counts into Rates

Many databases contain counts: number of purchases, number of calls to customer service, number of times late, number of catalogs received, and so on. Often, when these tallies are for events that occur over time, it makes sense to convert the counts to rates by dividing by some fixed time unit to get calls per day or withdrawals per month. This allows customers with different tenures to be compared.

When calculating events over time, you must be sure that the time frames line up. One common mistake is to define a variable such as events per year without making any adjustment for customers who have not yet had a full year of tenure. A customer with ten events in six months of tenure is experiencing events at the same rate as someone who experiences twenty per year; the metric should reflect that. The sidebar, "A Cautionary Tale," provides another example of how things can go wrong. In that case the problem was that two different data sources were combined without adjusting for the fact that they included different amounts of history.

A CAUTIONARY TALE: LONG-TIME SUBSCRIBERS DON'T COMPLAIN MUCH?

Calculating rates involves combining two different variables, which are often from different systems. For instance, calculating the complaint rate involves dividing the number of complaints (which comes from customer service records) by the customer tenure (which often comes from marketing sources). It is wise to pay careful attention to metadata to be sure that the sources describe the same time period.

This point was driven home to the authors by an embarrassing mistake during a customer segmentation project for a newspaper. The project used k-means clustering to create segments based on a subscriber signature. The customer signature included a complaint rate variable defined as the total number of complaints the subscriber had ever made divided by the subscriber's tenure. The complaint rate turned out to be a key variable for distinguishing between the clusters.

One of the clusters had very low complaint rates. It also had a very high average tenure. This led to much discussion of cause and effect. Could it be that people who rarely complain are getting better delivery service (the complaint categories were mostly about problems with delivery: wet papers, late papers, missed deliveries, missing sections) and therefore sticking around longer? Could it be that passive types, who never call to complain, also never call to cancel their subscriptions? All these explanations, and more, provide possible explanations for the phenomenon.

Alas, what was really happening was much less interesting. The "complaint rate" did not actually provide any information about customers. The complaints data had only been kept for two years, so "total number of complaints" was actually "total number of complaints *in the previous two years*." Some of the subscribers had been around for decades. Dividing complaints by tenure meant that anyone with a long tenure appeared to have a low complaint rate.

WARNING   When combining data from multiple sources, you must be sure that they contain data from the same timeframe.

Relative Measures

Another common situation is variables stored as counts of members of particular categories: number of men and number of women in the student body; number of members in each level of a loyalty program; count of multi-family homes or people with master's degrees in a town. The trouble with counts is that they all tend to rise and fall together. A large university has more men *and* women than a small college; a big city has more college graduates than a small town, and so forth. In such cases, there is more information in the percent of students who are male, or the percent of homes that are multi-family.

A percentage is an example of a relative measure, such as the count of some particular category relative to the count for all categories. Another common way of expressing relative measures is as a proportion of some monetary value such as the size of the economy. An example is military spending as a proportion of gross domestic product. Other examples of relative measures include z-scores, which are relative to the average value for a group, and percentiles, which give a ranking relative to other members of a group.

Relative measures are defined with respect to some total. If there are N categories, knowing the value for $N-1$ of them is sufficient to determine the value of the remaining category. If you know the percent of total revenue received from 49 out of 50 states, whatever they do not account for must have come from the 50th. Chapter 15 has a story in it that illustrates how this can become misleading when the number of categories is low. For many towns, census data shows a strong negative correlation between the percentage of African-American residents and the percentage of Hispanic residents. In fact, if these are the only two groups, knowing the percentage of either one means you know the percentage of the other, and they are inversely proportional to each other.

Replacing Categorical Variables with Numeric Ones

Numeric variables are sometimes preferable to categorical ones. Certain modeling techniques — including regression, neural networks, and most implementations of clustering — prefer numbers and cannot readily accept categorical inputs. Even when using decision trees, which are perfectly capable of handling categorical inputs, there may be reasons for preferring numeric ones.

The handset churn rate described earlier in this chapter is a case in point. Consider what would happen if a decision tree used the handset model name rather than the handset churn rate. The decision tree would do well at first, perhaps even better than the one using the handset churn rate. The decision tree algorithm would, in effect, invent the handset churn rate variable by grouping handsets according to the proportion of churners for each handset in the training data. Over time, however, the categorical model will decay quickly as new handsets are introduced and formerly well-regarded handsets lose popularity. The model built on the historical churn rate is more stable because even as handset models come and go, it remains true that subscribers with handsets associated with high churn are more likely to leave.

Replacing categorical variables with numeric ones is often a good idea, but how?

What Not to Do

A common mistake of novice data miners is to replace categorical values with arbitrary numbers. Table 19-1 shows the first few rows of a table where the states of the United States have been listed in alphabetical order and enumerated. The problem is that this enumeration creates spurious information that data mining algorithms have no way of ignoring. According to this table Alaska is very close to Alabama and Arizona. This is meaningless, but that is what the numbers say, and data mining techniques cannot ignore what the numbers say.

Table 19-1: An Enumeration of the States

STATE	CODE
Alabama	1
Alaska	2
Arizona	3
Arkansas	4
California	5
Colorado	6
Connecticut	7
Delaware	8
Florida	9
Georgia	10
Hawaii	11
Idaho	12
...	...
...	...
...	...

Remember, the reason for putting information in a numeric form is to make it available for modeling. However, the data mining techniques understand the numbers, not the original context. Assigning the values arbitrarily does not convey any information to the data mining technique. It merely provides a number that might as well be random.

Using Indicator Variables

Another popular approach is to create a separate binary variable for each category. A 1 indicates that a category is present and a 0 indicates that it is not. This works well when you have only a few categories, but to represent U.S. states this way would require 50 indicator variables, and that is before dealing with Puerto Rico, the District of Columbia, and Canadian provinces, all of which are typically present in a U.S. company's customer data.

This explosion of variables is undesirable because most modeling techniques work better with fewer rather than many variables, particularly when the many variables are quite sparse (that is, usually take on the value of 0).

If the important information contained in 50 variables, one for each state, could be expressed with fewer, it would be an improvement. Chapter 20 discusses ways to reduce the number of variables while retaining most of the information they contain. Here the goal is to avoid creating so many in the first place.

Replacing Categorical Variables with Numeric Descriptors

Often, the most satisfactory approach to categorical variables is to replace each one with a handful of numeric variables that capture important attributes of the categories. Of course, what counts as important depends on the target variable. Depending on what is to be predicted, the important characteristics of a handset model might be its price, its weight, the number of months it has been available, its popularity, the number of "apps" available for it, and/or its battery life. Similarly, a geographic location, such as a county, can be described by its population, its population density, its altitude, its latitude and longitude, its median income, its annual rainfall, or the proportion of radio stations with a country music format.

These numeric descriptors describe the different categories. They can also be quite useful. A decision tree might group several geographic codes, such as DC, MA, MD, CO, and VA, for a split. While the two may be equivalent, this is less informative than a split that says "more than 34 percent of adults have a college degree." Numeric descriptors often result in models that are more stable and easier to understand.

Binning Numeric Variables

There are also times when converting a numeric variable into a categorical one is desirable. For one thing, some data mining techniques, such as table lookup models and naïve Bayesian models, only work on categorical data. Binning, also called *discretization*, means dividing the range of a numeric variable into a set number of subranges (the bins) and replacing each value with its bin number. This can also be a powerful way of dealing with variables with skewed distributions — because the outliers are all placed together in one bin.

The three major approaches to creating bins are:

- Equal width binning
- Equal weight binning
- Supervised binning

These all place numeric values into ranges. The difference is how the ranges are defined.

Figure 19-1 is a histogram showing the distribution of months since the last purchase for a group of catalog customers. Most customers have made a purchase within the last couple of years. In fact, because the data was collected in the fall, and many customers purchase only in December, the tallest bar is for customers whose most recent purchase was 10 months ago.

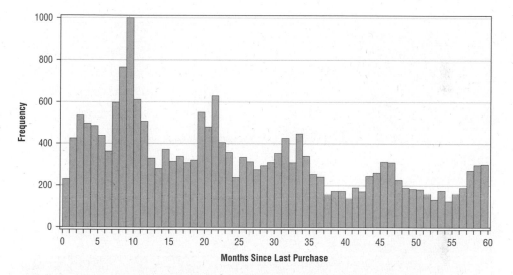

Figure 19-1: Most customers have made a purchase within the last two years.

Months since last purchase is a likely variable to include in a response model because people who have recently made a purchase are more likely to respond. Table lookup models like the RFM cubes described in Chapter 6 are popular in the catalog industry. The first step in building the cube is to discretize the recency variable; in this case, months since last purchase.

Figure 19-2 compares two possible approaches. The first creates five equal width bins. Because the customer with the longest time since last purchase was last seen 271 months ago, each of the five equal-width bins is 54 months wide. This means that more than three-quarters of the customers in the sample (36,856 out of 48,356) are in the first bin. The charts, which were produced by the SAS Enterprise Miner binning node, show something slightly different, The height of each bar represents the count of responders ("events") in each bin. This choice of vertical axis makes good sense for the equal weight bins — because all bins have the same number of customers, differences in height reflect differences in response rate. It makes less sense for the equal-width bins, so in the spirit of this chapter, let's derive the corresponding response rates. The response rate in the leftmost of the equal-width bins is 6.5 percent, which is just a little higher than the population average. The four other bins do have lower response rates, as expected, but they don't contain many people. The rightmost bin contains only 130 customers. Their response rate is 2.3 percent.

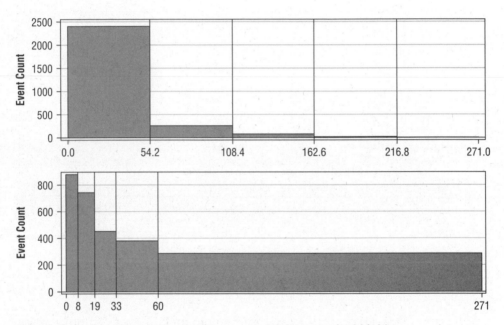

Figure 19-2: Quantiles are generally more useful than equal-width bins.

The second approach produces equal weight bins — five quintiles, each with approximately 20 percent of the customers. Because the height of the bars represents the number of responders, clearly the higher quintiles have higher response rates. The top two quintiles have higher-than-average response rates of 10.5 percent and 7.0 percent. The bottom three quintiles have lower-than-average response rates.

The quintiles provide a more useful binning than the equal-width bins, but there is no guarantee that the quintile boundaries are optimal in terms of separating high-response groups from low-response groups. Figure 19-3 shows one way to address this. A balanced sample of 50 percent responders and 50 percent non-responders was used to build a one-level decision tree with five-way splits. The five leaves of the tree are chosen by the decision tree split criterion to maximize the difference in response rate. Because months since last purchase is the only input variable provided, all the splits are on it. This is an example of *supervised binning* where a target variable is used to pick bin boundaries.

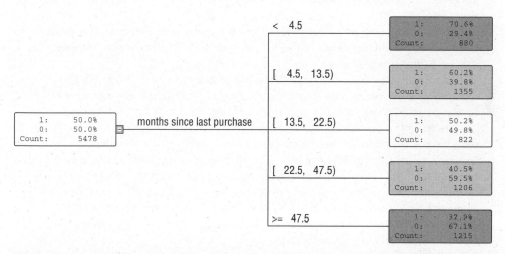

Figure 19-3: A decision tree with a single input variable provides supervised binning.

This approach to supervised binning uses information about the target variable to reshape the input variable so it can do a better job of predicting the target variable. If that sounds circular, it is, and for that reason, it might or might not work. You could find a binning that is optimal for this particular dataset, but will not generalize to any other. On the other hand, equal width and equal weight bins don't even try to find optimal boundaries with respect to the target. To the extent that a stable pattern actually exists, supervised binning has a chance of discovering them. This issue is discussed in more depth in the sidebar "Why Using Information from the Target Is Cheating, and Why It Might Work Anyway."

WHY USING INFORMATION FROM THE TARGET IS CHEATING, AND WHY IT MIGHT WORK ANYWAY

When creating a variable such as handset churn rate or county response rate, you should not use values of the target variable from the current training data. To do so would break a cardinal rule of modeling by creating input variables that use information (who responded or who quit) that would not be available when the model is applied to predict that very thing. Using information from the future is cheating, and yet, this is exactly what a typical decision tree algorithm does when faced with a categorical variable with many levels. It is also what the supervised binning example in Figure 19-3 does.

When a decision tree makes a split on categorical variables, it separates the categories into two groups based on the target. Are these groups of values cheating, because they were formed using information from the target? Or is this okay?

The answer depends on whether there is a real effect *that is stable over time*. If such an effect exists, what month you look for it in doesn't matter; even a future month will do.

Consider two made-up scenarios. In the first scenario, each month the marketing department chooses a letter of the alphabet and anyone who lives in a state beginning with that letter gets a half-price offer. If the training data is from the month of the "I" campaign, a decision tree will notice strong response from Indiana, Illinois, Iowa, and Idaho and group them together on the high-response branch of a tree. The split generalizes well to the validation set, which is just another sample from the same month, and the resulting model performs well on the test set. When deployed to predict next month's response, it fails miserably because next month's special offer goes to "M" states and the bulk of responders are from Maine, Massachusetts, Montana, Maryland, Minnesota, and Michigan.

In the second scenario, there is no change in marketing strategy from month to month, but because of the nature of the product (cross-country skis or surfboards, perhaps), it has always been more popular in some places than in others. This effect turns up every month, and a model that incorporates it will generalize well from month to month.

Methods such as supervised binning and grouping categories by target response are gambling that whatever pattern they detect is caused by an effect that is stable over time. This might or might not be true, so these methods might or might not work. No amount of validation data can help, unless it comes from a different time frame. The validation set usually comes from the same time frame as the training set and only guards against overfitting patterns that are due to sample variation; it cannot protect against overfitting on patterns that are due to effects that vary over time.

Combining Variables

One of the most common ways of creating derived variables is by combining two existing variables to reveal information that is not provided by either on its own. Often, variables are combined by dividing one by the other as in the price/earnings ratio or teacher/pupil ratio, but products, sums, differences, squared differences, and even more imaginative combinations also prove useful. This section starts by looking at a few well-known examples and then suggests ways of spotting good opportunities for creating your own combinations.

Classic Combinations

Some derived variables have become so well known that it is easy to forget that someone once had to invent them. Insurance companies track loss ratios, investors pick stocks based on price/earnings ratios, and retailers track year-over-year same store sales. The business world isn't the only place where variables get combined. Some of the best-known examples come from medicine, sports, and weather reporting. Thinking about these classic combinations and what makes them effective is a good way to begin.

Body Mass Index (BMI)

Anyone who has ever read a diet book (or even a brief magazine article on maintaining a healthy weight) has heard of the BMI measure, which was invented by the 19th century Belgian astronomer and mathematician Lambert Quetelet. He was interested in applying techniques, such as least squares, which were already in use in astronomy, to problems in the social sciences. This was the beginning of the field that he called "social physics" (what is now called sociology).

In 1844, Quetelet studied the measurements of 5,000 Scottish soldiers and invented the body mass index. It is defined as weight in kilograms divided by the square of height in meters, so it is measured in units of kilograms per square meter. A data mining consultant who is 1.8 meters tall and weighs 86 kilos has a body mass index of 26.5. Because anything more than 25 is considered overweight, he should consider a visit to the gym upon completion of this chapter.

Figure 19-4 is taken from an article on a National Institutes of Health website (www.ncbi.nlm.nih.gov/pmc/articles/PMC1890993/) summarizing data from two national surveys (which are labeled in the figure as SHIELD and NHANES) done in the United States. The chart shows the prevalence of Type II diabetes by BMI range. Clearly, there is a strong correlation between body mass index and diabetes.

For the purposes of this chapter, the most important thing to note is that BMI is not measured directly, and the two variables used to calculate it are not, individually, strongly correlated with diabetes. Height is not a predictor at all, and weight is a fairly weak one. It is the relationship of weight to height that captures the important notion of obesity.

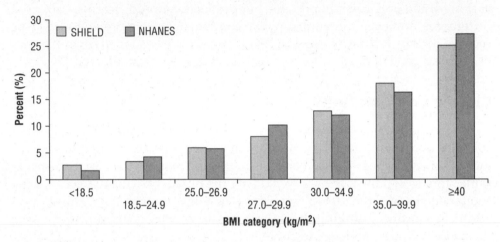

Figure 19-4: Type II diabetes is strongly correlated with body mass index.

Why is height squared? Because the metric should have a similar value for healthy people of any height, and weight does not increase linearly with height (nor with height cubed, as might be expected). A weight of 45 kilos is considered healthy for a woman 1.5 meters tall. That is a ratio of weight to height of 30. But a 1.8 meter woman should weigh about 65 kilos, which is a weight to height ratio of around 36. The weight to height squared ratio for both of these women is 20.

Weight should be proportional to volume. If people were spheres, our weight would be proportional to the cube of our height. If we were cylinders who got taller without getting wider, our weight would be proportional to our height. Because we are somewhere between cylindrical and spherical, using the square works well. BMI illustrates two things to consider when creating a derived variable: finding variables with important relationships and choosing a scale that makes comparisons easy. In this case, a BMI of 20 is good and a BMI more than 30 is considered obese, regardless of the person's height.

On-Base Percentage and Slugging Percentage

In 2003, Michael Lewis performed a seemingly impossible feat — he wrote a best-selling book, *Moneyball: The Art of Winning an Unfair Game*, whose heroes are statisticians. Actually, even more than Bill James and other baseball statisticians, the book celebrates the power of some of the derived variables they created. Baseball has always been crazy about stats. Alas, stats such as batting average, that baseball has tracked for more than a century, are not the best predictors of success on the field. Teams such as the Oakland Athletics that were early adopters of the new statistics used them to spot and recruit undervalued college players. This allowed a small-market, low-budget organization like the A's to field teams that competed successfully. Of course, it didn't take long for the richer teams to catch on, and money plus statistics still beats statistics alone.

Tradition is very important in baseball, so unseating a long-reigning champion, even one as clearly flawed as batting average, is very hard for a challenger metric. One problem with the traditional batting average is that a hit is a hit is a hit when, in fact, a double or triple is more valuable than a single.

A second problem with batting average is that a hit is only one of several ways for players to reach base. It is not only in business that people tend to manage what is measured. Recruiting players based on their batting average meant that some players who generated more runs were overlooked. That is the flaw that the new metrics were designed to correct.

Two of the new metrics are slugging percentage (SP) and on-base percentage (OBP). Neither is strictly speaking a percentage. Slugging percentage remedies the problem with batting average by counting the number of bases taken instead of the number of hits. The denominator is still the number of times at bat.

The definition of OBP is a bit more complicated:

$$OBP = \frac{H + BB + HBP}{AB + BB + HBP + SF}$$

In this formula H = hits, BB = bases on balls, HBP = times hit by pitch, AB = times at bat, and SF = sacrifice flies. Unlike the batting average, which takes only hits into account, the OBP numerator includes most of the usual ways a player can get on base. Before the adoption of the OBP metric, players with patience and a "good eye" were undervalued.

> **TIP** Every derived variable is essentially a hypothesis that the relationship it embodies will help explain the target. Like other hypotheses, this can be tested against past data.

New metrics such as on-base percentage, slugging percentage, and dozens of others gain acceptance because of their predictive power. They are designed by people with good intuition for the game and then tested on historical data to see how well they explain past outcomes. You can use the same approach when creating your own derived variables. Each derived variable reflects a hypothesis about what might explain some outcome of interest. The hypothesis can be tested by using the new variable in a model and measuring its effectiveness.

Wind Chill Index

A cold day feels colder when the wind is blowing. Everyone knows that, but how can the idea be captured in a useful way to help people know how to dress before setting out for school or work? Scientists might be happy with a measure that captures what is really going on, namely that wind increases the rate of heat loss. Indeed, one version of the wind chill index is reported in units of kilocalories per hour per square meter, but that doesn't really capture what a cold day *feels* like.

The first formal wind chill measure was defined by Paul Siple, an Antarctic explorer who represented the Boy Scouts on Admiral Byrd's expeditions to the seventh continent and returned there several more times as a researcher. The index was based on how long it took a bottle of water to freeze on the roof of the hut at the expedition's base camp. Figuring out the seconds to frozen bottle of water doesn't seem much more useful than units of kilocalories per hour per square meter in measuring how cold something feels.

In the 1960s, meteorologists began reporting the wind chill equivalent temperature, which was the temperature at which the bottle of water would freeze as fast in still air as it does under current conditions. This was a step in the right direction, but tends to overstate how cold the weather feels because there is rarely a complete absence of wind.

In 2001, the U.S. National Weather Service adopted a new model using the heat transfer rate for a bare face facing a 3.1 mph wind as its baseline. The formula is:

$$T_{wc} = 35.74 + 0.6215T_a - 35.75V^{0.16} + 0.4275T_aV^{0.16}$$

where T_{wc} is the air temperature in degrees Fahrenheit and V is the wind speed in miles per hour.

Other formulas are used in other countries. Some are meant for warm weather. Some take humidity into account. All are trying to capture the deceptively simple concept of how cold does it *feel*. In the end, precisely capturing something as subjective as a feeling is not possible. At any large gathering in a room with the thermostat set at 72°F, you will see some people pulling on their sweaters and others removing theirs.

Similar problems come up in marketing. What is a good measure for brand loyalty? Customer satisfaction? Buzz? These are all things that marketing efforts are designed to influence, so having good metrics for them would be nice. Currently, no universally accepted measures exist, so you have the opportunity to derive your own.

Combining Highly Correlated Variables

In business data, having many strongly correlated variables is not unusual. Amount paid this month is likely to be very close to amount billed last month. Total revenue is highly correlated with number of orders and so on. Often several families of related variables all tend to vary together. You learn more about this issue in Chapter 20. Usually, having a model include more than one untransformed variable from each family does not make sense. For some kinds of models, such as decision trees, additional highly correlated variables, while not helpful, do not cause much trouble. For others, such as regression models, highly correlated variables are actively harmful.

After you select the best representative of each family for inclusion in the model, should you ignore the rest? Not necessarily! The differences within families can be very revealing. Depending on the nature of the variables involved, these can be captured as differences, ratios, or degrees of correlation.

Differences between Nearly Synonymous Variables

Catalog and online retail data often contain two fields that nearly always contain the same value. One is *original order value*, which is the total value of the items ordered. The other is *net order value*, which is the total value of items ordered after taking into account returns and items not supplied because they were out of stock. In one typical sample of 50,000 customers, the correlation coefficient for these two variables is 0.993, which is very high and suggests that one or the other variable should be dropped. The better variable to drop in this case is net order value, because it has a time lag component to it. You know the original order value for orders placed last week; however, not all returns have come in, so the net order value is not yet known.

This discussion, though, is not about removing one of the variables. It is about the value of having both of them despite their being highly correlated. For the 50,000 customers, the average original order value is $196.67 and the average net order value is $187.86. Of course, the net order value is smaller, because items are removed from the order, reducing the value.

These averages conceal something interesting. For the vast majority of customers, the two figures are identical; most customers have never failed to receive what they ordered or returned merchandise for a refund. So, for the vast majority of customers, the net order value provides no additional value beyond original order value. However, a handful of customers have ordered thousands of dollars worth of merchandise and returned nearly all of it. For these customers — admittedly a small minority of the total — both variables are important for characterizing them. Retailers have a name for such customers: *renters*. A derived variable, the difference between original order value and net order value, highlights this highly unprofitable behavior. In general, when two things are usually equal, the few cases where they are not may indicate something of interest.

TIP When two variables are equal most of the time, the few places where they disagree may be very informative.

Usually, when two variables are this highly correlated, one of them should be eliminated, but as this case illustrates, it is worth thinking about whether there is some way that both can contribute.

Ratios of Highly Correlated Variables

Large universities all have more students than small colleges. They also have more professors. Either variable is sufficient to establish whether an institution is large or small, so there is no point in using both for that purpose. Instead, use the number of students to indicate the size of the institution, and the number of students per professor — an important ratio that may vary quite independently of an institution's size — as a measure of the amount of individual attention students can expect. This opportunity presents itself wherever highly correlated variables exist. Amount paid is highly correlated with amount billed; the ratio shows the proportion of the billed amount that has been paid.

What makes a good combination? The derived variable should have high variance (otherwise it is not adding new information) and it should be independent of its constituent variables. Achieving the second goal may require some transformation by trial and error. The following section works through an example of deriving a variable that relates rents and home values.

Example: Deriving a Variable for the Relationship of Rent to Home Value

Figure 19-5 is a scatter plot of two variables that are clearly related to one another. The data comes from the 2000 census. It describes the 1,006 towns in the state of New York. Among the variables describing each town are the median home value and the median rent, which are shown in the scatter plot in Figure 19-5. Not surprisingly, these variables tend to move together, and their correlation coefficient is 0.79. The scatter plot shows that most towns cluster fairly close to the point where homes cost about $100,000 and monthly rents are around $600. It is also clear that the points are spread out enough that many towns are far above or below the best-fit line. This means that there is additional information in the ratio of rent to home value.

The scatter plot also suggests that before rushing to create the derived variable median rent divided by median home value, you should think about what to do about the several towns where the median rent is zero (the little circles on the X axis). One example is the rural town of Duane in Franklin County in the Adirondacks, where 100 percent of households own their homes — 55 percent of these with no mortgage. No households pay cash rent. Saying that the median rent in Duane among the entire population is $0.00 because that is the amount of rent that everyone pays is clearly technically correct. However, the Census Bureau defines the median rent only among people who pay rent, and among this population the value is undefined. On the other hand, for rent as a proportion of home value to be meaningful, it should be based on actual rents paid. If anyone in Duane were to retire to the Sun Belt and rent out his North Country home, he would presumably expect to be paid a non-zero rent.

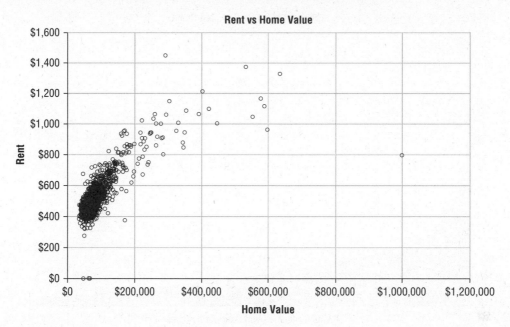

Figure 19-5: As median home value increases, so does median rent.

You have several possible choices on how to deal with the unfortunate lack of renters in some towns:

- Impute a likely median rental value for Duane by using the value for Franklin County as a whole, the next step up in the geographic hierarchy.

- Combine information from nearest neighbors, as defined by other census variables, to impute a median rent for Duane.

- Build another type of model to estimate median rent, based on towns that have renters, and use this model to impute a median rent.

- Leave the value of the derived variable undefined for towns where the median rent is $0.00.

- Accept the value 0 for the new derived variable on the grounds that it is rare enough not to cause problems.

The last two choices require the least work, so the next step is to justify using one of them by looking at the distribution of households paying no rent across the state. Figure 19-6 shows that in the vast majority of towns, the vast majority of households do pay rent. This suggests that the ratio of rent-to-home value is meaningful for almost all towns.

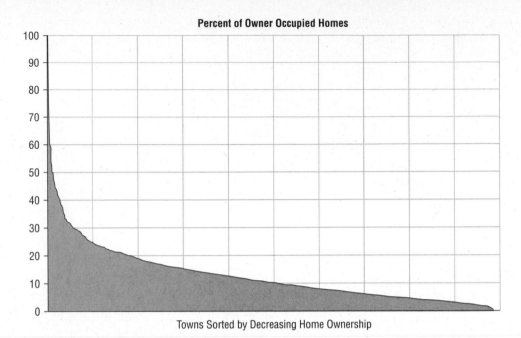

Figure 19-6: Although there are a few towns where no one pays rent, in most towns, many households do pay rent.

The new variable has a minimum of 0 (in the towns where no one pays cash rent), a maximum of 0.0143, an average value of 0.0065, and a standard deviation of 0.0017. Although both monthly rents and home prices are measured in dollars, the ratio has no units and its values have no intuitive meaning. Standardizing the values by centering on the average value and dividing by the standard deviation yields more intelligible values. After this transformation, one can clearly see at a glance whether the ratio of rent-to-home price in a town is above or below average and by how much.

To be useful for modeling, a new variable should capture information that was not readily available from the existing variables. If a newly created variable is highly correlated with an existing one, it probably does not add much information overall. This rent-to-home price ratio meets this requirement well for the majority of towns where home prices are under $100,000, but doesn't add much information for the wealthier towns.

Figure 19-7 plots the standardized rent-to-home price ratio against home price after removing the towns with no renters. For the more than three-quarters (776 out of 1,006) of towns where the median home value is less than $100,000, the variance is fairly large. These towns have standardized rent-to-home price ratios ranging from –3.82 to 4.61. In contrast, the relatively few towns with median home prices above $200,000 have standardized rent-to-home price ratios all within a narrower range and almost all are at least one standard deviation below average. Because the ratio varies quite a bit for the most typical towns, it is at least potentially useful as an explanatory variable for modeling.

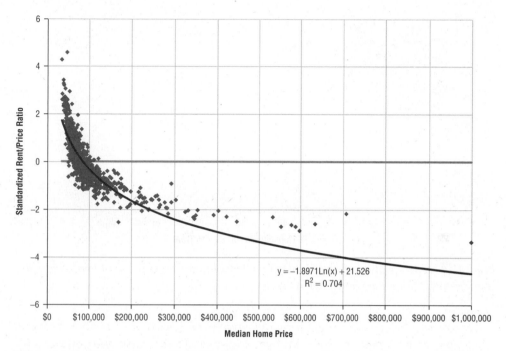

Figure 19-7: Most of the variability in the rent-to-home price ratio is in towns with lower median home prices.

The fact that the more expensive towns have lower rent-to-home price ratios is interesting in itself. Apparently, rents do not rise at the same rate as home values. The median home value in Scarsdale, the town with the highest median rent, is more than 20 times that of the town with the lowest median home value; its median rent is only about seven and a half times the lowest median rent. One interpretation is that there is almost no limit (other than financial resources, of course) to what people will pay for a home, which may be viewed as an investment, but there is a limit to how much they will spend on rent, which is viewed as an expense. Geographically, the towns with the highest home values and the lowest rent-to-home value ratios are clustered in the south-east near New York City.

Figure 19-8 shows the distribution of renters and owners across towns in the state of New York. There are towns where 100 percent of households are renters and towns where 100 percent of households are owners. It is natural to wonder how the proportion of renters in a town interacts with the rent-to-home price ratio. Figure 19-8 shows that there is no obvious relationship between the percentage of renters and the median rent–to–median home value ratio.

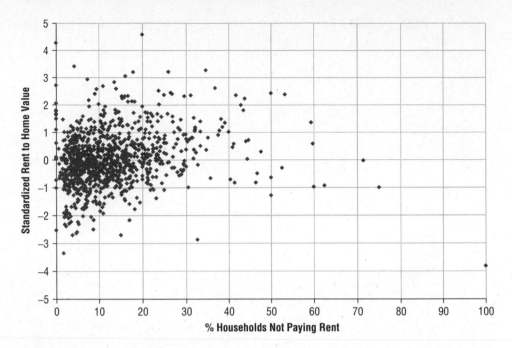

Figure 19-8: No relationship appears to exist between the percentage of owners and the median rent–to–median home value ratio.

Of course, the reason for creating derived variables is the hope that they will have predictive power for other things of interest. In this case, the new variable is correlated with several other potentially interesting variables in the data set such as the percentage of people with a four-year college degree.

More commonly, economists are interested in how this ratio changes over time rather than how it varies from place to place. Rents tend to move slowly, and only in response to changes in supply and demand. Home prices are more volatile because prices are determined partly by what a property can earn in rent, partly by the relationship of rents and ownership costs, and partly by speculative investment based on an expectation of higher real estate prices in the future. Home prices rising faster than rents may indicate that a speculative bubble is forming.

The Degree of Correlation

One very interesting thing to look at with correlated variables is whether the degree or direction of correlation is different in different circumstances, or at different levels of a hierarchy. For example:

- For new customers, credit score and involuntary attrition are strongly correlated, but the correlation is weaker for established customers.

- For towns within 10 miles of Boston, the *Boston Globe*'s penetration rises with distance; beyond that, it declines with distance.

- For people under 18, age and height are highly correlated; for older people it is not.

Professor Andrew Gelman, who teaches statistics and political science at Columbia University, gives a fascinating example in his book *Red State, Blue State, Rich State, Poor State*. The book examines an apparent paradox in U.S. elections: For several decades now, despite having policies designed to benefit the wealthy, Republicans do better in poorer states, while Democrats, despite policies designed to benefit the less wealthy, do better in richer states. The book is about the 2004 election, but this pattern continued in 2008.

It is easy (but wrong!) to look at a map of the United States colored red for Republicans and blue for Democrats and conclude that richer *voters* are more likely to support Democrats and poorer voters are more likely to support Republicans. The state-level correlation leads to misleading stereotypes of "rich, latte-sipping" Democrats and "NASCAR dad" Republicans. Aside from the obvious danger of trying to represent groups as varied as Republicans or Democrats by a single "typical" member, the characterization is simply wrong. In truth, the richer the voter, the more likely he or she is to vote Republican. This correlation holds true for the country as a whole and within each individual state.

As shown in Figure 19-9, what *does* vary from state to state is the strength of the correlation between income and tendency to vote Republican. In poorer states, such as Mississippi, the correlation is very strong; richer voters there are much more likely to vote Republican. In richer states, such as Connecticut, the correlation, though still present, is much weaker. Middle income states, such as Ohio, are somewhere in between. The strength of this correlation is a good predictor of which party will get a state's electoral college votes.

The regression equations for the probability of voting Republican as a function of income have different intercepts in different states, as well as different slopes, but the intercepts turn out to be quite close to one another. As the chart shows, poor people in all three of the states shown have a similar probability of voting Republican. The big difference between states is how likely middle income and rich people are to vote that way.

WARNING   Beware of the *ecological fallacy*. That is the statistical term for the common mistake of assuming that differences between members of different groups follow the same patterns as differences between group summary statistics such as averages.

The assumption that because richer states are more likely to vote Democratic, then richer voters are also more likely to vote that way is an example of the *ecological fallacy*. The mistake is to assume that a relationship that holds between groups at a summary level such as the average will also hold at the level of individual members of the group. This would be true if all members of the group had the average values for their group, but in fact, each group has its own distribution, and many different distributions have the same average. If two high schools have the same number of students and the same average SAT score, can you predict that they will produce the same number of National Merit Scholars? The answer is "no" because school A might have a large number of very high achievers balanced by an equal number of very low achievers, while students at school B might all cluster near the average. It is entirely possible that the school with the most high achievers does not have the highest average score.

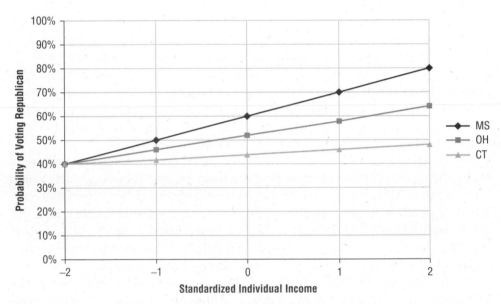

Figure 19-9: Probability of voting Republican as a function of income for several states.

Extracting Features from Time Series

Whole books are available about time series analysis. This is not one of them, but knowing how to capture some of the most important features of a time series so that the information is available to modeling techniques not specifically designed for dealing with them is important. Several of the sample customer signatures in Chapter 18 include time series at the customer level. For the fax service subscribers, it is faxes sent and received over the course of their tenures. For the catalog shopper, it is quarterly spending over a series of calendar quarters. This chapter uses that same catalog data to demonstrate two of the most important features of any time series — trend and seasonality.

A difficulty with the time series of quarterly spending is that, at the customer level, it is very sparse. Any one customer has very few quarters with a purchase. In fact, the most common number of purchases for a customer to have made is one. It doesn't make much sense to talk about a customer's spending increasing or decreasing over time when only a single data point exists, but adding up the spending of all customers produces a time series of total spending by quarter that works well to illustrate trend and seasonality.

Trend

Figure 19-10 shows quarterly sales for a small retailer over five and a half years. Clearly, sales are increasing over time, but how should that information be captured in a derived variable or variables? One simple measure is the difference between the ending value and the beginning value. In this case, $237,622.77 – $175,472.77 = $62,150.00. The fact that this number is positive indicates that sales are going up, but it doesn't capture any information about the rate of increase. Another idea would be to use the slope of the line connecting the two end points. The slope is simply the change in y ($62,150) divided by the change in x which is 22 quarters. The slope of the line connecting the series end points is 2825.

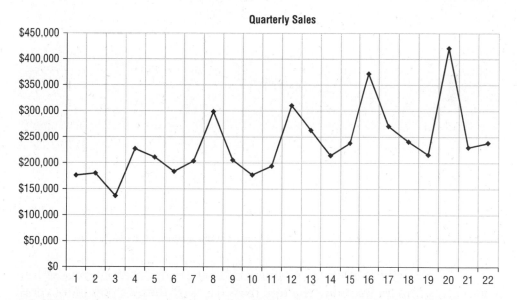

Figure 19-10: Quarterly sales for a small retailer show seasonal fluctuations but an overall increase over time.

Any two points define a line, but are the first and last quarters good points to choose? Because this is retail data, and because the series ends in a different part of the year from where it starts, the answer is "no." The data starts with first quarter sales in one year and ends with second quarter sales in another. Because of seasonal effects, it is generally a good idea to compare sales in a particular quarter to the same quarter in other years. This particular series has six first quarter to second quarter pairs, of which two go up and four go down, so the mismatch in quarters may not matter much. Comparing first quarters with fourth quarters would be much more of a problem, as discussed in the following section.

TIP When calculating a trend, always use complete years to eliminate seasonal effects.

Calculating a slope based on just two points is appealing because of its simplicity, but it does ignore a lot of data. An alternative is to use the slope of the best-fit line, which is described in Chapter 6. Figure 19-11 shows two best-fit lines — one using all the points and one using only the five complete years.

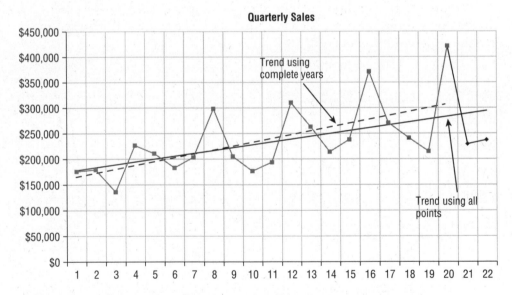

Figure 19-11: The growth trend can be captured by the slope of a best-fit line.

Both of these best-fit lines are steeper (have greater slope) than the line connecting the end points. The one that uses just the five complete years more accurately captures the overall trend, even though it uses less data. When all the points are used, the first and second quarters of the year are overrepresented.

Seasonality

Another very obvious feature of the sales data is that fourth quarter sales are stronger than any other quarter. This pattern, while obvious to the human eye, will not be picked up by a model without a little help from derived variables. At a minimum, there should be a variable that records whether or not a particular date is in the fourth quarter. Even better would be a variable that records which quarter of the year it is. Depending on the modeling technique used, this could be a categorical variable with nominal values "Q1," "Q2," "Q3," and "Q4" or four binary flags, one for each quarter. Just identifying the fact that quarters exist is a big help. A regression model to predict revenue would likely include the Q4 flag with a positive coefficient.

With a little more work, it is possible to represent the quarters in a way that provides any data mining technique with an even stronger hint. Instead of representing each quarter by an arbitrary string or a binary flag, represent it by its expected effect on revenue — how much more or less revenue is expected because of the season. The only difficulty is untangling the effect of seasonality from the effect of trend. After all, first quarter sales in the fourth year are considerably higher than fourth quarter sales in the first year. The standard way of dealing with this problem is to subtract the trend line from the data to create a *stationary* series — that is, a series with no systematic change in average or variance. The values of the stationary series tell how far above or below the trend line the corresponding revenue values are. This has been done in Figure 19-12.

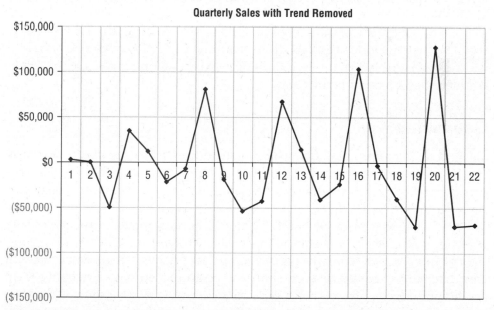

Figure 19-12: After removing trend, capturing the effect of seasonality is easier.

Based on this data, the quarters can be represented by their average difference from the trend line:

Q1	–10,633
Q2	–37,312
Q3	–38,923
Q4	82,837

This is an example of replacing a categorical variable with a numeric one that captures something interesting about the categories — in this case, how much better or worse than average each quarter is. This single variable provides a regression model with as much information as four indicator variables, one for each quarter.

Extracting Features from Geography

Location, location, location. It's not only in the real estate business that location matters; geography is important in many applications. The trick is to figure out what aspects of a location are important for a particular problem. Is it the latitude? The altitude? The temperature? The population density? The income level? The dominant local industry? Any or all of these could be important, and all of them can be looked up somewhere. Lookup tables are the key to making use of geographical data. Lookup tables exist at many different levels. In the U.S., these include five-digit ZIP codes, nine-digit ZIP codes, census tracts, census block groups, counties, and designated marketing areas (DMA). Other countries have similar hierarchies.

Geocoding

Geocoding is the process of translating an address into its actual coordinates on the surface of the planet. A number of companies offer this service on a commercial basis. For smaller batches of addresses, you can make use of free services, such as those offered by the University of Southern California at `https://webgis.usc.edu/` or Google maps. The physical coordinates of an address are useful for computing the distances or estimated travel times between locations. As an example, geocoding the address of service establishments where a credit card has been used allows each charge to be annotated with a distance from the home address. This makes it possible to derive variables such as the total amount spent in restaurants more than 50 miles from home.

The reverse process is also useful. Smart phones, GPS navigation systems, and an increasing number of other devices, are able to report their location to within a few yards. Geocoding services can translate these geographic locations into cartographic ones such as street names, towns, and counties.

Chapter 14 contains a case study about finding clusters of similar towns in eastern Massachusetts and southern New Hampshire for the *Boston Globe*. The clusters ended up using purely demographic variables, but along the way, a couple of geographic variables were derived in the hope that they might prove useful. Specifically, it was thought that the distance from Boston and the direction might be important.

A good way of capturing this information is using something called *polar coordinates*. In the Cartesian coordinate system — the one with the X and Y axes — each point on the place is described by its distance in the horizontal and vertical direction from the origin. In the polar coordinate system, a point is also described by two variables — its distance from the origin and its angle from a fixed line through that central point. For Boston, the origin is obvious: In 1858, Oliver Wendell Holmes called the Boston State House the "hub of the solar system." Later generations of Bostonians, less modest than Dr. Holmes, have amended that to "hub of the universe." For the clustering project, polar coordinates were the distance from the state house and the compass direction from its golden dome of the state house in degrees. X and Y coordinates such as latitudes and longitudes can easily be converted to angles using the arcsin function from trigonometry.

The motivation for using polar coordinates was that Bostonians attribute different characteristics to towns on the North Shore, South Shore, Cape Cod, and so forth, and polar coordinates could capture those differences. The variables were potentially useful. However, Boston has competing "rings" that also behave similarly. Median home price, for example, increases with distance from the city for a few miles and then decreases again. With just a couple hundred towns to work with, teasing out the different geographic patterns was not feasible.

Mapping

One reason for geocoding is to be able to place things on a map. As anyone who has used MapQuest, Google Maps, or a similar website knows, sophisticated geographic information systems (GIS) are available that can produce very accurate maps annotated with anything from traffic volume to political party affiliations.

For the rest of us, a simple scatter plot or bubble plot of ZIP code–level latitude and longitude makes a crude, but surprisingly effective map. Figure 19-13 shows penetration by ZIP code for an Internet fax service. It also shows how sparse the population of Alaska, the largest state by area, is. The map was created by using the latitude and longitude of each ZIP code's center point. No adjustment has been made for the fact that one degree of longitude is not exactly the same distance as one degree of latitude or for the fact that the world is not flat and lines of longitude are closer together in Alaska than they are in Puerto Rico or Hawaii. Nevertheless, this is recognizably a map of the United States.

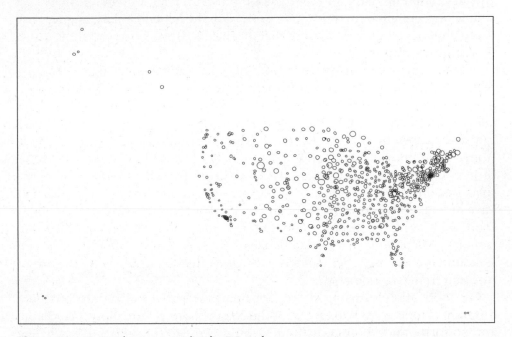

Figure 19-13: Product penetration by ZIP code.

ZIP codes with no subscribers are not represented on the map. The map clearly shows that the company has the most subscribers where there are the most people, where ZIP codes are close together. But some of the largest circles are in rural areas; these are places where a high percentage of a small population subscribes to the service.

Using Geography to Create Relative Measures

If a home sells for $200,000, is that a lot or a little? The answer is different if the home is in Scarsdale, New York, or in Opelika, Alabama. Income, temperature, rainfall, and percentage of immigrants in the population all vary quite a bit as well. For marketing purposes, a household's wealth relative to its neighbors may be more important than its net worth measured in dollars. One useful transformation is to calculate z scores for such measures using the average and standard deviation for the local area rather than for the country as a whole.

A localized home price z score of –2 means "way less expensive than most" in both Scarsdale and Opelika.

Using Past Values of the Target Variable

When historical data on the target variable is available and varies by region, past values of the target variable projected on geographic region can be a very good predictor. Regions that have responded well to a particular offer in the past are likely to do so again. This is just a variation on the theme of replacing categorical variables such as counties and ZIP codes with numeric values that describe them. In this case, the description is in terms of the target variable. When using past values in this way, care must be taken that the values really are from the past; that is, not just from before the model is created, but from before the values of the target variable were collected. This can be tricky to ensure for summary variables such as total lifetime orders, which may have been updated to reflect the responses recorded by the target.

WARNING   Past values of the target variable can be very powerful, but you must make sure that the values are really from the past. Otherwise, the derived variables you create will already contain the information they are intended to predict. You may get great "predictions" on the test set (which is a sample from the same population as the training data), but disappointing performance when the model is deployed.

Using Model Scores as Inputs

Any model score can be thought of as a summary of what its input variables combine to say about the person (or town or property or whatever) who has been scored. If the score was produced by a directed model, the summary is with respect to a particular target variable, but it might contain information that is useful for other purposes as well. If, for example, customers have already been assigned to customer segments, perhaps by an undirected clustering model, and already have scores indicating probability of default, both of these scores are good candidates to be input to a customer value model.

One familiar example of using model scores as input is the FICO score, a popular measure of creditworthiness named for Fair Isaac, the company that developed it. This indicator of general creditworthiness can be combined with more specific data to model the chance that someone will default on a particular offer of credit. The FICO score is clearly identified as a model score, but many of the fields available for sale from outside data vendors are, in fact, estimates produced by models.

Handling Sparse Data

A particular challenge for modeling is making use of the information in sparse variables. For example, depending on how they are counted, a bank might have 30 or 40 different consumer products. For each customer, it would be nice to record several fields for each of these products:

- Current balance
- Account tenure
- Time since last activity
- Transaction rate
- Slope of the balance trend

Plus, there are additional special fields that are specific to a particular type of product, such as time remaining on a certificate of deposit, or current balance to original amount ratio on a loan. The problem is that even if all products are equally popular, any one customer has only a few of them. This is different than the problem of rare ZIP codes that was handled with an "other" category in Chapter 18. In the customer signature, the rows are sparse because each customer is missing many products and the columns are sparse because each product only has non-null values for a minority of the customers. Most modeling techniques are not able to handle data like this. On the other hand, simply throwing away all this information would clearly be wasteful. The answer is to use a small number of dense variables to summarize information from many sparse ones.

A simple first step is to create derived variables for the total number of accounts and the total balance across all accounts. The total number of accounts is a measure of the breadth of the customer relationship and is likely to be predictive of the longevity of the relationship and receptiveness to additional products. The total balance is a better indication of customer value than the balance in any individual account. So, these variables are certainly useful, but they do not capture *which* accounts each customer has.

Account Set Patterns

The most common way of capturing the pattern of accounts a customer has is to create a separate indicator variable for each account type. This method introduces as many variables as there are account types and often the goal is to use a small number of variables to summarize information from many.

An alternative is to give a name to each possible pattern of account ownership so a single categorical variable can be used to describe each customer's pattern of ownership. Instead of actually thinking up names like "checking and savings and line of credit" and "checking and savings and car loan," simply giving each pattern a code is sufficient.

As with ZIP codes, you should treat these values as categorical even though they may look like numbers, because their ordering has no meaning. One comparison that *is* meaningful is equality. Two customers with the same account set pattern code have exactly the same accounts. Depending on how the account set codes are generated, it may be possible to define a distance function for them so, for example, a customer with checking, savings, and a car loan is closer to someone with checking, savings, and a home improvement loan than to someone with just a credit card. In the simplest case, however, two account set patterns are either "same" or "different." That is enough to be useful. Customers with the same account set pattern can be considered neighbors for memory-based reasoning. As with any segmentation scheme, the account set pattern can also be used as input to a decision tree or other directed model.

Binning Sparse Values

The original sparse values in the earlier banking example capture much more about each account than whether it is present or absent. For those that are present, there are variables for balance, tenure, and other important features. How can this information be added to the present value pattern? You cannot invent a code for every possible combination of balance amounts and tenures — there are far too many possible combinations. The solution is to reduce the number of possible values by putting them into bins labeled "high," "medium," and "low" or even simply "above average" and "below average."

An economical coding system is simply to enumerate the distinct patterns actually present, giving each a number from 1 to however many there are. This scheme leaves the code 0 open to represent any patterns that may be encountered in datasets to be scored that have never been encountered in the training data.

Throughout the book, you can find many examples of converting categorical variables such as counties, ZIP codes, and model numbers into nice continuous variables that provide more information. Binning goes the other way; in a sense, binning destroys information in order to save it. Knowing which balances are high and which are low is better than giving up on using any product-level balance information at all.

Capturing Customer Behavior from Transactions

As discussed in Chapter 18, part of the data miner's art is to create rich customer signatures from data that, at first sight, appears to have few features. This challenge comes up repeatedly when working with detailed transactions. Every click on a hyperlink produces a record with the destination, referring page, date and time, and not much else. Every item scanned in a supermarket produces a record with the store, lane, cash drawer open time, product code, and not much else. Every telephone call produces a call detail record (CDR) with the originating number, the number called, the start date and time, duration, billing rate in effect, and a few boring technical details about how the call was handled. It is the same with bank transactions, credit and debit card purchases, highway toll payments (when made by transponder), SMS messages, key card swipes, and transit pass uses.

Widening Narrow Data

Transaction logs tend to have many rows, but few columns because not very much data is recorded for any one transaction. Customer signatures, on the other hand, have only one row per customer, but many columns. One important data mining task is to turn narrow transactions into wide signatures. When many transactions can all be tied to the same customer, they provide enough information to populate many fields in a rich customer signature. As an example, when a supermarket loyalty card is used, a particular customer is linked to each of the scanner transactions described earlier. For every item that passes over the scanner, along with the store number, lane number, cash register open time, and product code, the loyalty card number is captured as well.

Any one of these records still does not provide much information. On a particular day, a particular customer's shopping included a particular item. It is only when many such records are combined that they begin to provide a useful view of customer behavior. What is the distribution of shopping trips by time of day? A person who shops mainly in the afternoons has a different lifestyle than one who only shops nights and weekends. How adventurous is the customer? How many distinct SKUs does she purchase? How responsive is the customer to promotions? How much brand loyalty does she display? When a competing brand is on sale, does she stick with her usual brand? What is the customer's distribution of spending across departments? How frequently does the customer shop? Does the customer visit more than one store in the chain? Is the customer a "from scratch" baker? Does this store seem to be the primary grocery shopping destination for the customer? The answers to all these questions become part of a customer signature that can be used to improve marketing efforts by, for instance, printing appropriate coupons.

Sphere of Influence as a Predictor of Good Customers

Once upon a time, a cellular phone company had a new product offering that it wanted to sell to its "best" customers. This product bundled together features such customers would want to have — features that are now regularly provided with typical phone contracts. Who were the best customers?

To answer this question, the company set up a marketing test. The marketing department had already defined good customers, using the business-as-usual methods. They hired an outside firm (which included the authors and former colleague Alan Parker) to find another definition of best customers. In some sense, the two groups were in competition.

Both groups started with essentially the same data: billing records that described each customer's usage during the month, marketing records that described the products and services used by the customer, and a small amount of demographic data. However, another important source of information was available as well — the call detail records (CDR) that describe each call made by each customer.

The standard measure of customer goodness was a measure called *minutes of use* (MOU), which is simply the total time that a user spends on the phone in a month. Clearly, better customers spend more time, and worse customers spend less time. However, two customers could have the same minutes of use and still have very different behaviors:

- Jane is on the road a lot, but speaks to her customers and perspective customers throughout the day, for short periods of time, adding up to 1,000 minutes each month.

- John works from his office and only uses his phone to talk to his wife and kids. He spends about 45 minutes a day talking to them.

Each of these customers has about the same minutes of use, but their patterns differ significantly.

What makes them different? The number of people to whom each customer talks in the month. For John, this number might be a handful, whereas for Jane is might be a few dozen, or even more than 100. This measure is called the *customer's sphere of influence*.

Intuitively, it would seem that sphere of influence would be a powerful descriptor of customer behavior. After all, keeping a customer happy who talks to many other potential customers is an example of guerrilla marketing. On the flip side, make such a customer unhappy, and the news will quickly spread through his or her social network of friends, colleagues, and acquaintances.

In the end, the marketing test showed the power of this variable. The measure for defining customer goodness that used sphere of influence achieved a 15 percent response rate on the marketing offer versus just 3 percent for the business-as-usual definition. A large sphere of influence is a powerful predictor, at least in this case.

An Example: Ratings to Rater Profile

In 2006, Netflix, an American movie rental company, did a great favor to data mining researchers and teachers by releasing a large data set of movie ratings. Netflix was not motivated by altruism. The company hoped for, and received, a substantial improvement in its system for predicting how subscribers would rate movies. Netflix offered a one million dollar prize for a 10 percent improvement in its chosen metric for evaluating ratings predictions. Thousands of graduate students, researchers, and just plain would-be millionaires from all over the world worked on the problem for years. By the time the prize was awarded to a coalition of teams from several countries in 2009, Netflix had certainly received its money's worth in free labor.

Recommendation is an interesting topic, but here what is important is how to turn a very narrow table of transactions into information-packed customer signatures.

The training data for the Netflix competition consists of 100,480,507 ratings that 480,189 users gave to 17,770 movies. Each row contains just four fields:

- User ID
- Movie ID
- Date
- Rating

A separate table links movie IDs to movie titles and release dates, but no other information about the movies is given, so clearly the ratings predictions cannot be based directly on attributes of the movie such as actors, director, language, or genre. Of course, it would be possible to look up those things, but the point of this section is that there is much to be learned from the ratings alone.

Sample Fields from the Rater Signature

The rater signature summarizes a subscriber's past rating behavior to capture traits that may help to predict future ratings. The signature fields can be grouped into three categories.

The first category contains fields that summarize the individual's behavior. Some raters tend towards the extremes, loving or hating everything they rate; others tend to rate everything close to the middle. Some raters watch only new releases; others rate mainly classics. Some raters (most, actually) have a burst of activity when they first make ratings and then lose interest.

The second category contains fields that compare the rater to the population. Does the rater make ratings more or less frequently than average? Are the rater's opinions more or less generous than average?

The third category contains segment IDs for several segmentations of the raters, all of which are based on their reaction to a small group of frequently rated movies ("the canon"). These IDs are exactly like the present value patterns discussed earlier. They allow scoring functions to make use of a kind of poor man's MBR without having to calculate hundreds of thousands of distances on the fly. Looking up how everyone else with the same segment ID rated a movie is simple. The canon consists of 64 of the most frequently rated movies that also have high variance in their ratings. A movie that is universally loved or loathed doesn't help, because everyone gives it similar ratings. Also, closely related movies that get very similar ratings, such as the three *Lord of the Rings* titles, are represented by the most frequently rated member of the group. There is nothing magic about the number 64. It was chosen so that a mask showing which movies were rated or loved or hated can conveniently be stored as a 64-bit integer. The sidebar "A Movie Rater Signature" shows the actual fields used in one version of the the rater signature.

A MOVIE RATER SIGNATURE

Fields that Summarize Past Ratings

- Total number of ratings
- Total number of ratings in first month
- Proportion of ratings in first month
- Ratings per month excluding first month
- Ratings per month trend including first month
- Ratings per month trend excluding first month
- Proportion of 1 ratings
- Proportion of 2 ratings
- Proportion of 3 ratings
- Proportion of 4 ratings
- Proportion of 5 ratings
- Average rating
- Standard deviation of ratings
- Proportion of ratings for recent release dates
- Average rating for recent release dates
- Average rating for non-recent release dates
- Ratio of 1 and 5 ratings to 2, 3, and 4 ratings

Continued

A MOVIE RATER SIGNATURE   (continued)

- Average time from release date to rating date
- Proportion of movies rated in the canon

Sample Fields from the Customer Signature that Compare Raters to the Population

- Population average minus rater average
- Population total ratings minus rater total ratings
- Population ratings per month minus rater ratings per month

Sample Fields from the Customer Signature that Assign Raters to Segments

- Rate Buddies — Bit pattern showing which members of the canon have been rated
- Love Buddies — Bit pattern showing which members of the canon were rated higher than the population average by a specified margin
- Love Buddies 2 — Bit pattern showing which members of the canon were rated higher than personal average by a specified margin
- Hate Buddies — Bit pattern showing which members of the canon were rated lower than the population average by a specified margin
- Hate Buddies 2 — Bit pattern showing which members of the canon were rated lower than personal average by a specified margin

The Rating Signature and Derived Variables

The reason for including the movie rater signature in this chapter rather than in Chapter 18 with the other sample signatures is that the rater signature consists almost entirely of derived variables. It illustrates what a large number of features can be extracted from a small number of fields describing transaction data. The rater signature makes use of many of the transformations described in the chapter. Raw counts of 1, 2, 3, 4, and 5 ratings have been transformed into proportions. The ratio of extreme ratings to 2, 3, and 4 ratings and the standard deviation of the ratings are different ways of getting at raters' tendency to stay near their average ratings. The trend in rating activity is captured as the slope of the line connecting the end points of a rater's activity and again starting with the rater's second month because many raters start off with a flurry, rating every movie they have ever seen and then settle into a pattern of just rating an occasional new one. Present value patterns for an important subset of influential movies are captured so that people with matching patterns can be treated as like-minded clusters.

This signature was used to test a wide variety of hypotheses about movie rating behavior using several of the techniques described in this book, including survival analysis, to predict how many ratings a person would make over time (and how many ratings a movie would receive over time) and a simple form of memory-based reasoning to predict how a rater would rate a movie not included in the training set.

Lessons Learned

Data often contains information that is not readily available to data mining techniques. As part of the data preparation process, the miner can bring this information to the surface by transforming existing variables in various ways and by creating new derived variables to capture important relationships.

Standard transformations to consider include standardizing numeric variables to allow comparisons between variables measured on different scales, re-expressing numeric values as percentiles to emphasize position, turning counts into rates to facilitate comparison between time frames, and turning counts into percentages to allow comparisons between organizations or segments that differ in size.

Derived variables often express a relationship between two existing variables using a simple formula such as a ratio or product, although sometimes more complicated formulas are called for. Many customer activities form time series such as quarterly spending and monthly minutes of use. Another important role of derived variables is to capture features of these series. A series can be characterized by its trend and by the frequency and amplitude of any seasonal patterns.

Most modeling techniques can handle numeric variables more readily than categorical ones. In fact, many techniques are only defined for numeric inputs. Therefore, translating categorical data into numbers is an important data preparation task, which involves replacing category labels with numeric measures associated with each category. For example, geographic variables such as state, county, or ZIP code can be replaced by latitude and longitude, median household income, or historic response rate as appropriate.

Sparse data presents special challenges. Many techniques are unable to make use of very sparse data. Fortunately, these variables can be salvaged by using summaries, account set patterns, and other encoding schemes to represent information from a large number of sparse variables in a small number of dense ones.

Transaction logs are the source for much of the data for business data mining. Individual transactions do not contain much information, but a collection of transactions contains many interesting patterns. Summarizing transactions in clever ways to turn them into rich customer signatures is up to the data miner.

Too Much of a Good Thing? Techniques for Reducing the Number of Variables

In data mining, having more data is often better. More data helps simplify problems by making it possible to build models and test their effectiveness without relying on sophisticated statistics or assumptions about distributions. More data helps avoid the problem of missing data, by making it possible to build more models. More variables give models more power, by making it possible to capture more nuances of customer behavior and to build stable models.

As any lover of dessert knows, more is not always better. The same may be true of data mining, particularly with regard to the number of variables. This chapter explicitly covers various methods for reducing the number of variables.

When you have many variables, the input data is likely to be sparse, meaning that many columns are dominated by just one or two values (such as zero or null). Some data mining techniques do not work well with a large number of variables. And many variables can increase the possibility of overfitting. These are some of the problems that can arise with too many input variables.

A common set of techniques for reducing the number of variables is to select the best input variables based on their ability to model the target. Some purists may think that using the target is cheating a little bit, but the method works well in practice, producing stable models. Many of these techniques have been touched on in early chapters. Chapter 6 introduces regression in the context of data mining, and the idea of forward selection of variables. Chapter 7 covers decision trees, and one of the powerful uses of decision trees is for selecting key variables. Chapter 8 discusses neural networks; the outputs of the hidden nodes in a neural network are another method for reducing the number of variables. This chapter revisits these topics, with the focus on variable selection rather than building models.

Principal components analysis is another technique that combines information from existing variables to create a reduced set of variables. Similar ideas go by names such as singular value decomposition and factor analysis. For readers with a strong math background, principal components can be described exploiting knowledge of linear algebra and matrices. Fortunately, a much friendlier geometric interpretation makes principal components as accessible as the best fit line.

The chapter covers several uses of principal components, including an innovative method for variable clustering. This method places variables in the leaves of a tree; variables attached to the same node are "as related" to each other as possible, proving a graphical view of variable relationships as well as a method for variable reduction.

Before diving into these various techniques, this chapter discusses the sparse data problem and other problems to help you better understand the need for reducing the number of variables.

Problems with Too Many Variables

Too many variables are both a blessing and a curse. More variables generally mean that more descriptive information is available, information that can be leveraged and used to build better models. On the other hand, they are a curse for a variety of reasons, discussed in this section. This section discusses three problems: the problem of high correlation among input variables, the increased risk of overfitting the data, and sparseness of the data set.

Risk of Correlation Among Input Variables

Many input variables implies that many variables are likely to be correlated with each other. A customer who generally spends a lot of money, spends a lot of money in any given month, and probably spends a lot of money over any given year — all of these might be input variables. This relationship among the input variables affects many different techniques, for both directed and undirected data mining. Earlier chapters discuss the importance of whittling down the number of variables for techniques such as regression and neural networks.

For decision trees, the effect is a more subtle. A plethora of variables that contain similar information may make understanding the decision tree more difficult because several variables might describe the same phenomenon. Some of the variables might describe the phenomenon clearly. For instance, to describe declining usage, the ratio of this year's usage to last year's being less than one clearly describes "declining usage." Other variables might happen to be correlated with this variable. For instance, recent usage being low would also be correlated with declining usage. These variables might be chosen by the decision tree, even though they have less descriptive power.

For clustering and MBR, having correlated variables among the inputs inadvertently overweights certain characteristics. For instance, if monthly spending and yearly spending are two dimensions, then "high-spending" customers are going to be close along both these dimensions — perhaps making them seem closer than they actually are. The result might be clusters (or MBR results) that really focus on just one aspect of the data, such as total spending.

A clustering example from Chapter 13 for a catalog retailer shows what can happen. In the example, the customer signature was simply the count of purchases in each department. The idea was to use k-means clustering to determine "natural" combinations of the departments, perhaps learning something about the merchandise and the customers at the same time. The result did provide learning, but more about sparse data and clustering.

Figure 20-1 shows the result from four clusters as a parallel dimension plot, so the cluster centers are the four curves. Each point on the curve is the proportion of the cluster that purchased from a particular department. Sadly, for the purposes of this example, the curves are all parallel to each other, indicating very little differentiation among the departments.

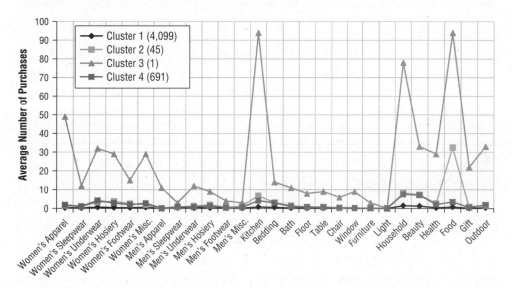

Figure 20-1: Because of sparse data, these four clusters are uninteresting, segmenting the customers into groups based on how much they have purchased. The one customer in Cluster 3 has made many purchases. The many customers in Cluster 1 have probably made only one purchase each.

Instead of providing insight about the departments, the curves segment the customers by the total count of purchases. The biggest cluster — corresponding to the line at the bottom of the diagram — consists of customers who made one purchase. Hmmm, one purchase is necessarily only in one department. The problem is that two customers, who have each made exactly one purchase but in different departments, are "close" to each other. Two such customers agree in almost all departments, because almost all values are zero. That is, someone who buys one product from women's apparel is very similar to someone who buys one product from gardening, because neither purchased from men's apparel, or women's shoes, or kitchen, or bathroom, and so on. They are close neighbors in "don't-buy-much" land.

In the end, customers who purchase from one department are similar to any other customers who purchase from one department. At the other end, customers who purchase from many departments are similar to other customers who purchase from many departments. The fancy clustering on two dozen input variables has produced essentially the same outcome as segmenting customers based on the total number of purchases.

Risk of Overfitting

Overfitting the original data is a potential problem with many data mining techniques. For the techniques that use a validation set, the risk of overfitting the data is small. However, more variables provide more opportunities for overfitting.

This is particularly true when using techniques such as neural networks and regression, where additional input variables result in additional degrees of freedom within the model itself. These degrees of freedom are an opportunity for the model to memorize specific cases in the model set, rather than generalizing from them in a way that creates stable models. For this reason, reducing the number of variables is an important part of using these techniques.

Decision trees are an example of a technique where this is not a problem, because decision trees choose their own variables, one at a time.

The Sparse Data Problem

One way to visualize data is as points in space, where each dimension is one of the input variables. Earlier chapters (on k-means clustering and memory-based reasoning) explain this geometric interpretation of data. These techniques also provide a good motivation for the sparse data problem. What happens when a given point does not really have any neighbors? The result is lonely data points, ones that have no neighbors to reinforce their patterns, loneliness that impedes data mining techniques from exploiting their information.

WARNING Even when you think you are using information in lots of variables, sparse data makes it difficult for data mining techniques to find interesting patterns.

Visualizing Sparseness

Technically, sparse data means that, in any given customer signature, most of the values are zero or some other specific value. Of course, there may be exceptions; even in sparse data, some customers have more robust customer signatures.

Visualizing sparse data can be difficult. People have evolved to see things in three dimensions, and three dimensions do not provide enough room to get good intuition on sparseness.

Figure 20-2 shows a two-dimensional scatter plot of some data. Is the data sparse? One reason to say "yes" is because the data shows a linear relationship and many areas in the scatter plot have few, if any, points. However, "sparseness" is a property most relevantly applied to the input variables, not the target variable. So, if Figure 20-2 has the target on the y axis, then it is illustrating a legitimate pattern in the data.

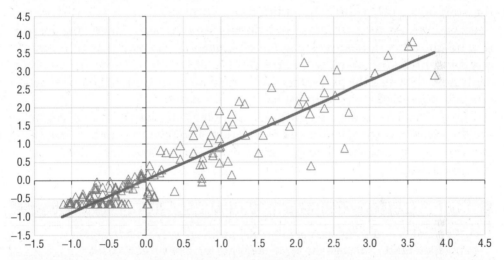

Figure 20-2: This data looks sparse in two dimensions, because of the many areas where there is no data. However, it is not sparse along just the X-axis.

On the other hand, if Figure 20-2 shows two input variables, then many areas in the input data space have no examples. This is a legitimate concern. One possibility is that the diagram does a good job of representing the input space. If so, then the two variables have a strong relationship — the R^2 value for the line is 0.87. Dispensing with one of the variables would probably have little effect on data mining results. Another possibility is that the input data is biased, so important relationships between variables are missing. Regardless, any model based on this data is unlikely to pick out important patterns involving both these variables because the information basically resides in one variable.

Independence

A key idea in the art of reducing variables is the idea of independence of the variables. If one variable can be expressed as a linear combination of other variables, then the first variable is not needed. For instance, Chapter 15 has a case study from a project where the data contained four ethnic variables describing the neighborhoods around grocery stores:

- Non-Hispanic African-American percentage
- Hispanic percentage
- Non-Hispanic White percentage
- Everything else percentage

Clearly, the sum of all these percentages is 100 percent, so all four variables are not needed for modeling. Any one of the variables is 100 percent minus the sum of the other three. In addition, such variables can lead to erroneous observations. As the percentage of Non-Hispanic African Americans goes up in a neighborhood, the percentage of Hispanics goes down. Far from saying anything profound about where people live, it says something trivial about arithmetic: because the percentages add up to no more than 100 percent, when one gets bigger, the others almost have to get smaller.

Closely related to the idea of linear independence between two variables are the ideas of orthogonality and correlation. The relationship between these concepts is explained in the technical sidebar, "Orthogonality, Correlation, and Independence."

ORTHOGONALITY, CORRELATION, AND INDEPENDENCE

Orthogonality and correlation are two ideas that are very closely related to independence, although the three ideas are not exactly equivalent. *Correlation* — or the lack thereof — was introduced in Chapter 4 as a statistical measure between two variables. Two variables that are uncorrelated are necessarily independent, but the opposite is not true. Variables can be independent and still have non-zero correlation.

Orthogonality is a geometric interpretation that may be a bit challenging to visualize. The geometric interpretation starts with each axis representing a different observation — not a typical way of looking at the data. The points in such a space are the variables. Because there are usually many observations, the *observation space* is a very high-dimensional space. The following figure shows an example of two variables, in a space for three observations defined by four variables. Notice that the values along each axis are standardized. This is helpful, so that each dimension is measured in the same units, standard deviations from the average, regardless of the original units.

This unusual space where each dimension is an axis and the points represent the variables provides a way to understand the concepts of orthogonality and independence. In the figure on the right, imagine connecting the variables to the origin so they represent vectors. When two points fall along a line that goes through the origin, then they are linearly *dependent* — the opposite of independent. When the vectors meet at right angles, then they are orthogonal, an even stronger condition than independence. When the vectors meet at another angle, the most common situation, then the variables are *oblique*.

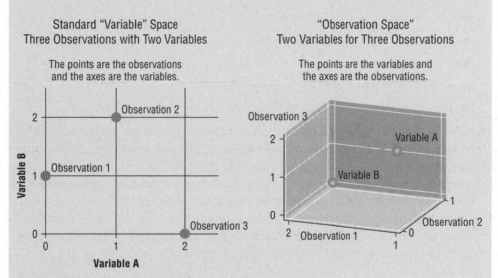

Standard "Variable" Space
Three Observations with Two Variables

"Observation Space"
Two Variables for Three Observations

The points are the observations and the axes are the variables.

The points are the variables and the axes are the observations.

In the variable space, each observation is shown as a point (as shown on the top), with the axes representing variables. In the observation space, each point represents a variable, with the axes representing observations.

The example used to illustrate these concepts only uses three observations, which is a far cry from the thousands or millions of observations available in most data mining applications. The example does not use two dimensions, because with only two observations, all variables are linearly dependent, because two points define a line. The concepts of orthogonality, obliqueness, and linear dependence remain the same, even as the data becomes too high-dimensional to visualize easily.

The nuances between these concepts are interesting — theoretically. For practical purposes, it is okay to interchange the terminology, although they are not exactly equivalent. The most general concept is linear independence between variables, meaning that variables should not contain information where one input variable can be defined in terms of other input variables. As one variable changes (say, goes up), another variable that is independent may stay the same, go up, or go down — and does all three as the first variable changes.

Linear independence may sound like a weak assumption, but it is actually a strong assumption, particularly as the number of variables increases. A particularly insidious and common situation is partial liner dependence, where variables are dependent on each other over a substantial subset of the model set.

For instance, low usage is a common predictor of customers leaving in many industries. Consider the case of a mobile phone company. When usage is low, the following variables are likely all to be true:

- Low minutes of use every month

- Low number of text messages every month

- Low use of Internet every month

- No complaints

- Low number of incoming calls every month

- Low number of outgoing calls every month

In other words, for this important subset of customers, all these variables are likely to be linearly dependent (because all are essentially zero). Such islands of linear dependence can pose challenges for modeling algorithms. However, they often suggest important behaviors or characteristics that can be captured in other variables.

Figure 20-3 shows a typical scatter plot for this partial linear dependence. Each point represents a ZIP code in the state of New York. The horizontal axis is the proportion of the ZIP code classified as urban. The vertical axis is the proportion that uses wood as the primary source of heat.

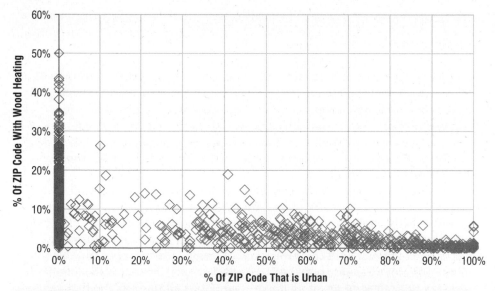

Figure 20-3: The relationship between the proportion of a ZIP code that is urban and the proportion of homes heated primarily by wood shows a partial linear relationship. The relationship between the two factors is quite different depending on whether or not the population is entirely rural.

Data points lined up vertically on the left indicate that many areas with no urban population have wood as their primary heating source (and many do not). With only a few exceptions, any urban population at all implies that fewer than 10 percent of homes use wood as their primary heating source. This scatter plot looks a bit like the capital letter "L" because these variables have an interesting relationship to each other. When the population is rural, then almost any proportion from 0 to 50 percent of homes may be heated by wood. When the population is urban, few homes are heated by wood, resulting in the low values stretched across the bottom.

Exhaustive Feature Selection

One possible way to create the best model, given a set of input variables, is to exhaustively try all combinations. This definitely creates the best model, but the number of combinations grows very quickly, as shown in Table 20-1 (the actual number is the two raised to the power of the number of input variables minus one).

Table 20-1: Exponential Growth of the Number of Combinations Needed for Exhaustive Selection

NUMBER OF VARIABLES	NUMBER OF COMBINATIONS
2	3
3	7
4	15
5	31
10	1,023
20	1,048,575
30	1,073,741,823
40	1,099,511,627,775
50	1,125,899,906,842,623

Exhaustive selection works for a small number of input variables. However, even a couple dozen variables have many millions of possible combinations. And as the number grows into hundreds of input variables, the value is simply too large even for the most powerful computers.

In the context of data mining problems with many input variables, using almost all the available computing power to select variables may not be the best use of time or computing power. Most techniques have various parameters that could also be tweaked over a range of values. A better use of time is to combine variables into new themes that capture interesting customer behaviors. Merely selecting a particular list is likely to be of much less value than cleverly combining the variables together, and selecting them using a less-than-exhaustive technique.

Flavors of Variable Reduction Techniques

Many techniques are available for reducing the number of variables for modeling and visualization. These techniques can be placed into four different categories, based on two factors. The first factor is whether or not the technique uses a target variable to select the input variables. The second factor is whether or not the technique uses a subset of the original variables, or derives new variables from them that maximize the amount of information (often at the expense of being able to explain the meaning of the reduced variables).

Using the Target

All the variable selection techniques explained in earlier chapters — such as forward selection in regressions and decision trees — use a target variable to select the best input variables. One consequence of this is that information from the target leaks into the model by affecting the choice of variables. This leakage is generally not important, particularly when using the training set to select the variables and a validation set to validate the model.

> **TIP** When building models using a training set and a validation set, you have little reason to be concerned about variable selection techniques that take advantage of the target variable.

However, the mere possibility of leakage poses a theoretical problem. This becomes a more practical problem when there are a large number of variables relative to the number of records in the model set and insufficient records to create a validation set. In such circumstances, the purist point of view demands that the target should not be used at all in selecting variables. For data mining purposes, this is overkill, because the focus is on building stable models that work on both the data used to build the model (the training set) and on unseen data (the test set).

Original versus New Variables

The second difference among techniques is whether they keep the original variables or replace them with new derived variables. The advantage of the original variables is understandability. Presumably, the original variables in the data — particularly when chosen as informative derived variables — are easier to understand than variables generated automatically by some variable reduction technique.

The subject of new variables is, to a large extent, the subject of principal components. Although there are other methods to combine variables, principal components are both theoretically appealing and useful in practice. The next section, though, starts the discussion with methods touched on in earlier chapters, methods that do not create new variables.

Sequential Selection of Features

The most popular way to select which of many input variables to use is by using sequential selection methods. That is, one variable at a time is considered for, either inclusion in or exclusion from the model.

Forward selection is the most common sequential selection method. Normally, the terminology implies some form of linear or logistic regression, although there is no reason why forward selection must be limited to these techniques. The only thing needed is a measure to compare different models using the same number of variables, and then to choose the best of the bunch (or at least the best based on the measurement being used).

The process of selecting variables can be separate from the process of building models. Using forward selection to select a subset of variables using a regression technique is perfectly reasonable, even when you plan to use the variables for some other purpose. In some sense, these variables are the "best" subset of variables to use in other situations, such as for inputs into a neural network or for visualizing the data as scatter plots.

The Traditional Forward Selection Methodology

This section describes the traditional method of forward selection, using linear regression as the modeling technique. One traditional measure is the R^2 value of the line, although other measures are used as well.

Start with no model. Well, in this case, no model means no variables in the model. However, the model does have a constant term, which is the average value of the target variable. Now, build a family of models, with each member of the family using exactly one of the possible input variables. Figure 20-4 illustrates an example with four census variables used to estimate the proportion of homes in a ZIP code whose primary heating is wood. Each of the scatter plots shows the best fit line for a particular input variable. The one that fits best is the first variable chosen by forward selection.

How well does a line fit a set of data? Chapter 4 explains the idea behind the R^2 value. This value quantifies how much of the variation in the target values is explained by the inputs in a linear regression model. So, an R^2 of 0.9 says that the input variable explains 90 percent of the variation seen in the target. Such a large value is usually quite good.

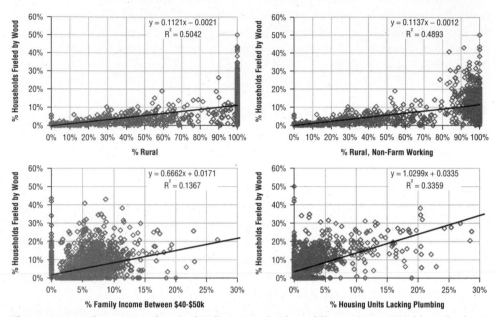

Figure 20-4: The scatter plots in this figure are for four different input variables. The best input variable is the one on the upper left, because it has the largest R^2 value.

The forward selection algorithm chooses the variable whose linear regression model has the highest R^2. Then, it repeats the process, adding in a new variable to the one already chosen. Once again, the variable with the highest R^2 is added into the model, and the process repeats.

The process continues, adding in one variable at a time, until one of two things happens. Typically, users specify a maximum number of variables, and forward selection stops at that number. A more automated way to stop is to say, "don't add another variable unless it makes the model better." Under most circumstances, the R^2 value will get slightly larger with each new variable — unless the new variable is 100 percent correlated with variables already chosen. For this measure, the algorithm uses a modification of the R^2 value, called the adjusted R^2, which punishes the measurement for using more variables. When the adjusted R^2 decreases, then forward selection stops.

Why isn't the variable with the second-highest R^2 in the first round always chosen for the second round? This question may seem naïve, but it is actually very important. The simplest answer is: the calculations just do not work that way. R^2 values are not additive in any way. So, adding the second variable to a model with the first variable might increase the R^2 of the model by a lot — or by nothing at all (it can't go down, though). If the two variables were linearly independent throughout their entire range, then the R^2 values would not depend on the order that variables entered the model. In the real world, it is very unusual for variables to be totally independent.

For instance, in the earlier example, the best input variable is the proportion of the ZIP code that is rural. Another variable — the proportion of the ZIP code that is urban — is just as powerful. However, when the rural percentage is included in the equation, the urban percentage no longer has any power. All the information has already been included.

TIP Don't worry about choosing the right measure for forward selection. There is more than one way to measure "best." However, all measures have the nice property that after a variable is chosen, variables that are highly correlated with it are unlikely to be chosen.

The choice of the R^2 statistic for choosing the variables is a very reasonable choice. However, other measures may be chosen. Another popular measure is the F statistic, which measures the likelihood that the best fit line is not constant (that is, that all the coefficients of the input variables are not 0). The difference between the F statistic and R^2 is subtle, and they might produce somewhat different results. Whatever the measure being used, however, after a variable is chosen, variables with similar information will not be included. The result should be a reasonable set of variables.

Forward Selection Using a Validation Set

Forward selection is a tried-and-true methodology. However, there is something slightly unsettling about it, due to its heavy reliance on a measure such as R^2, which is measured on the training set used to generate the models. Chapter 6 shows examples where the R^2 value is zero, and yet the examples exhibit clear patterns.

An alternative approach takes advantage of some key data mining ideas. The process of building data mining models uses a model set that is partitioned into training, validation, and test sets. Forward selection only uses the training set, both for building the models and for evaluating them. Logically, validating different candidate models is the purpose of the validation set.

And that is how forward selection with a validation set works. At each step, another variable is added into the model to create a family of models. The best model is chosen. In this case, the best model is determined empirically, by how well it works on the validation set. For linear regression (which has a numeric target), the measure is the sum of the squares of the differences between the actual and the predicted values. For a logistic regression, it is the proportion correctly classified.

The overall process is to build a regression model for each variable using the training set. Each of these models is evaluated by using the error rate on the validation set. As additional variables are considered for inclusion in the model, the validation set is used to determine which is the best.

Stepwise Selection

Stepwise selection is like forward selection, just slightly different. Instead of only adding one variable at each stage, stepwise also considers removing variables. This increases the number of possible permutations of variables being considered. In practice, removing a variable is rare. However, it is possible and stepwise is a very reasonable and effective modification to the forward selection process.

Forward Selection Using Non-Regression Techniques

The idea of testing one variable at a time and adding the best into the model is a good idea that can be applied to other directed data mining techniques. Undirected data mining poses a problem because, fundamentally, human judgment is needed to evaluate the results. Some form of automatic measurement could be used, such as the size and compactness of clusters, but it is unclear how useful this measurement would be.

Forward selection makes much more sense with other directed data mining techniques, notably neural networks. Academic research has focused on feature selection for neural networks, and forward selection is one possible method. Although data mining tools do not typically have the capability built in, you could approach the problem manually.

There is one philosophical objection to using forward selection in this case. The strength of neural networks is in their ability to take advantage of local phenomena in the data — patterns that are apparent in parts of the data space but not consistent throughout the space. These local phenomena may involve different variables in different areas, so a global set of variables does not exist. Similarly, selecting variables one at a time may highlight one particular area, overlooking other areas.

In practice, the authors have found that using forward selection with logistic regression to select the variables works well for selecting variables for a neural network. That is, use the logistic regression to select variables using forward or stepwise selection, and then use these variables as inputs for the neural network. Although there are theoretical reasons why this might not produce an optimal set of variables (the local versus global phenomena problem), in practice it seems to be a reasonable method.

Backward Selection

Backward selection is the opposite of forward selection. All the variables are initially included in the model, and variables are removed one at a time. Under some circumstances, backward selection works better than forward selection. In particular, when two or more variables combine to be highly predictive and the variables individually are not very predictive, then backward selection may work better than forward selection. Although such variables can be contrived in the lab, this situation is rare in practice. Typically, the original variables do have some predictive power, although the combination may be more predictive than the parts. For data mining problems, the authors do not recommend backward selection for several reasons.

First, there are many variables. Historically, backward selection would be applied to, at most, a dozen or so variables. Data mining problems can easily have hundreds of variables, all correlated with each other along parts of their ranges. Such variables tend to produce lousy regression models.

Second, the measure for removing variables is based only on the training set. A backward regression model that uses a validation set should produce results similar to a forward regression model.

The third reason is that backward selection simply may not work with non-regression techniques. It is unreasonable to feed hundreds of variables into a neural network, and then remove them one by one, because the training time for a neural network is related to the number of input variables, and highly complex networks are less likely to converge on the optimal solution.

Undirected Forward Selection

Forward selection of variables is typically associated with directed data mining techniques, such as linear and logistic regression. However, forward selection techniques can also work without a target variable. Such techniques choose a small set of variables to start, and then add variables one at a time, based on some measure of similarity (or dissimilarity) to the variables already chosen.

An example of such a technique starts with the two variables whose correlation is closest to zero. In some sense, these variables "span" the possible input space as much as possible, so they should be good for modeling and visualization purposes.

Additional variables are added, one at a time, based on the correlation to the existing variables. The correlation between each candidate variable and each variable already chosen is calculated. The candidate with the smallest maximum correlation is then added into the set of variables. The selection can stop either when all the variables are used up or when some stop criterion is met.

There is nothing special about the correlation measure, in this case. Other appropriate measures could be used.

Other Directed Variable Selection Methods

Forward and stepwise selection are very powerful methods for selecting variables. However, these techniques are associated with regression, meaning that the variables that they find are selected based on their globally optimal properties. This may sound good, but often variables are important in local regions, but not everywhere. Regression-based techniques are not able to find these variables. Instead, more flexible techniques such as decision trees and neural networks can be used.

Using Decision Trees to Select Variables

Chapter 7 introduces decision trees as a modeling technique. It also mentions that they are a very good method for selecting variables for other techniques (notably neural networks). In fact, decision trees are such a powerful method that some tools make it very easy to use the variables chosen by decision trees in subsequent models. Figure 20-5 shows an example in SAS Enterprise Miner of a decision tree choosing variables for a subsequent neural network model.

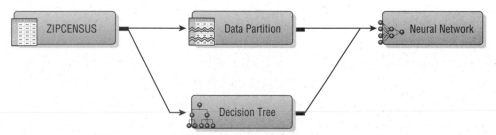

Figure 20-5: This picture shows an SAS Enterprise Miner diagram that uses a decision tree node to select variables for a neural network node. The data "flows" across the top part of the diagram from the source, through the partitioning node, to the neural network. The data also goes to the decision tree node, which builds the tree and passes the variables used to the neural network.

Why Is This Different From Forward Selection?

At first glance, decision trees seem very similar to forward and stepwise selection in regression. After all, the decision trees start with all the data at the root node and search for the best possible splitter among all the possible variables, and then choose the split (variable) with the best purity measure among the children. The decision tree chooses a variable, as well as a split value for that variable (or a set of values for a categorical variable).

This is quite similar to how forward selection starts. Forward selection builds a separate model for each possible variable input, and measures how good that model is. Forward selection does not have the notion of a split value, but it does have a notion of goodness of fit. A decision tree purity measure can be defined that always chooses the same first variable as forward selection.

At the first step, forward selection and decision trees are quite similar. The differences arise with the subsequent steps.

The decision tree continues by splitting the data into different parts, and then repeating the process on each split of the data. The next best variables (and typically a different one for each child) are the ones that work best on each child's *subset* of data. This is quite different from forward selection, where each subsequent model is built on the *entire* data set. The decision tree method chooses the next variable that works best on a subset of the data; forward selection chooses the next variable that works best overall on the data.

Also note that forward and stepwise selection produce a nice list of variables, ordered by their importance for improving the model. A decision tree does not naturally produce such a list. The list could be ordered by the size of the leaves in the tree where the split occurred, but this is an ad hoc approach to the ordering.

Which produces the better set of variables? As with many things in the data mining world, there is no right answer; fortunately, computers are fast enough and tools are efficient enough that you can try both. Table 20-2 compares the top seven variables chosen by forward regression and decision trees, based on the ZIP code level census data using wood heating as the target (a numeric target is not a great choice for a decision tree except when using the tree to select variables for another technique).

Table 20-2: A Comparison of the Variables Chosen by a Decision Tree and Forward Regression

VARIABLES CHOSEN BY REGRESSION		VARIABLES CHOSEN BY DECISION TREE	
VARIABLE	IMPORTANCE	VARIABLE	IMPORTANCE
hhuoplumbinglacking	1.000	longitude	1.000
pruralnonfarm	0.968	hhuoplumbinglacking	0.992
longitude	0.612	prural	0.641
latitude	0.350	hhuoplumbingcomplete	0.352
hhperson2fnonfamily	0.310	hhumedianyear	0.228
faminc010_015	0.288	latitude	0.196

The comparison between these variables is interesting. Both decision trees and regression provide a mechanism for measuring the importance of the variables. The first three variables are essentially the same, but in a different order. These specify that rural areas in the east with many homes that lack adequate plumbing are the most likely to be in ZIP codes that have many homes heated by wood. (Presumably, rural areas in much of the west either do not need heating or they lack trees to supply wood.) However, the decision tree chooses longitude first and the regression chooses the lack of plumbing. As the list progresses, the variables become different.

The lists do have one major difference. The regression variables are all different from each other. On the other hand, the decision tree chooses two variables that are essentially the same in terms of information content — percent of homes with plumbing lacking and percent of homes with complete plumbing. This is a consequence of different parts of the tree choosing the best variable, regardless of choices made elsewhere in the tree.

> **WARNING** When using decision trees to select variables, be aware that decision trees can select variables that are highly correlated with each other. Either eliminate such variables before building the tree, or test for correlation before using the variables in another modeling technique.

Decision trees can also suggest variables that interact with each other, which can lead to ideas on ways to combine them. In a sense, forward selection produces variables that work best globally — but they may miss interesting local features in the data. Because neural networks do a good job taking advantage of local phenomena, decision trees might be a better variable selection method. However, be careful not to include highly correlated variables chosen by the decision tree.

Categorical versus Numeric Inputs

One of the strengths of decision trees is their ability to handle both numeric and categorical input variables. As a result, the variables chosen by decision trees may be of any type.

On the other hand, some analytic techniques have a definite preference for numeric input — techniques such as neural networks, regression, and k-means clustering (and a few such as naïve Bayesian have a preference for categorical input). That means that when choosing variables, you want to eschew categorical variables.

The real problem with categorical variables is that not many techniques know how to handle them. As discussed in Chapter 18, each possible value of a categorical variable can be replaced with a flag. However, this multiplies the number of variables and contributes to data sparseness. A better approach is to replace categorical variables with useful information about each possible value.

Variable Reduction Using Neural Networks

Neural networks are more often the target of variable reduction techniques rather than the method themselves. Of course, forward and stepwise selection are reasonable methods to use with neural networks.

An interesting approach using neural networks goes back to the topology of the network. Remember, the hidden layer contains nodes sandwiched between the input layer and the output layer. One way to think about the nodes in the hidden layer is that they become detectors for patterns in different parts of the input space. As the neural network trains, the each node in the hidden layer may become a detector for a particular pattern in a particular area. The patterns themselves are a secret of the neural network. The outputs from the hidden layer can then be used as a set of reduced variables for the original data and used for other purposes, such as data visualization.

Scoring the hidden layer provides a way to reduce the inputs going into a neural network. As with most facets of neural networks, there are no guarantees that the hidden layer operates in this fashion. However, this is an example of a directed variable reduction technique that creates new derived variables from the input variables.

Principal Components

Principal components offer an alternative method for reducing the number of variables for analytic techniques. Principal components have certain optimal characteristics that make them very powerful. At the same time, the components themselves do not necessarily mean anything. They are like the intermediate values from the hidden nodes of a neural network — useful, but not necessarily informative.

This section introduces principal components, by starting with their relationship to linear regression. The section touches on some of the statistical background and their relationship to singular value decomposition, a similar method. Principal components are useful in other ways besides reducing the number of variables. They provide a powerful way to visualize data in a low number of dimensions, such as on a scatter plot. The place to start, though, is with the geometric definition of a principal component.

What Are Principal Components?

Principal components can be understood in various ways. Typically, they are introduced with the language of matrix algebra or described by a statistical definition. For instance, the statistical definition of the first principal component is that, of all possible linear combinations of the inputs, the first principal component is the one that maximizes the variance of the projection of the input points onto the line. So much for the fancy terminology. The geometric interpretation is much more intuitive for understanding the basic concepts.

Geometric Definition of the First Principal Component

Much earlier in this book, Chapter 6 introduces the idea of the best-fit line. The basic definition — in two dimensions — is that of all possible lines that could be drawn, the best-fit line is the one that minimizes a certain function. That function is the sum of the squares of the *vertical* distances between the line and the data points. Figure 20-6 shows a typical best-fit line, along with the distances to the data points.

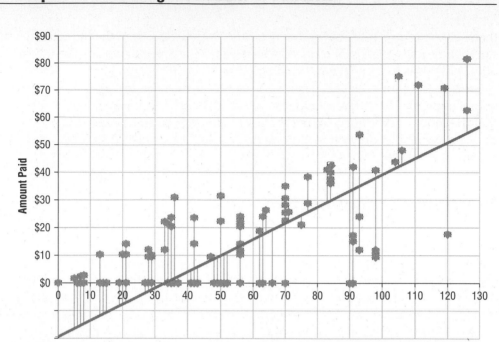

Figure 20-6: The best-fit line minimizes the sum of the squares of the vertical distances from the data points to the line.

This is a simple definition, that people accept without thinking much about. However, the best-fit line depends on the definition of "best," and other definitions are possible. For instance, if the measure is the sum of the distances — rather than the squares of the distances — then the technique is a called *robust regression*. Robust regression is less sensitive to the influence of outlying data points. Because the square of the distance is usually much larger than the distance itself, ordinary least squares regression is more sensitive to outliers.

The first principal component is another slight variation on the theme of the best-fit line. This is defined as the sum of the squares of the distances from the line to the data points. Not the sum of the squares of the vertical distances, but the actual distances themselves. Figure 20-7 shows the first principal component and the associated distances.

The first principal component is usually different from the best-fit line. At first, this may be counterintuitive. After all, isn't the best-fit line "best"? And if it is best, why isn't it the first principal component? Well, there is no such thing as "best" in isolation, only "best" with respect to a particular measure. For what is commonly known as the best-fit line, the measure is the squares of the vertical distances. This makes sense because the vertical axis represents the target variable — the quantity the model is trying to estimate. In that context, vertical distance is the error in the estimate. Principal components are best for another perfectly reasonable measure, the sum of the squares of the distances. This measure treats all dimensions as equally important instead of singling out a target variable.

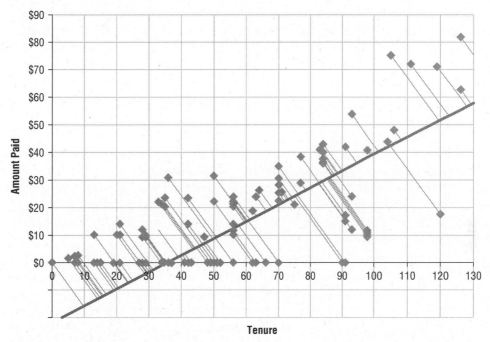

Figure 20-7: The first principal component is the line that minimizes the sum of the squares of the distances from each point to the line.

Properties of the First Principal Component

Although the first principal component seems a lot like the best-fit line, there are crucial differences between the two.

The definition of the best-fit line specifies that one of the directions is special — the direction that defines "vertical," because this is the direction used for calculating the distance from a point to the line. Typically, this distance is along the target dimension. For the first principal component, there is no special direction, because the shortest distance is used. What this implies is very important: target variables should not be used for the principal component. Principal component analysis uses only input variables.

TIP Principal components only make sense on input variables. Fortunately, most tools automatically exclude target variables from the calculation.

The second observation is related to the first. For the best-fit line, the residual for each data point is the distance along the vertical dimension between that point and its projected value on the line. The residuals are simply numbers, and one way to understand them is by understanding their distribution. For a good model, these residuals should have a normal distribution.

The residuals for the first principal component, on the other hand, are not numbers, because they have a direction associated with them as well as a length. There is no simple statistical measure to apply to vectors. However, as the next section describes, this is really an opportunity.

From the First Principal Component to the Next Principal Component

The residuals of the first principal component are vectors — they have a direction as well as a size. That means that the residuals cannot be understood using basic distributional statistics. However, it opens up another opportunity: plot the residuals vectors as points in space. What is a reasonable thing to do to points in space? You might have guessed: calculate their principal component. This is called the second principal component.

The second principal component can beget a third, and so on. But not indefinitely. The process has to stop. Eventually, the residuals are just points on a line, and there are no more principal components after that one. There are, at most, as many principal components as there are dimensions in the original space. Or, equivalently, there are, at most, as many principal components as input variables for the records.

There can be fewer principal components than the number of input variables. This occurs when some input columns can be written as linear combinations of other input columns. In fact, calculating the number of principal components is one way to measure the dimensionality of the input space.

Properties of Principal Components

The principal components for a given set of data have one very interesting property: they are orthogonal to each other. Geometrically, that means that the principal components all meet at right angles to each other, a stronger condition than merely being linearly independent. This very powerful property makes principal components powerful inputs into other statistical techniques.

Each principal component itself is a vector, which is usually normalized to have a length of one. Even so, principal components do have a length associated with them. This length describes how much of the information in the original data the principal component captures — analogous to the R^2 measure for linear regression.

The full set of principal components captures all the information in the original data. However, is it possible that many fewer principal components can capture almost all the information? This is a key idea in using principal components for variable reduction.

Figure 20-8 shows a chart called a *scree* plot. This curve starts at 0, when no principal components are included. Then it increases, bowing upward in the same way that cumulative gains charts bow upward, finally arriving at 100 percent when all principal components are included. For this data, the first 20 principal components capture about 70 percent of the information in the original data.

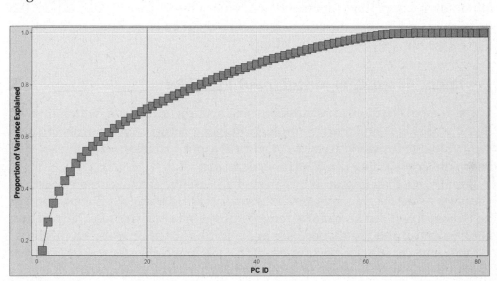

Figure 20-8: A scree plot shows the amount of information included in the first *n* principal components.

Principal components are somewhat sensitive to rescaling the dimensions. When all dimensions are changed in exactly the same way — say all the values are doubled — then the principal components remain exactly the same. To visualize this geometrically, imagine that each data point is a point in a multidimensional space. To this image, now add in the axes, with units on them. Now, if the units are doubled along all the axes at the same time, then all the points shrink in all dimensions, remaining the same shape, and hence having the same principal components. However, rescaling only one dimension does affect the shape, and that in turn affects the principal components.

Standardizing the inputs divides each dimension by a different factor. This affects the overall shape of the data and the structure of the principal components. In fact, when doing principal components analysis, doing the analysis on standardized inputs is recommended. Standardization eliminates the units along the different dimensions, and measures everything the same way, in standard deviations from the average.

TIP Because principal components are sensitive to the dimensions used for describing inputs, measuring all variables in the same units, by standardizing the inputs, is a good idea. Fortunately, most tools that compute principal components do this automatically.

In addition, principal components can be very sensitive to sampling considerations, particularly when the sample is defined in terms of the input variables. So, eliminating outliers does affect the principal components. On the other hand, although oversampling data based on a binary target variable does affect the principal components, the effects are not likely to be large, because the target variable is not used for the calculation.

Comment About Categorical Input Variables

The principal component calculation is an arithmetic formula, which implies that it works best on numeric inputs. However, principal components are also very valuable for working with categorical input variables, when these have been converted to flag variables for each level.

Usually, such an approach has a problem, because it generates very sparse variables — the flag variables are almost always zero. However, principal components counteract this problem by reducing the number of variables. This feature is very useful, and one that you see again in Chapter 21 on text data mining.

One caution: although you can use principal components for flag or indicator variables, that does not mean that the resulting principal components are always useful. Often, when only using categorical inputs, the authors find that reducing the number of variables is difficult. Figure 20-9 shows an example of the total variation captured by a set of flag variables for product purchases. Notice that this curve does not bow upward very much, indicating that the principal components do not efficiently capture the information in the variables. For instance, choosing 20 principal components accounts for about 80 percent of the variation in the input data — but 20 out of 27 is 74 percent of the variables. Not much improvement at all.

Principal Components Example

Each principal component is a linear combination of all the inputs for each record. That means that each one is a big equation that is the sum of coefficients times input values. Such formulas are most easily calculated for numeric inputs.

As an example, the Census Bureau provides a handful of variables that describe the highest level of education achieved by individuals in a ZIP code (or other census geographic unit):

- POPEDUNOEDU: Percent of population with no education
- POPEDUNOHS: Percent of population with no high school

- POPEDUSOMEHS: Percent of population who have some high school
- POPEDUHS: Percent of population who have graduated from high school
- POPEDUESOMECOL: Percent of population who have some college
- POPEDUASSOC: Percent of population with associate degree
- POPEDUBACH: Percent of population with bachelor's degree
- POPEDUMAST: Percent of population with master's degree
- POPEDUPROFDOCT: Percent of population with doctorate or professional degree

These variables are mutually exclusive, so a person gets counted only in the one indicating his or her highest level of education.

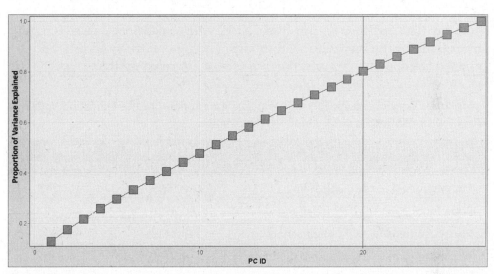

Figure 20-9: In this example with 27 flags, the scree plot for the principal components is not steep, indicating that the principal components do not efficiently capture the information in the original data.

Including so many variables in a model is overkill. After all, these variables are redundant because the sum adds up to one. One way to handle this situation is to reduce these variables to a single variable by taking a linear combination of them that represents in some way how educated the ZIP code is. One way to calculate this measure would be to arbitrarily assign coefficients on how well each group contributes to the "educatedness" of the ZIP code. So, the first two groups might have negative coefficients because these are associated with lesser education. Perhaps graduating from high school would have a zero, and then the more educated groups would have larger coefficients.

Such an approach does produce an education measure, but it would be arbitrary, because the coefficients are arbitrary. A better idea is to assign values based on the first principal component of the education variables. The advantage of the principal component is that human judgment does not cloud the process. That is, the principal component does not know about our preconceived notions of educatedness. After generating the principal component, though, you should check that it makes intuitive sense.

The first column in Table 20-3 contains the coefficients generated by this data. Notice that for the most part, they do conform to the intuitive ideas. Coefficients for the less-than-high-school groups are all negative and coefficients for the have-some-college groups are all positive. The list of coefficients does have a couple of anomalies. No reported education has a larger (less negative) coefficient than other not-as-educated groups. Perhaps areas with relatively high education have populations that report no education (perhaps due to inaccuracies in the census data collection process or to a misunderstanding of the education question by more educated people). At the high end, the coefficients are all the same, but the coefficient for finishing college with a bachelor's degree is slightly larger than for the more educated groups. The general trend is clear, and this principal component captures the idea of how educated a ZIP code is.

Table 20-3: Coefficients for the First Principal Component for the Education Variables, Weighted by ZIP Code and Weighted by Population

VARIABLE	DESCRIPTION	COEFFICIENT UNWEIGHTED	COEFFICIENT WEIGHTED
Popedunone	No Education	−0.1609	−0.2313
Popedunohs	No High School	−0.3526	−0.3601
Popedusomehs	Some High School	−0.3415	−0.3970
Popeduhsgrad	High School Graduate	−0.3402	−0.3202
popedusomecol	Some College	0.2016	0.1163
Popeduassoc	2-Year College Degree	0.2010	0.1770
Popedubach	4-Year College Degree	0.4701	0.4444
Popedumast	Master's Degree	0.4206	0.4221
popeduprofdoct	Doctorate or Professional Degree	0.3720	0.3690

Another possibility, which is always worth considering when using summarized data, is that small areas dominate the calculation. That is, thousands of ZIP codes have small populations, and their particular percentages may dominate the calculation. Principal components can also be calculated by weighting the data points. Table 20-3 has the principal component coefficients when the ZIP codes are weighted by the population used for the education ratios (that is, adults 25 years of age and older). Weighting by population has little impact on the coefficients.

Using the principal component is simply a matter of doing the calculations, multiplying the value of the appropriate variables by the coefficients and adding them up to get the result. One property of the resulting values is that their range is as large as possible. You already encountered this property in the statistical definition of the first principal component. Having a large range of resulting values is basically another way of saying that the variance is maximized.

PRINCIPAL COMPONENTS AND MATRICES

The main text introduces principal components using geometric ideas. However, a deep understanding of the subject requires learning about the part of mathematics that deals with matrices: linear algebra. This aside explains some of the basic concepts. In particular, principal components are related to an important idea in linear algebra called *singular value decomposition*.

The discussion starts with vectors. A vector simply connects the initial point to any point in space. For the purposes in this chapter, vectors all start at the origin, the point whose coordinates are all zero. A vector with two coordinates is a point in the plane; a vector with three coordinates is a point in three-dimensional space, and so on.

A vector is not only a point; it can also represent a transformation. The vector (2,1) is a point. Another way to think of it is as a recipe that can be applied to any point. The recipe says to move the point two units in the X dimension and one unit in the Y dimension. Consider a set of points in the plane that represent some polygon or other shape. "Applying" the vector (2,1) to this polygon would move the shape, by moving each point two units horizontally and one unit vertically. In this case, "applying" corresponds to vector addition.

A matrix is a rectangular array of numbers; a square matrix has the same number of rows and columns. One of the operations defined on matrices is multiplying the matrix by a vector. This produces a new vector, where each of the values in the new vector is calculated by taking a row of the original matrix times the values in the original vector and summing them up. A matrix can be multiplied by any point or set of points using the same calculation. A matrix transforms the points in some very particular ways. As an example, consider the following matrix:

$$\begin{matrix} 2 & 0 \\ 0 & 0.5 \end{matrix}$$

The calculation for any point results in a new point:

New X value = 2 * X value + 0 * Y value

New Y value = 0 * X value + 0.5 * Y value

Continued

PRINCIPAL COMPONENTS AND MATRICES   (*continued*)

Geometrically, this says: Move each point so the X value doubles and the Y value halves. Visually, this transformation stretches a set of points in the X direction (by a factor of 2) and squashes it in the Y direction (by a factor of 0.5).

Matrices can also express rotations and mirror images, in addition to stretches. For instance, the following matrix creates a mirror image of a point along the diagonal line by swapping the X and Y values:

$$\begin{matrix} 0 & 1 \\ 1 & 0 \end{matrix}$$

More complex matrices have more complex interpretations. In higher dimensions, the results are even harder to visualize.

What does this have to do with principal components? Well, it turns out that if you have a complicated series of actions on points that consist of stretches, rotations, and mirror images, then such a sequence can be expressed as a transformation by a matrix. And with such complicated transformations, an amazing thing happens. There are particular directions where points are simply stretched (or squashed), but they do not get rotated anywhere else. In the first matrix example, these directions are along the X and Y axes. In the second example, the direction is the diagonal line.

These directions are more than a novelty. Through a rather amazing result in linear algebra, these directions and the squashing or stretching factor basically define the matrix. And this is true for even non-square matrices. Understanding these directions and the stretching or squashing factor is the subject of *singular value decomposition*.

For a matrix where the entries are all real numbers (as opposed to complex numbers), there is a mathematical way to find these special directions. The mathematics uses a lot of terminology from matrix algebra. With that warning, the singular directions are the eigenvectors of a matrix formed by taking the square root of the product of the original matrix times its adjoint (don't worry if you don't understand that). The singular values are the eigenvalues of the same matrix. The important point here is that the singular values are interesting from a geometric point of view and they can be calculated using various concepts from matrix algebra. For square matrices consisting of real numbers, the principal components are the same as the singular values.

How do these all get calculated? Well, it turns out that the square root of the product of any matrix times its adjoint is equivalent to what statisticians call the *correlation matrix* — a square matrix with one column and one row for each input variable, where the value in each cell is the Pearson correlation (the "r" in R^2). An alternative way of defining principal components is that they are the eigenvectors of the correlation matrix. This particular definition is derived, though, from the concepts of singular value decomposition and matrix algebra.

Singular value decomposition and principal components analysis are essentially the same thing. They are arrived at in different ways, from matrix algebra or from statistics, and they use different terminology but the concepts are essentially the same.

Principal Component Analysis

Principal component analysis (PCA) refers to using principal components specifically for analytic purposes. A deep understanding of principal components requires some knowledge of matrices and linear algebra, as discussed in the sidebar, "Principal Component and Matrices." However, for understanding PCA, a deep knowledge of matrices is not needed.

Reducing the Number of Variables

Principal components have been introduced as a mechanism for reducing the number of variables for both undirected and directed data mining techniques. There are two common ways to use principal components in this way. The first is to devise principal components for all variables, and to select some number of these for modeling purposes. The second is to follow the example used for the education variables by using principal components to summarize a subset of variables within a particular domain.

A key idea in PCA is that it can describe the proportion of variance explained (also called the *cumulative proportional eigenvalue*), which was illustrated earlier in the scree charts in Figures 20-8 and 20-9. Another way of describing this proportion is that it describes how much of the information in the original variables is contained in some subset of the principal components. The principal components are ordered from the most informative to the least informative. A scree chart can be used to see the principal components that account for 20 percent, 50 percent, or 80 percent of the information in the original variables.

After the principal components are defined, the final step is to transform the original data so it contains the principal components rather than the original variables. Do note, though, that the principal components themselves do not necessarily lend themselves to explanation. One exception can occur when using them only within a particular domain. The example using education variables by ZIP code has an explanation: the principal component seems to measure "educationness." This interpretation requires human judgment about what the results mean; the interpretation is not automatic.

Understanding Input Variables

Typically, each input variable contributes to each principal component, because the principal component is a linear combination of all the variables. The coefficient could be zero for a particular input variable in a particular principal component, but that is a rare occurrence. These coefficients provide information about the impact of the input variable on any particular principal component.

The coefficients behave similarly to the coefficients in linear regression. The key to making the coefficients more understandable is to standardize the original variables — remember, standardization transforms a variable into z-scores by subtracting the average value and dividing by the standard deviation. With the standardized variables, the coefficients on the principal components can be interpreted as how strongly each input variable contributes to the particular component.

Figure 20-10 shows a picture of some of the variables used for a principal component. The idea is that the variables are ordered by the size of their contribution to the component. The tall variables on the left are all related to the size of the ZIP code — number of housing units, number of adults over 25 years of age, population, the number of families, and so on. Similar variables cluster together at the top. Some of the variables with very small coefficients are longitude and the proportion of the ZIP code not on public assistance, which are very different from the variables with large coefficients.

Later in this chapter, the section on variable clustering extends this idea to finding groups of variables that are related to each other.

Data Visualization

Another important use of principal components is for data visualization. Consider the data as a scatter plot in many, many dimensions. Unfortunately, such a scatter plot cannot be pictured on a two-dimensional page. Principal components enable us to make a good picture, in this case.

The first principal component is a good tool for visualization. The principal component is a vector, which means that it provides a vantage point for viewing the data. An example would be viewing the planets from the earth. Sometimes, all or many are visible in the night sky. On rare occasions, they might even all be in a small fuzzy area of the sky.

Such a vantage point would be a very bad viewpoint, because the planets are in a very small area. A much better viewpoint — or dare we call it a "principal component" — would be when the planets are spread out as far as possible across the sky. When the planets are spread out, distinguishing among them and finding relevant patterns is much easier. This is what statisticians mean when they say that the first principal component is a projection that maximizes variance — it maximizes the spread of the variables.

One dimension is not so interesting. Two dimensions start to get more interesting, because they form a nice scatter plot. If the first principal component is in the "best" way of looking at the data (to spread it out), the second principal component is the second-best vantage point. Together, this should make an interesting plot.

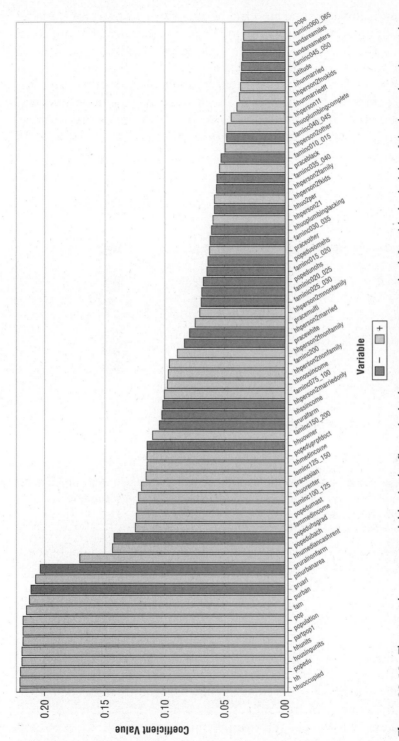

Figure 20-10: The most important variables in the first principal component are on the left, with the height of the bars showing each variable's contribution (the chart continues to the right, with variables that have smaller coefficients falling off the chart). Lighter shading is positive; darker shading is negative.

Figure 20-11 takes this idea one step further. It shows scatter plots created pairwise for the first four principal components for a data set with many variables. In this plot, there are no scatter plots along the diagonal because the points would all be on a line (the X and Y axes would be the same). The first scatter plot in the first line is the first principal component on the Y axis and the second principal component on the X axis. The next one has the third principal component instead. The different shading corresponds to a response variable. Because the response is a target for directed data mining, it is not included in the principal component calculations.

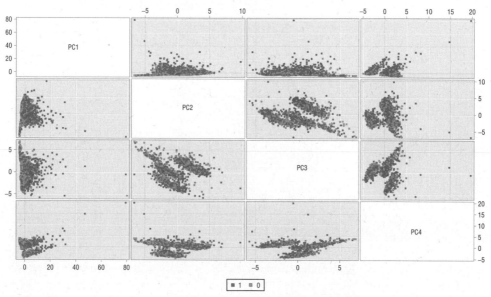

Figure 20-11: These scatter plots show the data along the first four principal components, plotted pairwise. The two charts on the upper left, for instance, are the scatter plot using the first two principal components.

These scatter plots provide a way to look at multidimensional data. In some cases, the points look like a big blob, albeit in an elongated ovoid shape. Interesting patterns do not necessarily jump out of such a blob. The shading of the response variable is included in the diagram, so it is possible for different parts of a blob to be shaded differently, suggesting important distinctions between responders and non-responders.

Other scatter plots show two or even three distinct components. These components suggest that two or three natural clusters might be in the data, natural clusters where the customers in each cluster behave differently from each other.

The groups in the scatter plot are a suggestion, a hint, and not a demonstration of the actual clusters. The planets in the nighttime sky might fall in an orderly line on occasion, from our viewpoint here on earth. This does not mean that the planets are actually in a line in the heavens; the line is an artifact of our viewpoint.

The two dimensions of the scatter plots in the example leave out many other dimensions. So, points that look close in these dimensions might actually be very far apart, when the other dimensions are taken into account. That said, the principal components are "best" in a particular sense, so further investigation is definitely warranted.

Factor Analysis

Factor analysis is set of statistical techniques used for reducing the number of variables that builds on principal components. The goal of factor analysis is to determine underlying explanations for the variables that might not be evident from the data.

For instance, a customer survey may ask customers about various attitudes regarding pricing, service, and convenience. A highly desirable goal would be to have a metric for all customers regarding sensitivity along these dimensions. Unfortunately, simply asking customers directly does not usually elicit the right information. Instead, survey questions might ask "Would you pay $5 more to receive an item one day sooner in the mail?" or "Would you cancel your subscription if you found a similar service for $10 less per month?"

In this case, factor analysis could be used to determine the factors that drive customers to respond to surveys in a particular way. The first step is principal component analysis, with some additional interpretation. The interpretation focuses on the variables that contribute most strongly to each principal component — either positively or negatively. For instance, in the example that uses variables describing education in a ZIP code, the variables representing more education contribute positively and the variables representing less education contribute negatively. This principal component is measuring the "education" factor for the ZIP code. Of course, given that only education variables were used, this interpretation is not surprising.

Traditional factor analysis goes beyond the basic principal components. The approach is typically to identify several of the most important components and then to modify them. Remember that one of the strengths of principal components is that the principal components are orthogonal to each other — that is, they meet at right angles. However, the first principal component contributes more information than the second, and so on. Factor analysis rotates the components so they no longer meet at right angles. Instead, the contributions are equalized. This rotation often makes finding interpretations more feasible.

TIP Factor analysis is useful in many domains. However, in the world of data mining, which is rich in data, other techniques are usually more practical.

The authors do not consider factor analysis an important technique for most data mining purposes. The technique was developed in the world of surveys, where the goal is to find underlying factors to explain survey responses. Customer data is typically much richer than survey data, including demographics, behavioral data, and rich transaction histories. The ideas behind factor analysis are useful, but a better approach is to explicitly define possible factors and develop separate measures for each one.

Variable Clustering

This chapter has covered the topic of selecting and reducing the number of variables. This section goes one step further. It introduces the notion that input variables have a structure that is useful for analytic purposes. Such a structure allows you to choose the number of variables for modeling, in the same way that agglomerative and divisive clustering methods allow you to dynamically choose the number of clusters.

This section introduces the notion of variable clusters with an example. It then explains two different approaches to building the clusters — one that is simple and one that is more sophisticated.

Example of Variable Clusters

An example is the best way to demonstrate the idea. Figure 20-12 shows a set of variables, connecting in a tree. The first seven variables, for instance, all combine into a single node. And all these seven variables are related to higher education or wealth — two phenomena that are highly correlated. On the other hand, the bottom seven variables are all related to the population of the ZIP code; these are variables such as the population, the number of housing units, the number of occupied housing units, and so on.

Where the variables are combined, a new variable is created with a made-up variable name (not shown in this diagram). These new variables are created using the first principal component of the variables feeding into them.

The horizontal axis is a measure of how much information is provided by the variables at that level. Obviously, if all the variables are included, then so is all the information in them. However, you can reduce the number of variables, sacrificing some information. For instance, five variables are sufficient to capture more than 60 percent of the information in the original set of variables, and two variables can capture more than 40 percent of the information

Another way of looking at the variable clusters is shown in Figure 20-13. In this method, the clusters are nodes in a graph, with the variables feeding into them. They are arranged so that closer clusters appear closer on the chart.

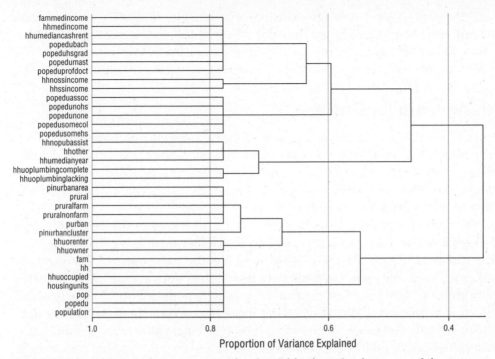

Figure 20-12: This tree shows an example of variable clustering for some of the census variables. The variables at the top, for instance, all indicate highly educated wealthy regions (or, equivalently, poorly educated, impoverished ones).

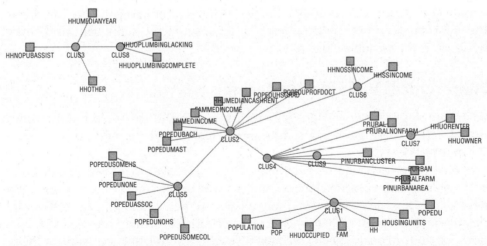

Figure 20-13: This cluster plot shows an alternative way of looking at the variable clusters as nodes in a graph that show relationships among the variables.

Different numbers of variable clusters are available, depending on how much information is preserved from the original variables. This is an example of hierarchical clustering, but at the variable level rather than at the record level. The power of this technique is the ability to choose the number of resulting variables.

Using Variable Clusters

Such clusters of variables are very useful for reducing the number of variables. The idea is to calculate one variable for each cluster. You can do this in basically three ways. The first is the manual method, where you choose the most descriptive variable in the cluster. This cannot be automated, because descriptiveness requires human interpretation.

The second method is to use the first principal component of the cluster. That is, generate the principal component on the cluster only using the variables in the cluster. The first principal component has the nice property that it can be generated automatically. Unfortunately, it lacks descriptive power. An interesting side effect of using the first principal component is the ability to measure how much information is lost by replacing the original variable in the cluster with the principal component. Technically, this is the eigenvalue of the first principal component divided by the sum of the eigenvalues for all principal components (the measure used in the section on principal components). Fortunately, any tool that provides principal components provides this measure.

The third method is to find the variable that has the most predictive power by using a statistical test. Various statistical tests could be used. Probably the most interesting uses principal components: simply use the variable that contributes the maximum amount to the first principal component. This variable is the most important variable for describing the principal component, and hence describing the variable cluster.

Hierarchical Variable Clustering

A simple approach to variable clustering is to build them from the bottom up, which is analogous to the agglomerative clustering method described in Chapter 14.

Such an approach requires two things. The first is a way to measure the distance between any two variables. The second is a way to combine two variables into a new variable, which can be used for subsequent agglomeration. As with many data mining techniques, there are many flavors of measure and combination functions for this purpose. The next section discusses a simple set of choices for them.

Correlation Variable Clustering

An intuitive measure of the "distance" between two variables is Pearson correlation, introduced in Chapter 4. Correlation is only defined for numeric variables, so this assumes that categorical variables have already been transformed into numeric variables such as the historical handset churn rate by handset, the market penetration by ZIP code, or average price of a product. The larger the correlation (or really, the larger the absolute value, because the correlation can be negative), the closer the variables.

Two variables can be combined by using their first principal component. After replacing the closest two variables with their first principal component, the variables themselves are then ignored. The process repeats using the principal component, until only one variable remains.

Example of Correlation Variable Clustering

Table 20-4 shows a sample of ZIP codes with five data columns:

- NOHHDIPLOMA: Proportion of the ZIP code who did not complete high school
- COLDEGREE: Proportion of the ZIP code who completed at least four years of college
- HHMEDINCOME: Median income for the ZIP code
- HHNOPUBASSIST: Proportion of households not on public assistance
- LANDAREAMILES: Area of the land portion of the ZIP code, measured in square miles

These variables are provided by the US Census Bureau.

Table 20-4: Example of Data for Six ZIP Codes

ZIPCODE	LANDAREAMILES	HHMEDINCOME	HHNOPUBASSIST	NOHHDIPLOMA	COLDEGREE
10011	0.6	$61,986	98.5%	3.5%	68.6%
33158	3.1	$118,410	99.3%	2.6%	60.6%
33193	13.7	$39,990	96.5%	10.5%	19.7%
55343	8.3	$44,253	97.0%	3.3%	38.1%
94518	5.6	$64,429	95.7%	4.7%	32.3%
98053	32.4	$96,028	99.4%	2.0%	57.8%

Table 20-5 shows the correlation matrix for the ZIP code variables. Notice that along the diagonal, all the values are one, because any variable is 100 percent correlated with itself. The table itself is symmetric along this diagonal, because variable pairs occur twice, once on the upper-right part of the table and once on the lower-right part.

Table 20-5: Correlation Matrix for Five Variables Used for Variable Clustering Example

	LANDAREAMILES	HHMEDINCOME	HHNOPUBASSIST	NOHHDIPLOMA	COLDEGREE
landarea-miles	1.000	−0.129	−0.012	0.019	−0.075
hhmedin-come	−0.129	1.000	0.327	−0.433	0.679
hhnopub-assist	−0.012	0.327	1.000	−0.129	0.163
nohhdi-ploma	0.019	−0.433	−0.129	1.000	−0.492
coldegree	−0.075	0.679	0.163	−0.492	1.000

The two variables with the highest correlation are HHMEDINCOME and COLDEGREE with a value of 0.679. This is not surprising because people with a college degree usually have higher incomes. Next, the principal component for these two variables is calculated and added back into the data. The process is repeated with the remaining three input variables plus the new cluster variable. The result is a tree structure that describes the variables, as shown in Figure 20-14.

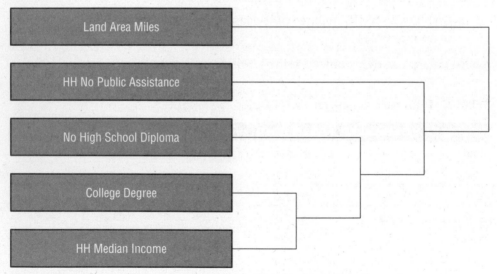

Figure 20-14: Tree structure for variables clustered using correlation and principal components.

The tree structure is useful in two different ways. First, it provides qualitative information about the variables. Variables that are close to each other share a common node low in the tree. Second, it provides a way of reducing the number of variables. A vertical slice through the tree provides a set of variables, consisting of input variables, cluster variables, or a combination of the two. By adjusting the location of the vertical slice, the number of variables can vary from one to the number of input variables.

Variations on Hierarchical Method

The hierarchical clustering method just described can be modified in a number of different ways. For instance, nothing is sacrosanct about using Pearson correlation for measuring similarity between variables. Another method, for instance, would be to break continuous variables into bins, and to calculate the chi-square statistic for the resulting contingency table and combine pairs that have the highest chi-square value. This method has the advantage of working with both numeric and categorical variables.

The first principal component is a very reasonable way of combining variables in each cluster. There are two way to calculate the principal component. The method described earlier builds it from the principal components of the variables going into the cluster. An alternative method is to build it from all the input variables going into those clusters, rather than from the summary principal components from the previous step.

Divisive Variable Clustering

Another approach to creating the variable clusters is to use a divisive method. This is actually the method used for the original example, using SAS software (using the Variable Clustering node in Enterprise Miner or the VARCLUS procedure in SAS). This section describes the ideas behind this top-down approach that uses principal components.

The basic idea is to look at the first principal components and the contribution that each variable makes to it. The variables are ordered from the most contributing to the least contributing. Then do the same thing for the second principal component.

Each variable has a measure of contribution to each of the first two principal components. Simply assign the variable to either the first principal component or the second principal component based on which it contributes to more strongly. This variable assignment becomes the highest split in the variable hierarchy.

The process repeats itself. Within each cluster, each variable is assigned to one of the first two principal components, based on its contribution to that principal component. This results in the next split in the tree, and so on, and so on until only two variables are left in each cluster.

The result is a hierarchical clustering of variables, using the ideas behind principal components. A natural extension of this idea is to reduce any particular cluster to a single variable, by taking the first principal component of all the variables in the cluster.

Lessons Learned

Data mining generally concerns itself with large data sets, both in terms of numbers of rows and numbers of variables. However, too much of a good thing may not be…good. Hence, there is a need for methods to reduce the number of variables.

Methods for reducing variables fall into four groups, based on two characteristics. The first characteristic is whether the method chooses the original variable or creates new variables. The second is whether or not the method uses a target variable for selection.

Early chapters have already covered several important variable selection methods that use target variables. Of particular importance are decision trees and forward selection in regressions. Each has its advantages and disadvantages. Decision trees are good at finding variables that interact and for finding localized effects. However, they can produce variables that are highly correlated. Regression, on the other hand, finds the globally optimal variables, but might miss important local phenomena.

Without a target variable, the most important techniques use principal components. The first principal component is similar to the best-fit line, in that it optimizes a certain measure. The difference is that the best-fit line minimizes the sum of the squares of the vertical distances; the principal component minimizes the sum of the squares of the distances.

Principal components can be used directly. They are not only good for variable reduction, but they are also very useful for visualization and data exploration. They lead to a technique called factor analysis, which is more useful in other domains than in data mining.

Finally, a collection of variables has a structure, and variable clustering finds this structure by grouping similar variables together. Variable clustering may be either agglomerative (bottom-up) or divisive (top-down). Either method produces a tree-like structure containing the variables and allowing the analyst to choose the appropriate number.

This chapter focused on the kinds of variables present in structured data. The next chapter dives into a considerably more complex realm of unstructured data as it covers the topic of text mining.

CHAPTER 21

Listen Carefully to What Your Customers Say: Text Mining

Since the dawn of the computer age, understanding human language has been a goal of computer science research. In 1950, just after the first invention of the computer, Alan Turing proposed a test for computer intelligence. He introduced the imitation game, which was at that time merely a thought experiment.

In this game, a person asks questions via instant messaging or chatting to determine which of two hidden responders is a "man" and which is a "woman." Two responders are in separate rooms from the questioner. One is a woman trying to help the questioner. The other is a machine, who is trying to confuse the questioner. Clearly, if the questioner identifies one of the responders as a computer, then the questioner knows the other is the woman, and the game is solved.

Turing, one of the greatest computer scientists of the twentieth century, introduced this machine in a paper called "Computing Machinery and Intelligence." Although the philosophical aspects of the paper are interesting, it is just as notable for the assumption that computers would be able to readily engage in conversation.

More than six decades later, computers can do amazing things that Alan Turing probably never considered possible — from the ability to control machinery to the analysis of what were then unfathomable amounts of data to reasonable translations from one human language to another to winning *Jeopardy*. And yet, almost half a century after the fictional HAL said, "I'm sorry Dave; I'm afraid I can't do that" in the 1968 movie *2001: A Space Odyssey*, computers still do not make good conversational companions.

Language is obviously a critical component of how people communicate and how information is stored in the business world and beyond. A lot of useful business information is stored in the form of text, such as:

- Comments on web pages that might tell you about your business and competitors
- Notes taken by customer service reps, doctors, mechanics, and so on that provide more information about real customer interactions
- Reports, encyclopedia articles, and the like that provide "fact" frameworks
- News stories that explain not only what might be happening, but how the facts are covered

Some estimates say that up to 80 percent of important information for businesses is stored in the form of text.

An astute reader might ask why such an important source of information is assigned to the last chapter of this book. Text data is an example of unstructured data, meaning that it does not fit into the neat idea of customer signatures, with specific features for each column. One approach is to extract features from the text, and then use any of the techniques described in earlier chapters. Other approaches are specific to text itself. The techniques used for text mining build on the ideas in many of the earlier chapters. The case studies in this chapter include memory-based reasoning, principal components, naïve Bayesian models, and expectation maximization clustering.

The chapter starts with an overview of the different types of text mining and text analytics. It then walks through several examples of text mining in the real world. The first is ad hoc query analysis, used to analyze a particular segment of customers. The second example uses text mining, along with MBR, to classify new stories. The third uses naïve Bayesian models to classify e-mail as "spam" or "not spam." The chapter introduces sentiment analysis and opinion mining. The final case study explains how DIRECTV has incorporated text mining into its business process, achieving interesting and actionable results along the way.

What Is Text Mining?

Data mining is the process of finding and exploiting useful patterns in data. Text is data, so it should be useful for data mining purposes. This section discusses various applications of analytics on text, some of which are more properly considered data mining, and some of which are just useful applications of text analytics.

Text Mining for Derived Columns

Perhaps the most common use of text mining is to add new derived columns into a model set; this is an example of converting unstructured data into structured features. Extracting derived variables is usually a matter of looking for specific patterns in the text. For instance, an address can be used to identify whether someone lives in an apartment by looking for an apartment number. What might this look like? If the address contains any of the following, then it is probably an apartment number:

- " Apt." in any case
- " #"
- Address line beginning with "Apt." or "Apartment"
- " Unit"

An `is_apartment` flag can be assigned based on whether or not an address matches these patterns. Such a flag might prove to be quite useful for modeling purposes.

> **TIP** Deriving columns from text is an example of directed data mining because you need to know what you are looking for.

Derived fields can, of course, be more complicated than merely searching for specific terms in a semi-formatted field. For instance, the language of a web page or text message can be determined from looking at the frequencies of words in the text. The "reading level" of an article can be determined by analyzing the grammar and vocabulary. The use of particular regionalisms and spellings can even say something about where an author was educated and where the author lives.

Beyond Derived Features

Deriving variables from text is one application area, but not the only one. Often, you don't know the exact features you are looking for in advance. One typical application is routing and prioritization. Chapter 11 on genetic algorithms has a case study of analyzing incoming e-mails. The goal is to determine whether the e-mail comment is a complaint (which needs to be handled quickly) or a compliment (which can be handled more leisurely).

This is one example of a routing application; there are many others. In the insurance industry, free-form notes help determine how to deal with the claim. Should the claim be:

- Paid immediately, because it has no cause for suspicion?
- Investigated thoroughly, because it seems suspect?
- Investigated with lower priority, because it might be fraudulent?

The insurance company cannot investigate all claims thoroughly, because that would be prohibitively expensive. Neither can they approve all claims, because that would open the floodgates to fraud.

Other examples appear in the media world. News articles, blogs, and the like appear continuously. Which readers would be interested in which articles? If someone has expressed a particular interest in a subject, whether the New York Yankees or the dollar-yen exchange rate or the latest celebrity divorce, how can you send appropriate articles to the interested reader, or be sure that such articles are visible on the user's customized web page?

Analyzing text directly for its content has several different flavors. One is *root-cause analysis*, which attempts to look at the root cause for customer communications. Another is *sentiment analysis*, where the goal is to understand the attitude of the writer toward the subject. A third area is simply clustering documents, as an undirected data mining exercise, to understand common themes and topics.

Text Analysis Applications

There are many useful text analysis applications that are not exactly data mining. However, these are useful both for understanding text mining and because these methods are often incorporated into text mining solutions.

Spell Checking and Grammar Checking

Everyone who uses a word processor or e-mail program is probably familiar with automated spell checking and perhaps grammar checking. Such tools help writers prevent simple mistakes.

Spell checking as an end goal is not really data mining. There is some overlap between them, however. When analyzing documents, particularly unedited documents, should you standardize the documents in spelling (to facilitate comparisons and search) or should you let the documents remain in their original style? This question does not have a correct answer, because it depends on the ultimate application.

Such tools can also provide information about the document — and hence about the author. What proportion of words is misspelled? What is the reading level of the document?

Translation from One Human Language to Another

An important application on text data is translation from one language to another. The early days of automated translation were filled with amusing anecdotes. A perhaps apocryphal story from the early world of machine translation tells the story of translating the phrase "The spirit is willing but the flesh is weak" from English to Russian and back to English again. The result: "The vodka is good but the meat is rotten."

More recently, machine translation has become much more adept, particularly with the entrance of Google into the business of translating web pages. Google takes advantage of the Internet, where millions of examples of pages are available in multiple languages. By building special-purpose software to parse these pages and to understand which phrases in one language correspond to which phrases in another language, Google has been able to build a powerful translation engine that works surprisingly well both for formal and informal communication. The results are understandable, although not quite what a native speaker would write.

Search

Perhaps the most common application of text analysis is in searching for documents, whether through the zillions of pages on the Web, through last year's e-mail, or the files on your hard disk. Searching for documents is a specialized task. Clearly, search engines start with text search. However, on the Web, they also take advantage of links between documents, what results people have clicked on in the past, and proprietary methods for maximizing click-revenue.

Searching can also be used for data mining. By producing a set of ordered documents in response to a query, search implements a similarity measure that can be used by techniques such as MBR and clustering. Later in this chapter is a case study that uses a metric originally designed for search specifically for classifying news stories.

Paying attention to search terms can also be very useful, particularly where search is an important part of a website. Amazon, for instance, pays careful attention to the search terms used on its website, particularly those that fail to find anything. It has gone so far as to have a daily meeting looking at the unusual terms that pop up. By paying attention to what customers were searching for, Amazon gets an early indication of trends occurring; for example, Amazon was the first retailer to pick up on the trend for Beanie babies (once upon a time) by paying attention to unusual search terms, which allowed Amazon to stock up on them.

TIP Tracking the popularity of search terms on the Web can provide very interesting information about what is happening in the marketplace.

Not all websites have search engines. However, most search engines provide the capability to see the popularity of search terms over time. Figure 21-1 shows a screenshot of Google Trends (www.google.com/trends) with one year's worth of popularity of the term *data mining*. This information has more than entertainment value. Ford Motor Company, for instance, uses information from search trends to enhance its near-term sales forecast. Its sales forecasting models are time-series models, built using standard time-series techniques. By including lagged search trends in the models, it has improved its near-term sales forecasts, according to Michael Cavaretta of Ford's Research and Innovation Center[1].

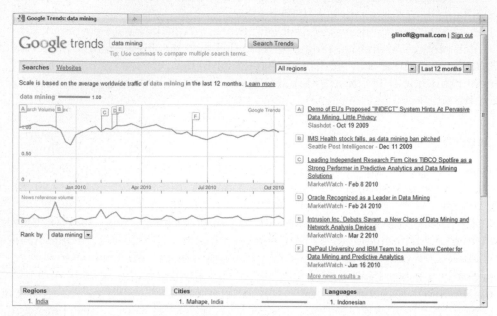

Figure 21-1: Google trends provides information about the popularity of search terms over time.

Summarizing Documents

Sometimes the goal is to summarize documents to understand their contents, in much the same way that an abstract on a scientific paper summarizes the contents of the research or the way that a review of a book on Amazon helps a reader determine his or her level of interest.

Summarization is sometimes useful on its own, to understand which of many large documents are most likely to be useful. The results of summarization do not need to be well-formed sentences and paragraphs. Tag clouds on websites that indicate the keywords associated with a particular page (often a blog) are an example of summarization that uses just keywords.

Similar to summarization is the challenge of visualizing the contents of a large set of documents. Text visualization often uses ideas from text mining, link analysis, and user-interface design to help users understand the contents of very diverse sets of documents. Even in the business world, such attempts at visualization can be useful. Imagine an application that visualizes the major themes of customer interactions, positioning them graphically for users to get a sense of what customers care about.

---

[1]Michael Cavaretta, 2008. *Sales Forecasting Using Google Searches*. Paper presented at M2008 in Las Vegas, NV.

Turing Test and Natural Language Processing

This chapter started by describing the Turing test. Such dialogue is an interesting text application. One could imagine the capability for a computer to converse as an important application in the business world. Voice automation is just starting, with robot vacuum cleaners that respond to cleaning orders, telephones, and household appliances that obey voice commands. However, natural language processing is still mostly a future application (Person: "Washing machine, start the wash later today when the electricity rates go down." Machine: "But the load has mixed whites and bright colors.")

The original Turing test had three participants. More commonly, a simplified version has a human chatting with either a computer or a human. Can the computer convince the questioner that it is human?

In 1966, a program called Eliza was the first to convince some of the people some of the time that it really understood their problems and could converse with them. This program, developed by Professor Joseph Weizenbaum of MIT, pretended to be a therapist. It was basically able to do three things. First, it could construct sentences and questions that were grammatically and colloquially correct. Second, it could rephrase comments the questioner made, picking out key words and asking questions ("What did you do this weekend?" "I visited my mother." "Tell me more about your mother.") Third, it would occasionally bring up topics that hadn't been discussed ("Do you like sports?"). These tricks were sufficient to convince some people that they were conversing with a real person.

Working with Text Data

Text generally requires more preparation than the structured data used for other types of data mining. After identifying the source of the text, the biggest challenge is to parse it into words and phrases.

Sources of Text

Text comes from many different sources, such as:

- E-mails sent by customers
- Notes entered by customer service reps, doctors, nurses, garage mechanics, and so on
- Transcriptions (voice-to-text translation) of customer service calls
- Comments on websites
- Newspaper and magazine articles
- Professional reports

The diversity of sources of text poses some challenges for data preparation. No single automated method understands scientific abstracts, call center memos, and human transcriptions — except, of course, for the human brain.

All the text associated with a given problem is called a *corpus*, from the Latin word meaning "body." A corpus, in turn, is comprised of *documents*. A document is a unit of text that all belongs together, as if in the same row of a model set. A document might refer to an e-mail, to a tweet, a sentence, to a news article, or a customer service comment. It is a convenient term for dividing the corpus into discrete chunks.

Different people use language differently. In spoken language, the same word can sound very different when spoken by a native speaker of the language versus someone who has an accent. A similar situation exists with written language. Is the language formal or informal?

Formal language follows (or attempts to follow) grammatical and spelling rules. Proper nouns are capitalized, sentences have punctuation, verbs and nouns agree, abbreviations are rarely used, and so on for all the different rules. Most published sources of information are formal.

Informal language is the stuff of e-mails, tweets, and spoken conversation. To give a simple example, consider the misspelling "isreal." Many people would assume that the space is missing so this should be "is real," and in many contexts, that is the correct interpretation. Consider instead blog postings debating topics on the Middle East. In that context, a better interpretation is probably the country Israel.

Words can have different meanings. Even worse, misspellings can refer to many different words. The process of finding out the correct meaning of a word is *disambiguation*. Fortunately, for many text mining purposes, disambiguation is not necessary.

Language Effects

Most of the discussion in this chapter centers on English as the language, which is the predominant language in text research. The choice of language, though, is not benign. Table 21-1 shows the term count and number of unique terms in various translations of the Bible. A term is any string of characters, generally separated by spaces or particular punctuation. So, "it's" would be a term as would proper nouns such as "Adam."

Table 21-1: Counts of Unique Terms and Total Words for Translations of the Bible[2]

LANGUAGE	UNIQUE TERMS	TERM COUNT
English	12,335	789,744
French	20,428	812,947
Spanish	28,456	704,004
Russian	47,226	560,524
Arabic	55,300	440,435

[2]Bader B. and Chew P, 2010. "Algebraic Techniques for Multilingual Document Clustering." In *Text Mining Applications and Theory*, page 23. (Michael W. Berry and Jacob Kogan, eds.). Wiley.

Why do such differences matter? The match between meanings and words (technically "lexical token" because these are based on the way the word is written) is not precise. In English, one word can mean very different things: "close" can be a verb meaning the opposite of "open" or it can be a preposition meaning "not far." Is a document that mentions "China" concerned with the country or with dinnerware? (In this particular case, capitalization can distinguish the meanings.) Clearly, one word is not sufficient for characterizing documents.

A word (or term) is generally considered to be sequences of characters separated by punctuation or spaces. As an example, this sentence has eight words. A verb in English, such as *have*, might have three or four different forms (*have, has, had*). In French, the same word has many more forms (*ai, as, a, avons, avez,* and *ont* just for the present tense, and dozens more forms when you include other tenses, moods, and genders). This greatly multiplies the number of unique words in other languages.

On the other hand, some languages are particularly good at combining multiple concepts into a single word. For instance, the German word *Schadenfreude* is a compound noun that translates into "pleasure derived from the misfortune of others." English would use six words whereas German would only use one (which may be why English speakers sometimes adopt the German word).

These pose challenges for the automatic understanding and classification of text documents, central challenges in text mining.

There are further complications for languages that are based wholly or partly on symbols strung together without spaces between words, such as Chinese and Japanese. Often one symbol acts as a syllable, rather than a letter or a word. Determining the exact meaning — something that humans (who know the language) readily do — is quite difficult for automated systems.

Basic Approaches to Representing Documents

Representing the documents in the computer is the first challenge in text mining. Documents can be stored just as they are, as text. However, this does not necessarily help the computer understand them. There is a continuum of approaches for understanding documents. At one end is the "bag of words" approach, where documents are considered merely a collection of their words. At the other end is the "understanding" approach, where an attempt is made to actually understand the document and what each word specifically means.

Bag of Words

The bag-of-words approach treats a document as a list of words. You may be surprised that the bag-of-words approach is viable. After all, the sentences "Man eats fish" and "Fish eats man" use the same words, but they mean very different things. In fact, for short sequences of text, a "bag of words" approach may not be sufficient. However, a longer document, such as a news story or even doctor's notes, often contain much redundant information that makes the words themselves useful for text analysis.

Natural Language Processing

At the other extreme of analysis are attempts to actually understand the text, creating models of what the text is saying. Technically, this is called *semantics*. This is difficult, because what words really mean depends on their context. Consider the two sentences:

- Time flies like an arrow.
- Fruit flies like a banana.

Both of these sentences could be of the form: noun, verb, preposition, noun phrase (such as the first). Or, both could be of the form: noun phrase, verb, noun phrase (such as the second). English speakers can distinguish between them, because we understand the meaning.

Another problem is ambiguity. Consider: "The turkey is ready to eat." Does this mean take out the knife and fork, Thanksgiving begins? Or does this mean the hungry turkey has his food? Much like a sentence that contains a pronoun with no antecedent, the sentence by itself does not contain enough information to determine the meaning.

Perhaps the earliest attempt to understand meaning was a program called SHRDLU created in the late 1960s by Terry Winograd at MIT.

SHRDLU was more than a program. It was a program that could communicate with people on one end (using typed commands and responses). SHRDLU controlled a block world, stored in the computer's memory, and shown on the screen. Users could type in commands, such as "place the largest block in the box." If the controller did not understand the command, it might respond saying, "I don't know which block you mean." Otherwise, SHRDLU would do the appropriate action. Users could even ask SHRDLU questions, such as "What is the pyramid supported by?"

Fast forward several decades and computer programs that can readily converse with people about just anything still do not exist. However, significant progress has been made in semantic understanding. For instance, call center applications can respond to simple questions, such as "What is my account balance?"

Representing Documents in Practice

These approaches represent the ends of a continuum. The bag-of-words is the most naïve approach, where even basic grammatical constructs are ignored. Natural language processing is at the other extreme, where, essentially, the computer understands the words, the relationships among them, and the concepts that they represent in the real world.

A handful of extensions to the bag-of-words approach make it more useful. Most of these can be automated, although the last, developing a lexicon, cannot.

Stop Words

Stop words refer to words that have little meaning. In this case, *meaning* refers to the ability to differentiate between different documents. For instance, virtually all documents in English contain the word *the*, and this word essentially has no meaning for typical text mining applications such as classification, deriving variables, navigation, and so on. (Curious readers might be amused by one exception to this, a short novel called *Gadsby*, which is written without the letter *e* and available at www.spinelessbooks.com/gadsby/.)

Stop word lists can be found on the Web, developed manually, or even found automatically. In the last case, this is the search for words that appear throughout the corpus, independent of any relationship to the documents. Although stop words are often common words (such as *of*, *through*, and *and*), less common examples include *nevertheless*, *differently*, and *furthering*).

Stemming

Stemming is the process of reducing words to their "stem," the base word or almost-word that provides the meaning without additional grammatical information. For instance, the word *stemming* would be transformed into the word *stem*, as would *stems* and *stemmed*.

The purpose of stemming is to better capture the content of a document. One customer complaint might refer to "late delivery" and another might say "not delivered on time," two phrases that have no words in common. Using stemming, they would have the word *deliver* in common.

Word Pairs and Phrases

Identifying word pairs and phrases is often important for understanding text. The rock group The Who is a famous example of what can happen with automated text processing. Most stop word lists would include both *the* and *who* on the list, so the phrase would disappear entirely from the document. This could be very problematic.

There are two solutions to this problem. The easy solution is to keep capitalized stop words, or at least capitalized stop words that are not at the beginning of the sentence. A more sophisticated solution is to search for common word pairs and phrases, and to be sure to keep these. Amazon's website for books has a section on "statistically improbable phrases" that it finds by looking for words that appear together more frequently than one would expect. For instance, the second edition of this book has such phrases as "undirected data mining," "automatic cluster detection," and "data mining environment."

Using a Lexicon

Most business applications of text mining involve a lexicon of one form or another. A lexicon is a list of words that are important. It might also include synonyms, so several different words might be combined into a single idea, including misspellings. For instance, "flight," "fl," and "flt" might all represent "flight" in airline comments.

Building a lexicon is often the most time-consuming part of text mining. Part of a lexicon may be available for an industry. However, each company also has its own language, used to describe its products, market, offers, and so on. This language should be part of the lexicon.

> **WARNING** Building a lexicon — the list of important words and synonyms — is usually the most time-consuming part of a text mining project.

Documents and the Corpus

One of the questions that arises when doing text mining is the relationship of each document to the overall corpus. There is often a desire to take a sample of all the documents, analyze them for important features, such as word phrases and stop words, and then move on. However, in the real world, a corpus is generally not static; new documents appear all the time. Although academic research may involve lots of work on static documents such as the Bible and Shakespeare's plays, in the real world, more and more text is produced every day, along with new words and combinations of words.

One of the case studies in this chapter assigns keywords to news stories. Because news is constantly changing, the relationship of different words to the classifications changes. Before September 2008, "Lehman Brothers" as a phrase would be associated with the investment bank and probably finance. After September 2008, the phrase would be more associated with the financial meltdown in 2008 and the subsequent recession.

> **TIP** In the real world, the lexicon is probably not static, and should be maintained over time.

Case Study: Ad Hoc Text Mining

Probably the biggest challenge in business is the unknown. Alas, the unknown happens all the time — competitors offer new products, economic conditions change, your marketing video goes viral on YouTube and is suddenly all over the Web and offline news. When something unexpected happens, how do you measure the impact on the business?

This case study is about using information gleaned from call center comment fields to understand the effects of a boycott on a media product. This type of analysis is typically ad hoc, because hopefully the same boycott does not arise very often. The same ideas were applied to other events, such as coverage of the Iraq war and the initiation of same-sex marriage announcements.

The Boycott

Once upon a time, a prominent media company was the target of a boycott for its coverage of the Middle East. The goal of the boycott was to get customers to stop their subscriptions. News of the boycott spread, and customers stopped in almost every state in the country. However, because it appealed to particular ethnic groups, there was a regional distribution. A higher proportion of stops were in the New York area than would be expected.

The boycott was sufficiently large that it caught the attention of the company. This immediately led to analytic questions, such as:

- How many stops can be attributed to the boycott?
- Who is stopping?
- Are they coming back?

These are challenging questions. Customers stop. But no stop reason code explicitly says "Middle East Boycott." Even if there were, it is doubtful it would be used correctly 100 percent of the time.

Business as Usual

When customers call in to stop, the call center personnel would apply one of about 100 stop codes to the call. The stop codes would specify things such as the stop being due to poor service, switching to another product, vacations, or the price being high. One of the stop codes was for editorial content.

The simplest way to track the boycott stops was to assume that all editorial content stops were due to the boycott. And, further, that all boycott stops received the right stop code.

If the information were really important, then the call center personnel might reinvestigate some of the stops by listening on the phone and having independent agents assign stop codes. Alternatively, they could do it after the fact by investigating the various codes. Either way, such an approach would be an intensive, manual effort.

Combining Text Mining and Hypothesis Testing

An alternative to a manual investigation was ad hoc text mining, with the goal of classifying the comment fields on calls by using a combination of text mining and hypothesis testing. The data itself was stored in an Oracle database. The ad hoc text mining effort used character functions inside the database.

> **TIP** For ad hoc efforts, the character functions inside databases can be sufficient. However, more advanced text mining typically requires more advanced tools, which are available in text mining tools, some data mining tools, and increasingly in databases.

The process started by looking at the editorial content stops, and reading the comments. One of the advantages of a boycott is that customers want the company to know why they are stopping. For instance, many comments were like:

- "Stopping due to anti-Israel bias"
- "Due to Mid East Coverage"

A handful of comments were quite ambiguous:

- "Due to Editorial"
- "Not balanced as far as ideas"

Most other comments were clearly not related to the boycott.

In the end, a handful of terms were identified that seemed highly correlated with boycott comments. For instance, the following terms all indicated boycott stops: " ISRAEL," " ISREAL," " ISREEL," " ISAREL," and " ISERAL." These terms all start with a leading space, indicating that they are the start of a word. All indicate that the comment is about Israel. The last four are misspellings.

In some cases, the terms could be confused with other types of comments. One of the rules looks for comments that have terms beginning with "MID" and containing "EAS." These would tend to indicate something about the "Middle East," capturing numerous variations on spelling. However, some of these were comments such as "Please refund remaining balance; customer quit in middle" or "Please use work address at Middlesex College." To prevent confusion, the full rule ignored comments that contained the word *please*.

In the end, fourteen rules were sufficient to identify virtually all the stops due to the boycott.

The Results

Because the volume of stops measured in the thousands, investigating many of the comments manually was possible. One day's worth of editorial content stops were investigated in detail in order to validate the rules. The rules did a very good job, missing only two obvious boycott-related stops due to misspellings ("Cancel Due To Middle E4st Coverate" and "Due To Nmiddle East Coverage").

Table 21-2 shows the results from this effort over a longer period of time. This analysis period had 4,893 total editorial stops. Of these, about 90 percent were, indeed, due to the boycott. However, focusing on the editorial stops missed an additional 1,200 stops that were classified from the comment fields.

Table 21-2: Boycott Stops with Respect to Stop Types

STOP TYPE	TOTAL	BOYCOTT	PERCENT
Editorial Stop	4,893	4,378	89.47%
Vacation	34,678	1,055	3.04%
Other	8,811	349	3.96%
Missing	6,083	292	4.80%
Total		**6,074**	

Beyond understanding the effectiveness of the boycott, the stops also fed into a special campaign to win back these customers. Correctly capturing the customers who stopped due to boycott was critical to the success of this win-back campaign.

Classifying News Stories Using MBR

This case study uses MBR (covered in Chapter 9) to assign classification codes to news stories and is based on work conducted by one of the authors. The results from this case study show that MBR can perform as well as people on a problem involving hundreds of categories and text data.[3]

The work for this case study was done for Dow Jones News Retrieval Service (DJNS). Although dating back to the 1990s, the problem of assigning keywords to stories and articles is still important. A more modern example is the word tags associated with many blog articles.

What Are the Codes?

Classification codes are keywords used to describe the content of news stories. These codes are added to stories to help users search for stories of interest. They help automate the process of routing particular stories to particular customers for e-mail and customized web pages. An industry analyst who specializes in the automotive industry (or anyone else with an interest in the topic) can simplify searches by looking for documents with the "automotive industry" code.

---

[3]This case study is a summarization of research conducted by one of the authors. Complete details are available in the article "Classifying News Stories using Memory Based Reasoning," by David Waltz, Brij Masand, and Gordon Linoff, in Proceedings, SIGIR '92, published by ACM Press.

DJNS maintained a team of knowledgeable experts (editors) who assigned the codes to news stories. The codes used in this study fall into six categories:

- Government Agency
- Industry
- Market Sector
- Product
- Region
- Subject

The data contained 361 separate codes. Table 21-3 shows the distribution of the codes in the model set.

Table 21-3: Six Types of Codes Used to Classify News Stories

CATEGORY	# CODES	# DOCS	# OCCURRENCES
Government (G/)	28	3,926	4,200
Industry (I/)	112	38,308	57,430
Market Sector (M/)	9	38,562	42,058
Product (P/)	21	2,242	2,523
Region (R/)	121	47,083	116,358
Subject (N/)	70	41,902	52,751

The number and types of codes assigned to stories varied. Almost all the stories had region and subject codes — and on average, almost three region codes per story. At the other extreme, relatively few stories contained government and product codes, and such stories rarely had more than one code in these categories.

Applying MBR

This section explains how MBR facilitated assigning codes to news stories for a news service. The important steps were:

1. Choosing the training set
2. Determining the distance function
3. Choosing the number of nearest neighbors
4. Determining the combination function

The following sections discuss each of these steps in turn.

Choosing the Training Set

The training set consisted of 49,652 news stories, provided by DJNS for this purpose. These stories came from about three months of news and from almost 100 different sources. The source of the story is important. Both *People* magazine and the *Economist* might have an article on the presidential inauguration; the language used in the two articles would be very different.

Each story contained, on average, 2,700 words and had eight codes assigned to it. The training set simply consisted of available stories, so the frequency of codes in the training set mimicked the overall frequency of codes in news stories in general.

Choosing the Distance Function

The next step is choosing the distance function. In this case, a distance function already existed, based on a notion called relevance feedback, which measures the similarity of two documents based on the words they contain in common. Relevance feedback, which is described more fully in the sidebar, was originally designed as a way of refining searches.

Choosing the Combination Function

Assigning classification codes to news stories is a bit different from most classification problems, which have a single best solution. News stories can have multiple codes, even from the same category. The ability to adapt MBR to this problem highlights its flexibility.

The combination function used a weighted summation technique. Because the maximum distance was one, the weight was simply one minus the distance. Weights would be big for neighbors at small distances and small for neighbors at big distances. For example, say the neighbors of a story had the following region codes and weights, shown in Table 21-4.

Table 21-4: Classified Neighbors of a Not-Yet-Classified Story

NEIGHBOR	DISTANCE	WEIGHT	CODES
1	0.076	0.924	R/FE,R/CA,R/CO
2	0.346	0.654	R/FE,R/JA,R/CA
3	0.369	0.631	R/FE,R/JA,R/MI
4	0.393	0.607	R/FE,R/JA,R/CA

USING RELEVANCE FEEDBACK TO CREATE A DISTANCE FUNCTION

Relevance feedback returns documents similar to a given document. You can think of it as putting a news article as the query for Google. The difference is that relevance feedback uses only the text in the document, whereas Google also uses link information.

Relevance feedback provides a measure of similarity of every document in a corpus to the query document. This similarity is the score, which can be used as the basis for a distance measure for MBR.

In this case study, the calculation of the relevance feedback score went as follows:

1. Stop words, such as "it," "and," and "of," were removed from the text of all stories in the training set. A total of 368 words in this category were identified and removed.

2. The next most common words, accounting for 20 percent of the words in the database, were removed from the text. Because these words are so common, they provide little information to distinguish between documents.

3. The remaining words were collected into a dictionary of searchable terms. Each was assigned a weight inversely proportional to its frequency in the database.

4. Capitalized word pairs, such as "United States" and "New Mexico," were identified automatically and included in the dictionary of searchable terms.

5. To calculate the relevance feedback score for two stories, the weights of the searchable terms in both stories were added together. The algorithm used included a bonus when searchable terms appeared in close proximity in both stories.

This approach is a modified bag-of-words approach. The modification is to give matches a boost when they appear close to each other.

The relevance feedback score adapted an already-existing function for use as a distance function. However, the score itself does not quite fit the definition of a distance. In particular, a score of zero indicates that two stories have no words in common, instead of implying that the stories are identical. The following transformation converts the relevance feedback score to a function suitable for measuring the "distance" between news stories:

$$d_{classification}(A,B) = (1 - score(A,B)) / score(A,A)$$

This is the function used to find the nearest neighbors.

The total score for a code was the sum of the weights of the neighbors having that code. The score for R/FE (which is the region code for the Far East) is the sum of the weights of neighbors 1, 2, 3, and 4, because all of them contain the R/FE, yielding a score of 2.816.

Table 21-5 shows the results for the six region codes contained by at least one of the four neighbors. For these examples, a threshold of 1.0 leaves only three codes: R/CA, R/FE, and R/JA. The particular choice of threshold was based on experimenting with different values and is not important for understanding MBR.

Table 21-5: Code Scores for the Not-Yet-Classified Story

CODE	1	2	3	4	SCORE
R/CA	0.924	0.654	0.000	0.607	2.185
R/CO	0.924	0.000	0.000	0.000	0.924
R/FE	0.924	0.654	0.631	0.607	2.816
R/JA	0.000	0.654	0.631	0.607	1.892
R/MI	0.000	0.654	0.000	0.000	0.624

Choosing the Number of Neighbors

The investigation varied the number of nearest neighbors between 1 and 11. The best results came from using more neighbors. The more typical problem is to assign only a single category or code, and fewer neighbors would likely be sufficient for good results.

The Results

To measure the effectiveness of MBR, DJNS had a panel of editors review all the codes assigned, whether by editors or by MBR, to 200 stories. Only codes agreed upon by a majority of the panel were considered "correct."

The two technical terms for measuring the effectiveness of such coding are *recall* and *precision*. Recall is to the percentage of the correct codes that were assigned, as a percentage of the correct codes. Precision refers to the percentage of correct codes as a percentage of codes assigned. For the original codes on the stories, the recall was 83 percent and the precision 88 percent (relative to the codes chosen by the experts). For the codes assigned by MBR, the recall was 80 percent and the precision 72 percent.

To translate these measures into terms that are, perhaps, easier to follow, consider 100 codes assigned to the stories originally. Of these, the original codes had 88 correct, with 12 incorrect and 18 missing. Of 100 codes assigned by MBR, 72 were correct, 28 incorrect, and 18 missing. (It is a coincidence that 18 are missing in both cases.)

Figure 21-2 is a Venn diagram that compares the results for 100 codes assigned by humans, ignoring the incorrect codes. MBR did not do as well as the most experienced coders; however, it did do as well as intermediate editors. Interestingly, MBR worked better with respect to the original codes on the story than with respect to the codes assigned by the expert coder. This may be because the original codes in the training set were not vetted by an expert coder.

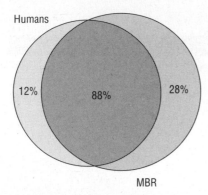

Figure 21-2: A comparison of results by human editors and by MBR on assigning codes to news stories.

From Text to Numbers

The examples so far have treated text as text. The MBR approach is based on a distance function that measures the similarity between two documents based on the words that they contain. The ad hoc approach is similarly word-based.

This section discusses an alternative way of looking at documents, which is to transform them into numbers. The idea of transforming easily readable, well-written documents into gobs of numbers might sound like something from an analytic horror movie, a Frankenstein approach that only its creators could really appreciate. On the other hand, this approach has proven quite useful. The remaining case studies in this chapter are based on this simple idea.

Starting with a "Bag of Words"

Documents contain words. However, for a person, just reading lists of words in a sentence doesn't make sense. Consider the following list:

- a
- a
- doesn't
- for
- however
- in
- just
- lists
- make
- of
- person
- reading
- sense
- sentence
- words

What is this list trying to convey? These words are from the second sentence of this paragraph, arranged alphabetically.

Although the exact meaning of the sentence is not evident in the list, the collection of words does provide some information. This collection of words is probably not about a political development, war, or history. A sentence about botany, sports, or fashion would probably contain a different set of words. In other words (pun intended), the vocabulary used to express ideas does provide information about the subject. It may also provide information about sentiment and other features as well.

Given that people do not understand language this way, it is remarkable that computers are quite successful using the bag-of-words approach. This approach to representing documents for text mining goes back at least to the 1980s.

Words with Multiple Meanings

Perhaps the biggest assumption in the bag-of-words approach is that each word has a single, unique meaning. English has many examples of words that have multiple and quite disjoint meanings: "mean," "close," "contract," "class," and so on. However, compared with some other languages, English does a fairly good job on the one-word one-meaning scale.

The case study later in this chapter on classifying spam e-mail applies the same approaches to English and Chinese e-mails. Interestingly, the technical approaches work differently in the two languages. One reason is that identifying words in Chinese is much more difficult than in English. In general, each Chinese character represents a word. However, it also represents a syllable. Several together might combine to form what in English would be a single word. This would be analogous to breaking apart a word like "together" into three separate words: "to," "get," and "her." Analyzing language syllable by syllable rather than word by word very well could change the approaches that work best in text mining.

Words with Many Forms

The opposite problem occurs in other languages. In English, a single word like "is" can have several different forms: "be," "are," "was," "were," and "been." In French (or Spanish or Italian), the various forms of "to be" are too many to fit into this short paragraph. Varieties depend on the tense (present, past, future), on the number (singular, plural), on the mood (indicative, imperative, subjunctive), and occasionally on the gender. Literally dozens, if not hundreds, of variations are based on such grammatical nuances.

The solution to this problem is stemming. In English, this is usually a simple matter of removing suffixes, such as "-s," "-es," "-ed," and "-ing" from words, and handling a few exceptions ("geese" becomes "goose"). Sometimes, prefixes are removed as well, such as "pre-," "post-," and "over-." The goal of stemming is to reduce the word in the text to its base form, so the same word can be found in many different places, regardless of grammatical inflections.

As discussed earlier in this chapter, English has fewer unique terms than the other languages, by a large margin, at least when it comes to translations of the Bible. This is because English has few word forms compared to other languages.

On the other hand, the languages with the most unique terms also often have the lowest overall number of words. What is said in English with several words becomes one word in some languages. A clear biblical example is in Genesis. In Hebrew, the first word is *barasheet*, which is translated into English as the phrase "In the beginning."

Ignoring Grammar

The bag-of-words approach also ignores the information provided by grammar and word order. For instance, the word *not* can drastically change the meaning of a sentence, depending on where it is placed in a sentence ("I did A but not B" is quite different from "I did B but not A"). The bag-of-words approach ignores such information.

Term-Document Matrix

Techniques that use the bag-of-words approach transform the bag of words into a giant table of numbers, the term-document matrix. The term-document matrix is a simple array, where each row represents a single document and each column represents a particular word. Typically, the number of words in a document is reduced through several steps:

- Fixing misspellings
- Removing common words and words with little meaning ("stop words")
- Stemming
- Replacing words with synonyms

The result is a vocabulary or *lexicon*, typically of several hundred to several thousand words that describe each document.

The cells in the matrix contain zero if the word is not in the document. Words that are in the document could simply contain the value one, indicating the presence of the word. Another possibility is the count of words in the document. More commonly, though, the value is the *inverse document frequency* or one minus the log of the document frequency. The inverse document frequency is one divided by the number of documents containing the term. Words in many documents have low values; words in few documents have higher values. One minus the log of this value behaves in a similar way. As Figure 21-3 shows, the term-document matrix captures this information in a matrix form.

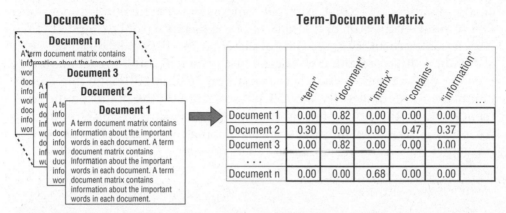

Figure 21-3: A term-document matrix contains information about the important words in each document.

Corpus Effects

Transforming a document into a term-document matrix seems to depend only on the document itself. However, this is not the case. There is some dependency on the corpus, meaning that the results can vary depending on other documents.

The first effect is the removal of common words. The definition of *common* depends on the rest of the documents in the corpus, so different words might be common in different groups of documents. Similarly, the definition of *rare* is also corpus dependent. A word that appears once in a sample of one thousand documents might not be included in the lexicon. In a corpus of one million documents, it might appear in a hundreds of them. A related issue is the synonym list. A larger corpus, for example, might suggest more synonyms.

The other dependency is within the term-document matrix itself. The values in each cell are generally related to the frequency of terms in documents. This, of course, depends on the corpus.

In practice, these effects are not large, so you usually do not have to worry about them. They can be an issue in some cases. You wouldn't want to use a collection of news stories to develop text mining methods, and then apply the methods directly to blog comments picked off the Internet.

WARNING   The collection of documents used to set up a text mining solution is important. Don't try to apply results from one type of document to a radically different type.

Singular Value Decomposition (SVD)

Principal components, introduced in Chapter 20, are a key idea when working with arrays of numbers, including term-document matrices. Chapter 20 describes principal components analysis using a geometric description of principal components. The first principal component is the line (in n dimensions) that minimizes the sum of the squares of the distance from each point to the line — not the distance in the vertical direction, but the actual distance.

An alternative definition is that the first principal component maximizes the variance of the projection of the points on the line. Although this sounds more complicated, it really is not. The "projection of the points on the line" means where the points fall on the line when connected by the shortest segment, as shown in Figure 21-4. "Maximizing the variance" means essentially that the points are as spread out as possible.

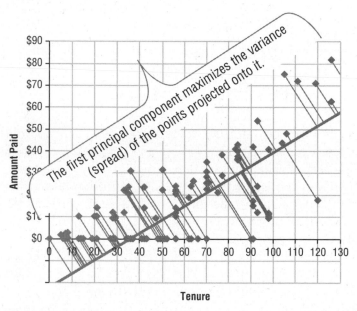

Figure 21-4: The first principal component maximizes the variance of the points on the projected line.

The alternative definition was first used by Karl Pearson when he investigated principal components for statistical analysis in the dawning years of the twentieth century. Mathematicians also approached the problem, but from a different perspective. Instead of points in space, mathematicians considered matrices, which are just lists of the coordinates of points, as shown in Figure 21-5. A matrix does not have to be a square; it can have different numbers of rows and columns.

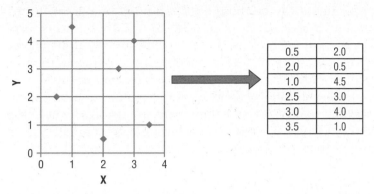

Figure 21-5: One interpretation of a matrix is that it is just a collection of points.

As mathematicians studied these matrices, they discovered some very interesting transformations. One of these transformations is a way to factor matrices, analogous to the way that numbers can be factored. Just as 105 can be written as $3 \times 5 \times 7$, a matrix can be written as the product of exactly three other matrices that are simpler than the original matrix. This process is called *singular value decomposition* (SVD).

It turns out that one of the matrices in the factorization has zeros everywhere except along the diagonal (this is called a *diagonal matrix*). The values on the diagonal are the *singular values*, which is where the technique gets its name. For analytic purposes, the two other matrices are more interesting. One consists of rows that are orthogonal to each other, and the other consists of columns that are orthogonal to each other. Orthogonality is a desirable property. In fact, one of these matrices consists of all the principal components of the original data. In other words, singular value decomposition is one way to calculate principal components.

If singular value decomposition is essentially the same thing as principal component analysis, why have two different names for essentially the same thing? The first reason is historical. Principal components come from statistical analysis, whereas singular value decomposition comes from mathematical analysis.

Another reason is related to subtle nuances between the approaches. Suffice it to say that although the basic themes are the same, there are some differences A final reason is one of emphasis. Singular value decomposition inherently recognizes that the columns of the matrix are different from the rows. Principal component analysis only works on square matrices, so rows and columns are similar to each other.

What Does SVD Have to Do with Text Mining?

Text mining uses singular value decomposition to transform documents into numbers, in the same way that principal components are used for more structured data.

Specifically, each document can be thought of as a point in a giant "term" space. A corpus can contain thousands of possible terms. These terms form a space, where each term is along an axis; there are thousands of dimensions. The data is quite sparse, meaning that most documents do not contain most terms. High dimensional sparse data is a big challenge in data mining.

The solution is to use the singular values decomposition to reduce dimensionality, in the same way that principal components are used. The last case study in this chapter from DIRECTV reduces the term-document matrix from thousands of dimensions to 50 dimensions.

Latent Semantic Indexing

When singular value decomposition is applied to text mining, it is often called *latent semantic indexing*. The idea behind latent semantic indexing is that each of the singular value vectors — principal components — represents a "theme" in the original documents. The position of the document along each of these dimensions measures the strength of the corresponding theme in the document. This description has a certain elegance and is quite similar to factor analysis discussed in Chapter 20. However, the themes themselves are not obvious, which is where the "latent" comes in.

Applying SVD to Text Mining

The magic of singular value decomposition is that it turns documents into points in space. This means that you can readily apply many of the data mining techniques already described in this book to the data.

For instance, the last case study in Chapter 9 on MBR uses a complicated definition of similarity based on the mutual content of words between two documents. An alternative approach is to transform documents into points, using SVD, and then use MBR directly on the transformed data.

After you make the transformation of the documents into numbers, MBR is not the only choice of technique. Decision trees and neural networks are also powerful choices. More traditional statistical methods such as regression or logistic regression are feasible.

The final two case studies in this chapter use SVD-based models for text mining. The first uses naïve Bayesian modeling and the second uses expectation-maximization clustering.

Text Mining and Naïve Bayesian Models

One day, computers will be able to read documents, understand what they mean and then answer questions about them, organize them, and explain unexpected patterns. That world does not yet exist. One of the challenges in text mining is simply that language provides many ways of saying the same thing. A human reading text understands these similarities, pretty much automatically. However, computers analyzing text must be given lots of hints about the content. Even then, the hints must be combined correctly — dare one say intelligently — in order to get sensible results.

What is needed is a data mining technique that can combine these hints into sensible predictions. Such a technique exists: naïve Bayesian models, introduced in Chapter 6. This technique is common in the world of text analysis.

Naïve Bayesian in the Text World

Naïve Bayesian analysis is an excellent way of combining evidence from features, even when many of the features are missing. In the case of text mining, the features are the presence of certain phrases. For the boycott example, the word "Israel" is a feature, as is the word "Middle East" and many other words. For that example, the presence of the word in the comment is sufficient to establish the purpose of the call.

Naïve Bayesian models work differently. It is a modeling technique used best for binary response modeling — that is, determining whether a document is or is not something. The example in this section is for classifying spam, where naïve Bayesian provides a score that estimates the probability that an e-mail document is spam.

As described in Chapter 6, it works by modifying the odds ratio, based on the presence of evidence. In a balanced model set (one with equal numbers of both types of categories — say spam and non-spam) the odds ratio starts out at one. When the feature is present, then the odds ratio is multiplied by some factor, either increasing or decreasing it. In the end, the odds ratio can be transformed back into a probability, using simple arithmetic.

Identifying Spam Using Naïve Bayesian

Identifying spam is a perennial battle for e-mail providers. Over the years, many different techniques have proliferated. However, naïve Bayesian has proven successful for this purpose. This discussion is based in large part on a paper[4] written by Professor Eric Jiang of the University of San Diego and on discussions with the author.

TIP Naïve Bayesian models are particularly well-suited to directed text mining applications, because they accumulate evidence and can handle missing values very well.

---

[4]Jiang, Eric P (2010). *Content Based Spam Email Classification using Machine Learning Algorithms*. In *Text Mining Applications and Theory*, Michael W. Berry and Jacob Kogan (eds). Wiley.

The Complexities of Spam Detection

For someone receiving unwanted and unsolicited e-mail, the content immediately seems to indicate the nature of the e-mail. Attractive women from Russia don't send enticing e-mails to strangers, in general. Pharmacies do not advertise to sell prescription drugs, and no one in Africa really wants to transfer millions of dollars into your bank account. Unfortunately, many people do receive romantic e-mails and do have financial discussions by e-mail. One of the authors was amused once when doing a project for Pfizer, and many of the e-mails landed in the spam mailbox. Pfizer manufactures Viagra, and the presence of that word clearly tripped spam filters, even when the discussion was analyzing usage of the drug rather than trying to sell it on the Web.

From the perspective of the e-mail service provider, an e-mail has more information than just the message itself. Of particular importance is the Internet service provider (ISP) address that sends it out. Large e-mail providers keep track of how many end users mark an e-mail as spam, and which ISP addresses these seem to come from. Too many spam e-mails from the same source, and the source is turned off: E-mails will no longer be accepted from there.

Finally, one person's spam may be another person's discount coupon or dating service. The same e-mail may be regarded differently depending on who receives it, particularly depending on how the e-mail sender obtained the person's e-mail address.

Content-Only Spam Analysis

Content-only spam analysis is particularly useful at the individual level. The e-mail provider can identify many messages as spam and put these in the spam folder. Sometimes the e-mail provider is wrong, and one of the spam items is really valid. Sometimes the e-mail provider misses some spam, and the user marks them as spam.

As time goes by (and very little time is needed, given the preponderance of spam), more and more e-mails are classified into these two buckets: Valid and Spam. Each user may classify things a bit differently. So, when e-mailing about technical analyses regarding Viagra and marking these e-mails as Valid, the term *Viagra* becomes less important as a marker of spam.

The data mining problem is: Given a set of a user's e-mail, how can a model distinguish Valid from Spam? This model would presumably start with the e-mail provider's best score for spam, and then modify it based on the characteristics in the e-mail message and the history of each individual person.

Building the model requires two steps. The first is finding a list of important terms, the lexicon for the analysis. The second is combining information from each e-mail to calculate a score. This is where naïve Bayesian modeling comes into play.

Finding Important Terms

Building the text mining model to identify spam follows typical text mining steps. First, available e-mails are parsed with *stop words* removed. Similarly, very rare words that appear in only one or a handful of e-mails are removed. Words that are too common or too rare are not useful for distinguishing valid e-mails from spam e-mails.

> **TIP** For many text mining applications, you want to remove both words that are too common and too rare. Too common words appear in all documents, so are useless for distinguishing among them. Too rare words occur in too few documents to be useful.

So far, the preparation of the text documents into bags of words is unsupervised. Next, a supervised phase occurs, where the frequency of each term in the spam e-mails is compared to the frequency in the valid e-mails. Only terms that have statistically significant differences in frequencies are kept. A typical test to use for this comparison is the chi-square test, although other statistical tests can be used. Basically, all the terms are given a statistical measure of how good they are for distinguishing between spam and valid e-mails.

The next step is to choose an appropriate set of terms. One way is to use a threshold (choose terms where the chi-square value is greater than 2, for instance). Alternatively, a specific number of terms can be used. In the end, only the terms that pass through this process are used for text analysis.

Building a Naïve Bayesian Model

Applying the naïve Bayesian technique is quite simple after the data has been prepared. Each term provides evidence, one way or the other, of an e-mail being spam. The naïve Bayesian model simply combines the results from each term as described in Chapter 6, arriving at a probability of how likely the e-mail is to be spam.

The Results

Figure 21-6 shows the results of the naïve Bayesian model based on the number of features (words) extracted from the email and used for the naïve Bayesian model. Not surprisingly, having more features tends to result in better and better models. Interestingly on this model set, which is rather small (fewer than 2,000 e-mails), around 750 features worked well.

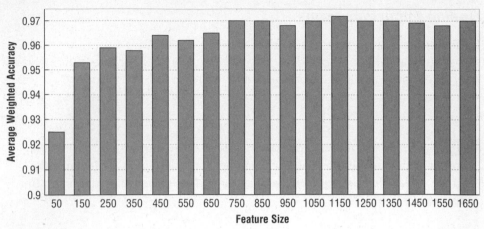

Courtesy of Prof. Eric Jiang, University of San Diego

Figure 21-6: The naïve Bayesian classifier tends to work better as more terms are added, although the improvement plateaus around 750 terms.

Professor Jiang then studied this approach in two different ways. One way was to study the effects of language, so he compared his spam-detector on e-mails written in English and Chinese. Second, he compared different methods for building directed data mining models from the features in the e-mails. These methods were:

- Logistic regression, with a boosting algorithm
- Support vector machines
- Radial basis function neural networks
- A specialized method using augmented latent semantic indexing, which is discussed in the sidebar "An Alternative Approach for Classifying E-mails"

For distinguishing spam in English, naïve Bayesian outperformed the other techniques when the models used significant numbers of features. This is not surprising, because naïve Bayesian is particularly well suited for large numbers of features.

Naïve Bayesian performed less well in two situations. For Chinese, it did not perform so well, probably due to specific characteristics of the Chinese language. The same character can mean very different things in different contexts (called *polysemous* in the academic language of natural language processing). This means that finding well-defined terms is much more difficult than in English.

Naïve Bayesian also performed less well when the classification problem was changed to include different weights for false negatives and false positives.

AN ALTERNATIVE APPROACH FOR CLASSIFYING E-MAILS

In his work on e-mail classification, Professor Jiang has proposed an interesting alternative approach for classification that has uses extending beyond this application.

The basic idea is to develop clusters for valid and spam e-mails:

1. Create two sets of principal components, one for the valid e-mails and one for the spam e-mails.

2. Create clusters in each space, using k-means clustering using both spam and valid emails.

3. Each cluster is assigned "valid" or "spam," depending on the prevalence of each label in the set of data used to create it.

Scoring new e-mails now entails:

1. Determining the distance to each of the clusters.

2. Voting on the category, using inverse distance to weight the votes.

3. The category with the most votes is assigned to the cluster.

In the language of text mining, this technique is described as "clustering in the latent semantic indexing space." Just remember that "latent semantic indexing" means principal components.

The basic approach is an interesting idea. However, it does not work as well as you might expect for a very simple reason: Spammers write spam e-mails to look like real e-mail. This problem is a challenging one. In essence, each cluster does a good job for its category, but members of the other category are also close to the center of the cluster.

To solve this problem, Professor Jiang augmented the clusters. For each cluster, he identified the e-mails in the other category that are closest to the cluster center. He then added some of these as new clusters into the set of clusters. Overall, just a few dozen new cases were added. The figure on the next page illustrates the basic approach.

Augmenting the results this way proved quite useful. In some situations, the augmented clusters in the latent semantic indexing space outperformed other methods, such as naïve Bayesian models.

Continued

AN ALTERNATIVE APPROACH FOR CLASSIFYING E-MAILS (*continued*)

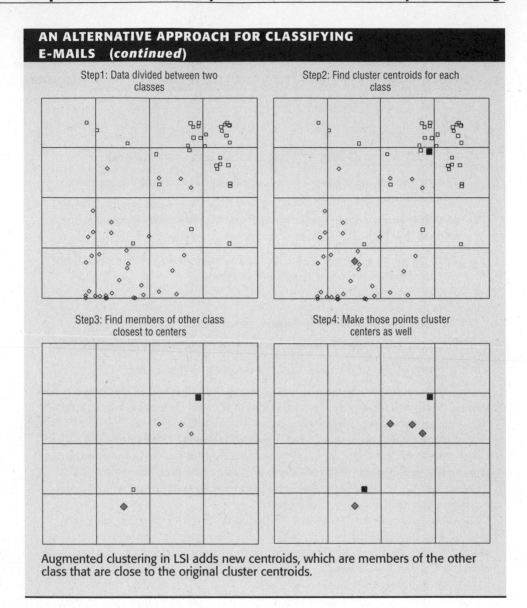

Step1: Data divided between two classes

Step2: Find cluster centroids for each class

Step3: Find members of other class closest to centers

Step4: Make those points cluster centers as well

Augmented clustering in LSI adds new centroids, which are members of the other class that are close to the original cluster centroids.

Sentiment Analysis

Sentiment analysis (sometimes called opinion mining) is another important application of text mining. The goal is to automatically peruse published sources of information and determine how people feel about something — a brand, a product, a celebrity, a stock. Among the more successful applications is for financial investment, where companies such as RavenPack use sentiment analysis to improve forecasts of equity prices.

What Sentiment Analysis Does

The purpose of sentiment analysis is to assign a sentiment score to documents or parts of documents. A sentiment score typically ranges from highly negative (–1) to neutral (0) to highly positive (1). Such scores can be used in a variety of different ways.

For instance, sentiment analysis has been used to predict who would win *American Idol*, an American television show in which the audience votes on the winner, using information gathered from social media sites on the Web. Attensity, which has a system for monitoring comments on the Web, has used its system to track the sentiment and volume of mentions for each of the contestants.

Uses of sentiment analysis go beyond merely predicting the winner of a talent competition. Brand managers cannot read all the comments and articles posted about their products. How can they keep track of market sentiment? One way is to track the overall sentiment for their products and their competitors. In particular, tracking sentiment over time helps them understand what happens in the market.

> **TIP** Sentiment analysis is a powerful way of keeping track of market perceptions. It is most useful when looking at sentiment over time.

A more detailed use, which is really still being researched, is to understand details of opinions within a product review or blog entry. This can be quite complicated, because multiple products might be mentioned, and a comment can have nuances of opinion ("I love the phone! I hate the battery!").

Another use is in the financial world. Many articles and analyst reports discuss various companies. Do these discussions have predictive value on the future price of a company's stock?

Basic Approach

Sentiment analysis generally uses published documents. These might be magazine and newspaper articles, blog postings, or comments posted on the Web. To a greater or lesser extent, these postings are attempts to communicate in complete sentences, using a minimum amount of jargon, non-standard abbreviations, and misspellings. Of course, such anomalies do exist, but they are less important than when using other sources of text, such as customer service comments or e-mails.

The basic idea is to:

1. Clean words in the document.
2. Find the topic of interest in the document.

3. Determine the sentiment of the surrounding words, sentences, paragraph, or document.

4. Apply the sentiment to the topic of interest.

Sentiment analysis can take a "bag-of-words" approach. However, this approach must usually be extended, because proximity to words describing the item of interest is also important, requiring a bit more care when handling the text.

For more complex analyses, such as finding all the opinions about a product in a blog entry or review, the language is more important. The simple example "I love the phone! I hate the battery!" shows the limitations of the bag-of-words approach. Natural language processing (NLP) takes into account the grammatical structure of the language and is used for more complex types of sentiment analysis. In some cases, the bag-of-words approach applied at the sentence level can yield good results.

This chapter has already covered cleaning documents. For sentiment analysis, one additional step is required. The words, phrases, abbreviations, and even pronouns used to refer to the item of interest must be identified to determine the sentiment of the surrounding words.

Using a "Psycho-Social" Dictionary

The more interesting part of sentiment analysis is its use of vocabulary. In the 1980s, researchers at Harvard created something called the "psycho-social" dictionary. This is a list of thousands of words, along with various nuances of their meaning, particularly with respect to attitudes.

The current version (which is available at `www.wjh.harvard.edu/~inquirer/ homecat.htm`) has attributes about words, in dozens of categories such as:

- Positive
- Negative
- Strong
- Weak
- Pleasure
- Pain

These categories have been researched and enhanced for many years.

As an example of what the dictionary contains, the word *deprive* is marked as "negative" and "strong," whereas *destitute* is "negative" but "weak." *Profitable* is "positive" and "strong," and *prosper* is "positive" and "weak."

These categories become the building blocks of sentiment. The more "positive" words in a document, the more positive the sentiment. Proximity is also important. The presence of more "positive" words near the target implies more positive sentiment.

Several thousand words have been categorized into these categories. The basic set of words consists of those occurring more than four times out of a million, in a large corpus of published documents.

The psycho-social dictionary can be used as a basis for mining sentiment in documents. The simplest measure would simply be the number of positive words minus the number of negative words in the document. A greater number of positive words implies a more positive sentiment.

This is only the beginning. The analysis can incorporate information from other categories as well, so "strong" positive would have a bigger influence than "weak" positive. This information can even be combined into more refined measures than just the number of words. By assigning a "positivity" score to each word that varies between zero and one, you can create a model set appropriate for using naïve Bayesian to combine the words into an overall sentiment value for the document. Naïve Bayesian is definitely not the only approach to opinion mining, but it is a common approach.

Some interesting successes have been achieved using sentiment analysis, both from the academic perspective and from the business perspective. For instance, several academic studies have shown that stock prices are correlated with the sentiment of articles written about them during earlier time periods. This information has also proven useful for investors. Unfortunately, companies that use sentiment analysis for investment are not willing to share case studies.

DIRECTV: A Case Study in Customer Service

DIRECTV is the leading provider in the United States of direct broadcast satellite service that distributes video, music, data, and more via satellite. It has been a leader in using data mining to understand its business, particularly what its customers are saying the hundreds of thousands of times that they call customer service every day.

This case study is not about a single project that used text mining for a specific purpose. Instead, it shows the power of data mining in transforming the customer service side of the business — a power made possible by text mining. The authors are immensely grateful to Dirk De Roos, leader of the customer care analytic team at DIRECTV, and John Wallace of Business Researchers, who worked with Dirk on text mining efforts. The work primarily uses SAS Text Miner and custom code developed by Business Researchers.

Background

DIRECTV competes against other multi-channel video programming providers, including satellite television as well as cable. By using satellites, DIRECTV is able to provide service throughout the United States with a minimum of blackout areas, including to remote areas that are "off the grid."

The customer service department receives hundreds of thousands of calls every day that are generally in one of four categories:

- Information requests, particularly about the cost of channels: "How much does Showtime and HBO cost?"

- Billing requests: "What is this charge?" "Change the bill to Spanish." "Change address."

- Technical requests: "Customer needs to have slimline dish installed."

- Retention requests: "I want to stop my service."

With a growing business and so many calls, the customer care department is concerned about three things:

1. Gaining a general understanding of what customers are calling about. In particular, DIRECTV wants to identify whether new problems are arising in the business.

2. The average duration of calls. Each second of talk time — on average — costs hundreds of thousands or millions of dollars per year.

3. Understanding and predicting call volumes, particularly for staffing purposes.

The Call Center Interface

The call center software utilized by DIRECTV was originally developed to facilitate customer relationship management. The goal of the software was twofold. First, the software needed to help agents effectively complete calls, record what happened on the call, and take effective action. Second, the software needed to help agents finish the calls in as short a time as possible.

The software was also designed to gather information for business purposes. For instance, there would be a way to track whether the call was a retention call, trying to retain customers who might leave. It also had a way to track upgrade calls, technical service calls, and so on. A key goal of the CRM system was to resolve problems on the first call — resulting in better service for the customer and more efficient use of the call center.

The software was designed to be efficient as well, with drop-down menus for the agents to describe the call. High-level drop-down menus led to lower level ones, and lower level ones to even lower ones, reminiscent of the proverb: "Big fleas have little fleas upon their backs to bite 'em; little fleas have lesser fleas, and so on ad infinitum."

To actually do their work, agents would identify the problem and then access other systems to schedule appointments, updating billing information, and so on. Agents could also type in comments, providing even more detailed information.

What Happened Over Time

The call center interface became the primary source of information about calls. To facilitate marketing efforts, drop-down menus became more and more important. Other departments would add items to the menus to better understand particular offers and products. These "add-on" items to the menus often survived long after the original need was gone.

The end result was confusion. As the menus became more complex, the agents focused on fewer and fewer menu items. In fact, just a handful of items out of several hundred accounted for the majority of calls. Not surprisingly, these items were also the top choices of the menus.

Having most calls assigned default codes greatly reduced the effectiveness of the information. The items on the menus were intended to provide insight into the calls. In the end, they did not.

Applying Text Mining

At this point, Dirk De Roos, contacted John Wallace to develop a system that would help DIRECTV better understand what was happening on the calls. The idea was to use the comments typed in by the agents to categorize the calls.

Using undirected data mining, the system would find clusters in the text. (More technical detail is provided later in this case study.) Although clustering is undirected, there were "directed" goals for the clusters. The resulting clusters needed to make sense, in one of three ways:

- Customer segment
- Root cause of call
- Sentiment

All of these are important parts of the customer interaction. All are presumably available in the information on the call.

Determining the Usefulness of the RV Segment

The initial effort resulted in some interesting clusters. For instance, one of the clusters was the Recreational Vehicle (RV) cluster. It could be readily identified by words in the cluster such as Winnebago, camper, or RV. Satellite TV is popular for such "roving living rooms" because cable and broadcast TV are not available everywhere the campers might roam. Presumably their calls to customer service represented the needs of this particular customer segment.

As a customer segment, the RV group is of interest. Of course, DIRECTV had already identified this group as an important customer segment and had in fact been directing advertising and promotions to this group.

From the perspective of customer service, the RV group was less interesting. This group did not provide insight into improving customer service or agent efficiency or even in understanding why these particular customers were calling. The RV segment was as likely to call about setting up the satellite dish, as about billing problems (because the customers were often away from home), seasonal rate plans, and other issues.

The presence of clusters such as the RV cluster led to the next conclusion. Text mining was producing interesting, but not actionable, results. In researching the problem, the analysts realized that the comments themselves were not providing enough detail about the calls. Without the detail, separating comments into useful clusters was simply not possible.

The second problem was the goal of the analysis itself. Understanding sentiment, customer segment, gathering marketing information, and assigning the root cause for the call are all worthwhile tasks. But trying to attack all of them at the same time did not lead to actionable results.

Acting on the Results

The first round of data mining demonstrated that clusters based on comments could be interesting. The real understanding was that the project needed to be more focused:

- Agent comments needed to be more complete and assigned to more calls.
- The target chosen for the analysis was the determination of the "root cause" of customer calls.

Effecting these changes required modifications both in the call center and in the analytic environment.

WARNING   Trying to accomplish too much in one data mining effort leads to disappointment. Instead, focus on a task that is feasible and develop a culture of constant improvement.

The call center interface was modified to encourage agents to include comments. For one thing, the comments became mandatory. Another was that the menu items were replaced with actions that occurred on the call. So if the agent changed a customer's address, then "change address" would be added onto the call record automatically.

These modifications turned out to be hugely successful. After the company retrained the agents to focus on typing in comments rather than using the menus, the average call duration went down by almost 5 percent, as shown in Figure 21-7.

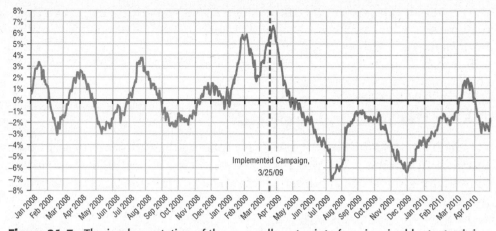

Figure 21-7: The implementation of the new call center interface, inspired by text mining efforts, reduced the average call duration by a noticeable amount.

To someone not familiar with call centers, this may not seem like a large number. Other efforts to reduce the duration of calls generally did not produce any long-lasting decrease at all. Furthermore, this decrease resulted in more complete data, because call center agents included more extensive comments. The decrease in call duration was an early and unexpected win for the text mining efforts.

Continuing Clustering

After working with the agents to clean up the comments, better data was available. The first task for using the improved data was to focus on root-cause clusters. Focusing on one type of clustering would allow DIRECTV to get more actionable results.

Better data and focus did indeed lead to better results. The clustering effort worked in tandem with cleaning and preparing the data — helping to determine what synonym lists to use, which stop words to include in the stop words list, and so on. The goal was to find a set of clusters that defined that "root cause" of the call. The end result was more than 100 clusters for different root causes.

One cluster, for instance, is about changing billing information, such as changing an address or phone number. It turns out that all comments in this cluster are about calls during which such a change was made, even though the clustering only uses information in the comment fields.

This does not mean that everyone who changed billing information is in the cluster, because other things might happen during the call. Perhaps the call is predominantly about satellite dish issues, and requires a service call. During the course of the service call, the customer says something like, "Oh, that's my landline phone number. Use my cell phone instead." The change of billing information is not the root cause.

In the end, more than 90 percent of the comments were able to be assigned confidently to a root cause cluster.

Taking the Technical Approach

Figure 21-8 shows the overall process for creating the clusters as described by Business Researchers. This process has several steps, almost all of them related to managing the lexicon and massaging the text. Only the last step uses data mining algorithms.

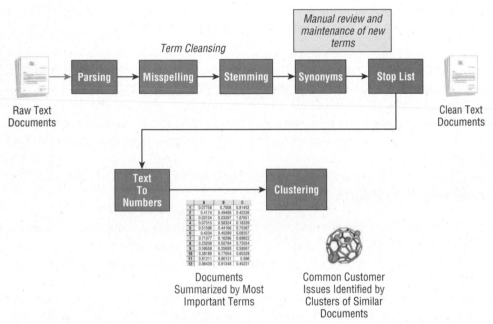

Figure 21-8: The process for building document clusters involves many steps to transform the data into a structure usable for analysis.

Parsing the Comments

The first step of the process to create clusters was to identify a set of comments for analysis and to parse them into terms — creating the model set. In general, parsing works by replacing punctuation with spaces, and then taking all terms between spaces. The bag-of-words approach works well for understanding agent comments, because the agents are not trying to write grammatically correct sentences. They are actually trying to quickly capture important ideas in the customer interaction.

There are some tricks in the parsing phase, because punctuation can be used in unusual ways. For instance, one agent might type in "Customer wants HBO and Showtime." Another might type in "Customer wants HBO/Showtime." In this case, the slash looks like punctuation. However, in other cases, a slash might be part of a word, such as "w/out." The trick is to handle these special cases by using special lists of terms that accept punctuation in the middle.

For the DIRECTV work, a random sample of about 400,000 comments was used, containing a total of about 7 million terms. These 7 million terms represented only 76,930 different unique terms, of which more than half (44,826) appeared only one time. Terms that are so rare that they appear only once are not useful for analysis.

Fixing Misspellings

Customer comments are typed in by real people with minimal or no editing. This means that misspellings are quite common. The problem of fixing misspelled words has been investigated almost since the dawn of the computer age. The sidebar "Spelling Suggestions Using Levenshtein Distance" discusses the basic method.

The automated task is simply a matter of constructing a valid dictionary and choosing the closest term. This is an iterative task, where you start with a dictionary and find the closest word to each word not in the dictionary. Some words are quite close (real misspellings) and some are quite far away (suggestions for new words to add into the dictionary).

In the case of DIRECTV, a standard dictionary is augmented with business-specific terms, such as the names of channels ("ESPN," "Showtime," and so on). Of the 32,104 non-unique terms in the sample comments, more than half were misspellings (or abbreviations). After taking this into account, the number of unique terms fell to about 22,000.

Stemming

Stemming transforms words into their root forms. For example, one comment might contain "Customer paid too much on last bill; money refunded." Another might say "Refunding overpayment." These two comments have no words in common, yet they are saying essentially the same thing. The stemming algorithm recognizes that "overpayment" and "paid" both have the root of "pay." Similarly, "refunded" and "refund" both have the root of "refund."

Stemming turns the two comments into "Customer pay too much on last bill; money refund" and "Refund pay." After stemming, the comments are not grammatically correct. On the other hand, comments similar to each other are much more likely to contain similar terms.

SPELLING SUGGESTIONS USING LEVENSHTEIN DISTANCE

Spell checking has become such a common feature of word-processing software that most people expect to see squiggly red lines underlining misspellings or alternate suggestions whenever they are typing text. These tools work very well for interactive spelling checkers.

The problem of finding misspellings is easier than the problem of suggesting alternatives. Finding misspellings is simply a matter of looking up words in a dictionary, while taking into account proper nouns and grammar (so "sister's" might not have to be in the dictionary).

For text mining purposes, automated spell checking is necessary. In addition, the dictionary of correct spellings is different from a standard dictionary. For instance, it might contain such useful phrases as HD, HBO, and NFL for the DIRECTV example.

This problem of finding alternative suggestions was first investigated in the 1960s by Vladimir Levenshtein when he was working at Moscow State University. He investigated a "distance" metric between two words. The idea is to count the minimum number of "edits" required to go from one word to another. An edit is one of three operations:

- Substitute one letter for another in the same position.

- Delete one of the letters.

- Add a new letter.

Sometimes, a fourth is added: transposing two letters (that is, going from "teh" to "the").

For instance, to transform "man" to "woman" requires two edits, adding a "w" in the first position and then adding an "o" in the second position. Of course, there are other possibilities, but two edits is the shortest transformation between the words.

Levenshtein also devised an algorithm for finding the fewest transforms. This algorithm is efficient enough that it can be run on large documents against a large dictionary in a short amount of time (computers have improved a lot since the 1960s).

The approach has also been refined, such as by giving different weighting to the first letter, breaking words into smaller pieces, and using context to determine the best alternative word.

Applying Synonym Lists

Synonym lists are words and phrases that are recognized in the text and replaced by a common synonym. These serve several purposes, including fixing misspellings and finding word phrases. The synonym lists used by DIRECTV also combined similar details into a higher level idea. For example, "Change address" and "Change phone number" both turn into "Change account info."

The lists can also be used to fix misspellings. For example, these might all be synonyms for Showtime (one of the channels offered by DIRECTV):

- Showtime
- Show time
- Show-time
- ST
- Showt
- Shwotme

The synonym lists turn these into a single word (in this case "Showtime"). Notice that the last term is simply a misspelling. Looking up the term in a dictionary of common words would come up with "snowmen," illustrating why common dictionaries must be augmented by domain-specific terms.

Using a Stop List

The stop list contains words that have minimal meaning, as discussed earlier in this chapter. Stop words can also be meaningful terms that simply do not distinguish between comments. The word *customer* occurs in many comments, but doesn't provide information about the root cause. Similarly, *television* and *TV* are not useful, because all DIRECTV customers are, presumably, calling about something related to their television. Almost all customers have high-definition TV, so *HD* is a stop word as well.

TIP The stop word list should remove words that might seem meaningful but are not likely to distinguish between documents. In the DIRECTV example, this includes *customer, television*, and *HD*.

The purpose of the stop word list is to remove words that do not distinguish between different comments, even when these words might seem meaningful. The synonym and stop list used by DIRECTV did not significantly reduce the number of terms in the document. The size of the vocabulary for the comments ended up having about 22,000 distinct terms.

Converting Text to Numbers

Figure 21-8 shows a step called "Text to Numbers." This chapter has already described term-document matrixes and the use of singular value decomposition (SVD) to transform documents into numbers. This technique was used in this case, using SAS's Text Miner software to calculate 50 singular value vectors for the clustering.

Clustering

The final step is clustering. As described in Chapters 13 and 14, many different clustering algorithms can find clusters in data. The clustering method used in this case was Gaussian mixture models (GMM), also known as expectation-maximization clustering. In fact, several different methods were tried, notably k-means as well as GMM. The clusters generated by the GMM algorithm tended to be better, based on subjective judgment of the resulting clusters. As described in Chapter 14, GMM does a better job of distinguishing between clusters that have oblong shapes.

Not an Iterative Process

Describing the process as a set of seven steps makes it sound like one of Julia Child's recipes. Like the recipes for fine French food, the steps of data mining are all interrelated and affect each other. Unlike the steps in such recipes (at least when Julia followed them), steps often need to be repeated and in different sequences.

The choice of dictionary for correcting misspellings has a big impact on the choice of synonyms later. The validity of the clusters, in turn, has an impact on the choice of stop words and synonyms. In fact, looking at preliminary clusters made it obvious that words like *customer* and *HD* should be part of the stop word list.

Continuing to Benefit

DIRECTV did not stop its text mining effort with a single set of clusters used for analyzing customer comments. On a daily basis, it "scores" new customer calls with the root-cause clusters, provided by data mining. Every six to twelve months, it dives deeper into the clusters, to determine whether the clusters are still working and whether new ones are needed.

The root-cause clusters have become more and more useful over time. In one case, DIRECTV was assessing the clusters by looking at average call duration over time. Normally, this would provide insight into where the customer service agents were doing a good job and where room for improvement might reduce the average talk time. It might also suggest new "hard" problems that are taking the agents longer to solve.

In this case, though, the clusters at the top of the list for increased call duration were all similar and related to billing. Changing a billing address had an increase in talk time. Providing a refund had an increase in talk time. Changing the rate plan had an increase in talk time. Most other clusters did not show an increase in talk time.

After investigating more, analysts found that the increase started in one particular month, rather abruptly. Further discussions revealed that there had been an IT "upgrade" during this period, an upgrade that slowed down the billing system. Without the benefit of root-cause clusters, such a change would probably not have been noticed — and the cost of the extra talk time would have continued until the next upgrade would (presumably) fix the problem.

Lessons Learned

Text mining is the application of data mining to text data, which can come from many different sources. Typical sources used in business include news articles, blog entries, comments on customer service calls, and e-mails sent in by customers.

The purpose of text mining may be to understand the documents, summarize them in some way, or to cluster them into similarity groups. Identifying a specific characteristic (such as finding which customers stopped because of a boycott) might be sufficient. In other cases, features extracted from text are combined with other data to build more traditional data mining models. Newer applications are being developed in the area of sentiment analysis and opinion mining, determining the attitude of the writer to what he or she is writing about.

The most challenging aspect of text mining is managing the text itself. At the extreme are two different methodologies. The first is the bag-of-words approach, which treats documents as unordered lists of their words. At the other extreme is the natural language processing approach, which takes into account the meanings and grammatical features of the language. There are many variations of both methods.

Processing the text for the bag-of-words approach usually involves removing stop words, common words, fixing misspellings, stemming, and replacing words with synonyms. The next step is to define the term-document matrix, which is a giant matrix with a row for each document and a column for each term. The cells generally contain the inverse term frequency of each term in the set of all documents.

The next step is the text equivalent of principal components, called singular value decomposition. This reduces the text to points in a multidimensional space, where more traditional data mining techniques can be used. Alternatively, naïve Bayesian models are often a very effective modeling tool.

As the examples in this chapter show, text mining has a very broad range of applications. The DIRECTV example provides an excellent illustration not only of text mining, but also of the virtuous cycle of data mining introduced in Chapter 1.

Index